Hellenic Studies 3

Greek Ritual Poetics

Greek Ritual Poetics

Edited by Dimitrios Yatromanolakis and Panagiotis Roilos

Published by

Center for Hellenic Studies
Trustees for Harvard University
Washington, D.C.
and
Foundation of the Hellenic World
Athens, Greece

Distributed by Harvard University Press
Cambridge, Massachusetts, and London, England

2004

Greek Ritual Poetics
edited by Dimitrios Yatromanolakis and Panagiotis Roilos

Published by Center for Hellenic Studies, Trustees for Harvard University, Washington, D.C. and Foundation of the Hellenic World, Athens, Greece

Distributed by Harvard University Press, Cambridge, Massachusetts and London, England

Volume editor: Christopher Dadian

Production: Kristin Murphy Romano

Cover design: Michael J. Horsley

Printed in Baltimore, Maryland, by Victor Graphics

Library of Congress Cataloging-in-Publication Data:
Greek ritual poetics / edited by Dimitrios Yatromanolakis and Panagiotis Roilos.
    p. cm. -- (Hellenic studies series ; 3)
    Includes bibliographical references and index.
    ISBN 0-674-01792-7 (alk. paper)
    1. Greek literature--History and criticism. 2. Literature and anthropology--Greece. 3. Rites and ceremonies in literature. 4. Greece--Social life and customs. 5. Literature and society--Greece. 6. Rites and ceremonies--Greece. 7. Ritual in literature. 8. Greece--Religion. 9. Ritual--Greece. I. Yatromanolakis, Dimitrios. II. Roilos, Panagiotis. III. Title. IV. Hellenic studies ; 3.
PA3009.G74 2004
880.9'3829138--dc22   2004016866

Table of Contents

Acknowledgments

This project started taking its present form in late 2001 and was completed in 2004. For his unstinting help with the production of the book we thank Chris Dadian. Many colleagues and friends have provided inspiration or valuable help, and have discussed with us diverse aspects of the book. We would like to thank Jacques Bouchard, Marcel Detienne, John Duffy, Pat Easterling, Walter Gilbert, Seamus Heaney, Albert Henrichs, Michael Herzfeld, David Lewin, Leonard Muellner, the late Robert Nozick, Elaine Scarry, the late Charles Segal, Alan Shapiro, John Shirley-Quirk, Laura Slatkin, Christiane Sourvinou-Inwood, Richard Thomas, Katherine Thomson, Helen Vendler, Jan Ziolkowski, and especially Margaret Alexiou, Gregory Nagy, and Peter Parsons.

Note on Transliteration

Absolute consistency in the transliteration of Greek words in a book that explores the ancient, medieval, and modern Greek traditions is almost impossible. Furthermore, accuracy and consistency in the transliteration of words of even a specific phase of the Greek language is equally chimeric. For instance, not only is our knowledge of the pronunciation of ancient Greek consonants limited, but, more importantly, it is problematic to adopt a transliteration system that assumes that archaic Greek was pronounced in the same manner as the Greek of the Hellenistic or the Roman periods, let alone the Greek of the Byzantine era. Changes in the pronunciation of ancient Greek seem to have occurred already in the Hellenistic period, and by the early Roman period, the changes were considerable. To avoid such problems, in this book we have opted for a transliteration system that reflects the internal orthographic tradition of Greek.

Part One

Ritual Poetics

One

Provisionally Structured Ideas on a Heuristically Defined Concept: Toward a Ritual Poetics[*]

for Margaret Alexiou

Dimitrios Yatromanolakis and Panagiotis Roilos

I

The aim of this book is to formulate an interdisciplinary and transhistorical *Problematik* of the embeddedness of ritual patterns of signification in cultural and sociopolitical discourses in Greek cultural contexts. Before embarking upon an analysis of the basic parameters of our use of the terms *ritual* and *poetics*, and, in particular, of the concept of *ritual poetics*, it is necessary to investigate the relevance of these terms and concepts to the Greek case.

First, some words about the "Greek case." The temporal scope of this book extends from Iron Age Greece to contemporary Greece. The hazard, and the challenge, of this exploratory attempt is obvious: it may create uneasiness, and perhaps expectations for bridging notorious gaps across periods *conspicuously* distant, both historically and culturally. Such a leap is not undertaken here. "Greek" is principally employed in this book as an overarching *linguistic* category. Instead of subscribing either to the detrimentally misleading dogma of linear diachronic continuities or to the equally monolithic and politically-charged dogma of absolute discontinuities,[1] our approach offers transhistorical, transcultural perspectives on the embeddedness of ritual patterns in broader cultural and sociopolitical discourses in different

---

[*] The order of our names here and elsewhere in the book reflects their original alphabetical order in Greek. An earlier version of this chapter, along with chapters three, six, and twelve, first appeared in Yatromanolakis and Roilos 2003.

[1] Continuity, often invoking and involving a variety of broader ideological issues, has been the subject of many a vehement debate in Hellenic Studies; for discussions relevant to the topic see Kyriakidou-Nestoros 1978; Herzfeld 1982; Danforth 1984; Vryonis 1978; Knox 1993; Alexiou 2002a offers a particularly balanced approach to the issue.

traditions of the Greek-speaking world. This exploratory enterprise puts emphasis on discontinuities and transformations across chronological and discursive boundaries. The diversity and volume of written records regarding ritual activities, whether religious or secular, actual or re-inscribed in other cultural discourses, is exceptionally rich in the Greek language. The Greek case, therefore, with its abundant material full of diverse continuities and discontinuities and their, more often than not, ideologically-informed reworkings throughout a period of around three millennia offers an admittedly challenging but fertile ground for comparative explorations and debates.

The second constituent of the notion of *ritual poetics* that is put forward in this chapter, the Greek-derived term *poetics*, is easily identifiable in the context of ancient Greek critical theory in its venerated surviving beginning, Aristotle's homonymous treatise. In the present book, however, *poetics* is mainly employed in light of its twentieth-century (post)structuralist developments. Although the term *poetics* retains here its aesthetic connotations, since on the one hand it is related to the semiotic, symbolic, and dramatic, that is, performative, dimensions of ritual, and on the other it is often used in association with the communicative patterns of aesthetic modes of communication, *poetics* should not be understood narrowly as a disinterested formalistic study of the structural patterns of such phenomena. Rather, it should be understood in a broader sense as the exploration of *dialogic* construction, subversion, negotiation, and conveyance of meaning in a number of interrelated social, cultural, and aesthetic domains of human experience and expression. We should make it clear from the beginning that *meaning*, which is employed here for want of a better term, is not perceived as necessarily intentional or directly encoded and decoded signification. In this respect, we find congenial Tambiah's view of *meaning* not as transmission of information but in the sense of pattern recognition and configurational awareness.[2] We would go even further and argue that *meaning* is not always constructed according to the mechanisms of the "logical logic" inherent in Western rationalistic thought. *Meaning* is rather perceived as a *practically* articulated process of communicative interaction, and its *poetics* is to be explored in such terms.[3] The diverse aesthetic, cultural, or sociopolitical discourses[4]/"texts" that *ritual poetics* aims to investigate are not self-contained and self-sufficient communicative systems but interact with each other in a persistent and ever re-invented heteroglossic game of exchanges and negotiations of symbolic

---

[2] Tambiah 1985a:139.

[3] Bourdieu proposes an insightful model for the study of the mechanisms of what he calls *practical logic*; see particularly his discussion in Bourdieu 1977:16–22; 72–95.

[4] *Discourse* retains here its Foucauldian connotations of positionality and power dynamics; see especially Foucault 1972 (especially pp. 21–117) and 1981.

and power capitals. While not necessarily refusing the help of structural analysis whenever pertinent,[5] *ritual poetics* is mainly interested in what has been called the "worldliness of the text,"[6] the "text"/discourse as situated within a nexus of what we would call *textural interactions* with other discourses.

Greek—ancient, medieval, and modern—uses a number of terms to describe a variety of symbolic actions commonly lumped together under the rubric of *ritual*. Our discussion of Greek terminology and the respective "emic" Greek concepts will focus here only on those aspects that we judge crucial for the illustration of the overall *Problematik* of *ritual poetics* that we propose in the present chapter. Τελετή and τελῶ are the most broadly encompassing terms employed in all phases of the Greek language to denote a range of primarily sacred ritual activities. Τελετή conveys an emphasis on the performative aspect of ritual, in the sense of acting out or, to use a concept favored by transformational generative grammar, in the sense of realization and completion of a traditional underlying system of mainly sacred ideas. Τελεῖν, from which τελετή derives, in marked contexts refers to solemn performances of traditional rites of passage or religious rites.[7] In the Homeric epics, for instance, the verb, in simple or compound form, is used with a noun in association with a rite of passage (e.g. τελεῖν τάφον, *Iliad* 24.60; ἐκτελεῖν γάμον, *Odyssey* 4.7). Often, τελετή in ancient Greek signifies a festival related to initiation

---

[5] Propp's "morphological" analysis of traditional Russian wondertales was the first influential systematic attempt at exploring the mechanisms of signification in prose from a formalistic point of view (Propp 1968); his approach was critically received by Levi-Strauss (see Propp 1984:167–189; in the same book see also Propp's response to Levi-Strauss, pp. 67–81). Todorov's and, in particular, Barthes' work offers more flexible paradigms for the study of narrative structures in fictional prose writing and of the conditions of literariness; see especially Barthes 1970 and 1987; Todorov 1981; Culler 1975 remains a helpful critical overview of major structuralist approaches to poetics; as for poetry, Jakobson's work is still most instructive; see especially Jakobson 1960 and 1987 (in particular pp. 121–144).

[6] The "worldliness of the text" is described by Edward Said in the following terms: "texts have ways of existing that even in their most rarefied form are always enmeshed in circumstance, time, place, and society—in short, they are in the world, and hence worldly" (1983:33–35). Such an approach to the text presupposes but goes beyond other theoretical models that have both alerted us to the restrictions of formalistic analyses that view text as a closed, autonomous system of signification, and shown ways to explore it instead in its dynamic interactions with its audience and the broader sociocultural conditions of the production of its "meaning;" cf., for example, the reader response and reception oriented theories (Iser 1974; 1978; 1989; Jauss 1982a; 1982b; Rifaterre 1983).

[7] Zijderveld 1934 contends that τελετή signified in general performance, achievement; the example that he adduces to substantiate his interpretation: καὶ πολέμου τελετὴ μονοήμερος ἐξετελέσθη (*Batrachomyomachia* [Battle of Frogs and Mice] 303) is, however, debatable, since a possible metaphorical usage of the term here cannot be precluded. On τελετή see also Rouget 1985:195–196; Versnel 1996. On the etymology of τέλειος, τελῶ, τελετή, see Waanders 1983 (on τελετή in particular see pp. 156–159).

rites; Athenaeus offers an interesting explanation of this meaning: τελετὰς τε καλοῦμεν τὰς ἔτι μείζους καὶ μετά τινος μυστικῆς παραδόσεως ἑορτὰς τῶν εἰς αὐτὰς δαπανημάτων ἕνεκα· τελεῖν γὰρ τὸ δαπανᾶν, καὶ πολυτελεῖς οἱ πολλὰ ἀναλίσκοντες καὶ εὐτελεῖς οἱ ὀλίγα (2.40d). Despite its fanciful semantic assumptions, this passage is significant for mainly three points. First, Athenaeus underlines the traditional character of the ritual event; its performance is situated within a temporal spectrum where the present and the past are linked through the reenactment of sanctioned ancient beliefs. Second, by associating the term with a verb that denotes consumption, Athenaeus points to the intricate socioeconomic dimensions of ritual performances. Third, the adjective that Athenaeus employs to describe the traditional character of the religious rituals, μυστική, leads us to some additional marked connotations that this term had carried since classical antiquity: more often than not, τελετή, usually in the plural, referred to the rites performed in the context of mystery cults.[8] The term preserved its religious associations in medieval Greek. In modern Greek, in addition to its sacred usage (e.g. Ἡ τελετὴ τοῦ Ἐπιταφίου), τελετή is widely employed in secular contexts with the generic meaning of ritual, ceremony: e.g. τελετὴ ἀποφοίτησης (commencement ceremony), τελετὴ ὁρκωμοσίας (inauguration ceremony), τελετὴ ἀπονομῆς βραβείων (awards ceremony), etc.

Δρώμενα, deriving from δρᾶν (the Doric equivalent of ποιεῖν, as Aristotle observes in his *Poetics* 1448b1) and often understood in juxtaposition with λεγόμενα (sacred, religious discourses), also alludes to the performative aspect of ritual in both senses, as a spectacle and as an enacted system of traditional or collectively communicated symbolic discourses. In the classical period, δρᾶν and δρώμενα seem to have been predominantly unmarked words meaning respectively "to do" or "to accomplish" and "deeds" or "acts."[9] Both δρώμενα and δρᾶν are widely employed with a ritual meaning from the Roman period onwards, especially in Plutarch and Pausanias, where they often refer to rites performed in mystery cults. Athenaeus (14.660a) and Hesychius, s.v., indicate that the verb (δρᾶν) was also understood in the specific sense of sacrifice. Frequently, the context in which these terms are employed suggests that the sacred deeds they describe were invested with specific symbolic meanings. This is made explicit in a

---

[8] On this see Burkert 1987:9–11.

[9] The epigraphical evidence (*Inscriptiones Graecae* I³ 4B.4 and 244C.11) for a marked ritual meaning of δρᾶν in the classical period discussed by van der Burg (1939:52) is inconclusive (I³ 244C.11) or based on restoration (I³ 4B.4). However, for a discussion of δρησμοσύνη ἱερῶν in the sense of "performance of ritual" in the *Homeric Hymn to Demeter* (476) see Richardson 1974:303–304. Cf. Kamerbeek's view on Sophocles' *Oedipos at Colonus* 1644 (Kamerbeek 1984:222). For the words δρᾶν and δρώμενα see the detailed discussion by Schreckenberg 1960:1–73 and 122–127, respectively.

passage from Eusebius, where it is stated that sacred rituals expressed symbolically ancient beliefs (οἱ περὶ τὰς τελετὰς ὀργιαυμοὶ καὶ τὰ δρώμενα συμβολικῶς ἐν ταῖς ἱερουργίαις τὴν τῶν παλαιῶν ἐμφαίνει διάνοιαν [*Praeparatio Evangelica* (Preparation of the Gospels) 3.1]). Plutarch juxtaposes δρώμενα and δεικνύμενα (that is, sacred objects that were shown in the context of initiation rites in mysteries; *De Iside et Osiride* [On Isis and Osiris] 352c), thus alluding to the multivocality and complementarity of the symbolic media employed in ritual contexts. Less often, δρᾶν is used in association with rites of passage. In a consolatory letter that he wrote to his wife after the death of their daughter Timoxena, Plutarch suggests to her that she should be brave and hold on to the composed manners prescribed for such occasions by tradition. In the case of an infant's death, he reminds her, old ancestral customs dictate that "people do not pour libations over their dead infants, nor do they perform for them any of the other rites that one is expected to perform for the dead" (τοῖς γὰρ αὐτῶν νηπίοις ἀποθανοῦσιν οὔτε χοὰς ἐπιφέρουσιν οὔτ' ἄλλα δρῶσι περὶ αὐτὰ οἷ' εἰκὸς ὑπὲρ θανόντων ποιεῖν [τοὺς ἄλλους] [*Consolatio ad uxorem* (Consolation to his wife) 612a; trans. Russell 1993, slightly adapted here]).

In all phases of the Greek language, primarily the religious, but also the secular, celebrations are denoted by the terms ἑορτή, ἑορτάζω and πανήγυρις, πανηγυρίζω, both having connotations of collective participation and of leisure, break from the everyday routine. In Christian literature and throughout Byzantium until today, the major Christian religious rite, the Mass, is described by the word λειτουργία. In ancient Greek, the term was predominantly used in the sense of public, religious or secular, service. Another highly marked term employed in formal Christian contexts is the word ἀκολουθία, which refers to all other religious ceremonies (e.g. Vespers, Midnight Office, the Hours, the funeral service).

Clearly, individual Greek terms tend to refer to specific domains of ritual activity. With the possible exception of the usage of τελετή (and τελετουργία) in modern times and particularly in formal contexts, Greek language does not provide an all-inclusive, broad term equivalent to *ritual* as it is regularly employed in modern English.[10] Our discussion of Greek terminology has focused on a number of major features of ritual behavior that call for further elaboration: (public) performance, collectivity, traditionality, symbolicity, order, solemnity, and a break from routine activities. Here we want to provide only some initial general comments to serve as directional markers toward the more detailed discussion of the *ritual poetics* that we undertake in the next part of this chapter.

---

[10] On aspects of ancient Greek ritual terminology cf. Calame 1991:196–204 and Graf 1996: 1318–1319.

Inherent in τελετή and δρώμενα is a sense of enacting, execution, and completion. The much discussed issue of the possible associations between δρώμενα and δράμα is beyond the scope of the present discussion. However, the point could be made that all these etymologically-related terms point to comparable semantic aspects of performativity. In rituals, performance is the *mimêsis* of a "script" of usually symbolic actions (δρώμενα συμβολικῶς) where the actors are also spectators.[11] Not rarely this double role of the participants entails both their ontological involvement with the enacted "script" and an epistemological distancing from the performed spectacle that invests their actions with a certain and varying, from occasion to occasion, reflexivity. This performance, as we will also see later, is executed through a variety of media, often employed with redundancy and in a specific order. Since, however, in such a performance the role of the actor coincides with the role of the spectator, the performative interpretation of the "script" does not preclude innovations or divergence. Deviations from established patterns remain recognizable as such in the context of the common culturally defined patterns of communication that the participants share. Often ritual performances tend to be assessed by their participants in terms of their expected performative efficacy[12]—in the sense *performative* is employed in speech act theory. This expected performative efficacy involves metaphorical discourses and actions that transfer the participating subjects from a specific initial position to the desired one.[13] In that respect it is not irrelevant, we believe, that τελετή is sometimes etymologically linked with τέλειος and explicitly described as a process at the end of which the individual accomplishes the desired perfection.[14]

---

[11] Rappaport views participation as a significant differentiating criterion between ritual and dramatic performance/spectacle (1999:134–137); such a polarization, however, should not be overemphasized. For a discussion of mainly terminological issues regarding ritual, drama, and spectacle cf. Gluckman and Gluckman 1977. The performative dimensions of ritual and its associations with theater have been the subject of several discussions in the fields of anthropology and performance studies. Tambiah has explored the performativity of rituals in his seminal article of 1981 (reprinted in Tambiah 1985a:123–166). Victor Turner synthesized the analogies between ritual events, drama, and social processes in his theory of "social drama"; see Turner 1969; 1974; 1982b; and especially 1987, where he emphasizes that performativity is an elemental feature of human expression and experience in general: "if man is a sapient animal, a toolmaking animal, a self-making animal, a symbol-using animal, he is, no less, a performing animal. *Homo performans* not in the sense, perhaps, that a circus animal may be a performing animal, but in the sense than man is a self-performing animal—his performances are, in a way, *reflexive*, in performing he reveals himself to himself" (81). Despite its universalistic overtones, Turner's model remains instructive in several ways. Schechner's studies on performance and ritual also offer interesting comparative material (Schechner 1985; 1988; 1993).

[12] On ritual efficacy see Rappaport 1999:108–113.

[13] Fernandez's discussion of the performative dynamics of metaphor in ritual contexts is most insightful; see Fernandez 1972; 1974.

[14] Plato *Phaedrus* 249C; also Maximus Confessor *Ad. Dion. ep.* 8. 6: τὰ μυστήρια . . . τέλη καὶ τελετὰς ἐκάλουν ὡς τελειούσας καὶ εἰς τὸ τέλειον ἀγούσας τοὺς τελουμένους.

Indications of a perception of ritual activity as solemn, collective business are preserved in the concept of λειτουργία. In ancient Greece λειτουργία was a serious enterprise, a service, offered for communally-defined sacred or secular needs, as it still defines the service offered to God both by the officiating clergy and the congregation—described precisely as λαός in the official liturgical manuals—who participate in the celebration of the Mass with prescribed antiphonic exchanges with the priest and with gestures of piety. Comparable are the connotations of the highly marked ancient Greek term ὄργια. Most probably etymologically related with ἔρδω, from which also comes the Greek word for work (ἔργον), this term was used in connection with mystery cults in ancient Greece[15] before its ideologically charged modifications with the advent of Christianity and throughout Byzantium, and its semantic "degeneration" in modern Greek, where it is encountered only in its metaphorical sense of sexual orgy and chaotic or sensational disorder.[16] Not unlike other premodern societies at large,[17] rituals are often perceived in traditional Greek contexts in terms of communal obligations and in association with economic activities, as the ancient λειτουργία and the aforementioned passage from Athenaeus indicate, and the Byzantine Mass less directly, but in comparable reciprocal terms, suggests in the prayer addressed to God: τὰ σὰ ἐκ τῶν σῶν σοὶ προσφέρομεν ("to you things of your things we are offering").[18] Notwithstanding their solemnity, religious festivities do not preclude revelry, dance, singing, or other ludic forms of social interaction and spectacles such as athletic and musical contests. As the term πανήγυρις (assembly; in contemporary Greek πανηγύρι) suggests, these are occasions for *collective* sharing and celebration of traditional cosmological values[19] often accompanied by forms of *collective* re-creation, in the sense of both amusement and creative rehandling of inherited forms of artistic expression.

In a famous passage, Thucydides presents Pericles taking pride in sharing with his compatriots the privilege of enjoying a great number of public contests and religious festivities throughout the year. These festivities offer the Athenian citizens

[15] For a detailed discussion of the ancient Greek meanings of the term see van der Burg 1939.

[16] It would be worth undertaking a systematic study of the ideological parameters of the "degeneration" of certain ancient Greek terms in medieval and modern Greek; Nietzsche's *Zur Genealogie der Moral* may offer an intriguing theoretical framework for such an exploration.

[17] Victor Turner observes that in parts of Polynesia people refer to annual rituals as the "work" of the gods, while in Bantu-speaking areas in Africa the same term is employed to describe the job of a ritual specialist, a hunter, a cultivator, or other workers (1977:39).

[18] On ritual reciprocity in ancient Greek contexts see Seaford 1994a; cf. Alexiou 2002b:328–332.

[19] The term "cosmological values" is used here in the sense Tambiah defines it: cosmology refers not only to sacred religious beliefs but also to any "unquestionable" sanctioned social, political, and cultural norms and conceptions that "compose the universe" of a specific society (1985a:129–131).

opportunities for relaxation and a break from ordinary tiring activities (καὶ μὴν καὶ τῶν πόνων πλείστας ἀναπαύλας τῇ γνώμῃ ἐπορισάμεθα, ἀγῶσι μέν γε καὶ θυσίαις διετησίοις νομίζοντες [2.38.1]). A different perspective is expressed by the so-called "Old Oligarch" in the *Constitution of the Athenians* who criticizes the Athenian's proclivity to festivities.[20] In Byzantium, the excessive revelry that often accompanied religious celebrations gave rise to severe condemnations on the part of Church officials. In the twelfth century, for instance, Balsamon would vehemently castigate his contemporaries for indulging in dances, games, and mundane economic exchanges on saints' days.[21] Ritual activities, in other words, are perceived as relieving breaks, or even ruptures, in the regular course of everyday time and, like dramatic performances, take place in specifically demarcated time and space. Even religious festivals constitute occasions for repose—what Strabo (1st c. BCE–1st c. CE) calls ἑορταστικὴ ἄνεσις (10.3.9)—and for ludic social and cultural interactions. In such ritual contexts, regular social norms are suspended or subverted and carnivalesque modes of expression may, in certain cases, come into play, thus informing the ritual process with a dynamic heteroglossia interlinking diverse domains of human experience and expression. This heteroglossia, in combination with the reflexivity involved in the role of the participants not as mere spectators but as actors in an enacted system of communicative codes, allows individuals room for flexibility and creativity. The role of individual agency on such occasions should be viewed in terms of a *continuum* defined at one end by rigidity (e.g. strictly prescribed religious rites like baptism, the Mass, etc.), and at the other by freedom and improvisation (e.g. carnival).[22]

Rituals are also viewed as repositories of collective memory and traditional modes of not rarely symbolic expression and communication. Since we will come back to this matter later in this chapter, suffice it to observe here that it is such a sense of traditionality (παράδοσις, Athenaeus; πάτρια καὶ παλαιὰ ἤθη, Plutarch; ἡ τῶν παλαιῶν διάνοια, Eusebius) that makes people perceive rituals

---

[20] [Xenophon] *Athênaiôn Politeia* (Constitution of the Athenians) 2.9.

[21] Rallis-Potlis, 3.465.6. Comparable is the attitude of Plato toward singing and dancing in religious contexts (see, e.g. *Laws* 652a1–674c7); cf. Henrichs 1998:52, 55. On aspects of the Church's criticisms against pagan spectacles and festivities in Byzantium see Magdalino 1990; also Roilos, forthcoming; on early Byzantium with an emphasis on John Chrysostom see Pasquato 1976; on πανήγυρις in Byzantium see Vryonis 1981.

[22] Carnival has often been employed as model case for the exploration of such dynamics; Bakthin's analysis of the carnivalesque, especially as undertaken in his *Rabelais and His World* remains influential (Bakhtin 1984); for a critique of the Bakhtinian approach and its applicability specifically to medieval European culture see the occasionally more moderate discussion in Gurevich 1988; for anthropological approaches influenced by Bakhtin's discussion of the carnivalesque see Kelly and Kaplan 1990:136–139.

as marked channels of cultural transmission and historical continuity, or as "promises about continuity."[23] Closely related to traditionality are the elements of repetitiveness, order, and formalization that often characterize ritual activities. Again, these features must be viewed not in absolute terms but in terms of a *continuum*. Perhaps the most rigid adherence to the formalization and repetitiveness of ritual reenactment is observed in prescribed religious rites like those that in the Greek Orthodox Church are precisely known as ἀκολουθίαι (services)—originally meaning *order* in the singular—or in secular political rituals like those described in a tenth-century Byzantine treatise attributed to the emperor Konstantinos Porphyrogennetos entitled Ἔκθεσις τῆς Βασιλείου Τάξεως, where τάξις also signifies order. Another issue that is explored in detail later in this chapter is symbolicity, which is often determined and legitimized by tradition, as the relevant passage from Eusebius, quoted above, suggests. For now, the point should be made that this feature contributes to a perception of rituals as enacted modes of communication and interaction among individuals who share more or less common cosmological ideas.

Our attempt to explore "emic" Greek terms and concepts has been inevitably, but also deliberately, selective and heuristic: if "reading" cultures entails "writing" cultures, that is, constructing textual discourses about other discourses,[24] one should be aware of the discursivity of one's own interpretive enterprise and try to eschew essentializing and definite verdicts, especially when exploring such extensive and notoriously "dangerous" fields as the Greek grounds—grounds full of gaps, continuities, discontinuities, transformations, and ambiguities. The discussion above, though, has addressed, we hope, some elemental features of ritual activity as mainly, but not solely, viewed in Greek contexts, features that can help us venture a working definition of ritual. Modifying Tambiah's apt description of ritual and being aware of the necessity of its adjustment to specific sociocultural contexts, we would define ritual as [the enacted process of a] "culturally constructed system of symbolic communication. It is constituted of patterned and ordered sequences of words and acts, often expressed in multiple media, whose content and arrangement

---

[23] Sally Moore and Barbara Myerhoff employ this apt phrase in connection with the significance of repetitiveness and order in ritual (1977a:17).

[24] The discursivity of an anthropologist's attempt at reading and reconstructing a culture has been the subject of a number of recent debates; on the "poeticity" of anthropological accounts see especially Clifford 1986a; 1986b; Rabinow 1986; Marcus and Fischer 1986:45–76. Such an awareness of the ethnographer's positionality has recently led to attempts at expressive experimentations in ethnographic writing; see the articles collected in Brady 1991, especially Tedlock 1991; Benson 1991; Bruner 1991; Turner 1991; cf. also Diamond 1986. Comparable is Heyden White's dismantling of the literariness of historiography and the mechanisms of "emplotment" in historiographic accounts (see in particular White 1978).

are [often][25] characterized in varying degrees by formality, stereotypy, condensation, and redundancy."[26] The performance of this process, almost always situated within a broader nexus of social and cultural discourses, is not impervious, we would emphasize, to alterations and manipulations on the part of individual or group agencies. As will be illustrated below in this chapter, such a possibility is linked with the culture-bound sense of ritual-making. This sense derives from the accumulation and communication of ritual experiences in a given society and may further inform other activities and forms of expression in this society as well as determine attempts at ritual experimentation. As with every definition, the notional constituents of our proposed working definition need further elaboration. These notions will be developed in the next part of this chapter, along with our elaboration of the proposed concept of ritual poetics.

II

Our analysis of ritual poetics presupposes an understanding of ritual as a dynamically enacted communicative system of collectively shared, or collectively marked out, cultural, religious or secular, constructs. Ritual employs a variety of symbolic and indexical media, both verbal and, mainly, representational—visual, sensory, acoustic.[27]

Greek—ancient, medieval, and modern—as well as foreign commentaries on ritual acts bear on the symbolic communicative function of ritual. Appearance and special dress, for instance, are invested with specific symbolic connotations in ritual contexts. In his treatise on Isis and Osiris, Plutarch offers a stimulating explication of the dress of the priests of the Egyptian goddess:

[25] This qualification is necessary if arbitrary universalizing approaches to ritual and ritual-making are to be avoided; illuminating, in this respect, are the cases of nonce rituals discussed in Moore 1977.

[26] Tambiah 1985a:128. The bibliography on ritual is vast. We have found particularly incisive the following studies: Bateson 1958; Goffman 1956; 1967; Turner 1967; 1969; 1982a; 1982b; Geertz 1973a; 1980; Bourdieu 1977; Fernandez 1977; Smith 1982; Rappaport 1984; 1999; Kerzter 1988; Staal 1989; Grimes 1990; Kelly and Kaplan 1990; Bloch 1992; Schechner 1993; for insightful critical overviews of the various attempts at defining and analyzing ritual see Bell 1992; 1997.

[27] As has been cogently observed, "the symbol is the smallest unit of ritual" (Turner 1967:19); however, Turner's full definition of ritual as "formal behaviour for occasions not given over to technological routine, having reference to beliefs in mystical beings or powers" (ibid.) is too restrictive to accommodate the multivalence of ritual as understood here. Rappaport's distinction between symbolic and indexical signification in ritual is useful, despite its bipolar rigidity: he connects the employment of symbols with the conveyance of what he calls "canonical messages" and the use of indices with "self-referential messages" (1997:52–68; on symbols in ritual cf. also Fernandez 1974:120–121; Leach 1976:9–24).

For she is wise . . . and discloses the divine mysteries to those who truly and justly have the name of "bearers of the sacred vessels" and "wearers of the sacred robes." These are they who within their own soul, as though within a box, bear the sacred lore about the gods clear of all superstition and pedantry [. . .]. [. . .] the fact that the deceased votaries of Isis are decked with sacred garments is a sign [σύμβολόν έστι] that this sacred lore accompanies them, and that they pass to the other world possessing this and nothing else. It is a fact . . . that having a beard and wearing a coarse cloak does not make philosophers, nor does dressing in linen and shaving the hair make votaries of Isis; but the true votary of Isis is he who, when the things that are displayed and performed in the ceremonies [δεικνύμενα καὶ δρώμενα] connected with these gods are conveyed to him according to the established tradition, uses reason in investigating and in studying the truth contained therein.

It is true that most people are unaware of this very ordinary and minor matter: the reason why the priests remove their hair and wear linen garments. Some persons do not care at all to have any knowledge about such things, while others say that the priests, because they revere the sheep, abstain from using its wool, as well as its flesh; and that they shave their heads as a sign of mourning, and that they wear their linen garments because of the color which the flax displays when in bloom, and which is like to the heavenly azure which enfolds the universe. But for all this there is only one true reason, which is to be found in the words of Plato: "for the impure to touch the pure is contrary to divine ordinance." . . . And it is from forms of surplus that wool, fur, hair, and nails originate and grow. So it would be ridiculous that these persons in their holy living should remove their own hair by shaving and making their bodies smooth all over, and then should put on and wear the hair of domestic animals. We should believe that when Hesiod said, "Cut not the sere from the green when you honor the gods with full feasting, / Paring with glittering steel the member that hath the five branches," he was teaching that men should be clean of such things when they keep high festival, and they should not amid the actual ceremonies engage in clearing away and removing any sort of surplus matter. But the flax springs from the earth which is immortal; it yields edible seeds, and supplies a plain and cleanly clothing, which does not oppress by the weight required for warmth (352b–e; trans. Babbitt 1936, slightly adapted here).

Plutarch articulates here an inchoate semiological approach to the dressing protocol of the Egyptian priests. His remarks make it clear that the specific topic in question is not a mere practical detail, but an important element of the cult of the godess bearing secondary connotations that are open to a variety of even allegorical interpretations. Different people, says Plutarch, find different meanings in such customs, but he prefers to offer an alternative, more moralistic, albeit equally symbolic, interpretation. The marked term σύμβολον that he employs in his comments highlights his understanding of the ritual detail he describes as an encoded message that needs to be deciphered.

In eighth-century Byzantium, the Patriarch Germanos composed a treatise on the sacred meaning of the Christian rites, notably the Mass, of the paraphernalia used for their performance, and of the architectonic arrangement of the typical Christian temple. In this work, Germanos pays special attention to the importance of the dressing protocol of the priests: each detail of their appearance, every piece of clothing, and every accessory is attributed a specific symbolic meaning. Germanos employs a diction that recalls formulaic expressions conventionally used in Christian allegorizations of biblical and ancient Greek literature.[28] His textualization of Christian rites, that is, his reading of ritual objects and actions as sequences of encrypted symbolic discourses, constitutes a paradigmatic example of medieval Greek ritual poetics. The implicit parallelism between ritual and text that runs through his extensive commentary is underlined by his employment of a variety of terms often encountered in Byzantine exegetical tradition: σύμβολον, αἴνιγμα, τύπος, (προ)τυποῦν, δηλοῦν, σημαίνειν, ἐμφαίνειν, μιμεῖσθαι, μηνύειν, ἑρμηνεύεσθαι. His reference to the haircut of the Christian priests is formulated in parallel, if more explicit, terms, as in Plutarch's account about the Isian votaries:

Τὸ δὲ ξύρισμα τῆς κεφαλῆς τοῦ ἱερέως, καὶ τὸ γυροειδὲς αὐτοῦ τμῆμα τὸ μέσον τῶν τριχῶν, ἀντὶ τοῦ ἀκανθίνου στεφάνου, ὅνπερ ὁ Χριστὸς ἐφόρεσεν. Ὁ ἐν τῇ κεφαλῇ τοῦ ἱερέως περικείμενος διπλοῦς στέφανος ἐκ τῆς τῶν τριχῶν σημειώσεως εἰκονίζει τὴν τοῦ ἀποστόλου Πέτρου τιμίαν κάραν, ἣν ἐν τῷ τοῦ Κυρίου καὶ Διδασκάλου κηρύγματι ἀποσταλείς, καὶ καρεὶς ὑπὸ τῶν ἀπειθούντων τῷ λόγῳ, . . . ταύτην ὁ διδάσκαλος Χριστὸς εὐλόγησε, καὶ ἐποίησε τὴν ἀτιμίαν τιμήν, καὶ τὴν χλεύην εἰς δόξαν, καὶ ἔθηκεν ἐπὶ τὴν κεφαλὴν αὐτοῦ στέφανον, οὐκ ἐκ λίθων τιμίων, ἀλλὰ τῷ λίθῳ καὶ τῇ πέτρᾳ τῆς πίστεως αὐτοῦ ἐκλάμπουσαν, ὑπὲρ χρυσίον καὶ τοπάζιον καὶ λίθους

---

[28] For a discussion of such allegorizations in Byzantium, with an emphasis on the twelfth century, see Roilos forthcoming.

τιμίους. Κορυφὴ γὰρ κακαλλωπισμένη καὶ στέφανος τοῦ δωδεκαλίθου οἱ ἀπόστολοί εἰσι, Πέτρα δὲ ὁ παναγιώτατος ἀπόστολος ὑπάρχει ἀρχιεράρχης τοῦ Κυρίου.[29]

The shaving of the head of the priest and the round shape in the middle of the hair stands for the thorny wreath that Christ wore. The double crown that the priest bears on his head is an icon of the holy head of Saint Peter. After Peter was sent off to teach the Word of the Lord and had his hair cut by those who did not believe in his sermons, . . . Christ blessed his holy head and made the dishonor honor and the humiliation glory, and put on Peter's head a crown not made out of precious stones, but, nevertheless, glowing more than topaz and gold and all of the precious stones, thanks to the stone and rock of his faith. For the decorated crown and wreath of twelve stones are the Apostles, and the most holy Peter, the first priest of Christ, is the real Stone (our translation).

In more recent times, Father Joseph François Lafitau, a Tylorian before Tylor with an exceptionally inflated imagination, offers some of the most idiosyncratic allegorical readings of ritual practices ever written, in an interesting account of the "customs of the American Indians compared with the customs of primitive times." In a predictable colonialist reversal of the evaluative connotations of the term "primitive," and often in a manner reminiscent of medieval commentaries, "American Indian" customs are viewed as telling survivals from primordial times and are assessed on the basis of their alleged parallels with, or even direct origins from, the venerated ancient Greek and biblical traditions. Perhaps the least unbridled excursion into "exotic" indigenous American life he undertakes in chapter eight of his work, where he describes "death, burial, and mourning" in a relatively systematic way. His account of mourning practices begins with some interesting remarks about the customary appearance of the mourners:

> The most essential law and the most outstanding sign of mourning was having the hair cut. For, as they initiated the dead or dying to the tomb by cutting off the hair consecrated to the deities of the nether world, so it was a kind of initiation and mystic death for the people nearest the deceased and who, having just reasons for regretting him, bore witness that it was not their fault that they did not follow him and that they would die as much as it was in their power to do so.[30]

---

[29] Migne, *Patrologia Graeca* 92.392D–393A.
[30] Lafitau 1977:241.

Van Gennep would have perhaps endorsed Lafitau's interpretation of this mourning ritual. Lafitau's further elaboration on the topic, however, is replete with a number of muddled references to Greek and biblical traditions with a view to substantiating his overarching thesis that the "American Indians" are directly related to ancient peoples, notably the Greeks and the Jews.

The symbolic communicative function of dress codes in secular rituals has been wittily commented upon by Thomas Carlyle. In an amusing twist of common expectations, he expressed the view that in political rituals appearance *is* the content or, to reverse Plutarch's wording in the passage discussed above, "a coarse cloak" *does* make philosophers, as the crown *does* make a queen or a king, and the color purple *does* make the Byzantine emperor: "Lives there a man that can figure a naked Duke of Windlestraw addressing a naked House of Lords? Imagination, choked as in mephitic air, recoils on itself, and will not forward with the picture."[31]

Special ways of dressing, hair-cutting, or tonsure could be viewed as constituents of a broader metaphorical ritual syntactic whole that is metonymically constructed out of interconnected unities of semantic polyvalence. The performance of such apparently minor ritual actions in both religious and secular contexts often becomes the occasion for negotiation of both symbolic, traditionally sanctioned meanings, and power relations. Tambiah has illustrated how the tonsure ceremony in Thailand can be transformed into a vehicle for the emergence of new sociopolitical meanings that are built upon a traditional vocabulary of verbal and representational symbols. His discussion of a historical royal tonsure ceremony that took place in 1866 illustrates the intrinsic manner in which conventional symbolism converses with "nonconventional implicatures" of broader political relevance.[32] The traditional symbolism of ritual objects and acts, in other words, is not impervious to innovative rehandlings that reorganize and reformulate established systems and channels of ritual communication and sociopolitical interaction.

The concept of *ritual poetics* addresses the interaction between the deep, socially and culturally defined structures of ritual and aesthetic ways of communication—*structure* being employed here as elsewhere in this chapter not with its static structuralist connotations, but in the sense of culturally identifiable forms of expression. Such an approach involves two main methodological steps: first, an exploration of the homologies between the two constituents of the concept, that is, the poetics of ritual and ritual as inscribed and manipulated in cultural, notably aesthetic, expressions; and, second and most important, the pervasiveness of the interpenetratedness of both in broader social and political discourses.

---

[31] Carlyle 1908:45–46 (quoted in Kertzer 1988:5).
[32] Tambiah 1985a:157–161.

The basic homology between ritual and cultural systems of communication, we contend, is their semiotic, often symbolic, character. The textualization of ritual encountered in an embryonic but paradigmatic form in Germanos' analysis of Christian rites finds a parallel but, no doubt more sophisticated, contemporary formulation in Geertz's interpretive theory of culture. Viewing cultural and social expressions as, on the surface, enigmatical systems of "webs of significance," Geertz offers a re-writing and reading of such phenomena as texts located in specific discursive contexts. The parallelism between textuality, or what we would prefer to call *poeticity*, and ritualistic modes of expression looms large in his discussion of the Balinese cockfight: "The culture of a people," he concludes, "is an ensemble of texts, which the anthropologist strains to read over the shoulders of those to whom they properly belong."[33] Geertz perceives and explicates the traditional cockfight as an art form: "an image, fiction, a model, a metaphor, the cockfight is a means of expression." Albeit not totally untainted by a rather colonialist interpretive essentialism,[34] Geertz's textualization of Balinese customs and culture in this specific essay alerts us to the discursivity of such symbolic communicative acts—and of the anthropologist's own interpretive "thick description."

In an unjustifiably neglected passage from Περὶ τοῦ μὴ χρᾶν ἔμμετρα νῦν τὴν Πυθίαν (On the fact that the Pythia does not now prophesy in verse), Plutarch articulates his own ingenious approach to the interconnection between poeticity and ritual practices, while at the same time addressing the issue of the culturally and historically determined position of the construing subject. His essay, which has the form of a dialogue, marks a crisis in traditional modes of ritual communication and interpretation in a period of cultural and historical liminalities. The unusual topic of his discussion is the decline of the old habit of recording the Delphic oracles in poetic discourse. How does the interdependence of ritual construction of meaning and its poetic conveyance affect the reception and evaluation of sanctioned religious and cultural values? This is the question that Plutarch's discussants are invited to explore. Commenting on the semantic dynamics and polyvalence of ritual objects, one of the characters in Plutarch's dialogue observes:

Ἀριστοτέλης μὲν οὖν μόνον Ὅμηρον ἔλεγε κινούμενα ποιεῖν ὀνόματα διὰ τὴν ἐνέργειαν, ἐγὼ δὲ φαίην ἂν καὶ τῶν ἀναθημάτων τὰ ἐνταυθοῖ μάλιστα συγκινεῖσθαι καὶ συνεπισημαίνειν

---

[33] Geertz 1973a:452.

[34] For an apt, although occasionally inadequately nuanced, critique of Geertz' analysis of the Balinese cockfight see Crapanzano 1986; cf. also Rabinow 1986:241–247; and Marcus' and Fischer's more balanced assessment of Geertz' overall theoretical contribution (Marcus and Fischer 1986:145–146).

τῇ τοῦ θεοῦ προνοίᾳ, καὶ τούτων μέρος μηδὲν εἶναι κενὸν μηδ' ἀναίσθητον, ἀλλὰ πεπλεῖσθαι πάντα θειότητος.

Aristotle said that only Homer could devise words possessing movement because of their vigor, but I would add that the dedications here are especially capable of moving and giving signs in accord with divine providence; and no part of them is empty or senseless, but all are replete with divinity (*De Pythiae oraculis* [On the oracles of the Pythia] 398a; trans. Russell 1993, slightly adapted here).

Clearly, ritual objects are invested here, as in Germanos' Christian allegorization, with a poetic vigor (ἐνέργεια) in both meanings of the Greek ποίησις: poetry and doing/making. They are viewed as units of a poetic, symbolic whole that articulate a dynamic performance of meaning. If we have been used to thinking of language and the world in terms of the performative potential of words or "how words do things," Plutarch's description helps us reflect on the ways in which things do (ποιοῦσι) not only other things, but also "words," symbolic discourses—how they articulate a semantic system open to various interpretations "in (semantic) accord with divine providence" (συνεπισημαίνειν τῇ τοῦ θεοῦ προνοίᾳ). By ascribing a similar semantic dynamism to both communicative systems, that is, poetry and ritual modes of expression, Plutarch highlights their parallel symbolic deep structures. It is our contention that ritual signification, not unlike poetic discourse, can be conceived of in terms of a projection "of the principle of equivalence from the axis of selection into the axis of combination."[35] Ritual context could be viewed as an overarching signifying system that invests its syntactical constituents, verbal or representational, with marked semantic connotations.

Nowhere in Plutarch's treatise is the interconnection between poetry, ritual prophesying, and ritual acts, and between cosmological values and their symbolic reenactment, more suggestively expressed than in a passage discussing the fate of Sibyl, the primordial oracular poetess:

Ὁ μὲν Σαραπίων ἐμνήσθη τῶν ἐπῶν, ἐν οἷς ὕμνησεν ἑαυτήν, ὡς οὐδ' ἀποθανοῦσα λήξει μαντικῆς, ἀλλ' αὐτὴ μὲν ἐν τῇ σελήνῃ περίεισι τὸ [καλούμενον] φαινόμενον γενομένη πρόσωπον, τῷ δ' ἀέρι τὸ πνεῦμα συγκραθὲν ἐν φήμαις ἀεὶ φορήσεται καὶ κληδόσιν· ἐκ δὲ τοῦ σώματος μεταβαλόντος ἐν τῇ γῇ πόας καὶ ὕλης ἀναφυομένης βοσκήσεται ταύτην ἱερὰ θρέμματα χρόας τε παντοδαπὰς ἴσχοντα καὶ μορφὰς καὶ

35 Jakobson 1960:358.

ποιότητας ἐπὶ τῶν σπλάγχνων ἀφ' ὧν αἱ προδηλώσεις ἀνθρώποις τοῦ μέλλοντος.

Sarapion recalled the verses in which she [the Sibyl] sang of herself: she foretold that she would not cease from prophecy even after her death, but would go round and round with the moon, as what appears to us as the face in the moon; her spirit, she said, would mingle with air and travel on for ever in rumors and voices, while from her changed body grasses and woods would grow on earth on which animals reared for sacrifice would feed, displaying in their organs all kinds of colors, shapes, and qualities from which men would prognosticate the future (*De Pythiae oraculis* 398c–d; trans. Russell 1993, slightly adapted here).

Sibyl's poetic prophetic voice is invested here with a cosmic, eternally recycled power, which is supposed to be incessantly reenacted in the context of ritual sacrifices. Her enigmatic poetic discourse, encoded in her regenerated body, crosses temporal and territorial boundaries to be repeatedly transcribed, performed, and decoded in each symbolic, spatially and temporally demarcated, ritual enactment. Ritual, like "inspired" poetry, interlinks different levels of human experience and imagination, and is acted out in a process of cosmic reciprocity based on a series of analogies between different levels of existence—plants, animals, humans, divine world, universe—and perceived in terms of temporal and spatial intersections—earth, air, planets, the past, the present, the future. The homology between ritual microcosm and universal macrocosm—the cycle of the seasons and the movement of the planets—corresponds here to the homology between the semantic structures of prophesying poetry and ritual. Plutarch's passage could be, therefore, read as a metaphor for the construction and communication of meaning in rituals: the repeated reenactments of ritual conventions, in the case under discussion the performance of ritual divination, is open to different rehandlings and receptions, not unlike the reenactments of traditional poetic structures.

It is our position that the performance of meaning in rituals can be perceived as the repeated reworking of established symbolic conventions parallel to the formulaic reactivation of traditional oral poetic patterns. More often than not, ritual acts are articulated as a series of polyvalent semantic building blocks drawn on a long established vocabulary of symbolic communicative patterns. This vocabulary tends to convey specific cultural connotations in specific ritual contexts in accordance with the overall semantic experience accumulated and transmitted within a particular tradition.[36] Ritual is characterized by dense and multilayered

---

[36] For an analysis of such modes of signification in Greek ritual oral poetry see Roilos 1998.

extratextuality that reaches out of each specific performative occasion to an all-encompassing semantic traditionality or to communally recognized modes of signification. The meaning of such traditional ritual units is almost intuitively perceived by the participants or observers in the same way that in traditional oral poetry the semantic value of a specific epithet, for instance, is exploited. Albert Lord employs a telling example to illustrate the construction and conveyance of "traditionally intuitive meaning" in oral literature: in Slavic oral poetry, the phrase "drunken tavern" bears, in addition to its apparent denotative significance, a traditional one. It does not mean only a tavern where men get drunk. It carries with it the culturally specific meaning of forgetfulness, often associated with one's entrance into the other world; it connotates death.[37] This "traditional referentiality"[38] does not imply a monolithic adherence of ritual practices to old revered conventions; rather, it circumscribes, we argue, the always negotiable paradigmatic boundaries of continuously renewed syntagmatic constructions of signification.

Not unlike oral literature, ritual is often composed or re-composed, while being performed.[39] Ritual, in other words, should be viewed in terms of its habitual embeddedness in traditional modes of symbolic communication. It is the importance of *habitus* for the acquisition of a sense of ritual that endows ritual activities with the power to transform themselves, to negotiate or transgress traditional meanings, to rearrange social dynamics, and to inform other domains of human activity. *Habitus* puts emphasis not on the product of an action as a finished entity but on the action itself, not on a specific ritual or, for that matter, on a specific product of oral poetics, but on the socially and culturally determined sense of ritual, on ritual-making and ritualization.[40] It is at the intersection of a habitually constructed sense

---

[37] Lord 1960: 66; Lord's model may be viewed as an exemplum of ethnopoetics in the sense this research area is defined in folklore studies and anthropology. We would consider ethnopoetics pertinent to the study of *ritual poetics* to the extent that it can illustrate aspects of parallel culturally-defined patterns of producing and conveying meaning in performative contexts; in this respect, we have found especially illuminating the work of Baumann (especially 1977; also Bauman and Sherzer 1974), Hymes (especially 1981), D. Tedlock (1983), and Sherzer (1990). On the notion of context in linguistic anthropology see Goodwin and Duranti 1992. Relevant, but more socially oriented and therefore more pertinent to our *Problematik* of *ritual poetics* is the pioneering work of Fernandez on poetic contests in rural Spain (Fernandez 1976–7) and the work of Kligman (1988). Music and dance are elemental constituents of ritual and poetic performance in traditional societies. Although dance is explored in this book, music is not addressed in a systematic way; on the interaction of ritual and music see especially Turner 1968; Rouget 1985; Basso 1985; also Pitts 1991; Sugarman 1997; McDaniel 1998; Yatromanolakis 2000.

[38] For the meaning of "traditional referentiality" in oral literature see Foley 1991:39–60.

[39] For the coincidence of performance, composition, and reception in oral poetry see Lord 1960; cf. also idem. 1991:76–77; 1995:11, 102–103; more flexible is Nagy's reformulation of this idea as re-composition-in-performance; see especially Nagy 1996b:7–38.

[40] On *habitus* see Bourdieu 1977 (especially 72–95; 143–158); see also Bell 1992:79–80.

of ritual-making (ποιεῖν) and a habitual re-enactment of this sense in other cultural and social discourses that ritual poetics should be located.

Such a habitual approach to ritual, which, to repeat, is often a traditionally structured communicative process comparable to oral literature—another traditionally constructed system of communication—contributes to our understanding of ritual as a culturally defined *form* of communication. It is ritual's predominant function as an *all-encompassing form* that makes it flexible, receptive to a variety of meanings and symbolic units, and, to go one step further, poetically interactive with other forms of social and cultural discourses. This accentuation of *form*, which functions as receptacle for various contents, or even defines the content, brings ritual close to aesthetic modes of expression like literature—especially drama and poetry. If poetry can be perceived in terms of an emphasis on the formulation of the message, in terms, that is, of aesthetic manipulation of common linguistic elements on the basis of parallelism, opposition, and divergence from the semantic and syntactical conventions of everyday use of language, the same holds true, we submit, for ritual. Ritual does not create semantic wholes out of nothing; it draws on common, everyday, or often traditionally defined, experiential elements and, by inscribing them into its demarcated performative frame, invests them with particular communicative value.[41]

This process of signification does not necessarily entail a communicative disinvestment, but rather a marked modulation of the common semantic connotations of the elements that are inscribed into each specific ritual context. To repeat an example already discussed: the cutting of hair performed in a ritual context is not a matter of personal hygiene or elegance, but a sign often invested with particular traditional symbolism. This act of symbolic sacrifice stands for the surrender of one's self to another beloved or revered entity, be it a god or a lost dear person, which surpasses oneself. Having your hair cut, perhaps once a month, at a barber shop is an unmarked habit. Having your hair cut in the context of Greek Christian Orthodox baptism is a marked sign endowed with particular symbolic significance. Wearing your Harvard or Oxford gown while regularly working in Widener or Bodleian library may be perceived as a rather eccentrically marked habit; wearing it in the context of the Harvard commencement or the Oxford *Encaenia* is a ritually marked act prescribed by the conventions of the specific ceremony. Poetry, and especially (post-)modernist poetry, also functions as a semantic frame that invests the elements it employs with marked semantic connotations. This assimilating

---

[41] Pertinent to our discussion here is Goffman's frame analysis (Goffman 1974); relevant also is the emphasis of linguistic anthropology on the notion of context; see Duranti and Goodwin 1992.
[42] Genette 1969:150–151.

function of what we would call framing in poetry—which, to be sure, is at work in other cultural phenomena as well—has been memorably, although from another perspective, illustrated by Genette. If one takes a prose passage from a newspaper and presents it as a poem, Genette argues, the aesthetic value, the communicative effect, and the conditions of signification of this piece undergo a radical transformation. New expectations are created for the readers and new strategies of reception and interpretation come into play. Such a journalistic passage would acquire a different communicative function if transcribed into the following format conventionally associated with poetic discourse:

> Hier sur la Nationale sept
> Une automobile
> Roulant à cent à l' heure s' est jetée
> Sur un platane
> Ses quatre occupants ont été
> Tués.[42]

Our emphasis on the importance of form in ritual does not entail, as we hope has been clear so far, an endorsement of the view that ritual may be conceived of as an absolutely senseless conglomeration of formal characteristics. Form in ritual, we maintain, functions as an overarching structural frame that shapes and conveys a series of semantic connotations. In that respect, we oppose Bloch's interpretation of any redundant, repetitive, and formalized media of expression in ritual, especially in ritual speech, as devoid of any semantic relevance. Albeit insightfully comparing ritual to art forms like song and dance, he rather arbitrarily maintains that art, like ritual, is an inferior form of communication.[43] Bloch adopts this neo-Cartesian, if not (neo-)Platonic—not in the technical sense of the term—approach to art and ritual with a view to substantiating his functionalist argument that ritual's often inflated formalization serves the reaffirmation of the political establishment. Let's take an example from Greece. The Greek Orthodox liturgy, which even today is performed in its original linguistic form(s), is highly repetitive, formalized, and distanced from everyday speech and hardly rationally understood in its entirety by its audience. Nevertheless, being embedded in a long tradition of religious and historical sentiment, the Greek Orthodox liturgy is far from devoid of any semantic function, which is not necessarily nor is it only conducive to the reproduction of a given authoritative—religious/ecclesiastical—order. In the end, Bloch's approach

---

[43] Bloch 1974.
[44] For ritual and European modernism see Korg 1995; for aspects of the ritualization of literary texts

validates and reproduces the hegemony of Western rationalistic ideological discourses over indigenous modes of signification.

If Bloch compares ritual to art in order to underline the alleged problematic communicative efficacy of the former, modernist poets such as Mallarmé and Eliot draw similar parallels in order to foreground art's multilayered semantic dimensions. Opposing the prevalence of materialistic values in post-industrial Western societies and aiming at a rehandling of primordial or "primitive" modes of expression—in ways, it should be noted, that do not always succeed in transcending some paradoxes inherent in their overall modernist re-evaluation of literary and socio-cultural establishments—they offer intriguing readings of art as ritual. Drawing mainly on Frazer's influential *The Golden Bough*, Eliot repeatedly comments on the interaction between art and ritual—not only implicitly in his creative work, notably in *The Waste Land* and *Ash Wednesday*, but also, and in more direct terms, in his essays. In a similar vein, Mallarmé insists on the significance of the dialogue between art and—mainly religious—rituals. The Catholic Mass represented for him the utmost form of solemn aesthetic communication, whereas he viewed art, especially poetry, in terms of religious and ritual experiences. If Plutarch and Germanos put emphasis on the poeticity of ritual acts and symbols, the poetic text in its semantic and material composition was considered by Mallarmé as the reinscription of ritual modes of expression.[44]

The interaction between aesthetic or cultural phenomena at large and ritual can be dynamically illustrated in terms of Victor Turner's analysis of liminal and what he calls *liminoid* forms of cultural communication. Reformulating van Gennep's seminal theory of rites of passage and building upon his tripartite structural description of such rites—separation, marginality (liminality), re-aggregation[45]—Turner offers an illuminating, albeit at times excessively functionalist, parallel reading of modes of symbolic expression in tribal and post-tribal societies. Turner's model is based on the middle stage in van Gennep's pattern. This transitional phase, which can be prolonged, entails a suspension or reversal of everyday concepts of time, space, and order. The rites performed in this betwixt-and-between stage are characterized by a tendency to inventiveness and ludic behavior. The participants in such rituals, who defy classificatory categories, are engaged in a

---

in pre-industrial Greece (in seventeenth-century Renaissance Crete) see Roilos 2002a; for the interactions between ritual and medieval and modern Greek literature see Alexiou 2002b (unfortunately the present chapter was near completion before the appearance of Alexiou 2002b, and as a result it has not been profited from Alexiou's analysis as much as we would have wished).

[45] For a recent critique of the universalistic character of van Gennep's (and Turner's) tripartite model see Crapanzano 1980.

communicative interaction that Turner calls *communitas* or "antistructure," that is, "a relation quality of full, unmediated communication, even communion, between definite and determinate identities, which arises simultaneously in all kinds of groups, situations, and circumstances."[46] The playful and inventive transgression of everyday spatiotemporal limitations and sociocultural norms enacted during ritual liminal phases and the concomitant sense of *communitas* is preserved, according to Turner, in post-tribal societies mainly in the form of aesthetic modes of communication (literature, painting, dance, etc.), as well as in aspects of leisure activities and optional social interactions such as sports and games. Liminoid phenomena, albeit often of a more individualistic nature than ritual processes in tribal societies, should be viewed as events holistically, interactively, and sometimes, we would emphasize, subversively located within the broader sociocultural context of their production and reception. Turner's views are pertinent to our discussion of *ritual poetics* to the extent that they can shed light on aspects of the dialogue between what we would call *deep structures* in ritual and cultural systems of communication, and to the extent that they escape their own functionalist limits.

Ritual poetics should be understood in terms of a dialogic exchange between diverse domains—ordinary, aesthetic, cultural, social, political—of human interaction and expression. The pervasiveness of ritual poetics, we argue, is not confined to specific unidirectional influences—how a particular ritual is re-interpreted in a particular "text" of aesthetic/cultural expression or social action, or vice versa. These one-way relations are of great, but not of definitive, importance for mapping out ritual poetics in a particular sociocultural context. Intrinsic to ritual poetics are mechanisms of mutual, and more often than not, homologically defined, assimilations of modes of expression on a deep level rather than on the surface. The semiological webs with which ritual poetics works presupposes an interweaving of homological patterns, modes, and tropes of expression, notably symbols and metaphors, as Plutarch's passage about the semantic vigor of ritual objects indicated in inchoate but suggestive terms. A trope of crucial importance for the formulation of such homologies is metaphor. In its original Greek meaning, metaphor (μεταφορά, deriving from the verb μεταφέρω) denotes transference, movement, and transposition from one field of experience to another. Metaphor is an inherently dynamic and dialogic trope, hence its expressive and performative value, as well as its ability to mobilize subjects across different epistemological, situational,

---

[46] This overoptimistic, even static, view of *communitas*, which has received several justifiable criticisms, is considerably downplayed by Turner's occasional explicit references to the dynamics of ritual processes and their power to act drastically upon established social orders; see in particular his comments in Turner 1987:24.

and ontological domains.[47] These homologies are not static but potentially nego-tiable, open to reinterpretations, and interwoven in intricate nexuses of heteroglossic dialogues.

Ritual poetics, in other words, is defined in terms of *interdiscursivity.* The homological associations through which this interdiscursivity unfolds are habitually enacted, we would argue, in the same ways that "symbolic systems [. . .] are the products of practices which cannot perform their practical functions except insofar as they bring into play, in their practical state, principles which are not only coherent—i.e., capable of engendering intrinsically coherent practices compatible with the objective conditions—but also practical, in the sense of convenient, i.e., immediately mastered and manageable because obeying a 'poor' and economical logic."[48] The heteroglossic and interdiscursive character of ritual poetics makes it, we contend, a more flexible and inclusive analytical tool than *ritualization* as defined by Catherine Bell.[49] Whereas *ritualization* refers to *ritualized* activities, profane or sacred, *ritual poetics* is concerned not only with such activities, but also with the dialogic interaction of a habitually constructed sense of ritual-making with a variety of domains of human action and expression—ordinary behavior, organi-zation of time and space in everyday life, art (literature, music, dance, architecture, painting), sociopolitical processes, and cultural discourses.

First, the interdiscursivity of *ritual poetics* can be explored in everyday patterns of behavior. Just as simple everyday speech genres interact with complex genres of verbal art,[50] ritual deep structures can interact with or be reinscribed into patterns of typical everyday activities. In traditional Greek society, the temporal and spatial organization of everyday activities is often structured in ways that parallel ritual demarcations of space and time. Midday and midnight, for instance, are invested with a sense of liminality comparable to the betwixt-and-between phase of tradi-tional rites of passage.[51] These hours are marked as potentially dangerous segments in the cycle of the day where regular activities, especially the ones performed outside the boundaries of domesticated space, must be either suspended or executed with utmost caution. Marking the threshold between the two twelve-hour halves of the day, these hours are perceived as rather timeless points of transition,

---

[47] For an illuminating study of the use of metaphor in ritual see Fernandez 1974.
[48] Bourdieu 1977:109. The "practical coherence" of symbolic systems, according to Bourdieu, does not exclude their "irregularities and even incoherences," since they are "both equally necessary because inscribed in the logic of their genesis and functioning," ibid.
[49] For *ritualization* see Bell 1992:88–93; 197–223.
[50] Bakhtin 1986:60–102.
[51] Ritual time suspends or inverts everyday time and it may be perceived as "dream time;" on this see Leach 1961; 1988:33–41.

ambiguous and abnormal—even water springs are said to stop running then. They are considered "voiceless" breaks in the course of the day, where human actions and especially human voice—an elemental differentiating component of human identity—are considered to be subject to the potential detrimental intervention of supernatural powers, notably the Nereids. Hence the belief that one who works out in the fields should remain silent at these "voiceless" hours, lest s/he attracts the destructive attention of such powers.[52] These patterns of spatiotemporal demarcations are not, however, impervious to ambivalence: for instance, the most "voiceless" hour can become the time for the most explicit pronouncement of the ultimate defeat of evil, as the celebration of the resurrection of Christ at Easter midnight suggests.[53] Comparable homological interrelations between spatiotemporal segmentations of everyday life and ritual patterns of behavior have been documented in other traditional societies. In Algeria, for instance, ritual rhythm patterns and metaphorical associations are echoed in the symbolic connotations of night and day, which are further reproduced in the rhetoric of social and political discourses.[54] Simple habits such as sharing food in everyday situations can also become occasions for the enactment of beliefs associated with marked ritualistic modes of signification. It has also been observed that the ritually-charged practice of scapulomancy performed by Cretan villagers on otherwise ritually unmarked occasions articulates "a genuine semiotic of social, ethical, and practical concerns."[55]

In addition to the parallelism between liminal and liminoid modes of communication, and to the homologies between everyday activities and ritual patterns, another *locus* for an exploratory study of aspects of *ritual poetic* interdiscursivity is the interplay between religious and ritualized secular modes of social and political behavior. Much discussion has been devoted to conceptual and terminological matters regarding the relations between sacred and profane rituals. Gluckman, for example, although himself among the first to speak systematically of ritualization, on the one hand in the sense of the often symbolic incorporation of secular relationships into rituals, and on the other hand in terms of the embodiment of ritual patterns of communication in social relationships, would reserve the term *ritual* only for events involving metaphysical religious concepts, while proposing the term "ceremonious" for ritualized forms of secular behavior.[56]

---

52 Such beliefs were current in the areas of Arcadia and Laconia in the Peloponnese at least until a decade ago (1991–1992) when one of us (P. Roilos) conducted his fieldwork on oral literature there.

53 On the organization of time in rural Greece in general see Hart 1991; for a discussion of comparable beliefs on the island of Naxos and their relevance to the negotiation of traditional moral values see Stewart 1991.

54 Bourdieu 1977:130–158.

55 Herzfeld 1985b:247.

56 Gluckman 1962; also Gluckman and Gluckman 1977.

His objections to a more flexible use of *ritual* have long been persuasively refuted by Sally Moore and Barbara Myerhoff, who have advocated the term and concept of "secular ritual," arguing that it also invokes unquestionable culturally specific axioms of a similar operational and conceptual order as sacred dogmas.[57] Moore has shown how political meetings in Tanzania in the 1970s manipulated symbolic and representational categories and practices comparable to those employed in sacred rituals. Similar are the results of Eva Hunt's analysis of the political ceremonies of the Cuicatec Indians of Mexico. The political processes she describes are organized around symbolic categories that reenact in a secular context isomorphic metaphors of hierarchy employed in religious rituals.[58] In his discussion of the Balinese ceremony of *negara*, Geertz illustrates the complex ways in which secular political order reproduces in performative terms cosmological ideas pertinent to religious ritual discourses.[59] If the symbolic organization of the Balinese polity makes it appear as a "theatre state," the same holds true to a great extent for the formulation of political order in the medieval Greek empire. Political power in Byzantium was performed in a highly theatrical manner, reenacting in homological symbolic terms ideas about divine and universal order. In the preface to the tenth-century treatise on court rituals attributed to the emperor Konstantinos Porphyrogennetos, it is stated that by describing in a simple spoken idiom and in traditional terms how the imperial power is governed by rhythm and order, the author also represents the harmony with which the creator moves the whole universe (καὶ καθωμιλημένῃ καὶ ἁπλουστέρᾳ φράσει κεχρήμεθα καὶ λέξεοι ταῖς αὐταῖς καὶ ὀνόμασι τοῖς ἐφ᾿ ἑκάστῳ πράγματι πάλαι προσαρμοσθεῖσι καὶ λεγομένοις, ὑφ᾿ ὧν τοῦ βασιλείου κράτους ῥυθμῷ καὶ τάξει φερομένου, εἰκονίζοιμεν τοῦ δημιουργοῦ τὴν περὶ τόδε τὸ πᾶν ἁρμονίαν καὶ κίνησιν).[60]

Comparable are aspects of the construction and public celebration of national identity in the modern Greek state: for instance, the Greek Independence Day celebrated on March 25, coincides, not fortuitously, with the holiday of the Annunciation of the Virgin Mary, whose religious symbolism informs the official— and common—patriotic discourses about the Greek Revolution.[61] Often the interweaving of *ritual textures* with patterns of sociopolitical discourse and behavior articulates discursive arenas where power relations are constructed, deconstructed,

---

[57] Moore and Myerhoff 1977b.
[58] Hunt 1977; on similar political rituals in Mexico cf. Vogt and Abel 1977.
[59] Geertz 1980.
[60] *De cerimoniis* (On ceremonies) I.4, ed. Reiske.
[61] For an analysis of comparable examples of the assimilation of sacred beliefs into political rituals in other cultures cf. Kertzer 1988.

reaffirmed, or subverted, and individual or group agents negotiate their position in the established social, political, or ideological order against, or in spite of, the counteractions of hegemonizing authorities, be these secular or sacred, directly (re)presented or indirectly inscribed in the cosmological values of a given society.[62] Ritual poetics, in other words, concerns itself with, and aspires to offer new insights into, the ways in which rituals or *ritual textures* as inscribed within other frames of human experience and expression interact with and act upon the formation, expression, and manipulation of diverse cultural and sociopolitical discourses.

III

The title of this chapter deliberately recalls the title of a much discussed article by Goody on ritual.[63] Albeit justified in opposing the arbitrary ad infinitum use of the term *ritual*, Goody rather lightheartedly discards the symbolic/communicative approach to the subject put forward by other influential anthropologists like Victor Turner. To his mind, the overuse of the term *ritual* has led to its semantic disinvestment. In an ingeniously polemical, albeit not necessarily convincing, spirit, Goody refuses to see ritual as enacted system of communication. One could perhaps counterargue that his own approach is not free from an overly rationalistic understanding of meaning and communication, which reactivates certain Western ideological stereotypes rather than elucidating aspects of indigenous conceptual systems. Nevertheless, his article, like any serious polemical attempt, remains tantalizingly heuristic, and this is perhaps its greatest merit.

The present chapter, and the book as a whole, have aspired to provide heuristic markers for the exploration of issues related to the interactions between ritual, society, and politics in different Greek cultural contexts, rather than definite answers. Such an investigation, we believe, necessitates an anthropological, crossdisciplinary perspective.

Some chapters of this book originate from a conference that was held at Harvard University in April 2001 and marked the retirement of Margaret Alexiou. This conference was generously hosted by the Department of the Classics at Harvard. A number of new and specially commissioned chapters were later contributed by scholars from a variety of disciplines—archaeology, classics, anthropology, modern Greek studies—who have worked extensively on aspects of the subject. Our goal has been to bring together different, occasionally even opposing,

---

[62] For a discussion specifically of ritual as actively involved in historical and social processes see Kelly and Kaplan 1990.

[63] "Against 'Ritual': Loosely Structured Thoughts on a Loosely Defined Topic," (Goody 1977).

methodological approaches from a number of disciplines. We believe that it is principally through their diverse theoretical orientations formulated more or less explicitly and in varying length and detail from chapter to chapter—that such interdisciplinary and transhistorical perspectives can contribute to the heuristic *Problematik* of the overall enterprise.

The book is divided into four sections according to overarching thematic/ conceptual categories, while within each section the chronological order—ancient, medieval, modern—has been preserved. Overlaps have not been avoided but occasionally deliberately kept with the intention of foregrounding interactions and transitions from one section to the other.

The first section focuses on ways of interconnectedness between ritual-making and other cultural systems of signification such as architecture, literature, and drama. Instead of focusing on specific ritual activities, the chapters in this section explore the *textural* interactions between ritual patterns and other forms of expression as these are conditioned by their broader cultural, social, and political frameworks.

Robin Osborne explores the interconnections between ritual practices and material culture in Iron Age and archaic Greece. Examining the intricate semiotics of monumental buildings and objects from that period, he proposes that they be viewed not as mere manifestations of political authority, but rather as integral parts of ritual processes enacted by each specific community as a whole. Monumentality in that context does not act as symbolic display and legitimization of the political power of some individual or group; it is rather to be understood in terms of the ritual enactment of communal social and cosmological values.

Dimitrios Yatromanolakis investigates the embeddedness of diverse *ritual textures* in the archaic society of Lesbos, as this is reflected in the songs of Sappho. Questioning the scholarly paradigm of constructing genre taxonomies for the poetry of Sappho, he explores the interconnections between archaic Greek lyric speech genres and ritual discourses. His chapter suggests that a significant aspect of the poetics of Sappho is the *interdiscursivity* of diverse ritual discourses and images embedded in the fragments' texture.

Moving to classical Greece, Richard Seaford proposes a new perspective on the appearance and formation of tragedy. He views tragedy as an overarching genre that incorporated a variety of preexisting genres that had been decontextualized and commodified after the rapid introduction of coinage and monetary culture in Athens in the early fifth century BCE. His investigation focuses on the ways in which monetization in the Greek *polis* of the archaic and particularly the classical periods and its political manipulation resulted in a reformulation of the traditional authority of ritual and in concomitant repositionings of literary culture.

29

In a wide-ranging chapter, Margaret Alexiou, drawing on the results of her extensive study of ritual and Greek literature, offers new ways of approaching the interaction between ritual and aesthetic expressions in post-classical Greek contexts. Her chapter explores the complex ways in which medieval and modern Greek ritual and aesthetic patterns have been transmitted and transformed through discontinuities and continuities across time, and have informed, in interaction with aspects of broader Greek cultural concepts, the production and composition of written and oral Greek literature.

Turning to modernist literature, Panagiotis Roilos investigates the underexplored area of the reinscription of indigenous systems of ritual communication in Greek modernist literature. Focusing on the work of Odysseas Elytis, the Nobel Prize winner for literature in 1979, he analyzes how textures of ritual discourses as reenacted in traditional cultural contexts and in Byzantine liturgy have informed the articulation of Greek modernism's critical stance toward the hegemonization of rationalistic Western European communicative and conceptual tropes.

The second section emphasizes the reenactment, inscription, or subversion of ritual patterns of expression, or of specific rituals, in literature. The chapters in this section analyze the ways in which repetition, ritual symbolic imagery, and the ritual construction of time and space inform, primarily but not exclusively, performative literary discourses.

Gregory Nagy explores the mechanisms of the reinscription of repetition, a ritualistic expressive pattern par excellence, in the Homeric epics. His focus is on the ways in which repetition informs the overall composition of the *Iliad*. His analysis of the poetics of repetition in the epic narrative shows that in the *Iliad* "the process of reformulation is in fact a reaffirmation of formulaic composition," which is reactivated every time the epic is re-performed.

Pat Easterling investigates the construction of time in drama and ritual. Focusing on Greek tragedy, particularly on Sophocles' works, she studies the narrative and performative mechanisms that define the inscription of ritual categories of time in dramatic texts. The reactivation of ritual time in Greek drama, especially the "co-existence of past, present, and future in the performative "now," is viewed in the nexus of interactions between performed text, audience, and established modes of ritual communication.

Albert Henrichs studies the embeddedness and the dramatic manipulation of ritual patterns in ancient Greek tragedy. The emphasis of his analysis is on moments of "ritual crisis" as depicted in the works of the three Athenian tragedians. Focusing on the tensions between ritual norms and deviations from ritual patterns mainly in Sophocles, he explores the intricate ways in which drama interacts with, and often undermines, the ritual expectations of the audience "by manipulating the performance of ritual, preventing rituals from being performed, or completely redefining the religious function and dramatic implications of a given ritual."

Christiane Sourvinou-Inwood offers a reevaluation of current interpretations of gender roles in ritual activities in classical Athenian society and their reinscription in drama. After an analysis of epigraphical sources, forensic speeches, epitaphs, laws, and iconography, she proposes ways of reconstructing the involvement of women in funeral rites in classical antiquity. Women's participation in the last phase of the funeral, the burial, as she shows, was limited and clearly differentiated from the more active role of men in the same ritual context. In tragedy, these gender boundaries, as well as the audience's corresponding expectations, were often subversively manipulated to convey a sense of abnormality and disorderedness.

John Duffy investigates a rich, but rather underappreciated, area of medieval Greek literature, the religious tale. The purpose of this genre, which, albeit central to the religious life of simple Byzantine people, remains, like other aspects of medieval Greek literature, unjustifiably marginal in modern scholarship, was twofold: to instruct its audience by portraying exemplary modes of behavior and to entertain them. Duffy's analysis, which draws also on parallels from the medieval West and modern Greece, focuses on the latter aspect and explores the subversive dialogue of such texts with sanctioned religious rituals, particularly the sacraments of baptism and the Eucharist.

In his second chapter, Panagiotis Roilos investigates the intricate ways in which established secular and religious Byzantine ceremonial discourses and performances are reenacted in the medieval Greek novel. Focusing on *Rhodanthe and Dosikles* by Theodoros Prodromos, one of the most prolific twelfth-century Byzantine authors, and exploring the Byzantine rhetorical concept of *amphoteroglôssia*, he illustrates how the parodic reinscription of sanctioned ritual modes of expression and power manipulation contribute to the multivocality of the genre.

Vangelis Calotychos focuses not as much on subversive reflections as on political refractions and narrative reactivations of traditional ritual discourses in contemporary Greek and Balkan literature and film. The theme of bridge-building, a common motif in Balkan oral literature often symbolically associated with rituals of sacrifice, is viewed in the context of the contemporary literature of the area as an overarching political metaphor connecting several areas of life—aesthetic, social, political—in Greece and the Balkans.

The third section focuses on the embodiment and narrative manipulation of ritual patterns in art and literature. The main emphasis is on the contribution of the reactivated or narrated ritual acts and forms to the production of meaning in literary, historical, and pictorial discourses.

Gloria Ferrari explores the interconnections between ritual metaphors, visual symbolism, and literary themes in classical Greece. Focusing on the parallel symbolic structures of two rites of passage, the funeral and the wedding, especially as they are depicted in literature, she investigates the embodiment of such analogies in the symbolic vocabulary of vase painting. The employment of "chthonian" imagery, caves and underground vaults, in a series of vase paintings is shown to function as an allusion to the metaphorical structures of the wedding ritual.

The ethnographic value of Herodotus' history has long attracted scholarly attention. Angus Bowie sets out to propose an alternative perspective on the study of the ethnographic passages in Herodotus' work: he examines the ways in which the accounts of the principally secular sociopolitical rituals of a number of Eastern peoples—Persians, Babylonians, Arabians, and Scythians—function as signifiers in the broader narrative context, contributing to the construction of the poetics of Herodotus' historical analysis as a whole and to the configuration of its ideological premises.

Ioli Kalavrezou explores the understudied subject of visual representation of dance in Byzantium. Dance, "as ritual and a form of communication," constituted an important element of public and private Byzantine life. In her chapter Kalavrezou studies the existing evidence and attempts to reconstruct the icono-graphic and occasional contexts in which dance was depicted in Byzantium. Focusing on the representation of dance in the context both of secular court and civic ceremonies and of religious biblical scenes, she explores the transformations of Graeco-Roman tradition in the medieval Greek visual vocabulary from early to late Byzantium.

Anna Stavrakopoulou addresses the manipulation of traditional rituals in Greek shadow theater. Focusing on the theme of the reversal of the wedding in a group of plays from the Whitman and Rinvolucri Greek shadow theater collection at Harvard University, she situates the embodiment of ritual elements in the specific "texts" within their broader performative framework.

Gail Holst-Wahrhaft looks at the ways in which traditional Greek "dance-events," often embedded within wider ritual frameworks in rural Greece, are embodied in specific modern Greek literary texts. Her discussion, based also on comparative material from other Mediterranean countries, centers on both the exoticization of dance and the ambivalent portrayal of the male dancer particularly in the work of Nikos Kazantzakis and Stratis Myrivilis.

The last section of the book focuses on the exploration of specific rituals and their embeddedness in broader sociocultural contexts. Here, emphasis is given to the interaction between ritual, history, and the formation of social and cultural discourses.

Ian Rutherford explores the semantics of an intricate ancient Greek ritual, *theôria* (a pilgrimage representing the community as a whole), which is directly connected with the political life of the city-states. Drawing also on comparative ethnographic material from India, he shows the mechanisms that allowed this ritual to incorporate structural and symbolic elements from both other categories of rites of passage and archetypical mythical discourses. Thanks to this interpenetratedness between mythical discourses and ritual enactments, *theôria* can be viewed as "a drama that enacts a rite of passage, a [political] crisis to be overcome, and a return and reaggregation into the city."

Charles Stewart's chapter acts as a bridge between pagan antiquity and Christianity. His focus is on "ritual dreams," the custom of incubation. Stewart investigates the transformations and changes that accompanied the development of incubation during the transitional period of late antiquity. In his analysis, he explores the ambiguities that marked the inscription and the negotiation of this ritual practice in the Christian imaginary and its interaction, on symbolic and pragmatic levels, with broader historical and cultural conditions.

Drawing on literary and historical sources from different periods of medieval Greece, Ruth Macrides looks at the underexplored secular ceremony of petitioning the Byzantine emperor. In her reconstruction of the particularities of this ritual, she examines its interconnections with other secular ceremonial practices performed at the Byzantine court and with sacred rituals. Petitioning the emperor, she concludes, should be viewed in terms of the reenactment of symbolic verbal and representational codes drawn simultaneously from traditional sacred Christian and profane ritual contexts.

Michael Herzfeld studies the mechanisms of the political and ideological manipulation of ritual practices by the hegemonizing ideological discourse of the "patriotic" discipline of Greek folklore. Exposing the cultural ambiguities embedded in a characteristically ancient genre of Greek ritual oral poetry, the "swallow songs" ("variants" of which are first found in Atheneaus and later in Byzantium), he explores the strategies of "taxonomic regimentation in Greek cultural history" and suggests that this was constructed by the educated élite of the modern Greek state to promote their ideological propagation of the Europeanness of the modern Greeks.

Speech act theory has alerted us to the ways "words do things." Laurie Hart modifies this model of investigation and addresses the question "how to do things with things" in ritualized and social contexts of signification. She does so by focusing on the architectonics of the interactions between the construction and the communication of social and historical memory, primarily as it is articulated by her informants in contemporary Northern Greece, and rituals of inhabitation. "The rituals of architecture," she concludes, "might better be thought about as attempts to rein in the unruly coexistence of recalcitrant things in space than as simple devices for the expression and reproduction of cultural order."

Jane Cowan explores the embodiment and renegotiations of social, ideological, and political discourses in the performative context of an underexplored contemporary male rite of passage in Northern Greece, the departure of young soldiers for the army. The performing "dancing, singing, drinking body" of the "little soldier," Cowan argues, becomes the locus for the negotiation of multiple gender, social, and ideological repositionings.

Thematic and methodological interconnections have been encouraged throughout the book. The present chapter offers a new *Problematik* of the interpenetratedness between ritual patterns of signification and aesthetic, cultural, and sociopolitical discourses in different Greek contexts. *Greek Ritual Poetics* aims to articulate an interdisciplinary, comparative heuristic model that, going beyond unidirectional schemata, approaches not "ritual" and "poetics" as autonomous essentialized categories but, instead, ritual textures and textures of sociocultural interaction as interwoven nexuses of ever re-invented negotiations of power capitals and *sêmansis*.

Part Two

Ritual Textures

Two

Monumentality and Ritual in Archaic Greece

Robin Osborne

No one familiar with the story of the competition that took place in the twentieth century CE to have the tallest building in the world will find it difficult to understand how peer polity interaction, in that phrase wished on us by Colin Renfrew and John Cherry in the 1980s, might lead to monumentality.[1] Anthony Snodgrass pointed out in his contribution to Renfrew and Cherry's volume that the fourth temple of Hera at Samos manages just to surpass the first temple of Artemis at Ephesos in ground area (6,038 sq m compared to 6,017) and that similarly the temple of Olympia Zeus at Akragas managed to surpass temple GT at Selinous with a ground area of 6,806 rather than 5,007 sq m.[2] It is very hard to think that the fact that the Parthenon, as well as being 10' 5-3/4" wider and 17' 7-7/8" longer than the temple of Zeus at Olympia also has columns that are a quarter of an inch higher is a product of anything other than direct competition. But to say that and to pass on is to miss what is crucial: it is clear that the casual passer-by will hardly have been in a position to notice slight differences of height, let along to calculate slightly greater ground areas. These are differences which acquire part of their power precisely because they are accessible only to the knowing; devised by architects at the very inception of the planning process, they achieve their political effect only by being disseminated as part of the "urban legend" that such monumental buildings construct around themselves and their creation.

But if in theory competition between rival communities such as that manifested in this way might bring about ever increasing monumentality, in fact competition of this sort can do very little at all to explain monumentality as such. Monumental Greek temple buildings did not come into being by inch-by-inch growth. Even if the appearance of one monumental building inspires other monuments that are even grander, the competitive urge will not explain the first monumental building. Fractional differences bruited with pride, or contempt, among the

---

[1] Renfrew and Cherry 1986.
[2] Snodgrass 1986.

knowing cannot account for the origins of monumentality. To put it concretely, peer polity interaction does not get us far with explaining the tenth-century monster building at Lefkandi or the appearance of the Sounion *kouros*.

Archaeologists who have considered monumentality in other contexts than that of early Iron Age Greek history, have noted a correlation between monumental architecture and the emergence of complex societies. Bruce Trigger, in the paper which leads off the *World Archaeology* volume devoted to *Monuments and the Monumental* published in 1990, draws attention to the way in which monumental architecture violates the law that human groups seek to conserve energy. He suggests that the conspicuous consumption that monumental buildings involve should be seen as a display of power, and that "the need to express power through the medium of monumental architecture may be greater during the formative stages of early civilizations."[3] In the same volume Tom Dillehay notes that past explanations of monumental architecture have seen it as a way of accentuating social hierarchy and élite control of non-élite behavior, whether in terms of marking claims to land or territory, justifying élite control over primary resources, or providing a super-active symbolic system that legitimizes internal social strategies, though he himself concludes by wanting to play down the importance of crisis and of centralized political systems and to emphasize the correlation with environmental diversity, population density, and agricultural potential.[4]

In this chapter I will look beyond merely architectural monumentality to monumentality more generally, that is, to the production of objects at a size significantly greater than any purely practical function that they might perform demands. I will argue that in the case of archaic Greece, at least, it is not to peer polity interaction that we should look for an explanation, but to the particular and peculiar role that the "larger than life" plays in ritual. For all the recent interest in ritual, the objects that are involved in ritual have been accorded remarkably little attention. Studies of ritual have been primarily concerned with what people do with ritual and what ritual does with and to people.[5] Such a concern is neither surprising nor reprehensible, but it neglects the ways in which rituals involve people not only with one another but with things. In ritual people do things with words, but they also do things with things. This chapter will represent an initial tentative step towards exploring the part that ritual plays in transforming things, and in particular in creating the material context which itself serves to encourage and sustain the assumptions lying behind the creation of the rituals in the first place. It is in as far

[3] Trigger 1990:127.
[4] Dillehay 1990:223, 238.
[5] Landmarks in recent study of ritual are provided by Bell 1992 and Bell 1997, which provide a thorough bibliographic survey. See also the next footnote.

as, and only in as far as, they are created in a ritual context that monumental objects present themselves as not merely indexical, signs of the out-of-the ordinary resources that have been marshalled, but as things that substantiate experiences which have *not* been involved in the monuments' production. Whereas in the case of non-monumental objects variations in size are often largely a matter of "noise," that is they carry in themselves no significance, with monumental objects the monumentality itself carries significance.[6]

I start at Lefkandi, with what is undoubtedly the first Greek Iron Age gesture of monumentality, the Toumba building containing the burial of a man, a woman, and four horses (fig. 1). Although the sequence of events is not entirely clear, Mervyn Popham's arguments for the order are strong.[7] The burials, themselves involving a monumental Cypriot bronze bowl, seem to have occurred first, and the building then to have been erected over the burials, and briefly equipped with storage jars etc. These were then removed, the thatched roof taken off, the posts pulled up or cut off at the ground, and between four and five thousand tons of earth brought in to bury the building in a great tumulus.

One way and another, all discussions of the Lefkandi Toumba building to date have focused on its political implications. On one side is the argument about the "heroic" nature of the burial, which goes back to Mervyn Popham's first revelation of the building to the scholarly world in 1982.[8] So, recently, Ian Morris has insisted on the parallels with the burial of Patroklos in the *Iliad* and on the metal funerary urn, the killing of animals (and perhaps humans), and the erection of a mound as hero-izing elements.[9] "The Lefkandians announced that the man under the mound was a hero, transcending the race of iron," Morris suggests.[10] On the other side is the matter of the sheer labor demanded by the building, the quality of workmanship in which it is notably high, and by the mound. That is the line that I took in *Greece in the Making*; "all of this implies . . . a mode of communal organisation such that one family, or some other very small group, were able to exploit the rest of the local society, and to extract from them such a surplus as to be able to afford a display such as this."[11] Irene Lemos has recently further advanced this type of explanation in

---

[6] Here as elsewhere in this chapter I draw inspiration, and some of my language, from Rappaport 1999. On noise and meaning compare Rappaport 1999:256, "what is noise in ordinary language is meaning in liturgy." Rappaport defines ritual as "the performance of more or less invariant sequences of formal acts and utterances not entirely encoded by the performers." My examples begin with what must be at the "less" end of "more or less invariant" and proceed to the "more" end.

[7] Popham et al. 1993; compare Lemos 2002:145–146.

[8] Popham et al. 1982.

[9] Morris 2000:235. See further Lemos 2002:168.

[10] Morris 2000:237.

[11] Osborne 1996:43.

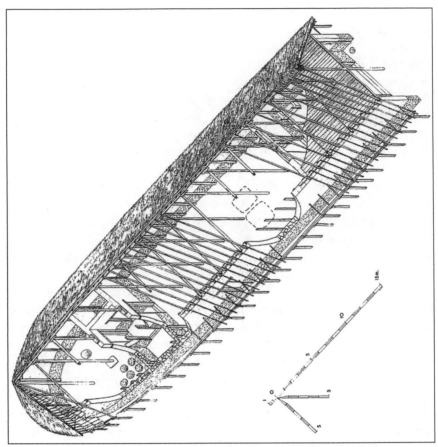

fig. 1 Reconstruction of Toumba Building, Lefkandi. *Courtesy of Dr. J. J. Coulton and the British School at Athens.*

drawing attention to the subsequent burials at the east end of the tumulus, suggesting that the Toumba building and its abnormal destruction were a deliberate "new start" establishing the foundation of an important lineage.[12]

Such a political emphasis fits well enough with those general theories about monumentality and the emergence of complex societies that archaeologists have trailed. But it does little justice to what is really *peculiar* about this case. What is peculiar is that this building appears to have been created and destroyed as part of a single act. That act cannot have been a simple functional one: disposing of corpses

---

[12] Lemos 2002:167–168.

does not demand the building and destruction of a house on any scale, let alone on this scale. We are dealing here neither with a monumental house nor with a monumental tomb. Since it was immediately buried, the Toumba building did not mark the creation of a long-lasting symbol of a ruling family, such as we might have taken the creation of such a building as a ruler's dwelling to have been. But since it had so complex a formation process, we cannot treat this as simply the creation of a tomb monument to a great past ruler, a monument which will overshadow all subsequent burials. The mound itself was indeed an impressive creation, but it is not one half of the story. What the archaeology presents us with clear evidence for is the devotion of very considerable effort to the creation of a building that was never used—the floors were so little walked upon as to be hard to detect in excavation—and but briefly seen. It is indeed the peculiarity of this sequence which has led Popham's critics to suggest that, notwithstanding the intensely burned areas of earth (which seem best explained as the site on which the cremation took place when no building was yet erected) and the absence of any sign of use, in fact the building was built for a ruler's habitation, but on the chance death of that ruler it was used for his burial, demolished, and itself buried. On my reading of the evidence, however, that makes poor sense of the archaeology as well as making the distinctive story of this building depend upon the chance timing of the ruler's death.

The peculiarity of the story must not be over-emphasized. Anthropologists are very familiar with societies in which material that has been created or accumulated is deliberately destroyed.[13] In some cases such destruction may be little more than a conspicuous expenditure of resources as a means conspicuously to display power, but in other cases this is an implausible reading. In northern New Ireland, *malangan*-sculptures are conceptualized as "skins" replacing the body of a deceased person, and themselves by their decay or deliberate destruction releasing the life force of that person so that it can be rechanneled to the living.[14] Closer to the Lefkandi example and more familiar to western experience is the creation of elaborate facilities and façades for carnival celebrations: here the destruction of the elaborate "stage set" upon which the carnival takes place is part of carnival's larger magnification and renunciation of excessive behavior to mark the arrival of a season of abstinence. One-off acts of excessive creation and destruction cannot be straightforwardly explained simply by reference to such calendrical rituals as carnival, however.

If we take seriously the very odd story to which the archaeology points, then what stands out is not that an individual is treated in a special manner, nor the massing of labor for a particularly hard task. What stands out is the way in which

---

[13] For some brief summary remarks see Bell 1997:120–128.
[14] See Küchler 1987:240; Küchler 1992.

the most elaborate of traditional burial practices is supplemented by an act of house-building that vastly exceeded in scale anything that had ever been known within that community. This elaboration is hard to contemplate unless we presuppose a determination on the part of the community as a whole to bear the labor burdens. Either of the monumental elements, the building or the mound, might on their own have been a product of labor coercion. Together, and together with the systematic demolition, they make the coercion model extremely unlikely. This is perhaps best seen by asking what exercises of coercion on a monumental scale might be good for. In a society where getting ordinary buildings built requires some coercion, getting built a monumental building that is going immediately to be demolished would become a display of conspicuous coercion whose effect could not be certain. If this act of building, demolition, and burial were merely a response to the contingent, then coercion would be inevitable. If the building, demolition, and burial were seen as consequential upon assumptions shared by the whole community, on the other hand, coercion ceases to be necessary. The actions become ritual actions performed by those for whom the performance means something— something other than an elaborate way of avoiding being lashed. What the building and its burial involve are a community going through something together. The mound at the end marks not just the place of burial of an exceptional man, but the record of an extraordinary communal experience.

In a trivial sense any monumental building which puts a heavy demand upon labor resources might be said to involve an "extraordinary communal experience." But the "community" involved in such laboring will often be far from co-extensive with the political community—for the great temples of the sixth and fifth century the labor will most normally have been servile or immigrant. Once the laboring becomes part of a ritual, the conditions of involvement become far different. Regardless of whose hands wielded the carpentry tools or the spade, the creation and burial of the Lefkandi Toumba building must have involved the whole Lefkandian community. Just so, indeed, the addition of funeral games turn the funeral of Patroklos from being something carried out by his close comrades to being something that involves the whole Greek army at Troy.

J.J. Coulton's careful analysis of the Toumba building leads him to suggest that ordinary domestic buildings must have existed on a somewhat similar scale. Only on that supposition is the elaboration of the plan of the Toumba building comprehensible: while the overall structure could be shrunk to the size of e.g. Nichoria House IV.1, the elaborate plan would make no sense at that scale. So, if the Toumba building was excessive in scale within tenth-century Lefkandi, it may have been grossly excessive only in rather limited features; Coulton himself points to the extent of the veranda as excessive.[15] For all that its size exceeds even the "monumental" hundred-foot temples of the eighth century, the sequence of actions that involved this building in a burial, even more than the size, are what render most appropriate the term "monumental."

If we can argue, as I have above, that size, in which I include the extent of the effort to construct the building in the first place, requires what I have called ritual to create it, then it is also the case that ritual encourages the monumental. Rituals both do things to and say things about their performers. Rituals also separate those who perform them from those who do not. In a different language, ritual makes holy, it sanctifies.[16] It creates sanctified linguistic transactions (as in wedding vows), but it also creates sanctified objects. Everyday objects may be used in rituals, but what the ritual creates is not everyday—if it were then the ritual would seem, and might be seen, to have achieved nothing. Many rituals create or leave no material marker, or the material marker which they create is incommensurable with other materials in the world. But the first two sorts of monuments with which I am concerned in this chapter—a house-like structure and pots—are commensurable with everyday items. For the visible product of a ritual to be indistinguishable from the visible products created and used in the course of non-ritual life would set up the risk of investing the ordinary with a significance which it could not support. Just as rules which are accorded sanctity need to be low in specificity if their sanctity is not to be threatened by changing circumstances, so objects which are accorded with sanctity need to be objects not open to confusion with everyday objects which might be or come to be used in very different contexts. Monumentality protects from "oversanctification."[17]

What I want now to go on to argue in what follows is that what is true of the Lefkandi Toumba building is also true of monumental buildings and objects in archaic Greece more generally. That is, that the monumental was created in, and only in, ritual contexts, and that it is the monuments' role in involving a community in a ritual, their role in focusing the community's ritual upon themselves, that explains the attractions of monumentality. Monuments are not simply a means of displaying power, they are themselves a means of creating social relationships, and they do so by directing attention not at some individual or group within a community, but by turning that attention beyond the living mortal community altogether, by distracting attention from political power rather than by displaying it.

[15] Coulton, in Popham et al. 1993:58–59.
[16] "The Holy and its elements are generated in and integrated by ritual," as Rappaport puts it (1999:24).
[17] On "oversanctification" see Rappaport 1999:440.

Robin Osborne

My second example of the monumental is not a built structure but a tomb marker, the monumental pots used as markers in late Geometric cemeteries. Or rather used as tomb markers in *one* late Geometric cemetery, the Dipylon cemetery at Athens. Ian Morris has repeatedly stressed how peculiar the Dipylon cemetery was: "this cemetery produced a spectacular haul of giant pots, with scenes of funerals and battles;" "about two thirds of all known Geometric funeral scenes come from the Dipylon and are the products of an artists conventionally known as he Dipylon Master and a small group of painters working in his style."[18] The Dipylon cemetery was not doing anything new in using pots to mark graves, that practice goes back in Athens to c. 900, but it was remarkable both for the frequency of so marking graves and for the size and decoration of the pots used as markers: Coldstream noted that "during the 200 years before c. 770, we know of only twelve Athenians to whom such respect was paid. Then, suddenly, 20 monuments were set up in the next 20 years."[19] The pots involved take two main forms, the belly-handled amphora and the krater, and stand more than a meter high: the belly-handled amphora reaches 1.55 m, the craters 1.22 or 1.23 m. Coldstream, again, notes that "they are too large to be useful in domestic life, and no potter would encumber his shop with them unless he was certain of selling them without delay."[20] The shapes are in fact shapes that are old ones and going out of fashion; Coldstream writes of the Dipylon Master that "in the belly-handled *amphora* he gave a final and glorious lease of life to a shape which was already obsolescent in his time."[21] All the pots are decorated with figure scenes, and these figure scenes are among the earliest in Athenian geometric art. All the pots have scenes of the laying out of the dead, and the kraters, at least, have further decoration which shows some form of action, in particular chariot processions and/or battles, with all the battle scenes appearing on LG1a kraters, believed by Coldstream to date to the decade 760 to 750. Of the kraters that ended up in the Louvre after the 1871 excavations, the richest of three sets of excavations of the cemetery, four of the five substantially surviving (A517, A522, A527, A530) feature ships, and ships also feature on three smaller Louvre fragments (A532, A528, CA3362).

Given the explosion of large marker pots in a single cemetery, and given the other signs of great wealth (gold bands etc.) displayed by tombs in that cemetery, it is not hard to see that emulation must have been playing some role in behavior here. This is a new cemetery opened up c. 760, adopted by the élite as a place apart where they can display themselves, and turned into a place where they

---

[18] Morris 1993:29 and 2000:297 respectively. For the original publication of the cemetery see Brueckner and Pernice 1893 with further reference.
[19] Coldstream 1968:350.

compete with each other in funerary display while as a group showing off their wealth and power to those who bury elsewhere. Such an explanation, however, like the purely political explanations of the Lefkandi Toumba building, does not really do justice to the peculiarity of the phenomenon. These monumental pots are clearly a form of conspicuous display, but they are not just any old form of conspicuous display.

These tomb markers are not just very large objects (fig. 2). Two features make these pots peculiar, and any explanation must make sense of those features. The first is that they take a form which is familiar and enlarge it to a size which is unfamiliar. If the Lefkandi Toumba building was an enlarged Lefkandi house then it was doing likewise. For a krater 1 m 23 cm tall to be appropriate we must be dealing with drinkers of unusual capacity. Enlarging the everyday in this way implies the larger than life. The second thing is the figurative decoration. Athenians were only just beginning to get used to the idea of figurative decoration on pottery, and yet here already are pots where figurative decoration is a dominant element—dominant in its placing in all cases, completely smothering the pot in many cases.

Some of those figurative scenes on these pots will have been very straightforward for any contemporary viewer to construe. The scenes of mourners at the bier of a dead man or woman are exemplary examples of economy of signification: the corpse is identified as dead by laying down on a fancy stand, the mourners identify themselves by raised hands tearing hair, all distinguish themselves as male or female by the presence or absence of a skirt. The viewer of these pots has no doubt that such figurative scenes relate directly to the circumstances that have led to their being placed in the cemetery. But the other scenes are different. They contain many elements which will always have been easily recognized. There are soldiers who identify themselves by their shields and spears, archers marked out by bow and arrow; chariots and ships which present characteristic profiles; dead and wounded men who appear horizontal rather than upright. But if most of the elements in these pictures are easy to construe, it is not at all so easy to link these elements together in any specific way, not nearly so easy to make them into a story. Whereas in the case of the scenes of burial the regularity of the ritual itself offered a template against which to measure the scene, we know of no similar regularities involving ships and soldiers. In the case of the burial, since all seems to conform to the template we adopt the explanation that the scene is a scene of the ritual. But neither we nor the original viewers can have any such template for the military scenes. All funerals follow a like course, but it is part of the essence of war that, however ritualized it may be in some respects, and we have no idea how far that was the case in the eighth century, the course of events is not predictable and the familiar elements may lead to very different results.

fig. 2 Attic Late Geometric krater, Athens National Museum 990. *Courtesy of Hirmer Verlag, Munich.*

These two "odd" features, the magnification of the everyday and the employment of prominent figure scenes, have an important effect on the impact that this cemetery makes. Regarded from afar it may seem only an excessive manifestation of a commemorative habit that some have indulged in for a long time. But it cannot be regarded from afar. The novelty of the size of the pots, and the novelty above all of their decoration, draws in the viewer. And the viewer then finds himself in the imagined company of the larger than life, joining in with the funerary ritual but also surrounded by signs of more or less regulated military activity. The funerary scenes have a conclusion, which is here in the cemetery, but the military scenes have no certain conclusion.

Unlike the Lefkandi Toumba building, the direct cost to the population of Athens in general of a few rich families indulging themselves in monumental burial markers was next to nothing. We are not dealing with a material imposition by a few upon the generality of Athenian inhabitants, even if the relationship between patron and potter or painter was not entirely free of coercion. But just as I wanted to insist that the Lefkandi Toumba building only made sense when seen as a ritual creation, so too I want to insist that we need to see these pots also in a ritual context. It is as the dead man is transported to the grave by the crowds of mourners that these marker pots make their most vivid impression. The pots do not simply commemorate the event, they magnify it. The figure who used a normal sized krater in life is furnished with a more than man-size krater in death. One way of understanding this is to invoke Victor Turner's association of liminality with "anti-structure."[22] The normal materials involved in life, and the imagery of the events of life, are redeployed, we might even say dramatized, in a special context so as to insist upon the structures of mortal life just at the moment when the individual abandons those structures, and crosses over the threshold into death, about which all that is known is that it is common to all.

These kraters do not simply magnify the domestic person, they magnify in particular the contributor to the defense of the community. The man who mixed it among infantry, who fought on land or sea with mixed success, is turned into a looming presence in death. The mourner, drawn in by the presentation of a world familiar to him from his present action, is made to face up to his duties in warfare as well as his duties in burial. The community that comes together in the funerary ritual is turned into a community that goes out to fight, whether as rower, archer, or hoplite. And all under the inspiration of these men who have become larger than life

---

[20] Ibid.

[21] Ibid.: 33–34.

[22] Turner 1969.

in death. In the *prôthesis* scenes one figure is marked out, the figure of the dead man. In the scenes of warfare, to the frustrations of the art historian who needs some order to hang a narrative upon, no single figure or group of figures offer themselves as different. Beneath the exalted person of the dead, no hierarchy is advertised. The power which the monumentality of the cemetery displays is nevertheless occluded in the rituals and the imagery. Here, as at Lefkandi, the very monumentality encourages displacement and misrecognition of the structures of power.

Monumental marker vases continued to be found in Athenian cemeteries throughout the eighth and most of the seventh century. Virtually at the end of the seventh cemetery the Dipylon cemetery would see the first Attic black-figure vase, the name vase of the Nessos painter, stand exactly as tall (1.22 m) as one of those LG 1a kraters. But just as in the eighth century sanctuaries took over from cemeteries as places in which conspicuously to dispose of wealth, so in the seventh and sixth centuries it is the sanctuary rather than the cemetery that primarily attracts monumentality. For the seventh century not only saw the introduction of stone temples with ceramic-tiled roofs, but also monumental votive offerings, in particular *kouroi*.

Like the pots in the Dipylon cemetery, both temples and *kouroi* lend themselves to a story of emulation. There is not much doubt that it was emulation of Egypt that inspired both stone built temples and *kouroi* in the first place.[23] Of Greek knowledge of colossal stone figures in Egypt we can have no doubt: it is upon the leg of the colossal statue of Rameses II before the temple of Abu Simbel in Nubia that Greek mercenaries scratched their names.[24] Nor is there much doubt, as we have already seen, that Greek cities came to compete with one another in the size of their temples. But neither for *kouroi* nor for temples will the story of emulation much help to explain the attractions of their monumental form. This is particularly clear for *kouroi* where, although the occurrence of more than one monumental *kouros* at Sounion and at the Samian Heraion (the "south colossus," known only from fragments, seems to have been comparable in size to Iskhys' *kouros* [fig. 3]) suggests some local competition, the trend over time is to abandon the monumental, not to cultivate it: most late archaic *kouroi* are of life size or just under life size.

So if the monumentality of the *kouros* is not to be explained purely in terms of emulation, in what terms is it to be explained? The first thing to note is that although *kouroi* will come to be used as grave markers as well as dedications, the *kouroi* used as grave markers seem never to have been monumental. Equally, although *korai* will come to feature alongside *kouroi*, and in the case of the Samian Heraion alongside monumental *kouroi*, no monumental *korai* are known. Monu-

23 The classic demonstration of the truth of the dependence of *kouroi* on Egyptian models, which was advertised by the Greeks themselves, is Guralnick 1978.
24 Bernand and Masson 1957:1–20; Meiggs and Lewis 1969 no. 7.

mentality then is not a feature of the representation of the free-standing human form, but a feature of *kouroi* alone, and then only some and in religious settings. In fact we know of only a small number of settings for monumental *kouroi*—the sanctuary of Poseidon and Athene at Sounion, the sanctuary of Apollo at Delos, and the sanctuary of Hera on Samos.

Although the monumental Sounion *kouroi* stand at the head of the history of the *kouros*, life-sized and monumental *kouroi* co-existed from the beginning.[25] The workshop that produced the two Sounion *kouroi* that measured in at just over 3 m in height also produced the New York *kouros* which is life-sized (1.84 m) and fragments suggest that other *kouroi* of the same period at Sounion were life sized or smaller. From the beginning then, the decision to "go monumental" was just that, a decision. It was not just that monumental *kouroi* naturally offered themselves for comparison with real men, they also offered themselves for comparison with life-sized *kouroi*. Just as the Dipylon marker vases were blown-up versions of familiar vase shapes so the *kouroi* were blown-up versions of familiar statue types. But whereas the size of an amphora or krater was essentially arbitrary, the size of a representation of a man was not. There was a proper size for a man to be, and though that might vary within limits, 3 m

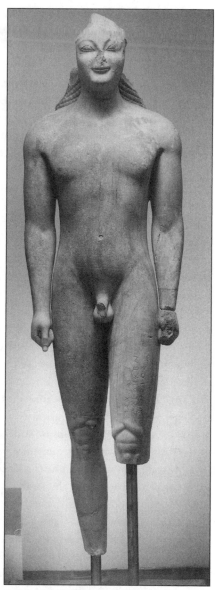

fig. 3 Iskhys' *kouros* from the Heraion at Samos. *Courtesy of the German Archaeological Institute, Athens.*

[25] The standard publication of *kouroi* remains Richter 1960. The most immediate presentation of the difference between monumental and life-sized *kouroi* is provided by Stewart 1990, Plate 43.

was off limits—and the 5 m of the Samian *kouroi* or 8.5 m of the Naxian *kouros* on Delos were well beyond the limit.

To come face to face with a life-sized *kouros* was to come face to face with a man. Funerary *kouroi* were to exploit that: when the *kouros* that marked the grave of the Athenian Kroisos bids the viewer to stand and weep at the tomb of a man who had died in the front line the sympathy the appeal assumes, and is predicated upon, the likeness of Kroisos' *kouros* to the viewer. That likeness involves not merely form, but scale: the mourner has to be able to relate to the *kouros* as he would to a real man, to come face-to-face at the same range as one would come face-to-face with a man. So too in the sanctuary. The one hundred plus life-size or just under life-size *kouroi* from the Ptoion sanctuary of Apollo offered the worshipper images of worshipper-sized men in the service of the god, the male worshipper had to be able to see in them substitutes for himself. A similar situation prevails in the case of *korai*. The *korai* grouped on the Athenian Acropolis, with their hands extended in offering, provided the image of human offering to the gods by themselves imaging the essential social exchange, the exchange of young women in marriage: these images had to be recuperable as the women whom men married.

It is against that background of the "standard" transaction made between the worshipping or mourning viewer and the *kouros* that the nature of the transaction with the monumental *kouros* has to be construed. It is not that one cannot come face to face with a 3 m or 5 m or even 9 m high *kouros*, for, as what photographers do itself clearly reveals, one can stand far enough away to regain the experience of exchanging gazes.[26] Rather it is that one cannot come face to face with such a *kouros* at the range at which one comes face to face with men (fig. 4). The conversation to which a variety of inscriptions on funerary *kouroi* invite the viewer cannot be had at the distance at which monumental *kouroi* need to be viewed. The male viewer cannot straightforwardly substitute himself for the monumental *kouros*. The very question as to what exactly this *kouros* is, or represents, becomes open to question.

Part of the power of the *kouros* as a dedication stems from the impossibility of distinguishing between man and god. Since gods have the form of men and since *kouroi* carry no attributes beyond a beardlessness that does not rule on status, the question as to whether the *kouros* in the sanctuary represents men to the god or the god to men is an open one.[27] The more closely a *kouros* mirrors a man in scale, the greater the presumption that it is upon a man that the worshipper's gaze has fallen. By contrast, the more a *kouros* assumes super-human scale, the more open the ques-

[26] I respond here to one criticism that has been offered (A. Stewart 1997:244) of claims that I have made in earlier publications (and originally in Osborne 1988) about the "mirroring gaze" of the *kouros*.
[27] A. Stewart 1997:63–70 wants to see a very specific social status represented by the *kouros*, but I fail to see in the nudity of the *kouros* any particular status signifier (compare Osborne 1997).

fig. 4 Reconstruction drawing of Iskhys' *kouros. Courtesy of the German Archaeological Institute, Athens.*

tion of his human status becomes. The worshipper who approaches Iskhys *kouros* on Samos and finds himself gazing at his thighs is not going to be moved with a frisson of recognition: either he turns his gaze upwards and becomes filled with awe or he retreats to a safe distance for exchange, but in either case the contrast with the pattern of behavior required on encountering a mortal man insists that this encounter is with something different. The monumental *kouros* establishes a clear distance between himself and the viewer, a distance that can only be breached by a worshipper prepared to approach in awe.

The 5 m high *kouroi* at the Samian Heraion certainly did not dwarf the successive temples of Hera in their midst, and the Sounion *kouroi* may have seemed only appropriate for the temple of Athena built there in the sixth century. That is, in both these cases the monumentality of the *kouroi* was not an isolated gesture but part of a larger program in and by which the gods were magnified. In the case of the Naxian *kouros* on Delos it is rather more likely that it towered above its immediate surroundings. Certainly in that case the associated inscription, declaring that this was an offering by the Naxians to Apollo and that the statue and base are of the same stone, makes clear the desire of the dedicators to have the scale of their achievement reflect glory directly back on them. If "the same stone" is understood to mean "the same piece of stone" and it is hard to think that it is worth saying if not, then the boast is in fact a false one. We might, however, take the Naxians' need to employ the dedicatory inscription to draw attention to their extraordinary power as itself a sign that without such an explicitly articulated claim the monumental *kouros* would not have automatically reflected back on them. Objects offered to the gods, the statements about power that these *kouroi* make are primarily statements about the power of the gods. It is important that not everyone can make such statements, but the display of human power remains implicit rather than explicit in these monuments, at least until explicated by an accompanying inscription. The monumental *kouros* dedications take their place alongside other dedications, dedications which may, for instance, by their own preciousness reflect upon the preciousness, and "buying power," of the gods. Like these other dedications to gods, the *kouroi* reflect primarily on the worthiness of the gods for such a dedication.

Michael Adler and Richard Wilshusen have observed that in small, politically non-stratified communities, social integrative facilities remain generalized in use, but that as the size of the interacting community increases, social integrative facilities of a more monumental nature tend to be constructed and used almost exclusively for ritual activities. In stressing in this chapter the link between monumentality and ritual, I want also not to lose sight of the specific social structural setting of those rituals. On the one hand, social factors alone will not directly produce monumentality. Monumentality does not arise simply through competition, whether between individuals or between groups or states. We are not dealing with gradual escalation of scale as a result of emulation. Rather we are dealing with the creation all at once of objects and structures that are out of scale and where being out of scale is part of their very nature. These are objects and structures not created for this world, but created as part of rituals which introduce men to the possibilities of a quite different world, whether of the dead or of the gods. But on the other hand, not all rituals produce monumental objects. The ritual creation of monumentality depends not on some change in the assumptions about the hidden nature of the world, some change in what Rappaport would call the Ultimate Sacred Postulates, but upon changes in the way those assumptions relate to the manifest world.[28] The creation of objects on a new scale should not be taken to imply new beliefs—in none of the cases we have looked at does any feature of the new monumental ritual suggest novel conceptions, and in the case of the Late

---

[28] Rappaport 1999:263 defines as "Ultimate Sacred Postulates" those "understandings, formal expression of which is largely confined to ritual" concerning the supernatural world.

Geometric Ia marker pots, continuity with past non-monumental practice is strong. Rather what is new is the expression of traditional beliefs in monumental ways. That expression is in part dependent upon the invention of new means of expression. So the Late Geometric marker pots can only do their job once there is a possibility of decorating them with figurative art, the monumental *kouroi* depend upon the acquisition of Egyptian technology. But desire as well as means are necessary, and that desire is only to be explained in terms of changing social, or sociopolitical, structures.

One of Rappaport's major concerns in *Ritual and Religion in the Making of Humanity* is with religion in adaptation. He argues that "sanctity has made it possible for associations of organisms to persist in the face of increasing threats posed to their orderly social life by the increasing ability of their members to lie."[29] This is, I think, an insight that can help us to see why the three examples of monumental object which I have reviewed in this paper were created, and why in none of the cases they resulted in a long-standing tradition. The argument is perhaps most straightforward in the case of the geometric marker vases and of the colossal *kouroi*.

Figurative art offered, in Rappaport's terms, a new technology of the lie. Here were a series of new signs which could relay the truth but which could also relay what was not true.[30] The kraters themselves display this. Their scenes of burial relay an event which the very presence of the marker vase in the cemetery confirms to have taken place. But their scenes of battle or chariot procession are not guaranteed in the same way: modern viewers cannot, and many, at least among contemporary viewers could not, be sure whether these scenes had a real life correlate. The way in which eighth-century individuals were aware of the possibilities of falsification that were opened up by new technology can be illustrated from that other new technology, writing. One of the earliest extensive examples of writing is the epigram written on a cup buried in the grave of a young boy at Pithecusae: it almost certainly began "I am the cup of Nestor," a joking, lying, allusion to a famous passage in the *Iliad*.[31] Making the outsize marker vases of the cemetery the prime location for the new art of figurative drawing encourages the assumption of a link between this form of representation and the sacred: figurative drawing is sanctified and as such its availability for the everyday questioned. It is not by chance that it

---

[29] Rappaport 1999:416.
[30] This is the feature of *mimêsis* that so concerned Plato in *Republic* 10 and which is already emphasized at the beginning of Hesiod's *Theogony* (lines 27–28), where the Muses tell Hesiod that they know how to speak what is true, but also false things that are like what is true. This passage suggests that the lying use of writing and other graphic signs was something of which Greeks were aware from the time they began to use them.
[31] Meiggs and Lewis 1969:no. 1.

will be another century and a half before pots show on them scenes of people using those pots.

The new technology of hard stone carving that made possible life-size statues of men and women can similarly be seen to have opened up a new possibility for the creation of the false. Now for the first time a statue might assume the size of a human being as well as general human form. What the placing and dominant forms of free-standing life-sized statues suggest is that this possibility was immediately brought into control. The restriction of freestanding life-sized statues to sanctuary and grave context, that is to ritual contexts, along with their restriction to a very limited range of forms—the naked and beardless *kouros*, the nubile *kore*, figures shown engaged in ritual actions (for example bringing a calf or a sheep to sacrifice)—all limit the possi-bilities of the lie. But monumentality clearly has a part to play here. The very possi-bility of producing "men" that are not man-sized raises issues over the status of men that are man-sized. The dedication of such monumental figures of human appear-ance in sanctuaries encourages the identification of the extra-ordinary man with beings that are not human at all, the anthropomorphic gods. And once the possi-bility that the referent is a god is opened up, the possibilities for falsely representing a human as other than he or she is is undermined. One of the things that is to be noted about the story of a woman passing herself off as the goddess Athena in the middle of the sixth century for political purposes, to assist the seizure of power by the tyrant Peisistratos at Athens, is that it occurs in the setting of a ritual.[32] The confusion here is not so much a matter of mistaking a woman for a goddess, but a confusion about the limits of the significance of ritual acts.

In the case of the Toumba building at Lefkandi, issues of representation do not arise in the same way. Yet the presence of a monumental building at the very beginning of the archaeological evidence for apsidal-ended dwelling structures must raise the question as to whether the new technology that these buildings involved did not similarly raise issues about the false images to which they might give rise. Should we not see here too a pre-emptive strike, the creation and destruction of a building on a previously unimagined scale which sanctifies the monumental building before it can ever become everyday? Certainly when apsidal-ended build-ings on anything like the same scale appear again in the archaeological record there is no doubt that they are cult buildings.

The traditional emphasis on the link between monumentality and complex societies has correctly perceived a connection, but has falsely taken the connection to be a direct one. Were the link direct, then it would be hard to explain why we do not simply meet monumental palaces or forts. But such direct gestures have the

[32] Herodotus 1.60.

disadvantage, as well as the advantage, of their specificity: for a ruler or ruling group to display power and superiority in so direct a way attracts envy and, equally riskily, emulation, encouraging resentment and encouraging socially divisive and dangerous insistence on hierarchy in other sectors of society. If one person or group can create the monumental, then another person or group can create an alternative monument. Or, in the equivalent of adding a negative to a verbal claim, destroy the monument that has been built. Once monumentality becomes possible, persons and groups with the power to create what is out-sized cannot forego that possibility, for that too would be to leave the field open to alternatives. But taking up that possibility in a ritual context is the adaptive option, the option which avoids the dangers inherent in the over-sanctification of the everyday. Ritual deployment not only involves (a substantial part of) the subordinate group, which can be made to own the monument even while being well aware of the power represented by the mustering of resources that has made that monument possible; it also grounds the monument not in claims to secular power but in the Ultimate Sacred Postulates. The visible, and undeniable, monument is made to attest to the invisible, and unfalsifiable; in doing that it occludes the real relations of temporal power which have made it possible, or rather transforms them from arbitrary and conventional to necessary and natural.[33] Far from being an in-your-face gesture, the attractions of monumentalizing lie in the ability of ritual to turn the human gaze away from the everyday.[34]

[33] I borrow, for one last time, from Rappaport (1999:407): "at the end of the last chapter I called attention to the remarkable structure embodied in the Holy and realized in ritual: the unfalsifiable supported by the undeniable yields the unquestionable, which transforms the dubious, the arbitrary and the conventional into the correct, the necessary and the natural."

[34] An earlier version of this chapter was given as a paper at a seminar in Corpus Christi College Oxford on "Monumentality." I am grateful to the audience on that occasion, and particularly to John Ma and to Nicholas Purcell, for a stimulating discussion, to Dimitrios Yatromanolakis not only for the invitation to contribute to this volume but for suggesting that I could clarify my ideas and argument by reference to Rappaport's work, and to Jaś Elsner for reading and commenting on a penultimate draft.

Three

Ritual Poetics in Archaic Lesbos: Contextualizing Genre in Sappho

Dimitrios Yatromanolakis

The study of ancient Greek literature and its sociocultural imaginary, not unlike the study of any area in the human sciences, is defined by paradigms.[1] In the case of archaic Greek literature and society, a marked evolution in scholarly paradigms characterized the nineteenth century, and, to a certain degree, continues to influence current research. The idea, for instance, that in the history of ancient Greek song-making traditions epic poetry appeared first, and that inevitably archaic lyric poetry was somewhat modeled on that epic tradition—"modeled" in the broader sense of adaptation, responsive dialogue, or refutation of what came before—is a "paradigm" that has endured for over a century. Although this idea has been undermined considerably, its impact on scholarship is still evident. Research on archaic Greek culture is occasionally marred by such paradigms, since scholars are used to "reading" ancient Greek poetic and sociocultural mentalities through specific, often overly culturally determined perceptual filters.[2] And perhaps the most precarious, but influential, paradigm is the concept that Western cultural systems are sometimes so imbued with the distant mentalities of the ancient Greeks that we can safely attempt to understand their societies "through our own eyes" rather than through the comparative eyes of "foreign cultures."[3]

This chapter examines an intriguing paradigm that has informed the investigation of archaic Greek tropes of lyric speech genres. My main "geographical" focus is archaic Lesbos, with a more specific emphasis on the cultural contexts in which

---

[1] The concept of "paradigm" in the context of speaking about fields of research was introduced by Thomas Kuhn in his influential book *The Structure of Scientific Revolutions* (Kuhn 1962).

[2] For such culturally determined "readings," see Sourvinou-Inwood 1991:3–23. For similar issues in "reading" archaic Greek poetry, see Parsons 2001:60–62; cf. Yatromanolakis 2001c:220–225 (revised form of Yatromanolakis 1998).

[3] For pathfinding recent discussion, see Detienne 2000 and 2001.

Sappho composed her songs. My broader concern, which can only briefly be touched upon in this chapter, is the concept of "genre" and its relationship to ritual in the so-called "lyric age" of archaic Greece.[4]

Ritual in Sappho has been a much-discussed subject. Since medieval times (and here I will not refer to the situation in antiquity since this is another, highly complex issue)[5] Sappho has been granted the role of a primarily ritual poet. She has been seen as—and called—priestess, sorceress, cult leader. Her alleged involvement in a sort of *Mädchenbund* has gained favor over time and was the subject of a remarkable, albeit highly speculative, theory by Reinhold Merkelbach.[6] Another, more recent scholarly approach sees Sappho as a fully-fledged "initiator" in ceremonies that follow all three phases of rites of passage proposed by Arnold van Gennep: separation, transition, and incorporation.[7]

I would think that, along with Alcman's *partheneia* or maiden songs, Sappho's songs are striking examples of "performative" discourse blending ritual and sexuality in the most elusive manner. Out of this blending comes our ever-increasing *aporia* about what might have been the social and cultural context in which these songs were composed. Archaic and classical lyric poetry is replete with significant ritual dimensions, several of which still need further—and perhaps more theoretically informed—investigation. The case of Archilochus and his possible ritual "stock characters," that is, the suicidal Neoboule and Lykambes, constitutes a question about archaic Greek poetry that resists consensus.[8] Ritual language in Alcman, Pindar, and Simonides is an equally intriguing area. Ritual occasion in Sappho (and Alcman) is perhaps the thorniest topic in current research on archaic lyric. In this chapter, I employ Sappho as a case study for an analysis of *ritual poetics* in archaic Lesbos.

Scholarly paradigms

From Welcker's 1816 "Sappho freed from a reigning prejudice" to Wilamowitz's reconstructed Sapphic innocence and Lesbian boarding schools, to Merkelbach's *Mädchenbund*, to Calame's choruses of young girls and pre-matrimonial education, to Hallett's Sappho raising the sensual consciousness of young women, to Gentili's

---

[4] I probe these concepts from a wider angle in my forthcoming book *Sappho in the Making* (Yatromanolakis forthcoming).

[5] For aspects of the earliest reception, see Yatromanolakis 2001a and 2004.

[6] Merkelbach 1957.

[7] Rösler 1992.

[8] See West 1974:27 and Nagy 1999:243–252; contra Rankin 1978, Gentili 1982, and Carey 1986. Cf. also Burnett 1983:19–23.

Sapphic cults of Aphrodite, influential models of "life and conduct" have been imposed on Sappho.[9] This is not the place to set out modern theories about Sappho's original audience. However, I should point out that in such reconstructions there is an underlying tendency to "attribute" genre categories to Sappho's fragments.

While scholarship on Sappho has become labyrinthine and arguments and polemics increase, the extant material that would provide some clues to our understanding of her work remains, I argue, in specific cases, underexplored. For example, partly following approaches current in the nineteenth century, twentieth-century scholarship, more often than not, attempted to see in the fragments of Sappho and the testimonia on her, references to the age of her companions and their role in the so-called "Sapphic circle."[10] This use of late *sources* as *evidence* for archaic realities is not confined only to discussions of the age of her companions, but also extends to the analysis of issues relating to the performance of her poetry.[11] The results of such inquiries are often based on late, post-Hellenistic sources;[12] earlier representations of Sappho have been persistently underexplored. More broadly, the ancient reception of Sappho has not received proper attention; the ancient sources have been approached with no systematic methodological or theoretical apparatus. The need to broaden our investigation is urgent. Sappho, I submit, should be revisited from several different perspectives. Such a reappraisal should also be based on a close analysis of her surviving textual corpus. Sappho's text has recently suffered from a curious lack of scholarly attention. Current critical editions do not incorporate new material, which would, to some extent, facilitate literary analysis. More importantly, many parchments and papyri were transcribed and edited—at times hastily—in the first half of the twentieth century. In their critical edition, Lobel and Page did not, in certain cases, re-examine the originals, but based their text on previous papyrological work by Schubart, Zuntz, and several other scholars.[13] In her monumental edition, Voigt has adopted the same practice

---

[9] Concerning the alleged involvement of Sappho in a cult association or teaching responsibilities, Denys Page has attempted to exorcise "these melancholy modern ghosts" (Page 1955:140), but there have been many opponents to such an attempt: see e.g. Murray 1993 (p. 327: "D. L. Page . . . denies a cult of Aphrodite in Sappho, wrongly in my opinion"). Traces of Welcker's influence (Welcker 1816) are still evident in e.g. Bennett's views (Bennett 1994).

[10] Starting with Welcker's *Sappho von einem herrschenden Vorurtheil befreyt* (Welcker 1816), see also Merkelbach 1957, West 1970, Rösler 1992, and Calame 1997:210–214, 231–233, 249–252.

[11] Yatromanolakis 1999a:185n28 and 184–187. In Yatromanolakis 1999a, I deliberately distinguished the concept of "sources" from that of "evidence."

[12] See above, n. 10; more recently, Lardinois 1994; cf. Lardinois 1996.

[13] To mention only a few cases of recent treatments based on autopsy, and of the most recent material: Malnati 1993, Yatromanolakis 1999b, Steinrück 2000, and Ucciardello 2001.

throughout.[14] In their turn, literary critics and cultural historians have based their (frequently influential) analyses on puzzling or inaccurate texts.[15] Theories on Sappho have too often rested upon further theories, all eventually based on the text that Lobel-Page and Voigt offer. And, as I mentioned above, literary testimonia on Sappho are still widely used to ponder questions such as the role of women in the "Sapphic circle" and in the society of archaic Lesbos.[16]

Genre and Ritual

In this chapter, I approach Sappho's poetics in terms of ritual and genre. I first examine current taxonomies of genre in Sappho in terms of the question of the ritual character of her poetry. In this context, I propose a new way of viewing the interaction between ritual and genre in Sappho's poetic discourse. First, I argue that the application of genre categories to Sappho can be misleading and that the existing fragments permit us to discern what we would call "genre" fluidity. Second, my analysis of the question of ritual and genre will lead to an examination of a couple of the longest and most intriguing fragments of Sappho. I primarily focus on her so-called "personal" and "cult" songs, which constitute the largest part of her slim textual corpus. The issue of genre in these songs is of particular significance in the study of Sappho, since there has been a marked tendency on the part of a number of scholars to define the sociocultural function of Sappho's poetry on the basis of genre categories.

One of the most complex features of Sappho's poetics is its polyphonic dimensions. So far as her fragments allow us to discern, Sappho assumes diverse poetic personae and constructs multi-faceted, ritualistic discourses. On a more basic level, the poetic voice is assimilated into different subject positions or explores the dynamics of other voices in the song. Such polyphony is evident in many of the fragments of Sappho:[17] for example, in fragment 1 V., apparently a complete song, the poetic subject, quoting Aphrodite's voice coming from the past, becomes Aphrodite, while in fragment 96 V. the multiplicity of the voices of the "internal audience" of the song becomes a metaphor for the ties that bind together its female characters.

These polyphonic dimensions may contribute to elucidating what I would call polyphonic ritual and genre discourses in Sappho's poetry. As noted earlier, in

---

[14] Lobel and Page 1955; Voigt 1971.
[15] Two striking and significant examples of such texts are fragments 94 and 96: an examination of Voigt's detailed critical apparatus of fragments 94 and 96 will demonstrate how difficult it is to determine which of the numerous different papyrological readings listed there is the most accurate.
[16] See e.g. the otherwise most insightful work by Calame (see above, n. 10).
[17] For the fragments of Sappho I use Voigt's edition; henceforth V. stands for Voigt.

both older and current research on Sappho a tendency to apply to her poems rigid categories of genre classification can often be discerned. One of the most influential and much-reiterated definitions of genre laws concerning archaic lyric poetry is that of Luigi Rossi, who has argued that during the archaic period literary genres followed laws that were unwritten, but respected ("leggi non scritte, ma rispettate").[18] More specifically, it has been assumed that Sappho, too, followed these unwritten genre laws, and, as a consequence, most of her so-called "personal" and "cult" poems have often been attributed "genre titles." Some examples will illustrate the point.[19] Fragment 2 V., preserved on a third-century BCE ostrakon, where Aphrodite is summoned to come from Crete to a supposedly holy temple,[20] has been given the definite genre classification of a "ritual song."[21] Fragment 17 V., with its references to Hera and maidens, has been seen as a "ritual hymn."[22] Fragment 140 V. has been analyzed as a "cult song" about Adonis.[23] For many scholars over the last two centuries, fragment 31 V. constitutes a wedding song. The list of such general genre taxonomies can be extensive in the case of Sappho's poetry. These constructed genre categories have led to further classifications of her poems according to their alleged ritual function. It has been argued that certain "ritual" songs allude to specific ritual occasions with which Sappho was associated. Based on this sort of tacitly accepted genre classification, arguments have been advanced with respect to a possible distinction between "ritual" and more "personal" songs; as a result, attempts have been made at a possible attribution of particular references and addresses to young girls and adult women to each of these song categories,

---

[18] Rossi 1971:75–77. I should note in advance that Rossi's perceptive discussion does not suggest rigid taxonomies for the work of individual poets. For literary genres in archaic Greece, see Harvey 1955 and Calame's thought-provoking views (Calame 1974). More congenial to my approach are the ideas explored from a different perspective and with a particular emphasis on the concept of *mimesis* by Nagy (1994–95b). Nagy insightfully suggests that "definitions of *genre* have to be related with questions of *occasion*," and that in archaic Greece "the occasion *is* the genre" (Nagy 1994–95b:11 and 13, respectively).

[19] Lardinois 2001 is a recent representative of the paradigm discussed in this chapter. However, this approach is by no means confined to Lardinois (see his references to earlier bibliography).

[20] See, among others, Gentili 1988:79 ("One such epiphany occurs at the moment of ritual invocation in the spot sacred to the goddess . . ."); Lardinois 1996:165.

[21] Lardinois 2001:77–78 ("the hymn was probably sung by a chorus of young women"; "Both this hymn to Aphrodite and the . . . song for Adonis [i.e. fr. 140 V.] suggest an intimate relationship between the goddess of love and young women, who're probably meant to adopt her as a model for their own budding sexuality").

[22] Lardinois 1996:165 ("These two fragments [i.e. frs. 2 and 17] together with fragment 140a (*the Adonis hymn*) suggest that at least some of Sappho's (choral) poetry was composed for ritual occasions, not unlike Alcman's partheneia"; my emphasis).

[23] This song "seems to have been part of a public celebration of the Adonia" (Lardinois 2001:77).

respectively.[24] Categories of genre have been closely connected with—and have sometimes subconsciously played a significant role in the creation of—alleged ritual roles that have been assigned to Sappho's companions and to Sappho herself. These constructed ritual roles, in turn, have verified the validity of genre taxonomies. This is indeed a case of a vicious circle of argumentation.

Let us for a moment go back to Rossi's broad definition of genre for archaic lyric poetry. Rossi argues that, in contrast with the Hellenistic period, during the archaic period literary genres followed laws that were unwritten, but respected. This presupposes the existence of the concept of genre laws (even unwritten) in the primarily oral societies of archaic Greece. But, although it might be argued that Pindar followed unwritten laws relating to encomiastic poetry and tried to meet the horizons of expectations of his audiences with regard to epinician poetry, Sappho's so-called "personal" or "ritual" songs do not suggest anything of the kind.

The various genre classifications of Sappho's poetry that I briefly discussed above betray an anachronistic imposition of modern scholarly analytical preconceptions on the fluidity and, I would stress, *interdiscursivity* characterizing verbal art in traditional and predominantly oral societies. Trying to define characteristics of different genres and draw clear-cut boundaries between them is an analytical method that has widely been applied in literary and ethnographic studies. As Dan Ben-Amos has remarked in a seminal article on traditional genres and genre taxonomies, scholarly discourse, by constructing tools and concepts, has often transformed cultural categories of communication into analytical models for the identification and classification of texts. Traditional genres have been approached "as if they were not relative divisions in a totality of an oral tradition but absolute forms."[25] It is my contention that genre criticism regarding Sappho's so-called "personal" or "cult" songs should not conform to such analytical classificatory

---

[24] Parker and, more explicitly, Stehle make the distinction between ritual and more personal songs, and attribute particular references and addresses to girls and adult women to each of these two categories, respectively: Parker 1993:325; Stehle 1997:267f. and 270. They both come to the conclusion that in Sappho's poetry the named female figures of the more "personal" songs are never characterized as *parthenoi* (young girls), while in the *epithalamia* (wedding songs) the *parthenos* getting married is never addressed by name.

[25] Ben-Amos 1976:215–216. Ben-Amos' article (originally published in *Genre* 2, no. 3 [1969], 275–301) provided a pioneering analysis of scholarly, analytical classification of ethnic genres as opposed to native taxonomies. Ben-Amos insightfully reminds us that "[t]he logical principles that underlie native taxonomy of oral tradition are those which are meaningful to the members of the group and can guide them in their personal relationships and ritualistic actions" (225). For traditional, oral genres and their interaction with cultural systems of metaphor and with performative tropes, see the syntheses in Roilos 1998 and 2002. Roilos 2002 explores the notion of "vocality" in Renaissance Greek poetry, a notion that would prove significant in a comparative study of oral traditions in ancient Greece and other traditional cultures.

models. Instead, the notion of genre in this period should be viewed, I argue, in terms of contextually determined communicative interaction between the performer and his/her audience.

In terms of ancient Greek literature, a more theoretically informed definition of genre has recently been proposed: "genre is a conceptual orienting device that suggests to an audience the sort of receptorial conditions in which a fictive discourse might have been delivered."[26] I would agree with much of this flexible working definition, but I would not subscribe to the use of the notion of "device," in terms of archaic Greece at least. Sappho's poetry was located within a larger framework of cultural exchange and interaction often enacted in particular performative contexts. In such a context, the audience would function as quasi co-author of the transmitted text, in the sense that its semantic and connotative dimensions, often embedded in traditional patterns of communication, were subject to a process of decoding based on shared, culturally defined, terms of communication and *indigenous frames of reference*. As in every context of communicative exchange, the participants—poet, audience—interact on the basis of what linguistic anthropologists would call "contextualization cues."[27] It is such cues that allow the participants to invoke simultaneously diverse frames of communication. In the case of literary compositions in archaic Greece, we could more preferably speak about flexible deep, but not necessarily strictly defined, structures of artistic or complex speech genres.[28] Genres in this early period were, I submit, cultural modes of communication, each dependent on specific contexts and, to some extent, on the poet's particular voice. Context is the defining factor in archaic genres.[29] Anthropological studies suggest that genre can be socially identified in diverse ways according to the different contexts in which it may be "located."[30] Further, for archaic lyricists genres are to a certain degree connected with style and should, therefore, be seen as lying

[26] Depew and Obbink 2000:6.
[27] Duranti and Goodwin 1992:5–7; Gumperz 1992 (cf. Gumperz's 1982 foundational work); Duranti 1997:19–20, 211–212.
[28] In the sense Bakhtin employs the term *complex speech genres* in "The Problem of Speech Genres" (Bakhtin 1986). Bakhtin speaks about simple and complex (that is, literary, scientific, etc.) speech genres, the complex, literary ones being in constant dialogue with other speech genres. Bauman uses Bakhtin's insights in his investigation of dialogue of speech genres in Icelandic legends of the *kraftaskáld* (Bauman 1992).
[29] Cf. Nagy 1994–95b, who pays particular attention to the concept of *mimesis* in terms of *genre* and *occasion*.
[30] See, among many ethnographies, the insightful work by Joyce Burkhalter Flueckiger (1996:26–49) on the middle Indian female festival tradition called *bhojalī*, which is celebrated in the Phuljhar periphery by unmarried pubescent girls who form ritual friendships, while in the Raipur heartland of Chhattisgarh this female festival tradition is celebrated by married women, who become possessed by the goddess they worship. The differences between the two performative contexts produce different receptions and formations of the song tradition associated with the festival.

at the intersection of traditionality and individuality. In other words, in archaic lyric poetry a merger of traditional speech genres and the individual speech genres "constructed" by the poet occurs. Archaic poets, often considered by indigenous interpretive frames of reference to be "masters of truth,"[31] could shape and re-shape particular genres and give them diverse formal and thematic features.

In the case of Sappho's "personal" (if we may use this term) and "cult" songs, our approach to genre should be broadened: allusions to possible ritual contexts cannot necessarily be taken as references to the actual performative context of a song. Instead, a closer look at Sappho's poetry suggests that a "literary" composition, as far as our surviving texts allow us to see, often constitutes a communicative, performative event that could absorb elements of diverse ritual discourses.[32] I submit that what characterizes Sappho's poetics is not conformity to any analytical delineation of genres, but interdiscursivity of diverse ritual discourses and ritual imagery. Her "literary" production should be perceived as a communicative aesthetic system, embedded in the broader traditional context of artistic communication in the society of archaic Lesbos that could often invoke ceremonial or ritualistic modes of expression. To go a step further, ritual discourses can become an integral feature of poetic genre without constituting contextualization cues, which point to specific contexts. For example, allusions in Sappho to different kinds of ritual imagery can inform her poetic discourse and affect its reception by an audience, but it is only the specific context within which the performance takes place that can ultimately help "decode" the genre of a particular song. As long as the context is unknown, it is precarious to assume that particular allusions imply specific contexts. I would argue that Sappho's songs are often polyphonic and dialogic, and that it is the interdiscursivity of ritual discourses and ritual imagery in them that constitutes a significant aspect of Sappho's poetics.

I will begin by discussing fragment 2 V., the fragment that has been preserved on a third-century BCE ostrakon, the so-called Florentine ostrakon of Sappho. I will then discuss one the longest songs, fragment 94 V.

It has been assumed that fragment 2 V. represents a cult song or hymn.[33] This suggests ritual and, to some extent, Sappho's role as a sort of composer of ceremonial songs for choruses of young girls. I would not think otherwise, had there been

---

[31] On archaic poets as "masters of truth," see Detienne's seminal study (1996:35–52, originally published in 1967 as *Les Maîtres de vérité dans la Grèce archaïque*); see also Nagy 1989 and Thomas 1995.

[32] I should spell out that I do not suggest that there occurs in Sappho *Kreuzung der Gattungen*. This idea would distance archaic genres from their communicative, interdiscursive dimensions that I propose.

[33] See above, nn. 21 and 22.

anything in the poem to suggest such genre classification. The fragment, as printed by Voigt, is as follows:

ια ..ανοθεν κατιου[σ | -
1   †δευρυμμεκρητεσιπ[.]ρ[ ] | .† ναῦον
    ἄγνον ὄππ[αι] | χάριεν μὲν ἄλσος
    μαλί[αν], | βῶμοι δ' ἔ‹ν›ι θυμιάμε-
4   νοι [λι]βανώτω‹ι›·
    ἐν δ' ὔδωρ ψῦχρο[ν]ı | κελάδει δι' ὔσδων
    μαλίνων, | βρόδοισι δὲ παῖς ὀ χῶρος
    ἐσκίαστ', αἰθυσσομένων δὲ φύλλων |
8   κῶμα †καταιριον·
    ἐν δὲ λείμων | ἰππόβοτος τέθαλε
    †τωτ...(.)ριν|νοισт ἄνθεσιν, αἰ ‹δ'› ἄηται
    μέλλιχα πν[έο]ισιν [
12   [ ]
    ἔνθα δὴ σὺ †συ.αν† | ἔλοισα Κύπρι
    χρυσίαισιν ἐν κυλίκεσσιν ἄβρως
    ‹ὀ›μ‹με›μείλχμενον θαλίαισι | νέκταρ
16 οἰνοχόεισα

Hither to me from Crete to this holy temple,
where is your delightful grove
of apple-trees, and altars smoking
    with incense;

therein cold water babbles through apple-
branches, and the whole place is shadowed
by roses, and from the shimmering leaves
    the sleep of enchantment comes down;

therein too a meadow, where horses graze, blossoms
with spring flowers, and the winds
blow gently [
    [   ]

there, Cypris, take . . .
pouring gracefully into golden cups
nectar that is mingled with
    our festivities.[34]

In this fragment, the poetic voice addresses Aphrodite and invites her to come from Crete to a delightful grove to join "the participants" in their festivities. Athenaeus, who quotes the last four lines (13–16), provides the following "Attic version" for these lines: ἐλθέ, Κύπρι,/χρυσίαισιν ἐν κυλίκεσσιν ἀβρῶς/συμμεμιγμένον θαλίαισι νέκταρ/οἰνοχοοῦσα ("Come, Cypris, pouring gracefully into golden cups nectar that is mingled with our festivities"). Athenaeus' text does not end with the word οἰνοχοοῦσα; it continues with the "deictic" phrase τούτοισι τοῖς ἑταίροις ἐμοῖς γε καὶ σοῖς ("for these friends of mine and yours"). The phrase "for these friends of mine and yours" may well have been part of Sappho's original poem. In such case, the "Attic version" attested by Athenaeus may possibly be connected with the Athenian "performative" transmission of Sappho's songs.

Even so, the song in this stanza (13–16) alludes to symposiastic contexts and drinking rituals, while in its first lines it evokes the atmosphere of a ritual invocation to the goddess. I argue that Sappho here uses diverse ritual discourses or imagery which allude to different ritualized, performative contexts. The song does not represent a cult hymn. Even the assumption that the reading ναῦον ("temple") in line 1 refers to a real shrine, which Aphrodite is invoked to visit, may raise objections. First, let us briefly consider the problems involved in reading poetic (and, by extension, cultural) "fragments." It would seem methodologically precarious to think that this "fragment" is a cult song or hymn, since: (a) we have neither its beginning nor its end; (b) more important, the setting may be imaginary; and (c) the *performative context* of the song may be different from the *descriptive context* of the song. A fundamental (but unjustly overlooked) problem in reading archaic lyric poetry is the fact that scholars often simply identify the *performative context* (which is in many cases unknown) with the *descriptive context* of a song, and then reconstruct the "realities" of a song, its poet, and, by extension, her/his society through the *descriptive contexts* she/he provides in her/his poetry. No doubt, the *performative context* of a song may sometimes be identified with its *descriptive context*. But, since Sappho often blends diverse ritualized discourses in the *descriptive contexts* of her songs, thus subtly

---

[34] The translation (slightly adapted here) is by Campbell (1982:57). Following Lobel and Page, Campbell prints οἰνοχόαισον, instead of οἰνοχόεισα, in line 16.

creating her own multi-faceted performative interaction with her audiences, it would be speculative to superimpose genre taxonomies on her poems and then attempt to identify "allusions" to ritual contexts in her songs. In other words, diverse ritual discourses are embedded in her songs, thus rendering any genre classifications rigid. Further, in contrast to what has often been assumed or taken for granted, it may be noted that the marked word ναῦον, even in the context of the first stanza, cannot lead us to any definite conclusions about the performative context of the song, especially since its "religious" connotations may be somewhat undermined by the actual conditions of the transmission of the fragment. The third-century BCE potsherd on which the song has been inscribed abounds with scribal errors, a fact that, I should stress, must be borne in mind when we attempt to approach—or emend—the text. It seems certain that the second half of the line reads .ΝΑΥΓΟΝ (or .ΝΑΥΓΟΝ),[35] while it seems possible that the uncertain letter before ΝΑΥΓΟΝ is Ḙ. The transmitted text is not ΝΑΥΟΝ. To be sure, ναῦον ("temple") is an emendation. It would, therefore, seem just as likely that, instead of reading the transmitted] ḘΝΑΥΓΟΝ as .ναῦον, we could read it as ἔναυ⟨λ⟩ον ("dwelling"), the majuscule letters gamma (Γ) and lamba (Λ) being easily confused. In fact, ἔναυ⟨λ⟩ον is an emendation that was originally suggested by Pfeiffer,[36] and has convincingly been defended by Lanata.[37] There seems to be, I believe, no reason to prefer the emendation usually adopted. If we accepted ἔναυ⟨λ⟩ον, the lines would read "Hither to me from Crete to this holy dwelling, where is your delightful grove of apple-trees." Thus, the marked connotations of the "word" (read: "emendation") "shrine" would somewhat retreat,[38] and the (imaginary) setting of the poem could, on a discursive/poetic level, be compared with the ἄλσος ("grove") that "Sappho" and the other female figure of fragment 94 V., to which I will now turn, apparently visited together.[39] The merger of diverse ritual discourses, that is, allusions to ritual

---

[35] For successive decipherments (by the editor princeps Medea Norsa, and later by Giuliana Lanata) of this line of the ostrakon, see Voigt's critical apparatus. Note that, given the difficulties of the text, Lobel and Page's critical apparatus is not as precise and detailed. For the results of a recent autopsy of the Florentine ostracon (=*PSI* XIII 1300), see Malnati 1993. Malnati does not discuss this reading.

[36] See Voigt's critical apparatus.

[37] Lanata 1960: 81. Diehl 1942 (pp. 32–33) prints ἔ]ναυ⟨λ⟩ον, considering it "potius quam ναῦον." Page does not discuss it in his commentary (Page 1955). In their critical apparatus Lobel and Page do not mention even as a possibility Pfeiffer's emendation. Voigt duly includes it in her critical apparatus.

[38] It should be stressed that ἄγνον in line 2 (let alone lines 3–4) suggests "a holy place," but my point here remains that literal interpretations of lines 1–2, especially based on an emendation (ναῦον) that has been taken as a clear contextual allusion, have led us to precarious genre classifications of this fragment and, hence, to circular arguments about *specific* ritual performative contexts in Sappho.

[39] Characteristically, West (1970:317) believes that in the context of the *locus amoenus* described in the fragment, "Sappho and her companions are enjoying a picnic."

contexts, in Sappho's poetry makes the identification of *specific* ritual occasions more difficult than most often assumed.

Let us now look at fragment 94. In this fragment, the vocative in line 5 (Ψάπφ') identifies the narrating voice as that of "Sappho." The other voice addressing "Sappho" speaks in lines 4–5. Our primary difficulty is knowing how much of lines 1–3 represents quoted speech. Specifically, who speaks—or is quoted in—the phrase τεθνάκην δ' ἀδόλως θέλω ("Honestly I wish I were dead")?[40] Since the first publication of the fragment in 1902, the attribution of line 1 has been the subject of intense scholarly debate. Restrictions of space do not allow me to elaborate on this issue.[41] I will only note that in these first five lines with quoted speech several instances of asyndeton occur.[42] As Aristotle and the ancient literary critic Demetrius observe,[43] passages with asyndeton involve inner strain and require reading aloud, since they belong to a more "hypocritic" kind of writing (they require acting). Certainly lines 4–5 (and, possibly, line 1) demand such a dramatic delivery.

[40] This is the first line of the fragment, and in lines 1–3 there are no unambiguous cues to help us recontextualize it. Attempts have been made to "reconstruct" the content of the missing glyconic that preceded line 1. Jurenka (1902:290) proposed the following: οἴχωκ' "Ατθις, ἄχυς μ' ἔχει. Edmonds (1928:240) envisaged a supplement more or less similar: "Ατθιδ' οὔποτ' ἄρ' ὄψομαι. West also (1970:318) believed that the name of the departing female figure must have appeared in the lost part of the poem. Along different lines, Robbins (1990:115), by analogy with Sappho fragment 95 V., suggested ζώοισ' οὐδὲν ἔτ' ἄδομαι. It should be noted that the first three of these four highly speculative attempts conform to the general scholarly tendency to suggest personal names as supplements to the gaps in Sappho's poems.

[41] Very briefly, if the line is to be assigned to one of the personae that, it seems, are involved in the fragment, there are three possibilities: a) to give the line to "Sappho"'s friend at the time of parting, b) to give it to the female narrator of this parting and commentator on the feelings that she herself communicates to the audience of the song, or c) to give the line to the speaking "Sappho" at the time of parting. The third possibility seems out of the question, since that would create, on the temporal axis of narrative, a great divergence between the "consolatory" dimension of "Sappho"'s quoted speech in lines 7ff. and her quoted poignant sorrow in line 1. The second possibility has so far been adopted by most scholars. Although Schubart, the editor princeps of the fragment, suggested that the line was spoken by the female figure who is leaving, in the same year Reinach (1902:65) set the course of future interpretations: "avec H. Weil j'attribue ces paroles à Sappho, non à son interlocutrice." If forced to choose between the two possibilities, I would be inclined to give the line to the departing female figure. Attributing the line to "Sappho" would presuppose a split in the persona of the narrator: if line 1 was spoken by her, the equation *narrator* (whose voice is heard for the first time in line 2) = *poet who is now* (line 1) *describing what her feelings are*, would not hold true. Of course, the reservation that any arguments on this issue may have a certain circularity must be kept in mind. One might hold, for example, that if we accepted the involvement of both an "objective" narrator and an "interpretive" one, the registers of voices in the fragment would be even more complex.

[42] In lines 4–5, which are spoken by the departing friend, we have two instances of asyndeton combined with end-stopping.

[43] Aristotle *Rhetoric* 3.12, 1413b, 18–22; Demetrius *De elocutione* (On Style) 193–194.

Further, I would argue that the use of intensely dramatic expressions, which contain weeping declarations, interjections, affirmations of pain, etc., suggests that this part of the song draws on the genre discourse of ritual lament. The idea of repetition that line 3 may indicate (πόλλα καὶ τόδ᾽ ἔειπέ [μοι, "often she said this too," or "she said much and this in particular") is also consistent with the characteristic use of repetition in threnodic songs, a "genre" with which Sappho was familiar. Such a tone seems appropriate for the expression of the departing friend's grief. If line 1 is assigned to her, too, we hear her wishing she were dead as she confronts the separation. The narrator quotes her words, then cuts them short (possibly she had used many expressions of this kind), then quotes the climax of her speech, lines full of agonized exclamation. This lamentation affects even the narrative of the narrator, who uses asyndeton to denote it (see line 3). The accumulated intensity of painful feelings leads to the intervention of "Sappho" in the rest of the poem.

Now, comparing this fragment to Erinna's *Distaff*,[44] Rauk has argued that the poem represents a lament, since, the reasoning goes, the invocation of memory in "Sappho"'s farewell (line 10) evokes standard characteristics of a ritual *thrênos*.[45] However, such an approach is not convincing: the style of "Sappho"'s long speech (starting with line 7 onwards) does not in itself evoke a mood of lament; especially lines 21–23 ("and on soft beds . . . you would satisfy your longing for tender . . ."), *if* they carry any sensual implications, resist inclusion in a ritual *thrênos*. As I have already indicated, an analysis of the first five lines suggests the use of genre discourses of threnodic songs. But I would further argue that if we now look at "Sappho"'s response, we can discern another kind of ritual discourse embedded in the narrative. This time it comes from the ritualized world of the *sumposion*. In what follows, I suggest that in the quoted speech of "Sappho" we see a ritualized sequel of symposiastic images subtly re-enacted.

From line 12 onwards, where the speaker "Sappho" reminds her departing friend of the intense experiences they have shared, "Sappho" invokes some abstract snapshots of the past, dreamlike images deprived of specific time, a significant characteristic of ritual time, as analyzed by the anthropologist Edmund Leach.[46] The snapshots that Sappho unfolds before her audience contain marked elements of symposiastic rituals. The garlands in the first snapshot constituted a basic feature of Greek *sumposia*. It may be significant for our fragment that they were considered to be the indication of the beginning of a banquet; they frequently appear in sympotic contexts in literature and vase-paintings. Further, the ὑποθυμίδες in the second

---

[44] Erinna fragment 401 *SH* (*Supplementum Hellenisticum*).

[45] Rauk 1989:110. Lardinois has recently argued that fragments 16, 94, and 96 "in fact represent laments that Sappho herself or young friends of the bride performed at weddings" (2001:83). Cf. also Lardinois' analysis of fragment 96 (2001:86–88).

snapshot (known as the garlands of the Aeolians and the Ionians, which used to be worn around the neck [Athenaeus 15 674c]), were typical *accessoires* of comasts and symposiasts, as a number of vase-paintings show. Even more so, the perfumes in the third snapshot are probably among those used in *sumposia* (see Pollux 6.104–105); the pouring of perfumed unguents on the body (especially on the head and the breast), the reclining of men on couches—usually propping themselves by their left elbow on cushions—and, in the end, possible heterosexual or homoerotic intimacy, are all well-known features of a *sumposion*.

It is also significant to note that personal recollection, used as the subject of a poem, might have a special place in sympotic contexts, where the personal memory could reflect the collective memory of the participants, and the poetic "I" and "we" could coincide with the personal experiences of each member of the assemblage.[49] In this fragment, as in fragment 2.13–16, Sappho evokes images of the *sumposion*. This re-enactment of symposiastic snapshots draws on cultural discourses and imagery relating to banqueting rituals.[50]

To go back to my original argument: This fragment has been "classified" as a ritual song. It has also, rather curiously, been proposed that the fragment indicates that there was genre sophistication in early Greek poetry, since it can be construed as a *propemptikon* of equal to equal (according to Menander the Rhetor's rhetorical classifications).[51] As I have argued in this chapter, genre taxonomies imposed on

[46] Leach 1961; 1988:33–41.
[47] See Blech 1982:64–72.
[48] Blech 1982:71–72.
[49] See Rösler 1990:232–234; cf. Schmitt-Pantel 1990:21.
[50] In the last fragmentary stanzas of the song, the snapshots refer to a shrine, a grove, dance, sounds.
[51] Specifically, in connection with this fragment, Cairns has posed the question whether there is generic sophistication in early Greek poetry. He maintains that the fragment suggests that there was (Cairns 1972:53ff.), since it could be construed as a *propemptikon* of equal to equal (see Menander Rhetor 395.12–17 ἕτερος δὲ τρόπος (sc. τῆς προπεμπτικῆς λαλιᾶς) ἂν γένοιτο, ἐν ᾧ δυνήσεταί τις ἐνδείξασθαι ἦθος ἐρωτικὸν καὶ διάπυρον περὶ τὸν προπεμπόμενον, . . . τῆς ἀξίας ὑπαρχούσης ἐφαμίλλου καὶ τῆς δόξης ἴσης τῷ προπέμποντι καὶ τῷ προπεμπομένῳ, ὡς ὅταν ἑταῖρος ἑταῖρον προπέμπῃ). Cairns has suggested that all the standard *topoi* that are used in this kind of *propemptikon* ('go' with good wishes, "remember me," statement of affection) are employed by Sappho. Even what normally follows the statement of affection as it has been described by Menander (398.26–29 εἶτα ἐπὶ τούτοις ἅπασιν ἀξιώσεις αὐτὸν μεμνῆσθαι τῆς πάλαι συνηθείας, τῆς εὐνοίας, τῆς φιλίας, καὶ παραμυθεῖσθαι τὴν ἀπόστασιν μνήμαις καὶ λόγοις) fits, according to Cairns, the content and form of Sappho's fragment. Furthermore, regarding the function of the first part of the fragment, where the departing figure's despair at being separated from "Sappho" (lines 1–2, 4–5) is described, Cairns has proposed that fragment 94 might be an example of a poem which incorporates a variant of a genre within a member of the same genre, that is, a kind of *suntaktikon* (the speech of the departing friend) is included in a *propemptikon* (the speech that usually follows the *suntaktikon*). However, it should be stressed that the attempt to detect (and draw so complex a picture of) the features of the genre to which a song belongs by adducing evidence from rhetorical sources from late antiquity is contrary to the song's very nature.

Sappho's poetry have become facts and ideas that we all take for granted and hardly pause to ponder. Instead, it is the *interdiscursivity* of diverse ritual discourses and ritual imagery that constitutes one of the most complex aspects of Sappho's poetics. More specifically, in her so-called "personal" and "ritual" poetry, Sappho does not conform to the analytical categories that have customarily been applied to her songs, but she draws on the "grammar" of diverse cultural and ritual discourses, such as cult hymns, the world of the symposium, and ritual songs of mourning, which construct a polyphony of genre tropisms. This fusion of multiple ritual and cultural discourses detected in traditional poetry deeply embedded in ritual can be discerned in many of her fragments.[52] And this kind of polyphony, in turn, suggests that the figure of Sappho may not easily conform to ritual schemes and constructed ritual functions that have been repeatedly attributed to her over time. Interacting with diverse cultural modes of communication and drawing from diverse ritual discourses, Sappho develops a symbolic discourse embedded in the *ritual poetics* of her society.*

[52] In that respect, the vexed question whether Sappho fragment 31 V. is a wedding song (and this is still the belief of a considerable number of scholars) is based on a rigid and essentialized understanding of Sappho's poetics. This also applies to our understanding of songs such as 1V., 44V., 44a V., 48 V., and 58V.

* This chapter constitutes a small section of a wider investigation into genre, ritual, and sociocultural discourses in archaic Greece. I owe a special debt to John Shirley-Quirk, whose *amitié* created this study.

Four

Tragedy, Ritual, and Money

Richard Seaford

Monetization and the Dionysia

The first thoroughly monetized society in history was, I believe, the Greek *polis* of the archaic and classical periods, partly through the adoption of coinage.[1] The result is a collision—and to some extent a synthesis—between two powerful social forces, the traditional authority of ritual and the new power of money. This should be, I suggest, a crucial element in the historical perspective on the unprecedented form of Athenian tragedy. What I present here is merely a sketch of a new way of thinking about tragedy, to be filled out by further research.

The City Dionysia belonged to the minority of Athenian festivals that was named after deities. Most of them were named (like most months) after activities or places. Another festival named after deity was the Panathenaia. The Greater Panathenaia (held every four years) and City Dionysia seem to have been the most spectacular of Athenian festivals, each embellished with a magnificent procession. They also stand out in a third respect: they both seem to have been considerably developed, if not founded, at some point in the sixth century, probably during the time of the tyrants (c. 560–510).[2]

These three features cohere. The occasion of the ancient[3] Ionian Dionysiac festival called Anthesteria (its name probably derived from ἀνθεῖν, to blossom[4]) was the opening of the new wine in February, roughly a month after the various rural Dionysia. The newer "City Dionysia," on the other hand (Διονύσια τὰ ἀστικά or Διονύσια ἐν ἄστει, in contrast to other Dionysia), occurred in late

---

[1] I describe some of the intellectual and cultural consequences of this much-overlooked fact in Seaford 2004.

[2] Parker 1996:75–77, 89–95 supersedes previous discussion.

[3] Thucydides 2.15.4.

[4] Deubner 1932:114.

March . Whereas the procession at the rural Dionysia seems to have accorded pride of place to the *phallos*,[5] the carrying of *phalloi* seems to have been only a relatively inconspicuous element—albeit the culmination of an aetiological myth (scholia on Aristophanes *Acharnians* 243)—in the magnificent procession at the City Dionysia.[6] Whereas it seems that most Athenian festivals centered on traditional *activity* (much of it connected with agriculture),[7] after which they are frequently named, the City (or "Great") Dionysia and the Great Panathenaia were entirely or primarily *civic* festivals in the sense that they give the appearance of having been designed (in the sixth century) to display the magnificence and coherence of the whole *polis* both to itself and to outsiders. In contrast to some other Attic festivals, both festivals were *open* (with their rituals visible to all), and both festivals contained mass consumption of sacrificial meat.

Accordingly, the later date chosen for the Great Dionysia (*Elaphebolion*, late March) coincided with the opening of the sailing season, and facilitated the presence of strangers (including Athenian allies) at the festival.[8] More specifically, there were—again as at the Great Panathenaia (held in summer)—poetic contests in which strangers competed. It was Hipparchos, son of the tyrant Peisistratos, who was credited with the institution at the Panathenaia of rhapsodic contests in the recitation of Homer. These rhapsodes moved between city-states (Plato *Ion* 530a1–2). Similarly, of the earliest known poets at the City Dionysia (writing, directing, and perhaps performing in dithyrambs, tragedy, and satyric drama) many are not Athenian: Lasos from Hermione and Simonides from Ceos, both invited by Hipparchos and both competitors in dithyramb at Athens,[9] the dithyrambic victors Hypodikos from Chalkis (509–8 BCE), Pindar from Thebes (497/6 BCE), Melanippides of Melos (493/4 BCE), and (somewhat later) Bacchylides of Ceos,[10] and the very early dramatic poet Pratinas from Phleios. The period also seems to have seen the migration of visual artists from eastern Greece.[11]

---

[5] Aristophanes *Acharnians* 202, 237–279; Plutarch *Moralia* 527d; Attic black-figure cup, Florence 3897.

[6] Among numerous references to the festival it is known only from a likely supplement to IG 1³ 46.11–13, an instruction to the Athenian colonists at Brea in Thrace to bring a *phallos*.

[7] For the agricultural orientation of numerous Athenian festivals even as late as the classical period see Simon 1983:11 (Bouphonia); 13–14 (Diasia, Pompaia); 17 (cults of Demeter); 21 (Thesmophoria); 35 (Eleusinina Mysteries); 35 (Haloa); 45–46 (Arrhephoria); 77 (Thargelia, Pyanopsia); 90 (Oschophoria); 92ff. (Anthesteria). See also Parke 1977:186–187.

[8] E.g. Aristophanes *Acharnians* 505–506; Aeschines *Against Ctesiphon* 43; Demosthenes *Against Meidias* 74.

[9] Aristophanes *Wasps* 1410; Lasos and Simonides competing with each other.

[10] Herington 1985:94.

[11] Andrewes 1982:409.

The rhapsodes competed for cash prizes (at least in the time of Ion of Ephesos: Plato *Ion* 535e4–6), although in some musical contests crowns were given as prizes instead. To attract poets and performers from outside Athens to the festivals was surely an aim of the Athenian tyrants. Hipparchos "invited Anacreon, Simonides, and the other poets to Athens" (*Constitution of the Athenians* 18; similarly pseudo-Plato *Hipparchos* 228c). The poets were no doubt influenced to come by money. There is in the sixth century evidence of the practice of offering skilled individuals sufficient money to lure them from their current patron. The most famous doctor of his day, Demokedes of Kroton, earned a talent (60 minae) a year from the Aeginetans, then 100 minae from the Athenians, and then two talents from Polykrates tyrant of Samos (Herodotos 3.131), who also patronized Anacreon (Herodotos 3.121).[12] About Simonides we are told that Hippias induced him to come to Athens by large fees and gifts (pseudo-Plato *Hipparchos* 228c), that he was the first poet to compose *epinikia* "for a wage" (μισθός),[13] and that he was too fond of money.[14]

The payment of (and prizes for) poets and rhapsodes was of course not the only expense incurred by the civic festivals. There were also, notably, processions and sacrifices and (especially at the Dionysia) choruses. There are several reasons for believing that in general the financing of civic festivals such as the Dionysia were met, or at least controlled, by the tyrants. Thucydides (6.54) says that the tyrants extracted only a 5% tax on produce and yet embellished the city (sim. Herodotos 1.59), carried out wars, and performed sacrifices for the temples (καὶ ἐς τὰ ἱερὰ ἔθυον). Herodotos adds other sources of income: in preparation for their final return to Athens, the Peisistratids received contributions of money (χρήματα), especially from Thebes,[15] and after his final return Peisistratos rooted his tyranny (ἐρρίζωσε τὴν τυραννίδα) by means of numerous mercenaries (ἐπικούροισι) and by means of revenue from Attica and from the Strymon river (1.61, 64). In the argentiferous area of Mt. Pangaion (near the Strymon) he "acquired money and hired soldiers" (*Constitution of the Athenians* 15: χρηματισάμενος καὶ στρατιώτας μισθωσάμενος). It is from about the middle of the sixth century that the first Attic coins appear (in silver).[16] Analysis of the silver of the very first Attic coins (*Wappenmünzen*) has revealed a different composition from that of the

---

[12] Cf. Stobaios 4.31. 91 V p. 767 Hense.

[13] Ancient scholia on Pindar *Isthmian Odes* 2.9 (Drachmann 3.214); cf. Cicero *De Oratore* 2.86; (etc., Kurke 1991:59).

[14] The earliest of numerous reports are Xenophanes fr. 21; Aristophanes *Peace* 698–699.

[15] I wonder whether this influenced the Athenian tragic representation of the Theban tyrant obsessed with money (Pentheus, Oedipus, Kreon).

[16] Kroll and Waggoner 1984.

subsequent owl-coinage, suggesting that the earliest coins were derived from Pangaion and the subsequent coins from Laurion in Attika.[17] The rooting of the tyranny owed much not only to Peisistratos' possession and control of a huge amount of silver but also surely to the ease with which coinage allowed him to distribute wealth to mercenaries, builders (on his civic projects), and (as loans: *Constitution of the Athenians* 16) to farmers, as well as to raise the 5% tax (Thucydides 6.54.4; 10% according to *Constitution of the Athenians* 16). All this promoted (as did his "traveling judges," ibid. 16.5) centralized—at the expense of local aristocratic—patronage.

A late fourth-century BCE text, the pseudo-Aristotelian *Oikonomika*, records various revenue-raising measures and financial tricks attributed to Peisistratos' son Hippias. One of these was to allow anyone about to serve as *triêrarkhos* or *phylarkhos* or *khorêgos* (or incur expense for any other such liturgy) to commute the service for a moderate sum (τιμῆμα) and to be enrolled among those who had performed liturgies (1347a). Despite the unreliability of much of the *Oikonomika*, Peter Wilson (2000:15) has recently argued that this passage does contain "a memory of ancient practice," albeit "in a form heavily coloured by contemporary arrangements." Hippias is described elsewhere as sensible and concerned with the affairs of the *polis*, in contrast to his aesthetically inclined (φιλόμουσος) brother Hipparchos (*Constitution of the Athenians* 18). The centralization of patronage (a step towards *state* responsibility) meant that aristocrats contributed money (and probably some of the prestige) to a central fund controlled by Hippias. This change was no doubt driven (at least in part) by the flexibility inherent in monetization (especially coinage). About premonetary *khorêgia* we have no direct evidence, but it must have been limited by the material resources, the organizing engagement, the ability to barter and acquire, to provide feasts for the chorus,[18] etc., of each individual *khorêgos*. The advent of precious metal money (especially in the form of coinage), with its condensed power of universal acquisition and payment, greatly facilitates the acquisition of goods (e.g. costumes) and payment of fees. It may even have contributed to the transition of *khorêgos* from chorus-leader (as the *khorêgos* could mean) to non-dancing organizer.[19] In the fifth century an Athenian *khorêgos* describes how, being busy, he could not look after the chorus himself, and so appointed a superintendent and three other men, one of whom had to "purchase or

---

[17] Kraay 1976:59n1; Wallace 1962; Gale, Gentner and Wagner 1980:30 note that analysis shows that an origin of the silver from Laurion for the *Wappenmünzen* is excluded.

[18] On this practice see Aristophanes *Acharnians* 1153–1155; Plutarch *Moralia* 349ab; Athenaeus 4654f.; Schol. Aristophanes *Clouds* 339.

[19] The ideological aspect of the development of the title *khorêgos* onto the financier is discussed by Wilson 2000: 115–116.

spend whatever the poet or any of the others told him" (Antiphon *On the Chorus Boy* 11–13). To be sure, this *khorēgos* seems apologetic for a—possibly unusual—lack of personal engagement, but the facilitation of such detachment by money did not necessarily diminish prestige.[20] Indeed, the commutation of the liturgy by paying a fee to Hippias' central fund may have seemed—to those who accepted the offer—merely a further instance of the blessings brought by monetisation. But what the centralization of the *khorēgia* must have produced was a huge sum of money under the control of Hippias, with all the power and flexibility to create a truly spectacular show, worthy of the new central festival of Dionysos and a worthy demonstration of the magnificence of Athens.

With the fall of the tyranny and the creation of democratic institutions, it seems that the expenses of the City Dionysia were divided between the center (the *polis*) and individual *khorēgoi*.[21] Under the democracy the organization of the Great Dionysia fell not to the *basileus arkhōn*, who administered the traditional festivals rather than the new creations (*Constitution of the Athenians* 3.3; 57.1), but to the eponymous *arkhōn* (ibid. 56.3–4). This innovation may have been designed to ensure that the festival did not fall under traditional (aristocratic) control. If it was introduced by the tyrants, we must remember that according to Thucydides (6.54.6) they took care to ensure that their own people held the magistracies.

Two events recorded by fifth-century historians suggest that the Athenian tyrants understood the political significance of festivals. The first is the use made by Peisistratos, on his first return from exile, of a very tall girl called Phye, whom he dressed as Athena and joined in a chariot, successfully putting about the rumour that he was being escorted back by Athena to the Akropolis (Herodotos 1.60). Whether we imagine the Athenians as manipulated dupes or as willing participants in a shared fiction, one of the cultural patterns evoked by this display is the festival procession escorting the arrival of a god in Athens.[22] It is in fact typical of stories about tyrants that they misuse festivals in order to obtain power.[23] The other event is the murder of Hipparchos, which occurred as a result of Hipparchos (in Thucydides, at *Constitution of the Athenians*18, his brother Thessalos), along with Hippias, insulting the sister of Harmodios by refusing her as a basket-bearer in the

---

[20] Wilson 2000:120.

[21] The *polis* took over payment of the poets (Wilson 2000:64–65), perhaps also of the large-scale sacrifices (cf. Parker 1996:129 with n. 25). Funding of the choruses by *khorēgoi* goes back to the earliest years of the democracy, probably earlier: Wilson 2000:13. The procession was funded by the private resources of 10 *epimelētai*, who were however by the time of the *Constitution of the Athenians* given money by the *polis* (56. 4).

[22] Connor 1987; Sinos 1993.

[23] Seaford 2003a. Add Thucydides 126.4 (Kylon fails to become tyrant at the festival of Zeus).

procession at the Panathenaia. The control over the festival that is implied by this incident appears also in the details that when the murder occurred Hippias was in the Kerameikos organizing the procession (Thucydides 6.57 διεκόσμει ὡς ἕκαστα ἔχρη τῆς πομπῆς προϊέναι), and that Hipparchos was killed while sending off (ἀποστέλλων) the procession at the Leokoreion (*Constitution of the Athenians* 18.3; Thucydides 1.20).

In the *Constitution of the Athenians* version Hippias is not in the Kerameikos organizing the departure of the procession but on the Akropolis to receive it. Peisistratos became tyrant for the first time by taking the Akropolis (Herodotos 1.59; *Constitution of the Athenians* 14.1); subsequently he was escorted back by "Athena" to the Akropolis (Herodotos 1.60); and the eventual fall of the Peisistratids meant their surrendering the Akropolis to the Athenians (*Constitution of the Athenians* 19.6). Whether or not the tyrants lived on the Akropolis, their control of it may have facilitated control of the treasury of Athena contained in her temple there, or rather of the "Treasurers of Athena."[24]

Let us now look briefly at the early development of the Greek festival. To begin with Homer: there are in the *Odyssey* two large-scale public sacrifices (or festivals). Firstly, Telemakhos and Peisistratos arrive at Pylos to find the Pylians arranged on the shore in nine groups, with each group sacrificing nine bulls to Poseidon. After their welcome at this huge sacrifice the Ithakans are invited to the palace of Nestor, where they participate in the sacrifice of a cow summoned from the fields (421) and sacrificed (382, 384) by Nestor. There is on the other hand no suggestion of how the eighty-one bulls sacrificed to Poseidon arrived on the shore, and the society described by Homer contains no indication of a centralized organization capable of assembling them. Athena prays to Poseidon to give glory to Nestor and his sons, "but then recompense for all the other Pylians together (σύμπασιν) for their glorious hekatomb" (58–59).

Secondly, in the background of Odysseus' return there is a "pure" public (κατὰ δῆμον) festival for Apollo (20.276–278; 21.258–259) on Ithaka, apparently Apollo *Noumenios* (of the new moon: 14.161–162; 19.306–307), a sacrificial festival open to all (20.156) and clearly meant to contrast with the scandalous eating of Odysseus' livestock by the suitors. The only indication of the provenance of the sacrificial animals is that "heralds drove the sacred hekatomb of the gods through the town" (20.276–277): clearly they are not provided by the monarch.

There was even in the classical period a traditional kind of festival in which much food was brought by the participants themselves.[25] An Attic instance is the

---

[24] *Constitution of the Athenians* 8.1; 47.1.
[25] Parker 1996:77–78; Gernet 1928.

Diasia, celebrated en masse but without any evidence of food provided by the *polis*.[26] Given that Greek sanctuaries did not on the whole own herds, sacrificial feasts at sanctuaries might depend on the contribution of individuals. Excessive numbers of animals contributed would be inconvenient, and from the eighth century onwards we find numerous durable substitutes—the durable parts of the animal, animal figurines, or equipment of the sacrifice such as spits and tripods. But even durable objects, in excessive numbers, may be inconvenient. The practice of substitution is extended to the substitution of *money* for objects in kind. And so for instance the victim's skin, to which the sanctuary frequently had a right, might be replaced by a monetary fee named after the skin.[27] The *pelanos* was an offering, in particular a kind of cake. But sanctuaries no doubt preferred money to a surplus of cakes, and *pelanos* comes to mean a monetary fee paid at a sanctuary, or even a *fund*.[28] In an (early Hellenistic?) Cretan inscription[29] payment is specified in staters, in triobols, and in *lebêtes*—presumably coins named after sacrificial cauldrons;[30] and this semantic shift from a particular sacrificial item to the generality of money is exemplified also by the origin of the name for a coin, obol, in the word for a spit (ὀβελός).[31]

This process of monetization contributes to the accumulation of coined or uncoined precious metal (money) in temple treasuries, which might contain, as at Athens,[32] the public funds of the *polis*. To Solon was attributed a written calendar of sacrifices, in which he seems to have laid down the prices paid by the Athenian polis for sacrificial victims.[33] However, as a durable store of wealth, precious metal (coined or uncoined) money can be used to fund ritual at any time. The performance of ritual is no longer dependent on communal tradition or the agricultural year (for instance

---

[26] Thucydides 1.126.6 (the scholiast takes ἐπιχώρια to mean cakes in the shape of animals); Parker 1996:77–78, who cites evidence for some meat provided by participating demes; agricultural fertility, Simon 1983:113–114.

[27] ἐς τὸ δέρμα (Sokolowski 1962:no.41.12–15); δερματικόν.

[28] Sokolowski 1969:5.36 (the Eleusinian first fruits decree, perhaps of the 420s); Sokolowski 1962:nos.13.19 (the first fruits decree of 353–2 BCE), 19.29–30, 35 (the Salaminians accord of 362–3 BCE); Stengel 1920:99; Ziehen in Pauly-Wissowa *Real-Encyclopädie der Klassischen Altertumswissenschaft* 19.250.

[29] *Inscriptiones Creticae* I.viii.5 (Melville Jones 1993:no.46).

[30] Guarducci 1944–1945:174, who compares Pollux 9.61 ("ox" as festival payment is two drachmas).

[31] Other names of coins (or of units of value or of precious metal) for which a sacrificial origin has been claimed are ἄγκυραι, πέλεκυς, and φθοῖδες: Laum 1924:107–109, 113–114, 124; Caccamo Caltabiano and Radici Colace 1992:153, 175–176.

[32] Gomme 1956:ad Thucydides 2.13.3 ἐν τῇ ἀκροπόλει; and especially Meiggs and Lewis 1969:no. 58; Harris 1995.

[33] Parker 1996:43–55; Seaford 2004:5§a (precious metal money, but not yet coinage, in the time of Solon).

the abundance of large quantities of produce at certain times of the year). Money transcends occasion. Moreover, the condensation of easily stored value in money allows the coordination of far greater expenditure on a festival than had occurred in traditional festivals, as well as allowing large sums to be controlled or possessed by a single individual—as I am suggesting occurred in the case of the Athenian tyrants.

This appropriation by an individual of the communal function of distribution is in fact found earlier—in the premonetary society described in Homeric epic, in which the right to distribute booty seems to belong nominally to the people but in fact to their leader.[34] There is a similar duality in the distribution of food, which is occasionally said to be distributed by the group as a whole, as at Pylos (*Odyssey* 3.66), whereas on the other hand wealthy individuals are said to hold feasts,[35] and food and drink are frequently distributed by the host or his henchmen.[36] This ancient duality acquires—with tyranny and its successor democracy, and with the monetization of cult (the interposition of money between the resourcing and the enactment of ritual)—a new form.

The return of the monied Peisistratos with Phye dressed as Athena occurred before the genesis of drama out of Dionysiac cult, but has been recognized as *theatrical*, "a ritual drama affirming the establishment of a new civic order."[37] Tyrants frequently misuse festivals to seize power, but Peisistratos—it is implied by Herodotos' narrative—does not wait for a festival but by his dramatic performance evokes the processional return of deity (as was enacted for instance at the Great Dionysia), outside the traditional calendar of sacrifices and for a purely political end. Similarly the founding (or development) by Peisistratos of a Dionysia in March "in the town," associated with the bringing of the god from the border of Attica with Thebes (Eleutherai), would be financed from the center, political in motivation, and devoted to *display*. Contrast the Anthesteria,[38] a festival of the old type, in which the participants themselves brought wine jars for the communal celebration of their opening.[39]

---

[34] Seaford 2004:2§e, 3§a; Borecky 1963.

[35] *Iliad* 9.70; 19.299; 23.29; *Odyssey* 3.309; 4.3; 14.250–252. Cf. *Odyssey* 8.387–420, where Alkinoos suggests (commands?) non-monetary gifts from the other twelve "kings" for Odysseus, who will soon narrate his adventures.

[36] Borecky 1963 traces a concomitant change in vocabulary from Homer to the classical period.

[37] Connor 1987:46.

[38] Of the other Dionysiac festivals Lenaia (the derivation of its name for λῆναι suggests maenadism) and Oschophoria we know nothing about this aspect.

[39] Old: Thucydides 2.15.4. Parker 1996:53 says of Anthesteria (and Diasia) "the contribution of the *demos* was in fact small." *Incriptiones Graecae* II² 1672.204 details some expenses of the Choes (including wine) for 329/8 BCE. Cf. Phanodemos FGrH 325 F12: "at the sanctuary *en limnais* the Athenians used to mix the wine for the god from the jars which they transported along there (τὸ γλεῦκος φέροντας τοὺς ᾿Αθηναίους) and then taste it themselves."

From Dithyramb to Tragedy

Everything above provides the context in which tragedy developed out of Dionysiac cult and came to be performed at the Dionysia "in the town." Of this development the three aspects with which I will be concerned are (a) of imitation out of action, (b) of audience out of participants, and (c) of a sequence of kinds of performance out of a single ritual. With (a) and (b) I will be concerned only briefly, as I have described them before.[40] My focus in this paper is on (c).

On (a) I observe merely that in the evidence for humans imitating deities in cult, exemplified in a sense by Phye,[41] the wearing of *masks* seems to have occurred especially in the cults of the mystery-gods Demeter and Dionysos.[42] The transformation of identity, a precondition of drama, is inherent above all in mystery cult. In the cult of Dionysos (including mystery cult) men might wear the masks of— and so be imagined as transformed into—satyrs. It was probably at the Anthesteria that men dressed as satyrs playing pipes escorted (an image of ?) Dionysos into the city.[43] And so it is no surprise to find Aristotle reporting that tragedy developed out of something like satyric drama (*Poetics* 1449a20).

(b) The presence of an *audience* rather than of *participants* is identified by Rappaport (1999:39–41) as a key criterion of drama (rather than ritual). In the development of a mass audience I would stress two factors. Firstly, there was the advent, at a burgeoning urban center, of a new kind of centrally coordinated festival, centered not on activity (such as the opening of the new wine) but on civic display. Even the escort provided by Phye merely *communicated* something to the masses (albeit with political *consequences*). Second, there was a mass desire to *see* the mystic celebration of the Dionysiac *thiasos*, a desire shared even by its male enemy Pentheus (Euripides *Bacchae* 471, 473, 812). To be sure, what the early audience saw was merely the dithyramb, an originally processional[44] hymn for Dionysos that combined mystic elements[45] (albeit such as would not profane the secrets) with public display: for instance, the choral *thiasos* of Bacchae as they enter the *orkhêstra* escorting Dionysos (back) to Thebes (85–87)—and in response to Dionysos' command that they make the city *see* them (62)—sing a dithyramb[46] that first calls

---

[40] Seaford 1994a.
[41] Connor 1987:45.
[42] Burkert 1985:186. Predramatic masks of Dionysos from Attica and Boeotia: *Lexicon Iconographicum Mythologiae Classicae* sub Dionysos (III 1) 424–425nn6, 11, 23, 24, 25, 26.
[43] Pickard-Cambridge 1968:12.
[44] Seaford 1994a; 241–243, 267–268.
[45] Seaford 1994a:268; Lavecchia 2000:11–12, 136.
[46] Seaford 1996: 155–156.

people out onto the street (68–70) and then, in a mystic *makarismos* ("blessed is he who . . ."), lists the blessings of mystic initiation (72–87).

(c) The details of this process are of course beyond recovery. But general considerations can be identified. One such general consideration, already identified, is the kinship of drama with Dionysiac mystic ritual. Another is the novel power of money.

Accepting Aristotle's remark that tragedy developed out of the leaders of the dithyramb (ἀπὸ τῶν ἐξαρχόντων τὸν διθύραμβον), let us imagine the dithyrambic performance from which tragedy developed. The dithyramb was a hymn for Dionysos, originally processional, and originally sung to escort the god into the community. The *thiasos* singing it was constituted by initiation into the Dionysiac mysteries, and the song contained mystic elements. As a hymn, it was likely to contain invocation of the god, and mythical narrative. The myths involving Dionysos are not numerous: the dithyramb certainly contained an account of the *birth* of the god and the accompanying thunder and lightning. The birth of the god was a typical theme of the hymn as well as being, in this case, associated with mystic initiation. The other main myth of Dionysos is about his overcoming of the resistance he frequently meets on being introduced into a new community:[47] this was narrated (it seems) in a Pindaric dithyramb.[48]

Much of this characterization has had to be gathered from various times and places, for alas no dithyramb has survived from the late sixth century. The closest we have to such a text are the fragments (some of them substantial) of the dithyrambs of Pindar. Three substantial fragments in particular have a Dionysiac content.

The papyrus fragment 70b starts by referring to the old processional dithyramb (πρὶν μὲν εἷρπε σχοινοτένεια) and describes a celebration by the Olympian gods of a τελετά of Dionysos. Τελετά can mean a festival but in a Dionysiac context is likely to refer to mystery cult, and almost certainly does so here, partly because it occurs inside a house (ἐν μεγάροις)[49] and so is unlikely to be a festival, and partly because the young men performing the dithyrambs are described as *knowing* what kind of τελετά of Dionysos the gods celebrate (<u>εἰδότες</u> οἵαν Βρομίου [τελε]τάν . . .).[50] It includes circular choruses (i.e. dithyrambs), the Great Mother[51] accompanied by *tumpana*,[52] a fire-breathing thunderbolt,[53] and—after the description of the various gods—the myth of Dionysos' birth.

---

[47] Resistance is shown by the Athenians, Pentheus, Lykourgos, the Minyads, the Proetids, Perseus, the neighbors of Ikaros.

[48] Perseus against Dionysos in fr. 70a Maehler: Lavecchia 2000:93–94, 103–105.

[49] So too the central mystic experiences of Pentheus take place within the house.

[50] Cf. Euripides *Bacchae* 73: τελετὰς θεῶν εἰδώς (undoubtedly of mystic initiation) with Seaford ad loc.; Lavecchia 2000:135. My translation adopts νεαν[ίαι, εὖ ε[ἰδότες (d'Angour 1997), but my argument does not depend on it.

The papyrus fragment 70c mentions a Dionysiac τελετά, springtime, ivy crowns, songs, and choruses, and contains an invocation (ἔλθε), almost certainly of Dionysos. And fragment 75 invokes the Olympian gods to the dance and to the *agora* in Athens, and goes on to praise Dionysos as celebrated along with Semele in springtime. It has been suggested that we might expect further references to the story of Dionysos' birth after the mention of Semele in the last line of the fragment.[54] Of the less substantial fragments, fr. 71 mentions the invention of the dithyramb, fr. 85 the second birth of Dionysos, fr. 335 the conflict between Dionysos and Lykourgos (possibly), and fr. 346 the Eleusinian mysteries.[55]

Pindar was competing in the dithyrambic contest at Athens at least as early as 497/6 BCE.[56] The dithyrambs of Bacchylides, which lack Dionysiac content, were, I imagine, written somewhat later. Even the fragments of Pindaric dithyrambs contain non-Dionysiac myths, and the invocation of gods other than Dionysos. The annual competition between twenty dithyrambs at Athens, to say nothing of performance elsewhere, created an even greater pressure for novelty of content than was exercised on tragedy.

The processional entry-song of Euripides' *Bacchae* is (as mentioned above) a dithyramb. It narrates two myths: the first—told immediately after the mystic *makarismos*—is about the birth (with thunder and lightning) and rebirth of Dionysos, and the second is about the invention of the *tumpanon* (drum). The thunder and lightning at the birth of Dionysos is in the parodos merely narrated, but in the second stasimon it is first *dramatically* described[57] (with Zeus imagined as addressing the infant Dionysos as 'Dithyrambos', 526) and then becomes a reality (594, 597–599, 623–624) as Dionysos in response to his thiasos' invocations makes his epiphany, in a scene that is full of evocations of mystic ritual.[58] The next choral song contains another mystic *makarismos* (862–912). Other choral songs

---

[51] Cf. Lavecchia 2000:138–143.

[52] Cf. Euripides *Bacchae* 78–79, 124–131; Pindar fr. 80? Actually we have in fr. 70b the phrase ῥόμβοι τυμπάνων: what is envisaged is unclear, but the ῥόμβος is a whirling instrument used in the mysteries.

[53] Cf. Euripides *Bacchae* 596–599; Seaford 1996:195–198; Lavecchia 2000:156–157.

[54] Van der Weiden 1991:186.

[55] On Dionysos associated with the mysteries of Demeter at Thebes see Lavecchia 2000:116–118.

[56] P. Oxy. 2438.9–10; van der Weiden 1991:186.

[57] The direct speech of characters in Bacchylides' dithyrambs and the mimetic nature of the New Dithyramb (van der Weiden 1991:12–13) are not necessarily a result of influence from tragedy.

[58] Seaford 1996:195–203. Add the use of trochaic tetrameters only at 604–641 (describing the mystic epiphany of the god) of *Bacchae*. Early in its history tragedy used this meter rather than the iambic (Aristotle *Poetics* 1449a21, *Rhetoric* 1404a30). It is common in the earliest extant play (Aeschylus *Persians*), and revived in late Euripides. In the fragments of Aeschylus it occurs only in an unknown play (fr. 296) and the *Edonians* (fr. 60: probably spoken by Lykourgos on the captured Dionysos).

81

invoke, besides Dionysos (556, 1017), Thebes (105), *Hosia* (Purity; 370), the spring Dirke (519), the hounds of *Lussa* (Frenzy) (977), and Justice (992). With 1017, the invocation to Dionysos to appear as a bull, compare the "hymn" of the Elean women invoking him to do just that (PMG 871).

We have three stages in the presentation of the birth-epiphany of Dionysos: narration in the entry-song, and then in the second stasimon dramatic description followed by enactment. That the description of the birth of Dionysos took a quasi-dramatic form already in the dithyramb is suggested by a fragment of a Pindaric dithyramb (85 Maehler) in which Zeus, during the birth of Dionysos from his thigh, shouts words (λῦθι ῥάμμα, "be released, stitching") that are the origin of the word "dithyramb."

As for the second mythical theme of the entry-song, the invention of Dionysiac musical instruments—this became the preserve of, and a common theme in, satyric drama as well as in the "new dithyramb."[59]

If we imagine the dithyrambic entry-song as the nucleus of tragedy, then the dramatization preserved in *Bacchae*[60] suggests that the earliest tragedy emerged through duplication of dithyrambic elements. The drama as a whole is framed by the resistance myth, which as one of the few other myths of Dionysos may well also have been a theme of the dithyramb. The extension is thus neither random nor arbitrary, but contained by the framework of the etiological myth, which for Dionysiac (and some other) cults involves resistance. So too in general the shape of tragedy tends to be *etiological*.[61] If so, then the action is an extension and amalgamation of the rebirth and resistance narratives contained in the dithyramb. We should add that the dithyramb was originally a *sacrificial* procession,[62] and that the killing of Pentheus is represented as a sacrifice.[63] Tragedy takes its name from the singers at the sacrifice of a goat.

If this is how tragedy began, we do not have to look very far for the first actor. He represented the god. In *Bacchae* Dionysos is brought into the city by the *thiasos*-chorus (85). The dithyrambic chorus *escort* the god and *invoke his epiphany*. Archilochus knows how to "lead off" (ἐξάρχειν) the dithyramb (fr. 120), i.e. to sing (improvise?) the solo to a choral refrain:[64] he is, like the tragic actor, attached

---

[59] Seaford 1994a:268.

[60] On the pronounced *archaism* of *Bacchae* see Dodds 1960:xxvi–xxxviii (and on its similarity to earlier Dionysiac plays see xxviii–xxxiii), to which add the trochaic tetrameter (see n. 58 above).

[61] Seaford 1994a; 2000:78–91.

[62] Seaford 1994a:241–242.

[63] Seaford 1996:index sub sacrifice.

[64] This is what the word means in Aristotle's contemporary Heracleides of Cumae FGrH 689.2 (Athenaeus, 145d). Cf. *Iliad* 24.721.

to the chorus but separate from it. Aristotle tells us that tragedy came into being from the improvisations of those who "lead off" the dithyramb (*Poetics* 1249a11: ἀπὸ τῶν ἐξαρχόντων τὸν διθύραμβον), and in the dithyrambic parodos of *Bacchae* it is Dionysos who is imagined as "he who leads off," (ἔξαρχος, 141). Pictures of the Dionysiac *thiasos* with their god predate drama.[65] It is very likely that at an ancient Ionian festival the *thiasos* of satyrs escorted their god into the city (in the Καταγώγια, cf. *Bacchae* 85: Διόνυσον καταγοῦσαι) with the god represented either by an image or by an impersonator.

The introduction of the *second* actor (attributed to Aeschylus) arises, I suggest, from the kind of myth celebrated by the incoming *thiasos*. Aetiological myth of Dionysiac cult frequently includes initial *resistance* to the introduction of the cult. What is the function of this theme? We may compare, for instance, the resistance exhibited by the bride to the transition effected by the wedding: it is through the display and triumphant overcoming of resistance that the inevitability of the transition is explained. Secondly, mythical resistance allows the new deity to inflict a punishment that remains as a warning to the people that they must not resist or neglect the god. At the City Dionysia there was enacted the arrival of Dionysos,[66] who, we are told, was not at first well received, with the result that the men of Athens suffered a disease of the genitals, from which they recovered only by honoring Dionysos with *phalloi*.[67] It is at this point in the festival enactment of the arrival of the god that we find the need for the second actor, to provide the *enactment of opposition* between Dionysos and the King, as occurs in *Bacchae*. Compare, once again, the older festivals of Dionysos at Athens. About the Lenaia we know very little. At the Anthesteria it seems likely that Dionysos, represented by an image or an impersonator, was escorted—in a cart shaped like a ship—by his *thiasos* of pipe-playing satyrs into the center of the city, where, within the *Boukoleion* (imagined to be the old royal house: compare extant tragedy) he was sexually united with the wife of the 'King' (*basileus*) *arkhôn*.[68] It seems that this ritual was associated in the classical period with the myth of Dionysos requiring Theseus (as prototype of the *arkhôn basileus*) to surrender Ariadne to Dionysos.[69] It is easy to see how easily

---

[65] *Lexicon Iconographicum Mythologiae Classicae* sub Dionysos (III 1) 451–452; Schöne 1987:12–22. Dionysos imagined as leader of the dance: Sophokles *Antigone* 114.7; PMG 1027d.

[66] Pickard-Cambridge 1968:59–61.

[67] Schol. Aristophanes *Acharnians* 243

[68] Cf. Euripides *Cyclops* 37–40.

[69] Simon 1983:97; Beazley 1963:1057.96 and 97; Pausanias 1.20 3; 10.29.4; Apollodorus *Epitome* 7–10; Hyginus *Fabulae* 41–43; Athenaeus 296a; Diodorus Siculus 5.51.4. Other similar myths are those of Dionysos, Oineus, and Althaia, and of Orion, Oinopion, and Merope (apparently narrated in a Pindaric dithyramb, fr. 72–74 Maehler: Lavecchia 2000:273–278).

the enactment of opposition between Dionysos (accompanied by his musical *thiasos*) and the King could have developed in front of the palace. I have elsewhere[70] pointed to the political significance of this opposition.

If tragedy originated in this kind of ritual, then a key question is: how was it *extended* beyond the performance of the ritual, both in time (to as much as about two hours) and in content (so as to include the complex imitation of an action or event)? For a relatively long performance, requiring from a large audience concentration on a variety of mythical incidents, a precedent had been set in the Homeric recitations at the Panathenaia. In early drama on Dionysiac themes the story may have been contained within the dithyrambic nucleus, so that the extension may have involved a certain amount of duplication, as we have suggested for *Bacchae*. As for the earliest tragedies about non-Dionysiac myths, we are of course limited by the near-absence of evidence. Nevertheless, the following considerations may be relevant.

Herodotos (5.67) reports that the Sikyonians honored the sufferings of Adrastus τραγικοῖσι χοροῖσι ("with tragic choruses"), and that the tyrant Kleisthenes transferred the choruses to Dionysos and the rest of the sacrifice to Melanippus, as well as abolishing the rhapsodic recitations of Homer. I will supplement the frequently observed general importance of this passage for understanding the genesis of Attic tragedy by emphasizing two interrelated points. The first is that the "tragic choruses" in honor of Dionysos must be to some extent a *mixture* of rituals (Dionysiac cult and hero cult). The second is that Kleisthenes was tyrant in about the first third of the sixth century. Herodotos reports the details that his chariot won an Olympic victory, and that after entertaining for a year numerous noble suitors (from throughout Greece) of his daughter, he sent them away with a talent of silver each (6.130). This excess of precious metal money[71] was no doubt fundamental to Kleisthenes' tyrannical power. As in the case of Peisistratos and his sons, we may infer that the concentration of huge sums of precious metal money in the hands of an individual allowed him unprecedented power to coordinate the activities of large numbers of people, simply by means of payment. Because money is one of the few things powerful enough to create a break with tradition, its possessor can transform cultural traditions to an extent inconceivable in, say, the premonetary world of Homer. The cultural policy of Kleisthenes of Sikyon had, according to Herodotos (5. 67–68), a political purpose.

[70] Seaford 1994a:266.
[71] Kleisthenes is contemporary with the Athenian Solon, in whose legislation silver money is important, in a period shortly before the introduction of coinage. Note also that a Sikyonian *treasury* seems to have been built at Delphi during the rule of Kleisthenes: Griffin 1982:106–108.

Besides reshaping Dionysiac festivals, this monetary power was able, we noted, to attract poetic talent from elsewhere. Periander, tyrant of Corinth, an older contemporary of Kleisthenes, had attracted from Methymna Arion, who according to Herodotos was the first known person to have composed, named, and produced a dithyramb, in Corinth. Arion also made a lot of money (χρήματα μεγάλα) on a trip to Italy and Sicily.[72] Presumably he was also attracted to Periander by money. When Herodotos writes that he was "the first to produce (διδάξαντα)" a dithyramb, this may imply that Periander was (one of?) the first to finance dithyrambic contests. And as for "the first to name" a dithyramb, this may imply that his dithyrambs circulated, *independently of the context for which they were written*. A single performance in a Corinthian contest would not necessarily require the dithyramb to be "named." The progressive *decontextualization* of poetry in the archaic period[73] seems to culminate in the figure of Simonides, who combined mobility, a wide variety of genres, and a reputation for money-grubbing that may reflect his being one of the first poets to treat poetry openly as a commodity.[74] Indeed, we have seen that according to an ancient tradition he was the first to compose *epinikia* "for a wage."

One of the many genres which Simonides produced was the dithyramb, and one of his many patrons was Hipparchos of Athens. Once a hymn to Dionysos sung in a specific context (in particular the epiphany or processional entry of the god), the dithyramb was more suited than some other genres—the wedding song, the epinikian, the lament, etc.—to be sung outside that context. The dithyramb was transformed from a processional hymn with traditional or improvised words into a hymn taught to a static chorus by its author (Arion, Simonides) in order to win a formal competition. Significantly, this process also meant the detachment of the hymn from its ritual function (to celebrate the advent of Dionysos) to an extent far greater than was possible for the wedding-song, for instance, or the lament, or the epinikian. The dithyramb at Athens had to be sung in a certain manner (with circular choruses, in a certain style, etc.), and originally at least with a certain content. But it was especially susceptible to thematic and musical *innovation*, and to judge from the surviving dithyrambs of Pindar and (especially) Bacchylides, lost all necessary association with Dionysiac myth. It was this freedom of development, unconstrained by ritual function, that (along with other of its characteristics) allowed it to give birth to tragedy.

---

[72] Herodotos 1.23–24; cf. Solon fr. 30a West.
[73] See most recently Ford 2002.
[74] On the reaction of Pindar to the new monetary economy see Kurke 1991.

The decontextualization of archaic poetry is implicit in the presence of foreign poets in tyrannical households, for instance the presence of Anacreon, Simonides, and others in the household of Hipparchos at Athens. An individual removed from his own *polis* and from his own kin is also removed from the specific kind of participation bestowed on him (by birth and citizenship) in the traditional occasions for song. To be sure, Simonides could find similar occasions outside Ceos, but to the extent that a song by him was a commodity it transcended occasion: it could for instance be sung in more than one dithyrambic contest. The decontextualization of archaic poetry, its production, and circulation independently of the context for which the poetic genres were originally produced (banquet, symposium, wedding, funeral, procession, victory, and so on), was a precondition for the genesis of tragedy. Tension between professional and unpaid citizen *performers* is perhaps reflected in the information preserved in Athenaeus (617bc) that 708 PMG of Pratinas (in my view from a very early satyr-play[75]) was written in reaction to *paid* chorus-members and pipe-players taking over the *orkhêstrai* (αὐλητῶν καὶ χορευτῶν μισθοφόρων κατεχόντων τὰς ὀρχήστρας ἀγανακτήσας).

The debt of tragedy to previous poetic genres—epic, elegiac, iambic, and lyric—was admirably described by John Herington (1985), notably in respect of *meter*. But there are in his account two glaring omissions. One is the absence of any attempt to explain the ubiquitous role played in tragedy by *ritual* (Herington, like others of his generation, seems to have suffered from total, uncritical aversion to the Cambridge school).[76] The other is the absence of *history*: there is no serious attempt to explain why tragedy came into being when and where it did. We must retain Herington's basic emphasis, that "tragedy is a *mixture*"[77] (even of dialects) while attempting to fill the gaps.

Tragedy as an Amalgam of Rituals

That the enactment or evocation of ritual is frequent in tragedy may seem obvious. First, it is important to distinguish between *enactment* (e.g. of the pouring of libations in Aeschylus' *Libation Bearers* or the epiphany of Dionysos in *Bacchae*) and *evocation* (e.g. of mystery cult in the experiences of Pentheus in *Bacchae*—for Pentheus is not actually initiated even in the fiction). And evocation may take the form of a fleeting allusion or, at the other extreme, of a basic structural similarity

---

[75] Seaford 1977–78.
[76] A similar criticism is made by Nagy 1994–95:45; for more detailed critique see Seaford 1994a:277–280.
[77] Herington 1985:110, 122, from Aristoxenos fr. 81 Wehrli = pseudo-Plutarch *On Music* 1136cd.

between the dramatic situation and the ritual (e.g. with the evocation of the *pharmakos* in the case of Oedipus—see below).

Our analysis of *Bacchae* has certainly not revealed all the rituals enacted or evoked by that drama (cf. e.g. πομπή-ἀγών-κῶμος and *pharmakos* at 961–966). But let us consider instead, in order to illustrate the general nature of the phenomenon in tragedy, the enactment or evocation of ritual in two Sophoklean and two Euripidean tragedies (I will come on to Aeschylus later), chosen merely because they are (apart from *Bacchae*) probably the best known, *Oedipus Tyrannus* and *Antigone*, *Medea* and *Hippolytus*. It is not my intention to list *all* the rituals evoked or enacted, but to give a sense of the variety of rituals involved.

The opening scene of the *Oedipus Tyrannus* evokes, it has been argued,[78] the Athenian *festival* of the Thargelia, in which two *pharmakoi* (scapegoats) were expelled and εἰρεσιῶναι (branches of laurel or olive garlanded with wool and hung with offerings) were hung on the doors of the sanctuary of Apollo. The evocation, though brief and largely visual, implies a basic structural equivalence between Oedipus and the polluting *pharmakos,* whose expulsion allows the well-being of the community. This is followed by a lengthy choral invocation of various gods (151–215), ending with Dionysos (209–215). Whereas the evocation of the Thargelia seems to embody Oedipus' relation to the *polis*, his relation to his kin is embodied in the horror into which his *wedding* and its associated imagery are retrospectively transformed (420–423), just as his self-blinding over the suicide of Jocasta is represented as a horrible wedding (1275–1285).[79] Finally, Oedipus *laments* antiphonally[80] with the chorus (1297–1368).

In *Antigone* the entry-song of the chorus, celebrating deliverance from warfare, ends with the desire for all-night dancing at the temples and "that Bakchios who shakes the earth may rule Thebes" (152–154). Antigone sings for herself, antiphonally with the chorus, a lonely *lament* which is also a *wedding song* (806–892), announced by a *hymn* to Eros (781–805).[81] Then the prospect of saving Antigone inspires from the chorus a *hymnic invocation* of the Eleusinian Dionysos (the final word is Ἴακχον), and the subsequent narrative of her death describes her "bridal-chamber of Hades" in a manner evocative of the Eleusinian *mysteries* (1204–1205).[82] Finally, Kreon *laments* antiphonally with the chorus (1257–1246).[83]

---

78 Vernant 1972:117–124; Guépin 1968:89.
79 Seaford 1987:119–120.
80 For antiphony in the ritual lament see Alexiou 2002a:131–150 (and on *Oedipus Tyrannus* see 166); Seremetakis 1991.
81 Detail is in Seaford 1987:108.
82 Seaford 1990:88–89.
83 On typical features of this lament see Alexiou 2002a:136.

Early in the *Medea* the chorus represent the death wish of Medea as the ritualized death-wish of the *bride* 148–153).[84] Later we see Medea performing the ritual of *supplication* on Aigeus (709–718). The *wedding* of Jason to Glauke allows Medea to send the fatal wedding gifts and the bride Glauke to adorn herself fatally. Medea's killing of her children is called a *sacrifice* (1054), which will be commemorated in a *polis festival* of Hera Akraia (1378–1383).

Early in the *Hippolytus* is a *hymn* (58–71) and *offering* (73) to Artemis. The nurse performs *supplication* on Phaidra (325–335). The fantasies of the lovesick Phaidra (198–241) seem to evoke *maenadism*. The chorus sing a *hymn* to ῎Ερως, with strong *hymenaial* content that includes mention of the thunderbolt that produced the birth of "twice-born Bacchus" (545–562). Theseus *laments* antiphonally with the chorus (811–855). There is an (apparently antiphonal) choral song which, accompanying Hippolytos' departure into exile (1103–1150), combines features of the *lament* and of the *propemptikon*.[85] Finally, Artemis establishes a *polis festival* in which maidens before their marriage will cut their hair and sing laments for Hippolytus (1423–1430).

The enactment or evocation of ritual is not necessary to the dramatization of these stories, but allows the tragedian to evoke the emotion with which the audience experiences the rituals in their own lives. Further, tragedy dramatizes *myth*, which frequently represents the kind of situation—notably transitions such as marriage and death—that is sufficiently fundamental to require ritualization. And so numerous myths are inherently suitable for dramatization that includes the enactment or evocation of ritual.

We turn now to the three earliest extant plays of Aeschylus, *Persians* (472 BCE), *Seven against Thebes* (467BCE), and *Suppliant Women* (of uncertain but late date, perhaps shortly after 467 BCE). Of course these dramas were written at least a generation after the institution of tragedy at the Great Dionysia. They may nevertheless be of some use to our reconstruction of the development of tragedy.

The chorus of *Seven against Thebes* consists of maidens, who are faced not only with the violence of the Argive siege but also with the opposition of their own king, Eteokles, who repeatedly tells them to be silent, so as not to spread panic (237–238, 262, etc.), and even to remain in their homes (232). As in *Bacchae*, the king tries to control the women of his own city, with the difference that whereas in *Bacchae* the female chorus are aliens, in *Seven against Thebes* they are Theban. The ritual activity of the chorus consists in supplicating the images of the deities (98, 185,

---

[84] Seaford 1987:122–123.
[85] Cairns 1972:284–285; Russell and Wilson 1981:304–305.

258, 265), repeated invocations of various deities, and lamentation, including *self-lamentation* "It is to be wept," they sing (333–335), "for recently reared maidens, plucked raw, before marriage to make the hateful journey from their homes."[86] This evokes the hymenaial *topos* of the bride as a fruit not yet plucked in marriage,[87] and the idea that for the bride departure from her natal home in the wedding is hateful, indeed "to be wept" by the bride herself.[88] Each maiden of the chorus sees her enforced departure from her home (no doubt for rape) in terms of her wedding, for it happens also at the wedding.

And so the chorus of maidens in *Seven against Thebes* associates the immediate prospect of suffering male violence with bridal self-lamentation at the (hateful) wedding, not unlike Antigone (Sophokles *Antigone* 806–891). In Aeschylus' *Suppliant Women* this is an organizing principle. I have set out this case elsewhere.[89] My point here is to suggest the importance, in the early development of tragedy, of *overlap* between different kinds of ritual. The transfer of "tragic choruses" from hero-cult to the cult of Dionysos (by Kleisthenes of Sikyon) implies a similarity between the two kinds of cult: both included *lamentation*.[90] For instance, the chorus of the *Seven against Thebes* call themselves θυιάς (maenadic) in the lament (835–836). But they also, we have seen, evoke *bridal* lamentation. And in the *Suppliant Women* bridal lamentation is central, with the result that many scholars have thought that the Danaids are simply rejecting marriage (rather than, as they in fact make clear, specifically marriage with their cousins). In this way traditional tragic lamentation can be preserved in—or may even have suggested to the poet—a new narrative. Another practice common to various rituals (hero-cult, mystery cult, the wedding, death ritual, and so on) is animal sacrifice: accordingly, murder in tragedy is regularly represented as animal sacrifice.

What I am suggesting is that the development of the thematics of tragedy is not governed merely by a kind of free market in attractive myths. There is a tradition of choral practice, including ritual practice, which was a factor in this development. On the basis of my view that *Bacchae* is a specimen of the earliest (Dionysiac) tragedy, let us compare it with Aeschylus' *Suppliant Women*. In both dramas a chorus of alien women, arrived from abroad accompanied by a single male protector, claims a link

---

[86] The manuscripts have κλαυτὸν δ' ἀρτιδρόποις (or -τρόποις) ὠμοδρόπων (or -τρόπων) / νομίμων προπάροιθεν διαμεῖψαι / δωμάτων στυγεράν ὁδόν (or -όδόν). I read ἀρτιτρόφοις (Schneider) ὠμοδρόπως (Lowinski).

[87] Cf. Sappho fr. 105(a); Seaford 1987:111–112.

[88] Seaford 1987:113–114. Comparative evidence: Nagy 1994–95:51, citing Vladimir Propp.

[89] Seaford 1987:110–119. Note especially 41, 62, 69–76, 104–106, 110, 144–153, 223–226, 335, 351–352, 663–666, 748–749, 788–792, 905, 998–999, 1031–1073, frr. 43 and 44 Radt.

[90] Seaford 1994a:319, 322–323, 398.

with the *polis* through an earlier sexual union between Zeus and a local princess, invokes accordingly the local site of that union (*Suppliant Women* 50–52, 118, 539–541, *Bacchae* 519–522), is confronted by the local king, and rescued from threatened violence. The Aeschylean trilogy may have ended, like *Bacchae*, with the establishment of ritual.[91] The marginality and vulnerability of the tragic chorus— either as old men (in eight dramas) or as women (in twenty-one dramas, often also slaves or foreigners)—is a regular feature of tragedy that I suggest derives in part from its Dionysiac association. Of extant tragedies only in Sophokles' *Ajax* and *Philoktetes*, and the anonymous *Rhesus*, does the chorus consist of vigorous males, albeit in each case soldiers or sailors far from home and dependent on their commander.[92]

The confrontation between marginal chorus and local monarch occurs in *Seven against Thebes* and in *Suppliant Women*. But what of the third (relatively) early extant drama of Aeschylus, the *Persians*? It is important that this is the only extant tragedy set entirely in a barbarian society antithetical to the *polis* (even the action of Euripides' *Trojan Women* is dominated by Greeks). This has enormous implications for its form, which is unparalleled in extant tragedy. Two rituals dominate the drama, persistent choral lamentation and the raising of Darius from the dead. In stark contrast to *Seven against Thebes* and *Suppliant Women*, the choral lamentation is no threat to the monarch. Indeed, quite the reverse. Early in the drama Atossa warns the chorus that her son Xerxes, not being responsible (ὑπεύθυνος) to the *polis*, will "even if he fails, rule this land just as before" (211–214), and then, after news of the disaster, instructs them to "comfort him and escort him into the house, lest he suffer an additional disaster" (530–531). The additional disaster can only be the resentment and freedom of his subjects (584–594). The drama ends with the chorus obeying her instructions: they escort Xerxes into the house with elaborate lamentation in perfect solidarity with the monarch. The antithesis with the values of the *polis* is given powerful and spectacular expression.

Another manifestation of the decontextualization—and consequent amalgamation—of rituals in tragedy is exemplified at *Bacchae* 1161–1162: the chorus of Asiatic maenads sing that the Theban maenads "have made your famous hymn of victory[93] into lamentation, into tears." The Dionysiac victory (975–976) seems to Agaue and the Theban maenads a triumph (1147: τὸν καλλίνικον) but is in fact to be lamented: the victory-song becomes a lament. The transformation of triumph into disaster is expressed as the unity of antithetical ritual utterances.

---

[91] Seaford 1987:115–117; Seaford 2000.
[92] Gould 1996:220.
[93] τὸν καλλίνικον κλεινόν (cf. 1148: τὸν καλλίνικον, ᾧ δάκρυα νικηφορεῖ). Compare, e.g. Euripides *Electra* 865, *Hercules Furens* 681.

This unity of opposites is not confined to *poetic* genres. Indeed, many Greek rituals contain a negative element, which is eventually overcome in the positive conclusion of the ritual. One function for the mythical initial resistance to a new cult may be (we noted earlier) to intensify and define the necessity of performing the cult, and may have been expressed in ritual. Similarly, the expression of initial reluctance in a rite of passage may intensify—and define the necessity of—its positive conclusion. An example of such initial resistance is the self-lamentation of the bride. Among the negative or sinister elements of the Anthesteria[94] was the practice of drinking separately and silently in commemoration of the presence of the polluted Orestes at the festival. Sometimes the opposition between negative and positive elements in a ritual may be encapsulated in a formula, for instance in the cry, *Eleleû Iou Iou*, expressing both triumph and consternation, at the Athenian Dionysiac festival of the Oschophoria (Plutarch *Theseus* 22 gives the contradiction a mythical explanation), or in the formula uttered in mystic initiation "now you died and now you were born" (νῦν ἔθανες καὶ νῦν ἐγένου).

Extant tragedy is—in contrast to, say, Homeric epic—intensely interested in this kind of contradiction.[95] Archaic poetry was generally created for a specific context (often a ritual context), or at least *as if* for a specific context. Indeed, this appropriateness for a specific context is sometimes expressed by the verb πρέπειν.[96] Plato maintains that before the Persian wars music was divided into several kinds: hymns, laments, paeans, dithyrambs (dealing with the birth of Dionysos), and nomes. But subsequently these genres were mixed up with each other, with the result that "aristocracy" gave way to "theatrocracy" (*Laws* 700a–701a). Plato is thinking of music, but the point could be extended to other features of the poetic genres.[97] Although a song composed by Sappho for a wedding may express ambiguous emotions (joy at the sexual union, sadness at the loss of the bride), there is no doubt of the ritual and of the genre to which it belongs. In its appropriate context (in real life) the wedding, and indeed all ritual, must end well. But the decontextualization of poetry in tragedy allows the ambiguity of emotion to be expressed in the *imagined unity* of opposed ritual genres. For instance, the frequency of the wedding song in tragedy results (we have argued) in part from its overlap with the bridal lament: in real life the bride laments, but is finally incorporated into her new home, and similarly in tragedy, say Aeschylus *Agamemnon* 681–770, the arrival of Helen in Troy is described as greeted by a wedding song

[94] Burkert 1985:237–242.
[95] See further Seaford 2004.
[96] E.g. Alkman 98 PMG; Ford 1992:13–15.
[97] Cf. Nagy 1994–95:48, "we may expect that the *theatrokratia* of Athenian State Theater had effected a radical stylisation in all ritual dimensions of choral performance."

which has various features of the lament,[98] which are appropriate because lamentation is a feature of the real-life wedding song. But here in tragedy they are appropriate also because of what will befall Troy as a result of the bride's arrival. The two opposed ritual genres interpenetrate, and in the end (in stark contrast to the real-life wedding song) *lamentation prevails.*

An example of how a sequence of rituals in tragedy may sometimes reflect real life occurs at *Seven against Thebes* 264–270. The chorus has agreed to be silent, and Eteokles responds by urging them to abandon their physical contact with the images of the gods, and "pray for better things," for the gods to be allies, and to sing "the Greek custom of sacrificial cry," the *paian*, that gives "courage to friends, dissolving fear of the enemy." Eager to transform dangerous collective fear into the collective confidence that brings victory, Eteokles urges the replacement of one kind of ritual song (barbarian lamentation, and supplication of the gods) by another more positive kind, the Greek *paian*. Similarly the lamentation for Agamemnon in Aeschylus' *Libation Bearers* looks forward to being replaced, on victory, with paians (342–344).[99] But because it also enlists the support of the dead, and creates the collective confidence required for the matricide, lamentation is in this tragic passage itself vital for the "victory"[100] and so can be described in the oxymoron "*paian* of the dead" (151).[101] Here a *sequence* (lament then *paian*) has become—or at least is formulated as—the *unity of opposites* typical tragedy. It is this move, I suggest, that is encouraged by the *decontextualization* of ritual in tragedy.

Numerous further examples could be given from tragedy of the unity of opposed rituals. Instead, I will conclude by re-emphasizing the counter-intuitive association of monetization with the genesis of tragedy.

The monetization of Attica, and especially the rapid introduction of coinage in the middle of the sixth century BCE, created under the tyranny the centralized, coordinating *power*—as well as the political *motivation*—to create a new kind of communal festival, devoted to *display* rather than to the fulfillment of a traditional function that was often related to agriculture. Monetization also increased the *decontextualization* of the poetic genres, and the commodification of song, by making it easier to detach poets from their communities by means of payment. The combination of decontextualization with *lavish display* before a large audience promotes the *amalgamation and confusion of genres* that Plato attacks in the sphere of music and that we have given examples of from the closely related sphere of

---

[98] Seaford 1987:123–127.

[99] This occurs in reverse at Thucydides 7.75.7.

[100] 478—the last word of the lament, also 148.

[101] See further Seaford 2004. For this paradox in tragedy, and the positive nature of the *paian*, see Rutherford 1994–95.

ritual. Uncontrolled by any specific ritual function, taking its life rather from the power of money to acquire any kind of goods or the services of any kind of performer—in these conditions of decontextualized lavishness the Dionysiac dithyramb was *extended* into the unprecedented amalgamation called tragedy, performed before a (probably unprecedentedly) huge audience It is no coincidence that tragedy was the first (and perhaps the only)[102] genre to be come into being after the (historically unprecedented) pervasive monetization of the Greek *polis*. It is easy for us to forget, as familiar as we are with the form of Athenian tragedy, quite how unprecedented was the tragic amalgamation of rituals.

Tragedy did not emerge out of a preconceived idea of its desirability and its form. But this does not mean that tragedy can in any way be *reduced* to monetization. Rather, monetization created the conditions in which tragedy could emerge.

Finally, it is critical to my argument that money also heavily influenced the *content* of tragedy. I regard tragedy as embodying a synthesis of (premonetary) myth with institutions (including money) of the *polis*. And I regard the isolating power of money as a precondition for the unprecedented isolation of the individual at the heart of Athenian tragedy.[103] What is sometimes called the "tragic hero" is in fact never called a "hero" in tragedy or in other ancient texts. Very frequently he is called a "tyrant" (τύραννος), reflecting the recent experience of the Athenians (and others) of tyranny. And tyranny, as one discovers form Herodotos, Plato, and others, depends on money. To be sure, this is not to deny the persistence of the man of money, as an influence on tragedy, into the democratic era. For instance, Peter Wilson has cautiously drawn attention to the analogy between the tragic individual and the *khorêgos*, on whose money the tragic performance depends.[104] This argument about the *content* of tragedy, which I have set out elsewhere[105] and do not have the space to repeat here, complements the argument set out in this paper about tragic *form*.[*]

---

[102] I exclude the passage of song from oral to literate form (e.g. epinikian, bucolic).

[103] The universal power of money potentially frees its possessor from dependence on others (even kin) and from the claims of reciprocity and religion. In tragedy the individual (unlike the Homeric hero) may be alienated from his nearest and dearest and from all gods. Money (even coinage) in tragedy: e.g. Aeschylus *Agamemnon* 1638–1639; Sophokles *Oedipus Tyrannus* 124–125, 380–386, 388–389, 542, etc., *Antigone* 295–301, 322, 1036–1039, 1047, 1055–1056, 1061–1071; Euripides *Bacchae* 257, 812, *Electra* 550–574; Seaford 1998.

[104] Wilson 2000:109, 111, 123, 148–149, 151, 157, 170, 194–197.

[105] See Seaford 2003a, 2003b, 2004.

[*] My thanks go to Peter Wilson for his helpful comments on this chapter.

Five

Not by Words Alone:
Ritual Approaches to Greek Literature[1]

Margaret Alexiou

What Is Ritual?

In *The Ritual Lament in Greek Tradition*, I suggest that the relation between lament and ritual provides a clue to the continuity and poetic quality of the genre in Greek tradition, and draw attention to the ritual connections inherent in ancient literary and modern folk laments. I state, "When this dynamic interplay of poetry and life was obscured in Byzantine learned tradition, the result tended towards a cold and formal literary exercise, divorced from popular language and culture."[2] My implied concepts of both ritual and literature here are, I now think, oversimplified. The lament is, by its very definition, performative and ritual; and, when not confined to wailings, poetic. That does not mean that Byzantine learned laments lack ritual contexts, as has been demonstrated in recent studies on the interdependence of literature, both religious and secular, and rhetoric, ceremonial, ritual.[3] Nor is the

[1] For my sister, Lis (Elisabeth Thomson, 14 December 1936—27 July 2000). Her quiet strength has been with me throughout the preparation of this chapter, inspiring my choice of texts, especially "The Dumb Violinist," and Flora Thompson. My interest in ritual began with my first book, Alexiou 2002a (first edition 1974). In my latest book (Alexiou 2002b), I attempt to redefine ritual and explore its resources from new perspectives. Ideas on ritual approaches to literary texts were further developed in a series of inter-related lectures given at the Universities of London (King's College), Birmingham, Oxford, and Cambridge, between March 1998 and February 2000, and assumed their present form in a lecture for Harvard University's Modern Greek Studies Seminar in November 2000. I give thanks to all participants in discussion, especially those I have argued and worked with over a period of some thirty years or so. Where possible, readers are referred to Alexiou 2002b for a fuller range of bibliographical references than constraints of space here permit. For putting the chapter onto the computer, I would like to thank Jean Day, of Dover, most warmly.
[2] Alexiou 2002a:50.
[3] Magdalino 1993:332–342, 426–430. On the ritual aspects of laments in Byzantine literature see Roilos forthcoming, chapter 1.

dichotomy between learned and popular so great as I maintained. The prioritization of "popular tradition" may be seen as an expression of "nationist demoticism," and far from even-handed, since scholars have accorded higher status to some folk genres than to others, depending on how easily they could be assimilated to visions of the continuity of Hellenism and the heroic struggles of the Greek people.[4] Whatever scholarly predilections may have been, modern Greek writers have absorbed into their poetry and prose at least as much from the less accredited folk genres, such as love songs, legends and tales, as from laments and historical songs.[5] Modern literature lay beyond the purview of my first book; but I shall argue that there is every reason now to explore ritual approaches.

In my latest book, *After Antiquity: Greek Language, Myth, and Metaphor*, I begin the third section ("Metaphor") with a chapter entitled "The resources of ritual."[6] I will now summarize and update my findings there so as to apply them in this chapter in somewhat different directions, including modern literature. Ritual is not a corpus of solemn activities undertaken by rural folk or by agents of religious institutions at times of ceremony and crisis. It is a profoundly analogical way of seeing, thinking, acting, and has inspired Greek writers and artists over many centuries. Ritual is an attempt by one or more persons, whether acting individually or in concert with others, to control the perceived outside world in relation to the self, and to organize that world by means of the associations of one's senses. It can inform ethical codes by modes of consensus beyond the rational and verbal, involving repetition, with rhythm and pattern but not without variation, of actions, gestures, sounds, and utterances. Anthropologists stress the communicative and performative aspects of ritual, sociologists and psychologists the interactive. Autistic and psychotic rituals are seen as redundant; yet their apparently meaningless "ritualistic" qualities afford insight into the emotional, neurological, and physiological bases of ritual—*how does it work?*

Drawing on ethnographies, clinical studies, field work, and my knowledge of autistic people (including my adult twin sons), I argue that ritual cannot be relegated to one or other sphere of public / private, sacred / secular. Rituals cross a continuum of flexible rules and transgressions, as we confront our mortal condition on three interacting levels. First, everyday life: activities within the household

---

[4] On "nationist demoticism," see Tziovas 1986; on the prioritization of certain genres within the canon of Greek folklore, see Herzfeld 1980 and Herzfeld 1982:97–122, 145–148; Alexiou 2002b:176–180.

[5] At a presentation of her Ἱστορίες γιὰ τὰ βαθειά (1983) for a Harvard Colloquium on Modern Greek Studies, November 1997, Jenny Mastoraki described her indebtedness to the *paramuthia* she had known since childhood.

[6] Alexiou 2002b:317–348; on metaphor and ritual in songs of the life cycle, 348–410.

or around the workplace, both autonomous and other (including the sacred). Second, stress and heightened emotional states, whether caused by adversity or success. Third, the life cycle and beyond: birth, marriage, death, afterlife. These three levels may be experienced concurrently. The mechanisms for dealing with them—or "coping strategies" as my autistic son Dimitri calls them—tend to revolve around the same bodily needs: food and drink, clothes and washing, home and abroad.

Links between these three levels of ritual, everyday and sacred, may be forged by analogy, not by words alone. For example, an elderly couple among Renée Hirschon's informants, refugees from Asia Minor, welcome her to share their simple meal at their home in Kokkinia. They silence her remonstrances at their trouble and expense with an upward glance at the icon of the Last Supper hanging above the table, with the words "As with Christ, so with us" ("Οπως ὁ Χριστός, ἔτσι κι ἐμεῖς).[7] Such simple gestures lend ritual grace to hardship and poverty. How aesthetic and religious dimensions merge in Greek Orthodox practice is expressed by another of Hirschon's informants, who exclaims as she prepares food and cloths for a local pilgrimage, "Our religion is beautiful" (Εἶναι ὡραία ἡ θρησκεία μας).[8] Aesthetic as well as moral considerations help to shape ethical codes that are based on concepts of reciprocity, relativity, accountability, and a sense of propriety (σωστό). The niceties are endlessly disputed (to the delight of all) according to criteria that operate in synthesis with the sphere of religion, but independently of it. Above all, before passing a negative judgment that is final, you must take account of the human propensity to err: "We are human, it could have happened to us" ("Ανθρωποι εἴμαστε, θὰ μποροῦσε νὰ συμβεῖ καὶ σὲ μᾶς).

Ritual is synesthetic and kinesthetic, hence its power to move us. It involves all our senses—sight, sound, smell, touch, movement—sometimes separately, sometimes together, its magic rooted in participation and performance, both public and private; not remote, but part of our daily transactions and interactions. Manifestations vary; but the interconnections between ritual and metaphor, indicated in my *Ritual Lament* as well as in *After Antiquity*, provide clues for the non-verbal as well as verbal paths of cultural transmission.

In his magisterial study of ritual and religion, Roy Rappaport argues for the centrality of ritual rather than belief in the formation, development and durability of religions, and explains the dynamics of change according to models adapted from

[7] Hirschon 1989:20.
[8] Hirschon 1989:21.

speech-act theory and cybernetics.[9] He suggests that ritual and liturgical forms, however arcane, tend to remain constant, whereas belief systems and dogma are prone to modification, revision, and disruption. If so, although references to Greece are few in his work, and limited to antiquity, the case for Greek ritual and religious forms, documented as they can be with archaeological and linguistic evidence across three and a half millennia, is compelling.

Although aware of the non-verbal qualities of ritual, Rappaport says little on the ritual uses of art, music, and dance, or on the relevance of ritual to the secular arts up to and including our own times. More research is needed on aesthetics, both as applied and interpreted in pre-modern times, and on how music and drama can be used to transform the repetitive, ritualistic mannerisms of autistic people into creative activities.[10] The implications are far-reaching. Ritual's capacity to switch back and forth from the mundane to the eternal, through sensations rather than by logical thought, and by means both shapely (εὔμορφος) and unshapely (ἄσχημος), draws from the same mainspring as the arts, but with less generic differentiation and specialization than is current in most modern art forms. To put it more crudely, ritual has always included dirt, shit, sex, blood, and violence, so as to set them up against their analogical opposites in creative tension. Ritual is inclusive, and knows few marginalized genres.[11] The Greek material, diversely represented both in folklore and pre-modern literature, can help to uncover the resources of ritual—even, in Rappaport's terms, the "making of humanity."

There is semantic support for the case that ritual is more enduring than belief. The Greek word πίστις includes, without marked distinction, the meanings belief, faith, trust, credit (as in τράπεζα πίστεως, "credit bank," not "bank of faith"). Πίστις is relative, shifting, dependent on reciprocal negotiation and exchange, rather than on unquestioning belief or unswerving faith. The dimensions of ritual are aesthetic and ethical, political and social, as well as religious.[12] Ritual is, above all, a matter of reciprocity: a process of negotiation and mediation by means of "things done" (δρώμενα), "things said" (λεγόμενα) and "things thought"

---

[9] Rappaport 1999. My own ideas on ritual, as formulated in *After Antiquity*, then in press, were independent.
[10] See Clethero 2000–2001. Her eleven years' experience of working with autistic adults—including some without speech—has not only brought purpose and hope into their lives, but also sheds fresh light on the condition of autism, and the creative impulse.
[11] On obscenity, humor, and the grotesque in folklore and medieval literature, see Bakhtin 1984a:1–144, 303–346. On ritual laughter, see Propp 1984:124–175.
[12] Although she does not use the term "ritual," Onora O'Neill expresses similar concepts, especially with reference to Sokrates' Athens, O'Neill 2002:63, 69.

(νομιζόμενα), as studies in the history of Greek religions, ancient, medieval, and modern, have shown.[13] Rappaport confirms the wider relevance of such a model.

Let me give a few brief examples, beginning with Chryses' imprecation to Apollo from the opening of Homer's *Iliad*. Outraged at Agamemnon's treatment of his daughter Briseis, Chryses prays to Apollo as Smintheus ("Mousegod"): "Hear me, if ever in the past I built you a shrine or burnt you fat thighs of a bull or a goat, grant me this wish: may the Danaans pay for my tears with your arrows" (I 33–42). Apollo's wronged priest, Chryses, stalks the shore in anger; his prayer to Apollo "Mousegod" is answered, and the ensuing pestilence sets in motion the final act of the Trojan War. A modern parallel to this type of imprecation ("if ever before, so now") occurs in a lament from Mani, where a mother reproaches Saint Dimitrios for failing to save her son—who bears his name—from drowning: "Saint Dimitrios, didn't we glorify you? keep your light burning? didn't my Dimitrios bring you three silver oil lamps? three painted doors . . . ? How then did you not help when the sea was rough and our boat sank?"[14] Both prayers form a process of exchange, negotiation, credit, debit, with the expectation of correct balance at the end. The process may bring trust, as at the end of the *Iliad*, when Priam and Achilles agree to exchange the bodies of their dear ones, including Hector's.

In other kinds of ritual, such as enchantment (μαγεία), or funeral rites for those whose bodies cannot be recovered, efficacy depends on the inclusion of a small physical item which represents the whole of the person or concept concerned, such as hair, nails, clothes, intimate belongings, a photograph.[15] Synecdoche of this kind is part of metonym, and integral to ritual. Viewed from this perspective, autistic rituals—often labeled "fetishistic"—can be better appreciated, even though we can only rarely glimpse what "whole" their small but treasured item may reveal to them.

I have touched on aspects of ritual that deserve more attention: analogy and metaphor, including synecdoche; reciprocity and negotiation; accountability and

[13] Jane Harrison sets out the dynamics of ancient ritual and religion, with illustrations from art and archaeology, literary and historical sources, Harrison 1922. George Thomson explores the ritual precursors of tragedy, Thomson 1941, 1966. On ritual and other ancient genres, including epic, see also Thomson 1949. Drawing in part on Thomson's work, Richard Seaford sees reciprocity as integral to ritual in his study of epic and drama in the city-state, Seaford 1994a. My own use of the term reciprocity in relation to ritual pre-dates my knowledge of Seaford's (1992, personal communication), and is based primarily on modern Greek sources and experiences, especially the work of Hirschon 1989:169–186, 213.
[14] For full text and translation, see Alexiou 2002a:170–171.
[15] On synecdoche in ritual, see Meraklis 1984:19: In an emigration ritual from Monolithi in Epiros, mothers place a coin in a μισιοκάρα (half-measure vessel) of water, and set it on the threshold for departing sons to spill as they step out of the household, to the words, "Όπως τρέχει τὸ νερό, νὰ κυλᾶ καὶ τὸ χρῆμα μέσα στὸ πουγκὶ τοῦ μετανάστη ("as the water flows, so may the money flow in the emigrant's purse").

trust. Most remarkable is its power to switch us, in an instant, back and forth between the mundane and the eternal, in space and time. Perhaps that is why we recall exactly what we were doing when we received an important but unexpected piece of news, good or bad: the instant is marked, through the senses, with everyday activities, however inappropriate. The ballad singer exploits this phenomenon with dramatic effect, as in a Thracian version of the Virgin's lament, where Mary Magdalene brings news of Christ's Crucifixion only to find Mary "washing in a silver bath"; or, in another version from Asia Minor, "sitting at her table eating."[16] The incongruities are more marked because of Christ's central role in baptism and the Last Supper.

And so we come back to the bodily needs and human activities around which ritual revolves: food and drink, clothes and washing, home and abroad. Greek Orthodox women, however humble, can experience such transcendental moments by virtue of their daily to-ings and fro-ings between household chores and tending of church, shrine, or tomb.[17] As to literature, the novel is perhaps the most flexible genre for constant interplay between mundane and cosmic levels of experience, as I shall argue in the closing section. Meantime, I shall survey four kinds of pre-modern texts that make the Greek literary heritage distinctive, inviting approaches through ritual.

The Liturgy

The liturgy is an obvious place to begin, given its central position in Greek Orthodox worship—private and shared, within and beyond the household—to high days and holy days, and life cycle rituals. From the hymns of Romanos the Melodist in the sixth century to the poetry of Odysseas Elytis in the twentieth, the Greek liturgy and its language have evoked far more than words by themselves can say or mean, as is the case with the King James "Authorized" version of the Bible for modern English. Sixty years after Sophie Antoniades published her meticulous and wide-ranging study, Antony Hirst has been one of the few to scrutinize in scholarly manner the liturgical sources and their uses by modern Greek poets.[18] Yet I would put his case the other way round. Modern Greek poets do not appropriate the liturgical language, pretending they are God. Rather, they bring God, and the language in which they worship him, into their poetry, just as Hirschon's Asia Minor refugees brought Christ to their dining table.

---

[16] For texts and translations, see Alexiou, 2002a:74–75.
[17] Hirschon 1989:17–22; Hart 1991:148.
[18] Antoniades 1939; Hirst, Ph.D. thesis submitted to King's College, London, June 1999.

Of liturgical texts, the 'Επιτάφιος Θρῆνος has long been in need of closer philological, linguistic, and literary study. Still a living part of the Holy Week liturgy, it had assumed more or less its present form by the fourteenth century, although much can be traced back to the sixth and seventh centuries.[19] Its lexical richness makes it difficult to date or define, with a high incidence of rare and exotic words, some seemingly peculiar to Hellenistic poetry. It is not the κοινή Greek of the New Testament.[20] The very strangeness explains its power and fascination, in Byzantine times no less than our own, reminding us that there is sensual delight in the sound and non-sense of words—much as my son Dimitri loves to chant over and over again the same old obscure words whether culled from hymns or his own invention, to variations on his own pentatonic tune. My father-in-law, Dimitrios Alexiou, as cantor in the village of Sklithron Ayias, Mount Pelion, knew the liturgy and much of the New Testament by heart. He may not have known how to construe New Testament Greek; but he had internalized the music of the liturgical language, and made it his own, in the manner of poets and singers rather than that of scholars.

There is much to explore in the resonances of the liturgy and its language in poetry and prose fiction. But there can be no question of appropriation: ritual and religious language belongs to all who hear, know it, as with the King James Bible or the Book of Common Prayer.

Seasons, Games, and Play

There is a rich and diverse fund of Byzantine sources on seasonal games and play, ranging from snatches of vernacular songs from the seventh century onwards to the more comprehensive narrative vignettes in Niketas Choniates' *Historia* (twelfth century). The materials have been adequately collected; but few scholars have paid attention to their potential value for the study of literature.[21] Of the ten or so song fragments I analyze in *After Antiquity*, primarily for linguistic purposes, I have selected one for summary and comment here, mainly because it affords insights into how song can mean in ritual, not logical, terms.[22]

---

[19] See Alexiou 2002a:65–68. On the Virgin's lament, see Alexiou 1975; Bakker and Philippides 2000.

[20] A preliminary listing of unusual lexical items includes: *drax, epirrainô, askis, peparmenon, pelekas*. The *Epitaphios Thrênos* deserves a full-length linguistic and philological study, of the same thoroughness as that of Grosdidier de Matons 1977:285–328: the *index nominum* illustrates the lexical wealth of Romanos, including a high proportion of ancient Greek vocabulary. On the New Testament and its linguistic legacy, see Alexiou, 2002b:43–65.

[21] The fullest compilation of sources remains Phaidon Koukoules' monumental work: Koukoules 1944–49. Literary studies include Alexiou 1999 and Roilos 2000.

[22] Alexiou, 2002b:81–95; 87–94 for text, transliteration, translation, and commentary.

The song belongs to the genre of "quête song," or "wassail song," performed by children to welcome the first appearance of the swallow as harbinger of spring, although its designation "swallow song" (χελιδόνισμα) is modern. Comprising forty-nine lines, it was recorded—apparently complete—in Latin script from Greek school boys, as performed in Rome for the Cornomannia festival, by Canon Benedict, for inclusion in his *Liber Politicus*. Extant in one manuscript from the twelfth century and two from the fifteenth, the text has been dated to the years between 1140 and 1143.[23] It has attracted much scholarly attention from philologists and folklorists, because of its affinities on the one hand with a text and custom cited by Athenaios (second century CE) alleged to go back to Rhodes in the sixth century BCE, and on the other hand with a corpus of modern seasonal songs (κάλαντα), many also from Rhodes. Here, then, is what we have been waiting for: the missing Byzantine link in the recorded history of a ritual song that goes back some two and a half thousand years!

Yet most scholars tend only to deplore the garbled nature of the Byzantine text, the impossibility of its transcription, translation, and interpretation. Having dealt elsewhere, and in some detail, with questions of word division, phonology, phonetic confusion possibly due to dialectal features, I will ask now, can sense be made of this text? Michael Herzfeld came closest to an interpretation some thirty years ago, not least because, as an anthropologist as well as a philologist, he perceived the levels of performative, non-literary context.[24] Here is my latest attempt to make ritual sense of this enigmatic but fascinating twelfth-century testimony.

The song is made up of three parts, and an epilogue. In the first part (lines 1–12), the boys address the "master of the house" (χαῖρε, οἰκοδέσποτα, χαῖρε). They banish February and usher in March, welcoming the communion between divine, human, and animal worlds. In the second part (13–35), the swallow responds to the boys' greeting, and there is a brief exchange: "Yes, I have built my nest here, I have seen the king, I have communed with the sky and stars." As for the boys, learning letters and respect for teacher are allusively linked to the coming of spring, the mercy of God, the palm and the Cross. In the third part (36–44), the boys respond to an implied threat of a beating from their master by reciting their numbers and letters in an acrostic that runs from alpha to iota. The epilogue

---

[23] Patala 1996.

[24] Herzfeld 1972. Roderick Beaton, by contrast, draws attention to the text's "excessively garbled nature," its "incantatory quality which seems to depend on the rhythm and sound of the words rather than on their meaning," and "the chaotic and inconsequential series of lines"; in the end, he casts doubt on the authenticity of the text, with the over-literary conjecture that "the Mr. Thwackum who taught the carollers the theory of financial gain also taught them the song from written song-sheets" (Beaton 1980:137–141).

(43–49) consists of acclamations, as master of the house, teacher, pope, and Christ are merged by a process of cumulative accretion in celebration of the Crucifixion. Here is an extract from my tentative translation:

> Let's begin to recite, Hail to all, thus:—Swallow, swallow, I have seen the king, once more I am here, the farmer is tilling, all things / with joy filling, with water and silt my tower I have built. Whip, / whip, might fights, they sang. Don't whip me on hands or on / arse-hole. Five, five, and five more, fifteen. You came out / wearing stars, you counsel and consort with the angels. / The world is awaiting you, joyful and fair. Rejoice, / good forty boys, running to school, learning your letters . . .

The text is problematic, but not nonsensical. With the ancient song, it shares the address to the swallow as harbinger of spring and abundance, and the hope that the boys will one day prove worthy of their elders.[25] With the modern κάλαντα, it shares formulaic and structural units, as well as themes.[26] Communion between human, animal, and divine spheres are explicitly linked to the cycles of seasons and stars. With contemporary Byzantine texts, such as the Ptochoprodromic Poems, the song shares a predilection for games and play, but with a serious purpose: the beatings suggest redemption through suffering; raucous humor and symbols, both sacred and secular, convey higher concerns.[27] The progressions are linked by contiguity and association, not by logic. As for the ritual itself, although condemned in the fourth century as "pagan" by John Chrysostom, it had been assimilated by the Church well before the twelfth century, and has been recorded, with many versions of the song, within living memory.[28] The significance of its endurance over time lies not in "continuity," but in the power and flexibility of ritual to adapt levels of belief and religious forms wherever it retains links with song and performance, in this case by celebrating the renewal of life in the calendar year: out with February, in comes March.

---

[25] The text is from Fabre 1905:173–174. On the ancient song, cited by Athenaios 8.359d–360d, see Petropoulos 1994:5–17.

[26] Herzfeld 1972:57–73, and appendix of texts. For references to other interpretations of the Byzantine and modern songs, see Alexiou 2002b:91–94.

[27] See Hesseling and Pernot 1910:Poem I, lines 172–197. Alexiou (1999:94, 97–102) situates the humor and satire of this episode in the context of seasonal games and play, often with the outcome of raising the dead. On forms of ritual play in twelfth-century Byzantine fiction, see Roilos 2000.

[28] Herzfeld 1972:1–56.

Words and Paintings: *Hysmine and Hysminias*

Seasonal rituals provide potent layers of meaning, not always manifest, in much Byzantine literary and artistic representation, sacred and secular.[29] Eustathios Makrembolites' *Hysmine and Hysminias*—probably also composed in the 1140's— is a love story in learned prose, and a conscious revival of the ancient genre. Perhaps the first fictional text to explore the awakening of human sexuality, male and female, it also celebrates the sanctity of Eros, the renewal of life, and its immortalization through art. Warring images of Fire (Πῦρ) and Water (Ὕδωρ) are used throughout to juxtapose the drives of sexuality with seasonal and ethical constraints, especially in the three extended *ekphraseis* drawn from the central panel of the garden frieze. Hysminias, the first consistent ego-narrator in the history of fiction, and Hysmine, whose precocious sexuality precipitates the action, are each by turns subject to trials of endurance, and triumph in the end through art. *Hysmine* exemplifies the Byzantine schema ΠΑΘΗ—ΗΘΟΣ—ΣѠΤΗΡΙΑ.[30] Sufferings test the moral courage of male and female protagonists, and lead them to salvation. It is a ritual schema familiar from the story of Christ and the saints' lives, but by no means restricted to Orthodox Christianity or to the sphere of the sacred, as we shall see from the παραμύθια (tales).

If we wish to appreciate Byzantine literature, we should pay close attention to the "word pictures," or *ekphraseis*, in the texts. Each of the three that frame the first part of *Hysmine* is strategically placed at key turning points, and in each, the multiple significations of the idyllic garden are evoked not only through literary and neoplatonic allusions, but by reference to contemporary manuals, artwork, or architecture.[31] Sosthenes' garden, so wondrous to behold and so evocative in its symbolism, remains within the horizons of twelfth-century Byzantine thought and practice. To cite the most relevant example for my present purpose, the third *ekphrasis* shows us a panel from the garden frieze: twelve men, each engaged on diverse labors of the year's cycle, beginning with a soldier and ending with an old man round a fire that reaches up from earth to heaven. They are—we infer—the twelve months, whose labors in the year's cycle are governed by three seasons—summer, cold, and spring. Contemplation

---

[29] Particularly "user-friendly" for literary scholars is Maguire 1981.

[30] On the Byzantine reception of Heliodoros, see Agapitos 1998:125–156; for a detailed discussion of the rhetorical appreciation and the allegorical interpretation of ancient fiction in Byzantium, see Roilos forthcoming, chapters 1 and 2.

[31] To the sources cited in my reappraisal of *Hysmine*, Alexiou 2002b:111–127, should be added those in M. H. Thomson 1955, and 1960, which show the specific, day-to-day functions of garden symbolism, as well as the spiritual qualities. For an extensive discussion of neoplatonic allusions in Byzantine fiction and their cultural and historical contextualization, see Roilos forthcoming, chapter 2.

by Hysminias and his friend, Kratisthenes, recalls the debates on the nature of Eros in Plato's *Symposium*. Yet the details can be matched exactly in a painter's manual, composed in simple Greek in the twelfth century, for the illustration of calendars.[32] Calendar cycles juxtaposing words and pictures became widespread from the eleventh century, with vernacular examples gaining in frequency from the fourteenth.[33] A major function of this much-loved genre was to accord due importance to each and every aspect of tillage and cultivation in its mundane and sacred aspects.

Each *ekphrasis* shows the ritual and cosmic dimensions of male and female initiation into sexuality. The Orthodox year began in March, and ended in February, whose representative is portrayed as the oldest and most important—albeit reviled— of the months, in accordance with interpretations of the twelve signs of the zodiac, between Pisces and Aries. August, six months later, marks the turning point between summer and winter. He is a naked bather, whose total immersion suggests baptism.[34] For humankind, the calendrical year sets up cosmic strife between Fire and Water. February's fire promises eternal renewal; but it must be tempered by waters (including tears) in August if it is not to consume itself. The *ekphraseis* signal the conflicts and oppositions that will be played out and resolved in the course of the book.

Several points emerge. First, we must look at all kinds of evidence, not just literature, if we wish to understand modes of composition, performance, and transmission in the pre-modern period. Stories were told in high and low forms, in *paraphraseis* and *metaphraseis* from the fourth to eighth centuries, and in non-verbal as well as verbal forms. Sculpture and painting, song and dance, have played their part; they are the very fabric from which literature is refreshed and refashioned.[35] By taking account of extra-literary sources, such as almanacs and garbled snatches of children's songs, we can imagine what might otherwise be dismissed as "non-senses indiscutibles," and glimpse the interplay between everyday activities and creative art.[36]

Second, modern literary genres and categories, such as novel, romance, or character, plot, may have little relevance for ancient and medieval texts, where boundaries are more shifting and flexible. The core genre in Byzantium, if any, is the προγύμνασμα (genre exercise), which honed and practiced rhetorical skills at all levels of composition, particularly in the craft of combining *êthopoiia* (imper-

[32] Polyakova 1971.
[33] Strzygowski 1888; Keil 1889; Eideneier 1979.
[34] Plepelits 1989:50–51.
[35] On lesser known literary modes of transmission, see Martlew 2000. For detailed parallels between Seljuc palace architecture and *Hysmine*, see Hunt 1984. On possible connections between *Hysmine* and papyrus fragments of the ancient story of Parthenope and Metiochos, also apparently known as ὀρχηστικὴ ἱστορία ("dance story"), see references in Alexiou 2002b:122–123.
[36] See Speck 1984:302–303, in response to the dismissive comments on Poem I by Hesseling and Pernot (1910:passim).

sonation) with *dialogos*, *diêgesis*, and *ekphrasis*, as in *Hysmine*.[37] Terms such as novel and romance are best avoided for pre-modern fiction, not least because they are not used by their authors and readers. If we try to avoid reading Byzantine texts through parachronistic spectacles, dismissive comments such as "this text has no literary merit" simply lose aesthetic meaning.

Third, where longer narrative is concerned, the ritual schema ΠΑΘΗ—ΗΘΟΣ—Σ(υ)ΤΗΡΙΑ may be adapted to themes pagan and Christian, religious and philosophical, whether erotic, military, or adventurous in nature. The scheme fits saints' lives as well as Digenes Akrites, Richardson's *Pamela* as well as Tolstoy's *War and Peace*—or Makrembolites' *Hysmine*. We need search no further for the origins of the novel, or strive to tell its true story.[38] It is a false quest.

One last point to close this section. From the texts surveyed so far, it is clear that fiction, in life as in literature, does not take place just on the level of everyday human reality, but stands in constant tension, interaction, and analogy with other, non-human forms of life and death, with the cycle of the seasons, and with the movement of earth and planets. Such cosmic dimensions transcend the limits of individual life and death. The Byzantine "swallow song" is not so far removed from the Orthodox liturgy and *Hysmine*, after all.

Telling Tales: *Paramuthia*

Let me continue my exploration of literary highways and byways by suggesting how orality and literacy have played in and out of the story of Greek fiction, in the form of *paramuthia*.[39] What are they? The Greek word is current in its present sense of

---

[37] See for example, Pignani 1983. On the role of *progumnasmata* in the composition of the Byzantine novel, see Roilos forthcoming, chapter 1.

[38] From the systematic discussion in Rohde's *Der griechische Roman und seine Vorläufer* (1914) to Margaret Doody, *The True Story of the Novel* (1998), historians of the ancient novel have been concerned with questions of Greekness, origins, and religion. If the term ritual, as defined above, is applied to the study of the novel and its precursors, then the apparent contradictions between secular and sacred, mundane and cosmic, may be more readily assimilated. As Doody has pointed out (1998:162–164), there is no reason to dismiss the concepts of religion and ritual as applied by, for example, Reinhold Merkelbach in his *Roman und Mysterium* (1962); however, a ritual approach does not necessarily preclude an historical or literary analysis, as Doody implies (1998:164).

[39] The first two pages of this section are condensed from Chapter 7 of Alexiou 2002b:211–265 to which the reader is referred for bibliographical references. I have included "The Dumb Violinist" for the first time to pay three personal tributes: to my sister, who was skilled on the violin but not one of unnecessary words; to Jenny Mastoraki, to whom I gave my only handwritten copy of the story in 1997; and to Jeremy Ballard, whose violin performance of the Larghetto from Dvorák's Sonata in G major, op. 100 (also known as "The Indian Lament") enraptured all 200 of us who attended Lis' funeral on 3 August 2000. The tale's proximity, both in date (1892) and mode, to the short stories of Vizyenos, Papadiamandis, and others, should also be noted.

"lying tale" since the seventeenth century. The verbal cognate, παραμυθέομαι, means "comfort; talk on the side," hence also "tell a tall story, divert," as at a funeral feast, which was also known since ancient times as *parêgoria, paramuthia*. The prefix *para-* suggests boundaries explored and transgressed, as appropriate for tales told to console the bereaved during the all-night vigil at the wake, when dirges are forbidden. Παραμύθια (tales of comfort) are the converse of μοιρολόγια (songs of fate), or laments.

Although tales seem to lack the obvious ritual context of the laments and wedding songs (pertaining to the life cycle), the occasions of performance, as described by Adamandios Adamandiou at the turn of the nineteenth and twentieth centuries, range from everyday (mothers and grandmothers, craftsmen and fishermen on night shift) to hardship and distress (cold, hunger, prison, war), to festivals, high days and holy days, and funeral wakes; that is, occasions coinciding precisely with the three levels of ritual I outlined in the first section of this chapter. Furthermore, tales are shared in a special and immediate way between teller and audience, however large or small, intimate or public. Tales invite us all to step outside the human bonds of everyday life, outside our time and space, even outside our own bodies, so we imagine we can become a fragrant tree, a variegated flower, or a dancing eel. That is why tales are magic, even when exchanged over such mundane chores as cooking, sewing, mending, washing dishes, or whiling away time on long journeys. Tales link our everyday activities and material anxieties with the divine and the cosmic.

Παραμύθια have been recorded sporadically from the 1840s, and began to appear in folklore journals and regional periodicals from the 1880s, although their appeal was, initially at least, to scholars of non-Greek origin rather than to Greek folklorists, who despised them as "mixed," neither uncontaminated oral tradition, nor purely Greek, nor historically accurate—and, we might add, most certainly not "politically correct." Many tales have Oriental connections, others contain elements seemingly lifted out of mythical compilations and chapbooks, such as the labors of Herakles, clashing rocks, the water of life. Literary "intrusions," from *Alexander the Great, Apollonios of Tyre, Halima (Shahrazad), Voskopoula*, and *Erotokritos*, were absorbed into the consciousness of audiences who heard extracts read out and debated, and then recast them into their own *paramuthia*. Tales are not inferior by contamination with foreign or literary elements, so long as they are assimilated into local narrative traditions.

A few brief references must suffice to indicate the more unusual features of the tales, as well as their thematic and narrative links with Byzantine and modern Greek fictional modes. "The Twelve Months" (1900) shows the twelve laborers of the garden frieze in *Hysmine* alive and well, each with his own distinctive personality— especially February and March—and quick to reward or punish, depending on

Not by Words Alone

how you greet or respond to them.[40] In "The Miller's Daughter" (1890), the humble protagonist wins a kingdom and judicial power thanks to her sense of justice and cosmic wisdom. Only she can solve the king's three riddles: What are the two that stand (τὰ δυὸ στεκούμενα)? What are the two that walk (τὰ δυὸ περπατούμενα)? What are the two that inhabit (τὰ δυὸ ἐνοικούμενα)? Heaven and earth, she replies, sun and moon, life and death.[41] Both stories illustrate the principle of ritual reciprocity, and the importance of non-human, otherworldly dimensions in the apportioning of justice. From "The Little Deer" (1899) comes the deliciously surreal passage where the tailor's apprentice, whose third impossible task is to weave a silken dress with sea, waves, and fishes woven into it, and to compress it into a hazelnut shell, is apprehended drunk, swimming naked in the dress he is about to complete.[42] The bemused little dialogues in this scene are as "unnecessary" to plot and character as *ekphrasis*, but audience and narrator are entranced. The apprentice fascinates because his source of magic is not revealed—God? the Devil? or the Nereids? And he makes those dresses so effortlessly, when in a drunken stupor, despite his master's abusive railings! Such strategies—and their social implications—have not passed unnoticed by modern Greek writers.

As R. M. Dawkins has observed, some tales may be "brought into the class of novels by being humanized."[43] Among the best examples is "The Dumb Violinist" (1892), which belongs to the tale-type where the protagonist, male or female, must make a dumb partner speak. The non-speaking partner—usually but not invariably of a higher social class—has been bewitched, and must be rescued by the other, not infrequently with the aid of a talking bird as intermediary.[44] "The Dumb Violinist" is different: there is no magic, just a poor fisherman's son whose violin consoles him until he chooses to end his wounded silence. Here is the story, in barest summary:

I.   A poor fisherman has no luck in fishing until one night his son Giannakis steals on board the boat. Next day a beautiful girl beckons Giannakis from the balcony of a rich house, and gives him three gold pounds. The next day, five gold pounds. She promises his father 300 gold pounds if he will let her have Giannakis for three years to educate him.

---

40 Kafandaris 1988:1, no. 92.
41 Kafandaris 1988:1, no. 70.
42 Dawkins 1950:186–188.
43 Dawkins 1950:389.
44 Examples include "The Silent Princess," Dawkins 1953, no. 48, and "The Aneraida," Kafandaris 1988:1, no. 40. For full text of Ὁ βωβὸς βιολάτορας ("The Dumb Violinist") see Δελτίον τῆς Ἱστορικῆς καὶ Ἐθνολογικῆς Ἑταιρείας τῆς Ἑλλάδος 1 (1892), 696–707. It is just one of many first-rate *paramuthia* that still remain to be recovered and enjoyed, especially from older and regional folklore journals.

II. Three years pass, Giannakis speaks many languages, and plays the violin like magic. Meanwhile, the girl's father, a shipowner, returns from America. She packs off Giannakis with money so he can return in disguise as a foreign prince to claim her hand. The ruse succeeds; but at the last dance of the grand wedding, she confides to a maidservant, "See, a fisherman's son is marrying a noblewoman." The wrath of God so willed it, and Giannakis heard.

III. Dumbstruck, he changes into his fisherman's garb, goes down to the shore, and boards a boat for Alexandria, where he works as apprentice to an Arab net maker. When he has proved his skill, he signals his desire for a fine violin, and his master buys him one. The fame of his playing reached the king in Cairo. Giannakis is appointed chief violinist in the kingdom, and word is sent out around the world that whoever can heal his dumbness shall have half the king's realm; but whoever tries and fails will lose his head.

IV. Back home, the girl is devastated. Hoping for news from travelers, she has a well built in the garden, with a statue of Giannakis playing the violin—the spitting image! One day, two sailors pass, and recognize the dumb violinist from Cairo. The girl dresses as a smart French doctor and goes straight there, sure she can get Giannakis to speak. She changes into her bridal costume but he won't speak, he just plays his violin. On the fortieth day, she is led out for execution. Just as the sword was raised to cut off her head, Giannakis lisps "THTOP!" He turns and says to her, "A fisherman's son was not unworthy to take a noblewoman in marriage. See how a fisherman's son can save a noblewoman from death?" There was the wedding of all weddings. The king had no children, now he found children.

Neither was I there, nor are you to believe me. I've said much, and that's enough. Good night to you, my neighbors.

"The Dumb Violinist" illustrates both the power and powerlessness of words. "Sticks and stones may break my bones, but words shall never hurt me" goes the English proverb, whereas Greek says the opposite, "Words have no bones but bones they break." Was Giannakis really dumb, or only pretending? As with the apprentice's magic, the narrator leaves the question open, allowing us to think that he is traumatized, not bewitched, first by his father's begrudging nature, then by the girl. She mocks him in a cruel aside at what should have been the supreme moment of their ritual bliss—the wedding dance. Her words rob him of speech, and he recovers it only to save her from death for his sake. But he could not have done so without his violin.

The tale was recorded in the 1890s from the island of Kastellorizo, then prosperous, now depopulated. It shows that tales are not stereotypes. Their meanings are recreated over time as they are handed on by tellers who exchange stories with other peoples, as well as with friends and family. Their appeal lies in narrative ingenuity, moral wisdom, and performative flexibility. Tellers may act out their life drama through assumed personae in fictionalized forms which do not disclose personal information or compromise the self in the eyes of the community. Tales may be related to the experiences of tellers and audiences in ways less obvious but more immediate than are envisaged by adherents of the historicist school. Persecutions and pursuits, disguises and hiding places, starvation and undreamed-of food, may seem fantastic to us. But they have been lived through at one time or another by those who shared in the making of παραμύθια, from the War of Independence (1821–28) to the turbulent aftermaths of World Wars I and II. Tales allow us to transcend, albeit momentarily, our mundane or traumatic reality. That is what lends them ritual qualities, rather than overt or perceived magic or religion.

Modern Prose Fiction

In "The Dumb Violinist," the narrative devices are those of the folktale, but the level of reality lies in the here and now. The girl is no princess, but the only daughter of a shipowner who makes his money in America, as did many islanders in the 1890s. She picks up Giannakis from the streets, toys with him, then packs him off, telling him what to do until she chooses to marry him. A very modern young lady. She has to suffer too.

Such tales stand at the cusp of orality and literacy, tradition and modernity, myth and fiction. Emigrants who left their villages with a treasury of such stories drew comfort from them as strangers in foreign lands, and thereby contributed to new fictional crossings. Georgios Vizyenos (1849–96), from Vizye in Thrace (then still part of the Ottoman Empire) composed four of his six stories between 1882 and 1885, when he was in London. "The Only Journey of his Life" (1885) owes most to the παραμύθια, in particular to a version of "The Clever Tailor's Apprentice," whose theme frames his story.[45] Vizyenos uses παραμύθια to lend ritual dimensions, taking us beyond story time. The narrator begins in the wonder-tale world of childhood, fed by his grandfather's παραμύθια, and closes with the death of grandfather and his world. The action is set between Istanbul and Vizye,

---

[45] Vizyenos 1980:168–201; translated by Wyatt 1988:153–183. For commentary, see Chryssanthopoulos 1994:111–129; and Alexiou 1993, where comparisons are cited from Byzantine literature, and from Blasket Island prose from the early twentieth century.

as he is summoned from the tailor's establishment at the palace to pay respects to his dying grandfather. In the interval between story time and narrating time, the narrator has learned to write.

The last *ekphrasis* in this story is an elegy for the passing of traditional patterns of settlement, cultivation, and burial.[46] The gap that separates narrator from grandfather is greater, because irreversible, than that between grandfather and grandfather's grandmother, who kept passing on her stories. Grandfather's peaceful end to the longest and most important journey—life itself—may prove beyond the narrator, as was the case with Vizyenos. Or with Hardy's Tess, whose tragic end is implied near the beginning of the novel by the juxtaposition of her own aspirations and those of her mother, which stretch back to the Jacobean past.[47] Ritual pauses, often marked by *ekphrasis*, halt the linear story but transport us to other times and places. The journey in Vizyenos' story is not literal, but a metaphorical and ritual passage, operating on several levels, between patterns stretching back across the generations to prehistoric and even prehellenic times, and modernity.

As with Vizyenos, so with Alexandros Papadiamandis (1851–1911): daily rituals, seasonal celebrations, songs, proverbs, and παραμύθια, form an integral part of his characters' world and consciousness. They provide diverse and conflicting lenses that leave narrator and author space for irony and pathos, and readers room for different opinions.[48]

Ethography, Modernism, and Modernity

Lest I be accused of restricting my fictional examples to "pre-modernist" texts, let me introduce my discussion of modern literature with some comments on critical terms and categories. Ἠθογραφία was coined on the analogy of the French *roman de moeurs* some time before the 1880s. Calqued from a European genre, it was used by N. G. Politis and others to classify fiction with a rural setting that depicted Greek ἤθη καὶ ἔθιμα ("ways and customs"), or rituals. By the turn of the century, the term had slipped into a pejorative ("folksy," "descriptive"), and has been

---

[46] Vizyenos 1980:196–197; Wyatt 1988:179–180.

[47] Hardy 1920:23–24.

[48] Papadiamandis 1981–88. Of the innumerable examples that could be given, the best known is from "The Murderess," 1903 (Papadiamandis 1981–88:vol. 3, 417–520), when Frankoyiannou interprets the appearance of the two little girls at the well as a sign of approval from Saint John, to whom she has just prayed, for her first act of infanticide. See above. The concept of ritual time and space might be a useful supplement to Gerard Genette's principles, as applied by Farinou-Malamatari in her meticulous analysis of Papadiamandis' narrative style, Farinou-Malamatari 1987; on irony in Paradiamandis, especially in his historical novels, see Roilos 2002b.

bandied back and forth uncritically against diverse writers from the 1870s to the 1950s.[49] The term should be dropped, not re-packaged as "folkloric realism" to include "all writers of the period." Which writers, what period, and where the realism? Rather, we should re-think the negative and unspoken associations of ethography with folklorism, naiveté, realism, patriotism, and false nationalism, particularly because it has been bandied about so uncritically against so many divergent prose writers between the 1870s and 1950s.

Most vehement in his criticisms of Greek prose fiction was Georgios Theotokas in the manifesto Ἐλεύθερο Πνεῦμα (*Free Spirit*) he published in 1929, as a 24-year old law student at Athens University. Calling for a "new national literature," he castigates Greek writers—especially prose writers—for their backward-looking provincialism and self-isolation from the liberalizing currents of western European thought. Greeks have accepted foreign influences, but what have they given back in return? Where is the Greek Anna Karenina, or Emma Bovary? Where are the social and moral voices of Charles Dickens or Fyodor Dostoyevsky? All perceived weaknesses are blamed on ethography.[50]

Despite much recent work on modernism, Theotokas' Europhile assumptions have gone largely unchallenged. They have even been reinforced. Beaton notes in the preface to his *Introduction to Modern Greek Literature* that Theotokas' manifesto ushered in a period "dense with literary innovation"; yet his concluding comments echo Theotokas' dismal pessimism that modern Greek literature "has given nothing back" in return from its borrowings from the west; and that "by 1993, despite some exceptions, it is not clear that much has changed."[51] Others have implied a lack of sophistication in prose fiction, particularly where folk influences can be detected: Dimitris Tziovas writes of "belated textuality" and "residual orality"; Gregory Jusdanis doubts whether modernism or post-modernism can exist as literary movements in Greece, given the incompleteness of its social and political modernization; Vassilis Lambropoulos cites "the continuing domination of fiction by the provincial concerns of ethography" as one reason for "Greek post-modernism as a marginal phenomenon."[52]

Sixty years after Theotokas' clarion call for young Greek intellectuals to seek closer links with Europe, Greece became a full member of the European Union (1989).

---

[49] Beaton 1994:68–69, no. 8. The origins and history of the term *éthographia*, its uses and abuses, have been itemized and debated from different critical perspectives for too long. For bibliographical details, see, for example, Vitti 1991:143–180; Beaton 1994:72–73, 99–101. Christophoros Milionis (1992) has argued most cogently that the term should be abandoned.

[50] Theotokas 1973:37, and chapter 3.

[51] Beaton 1994:9 and 368.

[52] Tziovas 1989; Jusdanis 1987; Lambropoulos 1988:50.

Now that monetary unification is also a reality, and further eastward expansion is envisaged, it is time to reassess Greece's role between east and west. That task is beyond my present scope. Suffice to say that Greeks today, and throughout their history, have a share in both. So far as fiction is concerned, oral and non-literary modes of performance and transmission have co-existed with literature since late antiquity, in papyri, the *metaphraseis* and *paraphraseis* of secular and sacred fictions (fifth to tenth centuries), and the florescence of literary genres in twelfth-century Constantinople. The consequent complexities and subtleties can only be obscured or over-simplified by modern labels and categories, for cultural attitudes are not necessarily consistent with demographic data. The Athenian experience of being catapulted, as it were, from the Middle Ages between 1821 and the present day into global post-modernism has been more than matched in today's third world. Such rapid transitions bring conflicts and tensions that seek expression in modes of fiction different from the nineteenth-century English novel. Furthermore, since the eighteenth century at least, the Greek mercantile diaspora has contributed to music, dance, and painting, among the vibrant multi-cultural cities of Asia Minor and Europe. As for popular culture, Greek songs, tales, dances—and moral values too—bear stronger affinities with those of the southern Mediterranean than they do with those of western Europe. Expatriate communities to this day tend to preserve these aspects of their identity, not least through the language, liturgy, and ritual of the Orthodox Church.[53]

Greece may be "imperfectly" modern, but its culture has always been cosmopolitan, and therefore anticipates the post-modern. Rather than deplore the paucity of precedents to the "novel," as perceived by modern critics, let us explore the diversity and difference of modern Greek fiction with some comparative examples.

What Is "Magic Realism"?

The term "magic realism" was coined in 1924–25 by the German art critic, Franz Roh, to describe impressionist paintings, and only subsequently adopted by literary critics to describe fictional attempts to present "strange occurrences in everyday contexts."[54] Less well known is E. J. Dent's use of the term "magical reality" as

---

[53] For general summary, see Alexiou 2002b:13–16. The question of modernity versus tradition has attracted much debate in studies over the past few decades. Juliet du Boulay saw the disintegration of traditional cosmology as part of the consequences of modernization (du Boulay 1974:257). Hart closes her study of rural Greece in transition with comments on the persistence of traditional values alongside modern ones, especially where "ritual and 'ordinary' practices and domains are very closely knit together in . . . daily life"; above all, she stresses the pervasive strength and flexibility of Orthodox faith and practice (Hart 1991:265–272). The tensions between tradition and modernity, as expressed in the life and work of one modern writer, are admirably explored in Herzfeld 1997b, esp. chapter 6.
[54] Carpentier 1995:106–107.

distinctive of masque and opera in the seventeenth century, a quality that makes up for the farcical, incongruous, and irrational plots with "the exquisite beauty of . . . emotional expression."[55] His comments, published a year before Theotokas' manifesto and a year after E. M. Forster's prescriptions and proscriptions on the novel, suggest that both the concept and term, "magical realism," was adapted from the non-verbal arts by literary critics. The blend of fantasy with realism may have seemed new in modern western fiction, but had always existed in traditions such as Greek, African American, Latin American, Indian, where stories are unfolded in song, dance, and embroidery, as well as by word of mouth in written prose and verse.

In some ways Theotokas was right: there is no Greek Anna Karenina. But is the "depth" or "roundness" of character deemed so indispensible by Forster a *sine qua non*?[56] Stratis Myrivilis' Smaragdi shares with Toni Morrison's Beloved a focus upon the grotesque, the shifting, the ambivalent. Are they real or ghosts, ξωτικά, or figments of fantasy? History, if not realism, is crucial to both, for both were created out of scraps of painful memories, ethnic displacement, myth and legend, that reach back to the early nineteenth century and beyond. Both come from nowhere, out of nothing. And both disappear from the consciousness of the living once their function has been served. Smaragdi resumes her place in the shrine of the Mermaid Madonna, whence it implied she came, out of an icon painted in magical colors:

Her voice was serious, quiet, decisive.

Fortis, who knew her, said no more about it. All at Skala and its neighborhood, and the villagers up at Mouria, had heard about it, spoken about it, and got used to it, that the girl had vouched herself to the Panagia.

Every day she would go up to tidy the shrine at Rachta, look after the lamp, and kneel in prayer before the strange icon.

And Our Lady the Mermaid would gaze back to her with slanting green almond eyes, motionless, shut up inside her mystery and her silence.

She held onto the boat in one hand and Poseidon's trident in the other, and her tail kept flipping, curly, bendy, strong.

The sea's voice rose, deep, serious, from the hollows.

(my translation)[57]

[55] Dent 1928:48.
[56] Forster 1927:103–118.
[57] Myrivilis 1949:486–487. See Alexiou 1990 and 2002b:310–334.

And from the end of *Beloved*:

They forgot her like a bad dream. After they made up their tales, shaped and decorated them, those that saw her that day on the porch quickly and deliberately forgot her. It took longer for those who had spoken to her, fallen in love with her, to forget, until they realized they couldn't remember or repeat a single thing she said, and began to believe that, other than what they themselves were thinking, she hadn't said anything at all. So, in the end, they forgot her too. Remembering seemed unwise. They never knew where or why she crouched, or whose was the underwater face she needed like that, where the memory of the smile under the chin might have been but was not, a latch latched and lichen attached its apple-green bloom to the metal. What made her think her fingernails could open locks the rain rained on. . . . This is not a story to be passed on.[58]

As with Vizyenos' "Journey," the story is passed on, in writing.

Both Smaragdi and Beloved elude us as "real characters." As the concluding passages make clear, each exists only as others see, hear, and speak of her. Her identity is defined not by an omniscient narrator, but disclosed unevenly through the diverse focalization of all participants and spectators. They do not speak with one voice; but their everyday gossip may take on the dimensions of choral voices— approving, censoring, prying, envying. As in Greek tragedy, anger and envy stalk characters and action, particularly at highly charged ritual moments and activities involving food and drink, clothes and washing, home and abroad.[59]

Both novels meet the five primary characteristics of magic realism, as listed by W. B. Faris, and most of her nine secondary specifications as well.[60] So do most παραμύθια, and many other pre-modern fictional texts. As a term, "magic realism" has flourished in fiction defined as modernist and post-modernist; but magic has always found room in literatures where oral traditions—and non-verbal ways of telling stories—have been passed on. And "realism"—do we really need it? Not if we heed two hallmarks of Greek fiction from time long past: melodrama and rhetoric. Exciting stories, sung and danced, are among the oldest modes of narrative perform-

---

[58] Morrison 1988:275.

[59] In *Beloved*, it was the envy and anger of neighbors, caused by the extravagant feast hosted by Baby Suggs, that triggered Sethe's infanticide; otherwise, neighbors would have sounded warnings of Schoolmaster's approach (Morrison 1988:136–138, 156–158). In the end it is Denver's silence in suffering that brings, through Ella, redemption for all, when these same neighbors act to exorcize Beloved.

[60] "Scheherzade's Children: Magical realism and post-modern fiction," in Zamora and Faris (eds.), *Magical Realism*, 167–180

ance, as in the ancient *parakatalogai*. Mimes and pantomimes were widely diffused throughout the Greco-Roman world, just when the fictions we now call novels were first recorded in writing. Critics disparage what they call melodrama in modern fiction, their favorite target being Tess' use of the carving knife to butcher Alec in Thomas Hardy's novel. If *Tess* lacks realism, it is arguably among the most ritual of English novels, where each phase in the protagonist's life and sexual maturation is juxtaposed with the changing seasons and the physiognomy of the landscape, as is implied in Makrembolites' *Hysmine*. There are echoes in *Tess* of Longos' ancient pastoral, *Daphnis and Chloe*, certainly known to both Makrembolites and Hardy.[61]

As for rhetoric, I have already indicated the importance of προγυμνάσματα (genre exercises) as fictional strategies in the twelfth century, when they were used to explore mood, character and scene in mythical, biblical, and historical contexts, as in Nikephoros Basilakes' ἠθοποιίαι (character sketches): What might Pasiphae have said when raped by Zeus in the shape of a bull? Or Hades when Lazarus was raised from the dead? I have analyzed elsewhere Vizyenos' use of *antithesis* and *ekphrasis*, two distinctively Byzantine rhetorical features, and have indicated above examples of *diêgesis* and *ekphrasis* in modern fiction.[62] My favorite example of *êthopoiia* is from Amanda Michalopoulou's *Wishbones*, an example of Greek post-modernism. We are at the dinner table, and there is yet another domestic dispute:

Σὲ λίγο θὰ ἀνοίξει τὸ στόμα του καὶ θὰ χαθῶ στὴ σκοτεινὴ του σπηλιά

In a short while he'll open his mouth and I'll be lost in its dark cavern . . .

At the end of the chapter we realize that the narrating voice is that of a tiny bit of spinach stuck behind the husband's wisdom tooth. Michalopoulou is funny

---

[61] Hardy divides the novel into seven Phases of Tess' life, from "Maiden" to "Fulfilment," covering six years in narrated time. Each phase is marked, sometimes contrapuntally, against the cyclical movement of the seasons and against the physical landscape of Tess' migratory labors and sufferings. By means of literary allusion, however, Hardy complicates the simple juxtaposition of man/nature. In Phase Three ("The Rally") Angel's idyllic pastoral courtship of Tess as milkmaid at Talbothay's is darkened by predatory imagery, and by his persistent reference to nymphs in Greek mythology, unknown to Tess and therefore mistrusted; but familiar to us, who know their fated end before we are told of Tess': "And the President of the Immortals, in Aeschylean phrase, had finished his sport with Tess" (508). As with Syrinx and other mythical paradigms from Longos' "pastorals of Daphnis and Chloe," so with Io—and Tess. John J. Winkler's dark reading of the ancient pastoral (Winkler 1990) affords greater insights into Hardy's mythical allusions than David Lodge's critical realist assessment (Lodge 1966:164–188).

[62] See Alexiou 1993 on Vizyenos, and comparative examples from modern Irish autobiography; on rhetoric and προγυμνάσματα in twelfth-century Byzantine literature, see Alexiou 2002b:96–148, for a detailed discussion of this issue, see Roilos, forthcoming, chapters 1 and 3.

because she draws on the serious language of the liturgy ('Ανοίξω τὸ στόμα μου, "I shall open my mouth") to play on poetic uses of high language.[63] If her technique is perceived as post-modernist, it is also worthy of the best Byzantine *progumnasmata*.

The novel emerged in eighteenth-century England and France. Themes, plots, and characters were borrowed from ancient fiction, as in Samuel Richardson's *Pamela* (1740) and *Clarissa* (1747–48). They were also adapted to masque and opera, where sung and danced elements were combined in musically innovative ways from the sixteenth and seventeenth centuries.[64] We know little about Byzantine modes of performance, although opera—not necessarily western—has been suggested as an analogue to the rhetorical theatre of twelfth-century Constantinople.[65] Features that were discarded in the European novel, as being inconsistent with the representational modes of realism, find perfect artistic and emotional expression in opera, as Dent indicated. Rhetorical laments add nothing to plot or character, but they make wonderful operatic arias that express conflicting feelings in ways beyond the power of words alone. The shedding of non-verbal modes in the novel has surely entailed a loss—a loss marked by Toni Morrison in her depiction of Cholly, who has abused his daughter, Pecola. We are reminded of the Greek tales, especially our dumb violinist:

---

[63] Michalopoulou 1996:148: Michalopoulou also parodies Odysseas Elytis' uses of the liturgy in his Τὸ "Αχιον 'Εστί, 6 ed., Athens: Ikaros, 1970 (1 ed., 1959).

[64] Doody 1998:279–300, charts the rise of realism, individualism, and the "feminization" of the novel in western Europe. On the non-realist directions of opera and masque, see Dent 1928.

[65] Magdalino 1993:353–354. He draws attention to the liturgical and iconic dimensions of Byzantine rhetoric and aesthetics, and to the "audio-visual resonance of words recited in a ceremonial context" where "verbal recitation was only part of a total orchestration, in which architecture, décor, dress, music and choreography also played a part." The extra-literary dimensions in the rise and transmission of the Greek novel opened up by these comments remain to be explored, although it is worth noting that the earliest modern examples depend on music and song for form and meaning, see I. K. 1989 and Pherraios 1971. Both comprise vignettes, or little love dramas, that exploit not the music of the rural "folk" (as yet undiscovered), but the ballad and cabaret of the urban salons of Constantinople, Smyrna, and Paris. Their appearance, as Beaton has pointed out, "coincides almost exactly, and surely not accidentally, with the reappearance in print of no fewer than four ancient and medieval Greek novels in prose, . . . produced by Greek publishers for a Greek readership, not as classical texts for the classroom" (1994:51). An interesting way to re-map the story of modern fiction might be to follow the leads of our female protagonists in their quest to maintain chastity, from Longos' Chloe and Makrembolites' Hysmine (technically virgins but by no means sexually innocent) to John Gay's Polly (no maiden she), Richardson's Pamela, and Mozart's Susanna, who, though servants like Hysmine at critical points, manage to thwart their masters' (and mistresses') overweening desires. Hardy's Tess, aware of her noble pedigree but indifferent to it, fails to resist the upstart Alec; yet despite her loss of chastity in Phase Two of the novel, through her *pathê* she earns the appellation "A Pure Woman," as in the sub-title.

The pieces of Cholly's life could become coherent only in the head of a musician. Only those who talk their talk through the gold of curved metal, or in the touch of black and white rectangles and taut skins echoing from wooden corridors, could give true form to his life . . . . Only a musician would sense, know, without even knowing that he knew, that Cholly was free.[66]

From the outset, the historical, cultural, and literary factors that shaped the emergence of the modern novel in Greece, as elsewhere, were conspicuously different from those operating in England and France.

Coda

I will close with three examples of ritual in the novel, one Greek and two English. As writer and painter, N. G. Pentzikis defies categorization. His *Architecture of Fragmented Life* (1963) tries to piece together into a book memory-slips of lives shattered by war and history, not unlike *Panagia* and *Beloved*, except that the result is just fragments, bits, and pieces with no beginning, middle, or end.[67] In *The Dead Man and Resurrection*, a beguiling novella written in 1938 and published in 1944, there is no plot or character; just a writer looking at a character gazing out of a window thinking of his beloved and contemplating suicide. The novella has been claimed as an early Greek example of interior monologue; yet the term fails to do justice to this polyphonic and multi-semic text.[68] There is only one speaker, it seems—the narrator; but through his eyes, ears, and nose we, the readers, see, hear, and smell in vivid detail the everyday life of the people who bring to life his γειτονιά (neighborhood) in Thessaloniki. Through his thoughts, we re-invent our own life in its cosmic and mundane dimensions. Through his evocation of texts and memories, we re-live an idyllic childhood of remembered house and garden, in an extended passage that recalls both παραμύθια and Byzantine ἐκφράσεις (pages 76–81). Half way through, the narrator decides to kill off his character (himself?); and does so, with gruesome semi-comic violence reminiscent of the παραμύθια. The relation between narrator and character remains obscure; but there is a narcissistic obsession with pools reflecting the opposite of what the gazer thinks is his image (as in the tales) . . . Then begins the *anastasê*. The narrator reconstructs himself, piecing bits and pieces together with scraps of everyday life, all collected

---

[66] Morrison 1972:125–126.
[67] Pentzikis 1963.
[68] Pentzikis 1987. On the complexity of "interior monologue" in Greek fiction, and its relation to modernism, see Beaton 1994:146–149, 257–259; Kakavoulia 1997.

and listed in litanies worthy of anyone with autistic spectrum disorder: names, papers, boxes, memories, stones, flowers, herbs.

On the literary level, resurrection lies in the written book. But with Pentzikis, the process is ritual, as defined at the outset of this paper: an attempt to control the perceived outside world in relation to the self, and to organize that world through the associations of one's senses. It is a continuum of rules for confronting the human condition on three levels—everyday life, adversity, and beyond: Ἀγωνίζομαι νὰ συμπεριλάβω ἀσήμαντες λεπτομέρειες ποὺ σημείωσα γιατὶ μόνο ἔτσι καταλαβαίνω ὅτι μπορεῖ νὰ λάβει κάποια ἑνότητα ἡ κομματιασμένη ἀπὸ τὶς καθημερινὲς ἀντιφάσεις ὕπαρξη ("I struggle to include insignificant details I noted, because only thus can I understand that existence fragmented by everyday contradictions can assume some kind of unity") (pages 53–54).

Is Pentzikis modernist? Yes, to the extent that he shares with modernist and avant-garde writers an opposition to Cartesian logic, as Eleni Yannakakis has argued.[69] Unlike her, I see Pentzikis' perception of time not as "circular and consequently static" (page 155), but as circular and thereby ritual, or spiral, each twist adding new levels of meaning. No, because "modernist" is too restrictive and reductive in its frame of reference, time-closed with the "pre-" and "post-," engendering arid legalistic disputes and incapable of encompassing the peculiarly modern Greek form of neoplatonism which inspired so much of his writing.[70] Ritual as a concept can be used to supplement conventional categories, movements, periodizations, just because it allows us to make comparative but specific connections between diverse literary texts that might conventionally be dismissed as unthinkable.

Through ritual, we can gain fresh insights into the English novel, by looking at recurrent themes and images linked not to character or plot, but to everyday activities and experiences, such as hair in Thomas Hardy's *The Woodlanders* (1887), or sleep / trance in *Tess of the d'Urbervilles* (1891). Two examples. Reference has been made to ritual features in the structure of *Tess*; but there is one scene that epitomizes the novel's capacity to create transcendental moments by switching between the mundane and cosmic. It is Tess' baptism of her dying infant, "Sorrow," an act, as watched by her younger siblings, that transforms her, in their eyes, into a goddess:

[69] Yannakakis 1997.
[70] Yannakakis 1997:160–161, cites Pentzikis' own references to neoplatonic texts and concepts, but without commentary. Research is needed on neoplatonic elements not just in Pentzikis, but in Greek fiction more generally. Vizyenos' inaugural dissertation for his appointment at the University of Athens is a careful commentary on Plotinus that also comprises a history of aesthetics; see Vizyenos 1995.

She did not look like Sissy to them now, but as a being large, towering, and awful—a divine personage with whom they had nothing in common (page 120).

Then comes the bunch of flowers she places on Sorrow's grave, in a neglected corner of the churchyard, so hard bargained-for with the village priest:

> What matter was it that on the outside of the jar the eye of mere observation noted the words "Keelwell's Marmalade"? The eye of maternal affection did not see them in its vision of higher things (page 123).[71]

Tess was published in 1891, set in a story time roughly contemporary with Vizyenos' short stories. Flora Thompson's *Lark Rise to Candleford* (1945) is a trilogy of novellas originally published separately (1939, 1941, 1943), at intervals during the Second World War, as was Pentzikis' novella.[72] Without sentimentality, nostalgia, or idealization, but with an historian's eye for detail, and a painterly talent for words, she brings to life the childhood world of Laura, based on her own experiences in rural Oxfordshire in the 1880s and 1890s. There is no attempt to set up a novelistic plot, characters, let alone love story, just a series of vignettes of people, places, ways of life, lovingly remembered. Rituals are built into the structure not, as in *Tess*, to frame the tragic heroine's life and death, but to chart the changes in Lark Rise, Candleford, and Candleford Green as lived by Laura between the ages of four and sixteen, and as perceived by Flora, who lost her beloved brother in World War I, during World War II. Here is where ritual time is most expertly exploited: it is cyclical, not linear, and anything but static, since the narrator's perspective shifts deftly back and forth between story time and writing time, childhood, and maturity, as in Vizyenos' "Journey." The similarities between Thompson's trilogy and Vizyenos' six stories are remarkable, both arguably "in search of a novel." Laura can also be viewed as Hardy's Tess in mirror image. Laura does not mention Tess, although she records the literary heroines she discovered for herself from the age of

---

[71] Tess' quasi-apotheosis comes about through the power of ritual enacted in mundane, poverty-stricken surroundings. In an attempt to show that even today, the novel has not lost its ritual and religious dimensions, Doody draws attention to the goddess / witch figure (1998:432–464). I would rather place emphasis on key themes and images, which link mundane activities with eternal meanings, such as food and drink, clothes and washing, home and abroad. In *Tess*, for example, horse, wagon, truck, carriage signify as vehicles associated with violation and murder, as in the d'Urberville myth, which echoes Aeschylus' use of the myth of the House of Atreus. In Morrison's *Beloved*, as in the closing passage cited above, a key image is water: rain, tears, sea, baptism, re-birth, drowning, slave voyages. Recognizing the resources of ritual allows us to read novels more poetically, according to both metonymic and metaphorical poles.

[72] Thompson 1973.

seven, from Richardson's Pamela to Thackeray's Amelia. Tess, her fate and world, were however, known to Flora, who does not allow her Laura to be a victim, making her choose an observer's perspective. Towards the end of the trilogy, after describing a club-walking scene at Candleford Green—much like the opening scene at Marlott where Angel did not dance with Tess, Flora intervenes:

> The heroine of a modern novel would have seized such an opportunity to go out into the throng and learn a little at first-hand about life; but this is a true story, and Laura was not of the stuff of which heroines are made. A born looker-on, she preferred to watch from the window. . . . (pages 446–447).

Where Hardy projects his sense of loss in rural life and values onto his beloved Tess, Thompson, like Vizyenos, makes the landscape and ways of life the focus of plot and character. All three writers chart a story of demise and loss, recorded in times torn by wars and ethnic conflicts—dark but not hopeless.

To return, in closing, to Pentzikis: neoplatonic dimensions are explicit in his later works, as in Vizyenos' stories and writings. They are not intrusive or extraneous, but flow—naturally and with feeling—from his dialogue with objects, texts, and paintings, past and present, Greek and European, and above all Byzantine. Makrembolites' neoplatonism in *Hysmine* achieved in the twelfth century a synthesis of pagan and Christian love. Pendzikis' neoplatonism, in the mid-twentieth century, underlines the interconnectedness, through our senses, of things, memories, and contacts with people and places. Thomas Hardy, Flora Thompson, and Toni Morrison, remind us that ritual still inspires literary texts, whether we dub them romantic, melodramatic, ethographic. They do not have to be Greek. I have not said the last word, but I hope I have encouraged others to explore ritual so as to broaden aesthetic criteria and enrich our understanding of literature.

Six

Ritual and Poetics in Greek Modernism

Panagiotis Roilos

In his intriguing discussion "on lyric poetry and society," Adorno notes that "the lyric work is always the subjective expression of a social antagonism."[1] Adorno's remark, I would submit, is especially valid for modernist and avant-garde poetry.[2] This social antagonism that he views as an elemental feature of lyricism can be perceived not as much on an objective level—the antagonisms inherent in a given society—as on a subjective level, that is, in terms of the modernist artist's position in the society and his attitude toward its dominant cultural and sociopolitical discourses.

The military etymological associations of *avant-garde,* a term that acquired its current cultural implications in France in the 1870s,[3] explicitly foregrounds modernists' polemic reevaluation of tradition and their subversive interaction with the established conventions of post-industrial society. Modernism protested against both the traditional modes of artistic communication and the commodification of social and intellectual life that had dominated post-industrial European society. And here lies one of modernism's major intrinsic contradictions: modernism manifests itself as a symptom of the very sociocultural conditions that it seeks to undermine. Further contradictions may be detected here: modernism, in its most militant avant-garde forms—dadaism and futurism—at least, turns against modernity by employing the expressive dynamics of its most celebrated ideological and material commodities—speed, technology, and a progressive rupture with the past.

On the other hand, in their attempt to undermine the logocentrism of post-Enlightenment European thought, modernists recover and reactivate forms of expression drawn from outmoded or suppressed paradigms of symbolic communication such as dream language and ritual. The latter choice, however, further

---

[1] Adorno 1991:45.
[2] I am following here the distinction between modernism and avant-garde proposed by Russell (Russell 1985:7–8).
[3] Calinescu 1987:108–116.

121

complicates modernism's inherent antinomies; the nonconformistic use of supposedly common symbolic systems such as dream language or, for that matter, traditional ritualistic patterns of expression, enhances the modernist artist's alienation and distance from his or her sociocultural surroundings. Despite, for instance, the propagation of dream language as the most common, and hence the most "democratic," symbolic idiom shared by all people of all social and cultural backgrounds everywhere in the world, an idea that in Greek literature can be traced from the fourth–fifth century CE with Synesius of Cyrene[4] to the twentieth century with Odysseas Elytis,[5] surrealism and other avant-garde movements have cultivated rather aristocratic modes of expression that deepen, instead of bridging, the gap between common language and artistic idiolect. The elitism of the modernist poet could not have been more blatantly expressed than in a manifesto entitled "Revolution of the Word" that was published in the review *transition*. There, it is arrogantly stated: "The writer expresses. He does not communicate. The plain reader be damned."[6]

Traditional patterns of ritual symbolism provided modernist poets with primordial codes of signification that had been marginalized or ignored in post-industrial European societies.[7] In that respect, the impact of the newly established field of ethnography, and in particular of James Frazer's seminal *The Golden Bough*, on their cultural explorations and aesthetic experimentations was crucial.[8] In a paper that he wrote in 1913, while he was still a student at Harvard University, T.S. Eliot attempted to explore the mystical nature of primitive rituals. In a review published ten years later, in 1923, he returned to the same topic with the observation that "all art emulates the condition of ritual. That is what it comes from and to what it must always return for nourishment."[9] Expressed by one of the most influential modernist poets, this approach to art should be viewed, I submit, in the

---

[4] Elytis 1987:207. I find Synesius' *On Dreams*, especially his emphasis on the relationships between literature and dreams, exceptionally pioneering. Synesius underlines the importance of unconventional dream imagery for literary experimentation in terms that foreshadow, in a sense, modernism's appreciation of dream language: "any one can see how great the work is, on attempting to fit language to visions, visions in which those things which are united in nature are separated, and things separated in nature are united, and he [the orator] is obliged to show in speech what has not been revealed. It is no mean achievement to pass on to another something of a strange nature that has stirred in one's own soul, for whenever by this fantasy (of dreaming) things which are expelled from the order of being, and things which in never in any possible way existed, are brought instead into being—nay, even things which have not a nature capable of existence, what contrivance is there for presenting a nameless nature to things which are *per se* inconceivable?" (trans. Fitzgerald 1930:355).
[5] Elytis 1987:207.
[6] Quoted in Poggioli 1968:38.
[7] For a discussion of ritual in European modernism see Korg 1995.
[8] On aspects of the impact of ethnography on modernism see Manganaro 1990.
[9] Quoted in Korg 1995:42.

broader context of modernism's critical dialogue with the dominant materialistic values of post-industrial societies; the tendency to approach, and furthermore, to *create* art as a substitute for, or in close relation with, ritual is a manifestation of modernist artists' wish to overcome their sense of alienation from the materialistic orientation of society. Poets such as Pound, T.S. Eliot, Mallarmé, Yeats, or Auden viewed ritual language as a refreshing and defamiliarizing symbolic idiom that could contribute to their aesthetic critique against the reification of cultural life in modern societies. For instance, Mallarmé perceived the work of a poet as a reenactment of ritual acts and symbols, where even the slightest material detail—the paper, the inkwell, or the signifying potential of the alphabet—carried specific ritualistic associations. He envisaged the performance of *Livre*, his magnum opus, as an all-encompassing ceremonial combination of drama, music, and dance—[10] a vision that finds its parallel in similar, but more interactive, performative attempts in postmodernist experimental theater.[11]

The reactivation of ritual textures of signification in modernist poetry can be interpreted, I contend, as an indication of the modernist artist's will to inform his literary product with the immediacy of traditional liminal systems of symbolic communication. Cultural activities in developed post-tribal societies, aptly characterized as "liminoid" activities by Victor Turner, are supposed to have retained aspects of the liminality of traditional rituals, since both play with and invert established structures of expression and modes of behavior. Such liminoid modes of expression have also preserved the sense of *communitas* and *flow* that, according to Turner, accompany the enactment of ritual performances in tribal societies.[12] In modernist liminoid forms of expression, though, *communitas* is often a highly elusive chimerical vision rather than an accomplished state of immediate communication between the artist and his/her audience. The association of liminoid phenomena with ludic recreation and leisure, as these concepts were developed in post-industrial societies, points to the individualistic, rather than collective, nature of artistic enterprises. In this respect, Adorno's discussion of lyric poetry proves once more instructively sensitive: "poetic subjectivity," he observes, "is . . . indebted to privilege."[13] More than anything else, the reappropriation of liminal structures of meaning in modernist poetry reaffirms, I would contend, both the paradoxical

---

[10] Korg 1995:10.
[11] On postmodernist theater and its connections with ritual performances see especially Schechner 1985; 1988; 1993.
[12] Turner develops his ideas about liminoid cultural phenomena in a number of articles and books; see in particular Turner 1977; 1982b; 1987.
[13] Adorno 1991:45.

Panagiotis Roilos

conditions of its production and consumption, and its agonistic and antagonistic program against established norms of viewing and expressing reality.

Developed as an idiosyncratic version of its European prototype and in a highly self-conscious juxtaposition with literary paradigms of the "glorious" Greek past, notably classical and, to a lesser degree, Byzantine literature, Greek modernism provides a challenging case for the exploration of the ideological and aesthetic manipulation of ritual symbolization in modernist literary discourse. Albeit sharing several pivotal principles/directions of European modernism—e.g. the adoption of aesthetic solutions that undermine sanctioned literary conventions, the emphasis on the idea of renovation and new dynamic beginnings that go beyond traditional modes of expression, and the advocation of the autonomy of art, directions systematically propagated for the first time in Greece in the manifesto of the movement, the *Free Spirit* by G. Theotokas published in 1929[14]— modernism in Greece indulged in a rather ethnocentric literary endeavor that aimed at the aestheticization of autochthonous cultural products, predominant among which, I would argue, were traditional ritual patterns of signification. The combination of imported European literary models and indigenous elements of expression characterizes the work of almost all of the representatives of the dominant group of Greek modernists, the so-called "Generation of the Thirties."[15] It would not be an overstatement to argue that no Greek modernist, or avant-gardist, for that matter, with the possible exceptions of the marginally idiosyncratic Kostas Karyotakis and the ex-centrically revolutionary Nikos Kallas, would have shared Marinetti's "irreverent" nonconformist declaration: "a racing car whose hood is adorned with great pipes, like serpents of explosive breath—a roaring car that seems to ride on grapeshot —is more beautiful than the *Victory of Samothrace*."[16] The idiosyncrasy of Greek modernism, though, should not be overemphasized. The interaction between introvert ethnocentrism and extrovert Europeanness is unique neither to the *Greek* case[17] nor to the specific historical moment in the

[14] Theotokas 1929.
[15] On the "Generation of the Thirties" in general see Vitti 1977, which is still a highly illuminating study of this period of Greek literature. On the terminological convention of "generation" see ibid.:46–49. Poggioli offers a helpful discussion of similar terminological issues, with an emphasis on the terms "school" and "movement"; in his discussion of modernism, he opts for the latter (1968:17–27).
[16] Marinetti 1971:41. The topos of the speeding car as an almost mystifying metaphor for modernism's progressive clash with tradition, though, was adopted even by moderate Greek modernists such as Theotokas (1929:69–70) and Seferis (in his poems "Automobile" and "Syngrou Avenue 1930"); in their works, though, the degree of aesthetic revolutionism that this image connotes in futuristic contexts is considerably minimized.
[17] Vitti notes that parallel ethnocentric tendencies can be found in the Italian and Spanish literature of the time, whose idealized, but politically more conservative, *italianità* and *hispanidad* can be compared to the "hellenocentrism" of Greek modernism (1977:78, 200).

124

Greek literature that was produced after the establishment of the Greek state.[18] And a view of Greek modernism as a cultural commodity belatedly and idiosyncratically "made in Greece" is helpful if, and to the extent that, it eschews the danger of reproducing, implicitly or subconsciously, hegemonizing Western European cultural and literary canons.

In this chapter, I undertake a preliminary investigation of the understudied issue of the reinscription of symbolic ritual discourses in Greek modernism. Often, the majority of Greek modernists and avant-gardists, both poets and prose writers such as Cavafy, Sikelianos, Seferis,[19] Elytis, Papatsonis,[20] Engonopoulos, Embeirikos, Ritsos, Vrettakos, Myrivilis, Kosmas Politis, Scarimbas, Pentzikis—to mention just a few—reappropriate predominantly indigenous patterns of ritual symbolization in order to articulate aspects of their poetics. My focus will be on the poetics of one of the most significant representatives of Greek modernism, Odysseas Elytis, the second Greek poet, after George Seferis, to be awarded the Nobel Prize for literature (in 1979). Starting his literary career in the mid-1930s as an eclectic proponent of surrealism, he experimented with several poetic styles and forms, drawing on a number of indigenous and foreign, especially French, intertexts. Although drawn to the theoretical principles of French surrealism, Elytis refused to endorse several of its aspects, notably the importance of automatic writing. Surrealism's subversive confrontation with Western models of rational thinking and expression, however, offered Elytis a poetic and ideological paradigm that enabled him both to overcome the expressive constraints imposed by established linguistic conventions and to view Greek culture without the rationalistic prejudices that had hegemonized European thought since the Renaissance and Greek intellectual life since the Enlightenment. Elytis found the thematic and expressive "otherness" that the French surrealists were searching for in indigenous literary and cultural paradigms and, frequently, in ritual modes of signification.

In this chapter, I explore the ways in which traditional patterns of ritual verbal symbolization were incorporated in Elytis' work and reconciled with his modernist aesthetics. More specifically, I try to show that his poetics can be viewed as the aesthetic development of a ritualistic and metaphysical perception of poetry that

[18] On this compare e.g. Vayenas 1997. For aspects of the tension between Europeanness and Greekness in nineteenth-century literature see Roilos 2003b. On Greek modernism in general see Tziovas 1997b and the collection of essays in Tziovas 1997a; cf. also Layoun 1990. For an interesting discussion of modernism and postmodernism in Greece from a Western European perspective see Jusdanis 1987; cf. also Roilos 2003a; on the "Greekness" of Greek modernism see also Robinson 1981.
[19] For an interesting discussion of the theme of Adonis in Seferis cf. Krikos-Davis 1996.
[20] I find Papatsonis an exceptionally intricate case, since his poetic discourse, which remains rather neglected by contemporary scholarship, is deeply immersed in a ritual intertext that is marginal for its Greek context, that of Roman Catholicism.

undermines conventional rationalistic approaches to reality. More often than not, Elytis' verbal experimentations—vestiges, no doubt, of his early affinities with surrealism—may be also seen as poetic reenactments of lost or suppressed traditional modes of symbolic communication.

In the introductory essay to his first collection of essays (*Open Papers*), Elytis connects his decision to become a poet with two intense mystical experiences that he had as a young man. The first was when he saw a papyrus of a poem by Sappho: the arbitrary correspondence between the sounds of the poem and their written encoding in the primordial script of the papyrus filled him with a metaphysical awe, comparable, as he says, only to his other mystical experience:

> I am trying to express with today's words the emotion I had then; I found it again only in the spells which I observed, with fear and unrestrained admiration, being cast by our old Cretan cook. There was of course the ritual aspect, the repeated crossings, the drops of oil shaken in water, the sizzling, burning hairs, and the icons sprinkled with basil buds. But above all were the words, strange, "madtrap" mother would call them, entirely unrelated to anything else I heard and incoherent, a transposition of dream into verbal idiom.[21]

The transgression of the semantic boundaries of language, as exemplified in the apotropaic utterances of the old Cretan woman, disclosed to Elytis not only the potential of ritual language, but also its association with a secret, mystical level of experience. This world is viewed in parallel with the realm of dreams: "a transposition of dream into verbal idiom." The lack of apparent coherence, the juxtaposition of several semantically incompatible words, constitute subversive forms of expression, which point to subversive ways of perceiving reality.[22]

In Elytis' aesthetic and philosophical system, not unlike Solomos' or Sikelianos' case, poetics can be seen as a subdivision of metaphysics; poetic discourse mediates between the tangible everyday world and a transcendental world where the destructive power of death has been surpassed. In his afore-mentioned essay, Elytis describes the basic axis of his metaphysics in the following way: "inside

---

[21] Elytis 1995:16. Elytis comments several times on his fascination with the unconventional verbal and representational symbolism of such similar ritualistic acts; e.g., see his poem 'Οδύσσεια (Elytis 1971) where the ritualistic language of a gypsy woman fortune-teller is juxtaposed with the metaphysical language of Western and Oriental mysticism; cf. also Elytis 1982:14.

[22] The correlation between dream language and incantatory or nonconformistic verbal patterns is an elemental principle of surrealistic writing that Elytis explores in an essay specifically dedicated to dreams. Elytis places special emphasis on the unconventional use of words in dream language; see Elytis 1987:203–253.

me, the meaning of Resurrection is inseparably bound to the meaning of Death, and very early on, in the secret region that is the antechamber of Birth."[23] This idea, which recalls the cyclical perception of time dominant in agrarian societies and associated with traditional profane and religious rituals, is implicitly or explicitly reenacted throughout Elytis' work, from his first poetic collection[24] through his last works. The ideal poetic system, according to Elytis, must be constructed on the basis of homological correspondences between verbal modes of signification and a ritualistic perception of nature and calendrical time. The essence of his ritual poetics is formulated in terms that recall Bourdieu's analysis of the habitual homologies between different areas of experience and expression in traditional Algerian society.[25] "Lyrical energy," as Elytis puts it, should reactivate on a "mythical" poetic level the structural principles of the organization of the Greek Othodox calendar, on the one hand, and the correspondences between nature and "intellectual concepts," on the other.[26]

This metaphysical background defines the ritualistic character of Elytis' poetry as a whole. In his ῎Αισμα ἡρωικὸ καὶ πένθιμο γιὰ τὸ χαμένο ἀνθυπολοχαγὸ τῆς ᾿Αλβανίας (*Song Heroic and Mourning for the Lost Second Lieutenant of the Albanian Campaign*) (1945), a poem inspired by the resistance of the Greeks against the Italians in the Second World War, a highly ritualistic structure is reenacted: the young hero is dead, and in the lamentation for his death, his present condition is compared to his previous life in a way that recalls topoi of traditional ritual laments.[27] The mourning is finally followed by the young man's symbolic immortalization. His glorification takes place in a scene reminiscent of Christian religious rites, especially the celebration of Christ's Ascendance. The composition of the *Axion Esti*, Elytis' magnum opus, which was also inspired by the Second World War, is based on a tripartite religious ritual model: Genesis, Passions, and Gloria. The ritualistic structure of the poem is further foregrounded by the use of Byzantine liturgical genres. At the beginning and throughout the poem, the poet assumes the persona of a prophet who undertakes to create the world anew. The topos of the poet-seer, which in modernist tradition can be traced back to Rimbaud, is informed here with predominantly biblical resonances. Alluding to the book of Genesis and to the first lines from the Gospel according to Saint John, the

---

[23] Elytis 1997:18. Elytis has expressed similar ideas elsewhere as well; e.g. see Ὁ κῆπος βλέπει (Elytis 1982; cf. also Elytis 1984, entry "Wednesday 1,b").

[24] *Prosanatolismoi*, published in 1939; see especially the poem "Dionysos."

[25] See Bourdieu 1977:130–158.

[26] Elytis 1987:450.

[27] On traditional topoi in Greek ritual laments see Alexiou 2002a.

127

poeta vates recreates the world by using the magical power of his words: "The silence I reclaimed to brood—germ-cells of letters and golden seeds of oracles . . . here's the asparagus, here's the rabe, here's curly parsley, ginger plant and geranium."[28] The poet invests his verbal utterances with the performative efficacy usually associated with divine powers in many religions. In the Vedic tradition, gods govern the world by means of the recitation of magical words, while in the Parsi religion evil is defeated thanks to the power of words to transform the amorphous chaos into orderly cosmos.[29] In a metonymical manner reminiscent of traditional magical incantations like those analyzed by Malinowski in his seminal study of Trobriand magic,[30] the poetic persona in Elytis' "Genesis" generates and formulates both his own identity and the universe that he inhabits. Through the power of his words, he creates life and transcends death: for, as he says in a diction provocatively echoing the New Testament, "he [the poet]," like Christ, "is Death and he is Life."

The ritual associations of the utterance of words is a recurrent motif in Elytis' work. In a later poem, from the collection *Three Poems under a Flag of Convenience* (1982), Elytis envisages a new metaphysical reality inhabited by novice monks like himself, as he puts it—another version of the motif of *poeta vates*. In accordance with the metaphysical orientation of the whole collection, which articulates a critique of the materialistic values of modern society, this space is situated beyond the profane world of everyday commodified interactions. In this sense, it is a liminal space where the novice monks are initiated into the mysteries of a transcendental, and, I would argue, neoplatonic world.[31] In his seminal work on rites of passage, van Gennep has shown that the liminal phase of rites of initiation is often marked by the physical separation of the ritual subjects from the rest of the community. During that period, the initiates are taught aspects of the cosmological values of their society often encoded in a secret language.[32] In a similar manner, the marginalized novices of Elytis' poem enunciate ritual utterances while performing a celebratory rite that glorifies nature, love, and poetry—the three most important constituents of Elytis' own poetic universe: ἀπ' τὰ μάτια μου πέρασε μιὰ χώρα/βράχων μὲ τεράστια μοναστήρια/καὶ μικροὺς δόκιμους Μοναχοὺς/ὅπως ἐγώ/τακτικὰ κομίζοντας κλώνους ροδιᾶς/κοριτσιῶν ἐσώρουχα διάφανα/κι ἄλλα τῆς τελετουργίας ἄχραντα/λόγια ὅπως "βοριάς", ἢ "θέρος" ἢ καὶ

---

[28] Elytis 1997:126–127.
[29] Tambiah 1985:27; on the divine creative speech act in biblical texts see Janowitz 2002:19–31.
[30] Malinowski 1984:428–463.
[31] Elytis has explicitly expressed his admiration for Plotinus; e.g., see Ὁ κῆπος βλέπει (Elytis 1982); also his reference to "Plotinus' nine steps" in his *Axion Esti*; and his brief essay on "The Divine Light according to Plotinus" (Elytis 1992:311–312).
[32] Van Gennep 1960:65–115.

"ἀέτωμα" ("From my sight passed a country/of boulders with high huge Monasteries/and little novice Monks like me/regularly carrying pomegranate branches/girls' diaphanous underwear/and other ritual immaculate/words like 'north-wind'/or 'harvest' or even 'pediment.'").[33] The words singled out here—βοριάς, θέρος, ἀέτωμα—are normally devoid of any mystical or religious associations. However, by being uttered by the utopian novice monks as "immaculate ritual" words and reinscribed in a broader ceremonial frame, these unmarked linguistic signifiers acquire mystical connotations. The de-secularization, so to speak, of common words here equals the performance of a ritual; as has been observed, "ritual is a complex of words and actions. It is not the case that words are one thing and the rite another. The uttering of the words itself is a ritual."[34] In this manner, a correspondence is established between the ritual character of the language employed by the young monks and the metaphysical, dream-like, liminal space of the ceremonial landscape. This liminal locus also circumscribes the discursive topos in which the poet constructs and inscribes his own personal mythology. In another poem, the topos of the marginal metaphysical space is transformed into a remote island inhabited by the poet himself. The name of this island, *Elytonisos*, explicitly alludes to the poet's *élitist* marginality.[35] The transference of words from their secular everyday usage to a ritual religious level can be paralleled to Elytis' frequent use of coined words that convey a sense of reality or sur-reality that conventional language fails to communicate. In "The Two of the World," a poem from the collection Φωτόδεντρο, which is also structured around the metaphysical antithesis between this and a transcendental, or again, to my mind, neoplatonic world of beauty, the poet envisages a paradisiac space where angels perform hymns in a new secret language: "There with the curly-haired elongated expressionless faces of angels gazing and chanting with accompanying guitars *oualali oualali* beneath the dry flowers on the lintel *oualali oualali.*"[36] The

---

[33] Elytis 1997:392.

[34] Leach 1966:407.

[35] Ἐλυτόνησος. Κοινῶς Ἐλυτονῆσι, Elytis 1974; here it would be appropriate to recall that "Elytis" is not the poet's real name, but a pseudonym, possibly alluding among other things to *élite* (on the possible associations of *Elytis* see Vitti 1984:18–19). The metaphor of Elytis' poetic persona as a hermit is employed elsewhere in his work; see, again, his poem Ὁ κῆπος βλέπει (Elytis 1982). Elsewhere, he portrays himself as an officiating *poeta vates* (1984, entry "Thursday 2"); cf. also his nostalgic admiration of the function of poetry in old "sacred ceremonial epochs" (1992:117). The image of the poet as seer is explicitly and persistently foregrounded in the *Axion Esti*.

[36] Elytis 1997:236. Cf. the following verses from the "Fire Sermon" of T.S. Eliot's *The Waste Land*: "O City, city, I can sometimes hear/Beside a public car in Lower Thames Street/The pleasant whining of a mandoline/And a clatter and a chatter from within/Where fishmen lounge at noon: where the walls/Of Magnus Martyr hold/Inexplicable splendour of Ionian white and gold/The river sweats/Oil and tar/The barges drift/With the turning tide/Red sails/Wide/To leeward, swing on the heavy spar./The barges wash/Drifting logs/Down Greenwich reach/Past the Isle of Dogs./*Weialala leia/Wallala leialala* . . ." (my emphasis).

transgression of the lexical boundaries of common language here reenacts the disjunc-
tion between normal and ritual language exemplified in the spells of the old Cretan
cook discussed above.

If, in the *Axion Esti*, the poet is the creator of the universe, elsewhere in Elytis'
poetry he undertakes to transcribe the mystical scripture that is supposed to have
been inscribed in the elements of the world. Nature offers the most polyphonic
encoding of these mystical meanings, and natural processes are described in the
metaphorical terms of a ceremonial process in honor of Φυτώ, a fictitious fertility
goddess.[37] The poet assumes, in these cases, the role of a hierophant who construes
and records the transcendental language of nature in his own privileged discourse.
He becomes, to recall the title of one of Elytis' most metaphysical poems, a "Leaf
Seer." The means of his interpretive transcriptions, the alphabet, is also viewed as a
microcosm reflecting entities from, and analogies with, the broader natural and
metaphysical cosmos:

> I learned to catch them in air and in water. But still, I don't know
>   how to speak them:
> A—White or cyan, according to the hours and positions of the
>   stars.
> L—Really wet. Like a pebble.
> G—The most lightweight; so your inability to pronounce it shows
>   the degree of your barbarity.
> R—A child's and, certainly, almost always of female gender.
> E—All air. The sea breeze takes it.
> U—The most Greek letter. An urn.
> S—Weed. But the Greek must sometimes also whistle.[38]

It has been observed that the Indian term for alphabet, *Devanagari*, means
"the abode of the Gods."[39] Although no direct Indian influences on Elytis could be
detected here, this example points to parallel systems of viewing symbolic systems
of communication and their metaphysical correspondence to the alleged semantic

---

[37] Elytis 1982:35; cf. also the following examples of sacralization of nature: "And everywhere in the
fountains and rosemary a confidential Our Father ascended before breaking into dew" (Elytis
1997:211); "roses with religious meaning/still existed then/hallelujah" (ibid.:373); "and the whole
slope all along the seafoam way over my head spoke oracles and susurrated with myriad mauve trem-
blings and cherubic little insects (ibid.:208).
[38] Elytis 1997:434; for some comments on this poem, especially on the Greek "idiosyncrasy" of the
letter Y (U) see Kopidakis 1991.
[39] Tambiah 1985:26.

structures of the cosmos. To my mind, in addition to certain modernist resonances,[40] Elytis' approach to the verbal signs and the world that they create or communicate, bespeaks also some impact of neoplatonic views of language. A twelfth-century Byzantine neoplatonic text underlines the relationship between words and metaphysics in comparable terms:

> The word *ennéa* (nine) consists of two *en* revolving around each other; the first *en* shows the soul's inherent inclination to multiplicity; it is for this reason that it takes rough breathing; the second *en*, reversely read as *ne*, indicates the soul's return to itself, this is why it does not take rough breathing.[41]

Elytis views linguistic sounds as symbolic signs inscribed in his own physical and poetic existence: "before the body/that I am existed/a sea came first/full of little white rolling/vowels rattling: alpha epsilon iota/you'd say that even then/in the posture I had before descending into the Mother/I was shouting with all my might/*aeí aeí aeí.*"[42] This rather neoplatonic correspondence between the poet's body and the aspired eternal repetition of his primordial mystical poetic discourse recalls the eternal recycling of the Sibyl's signifying body as described in Plutarch's dialogue on the Delphic Oracle.[43] Like the Sibyl, the poetic persona in Elytis' poem reproduces the meanings that are supposed to have been inscribed in the world. By doing so, he rearticulates both this mystical universal scripture and the mythology of his own poetic identity.

This image of the poet as receptacle of mystic transcendental knowledge is explicitly reproduced in Elytis' description of a fictitious prophetess in his *Open Papers:*[44]

> She is beautiful! Beautiful! Right angel fragrant all over from rosemary. In a few hours she drank all my darkness, down to the last drop. At dawn, when I opened my eyes, she stood turned to the East, a wet, transparent

---

[40] Rimbaud's "Voyelles" is a highly probable intertext; cf. also Mallarmé's mystical view of the alphabet (see above n. 9).

[41] Gaisford 1820:548–549. For a discussion of this text in particular and of neoplatonic allegorizations in Byzantium in general see Roilos, forthcoming; cf. also Michael Psellos' allegorization of the Greek alphabet published in Duffy 1992:120–141.

[42] Elytis 1997:379.

[43] Plutarch, *De Pythiae oraculis* 398c–d. Cf. also Elytis' poem "The Garden Sees," where he speaks of the "body's Sanskrit" (Elytis 1997:373).

[44] For a discussion of the image of this fictitious sorceress see Yatromanolakis 2001b; cf. also Yatromanolakis 2002.

pebble raised in two fingers. She studied it like a prophet, I remember, and said: Νάγ᾽ ἰωδόσσα ἤνὶς μυριόλεον ἐνιπέσσα/᾽Ἰτόεν οὐ κιλδάνα. Συμβιδὶ δ᾽ ἄς. Παμφώετις.

Elytis offers the following "translation" of these nonsensical lettristic Greek sounds: "I'll give you a skin people can see through. You'll have no secret. You'll belong to everyone. All light." The initiation of the poet into the world of secret sounds is concluded with a new oracle: ᾽Αλλότερος ἢ θὶν παρὰ σαλτὸς ἰαῖος. Κιδάναν φέρ᾽ ἄλκαν/᾽Υμμήταον, ἰμίπαμπον/παμβωετὶ νικώτερον/σχὰς ὀλλεπίων λύκτωρ κὺν θαλτὸς οὐ ἰατός. Παιδόεν ἰρισίμας, Θόης, θόη. Θμώς. The last oracle is offered by Elytis with no translation: it remains an itinerant signifier devoid of any specific rationalistic significance, conveying, though, the sense of a lost, and re-covered, *Urtext* of poetic and metaphysical truth. This invented *Urtext* of sound symbolization, formulated exactly like the previous oracle in a diction that preserves more or less the morphological structures of the Greek language, recalls the linguistic patterns of magical spells preserved in ancient papyri. Two of the last three words of the concluding oracle, *thói-tmós,* are repeated in one of Elytis' most explicitly meta-poetic poems, whose title is characteristically "Three Times the Truth." The "truth" of the world is cryptically reduced and encoded not in words but in onomatopoetic sounds and in ideophones—symbolic sounds.[45] These words are invested with oracular, metaphysical powers:

> I lived on nothing . . . Something something something demonic but that could be caught in a net in the shape of an Archangel I was raving and running I reached the point of imprinting the waves from the tongue to the hearing Hey black poplars I cried and you blue trees what do you know of me? *Thói Thói Thmós.* Hey? What? *Ariéo éthymos thmóos.* I didn't hear what is it? *Thmós thmós ádhysos.*

Onomatopoetic verbal signs, as Demetrius maintains, are not "existing words but words which are only then [at the moment of their articulation] coming into existence" (94; trans. Innes 1995). The user of such words, Demetrius continues, "is like those who originally created language" (ἔοικεν γοῦν ὁ ὀνοματουργῶν τοῖς πρώτοις θεμένοις τὰ ὀνόματα [ibid.]). By inventing these new words, whose utterance is emphatically repeated three times in the poem (to convey three times the truth of the world?), Elytis imitates the act of the primordial creators of language (οἱ πρῶτοι θέμενοι τὰ ὀνόματα). His coined words "are coming into existence" at the very

---

[45] Cf. Elytis' admiration for what he calls "sound imagination" in the poetry of Andreas Kalvos (Elytis 1987:86).

moment of their enunciation and articulate a highly "esoteric" discourse provocatively imposed on the readers as a riddling signifier open to multiple interpretations.[46]

In a polemical essay where he attacks Western rationalistic thinking and the materialistic orientation of modern society, Elytis argues that by conveying an alternative view of "the truth" of the world, poetic discourse can transcend the boundaries of commonsensical views of the world and defeat even death. "Death," he declares, "exists only there where words cannot give new birth to things."[47] This idea is lyrically developed in a poem from *The Elegies of Jutting Rock*, one of Elytis' last collections, published in 1991, five years before his death. Here, Elytis resumes the ritual function of a seer who employs his secret linguistic code to exorcize death. The poem, whose title "Verb the Dark" alludes to Heraclitean ambiguity, could be read as a self-referential commentary on Elytis' own aesthetic and metaphysical systems. The poet employs a biblical image to refer to himself: he is "like an angel on the tomb who trumpets white fabrics." He speaks a language that is not understood by profane ears. He is a practitioner of *glôssalalía*:[48] "I am of another language, unfortunately, and of the Hidden Sun so that those unaware of celestial things know me not," he declares in a diction that recalls conventional topoi in Greek allegorical exegetical tradition. Used to inverting the rules of ordinary language and playing with them, at his imminent encounter with death, he gathers his poetic power against it:

> So now accustomed to make iotas smaller and omicrons bigger/I contrive a verb; like a robber his passkey/A verb with a proper ending—something that darkens you on one side/until your other side appears a verb with very few vowels/but many rusted consonants kappa or theta or tau/bought for bargain prices from the warehouses of Hades/because, from these places/you slip in more easily like Darius' ghost to terrify the living and the dead. Let heavy music be heard here./And the now lightweight mountains be transposed./Time to try my key./I say: *katarkythmévô*.

The utterance of the "dark verb," accompanied by the solemn performance of music echoing analogous instances of Greek surrealistic rhetoric, equals a reenactment of the synesthetic performative frame of a ritual. Todorov has observed that

---

[46] Cf. Malinowski's observation that onomatopoetic words play a central role in Trobriand magic (1984:447, 452).

[47] Elytis 1992:177; cf. 1985:41–45. For Elytis' polemical attitude to the commodification of modern life and his celebration of the transformative power of words see, for instance, also Elytis 1982:14; 1987:116–117; 1985:XI; 1998:34.

[48] On aspects of *glôssalalía* in Elytis see Belezinis 1999:91–131; on aspects of the use of poetic metalanguage in Elytis see Babiniotis 1991.

magical words function as micro-narratives: more often than not, he argues, the most important constituent of incantatory discourse is a verb denoting some change of state. Todorov further maintains that the narrative which is articulated in condensed form in a magical incantation does not refer to an *actual* action, as other narratives do, but to a virtual one. In Elytis' poem, though, by being inscribed in the specific poetic discourse, the coined magical word functions as a micro-narrative that relates, or rather performs, not a virtual, but an *actual,* action.[49] The poet's speech act transforms the pragmatic conditions of his world: in a highly ritualistic context where the Aeschylean scene of Darius' apparition is reversed rather than imitated and the Byzantine theme of Christ's Descendance into Hades is subtly reenacted, the poet unlocks the mysteries of death by employing the power of his own mysteries. The poet conquers death by spreading the nets of his magical spells: albeit ultimately dark, κατ αρκυθμεύω, Elytis' coined verb, may allude to the ancient Greek word for hunter's net: ἀρκύς.

Archaism seems to be an elemental characteristic of ritual, especially incantatory, discourse all over the world.[50] Tambiah discerns three categories of verbal signs used in traditional ritual settings in Thailand. First, there are occasions where a dead sacred language is employed; this idiom is understood only by the majority of the officiating monks. Second, there are rites performed in common language, which is understood by all the participants. Third, there are rituals where a secret register is used by the ritual expert.[51] If a parallel between these types of ritual language and Elytis' re-creative and ludic appropriation of the archaizing morphological and lexical elements of the Greek language could be drawn, it might be argued that Elytis' verb is a combination of elements of the first and third categories: it is a secret verbal sign based on an ancient linguistic register. Despite its obscure etymological and semantic associations, this word functions as a sound symbol comparable to the secret language spoken by the beautiful sorceress who gave Elytis the inspirational dark oracles. Elytis reenacts here the ritual act of his fictitious sorceress and articulates a cryptical ideophone that consists of four phonetic segments: κατ-αρκυ-θμ-εύω.

Linguistic anthropology has drawn our attention to the ritual connotations of such sound patterns in traditional societies. Bantu languages, for instance, make extensive use of ideophones that do not fit the conventional lexicon. The phonetic

---

[49] Todorov 1973:44.

[50] On the idiosyncratic conservative character of ritual language in general see Bloch 1974; cf. also J. Fox 1974.

[51] Tambiah 1985a:22–23.

segments of Elytis' ideophone, which, drawing on linguistics, I would call phones-themes—that is, segments that convey acoustic symbolic connotations[52]—point to corresponding lexical or morphological prototypes. Although Elytis' verb remains tantalizingly obscure, the allusiveness of its components is highly evocative: the phonestheme -θμ- , in particular, recalls not only the last word of the second unde-cipherable oracle that the prophetess gave to the poet in the visionary scene I described above, but also the usage of the same word in the poem "Three Times the Truth." The apocalyptic imagery (the angel), the possible metaphorical reference to the net (ἀρκύς), the ideophone θμός, and the word ἄδυσος, a quasi allophone of ἄβυσσος (abyss, Hades), which are used in that poem, all these point, I believe, to complex internal intertextual associations between this dark verb, the secret language of the archetypical sorceress who gave Elytis his initial poetic inspiration, and the reactivation of this language in the self-referential poetic discourse of "Three Times the Truth." The utterance of the ultimately undecipherable "dark verb" does not refer to any specific signified. It remains an elusive signifier whose only identifiable point of reference, the subject who utters it—the fictional persona of the *poeta vates*—is situated not outside, but within, the act of its enunciation. Along with the utterance of the cryptic ideophone, this subject articulates his own poetic myth that differentiates him from the rest of the world and its commodified modes of commonsensical communication.

The poem ends with an apocalyptic vision that reveals to the poet a new level of existence. The reader, entrapped in his materialistic preoccupations, is reluctantly invited, but in the end unable to participate, in this revelatory experience. The keyword for the transcription and the decipherment of this experience is supposed to be the exclusive privilege of the modernist poet:

> Friend you who hear, can you hear the distant bells
> Of the citrons' fragrance? Do you know the garden's corners where
> The dusk wind lays its newborn? Have you ever dreamt
> Of a boundless summer where you could run
> No longer knowing the Furies? No. That's why I *katarkythmévô*
> That the heavy creaking bolts give way and the great gates open
> Into the light of the Hidden Sun for a moment, so our third
>   nature can become manifest
> There's more, but I shall not say it . . .[53]

---

[52] For a discussion of the category of phonestheme see Duranti 1997:205–207.
[53] Elytis 1997:534.

꘠

In conclusion, ritual language, in exactly the same manner as dream imagery, provides Elytis with a non-rationalistic model of symbolic communication that undermines established linguistic conventions. This model of communication is appropriate for his poetic interpretation of reality and his poetic construction of a sur-reality, since poetry, too, can be defined in terms of the transgression of ordinary language. As in spells and dreams, in poetry as well, and in particular in Elytis' modernist poetics, the rules of everyday discourse are often suspended or inverted. Viewed from this standpoint, all of these forms of symbolic expression—ritual, dream, and poetry—occupy, I argue, parallel *liminal* spaces all along the spectrum of human discursive experience. In Elytis' work, poetry's inherent liminality is enhanced by the appropriation of indigenous ritualistic modes of expression that polemically communicate or create a second, metaphysical, level of experience. This *liminal* level of experience is situated beyond the communicative and conceptual norms adopted by modern materialistic society. For Elytis, this liminality is the poetic topos par excellence. Ultimately situated (or enmeshed?) in a between-and-betwixt communicative and existential modality—provocatively linked with the fictitious locus of Elytonisos in Elytis' homonymous self-referential poem—the aestheticizing and aestheticized poetic subject indulges in an *él(y)itist* re-creation of a discursive *topography* where indigenous patterns of ritual symbolization subtly perform the articulation of this subject's own personal mythology.

Part Three
Ritual Reflections

Seven

Poetics of Repetition in Homer

Gregory Nagy

In Homeric poetry there are references to ritualized repetition, as in descriptions of antiphony in the context of ritual lamentation. Such repetition is a matter of performance, not only composition. This observation applies not only specifically to ritualized repetition but generally to the Homeric phenomenon of "repeated utterances."

This argument is part of a larger project, which is to show that Homeric poetry is a medium of oral poetry. That project is exemplified in a 1996 book entitled *Poetry as Performance*, where I argued that the text of the Homeric poems, that is, of the *Iliad* and the *Odyssey*, is derived from a system that needs to be distinguished from the text itself—or, better, from the Homeric textual tradition that editors try to reconstruct as a single Homeric text.[1] The text of Homer is merely the surface. Underneath that surface is the system that is Homeric poetry, which needs to be analyzed on its own terms, as a system. This system, I argued, reveals a medium of oral poetry. My task here is to take the argument further by showing that the phenomenon of repeated utterances in the Homeric textual tradition is explainable in terms of this system, that is, in terms of oral poetry.

Essential for my argument is the idea that Homeric composition comes to life in performance. In oral poetry, performance is essential to composition: the composition of oral poetry is a matter of recomposition-in-performance.[2] If it is true that the Homeric text derives from oral poetry, then the phenomenon of repeated utterances is itself a matter of performance, not only composition.[3]

In some cases of repeated utterances in a ritual context, it is obvious that the repetition is a matter of performance, as in Homeric descriptions of ensembles of mourning women whose ritual laments echo the lament of the woman who initiates the mourning.[4] In other cases, however, the dimension of performance is less

---

[1] Nagy 1996b.
[2] Nagy 1996b:chapters 1–3.
[3] This observation about Homeric poetry applies also to Hesiodic poetry and beyond. In a future project, I hope to undertake such an application.

obvious. Least obvious to the modern mind is the idea that the actual "quoting" of a speaker is itself a matter of performance in oral poetics. A most convincing demonstration of this idea is offered by Richard Martin.[5] From the standpoint of oral poetry, the "quoting" of a speaker's utterance is not just a repetition of that utterance: it is also a performance—a reperformance—of that utterance. A repeated utterance, then, is a reperformance of a notionally original utterance. The same goes for any further repetition: it is a matter of further reperformance.

Here I find it most relevant to apply the intuitive formulation about repetition by Kierkegaard in his *Repetition* (1843): "The dialectic of repetition is easy, for that which is repeated has been—otherwise it could not be repeated—but the very fact that it has been makes the repetition into something new."[6]

With this formulation in mind, I now proceed to analyze examples of repeated utterances in Homeric poetry. These examples, I argue, show that repetition in Homeric poetry is not just composed but also performed.

These same examples have already been analyzed in a work by Tormod Eide, who views the phenomenon of repeated utterances in terms of "reformulated repetitions."[7] Although I disagree with Eide's conclusions, I find his analysis a most enlightening point of departure for my own analysis (references to his work will hereafter be marked shorthand by way of his initials, "TE").

TE summarizes his conclusions this way (p. 97): "strained grammar, narrative inconsistency, and anomalous word forms can sometimes be ascribed to the rephrasing of preexisting lines." He makes a distinction between "reformulated repetition" and "formulaic repetition" (p. 98). He thinks that "reformulated repetitions" do *not* belong to "the poet's 'gemeinsames Versgut,'" which he equates with oral poetry and which is characterized by "formulaic repetition." I argue, by contrast, that the phenomena he describes can indeed be explained in terms of oral poetics.

According to TE (p. 97) there are two categories of reformulated repetitions: (1) reported message and (2) the carrying out of a command, request, wish. To facilitate the discussion, I substitute for "carrying out" the expression "following through," as a paraphrase for the Homeric expression *tetelesmenon estai*, in the sense of 'it [= whatever has been said formally] will reach its due *telos*'.[8]

---

[4] I draw special attention to the repetition marked by the Homeric expression *epi de stenakhonto gunaikes* 'and the women lamented in response' (*Iliad* 18.315; 22.429, 515; 24.722, 746). See also in general Alexiou 2002a:64, 84–85, 90, 93–94, 96–98, 135–136, 156–159, 166–175, 168–169, 180.

[5] Martin 1989. See also Bakker 1997.

[6] Kierkegaard 1983:149. For an application of Kierkegaard's formulation to oral poetics, see Nagy 1996b:52 (cf. also 100–102).

[7] Eide 1999:97–139.

[8] See for example *Iliad* 2.257, in the ritualized context of a prophecy uttered by the seer Calchas.

TE elaborates (p. 97): "In both categories the repeated version entails changes primarily of the verbs and pronouns, changes which would often disturb the metrical pattern." I draw attention to the use of the word "version" in this formulation. A problem here, I suggest, is that there is no way to decide which of any two or more "versions" is "the repeated version." In terms of any formulaic system reflected by oral poetics, we cannot assume that any given "version" is the basic "version." TE's wording "changes which would often disturb the metrical pattern" invites questions. It is therefore most helpful that TE (p. 97) poses his own questions: "What does the poet do then, and how well does he do it? How often does the reformulation lead to grammatical irregularities? How often does the poet simply drop recalcitrant lines, and how does this affect narrative consistency? <u>Does the poet's treatment sometimes indicate recourse to writing?</u>" TE's own answer to the last question, as underlined, is "yes."

I propose that this line of argumentation needs to be confronted with two observations about oral poetry: (1) formulaic language is a system and (2) this system generates forms for the present, for the here-and-now of composition.

Much depends on how oral poetry is understood in the first place. Let us take for example this formulation (TE pp. 97–98): "If the poet in the passages I discuss commits what to a modern reader would count as a blemish, it is not necessarily from lack of ability, but because he did not care, and did not need to care. The Homeric poems were not created for readers or scholars. Nor should we forget that the listeners' thrill of hearing an impressive or dramatic passage repeated word for word would outweigh minor discrepancies introduced by the repetition."

Such a formulation underestimates the potential artistry inherent in oral poetry. From the standpoint of oral poetics, the "thrill" is not only in hearing a *notionally* word-for-word repetition of what has just been heard but also in apprehending the changes that are being made within this repetition. For example, there are changes required by the *shifting* of first / second / third persons in pronouns and verbs as the composer recomposes.[9] The artistic bravura is not just a matter of recomposition: it is a matter of recomposition-in-performance. An aspect of this bravura is the skill of *shifting* from one person to another in performing a set of repeated sequences requiring the deployment of different persons in pronouns or verbs.[10]

---

[9] On the linguistic term *shifter* as applied to "shifting" from one person to another in the three persons of pronouns and verbs, see Jakobson 1971:130–147.

[10] For a particularly valuable collection of examples, see Blackburn, et al. 1989; see especially Claus ibid.:55–74. At 74, Claus examines "a transition from a story *about* a spirit, to one told *to* a spirit, to one told *by* a spirit," and he adds: "Accompanying these transitions are shifts in verbal style: from the third person pronominal referent, to the second, to the first. There are also changes in the behavior of the performers and the audience." Another kind of performative bravura in shifting involves the movement from nominative to vocative. In a forthcoming study, I will examine the

TE's first test case is *Iliad* 3.67–75 ~ 86–94 ~ 136–138 ~ 252–258 (p. 99): "Paris suggests to Hector that the war be ended by a duel between Paris and Menelaus [passage A = 3.67–75]; Hector then passes on the suggestion to the men [passage B = 3.86–94]; the news is brought to Helen by Iris [passage C = 3.136–138], and, finally, the herald Idaeus summons Priam to descend on to the plain and conclude the pact [passage D = 3.252–258]."

A revealing aspect of TE's analysis is where he says (p. 99): "Hector's speech ends abruptly [passage B, after line 94], with no indication as to the future course of action that is to be sanctioned by the oath-taking, corresponding to the ending of Paris' speech [passage A, 74-75]. Kirk's explanation, that Paris' last two verses may have been dropped 'because Hektor does not feel it necessary or diplomatic to elaborate on terms of departure at this stage'[,] may seem too refined."[11] I suggest that there are problems even in saying that the last two verses of passage A were "dropped" in passage B. It is as if we were dealing with some pre-existing text that became a new text in the process of repetition. I propose that the renovation is a matter of recomposed performance, not rewritten text. TE continues (p. 99): "Two manuscripts and a papyrus omit also v. 94 [in other words, Hector's speech now ends after verse 93], and thus give a more natural ending to the speech. One may suspect that this was the invention of the original composer, and that the line [verse 94] was inserted later by a singer / rhapsode who noticed that one more of Paris' lines could easily, from a metrical point of view, be included in Hector's speech. Sometimes it is metrical adaptability rather than appropriateness that guides the composer in deciding what to include, what to leave out in the repetition" (underlines mine). I find it difficult to accept the distinction made here between "the original composer," who judiciously cuts the speech after verse 93, and the less judicious later "composer" who may decide to keep on going with the speech merely because the meter makes it easy for him to keep going. I draw attention to the assumption that the speech as conceived in passage A must be the basic speech.

After entertaining an alternative possibility, that "the line [verse 93] was omitted by somebody who saw that the line as it stands was unsatisfactory without a continuation" (p. 99), TE proceeds to examine passage C, where we see one single verse conveying the same general idea that we see conveyed by two verses in passages A and B. TE adds, and I agree with him, that this single verse in passage

---

phenomenon of narratives addressed to the second person agent of the narration, as in the case of Patroklos and Eumaios in the *Iliad* and *Odyssey* respectively. See also Nagy 2001b:xxii.

[11] For the *Iliad* commentary used by TE, see Kirk 1985.

C "is more suitable to a private conversation between two women" than the two verses in the corresponding passages: "the mention of *ktêmata panta* is dropped, and the neutral *gunaika* is replaced by the more affectionate *philê akoitis*" (TE p. 100). I disagree, however, with the textual implications of TE's analysis. I maintain that the adjustments required by different situations occasioned by repetition can be counted as examples of virtuosity in the art of recomposition-in-performance.

But what are we to do with the κε of passage C verse 138? Is it a lapse in artistry? This form is syntactically anomalous, in comparison with the corresponding κε of passage A verse 71 and of passage B verse 92. TE offers this explanation (p. 100): "We see that the constraints laid upon the poet when composing by this kind of recycling process may overrule both Greek grammar and narrative coherence." My work in formulaic analysis leads me to a different interpretation: "this kind of recycling process" is not restricted to "reformulated repetitions" and in fact it pervades the entire formulaic system of Homeric poetry. In general, I hold that the formulaic system of Homeric poetry has a grammar of its own—with rules as well as licenses that differ in part from those of everyday language.

In passage D, the formal problems of adapting the "same" wording that we saw in passages A, B, and C seem to be compounded. Particularly problematic for TE is the case of "a line with no change in wording, but with a different syntactical relation to the preceding [line] in order to achieve the join." For the first time, TE overtly applies to such a phenomenon the description "non-formulaic" (p. 101). We see here an explicit statement of what has in fact been the view of TE all along, that "reformulated repetitions" are symptomatic of non-formulaic composition. I see no justification for such a view.

Rather, I propose that the process of reformulation is in fact a reaffirmation of formulaic composition. In order to reaffirm or even clarify the meaning of something that has been "quoted," the "quoted" words may need to be quoted again, that is, performed again. I am using the word "quote" not in a textual but in a performative sense. Once a given formulation has been performed as a speech act, that is, once it has been "quoted" in performance, it becomes eligible to be "quoted" anew.

The idea of performance as a speech act is especially relevant to cases where we can identify a ritual as the overt referent in a set of reformulated repetitions. One such case is *Iliad* 6.87–101 ~ 269–278 ~ 297–310. Let us begin with the first in this set composed of three passages: in 6.87–101, Helenus, who is speaking here as a seer, "instructs his brother Hector to withdraw to Troy and beg their mother to gather the Trojan women in Athena's sanctuary to make offerings to the goddess in the hope that she will have pity on them" (TE p. 103):

A *Iliad* 6.87–101

"Εκτορ ἀτὰρ σὺ πόλιν δὲ μετέρχεο, εἰπὲ δ' ἔπειτα
μητέρι σῇ καὶ ἐμῇ· ἣ δὲ ξυνάγουσα γεραιὰς
νηὸν 'Αθηναίης γλαυκώπιδος ἐν πόλει ἄκρῃ
οἴξασα κληῗδι θύρας ἱεροῖο δόμοιο
90   πέπλον, ὅς οἱ δοκέει χαριέστατος ἠδὲ μέγιστος
εἶναι ἐνὶ μεγάρῳ καί οἱ πολὺ φίλτατος αὐτῇ,
θεῖναι 'Αθηναίης ἐπὶ γούνασιν ἠϋκόμοιο,
καί οἱ ὑποσχέσθαι δυοκαίδεκα βοῦς ἐνὶ νηῷ
ἤνις ἠκέστας ἱερευσέμεν, αἴ κ' ἐλεήσῃ
95   ἄστύ τε καὶ Τρώων ἀλόχους καὶ νήπια τέκνα,
ὡς κεν Τυδέος υἱὸν ἀπόσχῃ 'Ιλίου ἱρῆς
ἄγριον αἰχμητὴν κρατερὸν μήστωρα φόβοιο,
ὃν δὴ ἐγὼ κάρτιστον 'Αχαιῶν φημι γενέσθαι.
οὐδ' 'Αχιλῆά ποθ' ὧδέ γ' ἐδείδιμεν ὄρχαμον ἀνδρῶν,
100 ὅν πέρ φασι θεᾶς ἐξέμμεναι· ἀλλ' ὅδε λίην
μαίνεται, οὐδέ τίς οἱ δύναται μένος ἰσοφαρίζειν.

About 200 verses later, Hector conveys this mantic formulation to his mother Hecabe:

B *Iliad* 6.269–278

ἀλλὰ σὺ μὲν πρὸς νηὸν 'Αθηναίης ἀγελείης
270 ἔρχεο σὺν θυέεσσιν ἀολλίσσασα γεραιάς·
πέπλον δ', ὅς τίς τοι χαριέστατος ἠδὲ μέγιστος
ἔστιν ἐνὶ μεγάρῳ καί τοι πολὺ φίλτατος αὐτῇ,
τὸν θὲς 'Αθηναίης ἐπὶ γούνασιν ἠϋκόμοιο,
καί οἱ ὑποσχέσθαι δυοκαίδεκα βοῦς ἐνὶ νηῷ
275 ἤνις ἠκέστας ἱερευσέμεν, αἴ κ' ἐλεήσῃ
ἄστύ τε καὶ Τρώων ἀλόχους καὶ νήπια τέκνα,
αἴ κεν Τυδέος υἱὸν ἀπόσχῃ 'Ιλίου ἱρῆς
ἄγριον αἰχμητὴν κρατερὸν μήστωρα φόβοιο.

Hecabe follows the instructions of A and B by proceeding to fetch a *peplos* from the storeroom. Then the instructions are followed further, in the form of a ritual performed on the acropolis of Troy:

C *Iliad* 6.297–310

Αἳ δ' ὅτε νηὸν ἵκανον 'Αθήνης ἐν πόλει ἄκρῃ,
τῇσι θύρας ὤϊξε Θεανὼ καλλιπάρῃος
Κισσηῒς ἄλοχος 'Αντήνορος ἱπποδάμοιο·

300 τὴν γὰρ Τρῶες ἔθηκαν Ἀθηναίης ἱέρειαν.
αἳ δ' ὀλολυγῇ πᾶσαι Ἀθήνῃ χεῖρας ἀνέσχον·
ἣ δ' ἄρα πέπλον ἑλοῦσα Θεανὼ καλλιπάρῃος
θῆκεν Ἀθηναίης ἐπὶ γούνασιν ἠϋκόμοιο,
εὐχομένη δ' ἠρᾶτο Διὸς κούρῃ μεγάλοιο·
305 πότνι' Ἀθηναίη ἐρυσίπτολι δῖα θεάων
ἆξον δὴ ἔγχος Διομήδεος, ἠδὲ καὶ αὐτὸν
πρηνέα δὸς πεσέειν Σκαιῶν προπάροιθε πυλάων,
ὄφρά τοι αὐτίκα νῦν δυοκαίδεκα βοῦς ἐνὶ νηῷ
ἤνις ἠκέστας ἱερεύσομεν, αἴ κ' ἐλεήσῃς
310 ἄστύ τε καὶ Τρώων ἀλόχους καὶ νήπια τέκνα.

TE (p. 104) argues that there are two important inconsistencies: "(a) in A and B Hecabe is requested to *promise* Athena a sacrifice of twelve cows, while in C the sacrifice will take place *autika nun* (308); (b) in A and B Hecabe herself is to give Athena the *peplos* and utter the prayer, while in C it is the priestess Theano who performs both services. . . . Instead of asking, 'Why does the poet change his mind?' we ask, 'Which of the three texts bears the mark of an adaptation?' We will immediately see that it is A that has excited commentators." In this case, TE (p. 105) supposes the poet "to be composing backwards," using C as the basis for the variations in B and A. From the standpoint of oral poetics, however, A B C are all variants, and all three have to be treated as multiforms.[12] There is a crescendo effect here, as the ritual details become ever more explicit.

In this case, the execution of the formulation results in failure for the ritual, in that the goddess refuses the offering. I submit that the crescendo in detail provides an explanation for the failure: Hecuba had in the end chosen as her offering to the goddess something directly connected to the cause of the Trojan War: the *peplos* that she chose is connected to the story of Helen's abduction by Paris. Thus the repetition of a formulation has in this case helped motivate the outcome of that formulation in the plot of the composition.

There are other instances as well where the plot of the composition is clarified by the poetics of repeated formulation. Let us consider *Iliad* 9.119–161 ~ 260–301, about which TE (p. 115) observes: "In the beginning of Book 9 Agamemnon describes . . . the gifts he is prepared to offer Achilles to make him surrender his anger. Odysseus, in his speech to Achilles, follows Agamemnon's words closely (264–299), and thus we have the opportunity of studying an unusually long and [illustrative] example of the reported message."

---

[12] For more on the terms "variant" and "multiform," see Nagy 2001a:109–119.

A *Iliad* 9.119–161

ἀλλ' ἐπεὶ ἀασάμην φρεσὶ λευγαλέῃσι πιθήσας,
120 ἂψ ἐθέλω ἀρέσαι δόμεναί τ' ἀπερείσι' ἄποινα.
ὑμῖν δ' ἐν πάντεσσι περικλυτὰ δῶρ' ὀνομήνω

ἕπτ' ἀπύρους τρίποδας, δέκα δὲ χρυσοῖο τάλαντα,
αἴθωνας δὲ λέβητας ἐείκοσι, δώδεκα δ' ἵππους
πηγοὺς ἀθλοφόρους, οἳ ἀέθλια ποσσὶν ἄροντο.
125 οὔ κεν ἀλήϊος εἴη ἀνὴρ ᾧ τόσσα γένοιτο,
οὐδέ κεν ἀκτήμων ἐριτίμοιο χρυσοῖο,
ὅσσά μοι ἠνείκαντο ἀέθλια μώνυχες ἵπποι.
δώσω δ' ἑπτὰ γυναῖκας ἀμύμονα ἔργα ἰδυίας
Λεσβίδας, ἃς ὅτε Λέσβον ἐϋκτιμένην ἕλεν αὐτὸς
130 ἐξελόμην, αἳ κάλλει ἐνίκων φῦλα γυναικῶν.
τὰς μέν οἱ δώσω, μετὰ δ' ἔσσεται ἣν τότ' ἀπηύρων
κούρη Βρισῆος· ἐπὶ δὲ μέγαν ὅρκον ὀμοῦμαι
μή ποτε τῆς εὐνῆς ἐπιβήμεναι ἠδὲ μιγῆναι,
ἣ θέμις ἀνθρώπων πέλει ἀνδρῶν ἠδὲ γυναικῶν.
135 ταῦτα μὲν αὐτίκα πάντα παρέσσεται· εἰ δέ κεν αὖτε
ἄστυ μέγα Πριάμοιο θεοὶ δώωσ' ἀλαπάξαι,
νῆα ἅλις χρυσοῦ καὶ χαλκοῦ <u>νηησάσθω</u>

Τρωϊάδας δὲ γυναῖκας ἐείκοσιν αὐτὸς <u>ἑλέσθω</u>,
140 αἴ κε μετ' Ἀργείην Ἑλένην κάλλισται ἔωσιν.
εἰ δέ κεν Ἄργος ἱκοίμεθ' Ἀχαιϊκὸν οὔθαρ ἀρούρης
γαμβρός κέν μοι ἔοι· <u>τίσω</u> δέ μιν ἶσον Ὀρέστῃ,
ὅς μοι τηλύγετος τρέφεται θαλίῃ ἔνι πολλῇ.
τρεῖς δέ μοί εἰσι θύγατρες ἐνὶ μεγάρῳ εὐπήκτῳ
145 Χρυσόθεμις καὶ Λαοδίκη καὶ Ἰφιάνασσα,
τάων ἥν κ' ἐθέλῃσι φίλην ἀνάεδνον <u>ἀγέσθω</u>
πρὸς οἶκον Πηλῆος· ἐγὼ δ' ἐπὶ μείλια <u>δώσω</u>
πολλὰ μάλ', ὅσσ' οὔ πώ τις ἑῇ ἐπέδωκε θυγατρί·
ἑπτὰ δέ οἱ <u>δώσω</u> εὖ ναιόμενα πτολίεθρα
150 Καρδαμύλην Ἐνόπην τε καὶ Ἱρὴν ποιήεσσαν
Φηράς τε ζαθέας ἠδ' Ἄνθειαν βαθύλειμον
καλήν τ' Αἴπειαν καὶ Πήδασον ἀμπελόεσσαν.
πᾶσαι δ' ἐγγὺς ἁλός, νέαται Πύλου ἠμαθόεντος·
ἐν δ' ἄνδρες ναίουσι πολύρρηνες πολυβοῦται,
155 οἵ κέ ἑ δωτίνῃσι θεὸν ὣς τιμήσουσι
καί οἱ ὑπὸ σκήπτρῳ λιπαρὰς τελέουσι θέμιστας.
ταῦτά κέ οἱ τελέσαιμι μεταλήξαντι χόλοιο.
<u>δμηθήτω· Ἀΐδης τοι ἀμείλιχος ἠδ' ἀδάμαστος,</u>
<u>τοὔνεκα καί τε βροτοῖσι θεῶν ἔχθιστος ἁπάντων·</u>
160 <u>καί μοι ὑποστήτω ὅσσον βασιλεύτερός εἰμι</u>
<u>ἠδ' ὅσσον γενεῇ προγενέστερος εὔχομαι εἶναι.</u>

B *Iliad* 9.260–301

260   ... ἔα δὲ χόλον θυμαλγέα· σοὶ δ' Ἀγαμέμνων
ἄξια δῶρα δίδωσι μεταλήξαντι χόλοιο.
εἰ δὲ σὺ μέν μευ ἄκουσον, ἐγὼ δέ κέ τοι καταλέξω
ὅσσά τοι ἐν κλισίῃσιν ὑπέσχετο δῶρ' Ἀγαμέμνων·
ἕπτ' ἀπύρους τρίποδας, δέκα δὲ χρυσοῖο τάλαντα,
265   αἴθωνας δὲ λέβητας ἐείκοσι, δώδεκα δ' ἵππους
πηγοὺς ἀθλοφόρους, οἳ ἀέθλια ποσσὶν ἄροντο.
οὔ κεν ἀλήϊος εἴη ἀνὴρ ᾧ τόσσα γένοιτο
οὐδέ κεν ἀκτήμων ἐριτίμοιο χρυσοῖο,
ὅσσ' Ἀγαμέμνονος ἵπποι ἀέθλια ποσσὶν ἄροντο.
270   δώσει δ' ἑπτὰ γυναῖκας ἀμύμονα ἔργα ἰδυίας
Λεσβίδας, ἃς ὅτε Λέσβον ἐϋκτιμένην ἕλες αὐτὸς
ἐξέλεθ', αἳ τότε κάλλει ἐνίκων φῦλα γυναικῶν.
τὰς μέν τοι δώσει, μετὰ δ' ἔσσεται ἣν τότ' ἀπηύρα
κούρη Βρισῆος· ἐπὶ δὲ μέγαν ὅρκον ὀμεῖται
275   μή ποτε τῆς εὐνῆς ἐπιβήμεναι ἠδὲ μιγῆναι
ἣ θέμις ἐστὶν ἄναξ ἤτ' ἀνδρῶν ἤτε γυναικῶν.
ταῦτα μὲν αὐτίκα πάντα παρέσσεται· εἰ δέ κεν αὖτε
ἄστυ μέγα Πριάμοιο θεοὶ δώωσ' ἀλαπάξαι,
νῆα ἅλις χρυσοῦ καὶ χαλκοῦ <u>νηήσασθαι</u>
280   εἰσελθών, ὅτε κεν δατεώμεθα ληΐδ' Ἀχαιοί,
Τρωϊάδας δὲ γυναῖκας ἐείκοσιν αὐτὸς <u>ἑλέσθαι</u>,
αἵ κε μετ' Ἀργείην Ἑλένην κάλλισται ἔωσιν.
εἰ δέ κεν Ἄργος ἱκοίμεθ' Ἀχαιϊκὸν οὖθαρ ἀρούρης
γαμβρός κέν οἱ ἔοις· <u>τίσει</u> δέ σε ἶσον Ὀρέστῃ,
285   ὅς οἱ τηλύγετος τρέφεται θαλίῃ ἔνι πολλῇ.
τρεῖς δέ οἵ εἰσι θύγατρες ἐνὶ μεγάρῳ εὐπήκτῳ
Χρυσόθεμις καὶ Λαοδίκη καὶ Ἰφιάνασσα,
τάων ἥν κ' ἐθέλησθα φίλην ἀνάεδνον <u>ἄγεσθαι</u>
πρὸς οἶκον Πηλῆος· ὃ δ' αὖτ' ἐπὶ μείλια <u>δώσει</u>
290   πολλὰ μάλ', ὅσσ' οὔ πώ τις ἑῇ ἐπέδωκε θυγατρί·
ἑπτὰ δέ τοι <u>δώσει</u> εὖ ναιόμενα πτολίεθρα
Καρδαμύλην Ἐνόπην τε καὶ Ἱρὴν ποιήεσσαν
Φηράς τε ζαθέας ἠδ' Ἄνθειαν βαθύλειμον
καλήν τ' Αἴπειαν καὶ Πήδασον ἀμπελόεσσαν.
295   πᾶσαι δ' ἐγγὺς ἁλός, νέαται Πύλου ἠμαθόεντος·
ἐν δ' ἄνδρες ναίουσι πολύρρηνες πολυβοῦται,
οἵ κέ σε δωτίνῃσι θεὸν ὣς τιμήσουσι
καί τοι ὑπὸ σκήπτρῳ λιπαρὰς τελέουσι θέμιστας.
ταῦτά κέ τοι τελέσειε μεταλήξαντι χόλοιο.
300   <u>εἰ δέ τοι Ἀτρεΐδης μὲν ἀπήχθετο κηρόθι μᾶλλον</u>
<u>αὐτὸς καὶ τοῦ δῶρα, σὺ δ' ἄλλους περ Παναχαιοὺς</u>
<u>τειρομένους ἐλέαιρε κατὰ στρατόν, οἵ σε θεὸν ὣς</u>
<u>τίσουσ'· ἦ γάρ κέ σφι μάλα μέγα κῦδος ἄροιο·</u>
<u>νῦν γάρ χ' Ἕκτορ' ἕλοις, ἐπεὶ ἂν μάλα τοι σχεδὸν ἔλθοι</u>
305   <u>λύσσαν ἔχων ὀλοήν, ἐπεὶ οὔ τινά φησιν ὁμοῖον</u>
<u>οἷ ἔμεναι Δαναῶν οὓς ἐνθάδε νῆες ἔνεικαν.</u>

TE (p. 115) continues: "We see . . . that the habit of reproducing as faithfully as possible (or necessary) the original [*sic*] speech, creates a strait-jacket that leads to some infelicities or inaccuracies. The infinitives *nêêsasthai* (279), *helesthai* (281), and *agesthai* (288), prompted by the (metrically equivalent) imperatives *nêêsasthô*, *helesthô*, and *agesthô*, are left with nothing to govern them. [. . .] The future indicatives *dôsei, t[e]isei*, for Agamemnon's *dôsô, t[e]isô*, also strike a false note, as the third person form does not convey the notion of intention or will that the first person does. In the mouth of Odysseus these sentences become prophecies rather than promises." But that is precisely the point. Ex post facto, from the standpoint of the rituals associated with the cults of later centuries, these sentences are indeed prophecies about Achilles as a cult hero.[13]

More important, the variation of 158–161 ~ 300–306 in Book 9 of the *Iliad* is essential to the master plot of the whole composition. In this case, all depends on the success or failure of Odysseus' reformulated repetition of Agamemnon's earlier formulation. If Odysseus' reformulation had been successful, he would have persuaded Achilles to accept the offer of Agamemnon, but such a success would have resulted in the failure of Achilles' own epic.[14] Odysseus' reformulation failed, in that he failed to persuade Achilles. This way, the epic of Achilles could succeed. Achilles' refusal to accept Agamemnon's offer will cause his perpetual sorrow over the loss of his friend, Patroklos, but it also leads to the success of his own epic: he will achieve an epic fame that is perpetual, like his sorrow.[15] Achilles speaks about this fame already in *Iliad* 9.413, repeating a prophecy he says his mother had told him, but this prophecy cannot become a reality until the full story is told, that is, until the whole *Iliad* is performed. Such a performance already presupposes a repetition—in fact, an eternal series of repetitions. The words of Kierkegaard's *Repetition* can be applied anew: ". . . repetition and recollection are the same movement, except in opposite directions, for what is recollected has been, is repeated backward, whereas genuine repetition is recollected forward."[16]

---

[13] Cf. Page:133 and 166.
[14] Nagy 1996a:142–143.
[15] Ibid.
[16] Kierkegaard 1983:131

Eight

Now and Forever in Greek Drama and Ritual

Pat Easterling

The relation between drama and ritual is an absorbing and complex question, too vast even to begin to address in this short chapter. All I attempt here is a preliminary sketch of just one of its many aspects, the way drama and ritual—and more particularly Greek tragedy and ritual—relate to time.

I was first made to think about this years ago when I came across an account by the neurologist Oliver Sacks of a patient he called the "lost mariner," a man whose memory of a large portion of his past—and of his identity—had vanished, and whose state of mind was only free from deep disorientation when he was attending a religious service, watching a play, or taking part in a game.[1] Of course I am not going to be claiming that drama and ritual are "the same," but the essential point for me is that in both cases witnesses, or participants, are imaginatively engaged, in the immediate present ("playing time"), in an enactment which inhabits its own time. Nor, I take it, do witnessing and participating have to be seen as strictly separate categories. The Greek notion of *theōria* in fact comfortably accommodates both, and religious festivals were the normal context not only for drama competitions but also for other events that in the modern world would be classed as secular entertainment: athletic and musical contests, torch and boat races, beauty competitions. . . .[2] This privileged segment of time is characterized by the paradoxical fact that it always happens now and (in principle, at any rate) *it is infinitely repeatable*: Sophocles' *Antigone*, or the Orthodox Vespers, can be performed/celebrated as often as people choose, or judge appropriate, but each performance/celebration is autonomous, and the sense in which it is happening now is not crucially dependent on playing time: it doesn't matter whether say *Oedipus the King* runs, as on average it does, for an hour and a half, or (as in the

[1] Sacks 1985:ch. 2.
[2] The distinction drawn between the two activities by Rappaport (1999:135-137) strikes me as over-nice, at least in relation to Greek tradition, for which see n. 31 below.

famous Harvard production of 1881, when frequent costume changes were thought important)[3] for more than twice as long.

In order to explore the complex and even contradictory implications of "now" we need examples, and there is much to be said for choosing plays and ritual sequences that have displayed long-term staying power. Most of my instances from drama are chosen from Sophocles, whose plays have an exceptionally distilled or concentrated quality, enabling successive generations and different cultures to adopt them as their own. I have taken my examples of ritual from mainly Greek sources, without feeling the need to choose between pagan and Christian.

1. When Is "Now"?

I have already mentioned playing time, the most contingent, and for my purposes least significant, aspect, though it would be wrong to underestimate the contribution it may make towards the concentrated effect of the whole event. A Greek tragedy typically restricts the action it presents to what can be imagined as taking place within a day (allowing some temporal elasticity with the help of the choral odes), but since the actual playing time is nothing like as long there is always some element of compression and selectivity at work in the presentation of the story.[4] Then there is reception time. The meaning of a particular play or ritual sequence is bound to be in some sense conditioned by the historical circumstances in which it is performed, whether or not what is witnessed is a first performance or a repeat. A revival of *Oedipus the King*, for example, in a city recently afflicted by an epidemic might have new and special resonance (just as the celebration of the paean after the Athenian victory at Salamis in 480 BCE might have special meaning for the participants and witnesses, even if the words were the traditional paean words). Ideally the performance will feel urgently, even uniquely, relevant, and also escape being "time-bound." It goes without saying that the play or the ritual event must be able to mean differently for different times if it is to survive for any other purposes than antiquarian study. *Antigone* is the paradigm case of a play whose political resonances have been repeatedly re-defined and re-applied.[5]

---

[3] See the Appendix to Jebb's edition of the play (Cambridge: Cambridge University Press, 1883) for a detailed account of this production, which inaugurated the revival of Greek plays in the United States.

[4] See Lowe 2000:164–169 for an interesting discussion, from the narratological point of view, of the treatment of time in Greek tragedy.

[5] For examples see Steiner 1984. For the reception of other Greek tragedies see e.g. Hall 1999:261–306 and Hall et al. 2000.

From the point of view of the participants/audience the "now" of the performance can be felt to have particular application to the life and contemporary situation of the whole community, or it may have a strongly subjective focus, inviting
the witnesses to identify with the experiences of individuals as they go through the
process of self-discovery, or maturation, or the passage from life to death; one might
think of Neoptolemus' learning process or rite of passage in *Philoctetes*, or the final
journey and self-discovery of Oedipus in *Oedipus at Colonus*. Similarly, long ritual
sequences, as in a festival covering several days, like the Thesmophoria or the services of Holy Week in the Orthodox Church, can articulate the congregation's
changing emotional experience as fully as a sequence of scenes in a play or sequence
of plays in a tetralogy.

   This emphasis on process leads to thoughts about "now" as incorporating the
past, a richly complex construct. To start with the most obvious points: the "now"
of *Ajax* and *Antigone* is in a sense the heroic age—the time of the Trojan War, or of
the expedition of the Seven against Thebes—brought before our eyes, but what is
most interesting is the way this evocation is achieved through language.[6] The
language of tragedy, a combination of the high style of Homeric and lyric poetry
on the one hand and the "modern" vocabulary of the fifth century on the other,[7]
creates a very special "now," which is both close to the spectators and at the same
time distanced from them. Ritual typically works in a similar way, using "timeless"
language not contingent on changes of idiom, interspersed with references to
contemporary people and events. So the Orthodox liturgy uses the Greek of the
New Testament and the Fathers (and until a generation ago Anglican services used
English largely of the seventeenth-century),[8] conveying a sense that the *longue durée*
of a particular form of worship is condensed into "now."

   Another way in which past is merged with present is through the very action
of repeating—in speech, song, or gesture—the patterns of behavior that are
observed as normal and meaningful in a particular culture. Lamentation, for
example, can give the individual a means of expressing the emotions stirred by a
particular loss and at the same time recall communal traditions and values, often by
providing a context for all those present to re-live their own experiences within a

---

[6] A major difference between ancient and modern production styles is that ancient directors did not
use costumes and settings to suggest particular periods and places. Tragic costumes and masks did,
however, signify that the action was happening at a time and place other than the "now" of the audience in the theatre.

[7] Recently analyzed by Donald J. Mastronarde in his edition of Euripides (Mastronarde 2002:81–96).
For Sophocles see also Budelmann 2000.

[8] It may be donnish prejudice, but I can't help feeling that the banality of much modern English
reduces the intensity of ritual events that have been linguistically updated in this way.

151

shared framework, as in the *Iliad* (19.301–302) when Briseis' lament for Patroclus is echoed by the women: Πάτροκλον πρόφασιν, σφῶν δ' αὐτῶν κήδε' ἑκάστη ("For Patroclus, yes, but each woman also | For her own private sorrows").⁹ It is not surprising that this was a favorite pattern with the Greek tragedians, who regularly appropriated the vocabulary, music, and gestures of "real-life" laments for their fictive situations.¹⁰

There is a more strictly narratological point to be made, too, about the past. Both drama and ritual contain many narratives of a time further back in the past from the imagined "now" of the enactment: events recalled by Oedipus and Jocasta, for example, from their earlier lives, or the foundation stories evoked in ancient cult, or the biblical narratives read in Jewish and Christian services, which though formally past are also part of the "now" of the happening. In drama such narratives are sometimes there because they are part of the lived experience of the characters whose present actions we witness. Sometimes, indeed, they represent the persistent threat of what has been done in the past: the guilt and shame generated by the deeds of Oedipus (*Oedipus the King* 1297–1415) or the unavenged killing of Agamemnon by Clytemnestra (*Electra* 86–120), go on having reality for individuals and communities, and remain part of an extremely uncomfortable "now," until some way is found of dealing with them, if it ever is.¹¹

Other people's stories, too, told as consolation or as object lessons, have a continuing reality within the dramatic present, as when the chorus in *Antigone* remember Danae shut up in her tower as an analogy for Antigone on the point of being imprisoned as a bride of death (944–954). This sense of continuity, through which the past remains alive, may be achieved through the syntax: so the psalmist's recollection of the past is enacted by worshippers as a first-person recollection now: Ἐπὶ τῶν ποταμῶν Βαβυλῶνος ἐκεῖ ἐκαθίσαμεν, καὶ ἐκλαύσαμεν ἐν τῶι μνησθῆναι ἡμᾶς τῆς Σιών ("By the rivers of Babylon, there we sat down, yea, we wept when we remembered Zion" Psalm 136 [137] vs. 1).

There is a good illustration of this merging of times in John Campbell's account of the celebration of the "Great Week" of Easter by the Sarakatsani shepherds of Northern Greece in the 1960s and earlier.¹²

---

⁹ Trans. Lombardo 1997. I am grateful to Robert Garland for reminding me of the relevance of this Iliadic example. Cf. Alexiou 2002a:40–41.
¹⁰ See Alexiou 2002a; Loraux 1990; Segal 1993; Seaford 1994a; Foley 2001.
¹¹ Lowe (2000:167) notes the creative use of messenger speeches by the tragedians: "by 472 [the date of our earliest surviving tragedy] Aeschylus is already experimenting with a radical form of messenger tragedy in which the entire story is relegated to secondary narrative. In *Persians*, all significant actions are deep in the past or months in the future. . . ."
¹² Campbell 1964.

. . . something must be said of the dramatic atmosphere which makes this complex of rites and customs quite unlike any others in the religious calendar. There is an air both of anxiety and anticipation. The historical events which the liturgy commemorates on the different days of the week are not treated as such. They are re-lived, people participate in them. They know what will happen: He will rise again; yet they are anxious. The women discuss the events in the present or perfect tense as they would the local gossip at other times. As the drama proceeds the women in chorus make their simple and troubled comments, "They have seized Him," "He is being judged," "Now they are crucifying Him"; and finally, at the critical moment of the service on Easter Day, "Christ is risen."[13]

The same point can be made about sentiments as well as narrative. Memories of the past may be condensed into sayings, inherited wisdom which can help to put the events of a particular drama in an authoritative context of interpretation and thereby suggest the power of the culture to transmit the lessons of history—or at least to affirm a sense of continuity and identity. When Deianeira at the opening of *Women of Trachis* recalls the "old saying" that one can't tell whether a person has had good fortune or bad until he's dead (1–2), her purpose is to refute the old wisdom (she knows her own fortune is bad already), but it turns out to be corroborated by her own story: she finds out, by suffering, that she was wrong, since there was indeed much worse to come. Painful or reassuring, the old truths contribute to the process of learning through time, which leads to questions about the future.[14]

The lessons of time, from the viewpoint of the individual human being, are necessarily harsh: coming to terms with "now" entails finding ways of dealing both with the threats of the past and its memories and with the inevitability of change and death. What has to be learned, in effect, is that time is a tragic force: the gods may be unaging and eternal, and nature's rhythms may be self-renewing, but human life-stories all have an inescapable ending.[15] In their different ways, tragedy and ritual dramatize the process of learning through time, and often through suffering, partly (as I have been suggesting) by collapsing past and present and

---

[13] Campbell 1964:347–348. Charles Stewart, who kindly drew my attention to this passage, points out that the forms σταυρώθη and ἀνέστη help to bring out the past-present meaning: Christ is now on the Cross, Christ is now arisen.

[14] For other examples cf. *Antigone* 620–625; Aeschylus *Agamemnon* 750–762 and *Choephori* (Libation Bearers) 306–314. The staying power of many such "sayings" is well attested by their survival in anthologies throughout antiquity and the Byzantine period.

[15] Some relevant passages in Sophocles are *Ajax* 646–683; *Antigone* 582–625; *Oedipus the King* 1186–1215; *Oedipus at Colonus* 607–628 and 1211–1238.

drawing on the power of old traditions of behavior, old stories, and old sayings re-inscribed in "now" and re-enacted through performance, and partly by confronting the future and its implications.

It would be artificial, after all, to restrict the model of "now" to past and present, without finding a place for the future and all that it may entail. A contribution to a recent book on global ethics by Philip Allott, who writes from the viewpoint of an international lawyer, states the existential issue very clearly:[16]

> We, human beings and human societies, are processes of becoming. We are what we have been and what we will be. What we have been, what we call our *past*, exists nowhere else than as an idea in our minds. What we will be, what we call our *future*, exists nowhere else than as an idea in our minds. What we call the *present* is the vanishing-point between the past and the future, a mere idea within our minds of the relationship between what we have been and what we will be. In the continuous present of our idea of our becoming, we present the past and the future to ourselves as a contrast between an actuality and a potentiality.

> In the continuous present of our idea of becoming, we can constantly re-imagine the actuality of our past, through the mental processes which we call personal *memory* and *social history*, but that is the limit of the potentiality-for-us of the past. Otherwise the past is beyond our power. And we can imagine, and constantly re-imagine, the potentiality-for-us of the future, imagining what we could become, what we will be. But, in the case of the future, the human mind understands its relationship to the future in the form of a strange paradox . . . We can make the future but we cannot determine it. What will be will be what we do, but not only what we do. The future will also be made by the willing and acting of other human beings and other human societies, and by all other organic and inorganic processes of becoming, as they actualize themselves within the becoming of the universe of all-that-is. So it is that the strange paradox of our relationship to the future is also a strange fate.

Both Greek tragedy and the rituals of Greek tradition show familiarity with the problems posed by the unknowability and uncontrollability of the future, combined, as it always is, with the certainty of the end (in terrestrial terms, at least) for each individual, and they find room for these complexities within the models of "now" according to which they function. In formal terms, both plays and rites are strictly bounded, set apart from ordinary life and ordinary time by their privileged

[16] Allott 2001:61.

status as discrete performances, and they may seem almost by definition to demonstrate the inevitability of closure. But the very fact that they are infinitely repeatable opens up the possibility of challenging or denying that inevitability. Funeral rites, whether accompanying real-life events or mimicked in drama, are a good example of insistence on individual endings combined with an implied acknowledgement of the meaningfulness and potential for continuing life of the society that is there to perform the ritual.[17]

What particularly interests me is the way in which some plays, using the logic of ritual, go further, in fact toward a kind of escape from time's usual imperatives, by building the notion of "forever" into the sense of "now." Without moving away from tragedy in the direction of comic wish-fulfilment, it is easy to find examples of modifications, if not explicit challenges, to the inexorable forces of change and mortality, and it is worth giving a little attention to their implications.

2. "Forever"

A first and most obvious category is memorialization: the promise, or prospect, of future remembrance, through commemoration in the words of the play or ritual. Cults of ancestors, or individual heroes, or saints, by naming and recalling the revered figure(s) perpetuate their existence in an ever-repeated "now" and look to continuation into an indefinite future. Greek tragedy uses some of the same moves. The Chorus in Euripides' *Alcestis*, for example, reflect on the power of the goddess Necessity ('Ανάγκη) and advise Admetus to bear the loss of his wife, for no amount of lamentation will bring back the dead, and even the offspring of gods are subject to the laws of mortality. But Alcestis, they go on, should be honored, not with a tomb as the dead are, but with the kind of monument the gods are given. "And passers-by will say, 'This was a woman who died in place of her husband, and now she is a blessed daimon.[18] Hail, lady, and give good things'. This is how she will be greeted" (985–1005).

In some ways this is an untypical case, because the Chorus' reflections on the power of Necessity turn out to be promptly contradicted by events: their song is followed (1006) by the arrival of Heracles bringing back Alcestis from the dead. But

---

[17] Participants sometimes explicitly remark upon the contradictoriness of this kind of ritual. Hecuba, in Euripides' *Trojan Women*, decks her grandson's corpse for burial in an elaborately choreographed scene (1207–1250), which ends with instructions to take the child's corpse and bury it in its "poor tomb": "for he has received the garlands that belong to the dead. But I think it makes little difference to those who have died whether a person gets rich ornaments or not. This is just an empty display for the living" (1246–1250). For parallels in "real-life" rituals see Danforth 1982:148–149.

[18] For the range of meanings of *daimôn* see Burkert 1985a:179–181. On memorialization more generally: Garland 1992:156–157.

this does not invalidate their use of the motif of commemoration, which they have already exploited at 445–454, when they predict that Alcestis' fame will be perpetuated by singers at festivals at Sparta and Athens (i.e. all over Greece). Aeschylus uses it too: in *Eumenides* (The Kindly Ones) Orestes, gratefully responding to acquittal by Athena, imagines what "the Greeks" will say about him in the future, adding: "And, for my part, to your country and your people | I swear an oath that in future for all time shall prevail (τὸ λοιπὸν εἰς ἅπαντα πλειστήρη χρόνον), | before departing now for home: | that no ruler of my country shall come here | to bear against them the embattled spear! | For I myself, who shall then be in my tomb, | shall visit those that transgress the oath that I now swear | with misfortunes that shall reduce them to perplexity , | . . . | But if all goes well, and if they always honor | this city of Pallas with the spear of allies, | then they shall have more favor from myself" (762–774).[19]

Sophocles' surviving plays include nothing so explicit, but there are more oblique ways in which future remembrance and power are adumbrated. In *Oedipus at Colonus* there is repeated reference to the benefits that Oedipus will bring to the Athenians (and harm to their enemies) through the presence of his body after his death (72–93, 287–288, 389–390, 401–402, 409–411, 459–460, 576–582, 621–623, 1518–1538); by implication they will perpetuate both his fame and that of his adopted city.[20] The praise of Colonus, Attica and Athens, which the Chorus sing at 668–719, after Theseus has offered Oedipus a home in their land, reinforces this sense of future permanence by its insistence on "forever" (the keyword is αἰεί/αἰέν, 682, 688, 704). Everything that is special and blessed about the place—the never-failing vegetation, the streams of water, the sacred and indestructible olive—are all emblems of the self-renewing strength of Attica under the ever-watchful eyes of the gods. This assertion of confidence in an unlimited future is counterbalanced, but not negated, by the famous meditation at 1211–1248 on the inevitability of human suffering, old age and death: "Not to be born is best" (1224–1225). There is also a different kind of memorialization when Polynices, cursed by his father, asks his sisters to bury him if they go back to Thebes and find the curses fulfilled. "The praise you'll get for doing that," he says, "will be no less than what you are earning now from caring for our father" (1410–1412), a clear intertextual reference, surely, to the already established fame of *Antigone*, first produced over thirty years before the composition of *Oedipus at Colonus*, and to the future renown of both plays.[21]

[19] Translation by Lloyd-Jones 1970.
[20] Cf. (on *Ajax*) Segal 1995:23.
[21] Again, irrespective of whether Sophocles, or (more likely) the director of a revival, was responsible for the last few verses of *Oedipus the King* as transmitted (1524–1530), the text gives us at least a sense of what actors and audiences valued: the climactic naming of a paradigmatic figure, whose doing and suffering are there to be remembered, even though what his story illustrates is the truth of the old saying "Call no man happy till he's dead."

Sometimes it is the visible stage action that gives the strongest indication of a link with the future. As in ritual, so in drama, what is shown is immensely impor tant, and we need always to be on the watch for what the surviving texts imply about the use of space and gesture.[22] Processions at the ends of some plays can best be understood as leading to the future, as in *Ajax*, where the honorific funeral procession, set in train by Teucer's speech at the end of the play, has been thought to carry intimations of future hero cult in Attica.[23] *Women of Trachis*, too, ends with a procession, which is to escort the dying Heracles to his pyre on the top of Mt Oeta; the precise implications of this scene may be disputed, but there is no doubt that it is making claims for the continuing significance of Heracles and his cult.[24] In *Oedipus at Colonus* the climactic moment when the blind old man leads the way into the grove is strongly marked in the text (1540–1550, 1586–1589) as a highly significant piece of action, leading to the mysterious event (the divine voice summoning him, and his subsequent disappearance) that will guarantee his posthumous power, but the vanishing itself is not even described: all the audience learns (at third hand) is the unspoken reactions of Theseus, its only spectator, as reported by the messenger: ". . . after a short while we turned and looked back, and Oedipus was no longer anywhere to be seen, but we saw the king holding his hand in front of his face to shade his eyes, as though he had had some terrible vision that he could not bear to look at. Then soon after we saw him salute the earth and the sky, the gods' domain, in the same prayer" (1647–1655). These are not "happy endings" in which time's destructive power is negated or the uncontrollability of the future forgotten, but the model of time they work with differs from that suggested by the endings of (say) *Antigone* or *Electra*, where the focus, respectively, is on learning the implications of one's actions (*Antigone* 1334–1353) and on the compulsions imposed by the logic of revenge (*Electra* 1483–1510).[25]

There is a general point here about resistance to closure: the enactment that is (partially) witnessed remains to be completed in people's imaginative lives, including those of generations to come. In literary terms this makes room for the reception process, and it helps to explain the adaptability of these tragedies to different periods and cultures. In ritual the question of belief is more pressing and the affirmation more explicit: "now" must merge with "forever" if the truth that is

---

[22] See in particular Rehm 2002.

[23] See Burian 1972; Easterling 1993; Henrichs 1993; Rehm 2002, especially pp. 137–138.

[24] See Easterling 1981; Stinton 1986; Roberts 1988; Holt 1989.

[25] The ending of *Electra* is strikingly unresolved: the play ends even before the death of Aegisthus, whose reference to the "present and future evils of the Pelopidae" (τά τ' ὄντα καὶ μέλλοντα Πελοπιδῶν κακά) that the house must inevitably see draws attention to the "strange fate," whatever it may be, that the future holds.

being represented is to have perceived continuing power. Over and over again the rite must be performed, and each time whatever is affirmed now must be affirmed for the future as well if the rite is to have efficacy: εἰς τοὺς αἰῶνας τῶν αἰώνων, "For ever and ever."

This takes me on to prophecy. Many tragedies use prophecy, often pronounced by a divine, or divinely inspired, authority, to link the present with the future, as when Athena in Aeschylus' *Eumenides* founds the Areopagus, which will be the Athenians' court of justice "in the future forever" (ἔσται δὲ καὶ τὸ λοιπὸν Αἰγέως στράτῳ αἰεὶ δικαστῶν τοῦτο βουλευτήριον 683– 684), or when Artemis at the end of Euripides' *Hippolytus* promises him a commemorative ritual, to be performed "through long age," "forever," by girls before their marriage: δι' αἰῶνος μακροῦ (1426), ἀεί (1428). There is no need, of course, for confident forecasts expressed in the future indicative to be taken as any more literally true than any other statement in a dramatic fiction; but whatever their significance for the "theological" interpretation of their respective plays,[26] they have a very clear function in relation to time, since the future referred to in these prophetic words was familiar to the original audience through their collective experience of the historical present and memory of the past (reception time). The Areopagus, founded by Athena in *Eumenides*, was a familiar institution for Aeschylus' contemporaries and for many succeeding generations, just as the Troezenian ritual in honor of Hippolytus seems to have been well known to Athenians (and was no doubt made even better known through the influence of Euripides' play).

Less precisely bound to history, and perhaps all the more easily transferable to other times and places because they are less explicit, are those expressions that lay claim to "forever" through wish, blessing or prayer, using the optative (and sometimes the imperative) rather than the indicative mood. So Oedipus, as he sets off on the final stage of his last journey, addresses Theseus with these words: "Dearest of strangers, may you have good fortune, yourself and this land and your followers, and in prosperity remember me when I am dead, for your success forever": ἀλλά, φίλτατε ξένων, αὐτός τε χώρα θ' ἥδε πρόσπολοί τε σοὶ εὐδαίμονες γένοισθε, κἀπ' εὐπραξίᾳ μέμνησθέ μου θανόντος εὐτυχεῖς ἀεί (*Oedipus at Colonus* 1552–1555). What is important to emphasize here is the extreme fragility of the human capacity to remember and to act on that knowledge. Oedipus' posthumous power, as hero, to help Athens will depend (as he has explained, 1518–1539) on the ability of the successors of Theseus to pass on the secret of his burial place at the time of their own deaths, as one succeeds another. So it is appropriate to pray and exhort, but hardly to assert the certainty of "forever." At the same

---

[26] Such predictions in Euripides have been very variously interpreted; see Dunn 1996.

time the wish or prayer can be understood by an audience watching the play as having relevance to them and their community.[27]

What I have argued so far has been fairly pragmatic. I have suggested that when a tragedian (and I have been thinking particularly of Sophocles) built the idea of the future, at its strongest the idea of eternity, into "now" he might do so by looking forward to the continuing presence of certain heroes in cult, to the continuing familiarity and significance of his plays in the experience of audiences, or to the (hoped-for) continuing existence of the community itself and its institutions. From time to time, one might add, the tragedians seem to use the language of mystic experience and to draw on the imagery of mystery ritual.[28] The relevance of such language to the notion of "forever" is that it is designed to efface time, change, and death by linking the here with the beyond. For the Eleusinian or Dionysiac initiate the revelation of what is to come after death is expressed in terms of present being, through what theologians call "realised eschatology."[29] One of the images that lends itself best to such interpretation is that of the journey, the path traveled both by the initiand and by the tragic sufferer.[30] In *Oedipus at Colonus* this constitutes the dominant image of the action: Oedipus travels on a perplexing journey, finds his mysterious destination, leads the way into the sacred grove, disappears from mortal view and achieves what is claimed to be a specially favored passing from life to death, but also remains in Attica as a protective presence. If this pattern can be seen as offering some echo of the experience or the aspirations of the initiand we may perhaps want to see it as one more hint of how a drama can offer escape from time's normal constraints. But I would hesitate to press the point further and insist on a specifically "mystic meaning" as the key to understanding; whatever intimations the plays may offer of the beyond, or of the escape from time, they do not lose sight of the tragic realities that shape human lives, and they do not rely on a cryptic interpretation.

There is much to be said, after all, for a humbler and more agnostic way of thinking about what might in some sense go beyond "now," by attending to the shared response of witnesses to performance/enactment. This point of view emphasizes the importance of the community's share in "now," whether as audience or congregation, or (better) as *theôroi* at a festival, the most appropriate model for the

---

[27] Particularly when a chorus performs a lyric sequence of prayer or blessing, the relevance of this performance for the audience on any given occasion (i.e. in reception time) is not difficult to sense. See, e.g., Aeschylus *Eumenides* 916–1020.

[28] For mystery language in Sophocles see Seaford 1994b, and on *Oedipus at Colonus*, Calame 1998. More generally on drama and mysteries: Bowie 1993; Seaford 1994a; Segal 1997; Lada-Richards 1999.

[29] Robbins borrows this term for a discussion of Pindar's third *Olympian* (Robbins 1984:219–228).

[30] See Lada-Richards 1999:87–90 for the journey in the context of mystery cult.

Pat Easterling

ancient material.[31] The essential point here, and the factor that makes it relevant to tragedy in particular, is the uncertainty of the link between "now" and "forever," given our necessarily limited grasp of the ways in which we as human beings relate to present and future. Belief in the continuity between "now" and "forever" calls, after all, for faith of some kind, in the divine, the community, or humanity more generally. Shared witnessing may indeed be the only thing that continues to make sense.

৯

The fact that the tragedians modeled some of their most intense sequences on "real" ritual, borrowing freely from patterns familiar in their contemporary world,[32] is confirmation—if confirmation is needed—that they were very well aware of ritual's power, and often took their cue from it. A particularly important aspect of this power, I have argued, was the special relationship of both ritual and drama to time, and the degree of concentration that the co-existence of past, present, and future in the dramatic "now" could achieve. Returning to Allott's image of the present as "vanishing-point" (p. 154 above), we can see the value of this kind of concentration for the suggestive enactment of one of the most problematic aspects of human experience.*

[31] For the importance of the witnessing community see Sourvinou-Inwood 1994.
[32] Cf. Easterling 1993; Henrichs 1994–95; Friedrich 1996; Lloyd-Jones 1998.
* I am grateful to Robert Garland and Charles Stewart for comments and suggestions on this paper.

160

Nine

Gendering the Athenian Funeral:
Ritual Reality and Tragic Manipulations

Christiane Sourvinou-Inwood

1. Problematik and Methodology

Tragedies commonly deploy ritual material, but they do not "describe" rituals. They manipulate ritual material in various ways to construct meanings for the tragedians' contemporary audiences, who shared the same ritual knowledge, and so registered changes from the norm as manipulations; for example, they registered a particular articulation of a ritual as a transgressive version of normality and this contributed to the construction of the perception that the world of the play was seriously disordered[1]—while a modern reader may be in danger of explicitly or implicitly assuming that this was a ritually acceptable variation of normal ritual procedure. Clearly, in order to understand how the deployment and manipulation of rituals constructed meanings for the audiences who shared the tragedians' ritual knowledge it is necessary to reconstruct as much as possible of that knowledge. More specifically, since what may appear to be a small deviation would register strongly in the eyes of the members of the community that produced a cultural artifact[2]— especially when it involves ritual, where the norm reflects the society's religious and cultural assumptions as well as common practices—it is necessary to reconstruct, and focus on, the details, and not only the main lines, of the ritual involved before attempting to make sense of the ways in which its articulation contributed to the creation of meaning.

First, in this chapter, I will explore one small aspect of Athenian ritual reality, which also involves assumptions concerning gender: the role of women in the death ritual; for this ritual element is often misunderstood in modern discourses, where

---

[1] For some discussions of manipulations of rituals in the creation of tragic meanings, see especially Vidal-Naquet 1972:133–158; Vernant 1972:99–131; Easterling 1988:87–109.

[2] See Sourvinou-Inwood 1991:12–13 with bibliography on iconographical divergences.

the specific roles of female participants are sometimes (implicitly or explicitly) blurred into generic, and so misleading, notions about the general involvement of women in the death ritual.[3] I will then consider some of the ways in which this element was manipulated in different tragedies to construct different meanings. Clearly, to avoid circularity and cross contamination from potentially fallacious assumptions, the reconstruction of the ritual reality must be kept separate from the tragic readings. In any case, and more generally, the fact that tragedies manipulate ritual material, and sometimes create transgressive variants, entails that tragic passages cannot legitimately be used as evidence in the attempted reconstruction of Athenian ritual practices; the methodologically neutral strategy is to disregard tragic passages in any such reconstruction, and consider the tragic articulations after the ritual has been reconstructed from other sources; that is, consider the relationship between the two, not simply absorb the reconstruction as part of the reading, but explicitly consider how that reconstruction relates to the reading of the passage and the tragedy that would be constructed if this ritual element is left out, replaced by a semantic blank.

Such judgments are inevitable culturally determined, and some modern scholars believe it is pointless to attempt what I am advocating here, a systematic attempt to reconstruct as much as possible the ancient perceptual filters and so the parameters within which ancient audiences constructed meanings. This postmodernist privileging of unknowability is symbiotic with the privileging of the modern reader's own subjective responses—which in fact postmodernist critics do not always present as such, for they often blur the distinction between their subjective modern readings and the ancient meanings, explicitly or implicitly making claims of "truth." I believe that this postmodernist approach, and the mindcast it has more widely generated, is mistaken; for, I have argued,[4] it is possible to reconstruct the main parameters that shaped the process of meaning creation by the ancient audiences in performance. Critics who do not accept this should be prepared to accept that the Athenians thought that the tragic characters believed that deities in epiphany were holograms. No critic would accept this, because it involves concepts alien to the Greeks. In other words, even postmodernists implicitly rely on the notion that we *can* reconstruct *some* ancient meanings if we take account of the ancient assumptions.

It is, then, impossible to deny that we can reconstruct at least some of the parameters determining the creation of meaning by the ancient audiences, who had

---

[3] For example, the view (which, I hope to show here, is mistaken) that in Sophocles' *Antigone* it was Antigone's duty to bury her brother was most recently restated by Dillon 2002:288.
[4] See especially Sourvinou-Inwood 2003 passim; see also Sourvinou-Inwood 1989a:134–148.

shared the tragedians' cultural assumptions and constructed meanings through perceptual filters shaped by those assumptions. For example, we know that in Greek mentality incest and cannibalism are negatively perceived, elements of negative disorder; so, if incest or cannibalism occur in the context in which the death ritual appears, we can be certain that that context was, at the very least partly, and in ways to be determined, negatively disordered. So, to reconstruct meanings as close as possible to those constructed by the ancient audiences we must attempt to reconstruct, as far as possible, the perceptual filters shaped by the cultural assumptions which those audiences shared with the tragedians, or at least reconstruct the important parameters that shaped them, and so the parameters within which the process of meaning creation by the ancient audiences took place. In this case, we need to reconstruct the ritual knowledge pertaining to the role of women in Athenian funerals from non-tragic sources.

Different types of evidence are available for the reconstruction of that ritual knowledge: texts containing legal prescriptions concerning women's participation in the death ritual; texts, especially forensic speeches, containing references to the death ritual and to rites of commemoration;[5] inscriptions, epitaphs, and funerary regulations; and images, representing aspects of the death ritual and the commemoration of the dead. Each of these types of evidence must be read in its own terms; for example, the images must not be implicitly assumed to be representing a documentary record of the ritual; their reading must be informed by the recognition of their character as imaginary articulations based on selections shaped by assumptions shared by the vase painters and their public. The evidence from the orators is most important in this reconstruction. The forensic context is, of course, far from neutral, but forensic contexts differ in one very significant way from those of the multivocal and ambiguous tragic passages: the fact that we know the function of the discourse in each speech entails that the parameters of manipulation can, up to a point, be reconstructed with a certain degree of certainty. The goals of the speaker, the presentation that is most conducive to the achievement of these goals, can be seen to be generating certain pulls in certain directions and to be conducive to certain types of manipulation and not to others; and, of course, for the forensic manipulation to work, the references to ritual matters, in however biased a manner they were presented, had to make sense in terms of the jurors' ritual knowledge and assumptions.[6]

---

[5] The fact that the evidence of the orators is much later than the tragedies is not a problem here; for in fourth-century perceptions the legislation pertaining to women's participation in the death ritual was ancient, ascribed to Solon. And, we shall see, funerary regulations passed at Ioulis in the late fifth-century under Athenian influence were comparable to that "Solonian" legislation.

[6] See Pelling 2000:17 for the type of questions that we can ask of these texts.

2. Reconstructing Ritual Realities

Legal regulations express and enforce a society's normative ideology, and so can help us reconstruct some aspects of that ideology. That is, though we do not know what, if anything, Athenian funerary legislation prescribed on the question of the gender of the person performing the burial, the legal prescriptions concerning the participation of women in the death ritual to which we do have access are articulated by the assumptions which determined all relevant prescriptive behavior, and so had shaped all aspects of women's participation in that ritual; thus, if correctly reconstructed, those assumptions can help us determine the specific roles of women in the burial.

The participation of women in the funeral was different from that of men, for it was restricted by law. According to pseudo-Demosthenes 43.62 a law ascribed to Solon prescribes, among other things, that at the funeral the men are to walk at the front and the women at the back and that women under sixty were not allowed to take part in the *prothesis*, the laying out of the corpse, or in the funeral, unless they were within a certain degree of kinship, *entos anepsiadôn*, first cousins once removed or second cousins or closer. Finally, that no woman was allowed to enter the deceased's house after the funeral, whatever their age, unless they were *entos anepsiadôn.*[7] There is no equivalent limitation for men. In the funeral procession men and women are spatially separated, with men occupying the hierarchically superior position, at the front. The fact that women had an hierarchically, and so symbolically, inferior position in the last stage of the death ritual makes it prima facie unlikely that a woman could have played the most important role, person who buries, in that part of the death ritual.

Late sources ascribe to Solon further prescriptions pertaining to female participation in death rituals. Cicero reports that women were forbidden to wail or lacerate their cheeks.[8] Plutarch's *Life of Solon* gives an extensive account—shaped through perceptual filters which cannot be assumed, and indeed are highly unlikely, to have been the product of the same death related assumptions as those of archaic or classical Athens, despite Plutarch's comment that most of these practices are also forbidden by "our laws."[9] According to this account, the funerary legislation of Epimenides had paved the way for that of Solon.[10] Epimenides made mourning

---

[7] On Solonian and other funerary legislation see most recently Dillon 2002:271 and n.16 with bibliography; Sourvinou-Inwood 1983:47–48; Sourvinou-Inwood 1995a:421, 439–440 cf. 370–371, 177–178n287; Sourvinou-Inwood 1997a:155–156, 163n63.

[8] Cicero *De legibus* 2.64 (cf. 59).

[9] Plutarch *Solon* 21.5.

[10] I have discussed elsewhere Epimenides' association with Athens (Sourvinou-Inwood 1997a:155–159). Here, I will say that refractions of a protracted crisis in the late seventh and early sixth century, and of the purification and religious reforms that followed, became crystallized in the tradition around Epimenides and Solon.

Gendering the Athenian Funeral

milder and suppressed the harsh and barbaric practices in which most women had indulged before.[11] Death related ritual behavior became more *praos* (mild, gentle)—contrasted to *sklêron*, hard, harsh (and *barbarikon*), explicitly associated with women before the reforms. Solon, in Plutarch's account,[12] legislated on women's public appearances, both during the death ritual and during festivals, controlling disorderly and undisciplined behavior; after mentioning restrictions on what women should wear and carry in public and the conditions in which they were allowed to travel at night, Plutarch mentions the prohibition of self-wounding, without specifying self-wounding by women—unlike Cicero; Solon also forbade the use of set lamentations and the lamenting for someone at another's funeral, the sacrifice of an ox at the grave, expensive grave clothes, and the visiting of graves of non family members except during the burial.

From an anthropological perspective, these regulations, most notably the prohibition of self-wounding, and what Plutarch describes as a change from harsh to mild behavior, lowered the ritual's tone; what is being described is a change from a death ritual with a high emotional tone to one with a lowered tone—perceived through the perceptual filters of a later commentator who considered the high-tone ritual inferior and barbaric because his own perceived ideality excluded emotional excess. In reality, the range of acceptable and/or prescriptive emotions at death rituals varies greatly in different societies, depending on whether that society over-plays the externalization of grief, in a high-tone death ritual, or underplays it, in a low-tone one.[13]

Another set of rules in which the participation of women in the death ritual is restricted, a funerary regulation of late fifth-century date from Ioulis in Keos,[14] was probably passed under Attic influence.[15] Besides setting out various other ritual rules, this regulation, like Solon's laws, involved a lowering of the ritual's emotional tone, since the funeral procession had to be silent and the bier covered,[16] and it also restricted the participation of women—as well the expenses allowed for the funeral. After the burial no woman is to enter the house of the dead except those who are polluted by the death, that is, the deceased's mother, wife, sisters, daughters, and in addition only a few others. Lines 18–20 are considered problematic, but in my view there can be little doubt that this regulation is prescribing that those women who

[11] Plutarch *Solon* 12.4.
[12] Plutarch *Solon* 21.4–5.
[13] See for rituals of high or low emotional tone and the complex ways they relate to actual emotions in different societies Huntington and Metcalf 1979:23–43.
[14] Sokolowski 1969:188–191, no. 97.
[15] Humphreys 1980:99. See also Garland 1985:37, 41–42; Dillon 2002:272–273.
[16] Sokolowski 1969:188, no. 97.10–12.

165

took part in the funeral must leave the grave before the men, that the men stay behind.[17] This would fit the perception that it was appropriate that the women's role in the burial should be limited and circumscribed. Be that as it may, it is clear that here also restrictions on the participation of women in the death ritual are set out in the context of regulations which lowered the ritual's emotional tone.

There was, then, a strong connection in all these regulations between the lowering of the tone of the death ritual and the prohibition of certain types of female behavior and/or restrictions in the role of women.

After his account of Solon's legislation Plutarch added[18] that most of these practices that it forbade are also forbidden by "our laws," which also specify that those (*tous*) who do such things are punished by the *gunaikonomoi*, the magistrates who supervise women,[19] because such mourning is unmanly and womanish. So in the perceptions articulating this account mourning practices like self-wounding, though womanly, may be indulged in by men, but they are forbidden to all. Plutarch presents this as more of an individual failing than a gender-based practice; indeed, in his time, when such acts were transgressive, that is what they were. But in the death rituals that preceded the legislation that made them transgressive such acts were first gender based, and second, and correlatively, not a spontaneous show of emotion by individuals, but symbolic behavior regulated by society, which channeled grief when that was experienced, generated it when not, and in any case amplified it as part of a release mechanism leading to adjustment. As we saw, the range of acceptable and/or prescriptive emotions at death rituals varies. Self-wounding belongs to high-tone rituals, silence during the funeral procession to not very high-tone ones. I argued elsewhere that archaic funerary regulations that lowered the tone of the death ritual and restricted its encroachment in the life of the community reflected, and were part of, a partial shift in the collective attitudes towards death that made it desirable to limit death's invasion of life.[20] In that context high-tone death rituals came to be perceived as undesirable, and became transgressive; new regulations restricted the participation of women and forbade certain ritual practices that the latter had formerly performed.

In order to determine what, if anything, these changes can tell us about the role of women in the death ritual that resulted from the changes, and the perceptions associated with it, we need to consider the relevant practices, most notably the self-wounding, as part of a high-tone ritual in which such practices were gender-

---

[17] See Humphreys 1980:99n3; Garland 1985:37.
[18] Plutarch *Solon* 21.5.
[19] On *gunaikonomoi*, see now Dillon 2002: 290–1.
[20] Sourvinou-Inwood 1983:47–48; Sourvinou-Inwood 1995a:440; cf. 370–371, 421, and n. 13; cf. also 177–178n287.

based, and try to reconstruct, as much as possible, the meanings that those elements, and the restrictions on their performance and on the participation of women, had in the eyes of the archaic and classical Greeks.

Self-wounding appears as part of a system of ritual practices in the death rituals reflected in the Homeric poems. The use of the Homeric poems in attempts to reconstruct the ritual practices and representations of historical societies presents serious problems. The relationships between texts and rituals and their associated mentalities is especially problematic in the case of the Homeric poems, which are the end product of a long tradition of oral poetry which began probably in the Mycenaean, conceivably in the Early "Dark Age" period. The world they describe, its material culture and social institutions, does not have a correlative in a real historical society, it is a conflated picture made up of elements that had originally belonged to different societies, from different periods, which were combined over the centuries during which the epic material was deployed and redeployed, expanded, compressed, and modified, by the bards who handled it, with each generation making sense of, and manipulating, that material through their own perceptual filters. The fact that the world of the poems was made up of elements that did not belong together in the audiences' realities helped distance it from that of the present, and this distancing helped construct the heroic age, which was a time in which sometimes men walked with gods. But the practices that make up the death ritual are consistent throughout, and appear deeply embedded in, the epics. The minimum that may be inferred from this is that these practices and mentalities had characterized the societies of eighth-century Ionia; the maximum is that they had characterized all the societies that had contributed to the creation of the Homeric poems over the centuries.

In the complex death ritual articulated in the Homeric poems men and women play different roles of different weight in each of its three phases.[21] In the first phase, immediately after the death, the mourners express violent grief. The women closest to the deceased fling themselves on the corpse, shriek and wail, beat their breasts, disarrange their clothes, tear their breasts, neck, face, and hair.[22] Male relatives and close male friends roll about in filth and put filth on their head, neck, and face.[23] Friends, and others not immediately affected, wail and lament. Then the corpse is washed, anointed, and clothed in clean clothes before it is laid out on a bier.[24] Both the women's self-wounding and the men's self-defilement are forms of self-aggression which allowed the mourners to release sorrow and anger, externalizing the grief in

---

[21] I discussed the Homeric death ritual in Sourvinou-Inwood 1983:37–43.
[22] See e.g. *Iliad* 24.710ff., *Iliad* 19.282ff., *Odyssey* 8.523–530.
[23] *Iliad* 18.22–31; 22.405ff; 24. 160ff.
[24] *Iliad* 18.346–355; 24.580–590; cf. also *Iliad* 7.421–431; 16.679–680.

concrete, but also symbolic, terms, as wound and dirt, and separating the mourners from normality and order—a separation which reflects the many-faceted separations brought about by death. The dirt which the men take on is a symbol, a material manifestation, of the pollution which attaches to death. This material symbolization allows the abstract concept of pollution to be articulated and manipulated, first embraced and eventually removed.[25] But the self-aggression displayed by the women takes a more extreme form, self-wounding, together with the disarrangement of dress (which in the Greek representations expresses the notion of disorder[26]) and flinging themselves on the corpse. Like self-wounding, flinging oneself on the corpse was not an uncontrolled emotional gesture but a regulated ritual act in a high-tone death ritual that could channel and express the traumatic feelings generated by the death, and generate or amplify such feelings when they were not felt, or not felt strongly. It also involved intimate physical contact with the corpse, which was perceived both as the metonymic sign for the whole deceased, and as decomposing matter symbolizing death and corruption.[27] Thus the women's gesture involved also their embracing death very directly. Self-wounding, besides providing emotional release and exter-nalizing grief and the symbolic separation of the mourners from normality, also articulated a partial identification with the deceased, objectifying the stated wish to join him. It is another manifestation of the mourners' embracing of death.[28]

Clearly, women embraced death, corruption, disorder, and pollution much more extremely and directly than men. This is correlative with the system of symbolic classification articulating Greek representations, in which the male-female opposition was one of the main axes representing other oppositions, and in which women stood for the other pole of the qualities which ideality associated with the male. Hence, where the male stood for, and was symbolically associated with, order, women represented disorder; the male was symbolically associated with purity, the female represented pollution. This is not to say that women were perceived as inher-ently and inescapably disordered and polluted; there was a spectrum of representa-tions, at one end of which it was believed that women were more prone to disorderly behavior, and there was always the danger of a woman being out of control, and this notion is correlative with pollution, and one, but not the only, way of representing women was as having a certain "affinity" with pollution.[29] Correlatively, when a

---

[25] On Greek ideas and practices concerning pollution, see Parker 1983. On the concept of pollution, see Douglas 1970. On material symbolization see Leach 1976:37–38.

[26] See e.g. Euripides *Phoenissai* 1485–1492. See Mastronarde 1994:553, 562–565 *ad loc.* For Andromache casting down her headdress on Hector's death, cf. also Griffin 1980:2.

[27] Metonymic sign: in Leach's terminology (Leach 1976, especially 31).

[28] For other cultures, cf. Salisbury 1965:63.

[29] See Parker 1983:100–101. Somewhat less nuanced is Carson 1990; see especially 158–160.

symbolic contrast was made which set into place this opposition order-disorder, order and purity belonged with, and were represented by, the male, disorder and pollution by the female.

Thus, the values of disorder, pollution, danger, and death articulated in the first phase of the death ritual are correlative with, and at the same time reinforced by, the women's dominant role. For women carried the main ritual weight in this first part of the death ritual, as seen both in their intense embracing of death and pollution and in the fact that they normally wash, anoint, and clothe the corpse, manipulating the focus of pollution and death. Patroklos' corpse was washed by the Myrmidons,[30] reflecting the assumption of kinship roles by companions in a military situation; but men never lacerated themselves, this was done for Patroklos by captive women, especially Briseis. This shows that while washing, which involves removing the pollution, could be done by men, self-wounding, which involved the strongest identification with the deceased, could only be performed by women. In this part of the death ritual, then, the pattern of ritual behavior involved accepting and embracing death and playing up its symbolic attributes, such as pollution, disorder and separation.

In the second part of the death ritual, the *prothesis*, the ritual weight was carried equally by men and women.[31] In the third part, which involved the funeral procession, the cremation and/or rites at the grave, and the burial of the bones or corpse,[32] the ritual weight is carried by men, correlatively with the fact that men symbolically represented order: as the plot of the ritual moves from playing up disorder and pollution and embracing death toward purging pollution, separation from death and restoration of a new order, the separation of the corpse, the setting up of a grave monument and the reintegration of the surviving group, the role of the actors on whom the values of pollution disorder and embracing of death had primarily drifted, the women, becomes less important, while the role of the men, who had also at the beginning embraced pollution, disorder, and death, but much less strongly, and who were symbolically associated with order, became dominant. These differential gender roles are deeply embedded not only in ritual, but also in the cultural assumptions articulating the Homeric epics, as is illustrated by the fact that when reference is made to mourners in the two epics these are always women, when to burial it is men that are mentioned.[33]

This consideration of the death rituals reflected in the Homeric poems strongly suggests, I submit, that women were not allowed to bury in classical

[30] *Iliad* 18.346–355.
[31] See Sourvinou-Inwood 1983:39.
[32] *Iliad* 23.155 ff., 249 ff.; 24.790 ff.
[33] See e.g. *Odyssey* 3.260–261; *Iliad* 11.394–395, 22.82–89, 18.339–340, 16.674–675.

Athens. For the fact that women embraced death and pollution much more strongly, and were more closely associated with those values, which were stronger in the earlier parts of the ritual, while men were symbolically aligned with order and played the dominant role in the final part of the ritual, which aimed at achieving the restoration of a new order and separation from death, entails that there is a very serious objection to the notion of a woman performing a burial: the values associated with women were not the values that were desired for, and enacted in, the final part of the ritual, the funeral procession and burial; those belonged to the earlier part of the ritual and they needed to be purged in the final part, which brought about a new order, in which the deceased is firmly separated from the living, among whom a new order is restored. This fits with the fact that the participation of women in the funeral was restricted by law.

That the same symbolic values and comparably correlative ritual behavior are associated with the two genders in archaic and classical Athens as in the world(s) reflected in the Homeric poems is shown by a series of arguments. First, we shall see that what evidence is available for the classical period shows that the roles of the two genders in the Athenian ritual were very similar to those in the Homeric death rituals. Second, the fact that funerary legislation forbade the self-wounding of women shows that in Athens also the practice of this extreme form of embracing death and pollution had been gender based, and practiced by women. Third, in the Athenian images of the archaic and classical period violent display of grief is limited to women.[34] Women are sometimes shown tearing their hair on the sixth-century black-figure plaques used to decorate the graves[35] and vases, and sometimes also in classical red-figure, and, to a much lesser extent, in white ground images, but never, to my knowledge, men. In representations of the *prothesis* men often appear in a formal group, apparently performing a lament and usually further away from the corpse; women surround the corpse, often touch it and tear their hair. Of course, the images are imaginary articulations, but the function of the plaques that decorated graves, and of at least some of the vases—those known to have been found in (or to be exclusively destined for) a grave context—indicates that those cannot have been transgressive manipulations. Indeed, this situation in the images is correlative with the fact that references to mourning in the orators seem limited to cutting one's hair and wearing black when it comes to men.[36] Self-wounding is not infrequently mentioned in tragedy, always as an action performed by women, and in

---

[34] On these images, see most recently Dillon 2002:275–288. See also Shapiro 1991:629–656.
[35] On funerary plaques, see Sourvinou-Inwood 1995a:218–219 and bibliography in n. 428; Dillon 2002:275–279, 364n31 with bibliography.
[36] See e.g. Isaeus 4.7.

contexts that suggest that this ritualeme is represented as normality.[37] This appearance of a practice which was forbidden by Athenian law, but which characterized the paradigmatic articulation of the heroic age in the Homeric poems, may be part of the tragedies' distancing from everyday normality, to the heroic age.[38] But this is less relevant to our concerns than the fact that when such behavior is articulated it is always ascribed to women—who are therefore represented as being associated with the same symbolic values as in the epics.

Another argument in favor of the view that the consideration of the Homeric death rituals strongly suggests that women were not allowed to bury in classical Athens is that since women's participation was greater in high-tone death rituals, and since the Athenian death ritual had a lower tone than the death rituals articulated in the Homeric epics, indeed the lowering of its tone was correlative with the restrictions in the participation and role of women, the fact that women did not bury in the Homeric death rituals entails that they would be most unlikely to bury in the Athenian death ritual.

Before I consider further the evidence from classical Athens I will try to set out the framework within which the question of women's participation in the death ritual should be considered, by trying to define what was considered to be normality and then the modalities of deviation from that normality, in order to try to determine, insofar as it is possible, the parameters of the acceptable.

Paradigmatic normality was for a man, and a woman, to be buried by their son, who also performed the *nomizomena*, the customary rites. Sons were obliged by law to bury their parents and perform the *nomizomena*;[39] not fulfilling this obligation was a very serious failing.[40] The mentality underlying this paradigmatic situation is the notion that ideally a son replaced his father as head of the *oikos*, the household, and in his membership of the *polis* and its subdivisions, and he would perform ritual activities in place of the father.[41] The son replacing the father as head of the *oikos* and the performance of the burial rites for the father by the son go together; this performance, among other things, articulates ritually the replacement of the father by the son as head of the *oikos*, and so also the continuity of the *oikos* that offsets and redeems the individual discontinuity of its successive heads. When a man did not have a son he often adopted one to be his heir, so that his *oikos* would

---

[37] See for example, Aeschylus *Choephori* (Libation Bearers) 22–28; Euripides, *Helen* 1089; *Suppliants* 50–51, 76–77, 87; *Electra* 146–149; *Phoenissai* 1351.

[38] See on the various and varying distances between the world of the tragedies and the world of the audiences Sourvinou-Inwood 2003:15–66.

[39] See e.g. Demosthenes 24.107; cf. Xenophon, *Memorabilia* 2.2.13.

[40] See, for example: [Demosthenes] 25. 54; Dinarchus 2.8.

[41] See e.g. Isacus 9.13: *anth' hautou*, in his place.

Christiane Sourvinou-Inwood

not become deserted, and to look after him in life, bury him and perform the *nomizomena* for him after his death. Contexts involving adoption, which mention what were perceived to have been the most important duties that a son owed his father, show that these concepts of continuation of the *oikos*, inheritance, care in life, burial and performance of the *nomizomena*, are often intextricably connected.[42]

A passage in Isaeus[43] presents the proper performance of the *nomizomena* for the deceased as virtually equivalent to giving him a son to perform them. The speaker claims that his opponents had inherited their brother's estate but did not give him one of their sons in (posthumous) adoption and his *oikos* became deserted. Having seen how shamefully they had treated their brother he asks, how could the man whose estate is at issue, Apollodoros, have expected them to perform the *nomizomena* for him, who was their cousin, not their brother? The notion of not performing the *nomizomena* and their reprehensible behavior towards their brother, which, above all, consisted in leaving him without an adopted son, are implicitly equated. So it was at least credible to the jurors that the proper performance of the *nomizomena* for the deceased could be presented, in a rhetorical polarization, as equivalent to giving him a son to perform them.

Of course, though the nexus of ideas centering on the adopted son replacing the father as head of the *oikos* is privileged in these contexts, there were also other reasons why adoption took place, especially inheritance within the family, and this is correlative with the fact that we know of a few cases in which a daughter is adopted. For example, in Isaeus 11.8–9 Hagnias adopted a niece before he left for an embassy to Persia, just in case something happened to him (as it did, he was put to death by the Spartans) and made a will saying that if she died (as she did), his estate should go to his half-brother. Theophon adopted his niece as he was dying,[44] leaving her a considerable estate, which her father, Stratokles, controlled for nine years. Presumably Theophon had appointed Stratokles as her *kurios*, legal guardian. All adopted girls would have had another *kurios* after the death of their adoptive father, who would also have taken over the ritual responsibilities that they could not perform, as they did the financial and other responsibilities from which a woman was excluded.[45] Thus, the existence of female adoptions does not diminish the importance of the ideological nexus: "a man adopts a son to bury him and perform

---

[42] See e.g. Isaeus 2.10, 15, 25, 36 cf. 2.13; 6.51; 7.30. cf. also [Demosthenes] 43.11; Isaeus 4.7.
[43] Isaeus 7.31–32.
[44] Isaeus 11.41.
[45] These girls would become *epiklêroi*, women whose father died without sons, through whom their father's estate was passed on; in order for this estate to remain in the father's family the right to marry her passed to her nearest male relative in a prescribed order (see Harrison 1978:10–12; 309–311; cf. 132–138; Leduc 1990:296–299).

the *nomizomena* as part of the mentality that a son replaced his father as head of the *oikos* and in his membership of the phratry, deme, polis." Nor does it show that women could bury and perform the *nomizomena* in the way that men could—any more than they could replace their father as heads of the *oikos*. Simply that, in certain circumstances, in which inheritance was privileged, and no desirable male adoptee was available, a female kinswoman was adopted.

The ideal, then, is for a son to continue the father's *oikos*, bury and perform the *nomizomena* for him—and for his mother, though with the mother no notion of replacement is involved. When there is no adult son the father, if he is alive, buries the deceased, otherwise a brother, or other male relative, or friends. Relatives had the legal obligation to bury,[46] friends volunteered. Plato[47] mentions that Kriton will bury Socrates, whose sons were too young[48]—not, it should be noted, Socrates' wife Xanthippe. In Isaeus 9 the speaker is the half-brother of the deceased Astyphilos, who had died as a soldier in Mytilene. The speaker's opponent claims that his son had been adopted by Astyphilos in a will. The speaker claims that when Astyphilos' bones were brought back to Athens the alleged adopted son did not perform the *prothesis* of the bones, nor did he bury them; it was Astyphilos' friends and military comrades who, realizing that the speaker was not in Athens, and the speaker's father (Astyphilos' stepfather) was ill, did the *prothesis* and all the other customary rites, and took the speaker's father to the grave.[49] The order of the people expected to bury someone, then, and perform the *nomizomena* was, in the absence of a son, a brother, a stepfather, friends.

Certain passages suggest that, as in the Homeric death rituals, so also in classical Athens, women played the dominant role in the first part of the ritual. For example, the fact that women wash the corpses is taken for granted in Plato (*Phaedo* 115 A).[50] In Isaeus 6.40, when Euktemon died his wife and daughters went to the house in which he had lived with a woman who had been either his second wife or his concubine—this is one of the points at issue—and were not allowed in. The speaker's

---

46 [Demosthenes] 43.57.

47 Plato *Phaedo* 115 D–E.

48 See Plato *Kriton* 45 C–D.

49 Isaeus 9.4. At 32 the speaker repeats that his opponent seized possession of Astyphilos' estate before performing *ta nomizomena* for him. Here again, there is a close and explicit connection between burying and inheritance.

50 In pseudo-Demosthenes 43.65, men and women are mentioned separately in connection with the taking care of the corpse and performing the customary rites: the formulation "we and our women" inherited the body of Hagnias when he died and performed all *ta nomizomena* suggests that it was probably shaped by assumptions in which the male "we" on the one hand and "our women" on the other played differential roles in the care of the dead—roughly speaking, the care of the corpse on the one hand and the performance of the *nomizomena* on the other—which, as it sometimes did, included the notion of burial.

opponents told them that it was not their business *thaptein* Euktemon. *Thaptein* means to bury, but also to honor with funeral rites, and this is what is meant here, not that the women could have buried Euktemon. For Euktemon certainly had grandsons to perform the burial, and may even have had a son—this is one of the issues in dispute; and, we saw, there is no doubt that burial was performed by the male heir when there was one. *Thaptein* here clearly covers the whole of the death ritual and refers to the performance of its first part, which was indeed the special responsibility of the women of the family, and which these particular women had gone to perform, and did perform when they entered the house (6.41). In the same speech, the performance of rites at the grave is inextricably connected with the status of heir: at 6.51 the speaker says that it was going to be either this woman's son who was to be heir to Philoktemon's property and would *enagizein*, perform sacrifice of *enagisma* type, and libations at the grave, or "this man," the son of Philoktemon's sister, whom he himself adopted. At 6.65 the customary rites for a woman are expected to have been performed by a husband, while her sons are expected to perform sacrifice of *enagisma* type (*enagizein*) and libations.

Let us now consider very briefly these customary rites. We hear of *enata*, rites performed on the ninth day after the death, of *enagizein*, offering sacrifice of *enagisma* type every year, of *enagizein* and all the *nomizomena*, *enagizein* and libations at the grave, offerings to the dead on the appointed day according to established custom, of rites performed on the thirtieth day after the death, and also of *kosmein* ("decorate," but also "honor") the grave.[51] Some of these rites were performed at the Genesia, the annual commemoration of dead parents.[52] So, whatever else may have been included in the category "the *nomizomena*," there can be no doubt that the visits and offerings to the grave, and the libations performed there, would have been part of these customary rites, which, according to the evidence we have seen, were performed by the male who had conducted the burial, above all, the male heir, with which, we saw, they are ideologically closely associated.

How, then, do we explain the fact that most representations of visits to the tomb and associated rites on white ground *lekuthoi*, a ritual shape offered to the dead in fifth-century Athens, involve women?[53] Indeed, women are also sometimes

---

[51] *Enata*: Isaeus 2.36, 37; *enagizein* every year: Isaeus 2.46; *enagizein* and all the *nomizomena*: Isaeus 7.30; *enagizein* and libations at the grave: Isaeus 6.51, 6.64–65; offerings to the dead on the appointed day according to established custom: [Demosthenes] 43.66–67: on the thirtieth day: Harpokration s.v. *Triakas*; Photios s.v. *Triakas*; Photios s.v. *kathedra*; *kosmein* the graves: Xenophon *Memorabilia* 2.2.13. See also on these rites: Humphreys 1980:100–101; Kurtz and Boardman 1971:147–148; Garland 1985:104–106, 166.

[52] On which see now Parker 1996:48–49 with bibliography. Cf. Humphreys 1980:100–101.

[53] See e.g. references and discussion with bibliography in Dillon 2002:282–288.

shown performing libations,[54] a rite which, we saw, is specifically said to be performed by the male heir and sometimes other males. Of course these images are not photographic records, they are imaginary articulations. However, their context and function determine their parameters of manipulation which we can reconstruct: the fact that they are offerings to the dead, and specifically images of familial piety,[55] entails that they cannot be representing transgressive rites, on the contrary they depict scenes of something customary or ideal. Leaving aside evidence from tragedy, the use of which would make the argument circular, there is also lexicographical evidence that indicates that women performed libations to the dead.[56] How do we explain this disparity between on the one hand the gender the images privilege as performers of these rites and, on the other the insistence on a male heir to perform the *nomizomena*? Indeed, how do we explain this insistence if women could perform the *nomizomena* at all?

Clearly, part of the answer must lie in the ideological nexus centering on the replacement of the father, since the notion of the male heir performing the customary rites is part of that nexus. But we need to make sense of the fact that the paradigmatic association of this heir with that performance suggests that he was deemed to be performing the *nomizomena*, while the images and other evidence represent as normative and/or ideal that women performed some of the ritual activities that made up those rites. In fact, the apparent contradiction disappears if we focus on the notion of the male heir replacing his father as the head of the *oikos* and try to make sense of the evidence through the filters shaped by Athenian assumptions about the *oikos*. For the death ritual and the *nomizomena* were *oikos* rites, and so (like other *oikos* rites, such as, for example, sacrifices to Zeus Ktesios) they took place under the "direction" of the head of the *oikos*, who had the ritual responsibility for them, and performed some himself—though other members of the *oikos* could also take part, as was the case in other *oikos* rituals, for example when the women performed the *ololugê*, the shrill ritual cry, at an *oikos* sacrifice. In the case of the death ritual, the male heir had the ritual responsibility, and the women of the *oikos* and the appropriate kinswomen played an active role in the ritual's first and second part and a more restricted one in the third, the funeral procession and burial, correlatively with the fact that in the symbolic classification articulating the ritual women represented disorder, pollution, and the embracing of death, while men represented the opposite values, which were the values required for the culminating part of the ritual and the restoration of the new order. After the burial, in

---

[54] For libations on white ground *lêkuthoi* see e.g. Dillon 2002:285.
[55] See Sourvinou-Inwood 1995a:324–325.
[56] *Etymologicum Magnum* s.v. *Enkhutristiai* says that *enkhutristiai* were the women who offered chthonic libations to the dead.

the new order, the importance of those values of order and disorder through which the death ritual was enacted would have receded, and the "nurturing" facet in the perception of women would have ensured a prominent role for women in the tending of the graves and performance of the customary rites—under the ritual responsibility of the male heir.

That there was such a thing as a ritual responsibility for the funeral and the *nomizomena*, and that others performed rites at the discretion of the man who had this responsibility, is shown by a statement in Demosthenes 44.32: the speaker says that there may be some excuse, though it was contrary to the law, for the dead man's father to have prevented "us" from performing any of the *nomizomena* for the deceased, for it is proper that charge for the burial (*tês taphês tên epimeleian*) should be given to the natural father, but after him also to "us," who were related to the dead man by adoption; but after the *nomizomena* (here clearly referring specifically to the funeral/ burial) had been performed, he had no right to deprive "us" of "our" inheritance.

The question then is whether a woman could have had the ritual responsibility for a burial and the performance of the customary rites.

Isaeus' eighth speech, *On the Estate of Kiron*, concerns the dispute between on the one hand the son of Kiron's brother and on the other the speaker and his brother, who claim to be the sons of Kiron's daughter by his first marriage. When Kiron died, each of the opposing sides had tried to perform the funeral rites as a means of establishing themselves as Kiron's heirs. The speaker claims that his actual opponent in the suit, Kiron's brother's son, had been instigated by someone else, the real villain, Diokles, the brother of Kiron's second wife. According to the speaker,[57] when Kiron, his grandfather, died, he presented himself at the deceased's house to carry away the body in order to bury it from his own house. But because his grandfather's widow begged him that he should be buried from that house, and said that she wanted to take charge of the body together with the speaker, and to prepare and adorn it, and as she was beseeching and weeping, he was persuaded to do as she asked. Thus, he went to his opponent and said in the presence of witnesses that he, the speaker, intended to bury Kiron from Kiron's own house since the widow, Diokles' sister, had implored him to. Diokles accepted this and said that, as he himself had bought some of the things needed for the funeral and had paid a deposit for the rest, he wanted to be reimbursed by the speaker, and they made arrangements to that effect. The present claimant had made no objection to these arrangements. Though the next day Diokles refused to be reimbursed by the speaker, saying that he had been reimbursed by the man who is now the speaker's

[57] In Isaeus 8.21 and following.

opponent, the son of the deceased's brother, the speaker says that he, the speaker, was not prevented from *sunthaptein* the deceased, burying him together with his opponent, but he helped with everything. But if Kiron had not been his grandfather, the speaker claims, his opponent ought to have prevented him from *sunthaptein*, while he himself had allowed his opponent to *sunthaptein* because he was the son of his grandfather's brother. He then says that the expenses for the burial were paid from Kiron's estate; but to avoid being accused of not having paid anything himself for the funeral expenses, he asked the interpreter of sacred law, and on his advice he paid for the *enata*, the ninth day offerings.

Clearly, the following assumptions concerning accepted practice underlie this piece of forensic presentation. First, the disposition of the funeral was entirely in the hands of the male heir, the nearest male relative, and the women's participation in the death ritual depended primarily on their relationship to the heir; even the widow of the deceased could only participate with the consent of this male. This demonstrates clearly the notion of ritual responsibility for the death ritual—and indeed for the *nomizomena* afterwards—which belongs to the male heir, or the nearest male kin who claims to be the heir. In this case the speaker claims that two potential heirs had taken joint responsibility. Second, the widow's request for participation was that she should be involved in the first phase of the death ritual, to take charge of the body together with the speaker and to prepare and adorn it. On the other hand, when the speaker's male opponent comes into play, the son of the deceased's brother, what the speaker says they did together was buried him. This differential participation corresponds to the differential role of men and women in the death ritual as outlined here. Finally, the fact that the widow's brother Diokles had bought some of the things needed for the funeral and paid a deposit for the rest sounds like a preemptive move on Diokles' part to ensure a role in the decision-making concerning the burial, and thus the disposition of the estate, since he undoubtedly knew that there were male claimants to the estate and so also claimants to the right to bury Kiron. But for him to do this on behalf of the widow whose *kurios* he, as her brother, became on her husband's death, it must have been the case that if there had been no male relative, some combination of the widow and her *kurios* would presumably have had to assume ritual responsibility for the burial—either the widow would have been assumed to have carried the ritual responsibility, or her *kurios*, or both.

In Demosthenes 41.11 the speaker's wife is the daughter of a man who had adopted a son, given him one of his two daughters in marriage, then annulled the adoption, arranged for that marriage to be dissolved, and married that daughter off to the speaker's opponent. The speaker claims (among other things) that his wife had spent a silver *mna* (a sum equivalent to a hundred drachmas) for her father at the Nemeseia and that his opponent, his wife's sister's husband, had not repayed the sum, which was his wife's share. The speaker's wife is here presented as the agent; this suits the forensic context, for he presents his case more sympathetically by juxtaposing his wife to his male opponent. Nevertheless, this may suggest that it had been the wife who had the ritual responsibility for the performance of the rites. It has been convincingly suggested[58] that Nemes[e]ia here is an early textual corruption for Genesia. In any case, whether the festival was the Nemes[e]ia or the Genesia, both were *polis* festivals.[59] It is possible that this may have entailed that as far as these rites for the dead were concerned there may not have been a notion of an individual ritual responsibility, and that women as well as men performed them under the ritual responsibility of the *polis*. If so, this would make offerings made during *polis* festivals for the dead different from *oikos* funerary rituals, in which the ritual responsibility was held by the head of the *oikos*. But it is in any case possible that in certain circumstances a woman, perhaps in combination with her guardian, may have had a share in the ritual responsibility for the customary rites, and perhaps also for the funeral and burial. The minimum role that a *kurios* would have played in such a burial would have been to take care of the financial transactions, since women were not allowed to conduct financial transactions above the value of a *medimnos* of barley.[60]

This notion of partial ritual responsibility may have been the assumption underlying Pherekydes' articulation of the version of the myth of Sisyphos that involved Sisyphos' wife performing *ta nenomismena*—if the formulation in the Homeric scholion that reports the story is reflecting Pherekydes accurately, on which we cannot be certain.[61] According to this version, before he died Sisyphos enjoined his wife not to send the *nenomismena* to Hades so that he, Sisyphos, could persuade Hades to allow him to come back in the upper world to request them, which he did, and then refused to return to Hades until he was old. However, it is also possible that the distancing effect of the other time and other place of the myth, and, above all, the abnormal situation preceding this event, Sisyphos having bound Thanatos who had been sent to get him as a punishment from Zeus, may have entailed that this was perceived as abnormal, that the wife's role may have been perceived as part of the nexus of abnormalities pertaining to death articulated in the myth of Sisyphos.

---

[58] Parker 1996:246 n101.
[59] On the Nemeseia, see Deubner 1969:219, 230; Parker 1996:103n5, 246n101, 254.
[60] Isaeus 10.10. See e.g. Harrison 1968:108n5, 236n3; Just 1989:29; Blundell 1995:114. For the cost of an Athenian burial, see now Oliver 2000:59–80.
[61] FGrH 3 F 119. On the myth of Sisyphos, see Sourvinou-Inwood 1986:47–55; Sourvinou-Inwood 1995a:67–70, cf. 88–89, 305, 311.

I will now consider the evidence of the epitaphs. Some epitaphs, in Attica and elsewhere, state that they were erected by a woman, often the dead person's mother.[62] Most epitaphs name the person who erected the grave monument, rather than the person who performed the burial. The two functions cannot be assumed always to have coincided, for some epigrams state that the grave monument was set up by the father and the mother of the deceased.[63] Since we know that, at least in Athens, the burial would have been conducted by the father—for when a close male is available he is the one who has the ritual responsibility for the burial—it is clear that in this case the ritual responsibility for the burial is not identical with the action of setting up the grave monument. Of course, a burial is terminated with the setting up of some sort of grave marker, normally a mound, and this stage had a very important symbolic significance.[64] But the inscribed grave monument was an optional extra, in the archaic period limited to the elites and associated with certain perceptions pertaining to the survival of the name of the deceased in memory,[65] and so it may have been perceived as a separate stage from the burial. Thus, its erection should not necessarily be taken as equivalent to performing the burial, as it was not in the case of the father-mother erections mentioned. Given the symbolic values enacted in the death ritual, the fact that the inscribed grave monument was erected in the world in which the new order after the death had already been established, and was not, as the burial was, part of the process that created the new order, in which the symbolism associated with the males needed to be dominant, would entail that its erection by a woman would not have been symbolically problematic. Consequently, when an epitaph says that a woman erected the grave monument it does not by any means follow that she had taken the ritual responsibility for the burial—certainly not on her own.

But the possibility cannot be excluded that such epitaphs may, at least sometimes, be reflecting a situation in which a woman had a limited ritual responsibility for the burial. In one fourth-century Attic epigram[66] the dead woman says, "thanks to my daughter's piety I was buried in the way that was appropriate to me." This formulation may be, but should not be assumed to be, a periphrasis for "my daughter buried me," for this would also be the most appropriate expression of the notion that her daughter had arranged for her to be buried by her (the daughter's)

---

[62] Attica: Hansen 1983:nos 35, 37, 94 (for two soldiers from Parion), 97; Hansen 1989:no 504. Elsewhere: Hansen 1983:nos 138 (Troezen); 157 (Thasos); 108 (in Euboea for an Aiginetan); 169 (Erythrai); 117 (Thessaly); 124 (Thessaly); Hansen 1989:nos 636 (Boiotia); 706 (Kos).

[63] Hansen 1983:no 25 with Guarducci 1961:159 (*ad* no 37); 119; Hansen 1989:no 693.

[64] See Sourvinou-Inwood 1995a:110–112 cf. 139–143.

[65] Ibid.: 278–279, 285–297.

[66] Hansen 1989:no 592.

kurios, for example, her husband, and so it is perhaps more likely to have been shaped by (and read through) parameters molded by the assumption that women did not bury, but at most held, or shared in, the ritual responsibility with the help of their guardian.

There is one case, from archaic Argos, which either belongs to this category of limited responsibility, or suggests a greater involvement of a woman in a burial. In the epitaph of Hyssematas,[67] a woman called Kossina, apparently his wife,[68] states that she buried him (*thapsa*) near the race course. But, of course, we cannot assume that the same practices pertained in archaic Argos as in classical Athens.

In these circumstances, we may conclude that the normative situation in classical Athens was that women played an important part in the first two stages of the death ritual, but not in the funeral and burial, where their role was restricted and rather passive. The ritual responsibility for the death ritual, usually referred to as the ritual responsibility for the burial and the customary rites, was normally assumed by a male, ideally by the son for his parents, with deviations involving other males. For a series of determining parameters make males the appropriate gender to perform the burial. First, the fact that the symbolic values enacted by the two genders in the death ritual require that the women had a dominant role in the early parts of the ritual in which death, disorder, and pollution were embraced, while the men played the dominant part in the funeral, above all the burial, which ushered in the restoration of a new order. Second, in Athens the paradigmatic normality is for a man (and a woman, but the paradigm is the symbolically central male self) to be buried by his son, who replaced him as head of the *oikos*; the performance of the burial rites articulated ritually this replacement and at the same time also the continuity of the *oikos* that offsets and redeems the individual discontinuity of its successive heads. Then, partly correlatively with this second aspect, the women's differential and subordinate position in the *oikos*; for, however significant their de facto role may have been, their normative position in the *oikos* was hierarchically inferior—in religion, as well as in everything else, while in public religion the role of women was complementary, not inferior, to that of men.[69]

We cannot exclude the possibility that in certain, very rare circumstances a woman may have had limited ritual responsibility for the burial, if no male kin or friends were available. But the determining parameters set out above would have made such involvement far removed from the ideal, which suggests that, since every woman had a *kurios*, it would have been that *kurios* who would have actively

---

[67] Hansen 1983:no 136 (last quarter of the sixth century).
[68] See Daley 1939:168.
[69] See on this Sourvinou-Inwood 1995b:113–116.

conducted the burial on the woman's behalf. For, I suggest, a maximum involvement of the gender that represents the wrong values for the final part of the death ritual, a woman both taking the ritual responsibility for the burial, and (to whatever degree) physically performing (even part of) the burial herself, was at the opposite pole from the normative and ideal—and so, I submit, would have been perceived as transgressive.

3. Tragic Manipulations

I shall now consider a series of tragic passages that involve women and the death ritual and try to reconstruct how the ancient audiences perceived the relationship between the manipulations of ritual material in those passages and their own ritual normality, and so try to reconstruct, as much as possible, what meanings they constructed out of those passages and how those meanings related to the meanings constructed in the rest of the tragedy.

I begin with two Euripidean tragedies which deal with the same story. In the final part of Euripides' *Trojan Women* the corpse of Astyanax is brought back to his grandmother Hecabe by Talthybios, the herald of the Achaeans, with a message from Andromache, who has been carried away by Neoptolemos before she could do anything for her son's corpse, so that she was not able (v. 1146) *dounai taphon* to her son. *Taphon* in this expression clearly refers to funeral rites in general; for what Andromache asks Hecabe to do for Astyanax on her behalf pertains to the preparation of the body: Hecabe is to clothe the corpse and crown it with wreaths. That is, she is asked to perform the ritual role that is traditionally performed by women in the first part of the death ritual, as, of course, she and the other women (the chorus) will perform the lament. Normally she would have had to wash the corpse first, but Talthybios tells her that he saved her one task (which she would normally have had to perform) for as they passed by Scamander he himself had washed the corpse. This is the same situation as we saw in Homer. The washing of the corpse is normally the women's responsibility, like the anointing and clothing, but it is sometimes also performed by men. Because there is pressure of time, no *prothesis* will take place, the second part of the death ritual is here elided, at least in Talthybios' words. But the most important thing is that he tells her that after she has decked out the corpse he and other Achaean men will bury Astyanax and put a spear as a *sêma* over the grave.

Here, then, it is the Achaean men, not Hecabe who will perform the burial, though Hecabe speaks of what she is doing as *thaptô nekron*; conceivably she might have been perceived to be carrying the ritual responsibility for the burial. But the fact that the actual burial will be performed by men makes this articulation normative, on my reconstruction of the gendering of Athenian funerals. This is correlative with the construction of the world of this tragedy and its women. For in *Trojan Women* the women in general and Hecabe in particular are victims, have suffered terrible losses, but they have not become abnormal women. The world of the play is disordered, sacrilege and other bad acts have taken place and will be punished, but it is not disordered in a way that implicates the Trojan women directly. On the contrary, Hecabe is colored positively throughout the play. This, I suggest, is correlative with the fact that, in this tragedy, burial is performed by men.

By contrast, in Euripides' *Hecuba* Hecabe becomes savage, and so do, to a somewhat lesser extent, the other Trojan women. Hecabe, with the help of the other women, took a savage revenge against Polymestor, who had killed her son Polydoros. They blinded him and murdered his sons. Her reason for desiring revenge was probably perceived to have been understandable, but the savagery of the revenge, especially given the fact that it was conducted by women against males, and captive women at that—a fact stressed by their victim, Polymestor[70]—inevitably would have generated in the eyes of the audience a negative coloring of abnormality and dangerous disorder for the women. Hecabe's savage abnormality is subsequently reinforced by the prophecy told by her victim that she will be transformed into a dog with fiery eyes and then disappear into the sea. This situation of disorder and abnormality is correlative with the fact that it is Hecabe herself that will bury Polyxena and Polydoros. Some of the earlier references to her performing the burial are not conclusive, but in verses 1287–1288 it becomes clear that Hecabe will perform the burial herself: Agamemnon's urging her *su de . . . steikhousa thapte*, "go and bury" the two dead, without any additional offer of help or other comment leaves no doubt about it. This happens at the very end of the play, after Hecabe has descended into savagery and her transformation which crystallized this image has been prophesied. The abnormality of her burying her children, which is correlative with, and in my view determined by, and expresses, this savagery and abnormality, takes place within the disordered world in which she started as a grieving mother and will end up as a dead dog.

Thus, the comparison between these two tragedies shows that the burial by a woman belongs to a context of abnormality, while the practices in *Trojan Women* belong to a context of normality.

In Euripides' *Medea*[71] also the notion of burial by a woman is correlative with abnormality—though a different type of abnormality. At vv. 1378–1379 Medea

---

[70] For example at vv. 1062–1065, 1095–1096.

[71] I set out my readings of Euripides, *Medea*, on which some of the statements that follow are based, in Sourvinou–Inwood 1997b:254–262, 294–296.

says that she will herself bury her sons—whom she had murdered—in the sanctuary of Hera Akraia. Burying in a sanctuary was abnormal, and here it is part of
the children's heroization, but most importantly, in the context of this burial Medea
announces the institution of a festival, as gods do in tragedy; for in this part of the
play, especially at vv. 1378–1388, Medea is strongly distanced from normality and
from "normal" women, distanced to the divine sphere.[72] The abnormality and
exceptionality of the context, then, is correlative with the fact that (on my reconstruction of Athenian ritual reality) Medea burying the children herself was
abnormal. Throughout the play Medea was a more or less ordinary woman, the
victim of male power, zoomed to, and distanced from, the two poles of feminine
behavior that were crystallized into the schemata "normal woman" and "bad
woman," ending up as a polarized version of the latter, killing her sons and
wreaking havoc on her husband's *oikos* and the male power establishment. Given
Greek values, she should now be defeated and suffer a terrible punishment. Instead,
she is distanced from normal women and zoomed towards the divine. This is, I have
argued,[73] a significant strategy in the construction of the complex network of meanings which created the ideological space in which Medea is both explored as a bad
woman and escapes punishment for her dreadful deed as part of a nexus of meanings pertaining to male behavior. On my reading, her announcement that she will
herself bury her children was another element of abnormality; it helped stress her
exceptionality and reinforce her distancing from the normality of ordinary women,
while perhaps it may also have helped reactivate the transgressive element of her
persona among the god-like distancing. It helps construct a significant meaning at
a significant place in the tragedy.

In Aeschylus' *Agamemnon*, after Klytemestra's murder of Agamemnon, the
chorus asks a series of questions which seem to be part of lamenting:[74] "Who will
bury him? Who will lament him?" and they also ask Klytemestra whether she, who
killed Agamemnon, would bring herself to lament him. In response she says, "we
will bury him," but not with laments from this *oikos* (vv. 1553–1554). "We" refers
to Klytemestra only.[75] Her burying Agamemnon would have been perceived to be
part of the negative abnormality of the context, the disordered world in which the
wife, who has, among other things, assumed characteristics that properly belong to
the male,[76] has killed her husband, an act which threatens the social order, and also

---

[72] Sourvinou-Inwood 1997b:259–261.
[73] Ibid.:254–262, 294–296.
[74] See Fraenkel 1950:731–733 *ad* 1541–1547.
[75] See ibid.:733 *ad* 1552f.
[76] See Aeschylus *Agamemnon* 10–11; Fraenkel 1950:10 *ad* 11; and see e.g. Zeitlin 1996:344.

specifically of an abnormal funeral with no laments. Lamenting is the part of the death ritual in which Klytemestra ought to have been playing a central role, and it is this that the chorus had asked her if she would perform. Her refusal to do so, perform her normative role, is correlative with her announcing that she will bury Agamemnon.

Euripides' *Suppliants* belongs at the other end of the spectrum; not only do the women not perform the burial,[77] they play a smaller part in the death ritual than was normally the case in ritual reality. At the beginning of the play, the chorus of mothers lament at the death of their sons while they are supplicating Aithra to plead with Theseus to retrieve their corpses for burial. Lamentation after the death is proper ritual behavior for women—though here it included self-wounding, (vv. 50–51, 76–77, 87) which, we saw, was forbidden in real-life fifth-century Athens, but may have been perceived as part of the distanced heroic age normality. At vv. 52–53 when they mention what they had not been able to do for their sons they say that they had not laid out their bodies in *prothesis*, nor do they look upon their graves. These are normative representations: the first was part of the family's women's ritual duty, burying (if my reconstruction is right) was the task of males, with the women playing a passive role.

But in this tragedy the women do not wash and clothe the corpses, for this, the messenger explains, was done by Theseus before the corpses are brought on stage (765–766)—a well disposed male washing the corpse instead of the women also occurs, we saw, in *Trojan Women*. Eventually, the corpses are brought on stage, and a lamentation takes place over them, the first *kommos*, a lament shared by the chorus and Adrastos (798–837). Adrastos gives a funeral speech, an *epitaphios* (857–917);[78] then a funeral procession takes the corpses to the pyres where they will be cremated, just offstage. It is Theseus, the king who retrieved the bodies and in whose land this ritual takes place, who conducts the funeral ceremony—which in this case does not include the burial of the ashes, since only those of Kapaneus, who was killed by lightning, will be buried there; the ashes of the others will be buried at Argos.[79] The mothers are not present at the funeral, correlatively with the fact that the chorus cannot leave the stage.[80] But the device for keeping them there (vv. 941–949a) involves the notion, put forward by Theseus in answer to Adrastos' invitation to the mothers to follow the biers, that the close sight of the disfigured

---

[77] I should note that *hôs nekrous thapsôsin* at 174 means "seeking burial," the release of the corpses and the performance of the death ritual including burial, not that they themselves would be doing the burying.
[78] On the funeral speech by Adrastos in vv. (857–917), see especially Pelling 1997a:230–233.
[79] See on this Collard 1975:411 *ad* 1185–1188a, see 341–342 *ad* 935.
[80] See Collard 1975:342 *ad* 940.

corpses would be intolerably painful to them; Adrastos, having first expressed surprise at the idea that the mothers should not touch the corpses of their sons, agreed when Theseus explained his reasons for suggesting that the mothers should not follow the corpses, adding that the mothers should embrace the ashes after the cremation.[81] This notion entails that the women had not handled the corpses when they had been first brought in, or at any time during the first *kommos*.[82] After the cremation the procession of the dead men's sons carry the ashes in funerary receptacles, over which they, as a secondary chorus, lament the final *kommos* together with the main chorus of the mothers (vv. 1114–1164).[83]

The women, then, play a smaller part in the death ritual in this tragedy than was normally the case in ritual reality. This may have been perceived to be correlative with the fact that the funeral of the Seven in this tragedy partly refracts the public funerals of the Athenian war dead,[84] in which the *polis* buried the dead and the family's role was limited. This more limited participation of the women would have been one of the elements that helped construct this complex refraction, with the difference that here, as opposed to the real life public funerals, women are not in the background; on the contrary, they articulate an important facet of the deaths, which is underplayed in the funerals of the war dead: the pain and grief of the dead men's families are here expressed strongly by the mothers, to a more limited extent by the sons, and most strikingly through the suicide of Euadne, Kapaneus' wife. Because these are Argives of the heroic age, this focus, and stress, on private grief, above all expressed by women, did not present itself as being in conflict with official Athenian ideology, which excluded from its rhetoric grief and lament for the war dead in favor of praise.[85] Nevertheless, in a context partly comparable to that of the Athenian funerals of the war dead, this tragedy articulated a representation in which the private pain and misery rather than the glory, are stressed, and the grieving women, who would have been perceived as comparable to the Athenian women who lost their men in war, are at the foreground.

These complex meanings do not make this burial any less paradigmatic—any more than they challenge the ideology of death in war; what they do is partly problematize it by stressing its darker side. For this burial, brought about as it was by

[81] See vv. 948–949 with Collard 1975:344 *ad* 947–949a.

[82] At vv. 815–817 the mothers say "Give my sons to me, that I may fold my arms about them and hold them in my embrace." And Adrastos replies at 818 "here they are before you" (Collard's translation [1975:314 *ad* 815–817, 315 *ad* 818]) but in fact they are not yet allowed to embrace their sons (see ibid.: 315 *ad* 818).

[83] On the secondary chorus, see Collard 1975:19. On the *kommos*, Collard 1975:390–396.

[84] See on this question Pelling 1997a:230–235. See also Bowie 1997:51–52.

[85] Sourvinou-Inwood 1995:191–195 with bibliography.

the virtuous intervention of Athens, above all Theseus, and conducted by Theseus, was paradigmatic, as is confirmed by Athena's appearance in epiphany: she urges Theseus to bind the Argives through an oath ritual in which they will swear that they and their descendants will never attack Athens, and orders the institution of sacred precincts in the place where the corpses were burnt.[86]

Antigone's burial of her traitor brother in Sophocles' *Antigone* is at the other end of the spectrum from the paradigmatic. I argued elsewhere[87] that in the eyes of the Athenian audience watching the performance of that tragedy, burial by Antigone, which turned out to have partly rectified an offence against the gods, would have appeared to have been wrong, since it had involved a manifold subversion of proper behavior. She broke the law and challenged the control of the *polis* over the funerary discourse, and the articulation which declared the disposal of the body of both those who died in the service of the *polis* and of traitors to be a public matter. So she also challenged the articulation of *polis* matters into public and private, she invaded and disturbed the public sphere in the service of her private interests. She also subverted her familial duty; first, because she said that she would not have acted in this way for a husband or a son, while in contemporary Athenian ideology her familial duty would have been much more compelling in those cases.[88] Then, because the head of the *oikos* to which the Athenian audience would have perceived Antigone to have become attached on the death of her brother Eteokles was Kreon, who became her *kurios*. Thus, her *oikos* duty was to obey Kreon. If the reconstruction set out here, according to which women did not bury, is right, Antigone's gender would have added to the subversive nature of her action. The person whose duty it would have been to perform the burial if Polyneikes had not been a traitor was Kreon himself.[89] Of course, when the man responsible for a burial does not perform it, it is up to others to do so. But even when no disobedience to the *polis* was involved, it has been argued here, such others would be men. It could be argued that, since no one else was prepared to do it, Antigone took this duty upon herself. This may or may not have been perceived as within the parameters of what was legitimate—most likely not, since, we saw, it is at the most symbolically transgressive end of the spectrum of a woman's involvement in a

---

[86] Cf. Collard 1975:417–419 *ad* 1211–1212.

[87] See especially Sourvinou-Inwood 1989a:134–148. See also Sourvinou-Inwood 1987–1988:19–35; Sourvinou-Inwood 1989b:141–165.

[88] See Sourvinou-Inwood 1987–1988:19–35.

[89] The fact that Antigone's choice was, at least prima facie, perverted, was expressed symbolically in the fact that the family whose interests she privileged above those of the *polis* is a perverted family. She and her brother were the products of an incestuous union. The brother she wanted to bury was killed by her other brother, whom he had killed at the same time. This negative coloration of the family whose interests Antigone privileged gave negative connotations to her actions.

burial. But even if it had not been perceived as actually transgressive, it was at the other end of the spectrum from proper womanly death related ritual behavior. It was certainly not the case that the audience would have perceived that to bury Polyneikes was Antigone's special duty or special area of competence.

Clearly, then, if my reconstructions are right the transgressive nature of Antigone's burial of her brother, which, I argued, was strengthened in the eyes of the audience by her gender, helped construct significant meanings; it helped construct the complex meaning that an action that had appeared to the Athenian audience to have been wrong, because it was a reversal of what was proper, ultimately turned out to have been right, because it reversed a cosmically important wrong. And this complex meaning helped construct one of the most important representations articulated in, and articulating, this tragedy: that the will of the gods in unknowable, and that the religious discourse of the *polis* is fallible— a meaning this last constructed at a symbolic distance, Thebes in the heroic age, with its ruler eventually distanced further though tyrannical statements.[90]

Once the righteousness of the burial of Polyneikes by Antigone was established in Sophocles' *Antigone*, the notion of Antigone burying Polyneikes became acceptable, so that in the inauthentic part of Aeschylus' *Seven against Thebes*, which depends on Euripides' *Phoenissai*,[91] not only does Antigone announce that she will bury Polyneikes[92] but also the semichorus announces (1074) that they will participate in the burial (*sunthapsomen*).

In Euripides *Iphigeneia in Tauris* the (as yet unrecognized and still destined for sacrifice) Orestes expresses the wish that his sister should lay out his corpse (627–635). In reply, Iphigeneia tells him that while that is not possible, she herself will place many offerings on his pyre,[93] and she will pour honey on it, and she will quench his ashes with oil. This means that she will personally take part in his cremation. Iphigeneia is here a priestess in a foreign land who performs human sacrifice. Indeed she is talking about the burial of such a human sacrifice. So the situation is sharply opposed to the audience's ritual realities. In this case, then, it is not transgressiveness that is articulated with the help of this ritual element of women performing, or taking active part in, a burial, but otherness.

In Euripides' *Helen* 1275–1276 the deployment of this ritual element is outside both these categories. For the plan devised by Helen and Menelaos to escape from Egypt and Theoklymenos involved the invention of a false rite of burial

---

[90] See Sourvinou-Inwood 1989a:146.
[91] See Hutchinson 1985:209–211 *ad* 1005–1078. In Euripides *Phoenissai* Antigone abandons her original intention to bury Polyneikes (see Mastronarde 1994:592–593 and n. 2).
[92] Cf. vv. 1027 and 1028.
[93] See Platnauer 1938:114 *ad* 632.

for a man whose corpse was lost at sea, an invention based on what was desirable or necessary for their successful escape.[94] Of course, for the plan to work Helen had to be on board, so it was necessary to claim that a wife (or a mother or child) had to "bury" the deceased. This representation, then, belongs outside the categories of transgressive behavior and otherness.

The construction of the matricide, and, correlatively, of the character of Electra, in Sophocles' *Electra* are extremely complex issues that cannot be discussed here. And yet they are crucial for the understanding of vv. 1138–1141, in which Electra laments over the urn which she believes contains Orestes' ashes (which in fact had been given her by the living Orestes), complaining that she did not wash his corpse, which we saw, was indeed part of the female role, and also that she did not collect his ashes and what was left of his bones from the funeral pyre, which, on my reconstruction, was not a role normatively performed by women. Also, at 1210 she intended to bury the urn with the remains. All I can say here is that the deployment of this element is correlative with the construction of Electra's character, especially through a series of intertextually constructed relationships, both of comparabilities to, and differentiations from, Antigone in Sophocles' *Antigone*, of which, I suggest, this reference to burying her brother is one instance.

4. Conclusions: A Summary

The reconstruction of the role of women in the Athenian death rituals suggested that the normative participation of women in the last phase of that ritual was limited and passive, and that it was symbolically important that the burial should be conducted by a male. In rare circumstances women may have had at least part of the ritual responsibility for a burial, in which they would have acted in conjunction with their guardian. For the Athenian audiences who made sense of the tragedies through cultural assumptions that included this ritual knowledge the performance of burial by women was one of the elements that helped construct, in the tragedies in which it appeared, the representation of a disordered world, or an otherwise abnormal situation, of one or other type of otherness. It helped create meanings the complexity of which is lost when modern readers assume a generic "important role for women in the death ritual" and elide distinctions that were important in the eyes of the ancient audiences who had shared the ritual knowledge through the deployment of which the tragedians had constructed those complex meanings.

[94] See Kannicht 1969:307.

Ten

"Let the Good Prevail": Perversions of the Ritual Process in Greek Tragedy

Albert Henrichs

Some twenty years ago Charles Segal published an essay titled "Greek Tragedy and Society" in which he comments from a structuralist point of view on the representation of cultural codes in Greek tragedy:

> Unavoidably, [the literary work] uses the codes that constitute the mental patterns of the society; and it could be analyzed, at one level, solely in terms of those accepted, normative codes. But at the same time it deliberately manipulates, distorts, or otherwise transforms those patterns in the special self-conscious structures—linguistic, psychological, societal—superimposed by its own internal, aesthetic coherence.[1]

The use of ritual by the tragedians is a case in point. All three tragedians construct complex dramatic scenarios that explore and exploit the conflict between ritual normalcy and deviations from the ritual norm.[2] In the eyes of the poets as well as their audience, the ritual norm is tantamount to what anthropologists like Victor Turner have called "the ritual process."[3] On a macroscale, the ritual process is the sum total of the scenarios of ritual activity sanctioned by a given society. On a microscale, it is synonymous with any performance of a given ritual that conforms to the ritual norms and expectations of that society. Implicit in the concept of ritual normalcy is the idea of a cultural consensus as to what constitutes proper ritual procedure and behavior in the context of a given ritual.

The central ritual of Greek culture was animal sacrifice.[4] In the case of animal sacrifice, ritual propriety required a process that encompassed the following three steps: the preliminary rites; the ritual killing of the animal; and in the prevalent type

---

[1] Segal 1986:24, originally published as Segal 1981a.
[2] See Zeitlin 1970.
[3] Turner 1969, 1982b; Bell 1992, 1997; Gladigow 1998.
[4] Burkert 1976, 1983:1–12; 1985a:55–59.

of animal sacrifice, the communal meal.[5] When the ritual process falls short of expectations and the norm is violated, scholars of tragedy speak of perverted rituals. Segal characterized the perverted ritual as "a recurrent feature of Greek tragedy."[6] It is certainly true that the tragedians were infinitely more interested in perverted rituals than in the ritual norm.[7] It is equally true that in order to sustain the very concept of ritual perversion, the tragedians incorporated a fair amount of ritual normalcy as a foil for the transgressive patterns.[8] The most frequent and powerful tragic instance of ritual transgression is the corrupted sacrifice, in which the ritual slaughter of animals serves as a metaphor for violence and murder. Prefigured in the Homeric accounts of Agamemnon's murder in the *Odyssey*, the motif of the corrupted sacrifice appears full-blown in the *Agamemnon* and is found with subtle variations in the majority of the plays of Sophokles and Euripides.[9]

In her recent study of tragedy and religion, Christiane Sourvinou-Inwood juxtaposes "the world of the audience" and "the world of the tragedy" as she explores the tragic tensions between the "religious content" of the tragedies and the "religious realities" experienced by the audience.[10] There is of course a third "world," that of the dramatist qua playwright, which incorporates and transcends both the inner frame of the play's action and characters and the outer frame of the Athenian audience and its religious experience. Throughout this chapter I am concerned with the tragedians as playwrights who manipulate the religious experience of their audience in order to create fictional ritual scenarios that serve their dramatic purposes.[11]

With a view to re-examining and refining current views on the tragic representation of ritual, I will offer a series of highly eclectic thoughts and observations on the *dramatic* function of ritual in all three tragedians. Aiskhylos and Euripides converge in their literal as well as metaphorical use of ritual and in their tendency to deliver in accordance with the ritual expectations of their audience.[12] Simply put, rituals that

---

[5] Van Straten 1995.

[6] Segal 1986:35.

[7] Zeitlin 1970:351–374.

[8] Easterling 1988, 1993; Jouanna 1992; Lloyd-Jones 1998. On the interplay of the real-life rituals familiar to the Athenian audience and the tragic tendency to create imaginary ritual scenarios that rely on polyvalence, ambiguity, and metaphor for their tragic specificity and dramatic effect see Easterling 1988:98–99 (= 1993:17), Krummen 1998, and Sourvinou-Inwood 2003.

[9] Zeitlin 1965, 1966, and 1970:271–277, 288–290, 315, 350–351, 355–358; Burkert 1966:116–121 (= 2001:17–21), and 1985b; Foley 1985: 17–64; Gibert 2003; Henrichs, forthcoming. On the Homeric precedent for the corrupted sacrifice (*Odyssey* 4.534–535, 11.410–411) see Henrichs 2000:180–182.

[10] Sourvinou-Inwood 2003:1–66.

[11] My emphasis on the dramatic function of ritual in tragedy is perfectly compatible with the integrity and importance of "the discourse of religious exploration" conducted by the tragedians and interpreted so forcefully by Sourvinou-Inwood.

[12] Henrichs 2000, on sacrificial rites.

have been announced will take place in due course. In the plays of Aiskhylos, the ghost of Dareios is conjured up, the suppliants take their seats by the altar, Iphigeneia is sacrificed (or so it seems), Elektra pours libations, Orestes is purified, and the *Semnai Theai* receive cultic honors.[13] In Euripides, the interplay of drama and ritual is more complicated and less straightforward, but the rituals are by and large performed as announced, if only with novel twists that go from the frivolous to the perverse, as when Elektra carries dishwater instead of libations while performing the ritual lament, Apollo belies the process of oracular consultation in the *Ion*, ritual purification becomes a stratagem of escape in the *Taurian Iphigeneia*, and Aigisthos is slaughtered over the animal victim in the course of a corrupted sacrifice in the *Elektra*.[14]

Sophokles has his own way with ritual. If his extant plays are at all representative, as they must be, Sophokles' approach to ritual as a dramatic tool is distinctly different from the patterns we find in Aiskhylos and Euripides. Unlike Aiskhylos, Sophokles tends to problematize even non-sacrificial rituals such as burial, libations, and purification. What is more, he systematically frustrates the ritual expectations of his audience in several of his plays by manipulating the performance of ritual, preventing rituals from being performed, or completely redefining the religious function and dramatic implications of a given ritual. The resulting pattern of acute ritual deviancy is unique to Sophokles, which explains why I will pay more attention to him than to the other two tragedians.

Ritual performance in tragedy has by definition more to do with words than with action.[15] Of the numerous rituals referred to by the tragedians, only lament, prayer (including its ritual antonym, curses) and supplication were regularly performed on the tragic stage.[16] By contrast, the three rituals most frequently

[13] Ghost of Dareios (*Persians* 598–851): Eitrem 1928, Rose 1950, Hall 1996:150–166. Suppliants crouching at the altar (*Suppliants* 188–196): Rehm 1988:301–302, Gödde 2000:151–153. Sacrifice of Iphigeneia (*Agamemnon* 218–248): Dowden 1989:9–47, Sourvinou-Inwood 2003:57n64, 232 (who argues that though Iphigeneia was a murder victim according to the characters in the *Agamemnon*, she actually survived in the ritual expectation of an Athenian audience preconditioned to her survival by Brauronian cult etiology). Elektra's libations (*Libation Bearers* 85–151): Henrichs 1991:168–169. Purification of Orestes at Delphi (*Libation Bearers* 1059 f., *Eumenides* 280–284): Parker 1983:386–388, Garvie 1986:348, Sommerstein 1989:124–125; Hoessly 2001:117–131. Cult of *Semnai Theai* (*Oidipous at Kolonos* 100, 158–160): Henrichs 1983.

[14] Nolan 1994: 177–179 on the Euripidean Elektra's shift "from a secularized role of water-carrier into a performer of lament;" Burnett 1971: 101–129 on Apollo in *Ion*; Wolff 1992 on rituals in the *Taurian Iphigeneia*; Henrichs 2000:187 and Sourvinou-Inwood 2003:345–350 on the corrupted sacrifice in Euripides' *Elektra*.

[15] Henrichs 2000:176–177.

[16] Foley 1993, Loraux 1998, and Alexiou 2002a on the ritual lament; Pulleyn 1997 on prayers and curses; Gödde 2000 and Naiden 2000 on supplication. Libations are normally performed verbally, as in Sophokles *Oidipous at Kolonos* 465–504, but in Aiskhylos' *Libation Bearers* they are poured on stage (Garvie 1986:81 on *Libation Bearers* 149).

dramatized in tragedy, sacrifice, burial, and the consultation of the Delphic oracle, were never performed in plain view of the audience. Altars appear on stage in all three tragedians, but they serve as places of refuge, not of sacrifice.[17] The sacrificial animals paraded across the stage of the *Eumenides* (The Kindly Ones) and the *Taurian Iphigeneia* merely establish a fleeting ritual presence before they head off to their ultimate destination offstage.[18] At the beginning of the *Libation Bearers*, Orestes offers locks of his hair to the Argive river-god Inakhos as well as to his dead father, an instance of ritual realism which is in keeping with the play's emphasis on the performance of libations and dirges for the dead.[19] Funeral processions impart a semblance of ritual closure to the *Seven*, the *Aias* and especially the *Trojan Women* and *Suppliants* of Euripides, but since the burials are not performed during the course of the play, the presence of corpses and urns ready for burial remains a mere ritual gesture similar to the procession of the sacrificial animals.[20] In the *Aulian Iphigeneia*, principal characters such as Agamemnon, Akhilleus, and Iphigeneia are conspicuously preoccupied with the preliminary rites of sacrifice— the wreathing of the victim's head, the sprinkling with holy water, the hurling of the barley groats—but the actual sacrifice in which an animal replaces the human victim takes place offstage.[21] In the *Ion*, dramatic momentum is to a large extent generated by successive attempts to consult the Delphic oracle in the course of the action. But Xouthos receives his deceptive oracular response behind the closed doors of Apollo's temple, a denial of full ritual disclosure which corresponds to the non-ritual role of the Pythia in this play.[22]

It follows from our brief survey that rituals consisting of actions as opposed to words or gestures are rarely performed on stage. Instead of being performed, they are normally described through words and thereby reenacted verbally. For the most part, ritual performance in Greek tragedy amounts to verbal reenactment of rituals either performed in the past or still to be performed in the immediate future. The sacrifice of Iphigeneia, for instance, is recalled in the *Agamemnon* and in the *Taurian Iphigeneia* as an event of the distant past while it is pre-enacted verbally in a series of proleptic performances in the *Aulian Iphigeneia*.[23] In the *Antigone*, the *Bakkhai*, and

---

[17] Rehm 1988; Poe 1989.

[18] Aiskhylos *Eumenides* 1006, with Taplin 1977:412; Euripides *Taurian Iphegeneia* 1222–1223.

[19] Garvie 1986: 50–51 on *Libation Bearers* 6–7.

[20] Aiskhylos *Seven against Thebes* 1068–1069; Garvie 1998:249–250 on Sophokles' *Aias* 1402–1420; Euripides *Suppliants* 1114–1175, *Tr.* 1119–1250.

[21] Euripides *Aulian Iphegeneia* 435–436, 675–676, 955, 1080, 1111–1112, 1470–1472, 1477–1479. See Aretz 1999:91–229.

[22] Burnett 1971:101–129; Zeitlin 1996:285–338.

[23] Aiskhylos *Agamemnon* 218–248; Euripides *Taurian Iphegeneia* 5–9, 175–177, 359–360, *Aulian Iphigeneia* 358–360, 528–533, 880, 1080–1084.

the Euripidean *Elektra,* various sacrificial rituals are reported by witnesses as recent offstage events.[24] They are conspicuous examples of rituals that are recalled and performed verbally. More than anything else, it is the verbal performance of ritual that constitutes the ritual dimension of tragedy. As Segal once put it, "verbal communication and ritual communication are isomorphic."[25] In some instances verbal performance of ritual in tragedy is comparable to the type of verbal enactment which John L. Austin called "performative utterance" and which he defined as one of several speech acts in which "the issuing of the utterance" is tantamount to "the performing of an action."[26] Applied to ritual performance in tragedy, the concept of performative utterance suggests that certain categories of verbally performed rituals such as oaths, curses, and ritual instructions derive their efficacy from the sheer power of the poetic voice. To put it differently, most ritual *drômena* or actions are conventionally translated into dramatic *legomena* or speech acts on the tragic stage.[27]

Tragedy approximates the actual performance of ritual most closely when the ritual in question has a distinct verbal component, i. e. when the *drômena* are accompanied by extensive *legomena.* Most examples of rituals that are more dependent on words and gestures than on action are from Aiskhylos and include the ritual lament, the evocation of the dead, oath-taking and curses, and prayers that are either self-sufficient or accompany non-verbal ritual acts. In all other cases the dramatic convention of tragedy reduces ritual action to a verbal account of the ritual performance. Whether actually performed onstage or merely reenacted verbally, ritual *drômena* are dramatic tools which are as effective as ritual *legómena.* To be specific, a description of a sacrifice has at least the same dramatic effect as the recitation of a prayer, the chanting of a hymn, or the swearing of an oath.

Within this conventional framework, each of the three tragedians adopted a different but fairly consistent mode of ritual representation. Aiskhylos makes the most literal use of ritual performance for its own sake. Four of his seven extant plays dramatize complex rituals such as supplication, ghost-raising, and the pouring of libations in fairly slow motion. He prefers ritual scenarios that have a strong chthonic flavor and create a genuine ritual ambience, with total integration of the visual, verbal, and rhythmic aspects of performance. In what turned out to be his most important and far-reaching ritual innovation, Aiskhylos introduced the epic concept of the corrupted sacrifice as well as the sacrificial metaphor to the tragic stage.[28] The figure of the Aiskhylean Elektra who hesitates to pour libations on behalf of her mother exemplifies

---

[24] Sophokles *Antigone* 998–1022; Euripides *Elektra* 774–858, *Bakkhai* 1043–1152, on which see Seidensticker 1979.

[25] Segal 1986:45.

[26] Austin 1975:6.

[27] On this distinction see Henrichs 1998 and Porta 1999.

[28] Henrichs 2000, and forthcoming; Gibert 2003.

the concept of a ritual crisis that defines her as a dramatic character with both an external and internal dimension—libations and revenge.[29]

In Aiskhylos, Elektra quickly reexamines her ritual priorities and pours the libations.[30] In Sophokles' *Elektra*, however, the ritual is never carried out, and no libations are poured. As a ritual alternative, Khrysothemis takes a lock of her own hair as well as of Elektra's and deposits them on the tomb. [31] Sophokles thus "took this moment of doubt which Elektra experienced in the *Libation Bearers* and twisted it into a rejection of the entire ritual."[32] Elektra's explicit rejection of ritual libations is a reflection of her unmitigated hatred of her mother and of her total dedication to the cause of revenge.[33] Her ritual scruples separate her from her sister in the same way in which her excessive mourning separates her from the chorus. In Aiskhylos, Elektra mourns in unison with Orestes as well as the chorus. In Sophokles, her mourning is solitary, and because it lacks the group participation characteristic of Greek mourning rituals, it is less ritualistic. Like all Sophoklean characters, Elektra is totally and relentlessly true to herself. Sophokles achieves this monolithic portrayal of Elektra through his manipulation of ritual. By making ritual performance an issue, he highlights its relevance for dramatic action. But by inventing the concept of ritual nonperformance, he at the same time opens new avenues in the construction of dramatic character.

The *Elektra* is not the only play in which Sophokles cuts short or redefines rituals that his audience was led to expect. In the *Aias* the hero is driven mad by Athena and slaughters a herd of cattle without due ritual process in the mistaken belief that he is killing the leaders of the Greek host.[34] After the humiliating blood-bath he announces his intention to go to the "bathing places" (654 *loutra*) by the seashore to cleanse himself with sea-water and to bury his polluted sword in the earth. But he never lives up to his ritual promise to rid himself of the pollution and its source (*apopompe*).[35] When he returns to the stage, he uses sacrificial language as he addresses the sword that he is about to turn against himself (815). He eventually makes good on his promise, but he does so in a way which is radically different from his initial announcement. The sword is buried in his body, not in the ground, and although Sophokles does not reveal the ultimate disposal of the ill-fated

---

[29] Henrichs 1991:168–169.
[30] Above, n. 13.
[31] Sophokles *Elektra* 328–471. On hair offerings in the cult of he dead see above, n. 19.
[32] I owe this formulation to Orah Burack, a student in my 1989 Harvard Summer School course on "Myth and Religion in Greek Tragedy."
[33] Sophokles *Elektra* 431–448.
[34] On the interplay of perverted animal sacrifice and violent death including suicide, of pollution and purification, and of hero cult and supplication in *Aias* see Easterling 1989:91–99 (= 1993:9–17); Henrichs 1993; Krummen 1998:301–316.

weapon, he leads us to believe that it was buried next to Aias' corpse along with the rest of his armor save his shield. Aias does achieve purification in the end, not from being cleansed by his own blood, as some interpreters believe, but through the "holy bath" (1405 *loutrôn hosiôn*) which is administered to his corpse as part of the funeral ritual and which cleanses his body from blood, his own as well as that of the slaughtered beasts and their herdsmen.[36] Instead of being performed in the literal sense, the announced rites of purification are deferred to a later point in the action. When they are finally performed, they have undergone a transformation which redefines their meaning and which changes our perception of Aias' ritual and social status. In the hands of Sophokles, ritual thus becomes a complex dramatic tool whose literal truth is denied while its validity as a metaphor is confirmed.

A similar pattern of ritual nonperformance can be found in the *Oidipous at Kolonos*. Oidipous arrives in Athens and trespasses on the sacred grove of the dread chthonian powers known as the "Reverend Goddesses" (*Semnai Theai*) or "Kindly Ones" (*Eumenides*). The trespassing is not merely accidental. The grove is the place where he is destined to die, and through his supernatural death he will be assimilated to the local goddesses and will receive cultic honors similar to theirs.[37] By entering the grove, Oidipous anticipates and achieves his own destiny. But in the eyes of the local citizens, he has committed a grievous offense for which he has to make ritual reparation. He has to perform wineless libations, which are described to him in meticulous detail by the chorus of local elders (466–484). The ritual prescription culminates in a prayer formula and is two dozen lines long; it is the most extensive account of a libation ritual not only in Greek tragedy, but in all of Greek literature.[38]

But is the ritual ever performed? By "advising" (464 *parainesai*) Oidipous to perform this ritual and by describing it in minute detail, the chorus has virtually enacted the ritual. In the eyes of the audience, it is as good as performed, and its actual performance by Oidipous should be a mere formality not worthy of the attention of the poet. But while fulfilling our ritual expectations on the verbal level, Sophokles completely frustrates them on the level of real action. Oidipous uses his age and blindness as an excuse and delegates the offstage performance of the ritual to his daughter Ismene, a rare instance of vicarious ritual performance.[39] It could be

---

[35] Krummen 1998:304; Parker 1983:229–230; Schlesier 1990.

[36] Segal 1981b:140; Easterling 1988:97–98 (= 1993:16).

[37] On the overall resemblance and ritual affinity between the *Semnai Theai* and the heroized Oidipous as recipients of "chthonic" libations see Segal 1981b:374–375, 396: Blundell 1989:257–258; Edmunds 1996:138–142.

[38] See the penetrating analysis of Burkert 1985b:8–14.

[39] Burkert 1985b: 11 comments: "Das Ritual ist autonom, es kann ohne weiteres stellvertretend durch einen anderen vollzogen werden." But parallels for such a vicarious performance are hard to find.

argued that the ritual situation envisaged by Sophokles is emblematic of the general role of ritual in tragedy. Ritual performance on the tragic stage is always mimetic and vicarious if seen from "the world of the audience" as opposed to "the world of the tragedy" and its characters.[40]

In terms of ritual propriety, the delegation of the libations to Ismene is an exceptional turn of events. Oidipous committed the trespassing, and he should be the one who repairs the damage through the performance of the ritual. By delegating the ritual performance to Ismene, Sophokles gets her off the stage. Once out of the picture, she is immediately abducted by Kreon, apparently before she was able to perform the libations (818–821). For all we know, the ritual is never performed, but Oidipous' intention to have it performed vicariously by Ismene sets off another crisis, which culminates in his confrontation with Kreon and with his Theban past. The ritual that was designed to resolve a minor crisis in the relationship between gods and mortals thus creates a crisis on the human level that has more profound consequences dramatically, both for the structure of the play and for the character of Oidipous.[41] From a dramatic point of view, Ismene's abduction that leads to the interruption of the ritual process is a *felix culpa* because it enhances the relevance of the libations by redirecting and redefining them, thus shifting the emphasis from the ritual status of the *Semnai Theai* to the ultimate identity of Oidipous.

We have to wait until the closing scene of the play before our ritual expectations are finally fulfilled. As in the *Aias*, the failure to perform one ritual is ultimately compensated by the performance of a different ritual that reconciles us with the character of Oidipous and with the role played by his daughters. Near the end of the play, an eye-witness recalls the last moments of Oidipous' life. Shortly before his miraculous death, he sent his two daughters "to fetch water for the ritual washing (*loutrá*) and libation (*khoaí*) from a running stream."[42] In connection with death, burial and the cult of the dead, the term *loutrá*, literally "bath(water)," refers either to the ritual cleansing of the corpse of the deceased—the "sacred" or "pure" ablutions of *Aias* 1405 (*loutrón hosíon*) and *Antigone* 1201 (*hagnón loutrón*)—or to libations poured on the tomb after burial (Sophokles *Elektra* 84, 434).[43] Exceptionally, in *Oidipous at Kolonos* the ablutions are performed by Oidipous

---

[40] On the distinction see above, n. 10.
[41] Segal 1981b:390; Krummen 1998:299.
[42] Sophokles *Oidipous at Kolonos* 1598–1599 κἄπειτ' αὔσας παῖδας ἠνώγει ρυτῶν / ὑδάτων ἐνεγκεῖν λουτρὰ καὶ χοάς ποθεν. Blundell 1990:104 comments: "Oedipus, with his daughters' help, prepared himself for death with the rites customarily performed at funerals: drink offerings, ritual washing, and dressing in funeral garments (1598–1603)."
[43] Stengel 1915, 1922:539–542; Parker 1983:35; Hoessly 2001:21–23.

himself moments before his death.[44] Throughout the death scene, Oidipous takes charge of his own destiny in a way which foreshadows his future status and power as a cultic hero. By adding the term *khoaí*, "libations," to the *loutrá*, Sophokles extends the ritual ambience of Oidipous' last ablution and assimilates it to the ritually marked libations which were customary in the cult of the dead as well as in that of the *Semnai Theai* and which figure so prominently as "holy libations" (469 *hierás* . . . *khoás*) in the play's first episode.[45] The ritual promise made there is at long last fulfilled as the play closes, but the function of the ritual is completely redefined in the process. By using the language of libation and by making Oidipous the performer as well as the recipient of the last ablution, Sophokles makes a statement about Oidipous which shifts the emphasis from the ritual performance to the dramatic character. This reorientation is the same as in *Aias*. A comparable shift occurs in *Oidipous the King*, where the initial emphasis on pollution from murder and on the need to exile the killer is reversed at the end of the play in the figure of the blind and polluted Oidipous who is granted permission to make physical contact with his children before he is denied exile and confined to the palace. Ritual propriety thus gives way to human compassion, to an inscrutable divine will, and to the ultimate realization that Oidipous' pollution from parricide and incest cannot be cured with ritual remedies.[46]

We have looked at three Sophoklean plays and found various patterns of the playwright manipulating ritual performance for dramatic purposes in ways unimaginable in Aiskhylos and not duplicated in Euripides. Elektra rejects her traditional ritual role as a libation-bearer, Aias does not keep his ritual promise, and Oidipous adduces old age and blindness as excuses for his refusal to pour libations. All three figures benefit from the rejection of their ritual roles: their dramatic character is enhanced, and their mission accomplished.[47] Two of the three, Oidipous and Aias, have rituals performed for them immediately before or after their death that take

[44] Ulrich von Wilamowitz-Moellendorff in Wilamowitz 1917:365 and Segal 1981b:389–392 on *Oidipous at Kolonos* 1598–1605. Like Sophokles' Oidipous, the Euripidean Alkestis (*Alkestis* 159–160) and the Platonic Sokrates (*Phaidon* 116a) also go knowingly to their deaths and wash themselves before they die. Burkert 1985b:13 and Blundell 1990:81 assume that Odipous was washed by his unmarried daughters, a scenario unsupported by the Greek text and unlikely for reasons of propriety.

[45] Stengel 1915:631 on *Oidipous at Kolonos* 1599: "Wasser, um die Leiche zu waschen und um dem Hingeschiedenen die Spende zu giessen." Similarly Krummen 1998:299: "Die Güsse der Reinigung werden zu Güssen, mit denen man den Toten wäscht" (a development which epitomizes the ritual shift in both the *Aias* and the *Oidipous at Kolonus*). But Oidipous was not one of the ordinary dead. As a cult hero he received chthonic libations similar to those received by the *Semnai Theai* (Henrichs 1983: 100).

[46] Sophokles *Oidipous the King* 1369–1523, on which see Segal 1981b: 244–248.

[47] Cf. Zeitlin 1970:369; Krummen 1998.

the place of the rejected rituals and redefine their function. In addition, Antigone's failed attempts to bury her brother and the failure of Oidipous in *Oidipous the King* to achieve purification and exile follow the same Sophoklean pattern of defining and enhancing a character's dramatic status by manipulating and abnegating the ritual process. The perversion of burnt sacrifices in the *Trakhiniai* can be interpreted along similar lines. If so, six out of the seven extant tragedies of Sophokles would follow a comparable pattern of a highly creative use of ritual to achieve distinct dramatic ends.

When Kalkhas in the parodos of the *Agamemnon* interprets the omen of the two eagles and understands its sinister implication, namely the need for a human victim instead of a sacrificial animal, he exclaims: "Let the good prevail" (τὸ εὖ νικάτω). In tragedy, ritual remedies usually fail, and instead of being the solution, ritual becomes part of the problem. That is why Kalkhas is so concerned, and why his words are apotropaic. The rituals of tragedy go easily awry, and that is what makes them so dangerous. While tragic rituals are a constant threat to the characters, they are an unqualified boon for the playwrights. Even more so than Aiskhylos, Sophokles recognized the enormous dramatic potential of the concept of the ritual crisis and put it to innovative use. While his characters struggle with rituals with which they don't identify and which they cannot control, the playwright reigns supreme over ritual processes that invariably work to his advantage. He is a ritual expert in his own right, and in his experienced hands the rituals of tragedy turn out to be exquisite tools over which the good of the playwright, the dramatic good that is, always prevails.[*]

[*] This essay reproduces the substance of one of my Sather Lectures, delivered at the University of California, Berkeley in the spring of 1990. I dedicate this version to the memory of Charles Segal, who heard it on May 12, 2001 during a celebration of his 65th birthday, which turned out to be his last. I am grateful to Panagiotis Roilos and Dimitrios Yatromanolakis for their patience; to Sarah Nolan for her acute comments; and to David Petrain for his last-minute help.

Eleven

Playing at Ritual:
Variations on a Theme in Byzantine Religious Tales

John Duffy

The ordinary inhabitant of Constantinople, at almost any period in the city's history, had the opportunity to become familiar with a great variety of religious and secular ritual, and much of it on a grand scale. Whether as a worshipper in Hagia Sophia, or a spectator in the Hippodrome, or as an onlooker at imperial processions through the streets of the capital, the Byzantine citizen was treated, if he wanted it, to a daily feast of liturgical and imperial ceremony. But even the peasant on the most remote country estate of the empire was never far from the local church which, on its own modest scale, staged all the services marking the passage through life, from baptism to the commemoration of the dead.

To say that the rituals and services of the Orthodox Church were important aspects of everyday life in Byzantium would be an understatement. They were part of the very fabric of the culture and as such, it is not surprising that they are fairly well reflected in the broad sweep of Byzantine literature, from chronicles to saints' lives, not to mention the multitude of special-purpose liturgical books that bear eloquent witness to the unbroken tradition of daily communal worship throughout the empire.

In this chapter I want to explore the topic of "ritual as reflected in literature" by going to a somewhat underappreciated corner of medieval Greek writing, to the religious tale, the διήγησις ψυχωφελής, "spiritually beneficial narrative" or "story good for the soul."

At a conservative estimate the number of these surviving stories is over a thousand. They are preserved sometimes in planned collections, such as the well-known *Pratum Spirituale* (The Spiritual Meadow) or Λειμωνάριον of John Moschus from around 600 CE,[1] but more commonly they are found widely scattered in groups or as individual items in special monastic books known as *pateriká*.[2] The

---

[1] See note 3 below.

[2] For a brief description of the genre, see *The Oxford Dictionary of Byzantium*, New York and Oxford: Oxford University Press, vol. 3, 1991; entry "Paterika."

degree of comparative neglect of this literature may be gauged from the fact that
even John Moschus must still be read in a late seventeenth-century edition.[3]
Fortunately, however, a small band of modern researchers have been doing yeomen's
work in the field. Since this kind of writing is a close relative of hagiography, the
far-sighted Bollandistes fathers in Belgium decided some years ago to collect and
catalog all tales of the type, with the result that special sections of their *Bibliotheca
Hagiographica Graeca*[4] provide some basic pieces of information, including tale title
and assigned number, incipit, desinit, edition, and manuscript sources, and even
variant versions of the same story. The Canadian based scholar John Wortley has
taken the work of the Bollandistes a step further. He is now putting the final
touches to an important new research tool, which he calls "A *Répertoire* of Byzantine
Beneficial Tales" and expects to make available to the public in the near future. The
work, developed single-handedly after many years of close study of the field, is both
a systematic listing and an index of more than a thousand stories. The index is an
invaluable indicator of subjects and motifs, making it possible, for example, to see
at a glance which stories over the centuries have treated the same or similar themes.

Wortley's *Répertoire*, to which he kindly gave me access in a pre-publication
copy, has proved very helpful for the subject of the present chapter. My focus will
be on the theme of young people playing at Christian ritual, a topic treated in a
small number of stories dating from the most fertile period of religious tale production, namely, the fourth to the seventh century.

We will begin, however, with an example that does not appear in the Wortley
list, presumably because it is presented by the source, Theodoret of Cyrrhus in his
Religious History, as an actual event connected with his own family; in any case it is
not fully developed as a narrative and did not enjoy an independent career outside
the text of Theodoret. It is instructive, however, as having the makings of a good
διήγησις ψυχωφελής and is of interest for the topic at hand because of its theme.
Chapter nine of the *Religious History*, written around the middle of the fifth
century, relates the following episode from the life of the holy monk Peter in the
city of Antioch:

One day a domestic servant, possessed by a demon, was brought to Peter for
help. The holy man said a prayer and, as part of the exorcism, forced the evil spirit
to confess why he had chosen this particular victim. "I was in Heliopolis," the
demon explained, "in the house where this man was working. The master of the

[3] The 1681 edition of J. B. Cotelier was essentially reproduced by J. P. Migne in vol. 87, part 3,
columns 2852-3112, of the *Patrologia Graeca* series (henceforth PG). For a complete English translation of the Migne text, along with twenty-four supplementary tales, see Wortley 1992.
[4] Henceforth BHG, an indispensable resource for all texts relating to Greek hagiography, third edition by
F. Halkin, 3 volumes, Brussels 1957; supplemented by a *Novum Auctarium*, ed. F. Halkin, Brussels 1984.

house was sick and, while the mistress was busy attending to him, the young maid-servants were entertaining themselves, telling stories about the lives of the holy monks of Antioch and the great powers they have against demons. Then the girls turned to pretending that they were possessed and raving mad. The next thing was, that servant put on a goatskin cloak and began exorcising them like a monk would. While this ritual was going on I was standing by the door, and not being able to bear the boasting stories about the power of the monks, I decided I would find out for myself. So I took possession of the servant in order to see how the monks might get me out of him. And now," he concedes in dejection, "I have learned my lesson and do not need another one. Since you have given the order, I will leave him straightaway." With that, concludes the hagiographer, he cleared off and the servant enjoyed his freedom again.[5]

As a story, the account of Theodoret does have engaging and sophisticated διήγησις elements. The saintly monk of Christian Antioch is pitted against a demon from the famously pagan Heliopolis (i.e. Baalbek); the evil spirit is not only expelled from his victim, but is forced against every instinct of his being to become himself, like a hagiographer, the narrator of a true account; and ironically the road to his downfall begins precisely when he hears the type of story about holy men in which he is destined to feature as defeated antagonist. Certainly there is novelistic stuff here. However, Theodoret does not linger long enough over any of the elements to draw out their potential. Even as a short story it is compressed too much and a full half of the demon's own account is reported as indirect speech. Add too the classicizing style of the Greek and the rhythmical prose, and it is easy to understand why the piece was not picked up and sent into circulation around the world of the beneficial tale.

By contrast, a story related in Latin by the Church historian Rufinus was taken over into Greek and included by John Moschus in his collection.[6] It concerns the renowned fourth-century bishop of Alexandria, Athanasius, and illustrates, among other things, the familiar hagiographic idea that God often sends signs foretelling a future saint's greatness. In this version we are told that one day, as he was looking out to sea, Alexander the bishop of Alexandria, saw a group of boys amusing themselves on the seashore, playing bishop and imitating church services. Paying closer attention he realized that they were performing secret parts of the divine mysteries and it disturbed him. So he sent some of the clergy to apprehend

[5] I have paraphrased the original Greek, which is edited (with French translation) by Canivet and Leroy-Molinghen 1977:422–424. For an English translation see Price 1985:85. I am grateful to Emmanuel Bourbouhakis for bringing the story to my attention in the first place.
[6] Moschus no. 197 = PG 873, 3084B–3085A.

the boys and bring them to him, which they did. Alexander interrogated the children, asking them about the game and the acts they were performing. Quite frightened, they admitted that they had picked the boy Athanasius as their bishop, had chosen clergy among themselves, and were baptizing some catechumens. Making further enquiries Alexander found out which children had undergone the ceremony and learned further that they had been baptized fully in accordance with church custom. The upshot of the episode was twofold: bishop Alexander decreed that those who had been given holy baptism had no need to receive the sacrament a second time, and he issued instructions that the young Athanasius and the companions chosen as presbyters and deacons be handed over to the care of the church for their education.

As a type of edifying tale the piece about young Athanasius would rank somewhere between the self-consciously literary performance of Theodoret and the unpretentious narrative storytelling that is usually on offer in Moschus and similar collections. In this case Moschus has openly borrowed from a written source, as he occasionally does,[7] and the translation from Rufinus' Latin has brought across a certain stiffness of style with it. Still, the storyline is worked out more completely than in Theodoret's description of Peter the monk, and there is a more extensive series of actions and reactions leading up to the dénouement.

And with the story, of course, comes the edification. Every διήγησις ψυχωφελής can be expected to have a point, a spiritual message; it is not invariably spelled out, but is often left to do its work silently on listener or reader. In the case of Moschus' retelling of Rufinus there is something more than the illustration of a hagiographical commonplace. There is an unmistakable interest in the ritual game played by Athanasius and his companions. There is an emphasis on the manner of performance. The Greek of Moschus says that "they carried out everything according to the custom of our religion";[8] in the fifteenth-century Latin translation of the *Pratum* by Ambrogio Traversari, who may have used a more complete Greek version, we have the additional sentence: "and they were asked what questions were put to the baptized and how they responded."[9] It would be a bit much to say that we have here a theological lesson on baptism, but there is surely a message about the gravity of the sacrament and the efficacy of rites performed with correct words and deeds.

---

[7] There is an excellent discussion of Moschus and his sources in Chadwick 1974.

[8] Op. cit. 3084D: κατὰ τὸ ἔθος τῆς ἡμετέρας θρησκείας πάντα ἐκεῖνα ἐτέλεσαν.

[9] Ibid. 3083D: "Tunc igitur diligenter inquirens ab eis *et quinam baptizati fuissent et quid et quomodo interrogati quidve respondissent.*"

This conclusion is nicely corroborated by the story that immediately follows it in Moschus.[10] It is a brief anecdote concerning Athanasius at a later stage in his life, when he was in fact bishop of Alexandria. A question was put to him about the validity of baptism performed on someone who lacked the faith. For his answer he cites the experience of a predecessor on the Alexandrian throne, Peter, who during a plague was faced with many people seeking baptism only out of fear of death. An angel appeared to Peter to deliver the following complaint: "How much longer are you going to be sending up here purses that are sealed, to be sure, but are entirely empty and have nothing in them?"[11]

The story preceding "Athanasius and his Companions" is an excellent representative of the style of narrative most typically on display in Moschus and in the genre as a whole.[12] It opens by identifying the collector's source, a certain pious Christian, George, the eparch of the province of Africa, who relates a marvelous event that took place in his original home province of Syria. It was in a village estate some forty miles from Apamea, where boys used to bring the flocks for pasture to the nearby mountains. One day the boys, playing like boys usually do, hit upon the idea of celebrating the Eucharist. So they appointed, from among themselves, a priest and two deacons; they chose a flat rock for an altar and placed on it some bread and a jar of wine. The priest proceeded to pronounce the words of consecration, which he happened to know by heart, and the deacons stood on either side using their headgear as fans. They had just completed everything according to church custom, and were about to divide the bread, when suddenly fire burst down from heaven and consumed everything, bread and rock altar alike, so that not a trace was left. Scared out of their wits, the children fell to the ground half dead, not able to speak or move a limb. When they failed to return to the estate at the usual time, their worried parents went searching, found them unconscious and carried them back home. Two days later, after their recovery, the children went back to the mountains accompanied by their parents and the owners of the estate, and were able to find some signs of the fire. Convinced by the evidence, the grownups hurried to the city and informed the bishop. He in turn with his clergy visited the site, got a firsthand report from the children and saw the evidence of the fire. As a result he sent the boys away to become monks, made the place into a monastery and built a church over the spot where the fire had descended. "And," says Moschus to conclude, "this same George informed us that he himself saw one of those boys in the monastery where the marvelous event occurred."

---

[10] No. 198 = PG 873, 3085C–3088A.

[11] Ibid. 3085D: ἕως πότε ἀποστέλλετε ἐνταῦθα βάλαντα ἐσφραγισμένα μέν, κενὰ δὲ πάντη καὶ οὐδὲν ἔχοντα ἔσωθεν;

[12] No. 196 = PG 873, 3080D–3084A. The corresponding number for the BHG is 1318x.

John Duffy

If Moschus' account of the young Athanasius, despite its coming straight from a written source, is several notches above that of Theodoret as a developed story, "The Boys of Apamea" is about as close as one can get to a complete folktale. It is certainly a model of the Byzantine διήγησις ψυχωφελής. It is fully self-contained; it has the seal of authenticity at the beginning and at the end—not only is the source, George, carefully identified but he is twice characterized as φιλόχριστος, a friend of Christ and Christians and, therefore, a reliable informant. Other details too serve the dual and complementary purpose of enhancing the listener's enjoyment and boosting the veracity of the account. The estate in Apamea is named,[13] its location is precisely noted, and the site of the miracle is said to be about a mile away in the mountains. Even the boys' wine jar is realistically described as "earthenware" (ὀστράκινον). As they stand around the altar, the two deacons used their φακιόλια (some kind of turban, presumably) to fan the air, just as deacons in church use fans over the oblation.[14] We are also informed, in a careful aside, how the pretending priest came to know the words of consecration—it was the custom in the church there for boys to stand in front of the sanctuary and to be the first to receive the Eucharist after the clergy. And since, in some places, the priests were in the habit of reciting the words of consecration out loud, the boys were able to learn them off by heart.

The edifying element of "The Boys of Apamea" centers on an important sacrament and its ritual performance. Once again it is not a lesson in theology. It is a simple story of an extraordinary event in which innocent children, having the necessary ingredients and knowing the exact ritual formulas, succeed in producing a miracle. The story does not spend time discussing whether or not that bread really turned into the body of Christ. No, it merely relates that when they had done everything in the prescribed manner and were about to divide up the bread, the fire descended and consumed everything. That by itself is an impressive reminder, for the believer, of the tremendous mystery and power of the Eucharist. And the spiritual point is strengthened when the bishop enters the picture. He formally recognizes the miracle, puts the boys in a monastery and has a monastery founded on the *locus sanctus*.

---

[13] Ibid. 3080D: τὸ Γοναγὸν καλούμενον. Once again, on a matter of detail, the Traversari Latin translation has an interesting addition. It specifies the town in Apamea from which George hailed: "ex oppido quod dicitur Thorax." The fact that a Slavic version of the story gives the place name as Terakus suggests that the town was identified in an earlier, if not the original, Greek version. See Widnäs 1966:184.

[14] For liturgical fans (ῥιπίδιον) see *The Oxford Dictionary of Byzantium*, vol. 3, entry "Rhipidion," 1790–1791. The use of fans at the oblation is also mentioned in Moschus story no. 150 = PG 873, 3016B.

The virtues of "The Boys of Apamea" as a tale made it an attractive item and led to its having a second, and even a third, career of sorts, outside the confines of the Moschus collection. We will now turn briefly to consider those developments.

Sometime in the eleventh century an elderly priest-monk from Amalfi in Southern Italy lived for a period in Constantinople, as part of the Amalfitan community in the Byzantine capital. This man, Johannes Monachus, was also a scholar of Greek and was involved in a number of translation projects. One of them, ostensibly undertaken at the request of a well-placed fellow Amalfitan, was to provide a Latin version of Greek religious tales. The result was the small book now known by the title *Liber de miraculis* (Book of Miracles), a gathering of forty-two *narrationes*, mostly from recognizable Greek collections such as "Daniel of Sketis," "Anastasius of Sinai," and above all of John Moschus.[15] Half of the book is taken from the *Pratum Spirituale*, including "The Boys of Apamea" under the heading "De sacrificio puerorum qui pascebant pecora." The versions by John the Monk are important evidence for translating activity and cross-cultural exchanges in the eleventh century between Byzantium and the West. And coming, as they do, several centuries before the translation of Moschus by Ambrogio Traversari, they are of considerable interest for the study of the original Greek text, especially since John seems to have stayed very close to his exemplar. In "The Boys of Apamea," for instance, the only difference of any significance appears at the very end where the Latin adds the detail that the bishop "at the proper time tonsured the boys and ordained them monks and priests."[16] Given the nature of John's translation style it would be a reasonable working assumption that the extra information reflects a variant in the Greek tradition of Moschus.

The treatment accorded to "The Boys of Apamea" on the Greek side, by contrast, is quite another matter. At a certain point in or after the seventh century the story was spirited away and grafted onto elements of an entirely different tale. Eventually the new transformation itself developed into two distinct versions, both of them duly recorded in the BHG and in Wortley's "*Répertoire*."[17] We will deal here only with the more elaborate of the versions. It was published in 1938 by Theodore Nissen as one of a group of "Unbekannte Erzählungen aus dem *Pratum*

[15] For basic information on J. Monachus one may consult the useful entry "John of Amalfi" in *The Oxford Dictionary of Byzantium*, vol. 2, 1062. The most substantial work to date on his life and activity will be found in the introduction to the edition prepared by Huber (Huber 1915).

[16] Ed. cit. 76, 31–33: "Tempore autem oportuno tondens pueros, monachos atque clericos ordinavit."

[17] The first version is BHG 1322n, which is assigned the number 486 in the Wortley *Répertoire*. The second is BHG 1076m (= Wortley 487) and was published by Karakallinos, on the basis of a manuscript in Austria (Karakallinos 1954:219–220).

Spirituale,"[18] but, as Nissen himself was the first to point out, this particular form of the tale could never have been part of the Moschus collection, since it reflects political realities in Palestine, namely an Arabic administration, that could only be dated after the year 638.[19]

In the Nissen version the source is recorded as a priest-monk from the New Lavra monastery, south of Jerusalem, who in turn heard it from some devout men (φιλόχριστοι ἄνδρες). The setting is no longer Apamea, but a Palestinian village; however, with the exception of one newly introduced element, the first part of the story unfolds very much as in "The Boys of Apamea" and the two accounts have a number of expressions in common, including the crucial phrase of the boys, "Come on, let's celebrate the Eucharist!" (Δεῦτε, ποιήσωμεν σύναξιν). The new element, superimposed for a reason that will become clear presently, is that one of the herding boys is Jewish, in fact a son of the local chief rabbi. He pleads to be allowed to take part in the Eucharistic ritual and is admitted to the game after being baptized by the pretending bishop of the group. The service goes ahead, the words of consecration are pronounced over the bread, the fire bursts down from heaven knocking the boys senseless, until they are eventually discovered and carried home by their parents, and, upon recovery, reveal everything that took place. At this point in the original Moschus tale, the reader will recall, we are about to enter the final phase and outcome. In this later remake we have heard only a quarter of the story, and what in Moschus was a well-rounded *narratio* is here merely the prologue to a much more elaborate drama. The scene quickly shifts to the home of the chief rabbi where we find the newly baptized boy turning against his old religion and adamantly refusing to eat the food offered by his father. The irate rabbi's immediate reaction to this apostasy is to plot the son's death, and the scheme develops into a surprising concatenation of people and events, involving the local Arab emir, the village bathkeeper who happens to owe the rabbi money, and a higher official of the Arab administration who turns out to be something of a deus ex machina for the boy. We cannot go through the intricate series of actions that have the boy, on three different occasions, sealed inside the blazing bathhouse furnace, only to be miraculously preserved, or the aftermath in which the father is condemned to be beheaded. We will leave this version with the observation that the kernel of the overwrought account of rabbi and son is directly inspired by yet another and much simpler original that was in circulation at least fifty years earlier. I am referring to the *Jewish Boy Legend*, in which a Jewish glassblower in Constantinople, angered by his son's partaking of the Eucharist with Christian

---

[18] This is the title of the article which appeared, with useful notes, in 1938 (see Nissen 1938); our story is no. 8, pp. 361–365. In another article, Nissen provides a German translation of the story (Nissen 1939:399–403) and a highly informative discussion of the relationship between the various versions.

[19] Nissen 1939:397.

schoolmates, throws him in the furnace of his workshop. The boy is miraculously saved, of course, and the father executed. That story, whose earliest extant telling is by the Church historian Evagrius, went on to have an astonishingly varied life in Greek, Latin and several Western European languages, throughout the middle ages,[20] ending up, at least geographically, in the British Isles. Jan Ziolkowski's edition of *Miracles of the Virgin* by Nigel of Canterbury contains a verse version in Latin.[21] And there are several surviving prose copies of the story in Medieval Irish.[22]

But we have digressed a little, and it is time to return to the main topic for some final considerations.

Children's games are, needless to say, a universal phenomenon and playing at religion can no doubt be attested in most societies. Still, it is particularly appropriate to be able to include here a comparative note from within the Greek tradition itself and to present some evidence that speaks for an element of continuity in this sphere between the worlds of Byzantium and modern Greece. The material comes from a wide-ranging article on religious toys and games in Greece and Western Europe over the course of the last three or four centuries, written by an historian of culture, Maria Argyriadi, who based the Greek part of her study largely on a decade of field research and oral reports from many different areas of Greece.[23] She was able to conclude that in the towns, cities, and particularly the villages all over the country children were involved, in various small ways, in looking after the local church. This meant that they were able to become very familiar with different elements of church ritual, which they then could imitate and turn into play. Some of her best evidence came from the recollections of priests.

One of them narrated the following account to her in 1991: "I remember as an altar-boy that inside the sanctuary I loved to blow the bits of charcoal in the censer, so much so that many a time I was swollen from the blowing. One of my favorite canticles was that sung at funerals, for which I was often scolded. In the early years of this century we children very often performed the baptism or the marriage of a doll. We used to quarrel about who should be the priest. Most times it would be the boy who would become a priest. He knew the psalms and could mimic the priest convincingly. He wore a sheet as a habit, chanted just like the priest and, in the end, it was he who took the much-sought-after title of godfather. The doll was baptised in a broken earthenware basin and we handed round ten-lepta coins as

---

[20] The most extensive study is still Wolter 1879.

[21] Ziolkowski 1986:62–64.

[22] The only fairly accessible Gaelic version can be found, with an English translation, in Stokes 1890:xx–xxii.

[23] Argyriadi 1993. Charles Stewart had the collegial kindness not only to bring Argyriadi's work to my attention, but also to send me a copy of the article.

John Duffy

martyrikia. The wedding crowns for the marriage ceremony were made of vine twigs and we used pebbles as pretend *koufeta.*"[24]

Another informant reported to her a story he had heard from an elderly priest-monk by the name of Ignatios: "one day in the 1920's, when Ignatios was a child, he and two friends were playing at being priests, in an attic in Pangrati. They had a glass of wine and a piece of bread, and they were celebrating mass in all seriousness, to the extent that at one point the glass filled with blood and the bread became meat. The boys were terrified. It was then that they decided to become clerics and follow the vocation of the priesthood."[25]

Those simple reports have the effect of bridging an enormous time gap and of making a vivid connection between ritual inspired forms of entertainment among children from two vastly different epochs.

The Byzantine religious tale is, by and large, a fairly uncomplicated affair, not an occasion for intricate structure or deeply hidden meaning. It reflects a world and a mentality in which men and women confront, with innocent faith, the mysteries of their earthly existence and their relations with the divine. Equally straightforward is the raison d'être of the tale. Its main, often declared, purpose is to edify; it also has a secondary, unstated aim, which is to entertain. In view of these considerations, one is reluctant to go hunting for profound conclusions. On the other hand, as latter day scientists we do have some obligation to look at the broader picture, and it is in this spirit that the following brief observations are offered on the small number of stories we have discussed.

A common element in all is the fact that the young people play at ritual only when they are by themselves and unsupervised—on the beach, in the mountain, or, in the case of Theodoret, when the mistress of the house is otherwise occupied. But there is no clear message that their activity is a serious transgression and deserving of punishment.[26] What we do see, from the episodes of baptism and celebrating the

---

[24] Argyriadi 1993:214. An editorial note (p. 220) explains that *martyrikia* are small tin-crosses or coins distributed by the godparents to the guests after a baptism; *koufeta* are sugared almonds given to the guests following wedding and baptism ceremonies.

[25] Argyriadi 1993:214.

[26] In discussing some episodes of ritual mockery in the religious stories collected by the twelfth-century Cistercian Caesarius of Heisterbach, A. I. Gurevich points to the important distinction made between the intentions of children and those of adults. In one instance where schoolboys baptize a dog in a river and, in so doing, drive the animal mad, Caesarius observes that the Lord was merciful towards the children because they behaved badly out of youthful foolishness. But in the account of two adults, one of whom made fun of the ritual of penitential ashes, punishment from God for this action was swift and severe. See Gurevich 1988:196–197. I am grateful to Panagiotis Roilos for making me aware of Gurevich's work and his treatment of these tales. In the edition of Caesarius (Strange 1851) the stories in question are in the second volume, nos. 45 and 53 of section 10. Perhaps we should see something of the same distinction in the account of Theodoret: the young servant girls pay no price for their fun, but the (older?) male servant becomes the target of the demon.

208

Eucharist, is that those "touched" by a miraculous event are handed over to the church. A similar thing occurs in one of the Greek versions of the *Jewish Boy Legend*, where the boy is made a reader (ἀναγνώστης) and the mother becomes a nun (ἀσκήτρια).[27] It is also the outcome in a Georgian story of a children's Eucharist, set in Byzantium, which relates that the "ministers" were ordained, each to the rank he had assumed in the make-believe.[28] Whether we are dealing here with an aspect of miracle theology or simply a tale motif, is not obvious to me.

What I would suggest, at the risk of making an artificial separation, is that the activity of the children and their fate belong more to the entertaining element of the stories. The spiritual point and edification, on the other hand, emanate from the focus on the sacraments of baptism and the Eucharist, two central rituals of transformation in the Christian Church. Beyond promoting the mystery and awesome power of the two sacraments, these tales do, as we remarked earlier, put a particular stress on the efficacy of ritual carried out in the proper manner, even when it is performed as child's play.

[27] See Mioni 1951:94.
[28] See Garitte 1966:420, no. 22.

Twelve

The Sacred and the Profane:
Reenacting Ritual in the Medieval Greek Novel[*]

Panagiotis Roilos

In this chapter I investigate the reinscription and rhetorical manipulation of sacred and secular performative and discursive ritual patterns in the twelfth-century medieval Greek novel. Despite its pivotal significance both for the narrative structure of these texts and for their extratextual interactions with their broader cultural context, the multilayered heteroglossia of the ritual discourses in the medieval Greek novels remains unexplored. My study here focuses on the rhetorical and parodic reenactment of aspects of Byzantine ceremonial court protocol in one of these novels, Theodoros Prodromos' *Rhodanthe and Dosikles*.

Although circumscribed by the strict and sometimes monolithic conventions of a long-established tradition, rhetoric in Byzantium always remained a potentially "double-tongued" (ἀμφοτερόγλωσσος)[1] art, which allowed its practitioners to exploit the ambivalences of language and, sometimes, even to undermine the

---

[*] This chapter is a modified version of Roilos 2000.

[1] Ἀμφοτερόγλωσσος is a term used by Tzetzes in his *Chiliads* in association with a rhetor's ability to manipulate the meaning of his words: Σερβίλιος ἦν ὕπατος καὶ Καῖσαρ τῶν Ῥωμαίων./Μεθόδῳ δὲ δεινότητος, ῥητορικῶς τῷ τρόπῳ,/ ἐκ Σερβηλίων τῆς γονῆς λέγω καὶ τὸν Σερβλίαν./ Ὡς εἴπερ ἄλλος ἤθελε, Σέρβον Ἡλίαν εἶπεν./Τοῦτο γὰρ ῥήτορος ἀνδρὸς καὶ ἀμφοτερογλώσσου,/καὶ πράγμασι καὶ κλήσεσι καὶ τοῖς λοιποῖς ὁμοίως/πρὸς ἔπαινον καὶ ψόγον δὲ κεχρῆσθαι συμφερόντως (Leone 1968:7.295–301); on the aristocratic family of Serblias in general, see *Oxford Dictionary of Byzantium*, s.v.). Tzetzes illustrates the character of rhetoric as ἀμφοτερογλωσσία (double-tonguedness) by means of his reference to the protean character of ψόγος (invective) and ἔπαινος (praise) which correspond to ψόγος and ἐγκώμιον, two of the most influential *progumnasmata* (rhetorical excersises) in Byzantine literary tradition. The ability of a *rhêtôr* to adapt the same words and ideas to different literary contexts with totally opposite functions points to the potentially playful character not only of rhetoric, but of literature in general. Such an *amphoteroglôssia* could be perceived as a Byzantine equivalent of the Bakhtinian *heteroglossia*. The notion of *heteroglossia* pervades the whole theoretical work of Bakhtin, especially his discussion of the novel, and is closely associated with his idea of dialogism. *Heteroglossia* refers to the multiple conditions that define the semantic value of a specific utterance on a specific occasion, at a specific moment; see especially Bakthin 1981:259–422.

authority of their models.[2] Rhetoric has invested Byzantine literature with a dialogic potentiality and an allusive intertextuality whose aesthetic appeal should be estimated not on the basis of our own criteria but according to the horizon of expectations of its original public—to the extent, of course, that these horizons can be reconstructed.[3]

The impact of rhetoric on the ancient Greek novel has been the subject of many discussions. Giangrande, for example, has argued that the origins of the ancient Greek novel should be sought for in the area of prose rhetorical paraphrases of erotic stories—in particular of Alexandrian love-elegies and epyllia.[4] Reardon, on the other hand, putting aside the thorny, and ultimately fruitless, question of origins, insists on the importance of rhetorical theory and practice for the composition of ancient Greek novels, arguing that "romance could be composed only as a form of rhetoric."[5] He puts special emphasis on epideictic rhetoric and *progumnasmata*, which, in his opinion, had contributed a great deal to the formulation of the literary taste and the aesthetic expectations of both the authors and the readers of ancient Greek novel.[6] The same holds true, I argue, for the twelfth-century medieval Greek novels.[7] As I have argued elsewhere, the twelfth-century Byzantine

[2] Some authors emphasize their own innovative divergences from the established tradition. See, for example, the cases discussed in Garzya 1973:7–8.

[3] If the appreciation of this kind of creativity demands considerable intellectual agility on the part of the general reader or even the specialized scholar, this by no means should be considered as an inherent flaw of Byzantine literature itself. In his notorious article on "The Hellenistic Origins of Byzantine Literature," for example, Jenkins expresses his negative view about rhetoric's impact on Byzantine literature in a vehement way, without trying to define its broader aesthetic and ideological parameters: "We have been compelled to pass an unfavorable judgment on Byzantine rhetoric, since it colored nearly every department of Byzantine literature and since honesty forbids us to regard its influence as anything but disastrous" (Jenkins 1963:46). For a brief review of previous negative assessments of Byzantine rhetoric see Hunger 1972:6–7. Hunger proposes a systematic model for the contextualization of the function of Byzantine rhetoric. For a comprehensive aesthetic and ideological approach to Byzantine rhetoric see also Beck 1969:91–101; Beck's overall attitude toward Byzantine rhetoric is actually more positive than what Hunger's criticism lets his readers think (Hunger 1972:7n5). For the importance of rhetoric in Byzantium in general see also Hunger 1981:35–47, and Kustas 1970:55–73.

[4] Giangrande 1962:152–154.

[5] Reardon 1991:84.

[6] Reardon 1991:87–89. Reardon rightly avoids, however, the one-sided analysis of the influence of rhetoric on the novel criticized by Perry 1967: 19n7. Cf. also Hägg 1983:107–108. For the role of rhetoric in the ancient Greek novel, see also Hock 1997:445–465. Hock notes that "despite the widespread acknowledgement of the important relation between rhetoric and the romances, little has been done to clarify this relation" (ibid.:450). Unfortunately, Hock's article as well is too general to address this problem in detail. Rohde was, of course, the first to study the impact of rhetoric on the ancient Greek novel (Rohde 1914:336–360).

[7] These texts, which were written in the twelfth century during the reign of the Komnenian dynasty, are also known as Komnenian novels. These are *Rhodanthe and Dosikles,* by Theodoros Prodromos; *Hysmine and Hysminias,* by Eustathios Makrembolites; *Drosilla and Charikles,* by Niketas Eugeneianos; and *Aristandros and Kallithea,* by Konstantinos Manasses.

novelists and their audience received and appreciated the ancient as well as their contemporary novels as predominantly rhetorical works; such an attitude of the Byzantine audience toward the genre of the novel is indicated by the manuscript tradition, the characteristics of the Komnenian novels themselves, and the overall aesthetic reception of the ancient Greek examples of the genre by the Byzantines.[8]

Rhetorical *amphoteroglôssia* allowed the Komnenian novelists to invest their works with a rich and ambivalent allusiveness. In what follows I try to illustrate the intricate ways in which rhetorical *amphoteroglôssia* enabled Theodoros Prodromos to reactivate aspects of Byzantine court rituals in an innovatively subversive and parodic manner. My focus is on Prodromos' fictional reconstruction of a formal dinner that takes place in the context of the ceremonial reception of an ambassador at the court of his enemy.

In his commentaries on Homer, Eustathios of Thessalonike (twelfth century) associates the description of banquets with the rhetorical *Idea* of *apheleia* (simplicity, naiveté).[9] More specifically, Eustathius argues, banquets, as events of everyday life, could be connected with *euteleia* as well (ordinary discourse), which is closely related to *apheleia* and associated with comic modes of literary expression.[10] It is in this comic vein of rhetorical *euteleia*, I argue, that Theodoros Prodromos reenacts conventions of the Byzantine court protocol in his novel.

In the fourth book of *Rhodanthe and Dosikles* Prodromos describes one of the most grotesque banquets in the whole tradition of the Greek novel. The banquet is attended by two enemies and serves a specific political agenda. Its context is as follows: Artaxanes, an envoy of the king of Pissa, Bryaxes, arrives at the court of Mistylos, the chief of the pirates who have arrested the two protagonists of the novel, carrying a letter from Bryaxes. In the letter, which has the form of an ultimatum, Bryaxes disputes Mistylos' rule over the city of Rhamnon: if Mistylos does not yield up the city, then Bryaxes will declare war against him. Although greatly upset, Mistylos does not express his agitation. He commands his *satrapês* Gobryas to prepare a banquet in honor of the Pissan envoy. The purpose of the banquet is to intimidate the guest.

In the description of this banquet Theodoros Prodromos demonstrates a unique dexterity in combining indirect references to contemporary Byzantine reality with

---

[8] For a more detailed study of both the rhetorical aspects of the Komnenian novels and the aesthetic reception of the ancient Greek examples of the genre by the Byzantines as documented by the manuscript tradition see Roilos 2000; and forthcoming.

[9] See Lindberg 1977:225–226.

[10] For the relation between *euteles* and *apheles* see Hermogenes' *De ideis* (On ideas), Rabe 1913:324–325. Demetrius speaks of the comic effect of *euteles*: τῶν δὲ χαρίτων αἱ μέν εἰσι μείζονες καὶ σεμνότεραι, αἱ τῶν ποιητῶν, αἱ δὲ εὐτελεῖς μᾶλλον καὶ κωμικώτεραι (128; cf. Lausberg 1960:521).

subtle allusions to literary tradition. As a result of this, the whole passage has been invested with a polyvalent ἀμφοτερογλωσσία that functions on several levels at the same time. Parody—possibly accompanied by satire—is the main device that Prodromos employs here in order to achieve this effect. The scene of this banquet should be viewed as an indirect glorification of the power of art in general, and Prodromos' own literary art in particular. Culinary art, rhetoric, ceremonial court poetry, religious liturgical poetry, mime, and secular rituals are all put together here and subordinated to the author's orchestrating and parodying creative art, in order to construct a complex literary artifact of a comic character, which only a special audience such as the one frequenting the twelfth-century Byzantine rhetorical *theatra* could have adequately appreciated.[11]

From the very beginning, the scene of the reception of Artaxanes reflects the prescriptions of Byzantine ceremonial protocol. In his description, Prodromos reenacts the formality and elaborate performativity of Byzantine court ceremonies.[12] The theatricality of the confrontation between the two main actors in this scene, Artaxanes and Gobryas, alludes to the highly ritualistic organization of the Byzantine polity as a "theater state," in the sense this term is employed by Geertz in his penetrating analysis of Balinese court rituals.[13] From the very beginning, the interaction between Artaxanes and Gobryas is presented in terms of a metaphorical discourse of ceremonial hierarchy. In accordance with the Byzantine court protocol and in a manner reminiscent of ceremonial symbolism in other cultures as well, the difference in status between the two men is metaphorically conveyed by means of their seating arrangement.[14] At the arrival of the Pissan envoy Mistylos sits on an elevated throne surrounded by his retinue. The author puts special emphasis on this detail: αὐτὸς δ' ἐπ' ὀκρίβαντος εἰς θρόνον μέγαν/ὑψοῦ καθεσθεὶς καὶ τιτανῶδες βλέπων,/τῆς σατραπικῆς στρατιᾶς εἰς τὸν θρόνον/ἱσταμένης κύκλωθεν εὐφυεῖ στάσει,/καλεῖν κελεύει τὸν σταλέντα σατράπην (4.16–20).[15] The titanic-like look of the barbarian leader contributes to the awe-inspiring effect of

[11] On "rhetorical theaters" in Byzantium see Hunger 1978:210–211; Mullett 1984:173–201; also the excellent discussion in Magdalino 1993:335–356; the latter contends that "*theatre* is in fact the key to understanding both the aesthetic and the social function of *high-style* literacy in twelfth-century Byzantine society" (ibid.:339).
[12] For Byzantine court ceremonies in general see Cameron 1987, where special emphasis on *De cerimoniis* (On ceremonies); also McCormick 1985. Specifically for the Komnenian period (the reign of Manuel Komnenos) see Magdalino 1993:237–248.
[13] Geertz 1980.
[14] On symbols of submission and hierarchy in political rituals in modern societies see, for example, Hunt 1977; on metaphors of hierarchy in a comparable ceremonial ritual context see Rosaldo 1968; on political rituals in general see Kertzer 1988.
[15] The references are to Marcovich's edition (Marcovich 1992); the translations of the Byzantine texts are mine, unless otherwise indicated.

his whole appearance. Artaxanes, on the contrary, bows his head in front of Mistylos' feet and gives him the letter.

The contrast in the positions of the two enemies corresponds, I believe, to the ceremony of the reception of foreign dignitaries at the Byzantine court. In his speech delivered on the occasion of the visit of the Sultan Kiliç Arslan II at the court of Manuel I Komnenos in 1161, Euthymios Malakes refers to a similar difference in the position of the two leaders. Euthymios interprets this difference as indicative of the Byzantine emperor's predominance over his visitor.[16] Illuminating information regarding this aspect of Byzantine court protocol is also provided by Western authors of the same period. In his account of the reception of Amaury I, king of Jerusalem, at the court of Manuel I in 1171, William of Tyre notes that the Byzantine emperor was seated on a golden throne wearing his imperial robes, while his visitor was seated on another throne lower than that of the emperor.[17] An indirect confirmation of the symbolic significance of the difference in seat can be drawn from Odo of Deuil's description of Louis VII's visit to Constantinople in 1147. Odo, whose overall account does not reveal a friendly attitude toward the Byzantines, does not spare the detail that the two sovereigns sat merely on two chairs, thus implying that no difference in status was imposed by the ceremony of the reception.[18]

---

[16] Πάλαι μὲν ὁ Δημάρατος ὁ Κορίνθιος, Ἀλεξάνδρου τὸ πρῶτον ὑπὸ τὸν χρυσοῦν οὐρανίσκον ἐν τῷ Δαρείου θρόνῳ καθίσαντος, μεγάλης εἶπεν ἡδονῆς στερηθῆναι τῶν Ἑλλήνων τοὺς τεθνηκότας πρὶν ἢ θεάσασθαι τὸν Ἀλέξανδρον ἐν τῷ Δαρείου θρόνῳ καθήμενον· ἐγὼ δ᾽ ἂν καὶ αὐτὸς οἰκειωσαίμην ἄρτι τοῦτο τὸ Δημαράτειον καὶ πολλῆς ἂν φαίην ἐστερῆσθαι τῆς ἡδονῆς τῶν ὑπό τινας Ῥωμαίων ἐκείνους, ὅσοι θανόντες οὐ πάρεισί γε νῦν ἰδεῖν τὸν ἑαυτῶν βασιλέα λαμπρὸν ἐνθάδε προθρονιζόμενον καὶ τὸν μέγαν τῶν Περσῶν ἀρχηγέτην αὐτῷ καλῶς ὑποποδιζόμενον. θέαμα τερπνὸν οὕτω καὶ ξένον καὶ οἷον οὐδέπω τοὺς ὀφθαλμοὺς τῶν Ῥωμαίων ἑστίασεν (Papadopoulos-Kerameus 1913:167.12–21; cf. Magdalino 1993:454, 242). It is worth noting that in this speech, Malakes refers to the sultan as *Persanax* as well (Papadopoulos-Kerameus 1913:167.25), a term encountered also in Niketas Eugeneianos' novel (5.338). For Eugeneianos' use of these terms cf. also Kazhdan 1967:109. For Malakes' speech cf. also Magdalino and Nelson 1982:132–135. In his description of the same event, Kinnamos offers the same information about the difference in the position of the two leaders: ἦρτο μὲν βῆμα λαμπρὸν καὶ δίφρος ἐπὶ πλεῖστον γῆθεν αἰρόμενος ἔκειτο, θέαμα λόγου πολλοῦ ἄξιον ... ἐφ᾽ οὗ καθῆστο βασιλεύς ... Κλιτζιεσθλὰν δὲ ἐπειδήπερ εἰς μέσους παρῆλθε, θάμβους ὅλος ἦν ... καθῆστο λοιπὸν ἐπὶ χαμαιζήλου τινὸς καὶ ἥκιστα ἐπὶ μετεώρου καθέδρας (Meineke 1836:205–206).

[17] William, Archbishop of Tyre 1948:380. In his description of the reception of Baldwin III by Manuel several years before this event (1159), William again puts emphasis on the same detail: Manuel was seated on a throne higher than that of his guest (ibid.:278).

[18] Given that Odo's view of the Byzantines was rather hostile, his description here must be less innocent than it seems at first sight, all the more since in his account of the same event Kinnamos explicitly notes that the Byzantine emperor was seated on his throne, whereas Louis on a little stool (Odo of Deuil 1948:59).

After he was received by Mistylos, Artaxanes was led by Gobryas to a hall specifically assigned for the reception of foreign envoys where the dinner would be served: ἐν δόμοις,/πρὸς τηλικούτων (sc. foreign dignitaries) εἰσδοχὴν τεταγμένοις (4.115–116; my emphasis). Again this detail does not depart from the strict protocol of the reception of foreign envoys at the Byzantine court.[19] From this point on, Prodromos, although continuing to allude to the psychological and subsequent political effectiveness of Byzantine ceremonial, proceeds to construct his own, more grotesque, version of it. Artaxanes is now served a "marvelous dinner" (δεῖπνον . . . πρὸς τὸ θαυμάσιον ἡτοιμασμένον [4.122–123]). This proleptic characterization of the banquet prepares Prodromos' audience for the unexpected event that follows: Artaxanes is served a roast lamb; when he tries to cut it, a flock of small sparrows come out of its belly and begin to fly above his head. Artaxanes is dumbfounded (ἦλθεν εἰς θάμβος μέγα [4.130]). Later, when he hears Gobryas' exaggerated interpretation of the incident, his surprise is transformed into terror (4.173–188; cf. 5.52).

The culinary marvel performed at this formal banquet has been rightly paralleled to the technological marvels demonstrated to foreign visitors at the Byzantine court.[20] Liutprand of Cremona (tenth century) relates his own experience of such demonstrations, whereas the author of the tenth-century Byzantine treatise *De cerimoniis* provides detailed prescriptions of their proper use in court ceremonial.[21] I would view this incident in Prodromos' novel, therefore, as a parodic example of ceremonial *conspicuous virtuosity*.[22] It has been pointed out that the motif of the roast lamb out of whose belly a flock of live birds flies finds a parallel in Petronius' *Cena Trimalchionis* (Trimalchio's

[19] Cf., for example, the description of "the reception" of the Saracenes in *De cerimoniis*, Reiske 1829–30:II. 584–585. The Greek word for "reception" that is employed in this treatise, that is, δοχή (ibid.: 583 and passim), recalls the similar term used by Prodromos in this scene: εἰσδοχή. *De cerimoniis* describes how the foreign envoys passed through several buildings before they arrived at the dinner hall where the emperor had prepared a feast for them.

[20] Hunger 1978:II.131–132; Beaton 1996:75; cf. Kazhdan 1983:13–27. None of these scholars discusses the issue in a systematic way.

[21] Liutprand was very proud of having not been intimidated by the display of such technological miracles at the court of Konstantinos Porphyrogennetos. He mentions a bronze tree with bronze birds that were chirping, metal lions that were roaring, and the impressive so-called "throne of Solomon." Liutprand, however, had already made enquiry about these marvels and he was not terrified (*Antapodosis* 6.5). *De cerimoniis* describes the throne and the other technological marvels at his court (Reiske 1829–30:II. 566–570). For the throne of Solomon and Byzantine court technology in general see Brett 1954:477–487; for the political manipulation of technological marvels at the Byzantine court see Trilling 1997: 17–230.

[22] Here, I use the apt term introduced by Trilling in his discussion of the political manipulation of technology at the Byzantine court; the second component of this term, *virtuosity*, refers to extraordinary skill, most usually artistic, while the second component, *conspicuous*, emphasizes the public display of such a skill (Trilling 1997:225).

Feast). Although, I would add, no evidence exists to prove that Petronius' text was available in twelfth-century Byzantium, this parallel illustrates, at least, the comic nature of the motif. However, no direct or indirect influence of Petronius on Prodromos is to be assumed. To my mind, the culinary marvel in Prodromos' novel can be seen as variation of the author's general interest in the motif of food that he manifests elsewhere too.[23] In any case, the studies that have suggested the parallels of this marvelous dish with either court ceremonial in general, as described by Liutprand and in *De cerimoniis*, or Petronius, fail to explore the comic character of this extraordinary incident and to view it within the broader context of the parodic subversion of the established Byzantine court protocol in Prodromos' novel.[24]

The first of these parodic elements is the demonstration of rhetorical mastery on the part of Artaxanes' host, Gobryas. In a long display of eloquence and in a comically supercilious twist of the topos of the structural homology between mundane political organization and divine universal order—a topos which is employed, for instance, in the most authoritative treatise on Byzantine court

---

[23] Prodromos does so even in contexts where one would not normally expect such an interest. In his *Life of Saint Meletios*, for example, he extolls the saint's spartan life by contrasting it to the alleged opulence of his audience. His enumeration of the dishes possibly enjoyed by his imagined reader takes a rather grotesque twist (Vasilevskii 1886:50). For a brief discussion of this *Life* and the issue of hagiographic writing in the twelfth century in general see Magdalino 1981:51–66. The whole description here recalls similar passages from the Ptochoprodromic poems, especially the ones on the poverty of the poet as a man of letters and the satire against the monks (Hesseling and Pernot 1910:III, IV; on the Ptochoprodromic poems see Alexiou 1986 and 1999). A special interest in food is documented in the works of other twelfth-century writers as well, such as Eustathios of Thessalonike, and might reflect a broader change in the diet of the Byzantines in this period (cf. Kazhdan and Epstein 1984:80–81; Kazhdan and Epstein, however, do not take into account the description in Theodoros Prodromos' *Life*).

[24] Beaton, for example, fails to view this episode in its broader context, while accepting the possibility of an allusion to *Cena Trimalchionis* unquestioningly (Beaton 1996:75). In his opinion, beyond the fact that Theodoros Prodromos composed poems for ceremonial occasions at court, "there is probably nothing in Prodromos' story that reflects the details of such ceremonies in the twelfth century" (ibid.); see, however, my analysis above, where I discuss the descriptions of analogous ceremonial occasions by twelfth-century Byzantine and Western writers. For the parallel with Petronius cf. also Hunger 1978:II.131. It should be also noted that the *Cena Trimalchionis* had a rather problematic manuscript tradition, on which see Smith 1975:xii–xiv. The similarity, however, between Theodoros Prodromos and Petronius remains intriguing. Is it a mere coincidence or is it to be attributed to some oral or another, yet unidentified, source? To the best of my knowledge, there is no study on the possible direct familiarity of twelfth-century Byzantine writers with specific examples of Latin literature. Salanitro's short note on a possible echo of Horace in Eugeneianos' novel is not convincing (Salanitro 1992:247–248). Intriguing are the similarities between Eugeneianos and Plautus identified by Giusti, who prefers to attribute them to an unidentifiable common source (Giusti 1993:221–223). On the other hand, as is well known, exchanges between the Byzantines and the Westerners were frequent in the twelfth century; cf. e.g. Jeffreys 1980:455–486; in this respect, it is worth noting that in his monody for his brother, Nikephoros Basilakes refers explicitly to the deceased's perfect knowledge of Latin (Pignani 1983:164–166).

protocol, the tenth-century *De cerimoniis*—Gobryas explains to the dumbfounded Artaxanes that the miraculous dish was prepared thanks to Mistylos' supernatural powers. Mistylos is so mighty that even nature succumbs to his will:

'Ορᾷς, ἔλεξε, παμέγγιστε σατράπα,/τοῦ δεσπότου μου τὴν
δύναμιν Μιστύλου,/ὡς ἐξαμείβειν ἰσχύει καὶ τὰς
φύσεις,/καιναῖς ἀμοιβαῖς καὶ τροπαῖς πολυτρόποις/τρέπων
ἕκαστα καὶ μεθιστῶν ὡς θέλει./ὁρᾷς τὸν ἀρνὸν ὡς κυΐσκει
στρουθία·/τῆς φύσεως μὲν ἀγνοήσας τὸν νόμον,/ὡς πτηνὸν
ὄρνιν πτηνὸς ὄρνις ἐκκύει,/ἀρνὸς πετεινὰ βλαστάνει τῶν
ἐγκάτων.

(4.134–143).

"You see," [Gobryas] said, ". . . the power of my master Mistylos, how he can transform even nature; . . . you see how the lamb gives birth to birds; ignoring the laws of nature, the lamb brings forth birds out of his entrails, exactly like the winged birds who give birth to winged birds."

Gobryas concludes his interpretation of the culinary marvel with an indirect threat against Artaxanes and his people: Mistylos could use his unbeatable power against his enemies in the war. He can even impregnate them with . . . puppies; he could make their bellies, although protected by armor, be pregnant with marvelous children (καὶ στρατιώτας ἄνδρας, ἀδροὺς ὁπλίτας,/σπάθαις σὺν αὐταῖς καὶ μετ᾽ αὐτῶν ἀσπίδων,/γεννήτορας δείξειε πολλῶν σκυλάκων,/καὶ γαστέρας θώραξιν ἠσφαλισμένας/ἐγκυμονεῖν πείσειεν ξένα [4.166–171]).

The Greek word for puppy, σκύλαξ, is invested here not as much with macabre connotations, as has been suggested,[25] as, rather, with comic sexual allusions. I find Hesychius' interpretation of this word pertinent to the overall atmosphere of the Prodromic banquet. Σκύλαξ, Hesychius observes, denotes a specific sexual position (Σκύλαξ· σχῆμα ἀφροδισιακόν, ὡς τὸ τῶν φοινικιζόντων; Hesychius, s.v.). Gobryas, in other words, underlines the prowess and omnipotence of his master by subtly alluding to his sexual potency as well, which can have a rather humiliating and unorthodox effect on his enemies.[26] Artaxanes takes Gobryas' threat at face value and

[25] Beaton, rather unconvincingly, argues that "the reader is presumably intended to decipher Gobryas' words as a punning allusion to worms (σκώληκες), to which the bodies of fighting men could indeed be said to 'give birth'—if they are killed" (Beaton 1996:74).

[26] Perhaps it is not fortuitous that the same word appears in Longus' novel as well, in the context of a homosexual's violent pass on the hero. Daphnis escapes Gnathon, the wanton homosexual, and runs away as a "puppy" (σκύλαξ; 4.12.3). Gnathon's desire and attack are described as violation against nature, another element that somehow recalls the paradoxical atmosphere in Prodromos' scene. That Prodromos was familiar with and influenced by Longus is beyond doubt. Suffice it to point out that the name of the Pissan leader, Βρυάξης, is almost identical with the name of the Methymnian general in Longus, Βρύαξις.

217

is scared to death. He asks Gobryas to spare him from such an ignominious pregnancy. Besides being terrified, Artaxanes is extremely bewildered. He cannot understand how men can get impregnated: "How can a man produce milk, if, as it is natural, the babies will need to be fed with milk? And, in any case, how can a manly general bear such a shame, giving, the poor fellow, birth to poor babies?" (Ποῦ γὰρ παρ᾽ ἡμῖν καὶ γάλακτος ἐκχύσεις,/εἴπου δεήσει φυσικῷ πάντως λόγῳ/γάλακτος ὁλκοῖς ἐκτραφῆναι τὰ βρέφη;/ἄλλως δὲ καὶ πῶς τὴν τοσαύτην αἰσχύνην/ἀνὴρ στρατάρχης καρτερήσειν ἰσχύσει/ἐγκυμονῶν ἄθλιος ἄθλια βρέφη [4.183–188]).

Around the ἀδύνατον of the culinary marvel and Gobryas' paradoxical claim, Theodoros Prodromos constructs a whole parodic argumentation greatly influenced by rhetoric. The topic under question is whether it is possible, and appropriate!, for a man to become pregnant and give birth to babies. The whole discussion of this topic should be read as a parody of the established rhetorical genres of "refutation" (ἀνασκευή) and "confirmation" (κατασκευή), which, according to Aphthonius, constitute the quintessence of rhetorical art.[27] The original form of the issue, however, as it is expressed by Artaxanes, has a rather mixed character, since it can be taken as close to the *progumnasma* of θέσις (argument) as well, whose character is by no means very different from *anaskeuê* and *kataskeuê*.[28]

In the diction of the traditional form of *thesis*, as it is prescribed by Hermogenes and Aphthonius, the question about the πρέπον (propriety) of a man's giving birth to babies could have been formulated as "should a man give birth to babies?"[29] Such a formulation of the topic would correspond to the πολιτικαὶ θέσεις, in Hermogenes' and Aphthonius' terminology (Rabe 1913:25; Walz 1832–36:I.108), or to πρακτικαὶ θέσεις, in Theon's terms ("practical theses"; Walz 1832–36:I.244). More specifically, in Hermogenes' system, this problem would be classified under the category of the *theseis* that examine an issue in relation to a specific category of people (αἱ κατὰ τὸ πρός τι λαμβάνονται) like the problem "should a king get married?" (εἰ γαμητέον βασιλεῖ [Rabe 1913:25]), since Gobryas and Artaxanes discuss the issue of giving birth only in relation with a particular group of people, that is men, and especially soldiers!

But the issue, as put by Artaxanes, has two sides: a "practical" side, which has been already mentioned, and a "theoretical" one, which is as follows: do men give birth to babies? If yes, how can they produce milk in order to feed them? These

---

[27] Τὸ δὲ προγύμνασμα τοῦτο (*anaskeuê*) πᾶσαν ἐν ἑαυτῷ περιέχει τὴν τῆς τέχνης ἰσχύν (Walz 1832–36:I.72); Aphthonius expresses the same view for *kataskeuê*: ἡ γυμνασία δὲ αὕτη πᾶσαν περιέχει τὴν τῆς τέχνης ἰσχύν (ibid.:77).

[28] In his discussion of *thesis*, Hermogenes speaks of how one can "refute" (ἀνατρέπειν) and "confirm" (κατασκευάζειν) the topic of the *thesis* (Rabe 1913:26).

[29] The topic of a *thesis* is usually expressed with the formula "should one . . . ?" (e.g. εἰ γαμητέον, εἰ ἀθλητέον, εἰ γεωργητέον [see Rabe 1913:25; Walz 1832–36:I. 109; 242]).

questions constitute the "theoretical" aspect of the *thesis* and correspond to what Hermogenes calls οὐ πολιτικαὶ θέσεις (Rabe 1913:25) or to the θέσεις θεωρητικαί in the system of Theon and Aphthonius (Walz 1832–36:I.180; ibid.:244). The physiological example of women's production of milk after delivery is mentioned by Aristotle in his *Rhetoric* as an example of true syllogism (1357b.15–16: τέτοκεν, ὅτι γάλα ἔχει); this example is discussed also in Stephanos' twelfth-century commentary on Aristotle's *Rhetoric*.[30] It is tempting to assume that here Theodoros Prodromos does not only parody the premises of this sort of syllogisms in general, but he also alludes to this specific example.[31]

Prodromos, however, seems to adhere to the demands of traditional rhetoric only to some extent, since he actually undermines and plays with the conventions of *progumnasmata*. His treatment of *thesis*, which, according to the theoreticians of the genre, involves the process of antithesis and solution (λύσις), of ἀνασκευάζειν and κατασκευάζειν, takes the form of a complex *anaskeuê* and *kataskeuê* indeed, but at the same time it defies an important rule of these two last *progumnasmata* prescribed more explicitly by Apththonius: one should attempt to refute not something that is absolutely clear or totally impossible, but something that is between these two extremes ('Ανασκευαστέον [καὶ κατασκευαστέον] δὲ τὰ μήτε λίαν σαφῆ μήτε ἀδύνατα παντελῶς, ἀλλ' ὅσα μέσην ἔχει τὴν τάξιν [Walz 1832–36:I. 72, 77]).[32] What really happens, though, is that Artaxanes and Gobryas are dealing here with an issue which is totally impossible (ἀδύνατον). Artaxanes' "problem" is dealt with in an *anaskeuê* of his views by Gobryas. As a matter of fact, this takes the function of a *kataskeuê* of an argument for the possibility and the ethical basis of men's giving birth to babies. Following the usual rhetorical practice, Gobryas' *kataskeuê* begins with a reprimand of Artaxanes' "irreverent" doubts, and proceeds to prove that there is nothing wrong with the whole issue. In order to substantiate his view, Gobryas adduces the example of Zeus, the god of gods, who gave birth to Dionysus and Athena. If Zeus did that, who, then, can call in question the morality of such marvelous deliveries?[33]

30 The syllogism is formulated here as following: αὕτη τέτοκε· γάλα γὰρ ἔχει· τὸ γάλα ἔχειν σημεῖόν ἐστι τοῦ τετοκέναι (Rabe 1886:264, 247.19–20).
31 For Prodromos' close familiarity with Aristotle cf. his short treatise Περὶ τοῦ μεγάλου καὶ τοῦ μικροῦ (On the great and the small) (Tannery 1887:104–119).
32 Cf. Hermogenes' similar prescription that τὰ δὲ πάνυ ψευδῆ οὔτε ἀνασκευαστέον οὔτε κατασκευαστέον (Rabe 1913:11).
33 Εἴπερ γὰρ ὁ Ζεύς, τῶν θεῶν ὁ βελτίων,/ὁ γῆν ἀνασπῶν καὶ τὸ πᾶν περιτρέπων . . . /ἔμβρυον ἀρτίφλεκτον εἰς μηρὸν μέσον/ἡμιτελεσφόρητον ἐρράπτειν θέλει/καὶ ζωπυρηθὲν ἐξάγει πρὸς ἡμέραν,/καὶ μητρικόν τι καὶ γυναικῶδες πάθος/ὁ τῶν Τιτάνων βασιλεὺς ὑποστέγει·/εἰ τὴν 'Αθηνᾶν ἐκ κεφαλῆς ἐκκύει,/ξίφει ῥαγείσης καὶ διχασθείσης μέσον,/πῶς αἰσχύνην φαίημεν ἀνδρῶν γηΐνων/ἃ τοῖς θεοῖς τίμια τοῖς οὐρανίοις [4.195–206]).

Panagiotis Roilos

The validity of the theoretical aspect of the issue, i.e. that men are able to give birth to babies, demonstrated by Gobryas' use of these mythological exempla, has been also already suggested by both the extraordinary dish served to Artaxanes, that is the "pregnant" roast lamb, and Gobryas' elaborate praise of Mistylos. Culinary art as exhibited in the specific ceremonial context—the marvelous dinner—and rhetorical art—Gobryas' elaborate encomium of Mistylos—function as a proleptical *kataskeuê* of the theoretical aspect of the *thesis*. The logically ἀδύνατον (impossible) of the *thesis*—a pregnant man—is abolished by means of the "real" δυνατόν (possible) of the culinary miracle that was just performed in front of Artaxanes' eyes. On this apparently *dunaton paradoxon* Gobryas bases the plausiblity (πιθανόν) of his rhetorical construction, employing a long series of paradoxes, which in their turn underline Mistylos' supernatural power. This encomium (4.134–172) does not follow the rules of ancient Greek rhetoric, but rather recalls the Byzantine ceremonial poetry performed on special occasions in honor of the emperor or other members of the Byzantine aristocracy. Prodromos himself was a prolific composer of this kind of poetry, which has been aptly described as "characteristically Byzantine."[34] Like this occasional poetry, Gobryas' laudatory speech exploits traditional rhetorical figures such as polyptoton, paronomasia, parechese, oxymoron, parallelism, repetition. On a first level, these rhetorical devices enhance the encomiastic character of Gobryas' speech; on a second level, however, they serve the parodic character of the whole scene, since they contribute to Gobryas' paradoxical argumentation.

Rhetorical *amphoteroglôssia* allows Theodoros Prodromos to appropriate, and even parody, the sacred discourse of religious ritual poetry as well. Gobryas' *kataskeuê* of the absurd *thesis* under discussion contains, I contend, some allusions to the miraculous birth of Christ. Gobryas' emphasis on the example of Zeus, the god of gods, giving birth to the androgyne Dionysus, and to Athena, a female god, sounds like a reversed, and not very reverent, version of the mystery of the Nativity. Instead of the theological *thesis* "how was the Virgin able to give birth to God," we are offered the playful theoretical *thesis* "how can a man give birth to babies and in particular to dogs?"

The abundance of antitheses, and especially of paradoxa and oxymora, in Gobryas' speech, may have been modeled upon several examples of religious poetry. The *Akathistos Hymnos* is the best and most famous of such examples, all the more since this hymn deals exactly with the Virgin and the mystery of her motherhood. Important in the *Akathistos* is the antithesis between rhetoric and religion, which revolves around the central issue of the birth of Christ. Mary's "miraculous childbirth" (ξένος τόκος) surpasses the power of rhetorical eloquence: "Before you, mother of

[34] Hörandner 1974:79.

God, we see wordy orators as voiceless as fish; they are at a loss as they say: 'How is it that you are still a virgin and yet had the power to give birth?' But let us marvel at the mystery and cry out in faith: . . . 'Hail to you who show the philosophers to be fools; hail to you who prove men of letters to be men of no wisdom; hail to you, for able disputers have been shown to be idiots; hail to you, for the fashioners of fables have been made to wither'" (Trypanis 1971:384) (ῥήτορας πολυφθόγγους ὡς ἰχθύας ἀφώνους/ὁρῶμεν ἐπὶ σοὶ Θεοτόκε./ἀποροῦσι γὰρ λέγειν τὸ πῶς/καὶ παρθένος μένεις καὶ τεκεῖν ἴσχυσας . . . /Χαῖρε φιλοσόφους ἀσόφους δεικνύουσα/Χαῖρε τεχνολόγους ἀλόγους ἐλέγχουσα./Χαῖρε ὅτι ἐμωράνθησαν οἱ δεινοὶ συζητηταί·/Χαῖρε ὅτι ἐμαράνθησαν οἱ τῶν μύθων ποιηταί [Trypanis 1968:36, ιζ'.1–11]).[35] While in the *Akathistos* the miracle of the Nativity surpasses the intellectual capacity of rhetors, in Gobryas' speech it is rhetoric, not less than culinary art, which manages to contrive a fake miracle. Gobryas' insistence on the miraculous "womb" of the lamb recalls an established image in hymnography: the μήτρα (womb) of the ἀρνός (lamb), a sanctioned symbol of Christ himself, functions as an allusion to the μήτρα of Christ's mother, the ἀμνάς (ewe/lamb).[36] Byzantine religious poetry offers many examples of a creative, although ultimately stereotypical, exploitation of the theme. In Romanos Melodos' second hymn on the Nativity, for instance, the Virgin addresses her baby in these words: "You are my fruit, you are my life . . . I have not experienced impregnation, I have experienced you as savior from the decay . . . since you left my womb keeping her intact" (Σὺ καρπός μου, σὺ ζωή μου . . . /Οὐκ οἶδα σποράν, οἶδα σε λύτην τῆς φθορᾶς/. . . ὡς γὰρ ἔλιπες μήτραν ἐμὴν φυλάξας σῷαν αὐτήν [Maas and Trypanis 1963:10.α'.3–9]).

One of the main points in Gobryas' eloquent encomium of Mistylos' power is the fact that the fire did not manage to burn the birds inside the "womb" of the roasted lamb: "Do you see, Artaxanes, most honorable among the satraps, how Mistylos transforms and governs over nature, the essence of fire he makes cool, the lambs he makes miraculous parents of birds, and only by means of his words he proves the just burnt, roasted womb to be the mother of unburnt babies, of winged embryos?" ('Ορᾷς, ἄριστε σατραπῶν 'Αρταξάνη,/ὡς ἐξαμείβει [Μιστύλος] καὶ τυραννεῖ τὰς φύσεις,/ψυχρὰν δὲ ποιεῖ τοῦ πυρὸς τὴν

---

[35] To my mind, the *Akathistos* might have been used as a model for the hymn for Mistylos performed later by the clown Satyrion as well.

[36] For the characterization of the Virgin as ἀμνάς see, e.g. Maas and Trypanis 1963:142.α'.1 (τὸν ἴδιον ἄρνα θεωροῦσα ἡ ἀμνάς); ibid.: 290.α'.3. The symbolism of the ἀμνός found its more explicit expression in religious art during the iconoclastic period, where Christ was really depicted as a sheep. The Council in Troullos, however, prohibited the use of this symbol in art; cf. the comments of the twelfth-century canonists Zonaras and Balsamon on this particular canon (Rallis and Potlis 1852–59:II.493–494).

Panagiotis Roilos

οὐσίαν,/ἀρνοὺς δὲ ποιεῖ στρουθοπάτορας ξένους/³⁷καὶ μήτραν ἀρτίφλεκτον ἐξωπτημένην,/βρεφῶν ἀκαύστων, ἐμβρύων καταπτέρων/ γεννήτριαν δείκνυσιν ἐκ μόνου λόγου [4.154–163]). The motif of the fire that burns without causing any harm recalls the miracle of καιομένη καὶ μὴ φλεγομένη βάτος, a traditional symbol of the Virgin Mary.³⁸ In hymnography, the paradox of harmless fire is employed to describe the mystery of the Nativity. Again in Romanos' second hymn on the Nativity, the Virgin says about her son: "Although being fire, he inhabited my womb and did not burn me, the simple woman" (Πῦρ ὑπάρχων ᾠκησέ μου/τὴν γαστέρα καὶ οὐ κατέφλεξεν ἐμὲ τὴν ταπεινήν [Maas and Trypanis 1963:14, ια'.3–4]). In Kosmas' canon on the Nativity the same image is employed to describe the miracle of the birth of God: "The cool furnace prefigured the nature of the supernatural miracle: it did not burn the Three Children, exactly as the fire of Divinity that entered the womb of the Virgin did not burn her" (Θαύματος ὑπερφυοῦς ἡ δροσοβόλος/ἐξεικόνισε κάμινος τύπον./οὐ γὰρ οὓς ἐδέξατο φλέγει νέους ὡς οὐδὲ πῦρ/τῆς Θεότητος Παρθένον, ἣν ὑπέδυ νηδύν [Cantarella 1942:I.120, 140–143]). The same image appears also in John of Damaskos' canon on the Epiphany: "Not being burnt, the Three Children of the Old Testament represent the womb of the Virgin, which, being sealed, gives supernatural birth" (Μήτραν ἀφλέκτως εἰκονίζουσι Κόρης/οἱ τῆς παλαιᾶς πυρπολούμενοι νέοι/ὑπερφυῶς κύουσαν, ἐσφραγισμένην [ibid.:114, 101–103]).³⁹ Here, as in Kosmas' canon, the comparison is between the fire in the furnace of the Three Children that did not burn them, a motif taken from the Old Testament, and the fire of God that did not burn the Virgin's womb. Prodromos gives this sanctioned motif a most grotesque twist: Mary's womb is transformed into the belly of the roasted lamb which, although dead, that is burnt, gives birth to birds. Furthermore, the image of the lamb's "womb" plays with the ideas of life (the live

³⁷ The same adjective, ξένος, is also used in the *Akathistos* to describe the τόκος of the Virgin; Trypanis 1968:35.ιδ'.1.
³⁸ See, e.g. Romanos' second hymn on the Annunciation, where the image of the miraculous bush is the *Leitmotiv*: Κατεπλάγη Ἰωσὴφ τὸ ὑπὲρ φύσιν θεωρῶν/καὶ ἐλάμβανε εἰς νοῦν τὸν ἐπὶ πόκον ὑετὸν/ἐν τῇ ἀσπόρῳ κυήσει σου, θεοτόκε,/βάτον ἐν πυρὶ ἀκατάφλεκτον (Maas and Trypanis 1963:289. *prooemium*, 1–4; cf. also ibid.:α'.1–2; 291.ε'; 293.ια', ιβ'). See also the second *troparion* of the first ode in John of Damascus' canon on the Nativity: ἤνεγκε γαστὴρ ἡγιασμένη Λόγον/σαφῶς ἀφλέκτῳ ζωγραφουμένη βάτῳ (Cantarella 1942:I.111, 6–7).
³⁹ Romanos offers a very powerful version of this motif in his first hymn on the Annunciation: Joseph says to the Virgin: "Ὦ φαεινή, φλόγα ὁρῶ καὶ ἀνθρακίαν κυκλοῦσαν σε·/κλίβανος πλήρης πυρὸς ἐγένετο ἡ ἄμεμπτος γαστήρ σου (Maas and Trypanis 1963:287.ιε'.3–5). It is noteworthy that the same motif in association with the metaphorical image of the lamb is also exploited in another poem by Theodoros Prodromos, in which he describes the symptoms of his illness: Πῶς ἐτεφρούμην τῷ πυρὶ καὶ πῶς ἀπηνθρακώμην/ἐξωπ[τημένος τῷ πυρὶ Θεῷ] ἀντεθυόμην/οὐχ ὥσπερ ἄμωμος ἀμνός, τίς γὰρ ἐγὼ καὶ τίνων/[ἀλλ' ὡς κατάρατος] κριὸς ἐξ ἁμαρτίας μέλας (Hörandner 1973:46.56–59).

222

birds) and death (the burnt belly of the lamb): life is preserved in death and the latter is followed by the former in a paradoxical way that exemplifies Bakhtin's understanding of the regenerative character of the grotesque.[40]

The possibility of a parodic appropriation of the discourse of religious ritual poetry by Theodoros Prodromos here is further corroborated, I contend, by some intriguing evidence provided by Prodromos' own commentaries on the abovementioned canons.[41] These commentaries elucidate the intricate intertextual allusions of the banquet scene under discussion in the most revealing way. To my mind, Prodromos' interpretation of the passages from John of Damascus and Kosmas leaves no doubts about his conscious appropriation of the hymnographic topos of harmless fire in Gobryas' speech. Commenting on Kosmas' canon, Prodromos observes: "Despite its fire, the furnace, which prefigures the Virgin's womb, did not burn the youths that it received; in our case [the miracle of the Nativity] He who was received into the womb did not burn the womb, although He bears fire, or rather, He is fire Himself" (ἡ . . . κάμινος ἡ τὴν παρθενικὴν τυποῦσα νηδὺν ἐκείνη τὸ καῖον ἔχουσα τοὺς ὑποδεχθέντας οὐ κατέφλεξε νέους. ἐνταῦθα δὲ ὁ τὴν μήτραν ὑποδεὶς καὶ ὑποδεχθείς, ἐκεῖνος ἔχων τὸ πῦρ, μᾶλλον δὲ πῦρ ὤν, τὴν ὑποδεξαμένην αὐτὸν ἀντιστρόφως μήτραν οὐκ ἔκαυσε [Stevenson 1888:52]).[42]

In his commentary on another *troparion* from Kosmas' canon, Theodoros Prodromos ridicules Greek mythology in order to prove the superiority of Christian theology. His analysis of Kosmas' canon sounds as a perfect *anaskeuê* of his own parodic *kataskeuê* in the novel. His main argument here is that the ancient Greek myths that speak about a male god, like Zeus, who gives birth to a child are altogether nonsensical. The theoretical *thesis*, therefore, "can a man give birth to a child?" is

---

[40] Bakhtin says that the notion of the grotesque encompasses the ideas of death, birth, and rebirth: "The grotesque image reflects a phenomenon in transformation, an as yet unfinished metamorphosis, of death and birth, growth and becoming. For in this image we find both poles of transformation, the old and the new, the dying and the procreating, the beginning and the end of the metamorphosis" (1984:24 and passim).

[41] It seems that the exegesis of the canons experienced a special flourishing in the twelfth century. It has been suggested that some of these commentaries were written as lectures for an academic audience (Demetracopoulos 1979:146–147). It should be noted that in the twelfth century similar commentaries were written also by Gregory Pardos, Zonaras, and Eustathios of Thessalonike (see Komines 1960:252). Prodromos' commentaries indicate that the commentators were familiar with each other's work (ibid.:251).

[42] Similar are his remarks on the excerpt from the canon of John of Damascus: Οἱ ἐπὶ τῆς Παλαιᾶς Γραφῆς ἀπυρπολήτως πυρπολούμενοι νέοι τὴν μήτραν τῆς ἀειπαρθένου εἰκονίζουσι Θεομήτορος, τὴν μετὰ τὸ ὑπερφυῶς γεννῆσαι ἐσφραγισμένην διαμείνασαν· πλὴν ἐκεῖ μὲν ἐν τῇ καμίνῳ οἱ παῖδες ἱστάμενοι ἀπείρατοι διέμενον τοῦ πυρός, ἐνταῦθα δὲ τὸ ἐναντίον ἅπαν· ἐντὸς ἔχουσα τὸ πῦρ τῆς Θεότητος ἡ Θεομήτωρ οὐ κατεφλέγετο· ὅπερ πολὺ ἐκείνου παραδοξότερον (Stevenson 1888:71).

subjected here to a totally different argumentation than that in the novel, and given, of course, a negative answer:

Ἐκ γαστρὸς δὲ γεγεννῆσθαι τὸν Μονογενῆ παρὰ Θεοῦ καὶ Πατρὸς λέγομεν, οὐχ ὡς σωματικὰς ὑπονοίας περὶ τῆς . . . ἀσωμάτου φύσεως ἔχοντες, οὐχ ὡς γαστέρα ἐμβρυοδόχον τῷ ἀνάρχῳ Πατρὶ καὶ ὠδῖνάς τινας καὶ λοχείας προσάπτοντες· Ἑλλήνων γὰρ ὁ ὕθλος οὗτος οἵτινες τοσοῦτον τοὺς ἑαυτῶν θεοὺς ἀπογυναικοῦσιν ὥστε οὐ γαστέρας μόνον ἀλλ᾽ ἤδη που καὶ κεφαλὰς καὶ μηροὺς ἐμβρυοδόχους τούτοις διδόασι. καὶ τὰς μὲν πελέκει διελόντες δυστοκοῦντος δήπου τοὺς θεοὺς καὶ τὰς ὠδῖνας οὐ στέγοντος θυγατέρα ἐκεῖθεν ἐξάγουσιν ἔνοπλον. τοὺς δὲ μηροὺς τὸν ῥαφέα λινὸν περιελόντες κραιπαλῶντα ἤδη καὶ ὑποβεβρεγμενον ἐξ αὐτῆς τῆς ὠδῖνος υἱὸν προΐσχουσι Διόνυσον.

(Stevenson 1888:48)

We say that Christ has been born by our God and Father not in the sense that we attribute bodily qualities to incorporeal God, nor that we attach to him a child-bearing womb and pains of child-birth. These are nonsensical tales of the ancient Greeks, whose gods are so effeminate that they are endowed not only with wombs but also with child-bearing heads and thighs. And breaking open with an axe the head of a god allegedly suffering in childbirth and not bearing the pangs of childbirth they produce thence an armed daughter. And removing the bands from the thigh [of Zeus] from these throes of childbirth they produce a son, the already intoxicated and drunk Dionysus.

This part of Prodromos' analysis of Kosmas' canon has been based, I argue, on Gregory of Nazianzus' homily on Epiphany (Εἰς τὰ ἅγια Φῶτα [On the Epiphany]; PG 36.336–358). In this oration, Gregory dwells extensively on the miracle of Christ's birth and opposes it to ancient Greek myths, which, as he notes bitterly, were not real mysteries, but illusions and misleading twaddle (ibid.:336). In the introduction to his speech, Gregory enumerates those ancient Greek stories that speak about miraculous births of gods, only in order to ridicule them:

Οὐδὲ Διόνυσος ταῦτα καὶ μηρός, ὠδίνων ἀτελὲς κύημα, ὥσπερ ἄλλο τι κεφαλὴ πρότερον· καὶ θεὸς ἀνδρόγυνος καὶ στρατὸς μεθυόντων, καὶ στρατὸς ἔκλυτος.

(PG 36.337)

These are not the same as the stories about the thigh and Dionysus, the incomplete fetus, or like the other story before about the head [of Zeus]; they are not about an androgynous god, or an army of intoxicated people, or a lascivious army.

Gregory of Nazianzus was one of the most appreciated Christian authors throughout Byzantium and his direct influence on Theodoros Prodromos is very probable.[43] To my mind, another source of inspiration could also be detected here: pseudo-Nonnos' commentary on Gregory's homilies. pseudo-Nonnos offers a much more detailed description of the ancient myths referred to in Gregory's homilies than Gregory himself. In his commentary on the birth of Dionysus, pseudo-Nonnos narrates how Zeus took the fetus from Semele first and then sewed it into his thigh (PG 36.1048; 1068–1069). The description of the same myth in Prodromos' novel follows the same sequence. Furthermore, pseudo-Nonnos' detailed description of Dionysus' company, Satyrs and Maenads, who indulge in revelry (PG 36.1068–1069), can be paralleled with the detailed description of the depiction of Dionysus and his entourage on a precious cup that was used during Gobryas' banquet (4.344–411).

Another fact should also be noted in respect to Prodromos' reference to the ancient Greek myths of Zeus' miraculous deliveries and its possible allusions to an established Christian topos. Four manuscripts from the eleventh and twelfth centuries preserve several illuminations to pseudo-Nonnos' commentary. Along with pseudo-Nonnos' text, these manuscripts also preserve Gregory's homilies.[44] Some of these illuminations present the story of Dionysus' and Athena's birth. In two manuscripts,[45] the birth of Dionysus is illustrated in three phases: in the first phase, Zeus takes the fetus from the womb of the dead Semele, who has been struck by the thunderbolt (cf. Prodromos' ἔμβρυον ἀρτίφλεκτον . . . ἡμιτελεσφόρητον [4.199–200]); in the second, he sews it into his thigh (cf. Prodromos' εἰς μηρὸν μέσον ἐρράπτειν θέλει [ibid.]) and in the last one, he delivers Dionysus as a baby (cf. Prodromos' καὶ ζωπυρηθὲν ἐξάγει πρὸς ἡμέραν,/καὶ μητρικόν τι καὶ γυναικῶδες πάθος/ὁ τῶν Τιτάνων βασιλεὺς ὑποστέγει [4.200–202]). In

---

[43] For example, in the twelfth century, Gregory Pardos observes that Gregory of Nazianzus had inspired many a melodist: τὸν γὰρ μέγαν φωστῆρα τῆς 'Ορθοδοξίας διδάσκαλον, Γρηγόριον δηλαδὴ τὸν Θεολόγον, ἅπαντες οἵ τε μελῳδοὶ καὶ οἱ περί τι τῶν ψυχωφελῶν καὶ θείων σπουδάζοντες διδάσκαλον ἔχουσι καὶ δογμάτων καὶ λόγων (cited in Komines 1960:248). Not rarely, Theodoros Prodromos himself refers to Gregory of Nazianzus in the commentaries discussed here; see, e.g. Stevenson 1888:34, 35, 44, 45.

[44] These manuscripts are the Τάφου 14 in Jerusalem (second half of the 11th c.), Vaticanus Graecus 1947 (11th–12th c.), Panteleimon 6 (11th c.), Paris Coislin 239 (end of the 11th c.); for the illuminations in these manuscripts see Weitzmann 1951:9–11.

[45] These are the Jerusalem and Vatican manuscripts (Weitzmann 1951:47–48).

two other manuscripts, only the third phase, that is, the delivery of the baby Dionysus, is depicted.[46] Athena's birth is illustrated only in the Jerusalem manuscript. She is depicted coming out of Zeus' head; in front of Zeus stands Hephaestus holding an axe (cf. Prodromos' τὴν ᾿Αθηνᾶν ἐκ κεφαλῆς ἐκκύει,/ξίφει ῥαγείσης καὶ διχασθείσης μέσον [4.203–204]).

It is tempting to assume that Prodromos was familiar with the iconographic vocabulary of such manuscripts, all the more since Gregory's homilies and pseudo-Nonnos' commentary were the main sources of inspiration in his construction of Gobryas' second speech. Perhaps Gobryas' reference to Zeus as the king of the Titans (ὁ τῶν Τιτάνων βασιλεύς [4.202]) may reflect such a familiarity, since in some of the above-mentioned manuscripts Zeus is really depicted as a Byzantine emperor (βασιλεύς).[47] Be this as it may, the literary evidence discussed so far— Prodromos' own commentary on John of Damaskos and Kosmas, Gregory's homily on Epiphany, and pseudo-Nonnos' commentary on it—indicates that in the scene of the ceremonial banquet served to Artaxanes and its rhetorical exploitation by Gobryas, Prodromos makes a parodic use of elements drawn from religious liturgical literature and especially hymnography.

The focus of this chapter has been on the ways in which Theodoros Prodromos, one of the most important twelfth-century Byzantine authors, combines a number of established performative and verbal ritual conventions to construct one of the most heteroglossic parodic scenes in the tradition of the Greek novel by exploiting the discursive dynamics of rhetorical *amphoteroglôssia*.[48] Drawing both from the long tradition of Greek rhetoric and his broader contemporary cultural context, he appropriates sanctioned religious and secular modes of ritual communication and expression only to subvert and parody them. The reinscription of ritual conventions in his novel contributes to the *amphoteroglôssia* of his fictional discourse as a whole. The pseudo-Aristotelean "nursing men," the suggestive image of the σκύλακες (puppies), and the marvelous ὀπτὸς ἀρνός (roast lamb) at Prodromos' grotesque banquet illustrate the dynamics of this *amphoteroglôssia* in the most dialogic possible way.

---

[46] The Panteleimon and Paris manuscripts (Weitzmann 1951:49).

[47] These are the miniatures in the Jerusalem, Panteleimon, and Paris manuscripts (Weitzmann 1951:47, 49). Perhaps an association between Zeus, the god of gods, and the emperor is also hidden in the indirect comparison of Mistylos with Zeus in the presentation of the former as ὑψοῦ καθεσθεὶς καὶ τιτανῶδες βλέπων (4.17–8; my emphasis points to the possibility of a deliberate association of Mistylos' titanic-like appearance with the characterization of Zeus as ὁ τῶν Τιτάνων βασιλεύς).

[48] For a detailed discussion of the intertextual response of Prodromos' novel to the ancient Greek examples of the genre see Roilos, forthcoming.

Thirteen

Human Rites:
Building and Bombing Bridges in the Balkans

Vangelis Calotychos

The Via Egnatia . . . was now called the *Road of the Balkans*, after the name the Turks have recently given to the entire peninsula, which comes from the word *mountain*. More than by the desire of the Ottomans to cover under one name the countries and peoples of the peninsula, as if subsequently to devour them more easily, I was amazed by our readiness to accept the new name. I always thought that this was a bad sign, and now I am convinced that it is worse than that.

Ismail Kadare, *The Three Arched Bridge*

The events of 9/11 and the pursuant United States "war on terror" rewrote world affairs in a new language. Cast aside in the instantaneous transition was the previous decade's language of barbarism that revolved around killing fields in a disintegrating Yugoslavia. The Balkans were, lest we forget, the topos through which, and on which, the West measured its (in)humanity at the end of the century. At a time of Western prosperity, intervention came about, and perhaps could only have only come about, in the heart of Europe—albeit the Other Europe—where alienness was sufficiently recognizable to be affecting. In the West's relation to the Balkans, "intimacy derives precisely from such a perception of similarity, while estrangement stems from the awkwardness and ill ease with which that similarity is greeted."[1]

Post-9/11, the "tinderbox" and "powder keg" of Europe, with its qualities of ethnic cleansing, bloodletting, and fractious regionalism, was consigned to the slag heap of metaphor. However, like the vampire often alluded to as a figure for the region, it is liable to return as it has done in the past.[2] And, along with the other Balkan catchword of the English language, "balkanization," it may come back to cut up into still smaller

[1] Fleming 2002:1229.
[2] Longinović 2002.

pieces that which has already been cut up pretty thoroughly. Until then, Mark Mazower has warned of how difficult it will be "to take a fresh look at the Balkans, without seeing them refracted through the prism of 'the Balkans' we have lived with for so long."[3] The region's identity *always already* originates in the language of its metaphorization.

One such fresh look from the field of cultural studies is a volume titled *Balkan As Metaphor*.[4] Its contributors treat "balkanism" as a "regime of knowledge production, [that] relies on figurative language and metaphor."[5] The first metaphor the editor Dusan Bjelic highlights in his introduction "Blowing Up The Bridge," is that of the "bridge." Like the bridge, the Balkans is oftentimes "dividing rather than connecting" and may be summoned to link East and West and signify the "in-betweenness of Balkan experience."[6] Throughout the 1990s, this in-betweenness has hung on the ubiquitous image of the bridge. Like many a television special, Balkan-wide collaborative project, and conference title, the volume in question depicts a bridge on its cover, which begs the question: why do Balkan writers and filmmakers, and those working on the Balkans, continually return to the bridge? In confronting the metaphorical language associated with the region, we might start studying one metaphor at a time, dismantling it one brick at a time. And maybe then rebuilding it. Do those *outside* and those *within* the region deploy this metaphor in the same way? What purposes does it serve in each instance? Is the exchange of the metaphor in contending sites worthy of metacritical investigation? Why is the theoretical consideration of the region's woes and the identity of its peoples undertaken in a ritual of building, destroying, or standing by or on bridges?

Balkanism

Large-scale transcultural interactions are nothing new. But today the allegorization of ways of life for the consumption of viewers, or readers, from afar are of a new order and intensity. The interactions of moving images and deterritorialized subjectivities in a global media age elicit ethnographic typologies for easy consumption. Consequently, in a facile manner, whole regions, countries, cultures, and peoples are often caricaturized and stereotyped, that image marketed, and they sometimes bombed.

Of all Balkan peoples, Greeks have been subject to, engaged in, and benefited from the weightiest and most durable of monumentalizing discourses, the Classical heritage. Rich in symbolic capital, it has much to contrast it with the discourse of

---

[3] Mazower 2000:xxx.
[4] Bjelić and Savić 2002.
[5] Bjelić in Bjelić and Savić 2002:15–16.
[6] Bjelić in Bjelić and Savić 2002:16.

balkanism, as Artemis Leontis has recently argued in an article that "bridges the Classical and the Balkan."[7] For, archetypically, while the Classical evokes a world that is bright and majestic, harmonious and with its emotion contained, whole even when it is fragmented, the Balkan is dark, brooding, and explosive; fragmented, or *balkanized*. While the classical is seen "as rising above the ordinary and raising people to a higher understanding of civilization . . . the Balkan is viewed as sinking below it, sucking people into a whirlpool of unnatural human hostility."[8] It comes as no surprise then that the most potent discourse of Greek modernity, the modernists' mythical method, the synthesis of classical and modern Hellenism, western Hellenism and Greek Hellenism, nativism and cosmopolitanism, went hand in hand with the repression of Greece's Balkan specificity. The turn to Europe and the project of liberal modernization following the Asia Minor debacle was built in part on a rejection of Balkan and Byzantine traditions as well as socialism.[9] When the Cold War plunged Greece into a Civil War, the communists were defeated, exiled, and repressed while they and other Balkan states faded behind the Iron Curtain. Greece's western trajectory was sealed.

With the tumultuous events of 1989 in Eastern Europe, Greek society, by then firmly rooted in Europe and trying to prove itself as something more than the "poor cousin" or "bad boy" of the European Union, reevaluated its relation to the Balkans and its peoples. Immigration from the Balkans challenged Greeks to acquaint themselves with the difference that lurked within their culture's own psychic and geographic borders. Despite the Karamanlis government's attempts to forge political links with Balkan neighbors in the 1970s and the socialists' cultural forays in the 1980s, with a folklorism as anti-Western as it was essentialist, the shock of 1989 found many Greeks totally unprepared to meet the challenge. Only after some missteps did Greeks eventually end the decade by venturing to enhance their very *European* profile by foregrounding their special relation to other Balkan peoples and even by championing the region's interests, in business and diplomacy, to their European allies—a bridge, you might say, to Europe.

Bridgespotting

The analysis of bridges undertaken here in a Balkan context privileges the specific conjuncture in Greek modernity described above and even overshadows a diachronically Hellenic context. Greeks today find themselves looking on as both insiders

---

[7] See Leontis 1999.
[8] Leontis 1999:641.
[9] Most typically, see Theotokas' famous declarations in his Τὸ Ἐλεύθερο Πνεῦμα (Free Spirit [Theotokas 1988 (1929)]). An English translation is available: Theotokas 1986.

and outsiders, situated both in the Balkans and among western Europeans. When thousands of Belgrade residents rushed onto the bridges over the Sava River in defiance of NATO bombing in April 1999, targets pinned to their shirts, most Greeks sided with their Orthodox co-religionists and largely opposed the NATO bombing. The Greek government also did not participate in the bombing. However, it did not veto the action and so allowed for the attacks to go forward. Intriguingly, despite popular resentment to the bombing and this policy decision, the government's approval rating in polls rose by 20 percent! The same people who heartily opposed the bombing realized that standing by NATO was the only pragmatic option for their government.

Such complexities make it difficult to determine where the state, the electorate, and the individual stand at any one moment. Before the Kosovo War, were you with the Serb police or the Kosovo Liberation Army? Were you for the bombing or against? After the war, were you with the minority Serbs or the majority Albanians in Mitrovica, on either side of the Ibar River? The linked question of perspective, whether one stands inside or outside the Balkans, is equally thorny. It calls forth the imaginary cartography of both the Balkans and Europe. The historian Maria Todorova has sketched the perspectives of Balkan people on their own self-ascription and their views of each other.[10] For Croats, the Balkans begin at the Serbian border; for Serbs, they begin in Muslim Bosnia or Kosovo; for Italians and Austrians, they begin in Slovenia; for the Germans, Austria is tainted with Balkan inefficiency and corruption (though it was overzealous German recognition of Slovenia and Croatia in 1991, states both south of Austria, that legitimated the disintegration of Yugoslavia and may have arguably drawn out the hostilities). In the early 1990s, the Greeks were Balkan dark horses to their European partners and European insiders in the eyes of their Balkan neighbors. As Slavoj Žižek points out, the imaginary projects on the territory in the same way that the conversion-symptoms of the hysterical subject does in Freud.[11] But this is not limited to an internal Balkan matter. Žižek cautions that there is also a "reflexive" politically correct racism from *without*—the liberal, multiculturalist perception of the Balkans as a site of ethnic horrors and tribal passions as opposed to the reasonableness of post-nation-state conflict resolution by negotiation and compromise in the West. In this discourse, the bridge becomes a convenient metaphor for superimposing a multiculturalist problematic of difference and its discontents on the region and even exploiting the discourse to justify military humanitarianism. The allusion to bridges aims conveniently to intervene in the issue of ethnic division and human rights.

[10] Todorova 1995. For how the pejorative associations of Balkan characteristics were deployed by the warring sides in the 1990s, see Bakic-Hayden and Hayden 1992.
[11] Žižek 1999.

Ideally, the cooperation of parties on both banks will secure the bridge's well being. Practically, when this is not possible or desirable, the bombing of some bridges facilitates building of new ones. Western policy subscribes to the adage that you need to crack eggs to make an omelet.

Certainly, there have been no few incidents to fuel the craze for bridges. The beautiful bridge of Mostar, built originally in 1566 by the Muslim architect Mimar Hayruddin, became like Sarajevo, a metaphor of desire for multicultural co-existence. The cover of the Penguin edition of Rebecca West's *Black Lamb and Grey Falcon* (1941), many westerners' first literary contact with the region, etches the Mostar bridge on our consciousness. Like the pounding of Dubrovnik, the bombing by Croat militiamen of the Stari Most, or Old Bridge of Mostar, which linked the eastern and western banks of the Neretva River on November 9th, 1993, *did* demand of us, as Leontis remarks, to ask rhetorically something searching of our common humanity.[12]

But all bridges are not equal. The NATO bombing of an ugly plate girder bridge over the Danube at Novi Sad in Serbia elicited only uncompassionate western media coverage. Built in 1956, it hardly deserved sympathy. Nor did the Serbs. Even where the Serbs were a minority, they could not claim "minority status." Places demand a certain mythologization or aestheticization to be lamented. However, this bridge *did* have a story to tell. It was built by German prisoners of war after World War II. Indeed the Germans rebuilt it, making up for their own bombing of it during the war that had just ended. By a quirk of fate, elsewhere on the May 22nd, 1999, Italian Army Engineers near the town of Pec in Kosovo exploded what was left of a road bridge hit by NATO bombs two months earlier. "We don't plan to destroy bridges," reassured Colonel Antonio Ligobbi of the Italian Army Engineers, "we normally plan to build them. And in this case it was necessary to destroy it before building a new one."[13]

Such uncanny repetitions suggest a Balkan folk tradition of building bridges where destruction and dismantlement are intrinsic to construction. One of the most famous ballads has variants all over the Balkans: "The Building of Skadar" or "Skadra" in the former Yugoslavia, "Master Manoli" in Romania, the "Legend of Rosafa" in Albania, "The Three Brothers" in Bulgaria, and the "Bridge of Arta" in Greece. In the Balkans the edifice may be a castle or monastery.[14] In Greek versions this edifice is always a bridge and it is given a different name in different versions— the Bridge of Arta, Larisa etc. As with historical songs on the fall of cities, "everything in the song[s], with the exception of the name . . . is traditional and found

[12] Leontis 1999:638.
[13] Tim Belay, The Voice of America, 22 July, 1999. *Dateline Report, Pec, Kosovo.*
[14] Translated into English and presented in Dundes 1996:3–12. Beaton 1980:120. On "The Bridge of Arta," see ibid:120–127.

with only slight variations in other contexts."[15] The song's dramatic action is initiated by work that cannot proceed:

Σαράντα πέντε μάστοροι κ᾽ ἑξήντα μαθητάδες
Γιοφύρι νεθεμέλιωναν στὴν Ἄρτα τὸ ποτάμι.
Ὁλημερὶς τὸ χτίζανε, τὸ βράδυ ἐγκρεμιζόταν.
Μοιρολογοῦν οἱ μάστοροι καὶ κλαῖν οἱ μαθητάδες·
"᾽Αλίμονο στοὺς κόπους μας, κρίμα στὶς δούλεψές μας,
ὁλημερὶς νὰ χτίζουμε, τὸ βράδυ νὰ γκρεμιέται."[16]

Forty-five master craftsmen and sixty apprentices
Were building a bridge on the river Arta.
All day they would build, at night it would fall down,
The master craftsmen lamented and the apprentices wept.
"Alas for our labors, what a pity all our toil,
All day we build, at night it falls down!"

This doing and undoing of construction recalls Penelope's handiwork in Homer's *Odyssey* and a tradition of rhapsodic weaving of tales, the spinning of yarns, the doing and undoing of narrative in a performative/oral culture of reformulated typologies. From folksongs down to the region's most well-known modern novel, Ivo Andrić's *Bridge on the Drina* (1945),[17] the bridge is associated with the story-telling of the peoples who live around it: "as . . . the great bridge arose, men began to remember details and to embroider the creation of a real, skillfully built and lasting bridge with fabulous tales which they well knew how to weave and to remember."[18] Predictably, Andrić's Ottoman-built bridge is: "an indispensable link on the road between Bosnia and Serbia and further, beyond Serbia, with other parts of the Turkish Empire, all the way to Stambul."[19] It lies between Austro-Hapsburg and Ottoman Empires and between nineteenth-century Bosnian servitude and Serbian nationalism. Its geographical liminality is typical of other bridges in the folk literature. One Greek historical song[20] laments how the Treaty of Berlin redrew the new Greek borders at the Bridge of Arta to leave a large part of Epirus in Ottoman hands and the Greeks of those "unredeemed" areas outside the borders of the Greek nation-state:

[15] Beaton 1980:96.
[16] The song was recorded in 1881. Politis 1978 (1914):131–133.
[17] Andrić 1977.
[18] Andrić 1977:27.
[19] Andrić 1977:14.
[20] Politis 1978:34.

Σ' ὅλον τὸν κόσμο ξαστεριά, σ' ὅλο τὸν κόσμο ἥλιος
Καὶ στὰ καημένα Γιάννενα μαῦρο, παχὺν σκοτάδι
Τὶ φέτο ἔκαμαν τὴ βουλὴ ὀχτὼ βασίλεια ἀνθρῶποι
Κι ἐβάλανε τὰ σύνορα στῆς Ἄρτας τὸ ποτάμι.
Κι ἀφήκανε τὰ Γιάννενα καὶ πήρανε τὴν Πούντα,
Κι ἀφήκανε τὰ Γιάννενα καὶ πήρανε τὴν Ἄρτα,
Κι ἀφήκανε τὸ Μέτσοβο μὲ τὰ χωριά του γύρα.

Clear skies and sun are upon the whole world,
And in wretched Iannina there is darkness, black and thick.
For eight royal powers have held council this year,
And they set the frontiers at the river Arta.
They have left Iannina and taken Pounta,
They have left Iannina and taken Arta,
And they have left Metsovo with its villages round.[21]

The line of separation is reinforced by the form and rhythm of this extract from the song, which depends largely on the juxtaposition of opposites across musical phrases. Margaret Alexiou finds similar features in the "Bridge of Arta." And this "habit of thinking in balances, antitheses, and parallelisms," as in ballads elsewhere, "operates not only conceptually and verbally . . . [but] extends to the moral and emotional planes." More generally, "the bridge signifies any liminal, and therefore dangerous, passage from one state to another (birth, marriage, death)" and often plays with the meanings of variable oppositions.[22]

In the Balkans of the 1990s, the injustice of separation was played out on the backs of those who migrated across borders for economic and political reasons. Sotiris Dimitriou's Ν' ἀκούω καλὰ τ' ὄνομά σου (May Your Name Be Blessed [1993]) which, incidentally, sports a photograph of a stone bridge on the jacket of its prize-winning English translation, considered this turn of events.[23] Three interlocking stories delve into a series of separations that mark three generations of an

---

[21] The translation is taken from Alexiou 2002a:96–97. Alexiou refers to the passage in a longer discussion of modern historical laments (90–101).

[22] Alexiou 2002b:192.

[23] Dimitriou, an Epirot author, employs a local rural dialect resistant to the Athenian reader's standard demotic. In an enterprising manner, the translator, Leo Marshall, explains in the translator's preface to his translation (xxi–xxiv) that he decided to convey this by building "on forms of expression (both lexical and syntactic) that have no specifically regional characteristics, but which are nonetheless rural in character and in many cases no longer in widespread use" (xxiv). Marshall rejects use of any one English dialect because it would unavoidably conjure up a whole set of sustained allusions and distract from the Greek context.

233

Vangelis Calotychos

Epirot family. The protagonist of the last story, Spetim, an economic migrant from Albania, struggles to survive in contemporary Greece. He endures the discrimination meted out to many an Albanian, even though he is, in fact, the grandson of a Greek-speaking woman once separated from her kin and forced to live on the wrong side of a redrawn Greek-Albanian border.

Consequently, otherness in the novella is a misrecognized sameness and truth is always somewhere else, on the other side of the bridge. In a famous scene from Theo Angelopoulos's film Tὸ Μετέωρο Βῆμα τοῦ Πελαργοῦ (The Suspended Step of the Stork [1991)], a colonel stands at the blue line on a bridge at the Greek-Albanian border. He lifts his leg and says: "If I take one more step, I will be somewhere else, or die." Faced with the gaze of a pair of Albanian guards across the bridge, the colonel suspends his leg in mid-air, only to lower it once more on the Greek side of the line. The scene, repeated later in the film, emblematizes the film's sustained meditation on borders. In another memorable scene, a refugee girl and her lover, whom she knew as a child but who is separated from her by the border, marry. They do so, each with their own wedding party on either side of a river. The only sound throughout is that of the rushing river roaring between them, a leitmotif in the movie that elicits fear even as it beckons each night. The rush of waters carries a compulsive desire to cross borders even while such passage presages the looming threat of death. The bridge becomes the liminal site for the resolution of dilemmas that both beckon and warn of the imminent danger involved in engaging with them. This function recalls van Gennep's well-known theory of rites of passage and its three phases of separation, margin (or *limen*), and reaggregation.[24] True to Victor Turner's discussion of the dangerous middle stage, "those undergoing it—call them 'liminaries'—are betwixt-and-between established states of political-jural structure. They evade ordinary cognitive classification, too, for they are neither-this-nor-that, here-nor-there, one-thing-not-the-other."[25] Angelopoulos' suspended step, like Dimitriou's protagonists with their hyphenated names, explores this stage. As extensions of the folk drama, these "liminaries" force the reader or viewer to question "the basic building blocks of symbolic complexes they had taken for granted as 'natural' units."[26]

Often this subversive effect is achieved by collapsing seeming oppositions. Recent fiction validates this view. In his short story "Kalamas and Acheron (1985),"[27] a second Epirot author, Christophoros Milionis, presents a river as the liminal site for the delineation of identity. The action takes place during the

[24] Van Gennep 1981.
[25] Turner 1977:37.
[26] Turner 1977:38.
[27] Originally published as: Christophoros Milionis, Καλαμᾶς καὶ Ἀχέροντας (Milionis 1985). Here, citations are taken from the English translation (Milionis 1996: 23–36).

234

Greek Civil War, when brother is pitted against brother (i.e. when kinship and sameness are denied). The protagonist is from a Communist village on the Kalamas River's west bank. He is troubled by news of atrocities committed on the eastern side of the river, "news that darkened the mind; that we had become worse than the Germans, that they were taking prisoners and making them dig their own graves. They would tell these things in this ambiguous way, and of course we all thought it was the others, and hated them even more."[28] Intrigue soon turns to terror when a fighter whispers to him that the perpetrators of these crimes were not from the right-wing resistance unit, "EDES," but "ours," communist EAM resistance fighters.[29] The news devastates this impressionable youth: "from that day, the hills undulating to the east and beyond to Kalamas looked different. That haze was not smoke from the mortars, nor was it morning mist—how can I put it? It was vapor from the Underworld. I came upon a book, an old school reader, and I read a poem by Lord Byron that was somewhat confusing: 'Here is Kalamas, black Acheron he.' Things had been mixed up so that Acheron and Kalamas became one."[30]

The allusion to Byron's own "somewhat confusing" footnote from Canto II of his *Childe Harold's Pilgrimage* (1812)[31] recalls a long history of locating Acheron. In antiquity, Acheron was the name of several rivers believed to be connected with the Underworld. Acheron ran through wild countryside and disappeared into a deep cleft. When it resurfaced near its mouth, it formed an unhealthy marsh in a barren land, the Acherusian Bog, which was understandably associated with the Underworld.[32] Kalamas, though located in the same area, was a separate river and was considered to be the ancient Thyamis that formed the northern boundary of Thesprotia, which separated it from Cestrine. Yet Byron's mistake—if that is what it is—might be excused as the Kalamas also has a waterfall that drops sixty feet and so might easily be mistaken for the Acheron.[33] In *Childe Harold*, Byron encounters there a landscape at once mythic hell and earthly heaven:

---

[28] Milionis 1996:25. EDES ('Εθνικὸς Δημοκρατικὸς 'Ελληνικὸς Σύνδεσμος [National Republican Greek League]), was a major resistance organization commanded by Napoleon Zervas and was the principal rival to ELAS. ELAS ('Εθνικὸς Λαϊκὸς 'Απελευθερωτικὸς Στρατός [National Peoples' Liberation Army]), the military arm of the EAM ('Εθνικὸ 'Απελευθερωτικὸ Μέτωπο [National Liberation Front]), the leftist republican coalition led by the Greek Communist Party, was the principal and largest resistance organization.

[29] Milionis 1996:26.

[30] Milionis 1996:26.

[31] Byron 1899:23, Stanza LI, line 6.

[32] See the relevant entries in Grimal 1986.

[33] See Longford 1975, especially pp. 37–39.

Dusky and huge, enlarging on the sight,

Nature's volcanic amphitheatre,

Chimaera's alps extend from left to right:

Beneath, a living valley seems to stir;

Flocks play, trees wave, streams flow, the mountain-fir

Nodding above: behold black Acheron,

Once consecrated to the sepulchre!

Pluto, if this be hell I look upon.

Close shamed Elysium's gates, my shade shall seek for none![34]

The collapsed opposites echo previous stanzas: at "monastic Zitsa . . . the distant torrent's rushing sound/Tells where the volumed cataract doth roll/Between those hanging rocks, that shock yet please the soul."[35] This conjoining of fear and rapture is typical of the sublime, which in Burke's then influential version referred to "that state of the soul in which all its motions are suspended, with some degree of horror. In this case, the mind is so entirely filled with its object, that it can not entertain any other, nor by consequence reason on that object which employs it. . . . Astonishment . . . is the effect of the sublime in its highest degree . . .The mind is hurried out of itself, by a crowd of great and confused images: which affect because they are crowded and confused."[36] For Byron, the mythic landscape on the border of Greece and Albania throws up everywhere the presentness of the Greek, or, the equally awesome and savage Albanian, wilderness. The mythic domain so cherished by Byron's traveling companion, Hobhouse, is countered by the savageness and newness of the present. In other words, the correlative of classical Greece, or "the imperatives of mythic consciousness," as one critic puts it, are counterweighed by "the equally valid ones of an [Albanian or even modern Greek] society which that consciousness [the western devotion to classical Greece] could not accept."[37] In this sublime moment, "here is Acheron, black Kalamas he."

Returning to Milionis' story, the protagonist winds up working for supporters of the enemy camp, EDES. Ten years later, it is amongst erstwhile foes in an office near the Acheron River that the group's chairman confesses to him: "The things our eyes have seen can't be forgotten. We became worse than the Germans. Do you hear, they made prisoners dig their own graves!" The protagonist's mind darkens as he asks whether the speaker is referring to "'our men?' No, 'ours . . . EDES men,'

---

[34] Byron 1885:69, Stanza LI.
[35] Byron 1885:68, Stanza XLVIII.
[36] Burke 1989:256/8. The extracts are taken from Burke 1757.
[37] I refer to the discussion of Childe Harold in Shilstone 1988, especially pp. 27–35.

said the chairman." The original trauma is relived, only the same signifier ("ours") holds different meanings for different speakers across different contexts. "Our men" are not the protagonist's in the original sense. Ironically, the Acheron of his imagination is not "of Pluto and Persephone," but "the other side, the invisible side . . . the other side of death."[38] It resides not in the Underworld, but in the world of the living. Acheron and Kalamas, EDES and EAM, the dead and the living have become indistinct.

Andrić's novel cited earlier uses the liminality associated with bridges to encapsulate the precariousness of distinctions drawn between sameness and difference, friend and enemy, life and death. The builder of this bridge, the Grand Vezir Mehmed Pasha, is a local born in a nearby village but whisked away by the Ottomans in his childhood to join the ranks of the elite Ottoman Janissary Corps. This practice of *devsirme* or *paidomazôma* entailed the enforced recruitment of non-Muslim boys for the Ottoman military and civil services. As a janissary, the boy is supposedly washed clean of his prior consciousness. Archetypally, the boy will return one day to his place of origin as conqueror of his own people. But blood does not become water and the hero is, at the very least, tormented by his actions and, more frequently, becomes conscious of his prior self. This narrative is something of a Balkan fixation.[39] In Andrić's *Bridge on the Drina*, the Vezir returns to conquer his hometown and memorializes this act by ordering the construction of a bridge that will unite the region with the main body of the Ottoman Empire. He hopes the edifice will bridge his two selves and cure him of "the same black pain which cut into his breast with that special well-known childhood pang which was clearly distinguishable from all the ills and pains that life later brought to him."[40] Unfortunately, though the bridge is completed, this desire remains unfulfilled as the Vezir "once again felt the 'black knife' in his breast" when a half-demented dervish assassinates him with a butcher's knife to the ribs.[41]

From the outset, the *vila* or spirits of the boatmen and the locals destroy "by night what had been built by day."[42] The conspiracy is thwarted only by the brutality of the builders' Ottoman foreman, Abidaga, who captures the rebels' leader, the Serb Radisav, and impales him on the bridge in one of Balkan literature's

---

[38] Milionis 1996:35–36.
[39] Some, like the Greek novelist Rhea Galanaki, employ this paradigm of the historical novel while subverting it (Galanaki 1987). An English-language translation is Galanaki 1996. On this, see Calotychos 1997.
[40] Andrić 1977:26. Galanaki's protagonist also considers himself dead in his first (Greek) life and reborn in a second (the Egyptian). As the novel progresses, it is clear that he is neither wholly dead in the one nor wholly reborn in the other. See Calotychos 1997:249–256.
[41] Andrić 1977:70.
[42] Andrić 1977:16.

most well-known scenes. However, Radisav's tortured body, "raised on high, hard and imperishable as a statue which would remain there forever," is resurrected.[43] And so Serb resistance, with its characteristic death in this life for reward in the next, reinscribes the bridge as a permanent monument for the locals' resistance. What began as a monument to the union of disparate parts of an individual and collective self, a polyreligious Empire, becomes the sign for the repression and self-contradiction on which such edifices, and empires, are built. This is what is at stake.

The region's folklore is embedded in Andrić's tale. In this material, the immurement of children or a beloved person appeases the spirits and allows for the construction of the bridge. In Balkan variants, the beloved is the foreman's wife. Such human sacrifice for the common good may not be the norm beyond the world of fantasy, as has been commented, but "ritual killing, whether by immuring or by slaughter and consumption of human, animal, and bird flesh, followed by burial of the bones, is a constant theme in the tales that leads to regeneration . . . it is still customary in Greece, as elsewhere in the Balkans, to slaughter a cock and let the blood run into the foundations of a new building, as it is among Orthodox Christians to roast and eat the Paschal lamb to celebrate Christ's rebirth. The community's life triumphs over individual death, on spatial and temporal levels, therefore the most precious being must be sacrificed in a reciprocal pact with God/Nature."[44] In Andrić's tale, the foreman's wife is substituted by the indigenous Serb. But not only by him. The torso of a young Arab, or "Negro," is accidentally wedged into the foundations of the central pier. Also, at an earlier stage in construction, the newborn, illegitimate twins of a "stuttering half-witted girl" are reputedly walled into the bridge. Again, the edifice becomes both symbol for the village and for the repression of ethnic, racial, and sexual otherness.

The obsessive return to the myth of the bridge constitutes a secular ritual that restates a set of social realities. "Ritual . . . veils the ultimate disorder, the non-order, which is the unconceptualized, unformed chaos underlying culture."[45] The danger underlying ritual lies in the ideals or imaginings that emerge from the attempt to paper over, or here build over them. In Freudian terms, the obsessive, compulsive ritual of return to the myth of the bridge recalls that that which is banished. Again and again, the bridge brings us back to the "inner alterity" that bedevils any claim to self-presence. The self-contradiction at the core of any one local identity's claim to primacy in the Balkans is also, by extension, a coda for the entire region's place in Western Europe. The Balkans remain on the borders of Europe, silent for

[43] Andrić 1977:55.
[44] Alexiou 2002b:192.
[45] Moore and Myerhoff 1977b:17. The article more generally discusses functions and attributes of secular rituals.

decades, marginal but never to be ignored, both "ours" and not "ours." Whenever this lesson is forgotten, the Balkans reassert themselves by firing a shot that is heard around the world.

Bombing Repetition

The bombing of the bridge at Novi Sad moved Belgrade residents to rush onto their city's bridges each night in mid-April, 1999, to prevent the NATO Allies from bombing them. Belgrade residents congregated on the bridge and swayed to the music of a nightly rock concert. Those crazy Serbs were confronting Charon as if in an Emir Kusturica movie, only without the manic gypsy rhythms of Goran Bregović's music.[46] The sacrifice of one's own in the bridge ballad suggested itself as the Serbs appealed to the Master Builder's sense of pity. One conventional myth-ritual thesis presents the ballad of immurement as a "survival from an actual practice of the past of offering a human sacrifice in order to appease supernatural spirits."[47] Oddly appropriate, for the *supranational* rather than *supernatural* entities presiding in 1999, the NATO forces firing from the heavens, demanded appeasement. The witnesses to justice from upon high, the *theôroi* of CNN-time, were ready to take their cues, instantiate the event and ordain the drama into discourse, and hence into being. In the minds of the western viewer, the Serbs' sacrifice, or their comeuppance, resonated with past sacrifices. It was typical, some observers intimated, of their suicidal makeup. After all, their most legendary song tells of how Tsar Lazar led the Serbs into battle against the Ottoman Turks in Kosovo Polje in 1389, and chose defeat with honor and a heavenly kingdom over a terrestrial victory.[48] As a result, the Serbs were condemned to endure 500 years of Ottoman rule. The ascendant Milosevic evoked this legend in 1987, at a Serb celebration for Kosovo Polje, and so invited myth to overtake reality. Now history was repeating itself in the province of Kosovo, where the Serbs were the minority and they portrayed the majority Albanians as "Turkish usurpers." That Milosevic's parents had both committed suicide made him an ideal successor to Tsar Lazar.

The Belgrade Serbs were standing on *their* bridge in real time. Repetition compulsion in life, in interpretation, and in history grants the event in its moment of iteration or experience a special poignancy. For knowing the event has happened before can offer both consolation in continuity and address the fatalism of consequence. In ritual, the "now" is infinitely repeatable. The ritual moment punctuates

---

[46] On the hypnotic, resistant anti-global strains of Bregović's music to Kusturica's films, see Gourgouris 2002:323–350.

[47] On this, see Dundes 1996:188.

[48] See Rebecca West's discussion of the legend in West 1941:906–917.

duration and by engaging linear time, it allays fears about its course, contextualizes it. At moments such as these, Victor Turner has argued, the community shares in the "now" by experiencing it in tandem with the sense of the threat of past actions once themselves in the "now," the "now" of those past moments.[49]

Of course, the defiance of Belgrade residents led neither to their immurement nor to the destruction of their bridge. In the end, their calculation suggests a postmodern understanding of how the politics around ritual can be made to work in one's favor. Ismail Kadare's *The Three Arched Bridge* is instructive on this point.[50] While Andrić's bridge has stood for centuries, Kadare's bridge has not. At the beginning of Kadare's tale, a ferryman carries people and goods across the river. Faceless and nameless forces impose a bridge on the locals and "the lineaments of a new order."[51] The bridge builders send an anonymous collector of folktales to learn from the narrator about the people's beliefs; they hire ballad singers; and pervert the tales of the inhabitants. Gjon the narrator is incensed when one hired collector of folktales provides "interpretations of legend . . . founded on baseness, betrayal, and disloyalty." But he also realizes that change is irreversible. The bridge is eventually built, but is, in the eyes of the residents, "superfluous, a stranger." To facilitate it, the authorities immure a villager, "the very stuff of legend poured over him." And, though the building of the bridge proceeds, and the boatmen as in Andrić's tale are replaced, eventually Gjon identifies this sacrifice *not* as a ritual, but as a "crime with only one purpose, to inspire terror." Agency, however, is never fully determined as Kadare intimates that control over legend is no simple matter: "These people had revived legend like an old weapon, discovered accidentally, to wound each other badly. It was nevertheless early to say whether they had really enlisted it in their service. Perhaps it was legend itself that had caught them in a snare, had clouded their minds, and had thrust them into the bloody game."[52]

Kadare's work amounts to a postmodern exposition of the politics of ritual and narrative, its manipulation—or here, its engineering—by economic, ethnic, and political interests. Guilt is not placed solely in the hands of conniving, external forces. Whether a ritual or a crime—and ritual here is a crime—those *within* the Balkan polity are aware of its workings by now and are a party to it. To a point, it is their responsibility to use this knowledge to unhand themselves from its grip. The last section of this chapter considers this question of agency, of blowing up the bridge, of escaping the narrative ritual.

---

[49] See, characteristically, Turner 1982b.
[50] Kadare 1997.
[51] Kadare 1997:101.
[52] Kadare 1997:125.

The Circle Is Not Round

Whether by discursive hegemony or local tradition, fictional representations of the Balkans in the nineties by foreigners and locals alike have tapped into this repetition compulsion. Gianni Amelio's film *Lamerica* (1994) considers an old Albanian man exploited by Italian con men in today's Albania. Their exploits lead to the old man's remembering that he was himself an Italian once lost behind enemy lines in World War II. Amelio's scenario resonates with themes and perspectives similar to Demetriou's novella discussed earlier. Emir Kusturica's *Underground* (1995) opens with the German bombing of Belgrade in World War II and so comments ironically on the more recent bombing of the city. Harvey Keitel's character of the filmmaker A. in Theo Angelopoulos' *Ulysses Gaze* (1995) searches for three reels by the filmmaker Manaki Brothers. He has viewed their extant first Balkan film, or originary gaze, which, incidentally, depicts weavers at work in Avdela in 1905. And so the tale begins. . . . His experience melds with the Manaki Brothers' own experience, as time frame and film frame meld in the narrative, and the beginning and end of the century elide into each other: "I used to dream this would be the end of the journey. But isn't it strange? Isn't this the way it always is? In my end is the beginning." The prescription is oddly familiar even if the economic, historical, and political circumstances that contextualize this repetition are engaged to differing degrees of depth and perspicacity from one film to the next. And while traditional psychoanalytic fare may have allowed the Balkan patient to interpret the symptoms of such age-old neuroses or rituals (as Kadare instructs), the postmodern reflexivity behind a knowing interpretation of such repetitions may even detract from the historical lessons to be drawn from them. It is important to go beyond these rituals to propose a radical model of agency. One example comes to mind.

Milcho Manchevski's *Before the Rain* (1995), winner of the Golden Lion at the Venice Film Festival, is also, typically, patterned on a cyclical structure. The film is structured around the idea that two opposing forces will circle each other, find themselves again, eventually collide, and when they do, conflict and death will ensue again. The film opens with the old monk Marko declaring, "It'll rain. The flies are biting. Come, it's time. Time never dies—the circle is not round." With only minor variation, this line is repeated in all three acts of the film; and Manchevski returns to the very first scene at the end. It is also the last scene. And in that scene, the monks look down to the valley below to remark that something is brewing. The open-endedness of the film lies in the viewer's foreknowledge of the trouble that will play itself out *after* the end of the film, a section which—the viewer knows only retrospectively after seeing the entire film—is featured in the first part of the film. It may be that rain will bring with it a further act of violence.

Or that an act of free will, a defiant response to intercommunal hatred, that has also taken place in the valley below prefigures another act of such empathy. This act will follow in the film's first part, i.e. the Slav Macedonian Kiril's compassion and love for the Albanian girl, Zamira. Such interethnic love will lead to Zamira's death, as it did for Kiril's uncle Alex in the third section.

But Manchevski authorizes the rewriting of a different ending for a new beginning. Beyond the narrative's open-endedness, in the midst of these opposing forces, Manchevski offers a third element—a rupture in the endless circularity of narrative. The time sequence of the film is purposely undermined by a single scene in which the protagonist's girlfriend in England, Anne, in the second part of the film, is handed photographs of her lover, the Slav Macedonian Alex's, shooting death near Ohrid. He is shot at the hands of his own Slav Macedonian family members. Temporally, this cannot be. Anne could not have seen these photos of Alex being killed; for they must have been taken *before* his death had taken place. The director has decided to interpose a break in the circle quite deliberately and leaves it to us to expose the potentialities of breaking time's circle in this manner. Will Anne do something about what has happened? About what *will* happen? Can we break the circle of violence? Or will we, even like Alex, return to do so and meet our death, only to push it round once more?

It is essential to confront what Manchevski himself terms as this "carefully designed quirk in the chronology" to discover how, in fact, this open-endedness "supplants the confining circularity."[53] Alex stands for a new paradigm of action and free thinking. Only an irrational break will destroy the inevitability of the endless cycle of conflict to always already come again—an act of free will contrary to the dictates of deeply ingrained logics of time, action, and the "rationale" of fate. Difference here in the chain of repetition functions not as a variation, but an illogical rupture in the very fabric, in the weave, of the text's tapestry. It does and undoes itself to highlight the potentialities derived by one who weaves the tale or makes the movie. After all, Alex the photographer scolds himself for once standing around and looking on as a militiaman answered his plea for something "to shoot" (with his camera) by shooting (with a gun) a prisoner of war in cold blood. Alex's decision to act and stem the tide of violence projects symbolically Manchevski's own plea for a dutiful recklessness that will break out beyond the forms of the dominant narrative ritual, its damning rationale, and simultaneously stem the tide of cyclical time. The film defies the patterned temporality of repetition and seeks a way out of the vortex of insistent narratives and metanarratives.

[53] Manchevski's comment is quoted in Iordanova 2001. While Iordanova admits that these "disjunctures" leave "a nice feeling of ambiguity" (79) and "leav[e] the viewer with a slightly dizzy feeling of open-endedness that supplants the confining circularity"(81), she does not get to grips with Manchevski's gesture.

Part Four

Ritual Embodiments/ Textual Positionalities

Fourteen

The "Anodos" of the Bride

Gloria Ferrari

In the fifth century there appears on Athenian vases a series of pictures, which Bérard in his study titled collectively *Anodoi*, or chthonian passages.[1] The theme unfolds in two distinct moments. Most vases show the point at which a woman emerges from the earth with the lower part of her body still underground in the same fashion as Ge, Earth herself, when she delivers Erichthonius to Athena or comes to the aid of her children in the Gigantomachy.[2] This scheme is adopted for the return of Persephone on the bell-*kratêr* in New York (fig. 1), where the fissure in the earth, out of which the Maiden arises, is drawn in detail.[3] In other cases it is difficult to say who the heroine is, but inscriptions tell us that, besides Ge and Persephone, she may be Pandora or Aphrodite.

There is one securely identified representation of Pandora as she rises out of the earth to meet her future husband, Prometheus' improvident brother, on a volute-*kratêr* in Oxford.[4] Epimetheus greets her with open arms, holding an oversize hammer or mallet in his right; Eros hovers above them. At left, Hermes moves towards them, a flower in his hand, looking back at Zeus, who stands at the far left of the picture. The mallet that Epimetheus carries connects this scene to others, in

---

[1] Bérard 1974. In this chapter the following abbreviations are used: *ARV²* = J. D. Beazly, *Attic Red-Figure Vase-Painters*, 2nd ed. Oxford: Oxford University Press, 1963. *Paralipomena* = J. D. Beazley, *Paralipomena: Additions to Attic Black-Figure Vase-Painters and to Attic Red-Figure Vase-Painters*. Oxford: Oxford University Press, 1971. *Beazley Addenda²* = T. H. Carpenter, *Beazley Addenda: Additional References to ABV, ARV² and Paralipomena*. Oxford: Oxford University Press, 1989.

[2] *Lexicon Iconographicum Mythologiae Classicae* 4 (1988) s.v. Ge nos. 5–8, 13–21, 23–27. In some scenes only the head of the woman is above ground, as in the tondo of the cup in Rome, Museo di Villa Giulia 50320, *ARV²* 840.60, *Beazley Addenda²* 296; Bérard 1974, pl. 12 no. 43. Whether archaic representations of colossal heads or busts are *anodoi* or merely abridged renderings of the figures is an unresolved issue; see Buschor 1937:5–7; Bérard 1974:43–51.

[3] Metropolitan Museum of Art 28.57.23, *ARV²* 1012.1; *Paralipomena* 440; *Beazley Addenda²* 314; inscribed Persophata.

[4] Volute-*kratêr* in Oxford, Ashmolean Museum G 275, *ARV²* 1562.4; *Paralipomena* 506; *Beazley Addenda²* 388. Except for the Eros, all figures are named by inscriptions.

245

fig. 1 Attic red-figure bell-*kratêr*. New York, Metropolitan Museum of Art, Fletcher Fund, 1928 (28.57.23).

which the emerging maiden is surrounded by satyrs wielding the same kind of instrument, as on the neck of a volute-*kratêr* from Spina.[5] In other *anodos* pictures Pans replace the satyrs with mallets, for example, on the Boston *skuphos* by the Penthesilea Painter.[6] A lost *kalux-kratêr*, once in Dresden, showed Persephone—

---

[5] Ferrara, Museo Archeologico T.579, *ARV*[2] 612.1; *Paralipomena* 397; *Beazley Addenda*[2] 268. Guarducci 1930, followed by Brommer 1944, and Simon 1982a:145–146, identified in the central figure Pandora. The scepter she holds, however, and the torch-bearer behind her, who resembles the Eleusinian *dadoukhos*, suggest that she is Persephone; see Bérard 1974:91–102.

[6] Museum of Fine Arts 01.8032, *ARV*[2] 888.155; *Paralipomena* 428; *Beazley Addenda*[2] 302; Bérard 1974, pl. 12, 42. Lexicon Iconographicum Mythologiae Classicae 2 (1984) s.v. Aphrodite no. 1158; 8 (1997) s.v. Persephone no. 249.

fig. 2 Attic red-figure *kalux-kratêr*. Once Dresden, Albertinum 350.
After F. Brommer, "Pan im 5. und 4. Jahrhundert v. Chr.," *Marburger
Jahrbuch für Kunstwissenschaft* 15 (1949/50) 22, fig. 25.

named by an inscription—arising in the presence of Hermes and surrounded by
leaping Pans (fig. 2).[7] Aphrodite, her name also inscribed, appears in the same
company on a *pelikê* in Rhodes, between an excited Pan and Hermes, who raises a
long whip in his right hand.[8] Scholars have plausibly identified Aphrodite also in
the scene painted on a *hudria* in Syracuse (fig. 3).[9] Eros bends to lift the woman,
in the presence of two white-haired solemn women, who each holds a scepter.
Behind Eros, a Pan crouches with arms extended, palms down, while an eager
Ares rushes in from the left. Other vases show the moment preceding the *anodos*.
A bell-*kratêr* in Berlin depicts the heroine in her underground cave, around which
are disposed an *aulos*-playing Eros, Dionysos, and two satyrs (fig. 4).[10] On another

---

[7] Dresden, Albertinum 350, *ARV*[2] 1056.95; inscribed Pherophatta.

[8] Rhodes, Archaeological Museum 12.454, *ARV*[2] 1218.2; *Beazley Addenda*[2] 349.

[9] Siracusa, Museo Archeologico 23.912, *ARV*[2] 1041.11; *Paralipomena* 443; *Beazley Addenda*[2] 320.
Lexicon Iconographicum Mythologiae Classicae 2 (1984) s.v. Aphrodite nos. 1178, 1305.

[10] Staatliche Museen 2646, *ARV*[2] 1443.6; *Beazley Addenda*[2] 378.

Gloria Ferrari

fig. 3 Attic red-figure *hudria*. Siracusa, Museo Archeologico 23.912. After *Corpus Vasorum Antiquorum* Siracusa 1 (1941) pl. 24.

bell-*kratêr*, the enclosure is ogival with regular outline, suggesting a *tholos*-like built structure rather than a cavern.[11]

This series of pictures is marked by consistencies that depend neither upon one particular myth or story, nor on the whim of the painter, but on the nature of the event and the genre of the representation. Although not all, many *anodos* scenes feature either satyrs or Pans. Following Guarducci, Buschor, and Simon,[12] most scholars believe that these refer to satyr-plays, some of which had a chorus of Pans in place of satyrs.[13] The evidence pointing to drama is considerable and, to my mind, decisive. On one example, the Eucharides Painter's *stamnos* in the Louvre, the hairy satyrs surrounding the *anodos* wear the phallic trunks of the actors in

---

[11] Malta, La Valletta Museum, *ARV²* 1436.7; *Beazley Addenda²* 377. See Bérard 1974:136–138, who aptly compares the rendering of the *tholos*-tomb of Glaukos on the cup by the Sotades Painter (British Museum D 5, *ARV²* 763.2; *Beazley Addenda²* 286), and points to a similar treatment of the enclosure on a *kratêr* fragment from an *anodos* scene, Oxford, Ashmolean Museum G 719, *ARV²* 1153.15; *Beazley Addenda²* 336.

[12] Guarducci 1930; Buschor 1937; Simon 1982a:145–146; 1989:197–203.

[13] A *kalux-kratêr* by the Niobid Painter, the British Museum Gr 1856.12–13.1, *ARV²* 601.23, decorated in two registers, shows on one side actors wearing the mask of Pan and the trunks of satyr-players, on either side of the *aulos*-player. Pickard-Cambridge 1968:185 and Webster 1970:24 suggested that a chorus of Pans was an alternative to the chorus of Satyrs. The register above is generally interpreted as the adornment of Pandora in the presence of the gods; see Reeder 1995:282–284. The pose of Ares, however, who rushes towards the central figure, and the chorus of Pans below call to mind the picture on the Syracuse *hudria* (fig. 3) and the possibility that she is instead Aphrodite; see Brommer 1937:14–15.

fig. 4 Attic red-figure bell-*kratêr*. Berlin, Staatliche Museen 2646. After F. Brommer, "Pan im 5. und 4. Jahrhundert v. Chr.," *Marburger Jahrbuch für Kunstwissenschaft* 15 (1949/50) 36, fig. 4.

satyr-plays.[14] Here, as on the volute-*kratêr* in Ferrara, the cast of characters includes the *aulos*-player, which is key in the identification of dramatic choruses.[15] Indeed, Pandora was the protagonist of a satyr-play, of which meager fragments survive, whose title suggestively features hammers or mallets: Sophocles' Πανδώρα ἢ Σφυροκόποι, *Pandora or The Hammerers*. From its title, we know that another satyr-play by Sophocles, the *Iambe*, had an Eleusinian theme and may well have included a satyric version of the return of Persephone.[16] Dramatic performances

[14] Louvre C 10754, *ARV*² 228.32; *Paralipomena* 347; *Beazley Addenda*² 199; Simon 1989.

[15] On this point see Brommer 1944:13, 49–54; Beazley 1955. On the *aulos*-player in vase-paintings of comic choruses, see Green 1985, particularly p. 98. Bérard 1974:93 maintains that the presence of the *aulos*-player is not enough to identify the scene as a dramatic performance, pointing to the fact that the figure is equally appropriate to a ritual performance.

[16] Sutton 1975a:351; Sutton 1975b. Bérard 1974:93–94, lists instances of Eleusinian scenes featuring satyrs on Attic fifth-century vases, which he believes illustrate ritual performances rather than drama.

may be enough to explain the currency of the theme on vases of this period, roughly from the 470s to the early fourth century, the heyday of the satyr-play.

Another recurring feature is the presence of instruments of percussion: the satyrs' mallets, the whip in Hermes' hand, and the gesture of the Pan on the Syracuse *hudria*, palms down as if to strike the ground with the flat of the hand. Bérard has argued most recently and convincingly that these should be explained in light of the practice of invoking the appearance of chthonian beings by striking the earth.[17] The hypothesis first was formulated by Jane Harrison, who compared the satyrs' action to a rite in the cult of Demeter *Kidaria* at Pheneus in Arcadia: wearing the mask of the goddess, her priest pounded the ground with rods (Pausanias 8.15.3).[18] The ritual may have a parallel in the performance by women reported by Pausanias 1.43.2 at Megara, at the rock called *Anaklêthris*, because there Demeter had called up her daughter. But instruments such as rods and mallets are not indispensable. For instance, Meleager's mother, Althaea, at *Iliad* 1.567–71, calls upon Hades and Persephone by beating the earth with her hands. The action described in the Homeric Hymn to Apollo, 333–340, bears an even greater resemblance to that of Pan on the Syracuse *hudria*. The passage describes how an enraged Hera prayed to Earth, Heaven, and the Titans who dwell under the earth that she may bear a child apart from Zeus. As she spoke, "she struck the earth with down-turned hand," χειρὶ καταπρηνεῖ δ᾽ ἔλασε χθόνα (333), as does the Pan in the *anodos* scene.[19]

The stomping of Pans around the rising figure, as on—as Bérard proposed— serves as well the purpose of arousing chthonian dwellers. Sophocles' *Ichneutae* (Trackers), provides a most relevant parallel. When the band of satyrs discover the tracks of Apollo's stolen cattle, they suddenly drop to the ground, attracted by the faint sound of Hermes' lyre emanating from an underground cave (249: νέρθε γᾶς). They will not leave before finding out "who is inside the roof," ἔνδον ἐστὶ τῆς στέγης (212), and their way of getting a response is to beat the ground with jumps and kicks (217–220):[20]

ἀλλ᾽ ἐγὼ τάχα
φ[έρ]ων κτύπον πέδορτον ἐξαναγκάσω
πηδήμασιν κραιπνοῖσι καὶ λακτίσμασιν
ὥστ᾽ εἰσακοῦσαι, κεἰ λίαν κωφός τις ᾖ.

---

[17] Bérard 1974, chapter 3.
[18] Harrison 1900:107.
[19] Bérard 1974:80.
[20] Text and translation from Lloyd-Jones 1996. On the motif of pounding the ground, see Zagagi 1999:208–211. On the staging of Cyllene's emergence, Jobst 1970:33–37; Maltese 1982:23–25.

But I'll quickly make the ground ring with repeated jumps and kicks, and force him to hear me, however deaf he may be.

The nymph Cyllene then comes out in a rage at the noise and the stomping, and eventually reveals that the child in the "vault," θησαυρός (282), below is Hermes, whom she is nursing. The nymph rising out of the subterranean cave among the satyrs finds an echo on several vases in our series.[21]

As regards Ge and Persephone, the *anodos* in each case is required by the mythical narrative. But the adoption of this figure for other characters remains a puzzle. Why is a chthonian passage, to use Bérard's expression again, appropriate to either Pandora or Aphrodite, indeed to both? Attempts to answer the question have taken two distinct paths. Following Buschor, Simon maintains that Aphrodite arises not out of the earth but out of the sea and that, likewise, Pandora comes up from the workshop of Hephaestus, located in the midst of Ocean in the cave that sheltered him after his fall from Olympus (*Iliad* 18.400–403).[22] But the action of beating the ground, which is common to the majority of the *anodos* scenes, strongly tells against this hypothesis. Moreover, there are no visual hints of the sea,[23] and fields and mountains, rather than the shore, are the habitat of Pan. Others have looked for a solution in chthonian aspects, located either in myth or in cult, that Aphrodite and Pandora, no less than Ge and Persephone, would possess. Although he dismissed the old idea that the rising of Pandora on the Oxford vase represents a pre-Hesiodic *Naturmythos* that featured Pandora as the Earth-goddess herself,[24] Bérard proposed what is in essence a new version of the chthonian hypothesis. In his view, the *anodos* scenes represent not drama or myth but performances by masked officiants in the cult of Demeter and Core, and in that of a primordial, "oriental" Aphrodite of the underworld.[25] The difficulty posed by Pandora, who is neither a divinity nor the object of cult, is resolved by postulating a confusion between "some chthonian goddess," to whom the name Pandora was applied as an epithet, and Hesiod's first woman.[26]

The common denominator to these otherwise disparate characters, I believe, is given by yet another theme that runs through the *anodos* scenes, that of marriage.

---

[21] Robert 1912:539–540; Buschor 1937:32; Simon 1989:200. A situation such as Hermes' in the play, that of a ward of the nymphs, might account for the representation of a youth in a cave, in the same iconography as that of the bell-*kratêr* in Berlin (above n. 10, fig. 4); London, Hope collection, Bérard 1974, pl. 10 no. 34.

[22] Buschor 1937:16–17; Simon 1959:38–49; *Lexicon Iconographicum Mythologiae Classicae* 1 (1981) s.v. Anesidora; 1982a:146; Loeb 1982b:785.

[23] See the critique by Bérard 1974, passim and chapter 9.

[24] Robert 1914:23; 1919:266–267.

[25] Bérard 1974:123–125, 160.

[26] Bérard 1974:161–166.

The allusion to the wedding of Pandora and Epimetheus is explicit on the Oxford *kratêr*. In the scene on the Syracuse *hudria*, Eros provides connotations of glamor, but the presence of Ares and his attitude suggest that, like Epimetheus, he sees his future bride for the first time. The imagery of the wedding has long been recognized in the picture of the return on the New York bell-*kratêr*. Core emerges out of the chasm, Hermes stands behind her, and Hecate, torches raised, leads her to her Demeter. Both Hermes and Hecate have important roles in the narrative of Core's abduction and return, but Hecate's gesture, a torch in either hand, unmistakably appeals to the iconography of wedding scenes. Here, as Reeder observed, "the bridal journey is inverted."[27] Aphrodite, Persephone, Pandora are all variations upon the paradigm of the *numphê*, the bride: Persephone is the bride of Hades; Pandora is the first mortal bride. As to Aphrodite, I turn to the account of her birth in the sixth Homeric Hymn:[28]

αὐτὰρ ἐπειδὴ πάντα περὶ χροῒ κόσμον ἔθηκαν,
ἦγον ἐς ἀθανάτους· οἱ δ' ἠσπάζοντο ἰδόντες
χερσί τ' ἐδεξιόωντο καὶ ἠρήσαντο ἕκαστος
εἶναι κουριδίην ἄλοχον καὶ οἴκαδ' ἄγεσθαι,
εἶδος θαυμάζοντες ἰοστεφάνου Κυθερείης.

And when the (the Horai) had fully decked her, they brought her to the gods, who welcomed her when they saw her, giving her their hands. Each one of them prayed that he might lead her home to be his wedded wife, so greatly were they amazed at the beauty of violet-crowned Cytherea.

It is my thesis that the "chthonian" circumstances of these figures are a property of the condition of *numphê*, rather than a quality specific to each mythical persona. That is, the visual image of the cave or underground vault, is the vehicle of a metaphor that structures the concept of a woman's betrothal, or *enguê*, and the wedding ritual itself.[29] This figure lends itself to comic exploitation, as in the satyr-plays from which the vase paintings discussed above draw their inspiration. But it is used most often to tragic effect in a metaphor, which, as has been suggested, was profoundly rooted in ancient Greek culture and long lived: that of the "bride of Hades."[30] The argument that follows relies in part on an analysis of the semantic

---

[27] Reeder 1995:13, 290.
[28] *Homeric Hymn to Aphrodite* 6.14–18; text and translation from Evelyn-White 1914.
[29] On metaphors embedded in lexical terms, see Ferrari 1990 and Ferrari 1997.
[30] Alexiou and Dronke 1971.

valence of the word *enguê*, which is presented in detail elsewhere and here will be summarized in its essential points.[31]

In the Athenian marriage the *enguê* was the agreement between a woman's *kurios*, her legal guardian, and her future husband, to whom she was thus promised.[32] This was a key step in that it established the legitimacy of children born of the marriage, and it preceded the *ekdosis*, the actual transfer of the bride to the groom, which was accompanied by rituals that could collectively be called *gamos*.[33] As Wolff demonstrated, the technical terms for the conveyance of the bride, *ekdosis* and *ekdidonai*, mean "to give out on loan."[34] The contractual metaphor implicit in these words, extends to the notion of the *enguê*. For no less than *ekdosis*, *enguê* is used for commercial transactions that require a guarantee, or the establishment of securities.[35] This meaning of "deposit" or security implies a metaphor of placing something (or someone), as it were, "*en guê*." Since antiquity this has been understood on the basis of an hypothetical etymological derivation of *enguê* from *guion*, in the sense of hand, the hollow or palm of the hand. Gernet's explanation has won favor that the term originally meant a solemn promise made on behalf of the family group, rather than the transferal of an object or person.[36] In his view, what is put in the hand is a pledge, signified by a handshake.

The palm of the hand, though, is only a particularly marked use of the figure that is implicit in a group of terms constituted by *guê, guia, gualon*, that of "hollow" or vault.[37] An analysis of the appearance of the word *gualon* in literary texts fully confirms Hesychius' definition of *guala* as treasuries, vaults, hollows,[38] and *guala* may also be said of cups and the canopy of heaven. A dominant image is the stony hollow or cavern, one that is suited to both the grave and the treasury. For example, in Pindar's *Nemean* 10, the Dioscuri, who share one life by spending each alternatively one day on earth and the other in Hades, are said to be in the caves of Therapne, deep under the earth, *en gualois*.[39] In Euripides' *Andromache*,

[31] Ferrari 2002, ch. 8.
[32] Wolff 1944:51–53. Vérilhac and Vial 1998, review of the history of scholarship on the *enguê*.
[33] Vérilhac and Vial 1998:229–258, argue unconvincingly that *enguê* and *ekdosis* are two words for one and the same act of "giving" the bride, which is, in turn, distinct from the *gamos*.
[34] Wolff 1944:48–51.
[35] Wolff 1944:51–53.
[36] Gernet 1917, particularly pp. 365–373; Harrison 1968:3–6. Sutton 1989 tentatively identified the *enguê* in the representation of an old king shaking hands with a youthful traveler on the *loutrophoros* in Boston, Museum of Fine Arts 03.802.
[37] Chantraine 1968–80:239.
[38] Hesychius s.v. γύαλα· θησαυροί, ταμεῖα, κοῖλα.
[39] Pindar, Nemean 10, 55–56: μεταμειβόμενοι δ' ἐναλλὰξ / ἁμέραν τὰν μὲν παρὰ πατρὶ φίλῳ/ Δὶ νέμονται, τὰν δ' ὑπὸ κεύθεσι γαίας/ ἐν γυάλοις Θεράπνας ("Changing in succession, they spend one day with their dear father Zeus, the other deep under the earth in the hollows of Therapne"). Text and translation from Race 1997.

the underground caverns at Delphi are both caverns and treasury, *guala* and *thêsaurous*, they are caverns filled with gold (1092–1095):[40]

'Ορᾶτε τοῦτον, ὃς διαστείχει θεοῦ
χρυσοῦ γέμοντα γύαλα, θησαυροὺς βροτῶν,
τὸ δεύτερον παρόνθ' ἐφ' οἶσι καὶ πάρος
δεῦρ' ἦλθε Φοίβου ναὸν ἐκπέρσαι θέλων;

See that man who moves along the god's caverns filled with gold, treasure-houses of mortals, who comes again with the same aims as he did when he came before, to sack the temple of Phoebus?

Here, as elsewhere, the meaning of *gualon* is akin to that of English "vault." In the same sense, the nymph Cyllene refers to her cave as a "treasury," θησαυρός (*Ichneutae* 282). The image of laying valuables in store in an underground treasury, is the one that structures the sense of *enguê* as "deposit," and suits its use both as guarantee and betrothal. The fact that the female is promised is cast in the figure of capital withdrawn from circulation and placed in the vault, from which she will taken out when the time comes to hand her over to the groom.[41]

Among the rites of the wedding day, the *Anakaluptêria* , or "uncovering" evokes the progress of the bride from figurative subterranean confinement into the open. It is doubtful that the word means a ritual unveiling, as most scholars now believe.[42] Our sources, however, leave us in no doubt that the emphasis was on "seeing": this was the name given to the day in which the bride was brought into sight of the groom, which was also called *Optêria*.[43] In this respect, its foundation legend, which survives in fragments of Pherecydes of Syros, is especially suggestive. The first *Anakaluptêria* was that of *Chthoniê*, the bride of *Zas* with the telling name "she who is under the earth." On the third day, *Zas* wove the whole world into a great mantle, which he offered to *Chthoniê*, asking her to unite with him.[44] When she receives the mantle, *Chthoniê* becomes the Earth, as we learn from another fragment of Pherecydes:[45]

Ζὰς μὲν καὶ Χρόνος ἦσαν ἀεὶ καὶ Χθονίη· Χθονίη δὲ ὄνομα
ἐγένετο Γῆ, ἐπειδὴ αὐτῇ Ζὰς γῆν γέρας διδοῖ.

---

[40] Text cited from Diggle 1984.
[41] Of particular interest here are Gernet's observations, in his essay on the mythical concept of value, connecting the idea of *thêsauros* as a "vault . . . dug into rock and covered with a lid" and the *thalamos*, where a wife or daughter would be kept; see Gernet 1968:129–130.
[42] See e.g. Oakley 1982:113. Vérilhac and Via 1998:304.
[43] Pollux *Onomasticon* 3.36; Harpocration, s.v. *Anakaluptêria*; Hesychius, s.v. *Anakaluptêrion*.
[44] Schibli 1990, Fr. 68.
[45] Schibli 1990, Fr. 14; translation by Freeman 1948.

254

Zas and Time existed always, and *Chthoniê*; but *Chthoniê* acquired the name Gê, since Zas gives the earth to her as a gift of honor.

Chthoniê then undergoes a transformation. With the great phâros, she receives the earth as her domain and becomes Earth herself. The mortal bride's own transformation into fertile ground, at her *Anakaluptêria* is stated in the classic marriage formula: "I give you this woman for the sowing of legitimate children."[46] Wedding rites then join metaphors of treasure to be entrusted and land to be cultivated. The two come together as well in the semantic range of words such as καρπός—fruit, children, but also profit—and τόκος, which is childbirth, offspring, and the produce of money lent, that is, interest.

I now come to the ways in which the figure of the subterranean *numphê* lends itself to tragic exploitation on the Athenian stage and in funerary epigrams, in the conceit that when a nubile maiden or a bride dies she becomes the bride of Hades.[47] Significantly and poignantly, the moment of death often coincides with her *Anakaluptêria* and the wedding procession. A striking and often cited example is Erinna's epitaph for Baucis (*Anthologia Palatina* 7.712), which tells us that she died as the cortege had reached the groom's house: her father-in-law lights the funeral pyre with the torches that had lit her wedding cortege; the *humenaia* turned into dirges. It has been observed that this powerful metaphor should be explained not in terms of literary conventions, but in terms of cultural poetics: "Most important, perhaps, was the sustained parallel in the ritual of the two ceremonies of wedding and funeral, which provided the poets with a wealth of comparisons and contrasts."[48] I suggest, however, that these pivotal correspondences do not establish an equivalence of marriage to death, but have the task of pitting one against the other as polar opposites.

The figure of the Bride of Hades or of a marriage in Hades draws upon the particular connotations of the persona of the *numphê* and of her role in society. Procreation is not just one of her tasks, it is the sole purpose of her existence. The death of the maiden precisely at the point at which she is readied to produce new life represents a violation of the natural order of things: sterility replaces fertility, as darkness replaces light.[49] To marry Hades is an oxymoron, like "sowing the sea," in

[46] E.g. Menander *Perikeiromenê* (The girl with her hair cut short) 1013–1014: ταύτην γνησίων παίδων ἐπ' ἀρότῳ σοι δίδωμι.
[47] Seaford 1990 interprets the imagery of imprisoned heroines, such as Danae and Antigone, in light of "the confinement of the unmarried girl in the dark interior of the female quarters" (78).
[48] Alexiou and Dronke 1971:838. The notion of a conflation of the wedding rituals with death rituals has become commonplace in studies of Greek tragedy; see e.g. Seaford 1987; Rehm 1994.
[49] On marriage and death as alternatives, see Alexiou and Dronke 1971:833–837. On polar opposites as alternatives, Lloyd 1971:93–94, 127–128, 134–137.

the proverbial expression.[50] The conceit of marriage to Hades is a particular instance of a topos that enjoyed as wide a currency in the ancient world as in the modern: that of the world reversed, where "the things of this world can be truly perceived only by looking at them backwards."[51] This is, in other words, an *adunaton* that turns on the opposition of life as generative power and death as its absence.[52] As in the case of the death of Daphnis in Theocritus' first *Idyl*, the order of nature is monstrously changed. Paradoxically, it is Eros who drags Daphnis to Hades; the song of the pastoral Muses comes to an end (132–136):[53]

νῦν ἴα μὲν φορέοιτε βάτοι, φορέοιτε δ᾽ ἄκανθαι,
ἁ δὲ καλὰ νάρκισσος ἐπ᾽ ἀρκεύθοισι κομάσαι.
πάντα δ᾽ ἄναλλα γένοιτο, καὶ ἁ πίτυς ὄχνας ἐνείκαι,
Δάφνις ἐπεὶ θνάσκει, καὶ τὰς κύνας ὤλαφος ἕλκοι
κἠξ ὀρέων τοὶ σκῶπες ἀηδόσι γαρύσαιντο.

Now bear violets, you brambles, and you thistles bear violets, and let the fair narcissus wave above junipers. Let everything be upside down and the pine tree bear pears, since Daphnis dies, and let the stag tear into the hounds and from the mountains let the owls rival the nightingales.

Where Daphnis said πάντα δ᾽ ἄναλλα γένοιτο, "let everything be upside down," in a marriage in Hades one might say that everything has been turned upside down. While Daphnis' death is configured as a series of reversals in nature, the horror of death of the bride is expressed by a metaphor of ritual inverted that relies on the sinister effect of familiar images and procedures turning into their polluted opposites, identical but backwards. It is a perversion of the wedding that torches that should have lit the voyage of the bride light instead her funeral pyre and that dirges replace wedding songs. The play of reversals hinges on the sequence of the proceedings. Both the transport of the bride and that of the corpse proceed in the dark, but the first takes place after dusk and the second before dawn.[54] Both ceremonies include a banquet, the symposium for the bride and the *perideipnon* hosted by the dead—but the first takes place before the sealing of the bride in her new home, and the second afterwards. Most significantly, the death of the bride

---

[50] πόντον σπείρειν; see Dutoit 1936:8–9.
[51] Balthasar Gracian, *El Criticón*, cited by Babcock 1978:13. On opposites in Greek thought and "polar expressions," see Lloyd 1971, Part 1.
[52] On the *adunaton* in Greek and Latin poetry, see Dutoit 1936; and Cocchiara 1981: 58–91.
[53] Text from Hunter 1999. On this passage see Dutoit 1936:31–34.
[54] On the stages of the funeral, see Alexiou 2002a, chapter 1. On those of the wedding, Oakley and Sinos 1993.

represents an inversion of the procedure leading from betrothal to wedding, from *enguê* to *ekdosis*. The figure of the bride-to-be as buried treasure is the key to this metaphor: just when she would be brought out, she instead is consigned to an underground vault, that is, her tomb, the *enguê* replacing the *ekdosis*.

The mythical paradigm for the many mortal brides of Hades is, of course, Persephone. The *Homeric Hymn to Demeter* insists on the fact that her father Zeus "gave" her to his brother and ruler of the Netherworld. Aidoneus carried her off, but Zeus gave her away, and it was Zeus who asked the Earth to make the narcissus grow as a snare for Persephone.[55] But Zeus' *ekdosis* results in a reversal of the sequence of uncovering and torch-lit procession sequence prescribed by the wedding ritual. Persephone's *Anakaluptêria* consists of her descent to the subterranean palace of Hades, not by the light of torches, never to generate children, her perennial sterility mirrored in the barrenness that Demeter imposes on the earth.[56] The play reversal is explicit in the representation of Core's return, as on the New York *kratêr* (fig. 1). If her wedding was an *enguê*, she emerges from it as though a bride to be given out, by the light of torches—not to her groom, however, but back to her mother.

In Sophocles' *Antigone* this conceit is deployed in a sustained manner, making use of the image of the cavern, the stony hollow. Creon's Thebes is the world upside down, where the dead lies unburied, where it is left to a woman to stand up for what is right. The king of Thebes is as well Antigone's present *kurios* and future father-in-law, since she is betrothed to his son Haimon. Creon should deliver her to the groom, but he does the opposite. Instead of "giving her out," Creon buries her in "a rocky cavern" (774), to which she is led as though to a bridal chamber—"the hollowed rock, death's stone bridal chamber" (1204–1205).[57] The exclamation of Antigone as she enters the cavern is deservedly the most famous expression of the metaphor of the grave as Hades' *numpheion* (891–894):

[55] Homeric Hymn to Demeter 8–10; 3: ἥρπαξεν, δῶκεν δὲ βαρύκτυπος εὐρύοπα Ζεύς; 30: Διὸς ἐννεσίῃσι; 79: ἔδωκ' Ἀΐδῃ. See also Hesiod *Theogony* 913–914.

[56] The widespread assumption that her marriage is a maiden's death as much as her death is a marriage to Hades has led interpreters to gloss over Core's sterility. See e.g. Foley 1994:82: "Thus, like Persephone, a young girl could be thought to undergo in her initiation into marriage a symbolic 'death' before emerging into a new life and fertility with a (generally) unknown husband in a strange household."

[57] Sophocles *Antigone* 773–776: ἄγων ἔρημος ἔνθ' ἂν ᾖ βροτῶν στίβος / κρύψω πετρώδει ζῶσαν ἐν κατώρυχι, / φορβῆς τοσοῦτον ὡς ἄγος μόνον προθείς, / ὅπως μίασμα πᾶσ' ὑπεργύγῃ πόλις ("I will bring her where the path is loneliest, and hide her alive in a rocky cavern there. I'll give just enough of food as shall suffice for a bare expiation, that the city may avoid pollution"). 1203–1205: καὶ τύμβον ὀρθόκρανον οἰκείας χθονὸς / χώσαντες, αὖθις πρὸς λιθόστρωτον κόρης / νυμφεῖον "Αιδου κοῖλον εἰσεβαίνομεν ("we raised a high mound of his native earth; then we set out again for the hollowed rock, death's stone bridal chamber for the girl"). The text cited is Griffith 1999; translation by Grene, in Grene and Lattimore 1991.

ὦ τύμβος, ὦ νυμφεῖον, ὦ κατασκαφὴς
οἴκησις ἀείφρουρος, οἷ πορεύομαι
πρὸς τοὺς ἐμαυτῆς ὧν ἀριθμὸν ἐν νεκροῖς
πλεῖστον δέδεκται Φερσέφασσ᾽ ὀλωλότων.

Tomb, bridal chamber, prison forever dug in rock, it is to you I am going
to join my people, that great number that have died, whom in their
death Persephone received.

Antigone's infernal wedding is emblematic of the world upside down over
which Creon rules. Tiresias reveals to him the monstrosity of his policies
(1068–1071):

> You have thrust one that belongs above below the earth, and bitterly
> dishonored a living soul by lodging her in her grave; while one that
> belonged indeed to the underworld gods you have kept on this earth
> without due share of rites of burial, of due funeral offerings, a corpse
> unhallowed.

This passage unambiguously proposes the death of the bride as a prime instance of
normative inversion and the polar opposite of the wedding.

No less than in the *Antigone*, the theme of the death of the bride as a reversal
of the natural and social order runs through Euripides' *Alcestis*. Admetus, returning
to his unhappy house after the burial, explicitly deploys the metaphor of marriage
to Hades (868–871):[58]

οὔτε γὰρ αὐγὰς χαίρω προσορῶν
οὔτ᾽ ἐπὶ γαίας πόδα πεζεύων·
τοῖον ὅμηρόν μ᾽ ἀποσυλήσας
"Αιδῃ Θάνατος παρέδωκεν.

There is no pleasure in the sunshine
nor the feel of the hard earth under my feet.
Such was the hostage Death has taken
from me, and given to Hades.

He soon afterwards evokes the images of his marriage day—the torches, the
wedding songs, when he led Alcestis by the hand into the same house, surrounded
by revelers—in a direct confrontation with the much changed present (915–925):

---

[58] Euripides *Alcestis* 868–871. The text cited is Diggle 1984, translation by Lattimore, in Grene and
Lattimore 1992.

τότε μὲν πεύκαις σὺν Πηλιάσιν
υὑν θ' ὑμεναίοις ἔστειχον ἔσω,
φιλίας ἀλόχου χέρα βαστάζων,
πολυάχητος δ' εἵπετο κῶμος,
τήν τε θανοῦσαν κἄμ' ὀλβίζων,
ὡς εὐπατρίδαι κἀπ' (Diggle: καὶ ἀπ') ἀμφοτέρων
ὄντες ἀριστέων (Diggle: ἀριστῶν) σύζυγες εἶμεν·
νῦν δ' ὑμεναίων γόος ἀντίπαλος
λευκῶν τε πέπλων μέλανες στολμοὶ
πέμπουσί μ' ἔσω
λέκτρων κοίτας ἐς ἐρήμους.

Then it was with Pelian pine torches,
With marriage songs, that I entered my house,
Holding the hand of my dear wife,
With loud rout of revelers following
To bless her who now is dead, and me,
For our high birth, for nobilities
From either side which were joined in us.
Now the bridal chorus has changed for a dirge,
And for white robes the costumed black
Goes with me inside
To where her room stands deserted.

No doubt, Alcestis goes to her death as a bride of Hades.[59] That is not to say that the play presents us with a conflation of marriage and death and of marriage ritual with death ritual. As in the *Antigone*, the two are related to one another as day to night. Alcestis' choice represents an inversion of the laws of nature, according to which the old die before the young. It is wrong for a child to die before his father. It is not Alcestis who should have given her life for Admetus, but his parents, as the bitter exchange between Admetus and his father Pheres makes clear. When Pheres appears at the funeral, Admetus rejects his sympathy, then disowns him (633–635):

τότε ξυναλγεῖν χρῆν σ' ὅτ' ὠλλύμην ἐγώ.
σὺ δ' ἐκποδὼν στὰς καὶ παρεὶς ἄλλῳ θανεῖν
νέῳ γέρων ὤν.

---

[59] Rehm 1994, chapter 6.

Your time to share my sorrow was when I was about to die.
But you stood out of the way and let youth take my place
in death, though you were old.

and later he says (665–666):

οὐ γάρ σ᾽ ἔγωγε τῇδ᾽ ἐμῇ θάψω χερί·
τέθνηκα γὰρ δὴ τοὐπὶ σ᾽ (Diggle: σέ).

This hand will never bury you.
I am dead as far as you are concerned.

A son who will not bury his father, an old man who clings to the sunlight past his time, a young woman who saves them both, like a hero,[60] the defilement of death upon the family are all symptoms of the profound disorder in which the house of Admetus has been thrown. The conceit that marriage to Hades is an inversion of the ritual, one that replaces the *Anakaluptêria* with the *enguê*, is the ground upon which its return to normality may be represented as a marriage. Herakles wrestles Alcestis away from Thanatos and, as Buxton and others have shown, leads her out of the tomb as though a bride.[61] She is a prize and he her *kurios*—"I won her fair and square," he says; his task is to persuade Admetus to take into his house, by the hand, as his wife. In the final exchange between Heracles and Admetus, the gesture of leading the bride by the hand is suggestively emphasized. Heracles insists that he take the woman in his hands, the right hand, and lead into the house, as he had done on the occasion of their first wedding (1110–1115). Like a new bride she appears extraordinarily young. The reverse world is thus itself reversed, as Alcestis' figurative perennial *enguê* in her tomb turns into the kind of *enguê* that ends in marriage.

Its happy ending and the fact that it was produced fourth in the tetralogy in the competition of 438, in place of a satyr play, have led critics to question the genre of the *Alcestis*—whether it is a true tragedy or a satyr play, or something in-between.[62] With the *anodos* of Alcestis we thus come back full circle to the pictures with which we began, an irreverent play on the figure of the bride-to-be, the beauty underground, pure gold, and, like the earth, unfailingly productive.[*]

---

[60] Garner 1988 argues that Homeric allusions and diction in the play cast Alcestis in the mold of the dead heroes of the epic, such as Patroclus and Hector. On gender reversals in the *Alcestis* see Foley 1992:142; Segal 1993, chapters 4–5.

[61] Buxton 1987; Halleran 1988; Foley 1992:138–140.

[62] See Sutton 1973; Buxton 1987:27–29; Garner 1988:58–59.

[*] The author thanks Laura Slatkin, Mary Ebbott, and Mark Turner for fruitful discussions, suggestions, and references.

Fifteen

Social and Religious Rituals in Herodotus' *Histories*

A. M. Bowie

This chapter considers the role in Herodotus' narrative of the accounts of the rituals and customs of those peoples—principally the Persians, Babylonians, Indians, Arabians, and Scythians—which he describes in detail.[1] For the purposes of the chapter, "ritual" will be defined in a broadest sense, to cover not just religious rituals but also social rituals of all kinds (in so far as these two can be distinguished), as will "poetics," which I shall use in the sense of the operation of a prose text.[2] I shall be interested in how these ethnographic passages operate within the economy of the narrative, not just as catalogues of (more or less accurate) facts about the races involved, but as signifiers in the narrative which contains them. The passages of ethnography will be found not to serve a single function, nor to be simply lists of facts which Herodotus was able to glean on his travels, nor constructs generated by the application of Greek schemata to foreign ritual. They do have the important function of differentiating peoples from each other in historically significant ways, but also the more important function of contributing to the historical analysis conducted by Herodotus' text. At times, we shall have to consider the "accuracy" of some of these passages, but this will not for the purpose of judging Herodotus' veracity, but of seeing what it is he does with the traditions he came into contact with.

The ethnographical passages have of course received a good deal of attention in the past. The most richly detailed and challenging study is that of Hartog,[3] who argued that the account given of the Scythians (and others) and their customs was constructed in accordance with Greek modes of thinking about the Other.[4]

---

[1] Reasons of space mean that it will not be possible to treat the Egyptian chapters, but see now Moyer 2002, who concludes "we must . . . modify the recent popular image of Herodotus the ethnographer, who does not discover, but rather creates through oppositional categories or 'grids' *barbaroi* useful to his overall project, in order to recognise the agency of the Egyptian priests and other non-Greek 'informants'" (88).

[2] Cf. Todorov 1977.

[3] Hartog 1988.

[4] On Herodotus' ethnographic work, cf. also Lachenaud 1978:405–632; Pritchett 1993; I have not had access to Bichler 2000; on sacrifice in particular, Gould 1994.

Rossellini and Saïd have also analyzed the complex manner in which Herodotus constructs matters of gender and sexual conduct among the more marginal peoples, and related that to Greek ideas in these areas.[5] Finally, Redfield gave rituals a crucial place in Herodotus' historical thinking about Greece.[6] He divides peoples into "soft" and "hard" according to their social customs. No "soft" people has defeated a "hard" people, but "hard" peoples are rendered "soft" by their conquests of the "soft."[7] Greece is at a crucial juncture between an original "hardness" and a potential "softness":

> Herodotus presents the critical comparison of cultures as itself a crucial element of Greek culture. . . . If Greece, having . . . reassimilated the softened and partly barbarized Ionians, is not to become soft at the centre, the solution must be found in this peculiarity of the Greeks. . . . Herodotus thus does more than exemplify the Greek form of civilisation, he makes a contribution to it.[8]

In this chapter, I want to shift the perspective from the Greeks to the Persians and to see what the ethnographic passages have to say about them and their empire. Herodotus writes for Greeks, but especially in the early books the ethnographic passages reflect more on the Persians than on the Greeks. Indeed, a justification for this change of perspective may be found in the fact that the first lengthy ethnographic passage concerns the Persians themselves: in it they are set up as a people of an in some ways idealized kind. Though Athenian tragedy in general represented the Greeks as superior to the Persians,[9] in the early part of Herodotus' work it is the highly organized world of the Persian aristocracy that stands out as meritorious, not least when it is, as we shall see, juxtaposed with a very different picture of the Greeks. In the later parts, the merits of the Greek world will be held up, but in the earlier books Herodotus would have us consider the world in the light of the rulers of the empire of which he was originally part.

Persian Customs: Persians and Greeks (1.131–153)

This passage on the Persians occupies a cardinal moment in the narrative: Cyrus and the Persians have defeated Astyages and the Medes and replaced the Median kingdom with the Persian. It will later become evident that ethnographic sections are

[5] Rossellini and Saïd 1978.
[6] Redfield 1985, especially pp. 109–118 on the opposition between "soft" and "hard."
[7] Cf. on this topic also Bowie forthcoming.
[8] Redfield 1985:117–118. Redfield's examination of "Greekness" in Herodotus, not as a given to be defined against the "Other" of non-Greeks, but as a dynamic character shaped by historical events and choices made in response to those events is revealing.
[9] Cf. Hall 1989.

not randomly situated but coincide with historically significant moments. Whatever the historical truth about this particular shift of power, this change of regime triggers, via an anachrony, a definition of the Persians by reference to their rituals and customs, which reflects more the status of Persia in Herodotus' time than in Cyrus'. This passage gives us our first real picture of the Persian race, which until this moment, has been merely a subject of the Medes, living in hardship in infertile lands and rising up against their masters in a rather speculative way. The only time they have appeared specifically as Persians was when Cyrus offered them, before the battle against Astyages, the choice of a life of hardship, symbolized by the clearing of thorny ground, or of luxury, symbolized by the banquet. The thorns characterized their previous lifestyle: recommending revolt, Cyrus says, "if you do not wish to obey me, you will have innumerable hardships like yesterday's" (1.126.5).

This ethnographic passage therefore transforms the Persians in a moment from poor men tempted by Cyrus' offer of the life of luxury into the grand and highly socially organized possessors of a mighty empire. This transformation is a purely textual one: it is not given as any sort of development, nor is it explained. The account itself is enough to effect the transformation in an instant and emblematic fashion, and this character of the Persians as a race is never explicitly qualified in the rest of the narrative. Ethnographic description thus elides narrative and causation. This is established as a paradigmatic time of Persian society, and this idealizing of Cyrus' era will have its apogee later in Xenophon's *Cyropedia*.

The description of their social customs characterizes the Persians as an orderly, hierarchical people, whether one considers the social rituals which are used between individuals, their broader construction of space within the empire, or the many more minor customs which Herodotus describes. Meetings between equals are marked by a kiss on the lips; between those slightly distinguished in rank by a kiss on the cheek; and between those of divergent standing by *proskunêsis* by the lower ranker (1.134.1). Social status is thus firmly marked in a public manner by greater or lesser physical intimacy, and each knows his place in a hierarchy which extends throughout society from top to bottom.[10] This hierarchization is then mirrored in their attitudes to other peoples in the empire:

> After themselves, they hold their immediate neighbors in the highest regard, then those who live the next furthest away, and so on in order of proximity; so they have the least respect for those who live furthest away from their own land. The reason for this is that they regard themselves as by far the best people in the world in all respects, and others as gradually

[10] On Persian kissing, cf. also Xenophon *Cyropaedia* (The Education of Cyrus) 1.4.27–28.

A. M. Bowie

decreasing in goodness, so that those who live the furthest away from
them are the worst people in the world. (1.134.2; trans. Waterfield)

Respect is thus granted according to distance from the center: the repetition
emphasizes the point. This attitude is said to be modeled on a Median principle,
whereby the Medes ruled everyone, but each succeeding nation also ruled over the
nation further out from it.[11] Again then, there are hierarchies in social thinking that
structure not just Persian society but the whole empire.

These descriptions reflect something of the Achaemenids' construction of
imperial space as found in their inscriptions and ideology.[12] The inscriptions sometimes list the countries of the empire by starting from the center and moving
outward east and west.[13] When Darius says, "This is the kingdom which I hold:
from the Scythians who are beyond Sogdia to Ethiopia, from Sind to Sardis,"[14] he
is setting out the furthest boundaries of the empire with Persia at its center. In
ideology and practice, the center of the empire is occupied by the King, and proximity to him denotes status. This can be seen for instance on the reliefs on the
Apadana stairway at Persepolis, where the King is accompanied by two high-
ranking officials in the central panel, and the people of the empire line up to bring
him tribute. On the other hand, the many races that are depicted on these reliefs
and others are not distinguished in any hierarchical way among themselves by, say,
size: an equality pervades the calm and ordered sequence of races, which are distinguished only by racial characteristics, clothing, or gifts.

This spatially-organized view of Persian society is paralleled in other Greek
writers. In Xenophon, the king's tent was at the center of the camp and his forces
were arranged around him, the most trusted closest to him.[15] In dining too, there
were various hierarchical systems: the king dined alone, with the most honored
diners in a room close by and the next most honored outside.[16] Xenophon gives
Cyrus a strict but shifting *placement* at table, which indicated where each man stood
in his estimation at any particular time.[17] Herodotus' and other Greek writers'
picture of Persian attitudes is thus clearly derived from Persian ideology, but not a
straight reflection of it. Nonetheless, it does embody the idea of the central importance of the Persian race.

[11] Herodotus may also mean that the Persians operated in the same way, but the interpretation of the last sentence of 1.134.3 is problematic.
[12] Cf. Briant 1996:184–196.
[13] Cf. for example DNa 3 (Persian inscriptions are numbered according to Kent 1953).
[14] Cf. DPh (cf. n. 13).
[15] Xenophon *Cyropaedia* 8.5.8; cf. 1–14, 2.1.25–28.
[16] Heracleides ap. Athenaeus 145–146; cf. Xenophon *Anabasis* (The Expedition of Cyrus) 1.8.25, 9.31.
[17] Xenophon *Cyropaedia* 8.4.3–5; cf. also Xenophon *Oeconomicus* (Discourse on Estate Management) 4.8; cf. Briant 1996:322–324, 948.

Persian society is also attributed with other marks of excellence and balance in various areas of social activity; not all of this is true,[18] which suggests we are dealing with a cultural construct to some extent. All prayers at sacrifice are not for the individual sacrificer, but for the King and the whole Persian race, "because the sacrificer is part of that whole Persian race" (1.132.2). Their religion and sacrifice generally have a simplicity about them that does away with temples, statues, altars, fire, libations, music etc. (1.132.1): indeed, they count men who anthropomorphize gods, thus confusing them with men, as fools; their gods are the elemental sun, moon, earth, fire, water, and winds (1.131). They are fond of wine and deliberate over it, but always deliberate again when sober to check their drunken decision, and vice versa (1.133.4); their education is pared down to warlike matters and telling the truth (1.136.2); no execution of a Persian or a slave is permitted for a single crime, but repeated crimes outweighing benefits may be seriously punished (1.137.1); patricide and matricide are denied (1.137.2); they avoid talking of forbidden matters; and shun lies and debt (1.138.1). They adopt foreign customs willingly, using Median clothes because of their elegance, Egyptian breastplates and taking in various luxurious customs from the rest of the world (1.135); foreign gods are also accepted (1.131.3). Their social solidarity is even symbolized in the fact that "their names, which reflect their physical size and their dignity, all end with the same letter, which the Dorians call *san*, and the Ionians *sigma*" (1.139). This is not of course universally true, but is another sign of the coherence of Persian society.

That every sacrifice contains the recital of a cosmogony (1.132.3), a description of how the world became as it is, seems to set the seal on this picture of an idealized Persian society, situated at the center of its universe.

This description of an ordered, structured, and in many ways highly moral society is then immediately juxtaposed to an account of the Greeks' behavior when Cyrus angrily rejected any notion of his forgetting their earlier failure to help him against the Medes (1.141ff.). This historical segment presents a significant contrast with the ethnographic section on the Persians. It is a picture of weakness: "the whole Greek race was weak then, and the weakest and most insignificant of the peoples were the Ionians" (1.143.2). The Greeks are also divided against themselves, and this is documented for each of the three tribal groups in Asia Minor— Ionian, Dorian, and Aeolian.

Twelve Ionian cities contrive to create an alliance centered on the Panionium sanctuary, but they exclude all the other cities (1.143.3), thus rendering that name somewhat ironic. Herodotus pours scorn on their pretensions to be purer and more nobly Ionian than the others (1.146), and generally stresses the heterogeneous

---

[18] E.g. altars and fires figure on Achaemenid art.

nature of those who call themselves Ionians (1.146–147).[19] A group of Dorian states treats their Triopian sanctuary in the same exclusive manner: "the Dorians of what is now the Pentapolis . . . acted in the same way. They ensured that they admitted none of the neighboring Dorians into the Triopian shrine, and even excluded those of their own number who breached the rules of the temple" (1.144.1). The contrast with Persian sacrificers who pray for the whole race is notable, as is the contrast with the Persians' general sense of ethnic identity, which is defined against other races, but not against other Persians.[20] Finally, amongst the Aeolians, similar internecine conflict is found. The Smyrnaeans took in some Colophonian exiles who, during a festival of Dionysus, proceeded treacherously to seize the city (1.150). Exclusion from communal rituals and the abuse of ritual activity mark out the fissiparous nature of the Greeks.

This section then closes with an explicit contrast between Persians and Greeks made by Cyrus himself, which focuses on differences in customs and specifically on Greek deceitfulness towards each other. Replying to Spartan threats he says:

> "I have never been afraid of the sort of men who have a place set aside in the middle of their city, where they gather and deceive each other with promises." . . . He cast this aspersion on all the Greeks because they set up markets and buy and sell in them. The Persians themselves are not accustomed to use markets, and indeed have no such institution. (1.153.1–2)

This contrast is not only functional in its immediate context, but looks forward proleptically to later history. Herodotus' account of the Ionian revolt is famously remarkable for its emphasis upon the weakness and divided state of the Ionians, which reaches its climax in the shambles at the battle of Lade, where there were instantly mass desertions and a comprehensive defeat (6.14–15): "I cannot tell for sure which of the Ionians were cowards and which brave in this sea-battle; they blame each other" (6.14.1). Indeed throughout the episodes of that book, there is a constant contrast between Persian and Greek in which the latter come off worst. This is true in religious matters: when Datis discovered a gold statue of Apollo, he was keen to return it to its shrine at Delium in Theban territory. He gave it to the Delians to deliver, but they did not bother (6.118). It occurs too in the juxtaposition of Darius' forgiving treatment of the revolted Milesians (6.20) and the Sybarites' failure to show any signs of grief at the destruction of Miletus, despite the

---

[19] Cf. 1.170 for further inability on the part of the Ionians to unite themselves.

[20] The making of such comparisons is in part encouraged by the similarity between Herodotus' remarks about all Persian names and all Ionian festivals ending in the same letter (1.139; 148.2).

mass mourning that Miletus entered into when Sybaris was captured by the Crotonians: "these cities have the closest relations of any we know" (6.21.1). The Persian tolerance and good treatment of others who opposed them[21] again contrasts with the scandalous behavior of the Samians in seizing the empty city of Zancle, whose inhabitants had invited them to live there after the defeat at Lade, and the equally scandalous behavior of their ally Hippocrates of Gela to whom the Zancleans turned for help (6.23–24). Herodotus attributes the fact that the three generations of Darius, Xerxes, and Artaxerxes brought more troubles to the Greeks than the twenty generations before Darius "in part to the Persians and in part to the wars for pre-eminence among the chief states themselves" (6.98.2). This fissiparous nature of the Greeks will dog them in the time of Xerxes' invasion, which makes it all the more surprising that the Greeks should have won.[22]

There is, however, a major irony, again with proleptic force. As Herodotus tells us, without comment, at the end of his account of the Ionians (1.148.1), the Panionium where the Ionians celebrated the Panionia festival was built in Mycale, which is exactly where the final Greek victory was won. The site which here paradoxically symbolizes Greek disunity, and which frames this original account of the disunited Greeks, will by a curious turn become the site of the Greeks' greatest victory.

Ethnography is thus used here to set up a fundamental opposition between the two peoples whose conflict will form the climax of the *Histories*. Persian order and centralism is opposed to a fragmented and disunited Greek world. The implied analepsis of the Greeks' final victory also poses the question of the significance of the victory of fractious states over a spatially and socially ordered society. In subsequent ethnographic passages, this view of the Persian world will again come up against a number of other societies who order their affairs very differently.

Babylonian Customs: "Gendered" Narrative (1.196–199)[23]

The second major passage about ethnographic matters is again associated with a victory by Cyrus. Indeed, if we count the brief description of the change in Lydian customs in 1.155–156 when, at Croesus' suggestion, Cyrus ordered them to abandon their weapons of war and to dress in a luxurious manner which permanently changed their bellicose nature, then each of his conquests of the main powers of the region, Media, Lydia, and Babylon, is associated with an account of

---

[21] Cf. Histiaeus (6.29–30), Metiochus son of Miltiades (6.41), and the Eretrians (6.119).
[22] On the importance of disunity in the depiction of the Greeks and their victory, cf. Immerwahr 1966:189–237.
[23] On Herodotus and Babylon, cf. Kuhrt 2002.

customs. Again, in a manner similar to but also slightly different from the change in the Persians in the last section, this change in the Lydians is instant, and not strictly "realistic."

What is striking about this passage about the Babylonians is how it and its surrounding narrative is "gendered": there is a dominance of the feminine both in the narrative and in the discussion of Babylonian customs. This may be contrasted with a masculine bias in the account of the Persians' own customs: women appear there only in the statement that "each Persian has many wives, but many more concubines" (*pallakai*; 1.135). This gendering then has the further function of preparing for Cyrus' subsequent death at the hand of the queen of the Massagetae, Tomyris.

The section on the capture of Babylon begins with a description of the spectacular physical aspects of the city, the techniques used in its building, and an account of two of its temples (1.178–183). Herodotus attributes the design and ornamentation of the city to the Babylonian kings, but he sets aside an account of this for his (either lost or never composed) "Assyrian narrative," and instead concentrates on two queens. He mentions but very briefly the famous Semiramis, who was in fact Sammuramat, wife of Shamshi-Adad V (who ruled Assyria in 823–811) and mother of Adad-nirâri III, for whom she seems to have been regent for about five years.[24] He tells at length however of one Nitocris, who has been variously identified, as Adda-guppi, the mother of Nabonidus (Nabû-na'id), probably Herodotus' Labynetus (ruled 555–539);[25] Zakûtu, also called Naquîa, wife of king Sennacherib (704–681) and mother of Asarhaddon (680–669), who rebuilt Babylon in a manner that somehow involved his mother; or simply as a doublet of the Egyptian Nitocris.[26] Who exactly she was is not important here: what matters is the focus on a female ruler. Herodotus describes at some length Nitocris' remarkable works of defensive engineering, conducted in expectation of a Median attack, and of her aquatic engineering and bridge-building, which made Babylon both safer and more convenient to live in. He ends with a trick which she prepared for any king of Babylon given to greed: she placed her tomb over the busiest gate, with an inscription inviting truly needy kings to open it and to take as much money as they required, with a warning against unjustified attempts to get the money. In a further victory of the female over a Persian king, Darius later fell into this trap: "this is the sort of woman they say she was" (1.185–188).[27]

This suppression of any account of the many great Assyrian kings and the raising to prominence of two queens is striking, but may be related to the ethno-

---

[24] Cf. Roux 2001.
[25] Cf. Röllig 1969.
[26] Cf. Kuhrt 1982:i, 539–554.
[27] Cf. Dillery 1992.

graphic passage which follows the brief account of Cyrus' capture of the city and the recital of the wealth of the country (1,188–195). If Persian customs largely elided women, those here recounted are mainly concerned with them (1.196–199). The customs are arranged in a simple pattern: their "wisest customs" and their "most shameful" surround short sections on other customs.[28] The most beautiful women were auctioned, and then the money raised was used to pay the men who were prepared to take the less beautiful: each woman was given to the man prepared to take the lowest sum. The most "shameful" was that all Babylonian women had once in their lives to sit in the sanctuary of Mylitta (Aphrodite) and go with any man who threw them money, however little; again the fates of the beautiful and the less favored are contrasted, the former getting home much before the latter. These two social rituals provide a curious contrast between careful arrangements for the proper marriage of women in society and a complementary disregard for sexual propriety.

The prominence of Semiramis and Nitocris as the sole named engineers of the city is thus mirrored by the emphasis on the treatment of unmarried and married women in Babylon in the ethnographic section. These powerful women, or at least Semiramis, who may have come to unite the characteristics of both in the literary tradition, fixed themselves in the Greek consciousness, probably through Iranian sources. The Medes and Persians start to feature in Assyrian sources around the end of the ninth century, precisely the time when Semiramis was regent, so that it has been argued that they may have remembered that their Assyrian masters were led in some way by a woman:[29] Herodotus' remarks on Nitocris' defensive works being carried out in expectation of a Median attack could be a reflection of this time (1.185.7). Whatever the truth here, in Greek writers after Herodotus, such as Ctesias, the legend of Semiramis was told at length and in some detail. It is as if the history of Babylon had, as a result of the activities of "Semiramis" and "Nitocris," become as it were feminized, the activities of the great male kings, so fulsomely detailed in the many royal inscriptions, being pushed into the background.

Herodotus' account of Babylonian rituals thus speaks very briefly about their medical practices, treatment of corpses, and their purification after sex, but devotes space to social rituals involving women. He says relatively little about religious ritual, but it is worth noting the only rite he discusses in detail involves the incubation in the temple of Baal of a single local woman, chosen for the purpose by the god, who visits the temple himself. Herodotus then provides parallels for this custom from Thebes in Egypt and Patara in Lycia (1.181.5–82).

---

[28] Cf. McNeal 1988.
[29] Roux 2001:157–160.

There is no evidence from Babylonian sources for customs concerning women such as Herodotus describes,[30] which suggests that the feminization of this part of the narrative is not simply the result of recording what he had heard: folktale is brought to bear to create a gendered narrative, pitting masculine Persians against "feminized" Babylonians. Cyrus effectively captures Babylon by matching the water-engineering of Nitocris and defeating her siege-defenses: "when he came to the lake, he did to the river and the lake almost exactly what the Babylonian queen had done" (1.191.3).[31] By diverting the river as she had, he enabled the troops to enter the city before the defenders had been able to make use of the postern-gates designed by her.

This superiority to women comes to an end however in the very next episode, his attack on the Massagetae, in which he is killed by the forces of Queen Tomyris, who mutilates his body. The episode is framed by ethnographic passages: at the start, Herodotus tells of the habit of the Massagetae of inhaling the smoke from a "fruit," probably cannabis, put on a bonfire until they are intoxicated (1.202) and, before concluding this part of his narrative, he briefly describes their sexual, funerary, dietetic, and religious customs (1.216). The function of these ethnographic passages would seem to be to mark out the importance of the Massagetae, the victors over Cyrus the Great: in this book only they, the Persians and the Babylonians (and to some extent the Lydians) have their customs described. As Cyrus conquers each people, the feminine element in the narrative grows: the transformation of the Lydians into effeminates is briefly noted; the Babylonian narrative is significantly gendered; and a queen brings about his defeat and death.[32] The more he conquers, the more the feminine predominates. The feminine at the margins thus, like Greek social disunity, confronts and defeats its Persian opposite.

Indian and Arabian Customs (3.98–117)

The third substantial ethnographic passage is the description of Indian and Arabian customs. Again, the importance of peoples is indicated by the presence of an account of their customs and indicated in the text: "the Indian race is by far the most populous of all the people we know, and they paid the most tribute, 360

---

[30] Kuhrt 2002:494.

[31] The concentration here on Cyrus as water-engineer contrasts with the balder account given in the Nabonidus Chronicle: "Cyrus did battle at Opis on the [*bank of*] the Tigris against the army of Akkad, the people of Akkad retreated. . . . On the sixteenth day Ugbaru, governor of the Guti, and the army of Cyrus entered Babylon without a battle. . . . On the third day of the month Marchesvan Cyrus entered Babylon. . . . There was peace in the city while Cyrus spoke (his) greeting to all of Babylon" (iii.12–20; cf. Grayson 1975:109–110; Pritchard 1969:306).

[32] Though Herodotus does not say so himself, later Greek tradition made the Medes a much more luxurious people than the Persians: cf. For example Xenophon *Cyropaedia* 1.3.1–12.

talents of gold-dust" (3.94.2); it was the most easterly land, rich in gold and unusual animals and plants. Similarly, "the Arabians were never reduced to slavery by the Persians, but were their *xenoi*" (3.88.1); they were free from tribute, but made a substantial gift of frankincense. Theirs was the most southerly land and filled like India with the most remarkable natural features.

This ethnographic account is, like the earlier ones, connected with an accession to power, not by conquest this time but still after a period of conflict. The context is the accession of Darius (3.83–88), which is immediately followed by an account of his organization of the administrative and fiscal aspects of the empire (3.89–97). The link between the historical situation and the ethnographic sections is that the latter are principally concerned with how the peoples, by means of a communally organized hunt, assemble the tribute whose collection Darius has organized. In the section on the Indians, though Herodotus interweaves description of the customs and habits of various tribes, the main part of the section is the account of the method used to collect the gold-dust. It is stolen from the "ants" (probably a kind of marmoset) which guard it, and ferried back by camels that can outrun the ants (3.102–105). Similarly, the Arabian section describes the remarkable ways in which they collect frankincense, cassia, cinnamon, and *ledanon*, a kind of fragrant resin. The collection of these spices involves engagement with the remarkable fauna of the area: frankincense is got away from winged snakes by burning storax resin, cassia is taken in defiance of savage bats, cinnamon is caused to fall from the nests of large birds, and the resin comes from the beards of goats. These activities then allow Herodotus to speculate on the nature of fauna at the ends of the world, including reference to the theft of gold from griffins by the one-eyed Arimaspians (3.116.1), which provides a link back to the start of this section. These chapters thus further characterize the Persian empire as orderly, wealthy, and in possession of all that the world can offer, down to the most remarkable things at the world's end. Men go to extraordinary efforts to fill the coffers of the King, as instanced by these Indian and Arabian customs.

This section on Darius' organization of the Persian empire closes with a custom which emblematizes the Persian control of these regions. The Persian King has taken control of rivers that used to irrigate the lands of peoples over by the Araxes river, south of the Aral Sea; he now keeps the water dammed up in a mountain-enclosed plateau. When the tribes need water they do the following:

> Since they are given no water they and their wives come to Persia and stand howling and shouting before the King's doors. The King gives orders to open the sluices that face the land of those who make their pleas most forcibly. When their land is saturated by the water, these

sluices are shut and he orders others opened for the other people who make a forcible plea. As I have heard, he opens the sluices having forced them to pay a great deal of money over and above their tribute. (3.117.5–6)

This is a simple emblem of the power of the King at the center of the Persian empire: all resources flow from that center, and the King determines to whom they shall flow, accordingly as people are able to show they deserve to have them.

Once again therefore the aspects of the ethnography on which Herodotus places most emphasis are those which relate most closely to the subject matter of the surrounding narrative, in this case the financial and administrative control exercised over their empire by the Persians. Like the "transformation" of the Persians on Cyrus' accession to the throne, these customs are associated with the very moment of Darius' own ascension. That Herodotus should in this context discuss the customs, flora, and fauna of the lands at the eastern and southern (and to some extent northern) edges of the world is entirely appropriate for the reign of a man who ruled an empire greater than Alexander's. At these margins, Persian rule is once more circumscribed, by the fact that it is not absolute, but satisfied by tribute and a measure of submission.

Scythian Customs (4.59–80)[33]

The grandeur of Darius' empire will soon find its limits however, when he decides, against advice, to attack the Scythians in the north, around the Black Sea. Echoes of Cyrus are to be heard. Shortly before this expedition, Darius also captures Babylon, pulling down its defenses "which Cyrus had not done when he earlier captured the city" (3.159.1). There is even a feminine element: the Babylonians had strangled their women so there would be enough food and Darius therefore imports large numbers to restore the population (3.159.2). Again, Herodotus describes how the Scythians like to crawl into felt tents, throw cannabis seeds on the fire, and howl with delight as they inhale the fumes (4.75),[34] which recalls the Massagetae, destroyers of Cyrus the Great. The Scythians do not destroy Darius, but nonetheless succeed in frustrating his desire to conquer them.

The dominant aspects of the early part of the account of Scythian habits are war and military prowess, which reflect upon the unwisdom of Darius' campaign.

---

[33] On Herodotus and Scythia, cf. Hartog 1988, with the criticisms of Pritchett 1993:191–226; Sulimirski and Taylor 1991; West 2002.

[34] Herodotus' account is substantiated by the discovery of tent poles, felt rugs, bronze cauldrons, and charred hemp seeds (Rolle 1989:93–95; Wolf and Andrashko 1991).

After describing how they sacrifice generally to other gods, Herodotus devotes space to a detailed account of the sacrifice to Ares. He is represented by an *akinakês* (a short sword), and animals and prisoners of war are sacrificed to him, the latter with their right arm severed (4.62). There follow the practices of scalping enemies and using their skulls as drinking-cups, especially at a yearly visit of the provincial governor (*nomarkhos*) when all those who have killed in battle drink together (4.64–66). Oath-swearing involves cutting oneself with an *akinakês* and drinking blood mixed with wine, and the rituals accompanying the burial of a king involve surrounding his tomb with fifty strangled horses and riders as a grim entourage (4.69–72). These customs well reflect therefore the fact that "by 500 B.C. [the Scythians] constituted one of the most powerful military forces in the known world."[35]

The military resistance of the Scythians to Darius' expedition is further mirrored in their resistance to the adoption of foreign customs (4.76–80). This is illustrated by the fates of two Scythians whose passion for foreign customs led to their deaths. First, there is the much traveled Anacharsis who, returning to Scythia, came across the rites of the Great Mother in Cyzicus. Having promised to institute her cult in Scythia if he got home safely, he duly carried out her rights secretly, but was observed and delated to the king, who came and shot him dead.[36] The Scythians now claim not to know his name, "because he traveled to Greece and adopted foreign practices" (4.76.5). A similar fate overtook king Scyles. Educated in Greek as a child, he always hankered after Greek ways, so much so that whenever a campaign brought him to the city of the Borysthenites, he would go inside and "take off his Scythian clothes and dress himself as a Greek. . . . He followed the Greek way of life and sacrificed according to Greek customs" (4.78.4). His end came when he insisted on celebrating the bacchic mysteries, despite the fact that a thunderbolt destroyed his house: he was informed upon, deposed and after a brief flight beheaded. "The Scythians are very keen on their own customs, and that is how they punish those who adopt foreign ones" (4.80.5). The examples involve Greek practices but the hostility to foreign customs generally is clear.

This refusal to adopt foreign customs stands in contrast to the Persians' welcome to all manner of them (1.135), and there is in Herodotus a polar opposition between the Persians at the heart of their empire and their opponents at the ends of that empire. We have seen such an opposition in that between male and female in the case of Cyrus' defeat at another margin, but it is here reinforced by a

---

[35] Sulimirski and Taylor 1991:547.
[36] An ostracon, the "Priest's Letter," dated to perhaps 550–530 and discovered at Olbia, tells of how "the altars are damaged again [...] of the Mother of the gods and of Borysthe(nes) and Heracl[es]": cf. Rusjaeva and Vinogradov 1991:201–202. This may reflect turbulent events connected with the two stories discussed here.

number of important passages on the nature of Scythian society and its rituals. The first is an ethnographic passage, unusually given by a character in the work rather than by Herodotus himself. When Darius expresses exasperation and contempt at king Idanthyrsus' constant refusal to stand and fight, the king replies as follows. He does not run from fear:

> What I am doing now is not far removed from my usual way of life during peacetime. . . . If we had towns we might worry about the possibility of them being captured, and if we had farmland we might worry about it being laid waste, and then we might engage you in battle quite quickly; but we don't have either. If you feel you have to get to fighting soon, there are our ancestral burial grounds. Go on, find them and try to ruin them, and then you'll see whether or not we will fight. (4.127.1–2; trans. Waterfield)

This description of the nomadic life and customs of the Scythians contrasts with the life of the Persians centered on their great cities,[37] a contrast which is made all the stronger by Idanthyrsus' point about the burial grounds. These are the only "center" which the Scythians have. The position of these tombs is significant.[38] The bodies of the kings are taken round all the tribes until they are come to the territory of the Gerrhoi, "the most remote of the tribes which they rule" (4.71.3): after the Gerrhoi, "no-one knows which lands the Borysthenes river runs through" (4.53.4). In other words, the "center" of the Scythian realm, where their most important rites take place is, in a curious reversal, at the very edge of their world.

The rites that are carried out here are also significant, in that they reinforce the sense of this burial area as a reversal of the Scythians' normal nomadic existence. Here alone, they create permanent "homes":

> They put the corpse on a pallet in the grave, and stick spears into the ground on either side of the corpse, over which they put wooden planks and then cover them with matting. In the space left in the grave, they strangle and bury one of his concubines, and his wine-pourer, his cook, his groom, his steward, and his messenger, along with horses, a selection of all his other effects, and gold cups. . . . They then pile up a great mound of earth over it all. (4.71.4–5)

---

[37] There were in fact significantly-sized fortified production centers in Scythia, and indeed their agriculture made very wealthy men of Scythian nobles through trade in corn with Greece. These features are more prevalent however in the "forest steppe," a rather more agreeable part of Scythia to the north of the steppe that Darius appears to be in: cf. Rolle 1989:110, 117–122; Kryzhickij 1991; Sulimirski and Taylor 1991:551, 580–589.

[38] Cf. imprimis, Hartog 1988:133–172.

In life, the king and his household wandered the steppe, but in death the household is recreated in static form.[39] But it is not only the dwellings that come to a stop here. After a year, fifty of the king's attendants and fifty horses are strangled, the horses are set up on half-wheels, their feet that once ran on the earth now dangling above it, and, as we have seen, a pole is pushed through them and a "horseman" is fixed to each horse (4.72). The king is thus surrounded by immobile rather than nomadic horseman. This center is the opposite not only of the world of the Persians, but also of the living Scythians.

Comparison with the archaeological evidence from the Scythian *kurgans* (burial mounds) in eastern Europe and the Ukraine is instructive for what Herodotus is doing here.[40] These *kurgans* are much grander affairs than Herodotus describes, in that massive wooden structures form the very heart of them, not just the roof, but he is right about the size of the mounds. His remarks about the burial of retainers are also authenticated by the archaeology. The *kurgan* at Arzhan in the Uyuk valley yielded the bodies of 17 human retainers, mostly elderly, as well as about 150 horses.[41] This corresponds to what Herodotus says about the rites immediately after burial.

However, archaeology has turned up nothing quite like the rites described in Herodotus as performed a year after the king's death. It is true that there is something at least as remarkable in *kurgan* 1 at Aul Ul' in the northern Caucasus, of about 500 BCE. On at least two levels in the mound were discovered the bodies of 360 horses (and there may have been many more), some of which were neatly arranged on the ground around the tomb. They were either laid out in rows on either side of wooden fences or placed in circles round vertical posts; the animals had been tethered before being slaughtered.[42]

The discrepancies between Herodotus and the archaeological evidence are instructive, because they suggest that Herodotus may not have been simply recounting Scythian burial customs as he had heard them, but tailoring them to structure his narrative. That he is transmitting actual knowledge of Scythian burial customs is made likely by the similarities we have noted between his account and the archaeology.[43] There has been much criticism of Hartog for perfunctory treat-

---

[39] The burial of ordinary Scythians reflects some of the features of the burial of the Kings. The body is again taken on a long journey round his friends for forty days before it is buried. The Scythians then purify themselves by creating a tent with poles and burning cannabis inside it (4.73).

[40] Herodotus is not very discriminating in his use of "Scythian," which can refer to a range of different tribes (cf. West 2002:439–441), so care must be taken in generalizing features of one area to another. The Ukrainian evidence of the turf in the tombs may be irrelevant to these particular Scythians, but the general point still stands.

[41] Rolle 1989:38–44.

[42] Rolle 1989:44–46; Sulimirski and Taylor 1991:568–573.

[43] The Ulskii *kurgan* is uniquely grandiose, so that its fame may well have spread and been generalized as typical; cf. Sulimirski and Taylor 1991:571.

ment of the archaeological evidence in favor of his structuralist analysis, but though the archaeology provides abundant evidence that Herodotus has not simply made his accounts up, there are still differences between it and his account. There are further points which might support this contention that Herodotus' account is not without a certain amount of shaping to fit the narrative. First, the archaeological evidence has qualified the traditional idea of the Scythians as warriors who fought simply by shooting arrows and running away, or by the evasive tactics described by Idanthyrsus. The graves have yielded actual and pictorial evidence that from the sixth century on there were heavily armed horsemen in Scythian armies.[44] They wore heavy scale armor on head, body, and legs, heavy belts to protect their loins, iron-plated shields, swords, spears, metal maces, and whips, all clearly intended for the kind of close combat depicted on vessels. Again, Herodotus' picture of the grave-mounds is of a static world, but the archaeology of the Scythian tombs suggests that the point of the Scythian burial rituals was to ensure that the king was able symbolically to ride the steppe and move his household in death as he had in life. This is suggested by the provision of horses, chariots, and drivers in the tomb, as well as of household goods and servants, and even more so by the fact that all the mounds in the Ukraine at least were filled, not with earth dug from around the area of the tomb, but with immense quantities of turf (now black soil) brought from some distance away, perhaps from a favorite area of the king's.[45] Herodotus' static nomads on horses whose feet do not touch the ground seem therefore constructed to emphasize his contrast between this place that he makes "central" to Scythia and the normal existence in the body of the country. He has interpreted the evidence in a way that suits better his analysis of history than the actuality of Scythian customs. The ethnography is again not purely descriptive therefore, but has a signifying function in the narrative.

In conclusion, where the Persian empire was one with a clear geographical orientation, Herodotus' Scythia is the opposite, a trackless waste without cities or agriculture, its people roaming its spaces, its only fixed point at its very edge. Darius' attempt to conquer this martial empire with a hole in the middle is doomed to failure. Persian spatial organization here comes up against its opposite, an undifferentiated world, in parts at least devoid of settlement and agriculture. Persia is again frustrated at the margins: it may have been a mistake to bother with such a land militarily, but ethnographically we are again confronted with a contrast which need not be read in a moral fashion but more neutrally.

[44] Rolle 1989:64–91, especially 66–69; Chernenko, in Rolle et al. 1991:131–135.
[45] Rolle 1989:32–34.

Other Customs

From this point in Herodotus' work, though the ethnographic passages are still thematically related to their surrounding narrative, they become rather less common and their relationship to the narrative less dynamic. Tribal customs are recounted when the tribes in question come to feature in the narrative: Darius conquers the Getae and Herodotus explains some of their customs. When the Scythian allies gather, their customs are duly listed (4.103–109). The passage on Thracian customs (5.3–10) comes naturally in the context of Megabazus' campaign in Thrace, and makes one particular point about the Thracians that, though they "use practically the same customs in all areas" (5.3.2), they are so divided politically that, when they could be the strongest peoples in the world, they are in fact hopelessly weak.

Aryandes' and Pheretime's expedition against Libya allows Herodotus to give a long list of the customs of more than twenty different named tribes and numerous others (4.168–197). Here the ethnographic descriptions largely take the place of historical narrative.[46] As we move ever further into Libya, each tribe is briefly characterized by items of dress, sexual customs, diet, religious customs, and so on. Yet again, we are taken to the end of the world, the last peoples mentioned being those who lived by the Pillars of Heracles (4.196), and once again Herodotus considers them from the point of view of their relationship with Persia: he frames his account with the remarks that "few of them are subjects of the king, and most care for him not at all" (4.168.2) and "these are the Libyans we can name, and of them the majority do not now nor have ever cared at all about the Persian King" (4.197.1). The limits of Persian influence are again emphasized. The final example is the only one of an ethnographic account of Greek customs, the description of the prerogatives of the Spartan kings in war and peace and on their death (6.56–60). This comes in the midst of the account of the feud between kings Demaratus and Cleomenes, which was a continuation of an original quarrel between the two houses and led to the latter's being deposed.

In the later books, comparison by ethnography is replaced by other devices. We have already seen something of this from Book 6, in its contrast of Greek and Persian, and as those two races come closer to their final conflict, there is a constant *sunkrisis* as their doings are juxtaposed in the narrative. Comparison is also conducted in a more direct manner, especially in the discussions between Demaratus and Xerxes (7.101–105, 234–237). There fear and loyalty to a monarch

[46] An exception is the centrally placed story of Jason (4.178–179).

are contrasted with devotion to law (*nomos*). The picture of the Persians has lost some of the gilt given it in the first passage we discussed, and when the matter is put to the test, it is *nomos* which wins out—in battle at least.

In the earlier books therefore, ethnographic accounts are not simply the recording of such information as Herodotus could glean from his travels and sources. The accounts of the Scythians' allies and of the Libyan tribes do look like that, but the earlier accounts are much more. They have a close thematic relationship to their narrative, but there is more to that relationship than a purely formalist one. Most importantly, they are part of the "poetics" of the narrative, which they not only adorn but also comment on. The ordered society of Persia at the heart of the world is set against a variety of marginal peoples whose characteristics are opposed to the Persian ones and who impose limit or defeat on Persian power. One of these margins is the Greeks, whose fissiparous nature inflicts a defeat as surprising as Tomyris' on the ordered world of the Persians. Herodotus' history stops at this point, but the later history of fifth-century Greece may prompted a wistfulness for the idealized picture of the Persians which Cyrus' first victory evoked.

Sixteen

Dance as Ritual, Dance as Performance

Ioli Kalavrezou

The role and place of dance in society has in recent years become a topic of interest and exploration especially in studies of cultural history. A growing body of literature in ritual studies, gender studies, and studies in theater and performance, especially in the ancient world, has made available the basis for further expansion into other fields and cultures.[1] Dance in Byzantium, however, has not yet received its proper attention.[2]

Dance is a universal form of expression recognizable by all when seen. What differs in each culture is the role and place of dance within that society and the manner of the actual performance. It is a social activity either through collective participation in the dance itself or through the visual experience of dancing by others. Because of the sequence of actions and the prescribed procedural rules dance can be characterized as ritual.[3] In western medieval societies it is especially attributed to women as a form of expression in contrast to the male art of verbal communication. It is a bodily articulation, a means of interaction through the body instead of through the word. As ritual and a form of communication dance uses a constructed system of culturally understood symbols to express meanings. Dance also contains what can be defined as temporal elements that in contrast to form cannot be depicted. These are the music, the melody, and the rhythm. So whatever image we have of a dance it is only but a moment captured and frozen in time of an action that is continuous and a form-in-the-making. It is only because of our experience with and memory of dance, either as participants or viewers, that we have the sense of an understanding of the performance in an image. Before any kind of analysis of dance as performance and as ritual can be undertaken for the Byzantine period, we have to establish for what occasions the dances were performed, what kind of

---

[1] E.g. Cowan 1990; Roueché 1993; Scodel 1993; Lonsdale 1993. For further general bibliography on dance and related themes such as gesture, body politics, gender and ritual, or social significance see Webb 1997.

[2] Two recent articles from different perspectives are Webb 1997 and Steppan 1997.

[3] Tambiah 1985a:118.

dancing was appropriate for these, and who danced and for whom. All these questions have barely been touched upon, and to answer them evidence from the textual as well as visual sources needs to be gathered and evaluated. The difficulty, however, with the gathering of any information on dancing in Byzantium lies in the fact that, as with other obvious and self-evident things in life, they do not get recorded or mentioned in the sources. Thus, the evidence is rather meager, with only few traces in the visual and limited comments in the textual record. Interestingly, two very good articles that addressed dance in Byzantium appeared in 1997: one by R. Webb, on "Salome's Sisters: The Rhetoric and Realities of Dance in Late Antiquity and Byzantium"; the other by Thomas Steppan, on the "Tanzdarstellungen der mittel- und spätbyzantinischen Kunst." The first is approaching the subject from the literary evidence and is focusing on the role and place of women; the second surveys the visual material in order to establish what is there.

This chapter focuses on the visual evidence, the pictorial documentation of dance, mainly from the middle Byzantine period, where the textual sources are especially brief, without trying at this point to either reconstruct the dances them-

fig. 1 Obelisk base, Constantinople: dancers and musicians at the Hippodrome, lat
fourth century. (Photo: author.)

selves or the experience of dancing. These rare depictions of dancing provide the physical evidence for the performed dances and offer a source for further analysis on the role that dance played in Byzantium.

Cultural conventions do change over time and caution needs to be applied not to draw conclusions too quickly, especially with a culture that has left so little information over so many centuries. As mentioned earlier, the Byzantine representations of dance as well as the textual references where dancing is mentioned are relatively few. To my mind, it is not a reflection on the limited occasions for dance in Byzantium. It is rather the result of the scanty surviving evidence, especially from the secular world, that has created this distorted impression. As much as we like to see the Byzantines as a society of devotion and piety, we should not forget that this society maintained customs and traditions that had their roots in the ancient Greek and Roman past.[4] Byzantium's inheritance is the classical Greek and Roman world and it existed not only in their literary and artistic traditions but also in their way of life and their relationship to, and knowledge of, nature and the world around them. Thus, when studying the Byzantine world and its expressions we are dealing with this Greco-Roman heritage within a Christianized society. Their religiosity did not prevent the Byzantines from adding to their life occasions of colorful pageantry and festive gaiety, although, as we know, the Church fathers, especially the voice of John Chrysostom, tried hard to condemn dancing.[5] However, Byzantium is known for its rituals and ceremonials. It is inconceivable that this culture, which surrounded itself with great festivities and celebrations and with monuments and objects of great beauty, did not add the same delight in pleasure to the activities in its everyday or ritual life. And as in most societies, so also in Byzantium, dances were performed and were associated with happy occasions and celebration.

It is most surprising to realize that of the most public performances of dance, either by professional dancers or by individuals that might join in the streets, we have the least images. These were civic occasions, such as the birthday of the emperor, the commemoration of the foundation of Constantinople on May 11th, the games and races at the Hippodrome, and imperial triumphs.[6]

---

[4] Weitzmann 1981; Mullet and Scott 1981.

[5] John Chrysostom is well known for his condemnations rather than praise on any type of dancing, private or public. His basic position was that the sight of a performer, mostly female, had a devastating effect on the audience, especially the male and his soul. He believed that the remembrance of a woman's sight, her gestures, the movements of her body, her glances, the dance itself, and even the words of the accompanying songs, contaminated a man's soul, which then could infect his household; see Webb's discussion (Webb 1997). But Chrysostom's is only one voice from the fourth century, and although famous and articulate, and with some reverberations in the later centuries, it did not succeed in preventing dance from being performed and enjoyed in Byzantium.

[6] Vogt 1967:II, ch. 79 (70).

The importance of this kind of dance in the public ceremonial life of Constantinople can be seen on a relief panel of the obelisk base in the Hippodrome of the late fourth century. It is one of the rare representations of such an event (fig. 1).[7] One of its sides depicts the celebration of victory. From his *Kathisma* the emperor, flanked by his family, senators, and other high officials, is ready to present to the victorious charioteer a wreath, which he is holding in his right hand. Below, at the lowest segment of the relief and actually the part that is closest to the viewer but the smallest in size—a visual marker of the lower status of this group in the societal hierarchy—female dancers are performing before the emperor and a large crowd, accompanied by two organs and flutes. The dancers vary in their poses: three can be seen on the left, two of which move rhythmically together, their waists slightly bent, holding castanets or rattles, and with one arm raised over their heads. On the right three figures holding hands as in a chorus line are accompanied by a fourth, who, with one arm raised over her head and possibly a rattle on the other, is leading the dance. The dance is performed at the high point of the celebrations, the presentation of the victory wreaths. A description of such a moment is found in the *Book of Ceremonies* of the tenth century for the day of the Anniversary of Constantinople at the Hippodrome. This composition is typical of the Byzantine mentality, which was able to create images that have simultaneously a symbolic nature as well as a literal, precise historical presence. The permanence of a monument like the obelisk required an image that would have had a lasting meaning in the public life and spaces of the Byzantine city. What is represented here is the imperial office, the senatorial class, the attending crowds, and a most precise representation of the dance performed on such occasions. What is missing is the actual victorious charioteer who in a monument of perpetual victory becomes unnecessary.

The other visual record of a similar civic celebration of victory is represented one thousand years later, in the early fifteenth century, on a tiny ivory box now at Dumbarton Oaks (fig. 2). It depicts the celebration of an imperial victory, most likely the taking of Thessaloniki by John VII Palaeologus.[8] Here, too, the emperor and his family are depicted as they are acclaimed victorious. A group of musicians with a variety of instruments stand together on one side while to their right two female dancers with veils in their hands dance independently. One holds her hands at waist level, the veil hugging her hips and legs. The other only visible from the waist up swings the veil above and behind her head. These images represent what could be identified as public performances of dancing at more or less an identifi-

---

[7] An additional image of dancing performed at the Hippodrome with further celebrants like singers, musicians, and a variety of acrobats can be seen in the frescoes decorating the staircase walls of the church of Hagia Sofia in Kiev from the first half of the twelfth century; Lazarev 1966:56–67, 236–24.

fig. 2 Ivory pyxis: dancers at an imperial victory, early fifteenth century. Dumbarton Oaks, Byzantine Collection, Washington, DC. (Photo: Dumbarton Oaks.)

able historical moment in time. Both are associated with victories and span the whole period of Byzantine history.

What are the other types of images depicting dance in Byzantium? Everyday household objects provide one rich source for dance imagery. That depictions of dance are commonly found as a decorative motif on, for example, bone carvings and textiles attests to the popularity and pleasure found in dance. Most of this material comes primarily from Egypt and dates from the fourth to the seventh century. The textiles are the richest source of imagery. They show a great variety of dancers, single, in pairs, or rows of chorus lines. They are the types known from antiquity, mainly figures from the Dionysiac revelers groups dancing freely, often holding noise makers, castanets, or wreaths, single or in pairs. They were part of the decoration of tunics, either as part of the frontal panel or at the hem, as well as on textiles for household furnishings. [9] Decorative borders of tunics allow for

[8] Oikonomides 1977.
[9] Maguire 1999, where many textile examples; Kalavrezou 2003:no.87, decorative ivory plaque with a dance scene.

283

fig. 3 Silver dish: Silenus and dancing Maenad, ca. 610-629. State Hermitage
Museum, St. Petersburg. (Photo: The State Hermitage Museum.)

a stage-like presentation of dancers. The dancers can also be shown as *putti*, a
popular variation on many of the decorative secular themes.

The surviving luxury objects of these early centuries give the best visual record
of the way dance was represented, still in its most classical form in this period. A
number of silver dishes with Dionysiac revelers from the Mildenhall treasure in the
British museum and a silver plate in the Hermitage with a Silenus and a Maenad (fig.
3) are representative of the dances of Dionysus and his retinue.[10] Although these two
dishes are close to three centuries apart—the first from the fourth century and the
other from 610 to 629—the dancers still dance with the gracefully free and ecstatic

---

[10] Weitzmann 1979:no. 130, p.151; Bank 1977:no. 84, p. 285.

fig. 4 Veroli Casket: detail of dancers on lid, tenth century. Victoria and Albert Museum, London. (Photo: after J. Beckwith, *The Veroli Casket*, London, 1962.)

poses and gestures of the Dionysiac revelers. Thus in its early period, although now a Christian empire, Byzantium still maintained the Greco-Roman world in its customs and traditions, and especially in its repertory of secular themes and forms. Whatever change took place over the one thousand years of its history was slow and took centuries to manifest itself, at least to us. The late antique themes found on luxury objects had a long life and we find its last vestiges well into the mid-Byzantine period. It can still be recognized in the well-known *putti* of the ivory and bone boxes of the tenth–eleventh century, who, among other mythological subjects, dance in the Dionysiac tradition. These are some of the last representations of this theme, now only shown in the guise of childish performers who, as in the earlier textile, through their small size, playfulness, and nudity transform these themes into a parody and remain purely decorative. The most famous examples can be seen on the lid of the Veroli casket (fig. 4).[11] Kicking one's leg back and high was part of the fun.

From the centuries that followed, especially from the second half of the seventh century to the second half of the ninth, there is very little visual evidence in general, and even after the ninth century the secular or profane world is much less represented. Most of the visual record of Byzantine culture comes from a religious context. Thus, when searching for evidence about dancing in Byzantium for the middle period we will also have to turn to the illustrations of religious subject matter, mainly manuscripts. The most impressive dancer of the ninth century is

[11] Beckwith 1962; *The Glory of Byzantium* 1997: no. 153, pp. 230–231.

fig. 5 Chludov Psalter: detail of Miriam dancing after the crossing of the Red Sea,
ninth century. Historical Museum, Moscow, Ms. gr.129, fol. 148v. (Photo:
The State Historical Museum.)

Miriam in the scenes of the Crossing of the Red Sea. Two manuscripts from the second half of the ninth century depict her in full pirouette with castanets in her hands raised above her head. In the Chludov psalter she is dressed in red and her long, black, partly curly hair is loose over her shoulders (fig. 5). In the Homilies of Gregory Nazianzus in Paris, a manuscript for imperial use, Miriam, dressed in white and with a long veil flowing over her head, leads the people of Israel.[12] This kind of dancing is reminiscent of the classical forms, but is most closely related to the public dancing as performed in the Hippodrome and depicted in the relief on the Obelisk base (fig. 1).

Beginning with the eleventh century, specifically in representations of secular subject matter, we can observe a clear change or shift in the visual vocabulary. This new visual language comes from the life of the court: among the figures that are now shown riding, hunting, fighting, and music making, we find also figures that are dancing. The scenes on such objects also include heroes that we can identify, such as Heracles and Alexander the Great. A representative example is a silver gilt bowl now in the Hermitage, probably from the twelfth century (fig. 6). Among twelve different figures that decorate the exterior of this deep bowl, under arches supported by columns with the Hercules knot, there is a female dancer. She has her arms raised, showing her long sleeves, and is shown jumping with one leg kicking toward the back. This is a pose that is typical of dancing in general but will become a standard feature characterizing the excitement and rhythm of the dance. There are a number of other silver containers that depict court entertainment which also include figures dancing, as, for example, on a lid from a vessel in the Hermitage, which has a male dancer with long sleeves accompanied by musicians and tumblers (fig. 7).[13] Dancing begins to be shown as part of the known pleasures of court activities and entertainment. Music making, dancing male figures, acrobats, entertainment in general is represented not in the form of the *putti* but with what appear to be contemporary figures, since their dress is clearly medieval. By the eleventh century, the straight mythological and Dionysiac vocabulary that was the tradition on objects of luxury is slowly disappearing and is replaced by this kind of new, and what I would label contemporary, courtly language.

This joyful world of luxury and riches not only finds expression in the representation of people but it incorporates also nature. Together with scenes from entertainment we see a lot of animals and plants covering the exterior of silver vessels. Clearly, there is a shift in the choice of subject matter with the introduction of new

[12] Brubaker 1999:57. The same type of figure can also be seen in the Paris Psalter manuscript (Bib. nat. gr. 139) from the tenth century, which in many of its images follows iconographic types from the Paris Gregory manuscript.

[13] Bank 1977:nos. 218–219, 220–224, p. 313.

characters that seem to derive from Byzantine epic and romance literature, as for example the famous story of Digenis Akritis. This world is well described in these texts, and here a few lines describing the dancing maidens in the festivities of the wedding feast from Digenis Akritis are appropriate:

fig. 6 Silver gilt bowl: dancer, twelfth century. State Hermitage Museum, St. Petersburg. (Photo: The State Hermitage Museum.)

fig. 7 Silver lid from a vessel: male dancer accompanied by musicians, twelfth century. State Hermitage Museum, St. Petersburg. (Photo: The State Hermitage Museum.)

What mind has quite the strength to tell what followed—
The wonderful reception by the Emir,
The lovely party given by his spouse,
The well-planned banquet and the right arrangements,
The endless spectacle of varied foods,
Servings of meat from countless animals,
The actors' changes, and the flutists' tunes,
The twirling dancing girls, their shifting feet,
The pleasure of the dances and strange music?
First one thing charmed and then, in turn, another.[14]

From the middle Byzantine period we do not have actual images of wedding feasts, and I do not consider here the representations of the Wedding at Canaa in church decoration, although this scene is the one that in later centuries provides us with the details of weddings and the material culture of everyday life musicians and dance.[15]

However there is an unusual scene that is quite revealing as to wedding celebrations and dance rituals. It is an illustration in the *Cynegetica* (On Hunting) of Oppian in the Marciana in Venice ms. Z 479 from the eleventh century (fig. 8).[16] The text at this point speaks of horses and describes the showing of a painted stallion to the mare. The presentation of the stallion is compared to a bridegroom who is dressed in his festive linen garments and is about to meet his bride. The hope is that the foal that will be conceived will be as beautiful. The illustration is divided into two registers. In the lower, a young man is bringing a stallion to a mare and a little to the side after the tree the same mare is licking the foal. On the register above a fancily dressed young man with a crown-like band on his head is being lead by a boy who is holding a candle in one hand and a perfume bottle in his other. Before him two dancing women, one with cymbals, the other with lit torches, lead the dance. Clearly, this is a moment when the bridegroom is led to his future bride like the stallion to the mare, a tradition that was still found in village life in Greece until twenty years ago. Wedding seems to have been the most common private ritual where dancing took place.

Except for these few silver vessels, where among the scenes of court entertainment and music making we find a few representations of dance, and the dancers on the famous Constantine Monomachos stemma (fig. 9) and the Artukid plate with

[14] *Digenis Akritis* Bk. iv, lines 883–892, p. 57; for a discussion of dance scenes in the medieval Greek novel see Roilos, forthcoming.
[15] For the middle Byzantine period the material is not as rich and everyday life and its material culture had not fully entered artistic representation.
[16] Oppian *Cynegetica* I. 333–346.

fig. 8 Manuscript of the *Cynegetica* of Oppian: bridegroom led by dancers, first half
of the eleventh century. Venice, Biblioteca Nazionale Marciana, ms. gr. Z 479,
fol. 12v. (Photo: Biblioteca Nazionale Marciana.)

the Ascension of Alexander, both in enamel, almost all other dance imagery comes
from manuscripts.[17] These manuscripts are either illustrated Psalters or Octateuchs.
The dance takes place and is depicted after two specific events from the Old
Testament: The Crossing of the Red Sea with Miriam leading the dance, as we have
seen in the Chludov Psalter, and the victory of David over Goliath.

The most famous image of dance from the manuscript tradition is the extraordinary dance composition in the Vatican Psalter gr. 752, dated to the year 1058/59,
of the dance of Miriam after the Crossing of the Red sea (fig. 10). [18] It is a full-page
illustration. The figures are arranged in a circle, where in the middle of it eight musicians are playing a variety of instruments: a flute, a viol, a drum, cymbals, a tuba, a
small and a large harp. These figures are probably part of the choruses of musician-
prophets who often surround David and assist in the composing of the psalms and
symbolize the *oktoêkhos,* the Byzantine cycle of eight modes, which forms the musical
basis for liturgical psalmody. The women are shown dancing in a flattened circle

---

[17] *Glory of Byzantium* 1997:no. 145, pp. 210–212, no. 281, pp. 422–423; Steppan 2000, which I
believe both to be Byzantine.

[18] About this manuscript and its unusual illustrations see Kalavrezou and Trahulia-Sabar 1993.

holding each other by their raised hands. They are depicted each one in her full stature, displaying not only their rich and colorful silk dresses, sashes, and hats, but also the precise reverse step they perform. Their brocade dresses with the pointed long sleeves mark them as women of the court of this period. Through this anachronistic image of contemporary women the artist here depicted the victory of the past as a victory of the present. He used contemporary imagery to refer to a past event instead of the traditional referential use of the classical past to represent the present, as was customary in previous centuries. This is a new way of approaching the depiction of present events. And I am certain that in this case a specific event should be sought for explaining this extreme, and very modern in conception, composition of a dance. What we can say is that this is a representation of a courtly celebration and a dance performed not by professional dancers, but by the women of the court themselves. This change in iconography, with the introduction of contemporary elements like the dress and possibly the form of dance, is what was also observed on the silver vessels where contemporary activities were directly quoted, and seems to be a phenomenon of the period in general.

The slow but observable change can be traced by looking at the various surviving Psalter and Octateuch illustrations of that scene. The earliest Octateuch, Vatican 747, from the eleventh century, has also the most classical dancing Miriam and companions (fig. 11). It is a free dance close to the Maenad's dance of the late antique period, with one of the women even shown with a naked breast.

By the twelfth century we can observe in a number of illustrations that iconographically the women dancers

fig. 9 The "Crown of Constantine Monomachos:" enamel plaque with dancer, ca. 1042. Magyar Nemzeti Muzeum, Budapest. (Photo: after The *Glory of Byzantium*, eds. H. C. Evans and W. D. Wixom, New York, 1997.)

fig. 10 Psalter: the dance of Miriam and the Israelite women after the crossing of
the Red Sea, ca. 1058-1059. Biblioteca Apostolica Vaticana, Vatican City,
Ms. gr. 752, fol. 449v. (Photo: Biblioteca Apostolica Vaticana.)

undergo a transformation (fig. 12). As can be observed from a twelfth-century
Octateuch,[19] the dancing figures have lost their free and Maenad-like movements
and gestures and the dance itself has become a more structured dance, closer to what
young women of the time looked like while dancing in public. It is with a late

[19] Vatican ms. gr. 746, fol. 20.

fig. 11 Manuscript of the Octateuch: Miriam and her companions dancing, eleventh
century. Biblioteca Apostolica Vaticana, Vatican City, Ms. gr. 747, fol. 90v.
(Photo: Biblioteca Apostolica Vaticana.)

twelfth-century Psalter from Mt. Athos in the monastery of Lavra, ms. B26, in the
illustration of the Canticle of Exodus, that this dance of formal regularity appears
with this scene for the first time. The young women hold hands crossed over the
bodies of the others and follow a regular step (fig. 13).

fig. 12   Manuscript of the Octateuch: Miriam and her companions dancing, twelfth
century. Biblioteca Apostolica Vaticana, Vatican City, Ms. gr. 746, fol. 194v.
Photo: Biblioteca Apostolica Vaticana.)

There are two points to be made here: First that by the twelfth century we see
iconographic changes introduced in the representation of dance. The second is to
realize that the Crossing of the Red Sea and the hymn or song sung by the Israelites
after their successful crossing and their victory over Pharaoh becomes the most
popular image of dance in Byzantium. It is found in the Octateuchs, as we have
seen, and in the illustrated Psalters, since it is included as one of the Odes or
Canticles at the end of the Psalms.

This particular event and its victory associations had become imperial paradigms from the time of Eusebius, who likened Constantine's defeat over Maxentius
at the Milvian bridge to the victory of Moses over Pharaoh on the Red Sea. This
biblical parallel with a contemporary victory and imperial triumph is still alive in
the minds of the Byzantines and is, for example, referred to in the *Book of
Ceremonies.* [20] Constantine Porphyrogennetos prescribes it as the chant proper for
an imperial triumph after a victory, for example, over the Arabs.

[20] Vogt 1967:II, 19; PG 112, col. 1138.

294

fig. 13   Psalter, Exodus Canticle: Miriam and her companions dancing, late twelfth
century. Mt. Athos, Megiste Lavra, Ms. gr. B26, fol. 26. (Photo: after *Treasures
of Mount Athos,* Thessaloniki, 1987, by permission of the Ministry of Culture
Greece, Tenth Ephoreia of Byzantine Antiquities.)

There are further eleventh-century literary texts, which, when describing imperial military campaigns, allude to the Crossing of the Red Sea. One is the *History* by Michael Attaleiates (c. 1020/30–85), describing troop movements led by the future emperor Nikephoros Botaneiates through a region occupied by Patzinaks. The other is a Lenten sermon by Michael Psellos, who describes a victory, most likely one of the emperor Constantine IX Monomachos, over the Patzinaks. Such comparisons of the living ruler to a biblical hero become commonplace and are thoroughly in the spirit of medieval Christianity. These illustrations of dance, therefore, should be seen as references to moments of liberation and triumphal victory and to public celebrations where dance was performed.

It is also my belief that certain illustrated Byzantine manuscripts, specifically the Octateuchs and some of the Psalters, although biblical, should not strictly fall under the category of ecclesiastical or religious books, but, rather, they should be viewed as texts that served a different function. The books of the Octateuchs from Genesis to the story of Sampson, and the story of David form the most secular part of the Bible. They should be considered books containing stories, epic-like in their narrative of great leaders, examples of figures that the Byzantines liked to draw comparisons to for their own images of leadership: Abraham, Moses, Joshua, Joseph. The book of Kings and the Psalter offer the great story of King David, the ideal king for Byzantine emperors since the seventh century. These Octateuch books abound in examples of heroism, leadership, and royal power—all supported by divine aid—and also of other life experiences like birth, death, sicknesses, and other difficulties of everyday life. Due to their secular nature as texts, I would, therefore, view the Octateuchs and some of the Psalters as repositories of images of public festivities and celebrations not found in other places. They provide us with the possibility to glance at mid-Byzantine music making and dance events with a more contemporary eye. From the visual evidence we can say that dancing took place during public ceremonies, then at the court at official events, and on private festive occasions such as weddings.

Seventeen

Wedding:
Re-Composing a Ritual in
Shadow Theater Performances[1]

Anna Stavrakopoulou

The shadow theater traveled from the Far East to the Mediterranean following the path trodden by silk merchants throughout the centuries.[2] After several transformations along the way, it arrived in the Hellenic geographical space sometime before the outbreak of the War of Independence in 1821 in the form of the Ottoman Karagöz.[3] The Ottoman Karagöz was a dramatic form whose practice was linked to the month of Ramadan. During the nights of Ramadan predominantly male audiences were entertained by the puppeteers, with comical stories set in urban or purely imaginary settings; the stylized cast was multiethnic and the stylized plots had developed through a process of assimilation of elements and motifs spread across the Silk Road, while the stylized visual and acoustical representation had borrowed heavily from sartorial and musical practices of the Ottomans.[4] To make a long story short, the first performances in the Hellenic geographical area were performed by multilingual Ottoman puppeteers in Turkish for multilingual ethnically mixed audiences.

Throughout the nineteenth century, performances of Ottoman Karagöz were frequently reported in areas belonging to the geographically restricted newly-established

---

[1] I would like to thank Sumi Furiya, Panagiotis Roilos, and Dimitrios Yatromanolakis for their insightful comments.

[2] For an overview of the itinerary of the shadow theater see Hadjipantazis 1991. The presence of the shadow theater in the Balkans is discussed in Puchner 1985.

[3] The presence of the Ottoman Karagöz in the Hellenic geographic space during the first half of the nineteenth century is confirmed by several accounts of European travelers. A multitude of shorter and longer references to Karagöz and Karaghiozis by Greek and non-Greek authors can be found in the annotated bibliography compiled in two installments by Puchner (1976–78 and 1979–81). For a historical survey of the information provided mostly by European travelers, see Myrsiades 1976, and L. and K. Myrsiades 1988. See also Biris 1952 for an account, which takes into consideration the history of the shadow theater in Greece as it was transmitted orally among puppeteers.

[4] For an overview of the Ottoman Karagöz, see And 1987.

Greek state; these performances, in Naphplio, Plaka, or Chalkida, took place in ill-reputed coffee-shops mostly in Turkish, and had all the expected oriental elements. If one judges by the articles in the local press, often these shows were obscene. By the last decades of the century a Hellenized version, the Greek shadow theater, or Karaghiozis, named after the main character, had fully developed.[5] The ethnic composition of the stylized cast was Turks, Albanians, and mostly Greeks from different geographical areas, the stylized plots combined inherited, reshaped motifs with an array of stories grounded vaguely on the recent history of the War of Independence, as well as dramatized current events,[6] the stylized visual and acoustical representation expanded along given patterns. During the golden years of the art in the twentieth century, the artists took advantage of various technological innovations to improve the quality of their productions, such as electric lighting, the turntable etc.

In this chapter, I will be discussing Greek shadow theater recorded performances from the Whitman/Rinvolucri collection, which was compiled in the 1960s and belongs to the Milman Parry Collection at Harvard University. Apart from being the only systematic corpus of recorded performances and an invaluable tool for the scholar of an oral tradition genre, the collection contains interviews with the artists about this practice, which include equally priceless information about the history of the genre.[7] Before I proceed with my discussion, I would like to clarify that in the case of the scholarship on the Greek shadow theater, the printed material preceded the recorded performances as evidence; thus many theories formulated about this exclusively performative genre have been based on written texts, the so-called Karaghiozis pamphlets, which were first published by publishing houses specializing in popular editions, in an attempt to exploit commercially the great popularity of the performances. Although during the first phases of this enterprise, famous puppeteers "signed" the printed plays, very soon skilled writers employed by the publishers undertook the regular production of an ever-growing number of pamphlets.[8] Hence, recorded performances are both rare and invaluable for a more accurate assessment of this oral traditional genre. In this article, in an attempt to reverse the previously adopted scholarly practice, I discuss extensively the performances and make only ancillary use of the printed texts.

---

[5] For a historical survey of the performances of the Ottoman Karagöz and the establishment of the Hellenized version of the shadow theater in Patras and Athens see Hadjipantazis 1984.

[6] At the end of the nineteenth century the Dreyfus trial, which had taken by storm not only France but all of Europe, had made its way to the stage of the Greek shadow theater (Hadjipantazis 1984:94).

[7] For a detailed description of the collection see Stavrakopoulou 1994:155–169. For an assessment of the collection see Stavrakopoulou 1999.

My focus will be the theme of the "inverted" wedding ceremony in order to discuss the transformations of the Ottoman Karagöz during the Hellenization process; also, by analyzing several variants of plays and by tracing the performative choices of different Greek puppeteers, I will make some suggestions regarding the oral tradition and its transmission from one generation to the next. To be more specific, I will examine performances culminating in a mock wedding ritual, as it is staged in the performances, in order to shed light both on the structure of the plays and on elements of assimilation and Hellenization in the Greek shadow theater. I will present recorded performances and compare them to earlier printed versions, both Turkish and Greek. My goal is to show how in an oral traditional genre repetition incubates change, and each performance is as dynamic as the society it mirrors.

When it comes to weddings in the Greek shadow theater, one of the most popular plays that comes to mind is the Wedding of *Barbayiorgos and Karaghiozis as the Bride*, about the wedding of two male characters. Despite its great success in the box office, the plot of this play can be studied only through five versions that have survived: two in a pamphlet form and three recorded ones.

Among the three versions of the *Wedding of Barbayorgos* in the Rinvolucri collection,[9] two are live performances; one by the puppeteer Michopoulos (R 20–21) and another by the puppeteer Yiannaros (R 48–49), while the third version is a dictated scenario by the puppeteer Vassilaros (B 4). All three share a number of common points in their plots, and the story is more or less the following:

An old man with a funny Greek last name[10] is the tutor or the father of a beautiful young girl with a well-rounded education. The time to marry her off has come and through one procedure or another, the lucky man chosen by the tutor turns out to be Barbayiorgos. Barbayiorgos is the maternal uncle of Karaghiozis and a shepherd by profession. He wears the traditional *foustanéla*, a kind of kilt established as

---

[8] For an extensive list of publishers, including the multiple series of pamphlets that were produced massively from the 1920s to the 1970s see Kassis 1985 and Chanos 1991. Both authors start a discussion on the history of popular editions in Greece; despite the fact that the impact of these editions was enormous both on the formulation of the audiences' aesthetics and on the thematology of oral traditional genres, the study of popular publications in Greece has just begun.

[9] The collection was compiled by three different collectors over nine years: the first tapes were recorded by Cedric Whitman (1916–1979) in 1962. The second and biggest set was collected by Mario Rinvolucri during the summer of 1969, and the last installment was made by Janet Beech-Braithwaite in February 1971. Hereafter the performances of the Whitman/Rinvolucri collection will be designated by an R, if collected by Rinvolucri, and by a B, if collected by Braithwaite, followed by the specific number of the performance.

[10] In Michopoulos' play his name is γερο-Ρέλιος, in Yiannaros he is γερο-Γιώργης Χουτρομπίγουλης (!), and in Vassilaros he is called κ. Πετηναράκης. From now on, I will use the initial of each player for each version: M for Michopoulos, Y for Yiannaros, and V for Vassilaros.

299

the traditional attire of Greeks after the War of Independence. Visually he is represented by one of the tallest puppets. He argues violently, the strength of his body compensating for the weakness of his mind. According to early Karaghiozis scholarship, he is one of the most important innovations the Greek artists made to the Turkish Karagöz.[11] The two main characters of the cast, Karaghiozis and his pal Hadjiavatis, have to go and fetch Barbayorgos, the bridegroom-to-be, who is in his bucolic quarters, up in the mountains. After the first meeting of the parties involved in this wedding, even those among the characters who had not reacted from the very beginning to this match realize that this union will have a disastrous outcome for the girl. Given that the girl has to be married by the end of the day and the guests have already arrived,[12] Hadjiavatis is trying to find a way out. The man who will run to the girl's rescue is no other than Karaghiozis. By undergoing a temporary gender change, he replaces the girl, "marries" his uncle and saves the situation. The Ottoman custom of veiling the bride is the way out of the impasse of the plot. It is the exchanges between the two men, when the "newlyweds" are about to consummate their marriage, that provide the funniest lines of the play.[13] This effort has a sad ending for the lustful shepherd, who, after discovering that his nephew is hiding under the virginal veil, has to leave for his village in a state of total humiliation.[14]

Compared to this basic plot, stripped down to the essentials, one of the three recorded versions is the closest, and the other two the furthest away from it. In the first version, the M version, the father is wearing Oriental clothes, while the daughter is dressed in a European outfit. Barbayiorgos is being coached to dance European dances for the occasion. This confusion of nationality could stand as a metaphor for Greece: from the Oriental phase it passed to the European one, with a *foustanéla* stop-over.

In the V and the Y versions the initial situation is set so as to provide more options. In these cases, the old man, after explaining a family tradition that wants the girls of the family to be married to men from the same geographical area, informs the audience that he has professionally successful siblings living abroad. At first one wonders what difference does having family abroad make, but later the

[11] Melas 1952–53; Biris 1957:661–668; and Ioannou 1978:vol. I, ξ-ξγ´.
[12] The guests being the regulars of the shadow theater: Nionios, Morfonios, Stavrakas etc.
[13] Although Marjorie Garber (1992:142) argues that "in a way all marriages, even heterosexual marriages, are 'mock marriages,' in their dependence upon certain aspects of sartorial tradition and 'ceremony,'" the situation between Karaghiozis and Barbagiorgos represents the "mock marriage" par excellence. Not only are they of the same gender, but they are also blood relatives.
[14] Moskof 1980:78–85 presents a historico-political approach to Karaghiozis and its interaction with Greek society, where he also deals—from his point of view—with the Barbayiorgos/Karaghiozis relationship. Nevertheless, because Barbayiorgos in the above article is equated with a deus ex machina, the continuous ridicule he has to undergo is overlooked.

usefulness of this situation becomes clear: once the shepherd has been rejected as a husband and before his ridicule, an uncle shows up from *xenitiá* (Cairo in V, America in Y) bringing along another bridegroom, who is rich, young and who meets the standards of every girl's dream in the sixties. This unexpected twist of fate sees that the graceful lady, who is not asked her opinion about this wedding, ends up properly married. Strangely enough, in the M version, one of the characters had enumerated the kinds of men who would best suit the girl, namely "a high rank official, a scientist, a doctor, a professor, a retail businessman, a ship-owner;" while these options never materialize in this version, they do in the V and Y variants, where indeed she marries a young businessman.

If we set aside this mismatched pairing, the biggest victim of this plot in all three versions is definitely poor Barbayiorgos, who is punished in such a heart-breaking way for no apparent reason.

The two printed versions of the play were "signed" by Markos Xanthos and by Kostas Manos. Ioannou, a scholar who reprinted the Xanthos version of the *Wedding of Barbayiorgos* in the 1970s,[15] believes that the Turkish original is the *Big Wedding* because in both plays there is a veiled bride.[16] Mystakidou, another scholar who has worked systematically on the Turkish Karagöz, has done a comparative study of another Turkish original according to her, *The Inverted Wedding,* and of the Manos version of *The Wedding of Barbayiorgos.*[17] Her detailed analysis reveals extensive affinities between the two plays that go beyond the veil; these affinities point in the direction of the Inverted Wedding as a possible model for the Wedding of Barbayiorgos.[18]

In the Turkish original, one notices a more consistent causality: the man who is being ridiculed there is a drunkard, and the fake wedding is staged by his family within the context of an original rehabilitation plan.[19] It is exactly because of the Ottoman tradition of the veil that the relatives of the drunkard can make this plan work. In all the Greek versions Barbayiorgos has no social flaws, since one cannot consider his mountain manners as deserving a punishment. Nonetheless, he is the one figure traditionally ridiculed in the Greek shadow theater.[20]

---

[15] Ioannou 1978:vol. 1, 1–45.

[16] Ioannou 1978:vol. 1, πη'-θ'.

[17] Mystakidou 1982:177–200.

[18] In the same volume there is a Greek translation of the Turkish play (Mystakidou 1982:281–310).

[19] In the translation of *Ters Evlenme* (Mystakidou 1982:292), it is clearly spelled out that "he [the drunkard] may understand how bad it is to drink, and repenting after his misfortune, he may stop drinking."

[20] In the *Marriage of Karaghiozis* by Mollas (which is the first Karaghiozis play ever to be published, and which appeared in a serial form in the newspaper *Akropolis* in 1918) as well as in the *Marriage of Morfonios* (mentioned by Kiourtsakis 1985:196) the bride also has to be veiled. Nonetheless, in these plays the veiled bride is an old woman.

In an attempt to explain the incongruities between the Turkish and Greek versions, one would have to examine the two published versions of the Greek play,[21] and consider them for the sake of this comparison as earlier *transcripts*. I am borrowing the term *transcript* as it is defined in recent Homeric scholarship as "[. . .] the writing down of a composition-in-performance not as a performance per se but as a potential aid to performance."[22] In both of these earlier *transcripts*, we find not only that father and bride were Turkish, but also that the mechanism that set the plot in motion was quite different. The father of the girl, who is a high ranking Turkish official, presents as many suitors to his daughter as possible, so that she can choose a husband, and the stock characters are a fraction of these hundreds of men that the girl is checking out. Mystakidou remarks very accurately that the Turkish officer and everything he represents are being ridiculed by this massive search for a husband.[23] That was valid in these earlier *transcripts*; however, as we have seen, in the performances recorded in the late 1960s father and bride are Greek and there is no massive search since the bridegroom has been chosen prior to the start of the play. This change of nationality of the main characters in the performances indicates that the Hellenization process lasted throughout the life span of the genre, since the printed versions precede the performances by a few decades: new elements were introduced slowly but steadily while the puppeteers were composing on a given pattern during the performances. While most scholars agree that the notion of composition in performance is the key to understanding the poetics of the Greek shadow theater,[24] no studies have been attempted so far about the rules determining the occurrence of new elements on a given plot. The process of Hellenization along with the sociohistorical transformations of Greek society, as they are reflected in the performances, provide useful evidence on some aspects of the poetics of change in the Greek shadow theater.

I mentioned earlier that two of the recorded versions present striking similarities on key issues. The artists in their interviews provide illuminating information on schools or traditions that existed, which determined the twists of the plot in the performances. Although many puppeteers tried to convince Rinvolucri, the interviewer, that they had not learned a lot from their teachers and that they had their

---

[21] The *Marriage of Barbayiorgos* in Ioannou 1978:vol. I, 1–45 and the *Marriage of Barbayiorgos* by Kostas Manos, which is used by Mystakidou (1982:177–200) for her comparison between the Greek and Turkish versions.

[22] See Nagy 1996a:36; the notion of the *transcript* in Homeric scholarship was also discussed in Nagy 1992:35.

[23] Mystakidou 1982:185.

[24] See Sifakis 1984 and Kiourtsakis 1981; both scholars were deeply influenced by Lord's *The Singer of Tales* (Lord 1960). The impact of Lord's compositional theory was invaluable particularly in the deciphering of the mechanism of composition in performance within the shadow theater.

own ways of performing—a comment frequently made by many in this immodest group of professionals—it becomes evident from the comparison of these two versions that your teachers' choices very often become your choices too.

The similarities between the two "sister" versions extend way beyond the plot; Karaghiozis, when he first hears about this wedding, fears the reaction of his uncle in case the plan falls through. In one version he says that "if you promise him a woman and you don't give her to him, everybody is going to be in trouble," and in the other we have an "updated" version of the same statement: "if the bride or the father-in-law change their mind you'd better go to the front line in Vietnam."[25] Apart from common stock one-liners, there is a stock scene in both versions, in which the duties of a shepherd's wife are specified, in a job-description "format." Barbayiorgos enumerates his future wife's duties: she will do nothing much, he says, only on Monday she will cut wood, on Tuesday she will put oil on the dogs so that they are clean of parasites, on Wednesday she will do laundry on the river bank, on Thursday she will sweep and clean their lodgings, on Friday they will curdle milk to make cheese and yogurt, on Saturday they will buy candy and on Sunday they will dance the *tsámiko* and have fun together (the example comes from the V version).[26] No such enumeration appears in the first version, perhaps because the performance is given in Athens,[27] while the other two have small provincial town audiences, which were more familiar with the above mentioned chores. From a performative point of view there is no doubt that Yiannaros' play is loaded with up-to-date and strictly local jokes. This is an asset that he has meticulously cultivated throughout his career and of which he is very proud (as he discusses extensively in his interview).[28]

---

[25] The first quoted passage comes from Vassilaros' and the second from Yannaros' performance.

[26] I have tried to render the original's tone and humor but for the sake of dialectic particularities I would like to quote it too: τὴ Δευτέρα θὰ κόβει ξύλα, τὴν Τρίτη θὰ ρίχνει πετρέλαιο στὰ σκυλιὰ νὰ φεύγουν τὰ τσιμπούρια, τὴν Τετράδη θὰ πααίνει νὰ πλένει τὰ σκουτιὰ στὸ ποτάμι, τὴν Πέμπτη θὰ παίρνει τὸ σάρωμα καὶ θὰ καθαρίζει τὸ μαντρί, τήν Παρασκευή, μαθές, θὰ πήζουμε τὸ γάλα γιὰ νὰ κάνουμε τρὶ καὶ γιαούρτες καὶ τὸ Σάββατο θὰ πααίνουμε νὰ ψωνίζουμε μαντολάτο κι ἀπ' ὅλα τὰ γλυκὰ καὶ τὴν Κυριακὴ θὰ παίρνουμε τοὺς ζουρνάδες νὰ χορεύουμε τσάμικο νὰ γλεντοκοπᾶμε.

[27] An interesting variation in the Michopoulos performance on another level has to do with the fact that Karaghiozis' daughter, Potoula, gets to be a bridesmaid during the wedding. This is an exception, given that Potoula is the only female child of Karaghiozis throughout the recorded material; it is possible that Michopoulos endowed Karaghiozis with a daughter to honor his own daughter.

[28] At the same time he is very self-conscious since he knows that his performance is being recorded; he is constantly asking the audience to be quiet, and he is frustrated because there are some dogs in the distance that are being recorded as well (φανταστεῖτε παιδιὰ τὰ σκυλιὰ τοῦ Σωτήρη θὰ πᾶνε στὸ Λονδίνο ν' ἀκουστοῦν στὸ ραδιόφωνο, he makes Karaghiozis say). Although on the one hand this shows a high degree of professionalism, on the other, it may mean that he has altered his performative style for the recording.

There is one more "prop" that requires further investigation, as it is part of wedding ritual in the Greek shadow theater: the veil. The veil has survived during the Hellenization process, because of its functionality. As Marjorie Garber notes in her work on Shakespeare: "the veil is to clothing what the curtain is to the theater. It simultaneously reveals and conceals, marking a space of transgression and expectation; it leads the spectator to fantasize about the real thing in anticipation of seeing it."[29] If what Garber says is true once for actor theater, it is twice as true for the shadow theater, where the screen is permanently there, and everything happens behind it. The audience gets the opportunity to have strong fantasies because, even if the veil of Karaghiozis is lifted by a horrified Barbayiorgos, the "anticipation for the real thing" never ends. At the same time, the *Wedding of Barbayiorgos and Karaghiozis as the Bride* stages a unique moment of theatrical "honesty": since men players always play the female parts, trying to be as womanly as possible, to actually see Karaghiozis pretending to be the bride—the blossoming woman—offers us a chance to have represented on the screen the permanent reality behind it. And this is what doubles the humorous power of the scene.

As far as wedding ritual is concerned, it is not surprising that the customary church wedding did not make it into these specific plays. The few weddings occurring during the performances have two main features: first, they give the opportunity to the puppeteer to stage a festive parade of people and vehicles with many exotic elements, which could be considered sometimes as "souvenirs" picked up during the westbound journey of the shadow theater (among donkeys, cars and motorcycles, the parade might include camels and elephants with princely Indian riders on their backs); secondly, they provide an ideal context to Karaghiozis to make a handful of jokes in which there is a confusion of wedding and funerary rites.[30]

There are very few weddings staged literally during a performance, in spite of the immense popularity of the play *Karaghiozis' Wedding* from the earliest stages of the Greek shadow theater. But, as a rule, the mother of the bride is excluded and never present, with minimal exceptions. The father of the bride is almost always a widower, who is utterly fond of his daughter. One would be surprised to discover that these three particularities—the lack of weddings staged during a performance, the exclusion of the mother of the bride, and the widowed father—are conventions

---

[29] Garber 1992:338.
[30] Kiourtsakis believes that "it is a typical carnival reversal that merges or, rather, identifies, on the speech level, the two basic functions of the bodily drama: marriage and death" (in Kiourtsakis 1985:209).

of Shakespearean theater too, thus betraying that otherwise very different conventional theater genres function along very similar lines.[31]

Before I conclude, I would like to attempt an explanation of the superior qualities of the young girl in the performances. The bride-to-be is the only educated member of the cast in the comedies; to be more precise, although her father, either in the form of an Ottoman dignitary or of a Greek wealthy gentleman, is usually a wise sage, his level of education is never commented upon. On the contrary, in the case of the young woman, her education is always considered out of proportion, she can read, she speaks foreign languages and, in general, she has deeply rational opinions.[32] And one wonders, why she was endowed with so many superior qualities? A likely explanation could be that the "casting" of the plays had from its origins as a goal to provide fantasies for men. First, in the Ottoman Empire we know that the audiences were strictly male; then, in Greece, although we know that women attended the performances, the point of view presented was predominantly male. A second possible interpretation—not so much of the origins of the situation, but of the results—is that the young girl represents modernity in the plays: she is cultured, she does not succumb to choices others make for her, and she reflects the progress of Greek society.[33] The Hellenization of the Ottoman Karagöz produced heavily "rehabilitated" female characters; in Karagöz the most prominent female figures were the *Zenne*, the neighborhood women, which were depicted as morally dubious, and socially quarrelsome, since they keep arguing with their husbands and lovers. In the Greek Shadow theater, some of those qualities have been absorbed by the wife of Karaghiozis, who holds a minor role in the plays. On the other hand, the leading female figure, the young woman, as she is embodied by the daughter of the most socially prominent male character of the cast, is virtuous, refined, and extremely educated.[34]

---

[31] "I have found no marriages (or funerals) staged literally in the plays of Shakespeare or his contemporaries; [. . .] the mother of the bride is a wholly excluded figure—as indeed she is throughout almost the entire Shakespeare canon " and "as in most of the father-daughter plays, the father here is apparently a widower with only one child, a daughter whom he loves possessively and has denied to several suitors." It is obvious, as can be seen by the remarks of Boose in Boose:1982:327 and 331, that there are striking similarities regarding the dramatis personae conventions of Karaghiozis and the Elizabethan theater.

[32] For an excerpt from a performance where all her scaringly impressive skills and education are enumerated see Stavrakopoulou 1994:225.

[33] Diametrically opposed to her modernity is Barbayiorgos' stale adherence to traditional mountain manners and values: he represents Greece's rural, uneducated past in contrast to her urban, cultured European future.

[34] On the subject of women in the Greek shadow theater, see also L. Myrsiades 1980. In this article, Myrsiades considers Karaghiozena, the wife of Karaghiozis, as the most important female character, and she mentions the role of the young woman only briefly. I believe that the role of the young woman deserves more attention, exactly because she was created to please the Greek Karaghiozis' audience.

I have dealt with numerous issues pertaining to the Greek shadow theater. I used a mocked wedding ritual as it occurs in the performances to discuss the origins of the genre and its continuous re-creation on the level of plot and stock characters, as well as the puppeteers and their modus operandi. Because of the interactive character of the genre, all the changes in the shadow theater reflect changes Greek society underwent from 1890, a date marking roughly the emergence of the fully developed Greek shadow theater, until the 1960s, when the recorded performances were collected. What becomes apparent even from the very small sample I have analyzed here, is that the modern Greek society was attempting to shape its identity by balancing and mixing all kinds of elements from Ottoman to Christian and from premodern to modern by weaving all these threads into one colorful tapestry.

Eighteen

The Body's Language:
Representations of Dance in Modern Greek Literature

Gail Holst-Warhaft

Dance can be many things in Greek life. It may be a manifestation of joy, flirtation, pride, sorrow, patriotism, gender, identity, resistance, religious ecstasy, or passion. Indeed, the diversity of traditional dances and the variety of their significance is so great that it is hard to generalize about Greek dance. The diversity is as obvious in anthropological studies as it is in literary description. The only constant may be the ubiquitous presence of dance and, at least until recently, its close association with the traditional rituals of Greek life.

Traditional Greek rural dance is a cultural performance embedded within certain sacred and secular rituals of village life.[1] The common aspect of all such ritual activities is order or pattern. Ritual activities impose a communal structure on individual, potentially disordered behavior. They may be considered from a functionalist perspective as a means of protecting the individual and the community from the dangers of chaos, but rituals may also give license to the community to indulge in otherwise unacceptable behavior. Within the patterned space of a wedding or funeral ritual, normal social controls and taboos are often suspended, allowing the community a temporary freedom, an exuberant excess whose performance is nevertheless monitored and prescribed by its own stylistic restraints.[2]

Until recently the performative aspects of most rituals were studied by anthropologists not so much for their own sake as for what they revealed about such traditional subjects as religion, political life, or gender relations. Victor Turner, for

---

[1] Here it is necessary to establish what we mean by ritual and to what extent dance constitutes a ritual activity. Margaret Alexiou notes that the absence of a common word for ritual in modern Greek suggests not that the practice is unrecognized or non existent; she sees it rather, as an "implicit recognition that ritual activities cross sacred and profane, civil and religious, and individual and social categories," Alexiou 2002b.

[2] As a number of observers have noted concerning the elaborate traditional activities surrounding death and mourning in Greece and other countries, such rituals impose a certain order on the chaos of death. See Alexiou 2002a; Padel 1995; Holst-Warhaft 1992, 2000.

Gail Holst-Warhaft

example, made use of his observance of Ndembu ritual[3] to develop his concepts of liminality and reversal in human action, and Clifford Geertz[4] related much of his analysis of Balinese culture to the spectacle of the cock fight. Over the last twenty years there has been an increasing emphasis on close observation of "performance practice" as a subject of interest in itself.[5] Goffman's use of the notion of a frame[6] that is imposed by people on a particular social activity has been a useful device for distinguishing the extraordinary, performative events like dancing from the ordinary events of daily life, recognizing them as both integrated into a broader social or ritual context and as discrete events.

Many of the studies of Greek dance in recent years by ethnographers, anthropologists, and dance specialists[7] have made use of the broader literature on performance practice and ritual, but there has been, as far as I am aware, almost no attention paid to the way dance has been portrayed in Greek literature. The preoccupation of contemporary anthropology with first hand observation, although perhaps a healthy response to the generation of "armchair anthropologists," may have had the effect of eliminating as irrelevant, or paying insufficient attention to, literary accounts of performance. But however distorted they may be by their artistic context, references to and descriptions of performance in Greek literature are generally made by keen observers, and many were made at a time when the context of performance was very different from the present. Not only that, but it is clear, at least in accounts of dance and music, that long before the anthropologists described the phenomena, Greek writers were keenly aware of the ritual dimension of dance.

Contrary to their prominence in tourist and ethnographic descriptions, portrayals of dance are not as common in Greek poetry and prose as one might expect (since traditional song texts are so intertwined with dance itself, they might be treated independently as a source of information on dance, but this is a rather different project and I do not propose to deal with them here). There are passing references to dance in a number of novels but few that deal with it in any depth. In this brief account of literary representations of dance, I shall not attempt a complete survey of these references, but concentrate on a handful of examples that underline the ritual and cultural importance of what is now described in the ethnographic literature as "the dance-event" in Greek society (Cowan 1990, Torp 1988). What

---

[3] Turner 1974, 1982a.
[4] Geertz 1972; "Person, Time and Conduct in Bali," in Geertz 1973a.
[5] See, for example, Hymes 1975; Beeman 1979; Bauman 1977, 1993; Goffman 1974.
[6] The notion is borrowed from Bateson. See Bateson 1955.
[7] Cowan 1990; Danforth 1989; Torp 1988, 1992; Tsouni 1987; Zografou 1993; Demas 1992; Coros 1983; Hunt 1993; Loutzaki 1991; Papagiotopoulou 1992; Savrami 1992.

emerges from these literary accounts is a common preoccupation with the extraordinary, even magical aspects of the dance, and with the male dancer, his temporary power and his vulnerability.

Kazantzakis' *Zorbas*

Because it has become an international cliché of what Greek dance is all about, and because it contains some of the most detailed passages on the subject in all of Greek literature, Kazantzakis' *Life and Culture of Alexis Zorbas* may be the ideal place to begin.[8] In some sense, Zorbas' dance, even in its original form, is a tourist account. Kazantzakis' portrait of Alexis Zorbas is full of contradictions. The foreign-educated, urbane Kazantzakis, or his persona, the narrator, is more of a stranger on the island of his birth than the Macedonian Zorbas. Both are temporary visitors, briefly coupled in the lunatic venture of a mine, but only one is capable of adapting to the local village conditions, and he is from the other end of Greece. The Cretan-born narrator remains as much a foreigner as if he were a visitor from London or Berlin. His admiring narrative of Zorbas' physicality, his sensuous enjoyment of the moment expressed to perfection in dance, reads like the account of an inhibited British traveler on his first trip to Greece who meets a colorful local character, drinks too much wine, and surprises himself by joining in the dance. Alexis Zorbas, on the other hand, may be a geographical misfit in Crete, but he could never be mistaken for a tourist. It is Zorbas' perorations on dance that inform the intellectual narrator, and so the reader, of the centrality of dance to the traditional Greek male psyche.

Zorbas and the narrator make an odd couple, whose strangeness is emphasized by their living in a hut at some distance from the village, but within earshot of it. In the first passage in the novel that refers to dance, Easter has arrived, and Zorbas has been on an errand of erotic mercy to the ailing Madame Hortense. What value would the Resurrection of Christ have, he asks, "if it weren't a signal for youth, joy, belief in the miraculous, and an old lady to become a wench of twenty again?" (276). The two men eat their Easter meal alone but from the village the sound of the lyra reaches them: "they're dancing in the village!" says Zorbas:

> Why on earth are we sitting here like a couple of cuckoos for? Let's go and dance! Don't you feel sorry for the lamb? To go to waste like that? Come on, let's go dance and sing! Zorbas is Risen! (276)

[8] Kazantzakis 1973.

Gail Holst-Warhaft

Zorbas' last remark underscores the peculiar nature of the two men's Easter celebration, and failure to dance after eating the Paschal lamb becomes tantamount to sacrilege. The narrator is not in the mood to dance and urges Zorbas to go alone; Zorbas then gives him a summary of his philosophy of life, the kernel of which is "Sea, woman, wine, and plenty of hard work," and sets off for the village. Left alone to contemplate Zorbas' brief sermon, the narrator is prompted to cast his normal inhibitions aside and sets off to seduce the beautiful widow.

The Easter dance, a ritual embedded in a ritual, is an extraordinary event in any Greek village. It is this, rather than Zorbas' now immortal dance on the seashore that reveals the full potential of the dance as a ritual event. The young shepherd who has taken the lead in the dance when the narrator enters the square, is an appropriately bizarre figure, who comes down only once a year from the mountains "to see people and to dance" (288).

> . . . a dark, virile (*varvátos*) young man of twenty, his thickly downed cheek not yet touched by any razor, his bare chest a thick forest of curly hair, he had thrown his head back, his feet beat the ground like wings, every now and again he turned his glance on some young girl and the whites of his eyes gleamed fiercely in the blackness of his face.

I was happy, afraid. (288)

When the narrator asks an elderly villager who the young man is, he is given an answer that leaves no doubt as to the dancer's supernatural qualities: "He's like the archangel, shameless fellow, who takes souls away."

The young man then shakes his head and calls out "like a hooked ram" to the lyra-player, βάρα ποὺ νὰ πεθάνει ὁ Χάρος ("play up, so Death will die"). We are told that the young people of the village have danced under the budding spring trees for thousands of years and will continue to dance for thousands more, their faces, "consumed with desire." The actual faces will change but "the essence, the One will remain the same."

Leaping high in the air, the young shepherd plucks the kerchief off his neighbor's head with the toes of his boots, a feat that is applauded by the men and causes the girls to shudder and look down in confusion.[9] But the young man, obedient to the rules of self-presentation in the dance, appears oblivious:

---

[9] Cowan (1990) has much of interest to say on the subject of hierarchy, evaluation, and gender in the dance.

310

Unspeaking, without looking at anyone, wild and disciplined, now resting his left hand on his lean, hard hip, went on dancing, fixing his eyes wildly and modestly on the ground (289)

At this moment, at its fierce climax, the dance is interrupted by an old man who calls out to the excited crowd that the widow has come into town and entered the church. In the scene that follows, the ritual of the slaying of the Pascal lamb is perverted by the stoning and stabbing of the widow, whose only crime is her manifest sexuality. The narrator even admits that in order to escape his panic, he has transformed the frightful scene into a necessary and ancient ritual, with its victim "almost smiling, in the sacred stillness of a symbol . . . as if the widow had died thousands of years ago and the curly-headed maidens of Knossos' Aegean civilization had died this morning" (296).

The barbarous murder of the widow, initiated by a ritually perverse dance, is exorcised by another dance, one that initiates the narrator into a ritual of bodily catharsis and cements his brotherhood with Zorbas. Again the Paschal feast, accompanied by a great deal of wine, ignites the dance, but it is not a local dance that Zorbas will teach the narrator; it is a dance that will become a pan-Greek symbol of masculine pride and emotion, a dance whose exclusive, "framed" space men will kill to preserve. As Zorba describes it, it is: "fierce, masculine [παλικαρίσιος]. The *komitadji* danced it before a battle" (342).

Zorbas begins his dance alone, his steps blending "wildly, joyfully," before the narrator clumsily joins in. Zorbas, in a gesture familiar to all observers of the *zeibékiko* (see, for example, Cowan 1990:1–2) then claps his hands in encouragement as his "boss" begins to catch on. Urging him on, Zorbas says, "To hell with the papers and pens . . . now that you're dancing and you're really learning my language, what won't we have to talk about!" (342). Dance has become an alternative language for the tongue-tied man of action, allowing Zorbas to express his deepest feelings: "I have a lot to tell you, but my tongue won't get around it . . . So I'll dance it!" (343). As he dances his ecstatic solo, the narrator sees him, on the shoreline, "as an old partisan archangel":

> Because this dance of Zorbas' was all provocation, stubbornness and rebellion. You'd think he was calling out "What can you do to me, Almighty? You can't do a thing to me, just kill me. Kill me, and I don't give a damn. I've had my revenge, I've said what I want to say. I managed to dance, and I don't need you any more" (ibid.).

Admiring his friend's performance, the narrator feels, "for the first time, the Daemonic revolt of man, defying weight and matter, the primal curse." In his dance

311

on the beach Zorbas inscribes "the dawn of human history." The scene ends with
the two men laughing and wrestling on the pebbled beach and sleeping in each
other's arms.[10]

The male ritual on the beach is ecstatic, defiant, liberating, and (if we can still
use the word without cringing) bonding. This may be the reason for the huge
success of the Cacoyiannis' film treatment, and what so many foreigners have found
enchanting about Greek dance. The scene is a vision of a lost paradise, a place where
two men can relate to each other emotionally and physically in an artful, cathartic,
masculine way. It is, of course, an artificial, literary/cinematic construct, but the
zeibékiko, the only solo male dance in the Greek repertoire, although one in which
other men participate as active spectators, had already become, in Kazantzakis'
lifetime, a pan-Greek symbol of masculine and ethnic identity.[11] However as
Kazantzakis was obviously aware, and as William Washabaugh[12] would later point
out in the case of the male flamenco dancer, and Jeffrey Tobin,[13] in that of the male
tango dancer, it is precisely in the most overtly masculine of postures that the ambiguities of sexual desire are revealed. The aggressive posture is combined with a
serenity, grace, and control, just as it is in the figure of the matador, or in the figures
of the bull-leaping young men from Knossos, which so fascinated Kazantzakis.

In the Andalusian bullfight or the mysterious bull-leaping activities of Bronze
Age Crete, we see an almost perfect metaphor for ritual itself: the enraged bull as a
chaotic force of nature, the matador/leaper/dancer as a tamer, controller and final
victor. And yet the flamenco dancer, like the matador and the *zeibékiko* dancer,
displays his power not so much to women as to other men, and in such a context,
power and control are not all that is on display. In the informal gatherings of *peña
flamenco* performers, called *juergas*, men dance provocatively with each other, cross-
dress, and shout the Spanish equivalent of πούστης (faggot) to one another.[14] This
is usually done after the wives have gone home and the men are alone. Similarly, in
the all-male *rebétika* circles of the hashish den, or the late night *bouzoúki* clubs,

---

[10] The setting of the dance on a beach may have added to the touristic appeal of Zorbas' dance, but,
as Alexiou notes (2002b:379), "down by the sea shore" is a common motif in Greek folk songs that
deal with love and death. Dance and music, in folk tale and song, often occur in marginal, "seductive" places, and the shore is, of course, a perfect metaphor for marginality.

[11] Cowan talks about the *zeibékiko* stance as "a 'potent image of masculinity" (1990:177) but she also
sees beyond this stereotype to the more ambivalent sexual subtleties of *zeibékiko* dancing and its
social function as a negotiation of power among men (see, inter alia, p. 189).

[12] Washabaugh 1998:39–50.

[13] Tobin 1998.

[14] Washabaugh 1998:45. Washabaugh is quoting fieldwork by Papavlou here, without a precise reference. Washabaugh also suggests that the classic male dancer's gesture of hoisting the hem of his vest
is a deliberate parody of a woman lifting her skirt.

dancing was often parodic and sexually ambiguous. As Washabaugh says: "The activities of men dancing in Greece, football in the United States, and story-telling on Providence Island are suggestive in more ways than one. It seems that males often create venues within which to play out complex relations of competition and bonding as a way of resolving the ambiguities of their gender" (1998:49). Kazantzakis' description of two men dancing a *zeibékiko* on the beach, before wrestling and sleeping in each other's arms, not only supports Washabaugh's remarks about the nature of male dancing, but also modern theories of the therapeutic effect of performance rituals.[15]

Myrivilis' *Vasilis Arvanitis*

In Myrivilis' novella *Vasilis Arvanitis*,[16] the eponymous hero is constantly overstepping the bounds of convention. Overstepping is both his glory and his downfall. In a passage that exemplifies his magical status as a hero, Vasilis' stepping is both triumphant and redemptive:

> Vasilis, with the nargileh in his hand, jumped—No! Flew like an eagle—over the gorge of Karini. Like an eagle and like an archangel he spread his wings and sailed through the air, over the bubbling water. When his feet touched gracefully upon the earth again it was with lightness and ease *as if he had just executed a dance step*. All you could hear were the silver chains which thundered on his chest and the ornamental gold coins which hung from his Cretan dagger. Not a single coal fell from the bowl of the nargileh (1943/1983:57–58; emphasis mine)

The motivation for Vasilis' miraculous leap is to appease his father and win back his approval, having shamed him in public. Vasilis has already proved himself a legendary hero, having slain a large snake with a spear at the age of sixteen. In case any reader may have missed the parallel with St. George, Myrivilis depicts the villagers staring up at the boy's disembodied head leaning over the edge of the roof, the site of his battle with the huge serpent:

> There was a hush as they watched. Only his head was visible, protruding over the edge of the roof. His face was alight—solemn and severe—and encircled by hair which shone in the sun like gold (17).

---

[15] As, for example, Moerman 1979.
[16] Myrivilis 1943. English translations are from Myrivilis 1983.

Gail Holst-Warhaft

Later adventures of the hero include the avenging of the death of an older hero, killed by the Turks, enforced exile, the killing of another "Dragon"—this time the leader of the Bulgarian *komitaji*'s, Karatassof, a triumphant return and the successful wooing of two beautiful sisters. Each of Vasilis' heroic feats, however, is tainted by his overstepping of the boundaries of tradition. The snake he kills is a σπιτόφιδο, a house-snake believed to bring good luck to the inhabitants of the house; to kill such a snake is generally believed to invite misfortune. Even Vasilis' behavior as a war hero is suspect. Having fought in the Macedonian war as an irregular on the Greek side against the Bulgarians, Vasilis later joins the Young Turks in their struggle against the Sultan, and is decorated for his bravery both by the Greek government and the new Turkish state. The hero's seduction of the two sisters known as the Lambrines, is not only shocking because they are unprotected orphan daughters of a mother who has also defied convention, but because Vasilis flaunts his conquests, hanging the medals he has won around their necks and dancing with them in public.

It was Vasilis' dancing that seduced the two sisters. Interestingly, Hathoula's description of the handsome dancer employs the same metaphor as the elderly villager in Kazantzakis' novel: "Oh, but he's so handsome, sister—as handsome as the archangel who takes men's souls."[17]

The scene of Vasilis' miraculous leap takes place in the context of the Feast of the Assumption in the village of Karini, during which it was customary to sacrifice a heifer. Vasilis walks at the head of the procession, leading the heifer, then wrestles it to the ground to be slaughtered by the butcher. Fiddles and lutes begin to play as the *rakí* flows. Then the dancing begins. At first the men dance "men's dances [παλικαρίσιους χορούς]—the *zeibékiko* and the *chasápiko*—and everywhere women and girls craned their necks to watch and admire them" (54). Then Vasilis, disobeying all social rules, suddenly walks over to where the women are sitting and leads his two mistresses, bedecked, like the heifer, with his war medals, one on a

---

[17] In this, as in many other portrayals of the seductive and extraordinary powers of Greek dance, comparison with its central position in Irish tradition is inevitable. To take an example from recent fiction, Eileen, the heroine of Jane Urquart's novel *Away* (1993), is seduced by the doomed hero Lanighan through the power of his dancing, a power that is not only erotic but rhetorical. The young man, who is about to plead, on behalf of the community, with the politician D'Arcy McGee, refuses to speak. When Eileen asks how Lanighan will make a petition to McGee if he won't talk, she is told by the Irish-Canadian captains: "Haven't you been watching? He'll dance. It's what he's been practising here all week . . . his petition to McGee." Eileen is baffled and asks how McGee will know what Lanighan is saying; the answer she receives is: "A true Irishman always knows what a dancer is saying" (1993:257). This is a wonderful example of how dance, for the Irish as for the Greeks, can "provide the individual with the ritual dramatic means to act out possible dialogues and conflicts between all contestants" (Alexiou 2002b:407).

blue Greek ribbon, one on a red Turkish ribbon, onto the dance floor. Despite their shock and disapproval, the villagers watch the dance open-mouthed: "Everyone in our village loves dancing, and beauty, no matter what the circumstance, comes to the heart of a man like the blessing of God" (55).

The shameless dance of Vasilis and the two girls insults the entire village and the invited guests, and his father is outraged. He sits puffing his nargileh, and as his son passes him he spits on the ground. For a moment Vasilis hesitates and withdraws, then he turns back, enters the coffee-house and orders the most elaborate nargileh in the cafe. Wrapping the tube around the stem he carries it carefully to the other side of the ravine and leaps.

Like his slaying of the snake, Vasilis' leap mimics an earlier mythical feat, the heroic leap performed on the same site by a magical hero called dayi-Panayotis who was said to have leapt across the Golden Horn at Galata, and who could "jump like a roebuck over the heads of the Turks who were after him" (52). Having emulated the feat of the legendary dayi-Panayotis, Vasilis presents his father with the magnificent nargileh, from which not a single piece of charcoal has fallen. The crowd goes wild with joy:

A new glory beat its wings over our village, a glory which would cause our friends to rejoice and make our enemies green with envy.

An old man from barba-Yannakos' [the father of Vasilis] group stood up and shouted as loudly as a bugle:

"May you live like the mountains, Eagle!" (58).

The scene closes with the hero's father smoking the proffered pipe and the feasting and music resuming.

Vasilis' heroic career ends on another feast day, appropriately the most solemn and splendid of the Orthodox year, the Friday of Holy Week, when the icons are taken from the church and carried in procession through the streets. On this awesome night, for reasons that are never explained, Vasilis, dressed in his rebel's uniform with pistol in hand, leaps in front of the procession shouting, "No-one passes here!" and orders the priest and his retinue to return to the church. The priest warns him that he is in mortal danger, saying, "God passes here." But the hero, in his deranged arrogance, responds: "Not even God will pass!" and fires his gun into the air. The crowd flees in panic and Vasilis sets off to see his two mistresses, unaware that a large irrigation channel has been dug across their street. In the darkness he steps over the edge, falls into the chasm and breaks his leg. Appropriately, the hero is undone by what he does excessively well. Having overstepped, he is felled by mis-stepping.

As he lies in agony in his mistresses' house a priest is brought to exorcise Vasilis' pain but the furious hero tells him that God has played him a dirty trick: instead of fighting like a man, he has tripped him up in the dark. "This is the way a real man fights," he tells the priest, and plunges a dagger into his own heart. Despite his defiance of the Church and his heretical suicide, Vasilis is given a heroic burial, his body placed upright in the earth as he had wished, his grave tended by his adoring mistresses, its constantly burning lamp a source of inspiration to the village and the narrator.

Dancing as Heroism and Danger: Vizyenos and Savvopoulos

Myrilivis' *Vasilis Arvanitis* offers us one of the most interesting treatments of dance in modern Greek literature. If we consider, and there is plenty of evidence in Greek and other traditions to warrant the assumption, that leaping and dancing, especially heroic male dancing, are intimately connected,[18] then we must say that the ultimate display of heroism is a form of dancing. Dancing is both heroic and dangerous, ritually prescribed and inclined to pervert the everyday rituals of Christian Greek life. There are a number of references to dance as dangerous and damaging in Greek literature, including Vizyenos' short story "My Mother's Sin,"[19] where the unfortunate heroine blames her failure to resist a final dance with her husband at a wedding for the death of her baby daughter. Having drunk a lot of wine and danced late into the night, the mother returns to nurse her baby in the bed and apparently rolls onto and stifles the child. The parents bury the baby secretly and for the rest of her life, the mother is haunted by her "sin."

The dangerous potential of the dance is very differently displayed in the passionate lyrics of Dionysis Savvopoulos' *"Makrý Zeibékiko gia ton Níko,"*[20] a song based on the true story of a fight in a *bouzoúki* club. The song is as much a social commentary on contemporary Greek life as it is about dance, but it tell us a great deal about the lore of the *zeibékiko*. The unfortunate Nikos, son of a Macedonian resistance fighter who went into hiding in the mountains, was isolated, as a child, because the villagers were fearful of associating with him. To escape the stifling atmosphere of the village and its watchful police, Nikos fled to Athens, but with no resources soon fell into a life of petty crime and served six

---

[18] This is not only true of the Greek folk tradition where the mythical hero of the folk song tradition, Digenis Akritas, straddles mountains, but also of Celtic folklore. The "seven league boots" of the British wondertale tradition enable heroes to travel vast distances just as, in Irish tradition, marginal and "mad" women lamenters are said to "leap" across the hills. (See Bourke 1988).

[19] Vizyenos 1980.

[20] Lyrics of the song, from the album Ἡ Ρεζέρβα can be found in Savvopoulos 1981.

years in jail. Fleeing again on his release, he settled in Thessaloniki, but was badly beaten up by the local police. He returned to Athens, where his fiancée was warned about him by the police and under pressure from her parents, broke off their engagement.

With nothing left to live for, Nikos heads for the "ghetto of the *bouzoúki* clubs," . . . ποὺ ἡ ἔκσταση ἐκεῖ ἀκόμα ζεῖ (where ecstasy still lives). His dream is to hear the songs and watch his young brother dance: τὸ ἀδερφάκι μου ὑψωμένο / νὰ τὸ κοιτᾶ στὸ χορό του μοναχὸ / καὶ κάτι νὰ παθαίνω ("my little brother grown tall, to watch him alone in the dance/ and to be turned on by something"). By ordering a dance for his brother Niko is displaying his own power and at the same time initiating his brother into the rites of manhood in the tough world of the σκυλάδικο (*bouzoúki* club).[21] But when the "order" is announced, and Demosthenios, Nikos' young brother, rises to dance, two policemen remain on the dance floor, turning their backs on him in deliberate provocation. When he reminds them it is his turn, they throw him to the floor, which is covered in broken glass, and Nikos, like an enraged bull, charges the dance floor with his knife drawn, killing policemen and bystanders in a frenzy. He escapes in the chaos, hides in a friend's house, and is betrayed by him. Beaten unconscious by the police, he is taken to jail and tried for murder. Savvopoulos' long lament for Nikos as the victim of a merciless, indifferent society, pays tribute to the Greek who seeks a last refuge, an "ecstasy" in music and dance, and defends his right to pay for it. The song ends with the lines, "Nikos is the sickness that saves us/ as it carries you further from your cell, Niko, to the sky of your music."

The space of the παραγγελιά (the dance for which a man has paid the musicians), is an inviolable one, particularly for the *zeibékiko*, and there are many tales of knife fights in *bouzoúki* clubs and other venues caused by intrusions into the dance space of another. The case of Nikos Kouyioumdzes made dramatic reading in the Greek press largely because police were involved and because it happened in the 1970s, decades after such fights were commonplace. To Savvopoulos, a man who was always conscious of the traditional theatrical aspects of his art,[22] Nikos' desire, even in his despair, to hear music and pay for his brother to dance lifts him beyond criminality to the realm of ritual victim. The songwriter imagines him in his cell as a "mythical animal," seeing him move in slow motion, "like a divinity unleashing her panic."

---

[21] On the phenomenon of *parangelia* and the conflicts that arise from it, see Cowan 1990:101–103, 109–112.
[22] See, for example, his 1979 interview with Grivas in Θεατρικά (in Savvopoulos 1981:27–31).

Gail Holst-Warhaft

Self-mutilation and the Burning of the Dancer

On the island of Mytilene (Lesvos) where Myrivilis was born, the *zeibékiko*, in various styles, usually danced by two men, was a common village dance, but not in its prototypical form, as danced by Muslim Zeybeks from Asia Minor. As he describes their dance, again in *Vasilis Arvanitis*, Myrivilis emphasizes the wild and terrifying nature of the true *zeibékiko*. The dancers are inspired by itinerant musicians from the Turkish mainland, who usually play the ντaούλι (large drum) and ζουρνά (folk oboe) for the hero, Vasilis, and his friends to dance. The villagers call them gypsies "partly out of contempt and partly because of their darker skins" (67). The outlandish costumes they wear and music they play mark them as orientals and outsiders, and yet they have a powerful allure, and when the young men of the village had drunk enough wine they would send for these eastern musicians. According to the author, it was "the ancient blood which would awaken within them and desire those primitive rhythms: a forgotten keepsake from the prehistory of our race whose ancient motifs would be revived by these echoes" (68).

What followed was a dance whose mysterious qualities were frightening to the children watching:

> Dark nostalgia would awake in their turbid souls and they would become serious and draw their daggers and draw their daggers to dance fearful Pyrrhic dances. "Hep! Hep!" they'd shout and their sharp knives would flash in the sun (ibid.).

As the slow *zeibékiko* progresses, the men dance together in a large circle around the musicians, but despite their drunkenness, their dance is controlled:

> Though drunk to the point of madness, the rhythm of the music would control their ecstasy with its strict discipline. We children would watch the pointed blades passing over their throats, behind their necks, across their chests, and below their knees. . . . Breathlessly we would wait for the *analyes* to begin. When their ecstasy had reached its peak they would raise their daggers and, with a shout, plunge them into their calves or their thighs. And they would continue their dancing (68–69).

Emphasizing the unnatural character of this spectacle, the author/narrator notes that "sometimes there wouldn't be a drop of blood on the knives." There were other strange aspects to the dance too. The dancers would circle around, arms extended towards the center; then, using only three fingers, they would pick up some earth, touching hands again in the center as they reversed the direction of the

318

dance[23] As Myrivilis comments: "The whole sequence had something of a secret and idolatrous ritual about it" (69) In contrast to the dancing of the hero, Vasilis, which may have its miraculous aspects but is the symbolic epitome of heroic action, the Zeybek dance is portrayed as a perverse ritual whose significance the narrator fails to understand.

Myrivilis' description of the *zeibékiko* invites comparison with the ritual healing dances of the *Anastenárides*, who enter a state of ritual possession and dance on a bed of hot coals. Danforth's detailed account (1989) of the *Anastenárides* notes the apparently miraculous aspects of the phenomenon, especially the fact that men and women can, while in a state of trance, dance on a bed of hot coals, without being burned. He also places his discussion in a broad comparative framework of spirit possession and religious healing (1989:54–63). A common aspect of many such rituals is the ambivalent nature of the "alien spirit" that temporarily inhabits the possessed person, transforming their personality. The effects may be, as in the Anastenaria, therapeutic, but they may also be the opposite, causing illness or psychological conflict.[24]

Dance as a prelude to violent action, including war, is a ritual activity common to many societies and cultures, from the Great Plains of the USA to the Black Sea. In an extreme and unusual example of the relationship between violence and ritual dancing, the Kululi people of the New Guinea highlands cause serious bodily harm to the male dancers in the Gisaro ceremony by thrusting torches into them as they dance. Kululi society is organized largely around elaborate systems of reciprocity that included prestation and headhunting. The climax of Kululi ceremonial life is the Gisaro, when four or more masked dancers in elaborate costumes sing and dance at the center of a crowd of their fellow villagers, many of whom hold resinous torches. As the singing and dancing progress, the villagers fall into a mood of deep and violent grief, which is carefully orchestrated by the order of the songs. When the tension reaches an unbearable point, men rush into the space of the dance to plunge their burning torches into the dancers' bodies.[25] Others wave axes, stamp, and bang. As Shieffelin observes: "*Gisaro* is a drama of opposition initiated by the dancers but played out by everyone."[26] The drama of the Gisaro is not perceived as antagonistic by the Kululi; it "has more to do with mutual understanding between friends and hostility between

---

[23] The symbolic nature of circling is evinced in many Greek charms, spells, dances, and rituals (see Alexiou 2002b:34). The line dances in which women participate are inevitably danced counterclockwise; the reversing of direction as well as the pinch of earth upset the usual pattern of circling.

[24] Crapanzo 1977:7; Danforth 1989:59–60.

[25] "This painful tension between grief, anger, intimacy, and violence becomes visible when someone from the audience angrily thrusts the torch out on the dancer's shoulder and then throws his arms around him, hugging him affectionately and wailing uncontrollably" (Shieffelen 1976:190).

[26] Shieffelen 1976:196.

enemies"(ibid.:203).[27] The dancers of the Gisaro ceremony "represent" the sorrows of the audience in the songs and dancing, causing a tension that is unbearable unless the audience can retaliate. The smashing of plates at the feet of dancers in Greece may be a much milder expression of this tension. Self-mutilation may be another form of tension-breaking, carried out by the dancers themselves as they reach a point of trance-like absorption in the dance. Self-mutilation was common in *rebétika* circles even in the 1960s; the self-mutilation of the *zeybek* dancers in Myrivilis' novel/memoir may also have the effect of satisfying a tension in the dancers themselves.

The Body's Language

There are many passing references to dance in Greek literature, but few writers deal with it as an important component of a novel or poem. Those who do, like Kazantzakis and Myrivilis, are keen observers who offer as much insight into the nature of Greek dance as any contemporary anthropologist. Their accounts remind us not only of the centrality of dance to Greek life, but of its extraordinary and magical qualities. The dancer is a figure of wonder, who can transfix the village with the sheer beauty of his movements, perform incredible feats, seduce, and provoke.

The dance is the body's metaphorical language, as Kazantzakis reminds us. It is the tongue-tied Zorbas' eloquence. For the language of the dance to be meaningful, it must be spoken in a social milieu that reads its symbolic discourse. Moreover, dance may have the potential to ritualize itself, according to its context, and to speak a new language for political effect. As has been observed, "the means by which ritual signals is symbolic: it performs functions and conceptualizes phenomena not directly related to the perceptual level of experience."[28] Dance is perceived and judged, but what it does, what the individual dancer expresses with his body, may only be expressible as another, verbal metaphor. As my neighbor said to me one night in a Cretan restaurant, when an old man took the lead in a *syrtos*: "The young men were talking to the birds. The old man is talking to the stars."

---

[27] The particular social and ritual situation that surrounds the dancers in the *Gisaro* ceremony, or the *Anastenaria*, might be considered in terms of Bateson's (1955) and Goffman's (1974) concept of the psychological "frame" imposed by humans on social activities. The rules of behavior, in ritual performance, are not the rules of everyday; they have their own set of conventions that are recognized by the community as appropriate to extraordinary activities.

[28] Alexiou 2002b:328. Speaking of flamenco, sociologist Gerhard Steingress notes that "traditional flamenco ritualized Andalusian popular music repeatedly for its nationalist or essentialist use" (Steingress 2000:17–18). Similarly, Greek modernist writer Kostas Tachtsis wrote of the way in which the *zeibékiko* became identified with "the spirit of the resistance" during the harsh period of the German occupation of Athens (Tachtsis 1977). According to Tachtsis, the *zeibékiko*, during this period, functioned as a collective symbol, a ritual that lost its power after the crisis had passed.

Part Five

Technologies of Ritual and Cultural Architectonics

Nineteen

In a Virtual Wild Space: Pilgrimage and *Rite de Passage* from Delphi to Sabarimalai[*]

Ian Rutherford

1. The Sabarimalai Pilgrimage

Every year up to 175,000 young men leave their homes in southwestern and southern India, in the areas of Kerala and Andra Pradesh, and make a long and arduous pilgrimage to the shrine of the young male deity Ayappan at Sabarimalai in the afforested mountains of Kerala. The pilgrimage is possible only during the forty-one or fifty-one days a year during which the shrine is open; and for the most part women are excluded.[1] The Sabarimalai-pilgrimage well illustrates two main social functions associated with pilgrimage by anthropologists and historians of religion. First, it may tend to foster a sense of shared identity among the participants, who are removed from their normal communities for its duration, the process labeled "communitas" by Victor Turner is described in his study of catholic pilgrimage in Mexico.[2] In the case of the pilgrimage to Ayappan, as Younger

---

[*] Earlier versions of this chapter were given as lectures at the University of Birmingham in November 1999; thanks to all who participated on that occasion; and at the conference "Seeing the Gods: Patterns of Pilgrimage in Antiquity," held at the University of Reading in July 2000. The final version was written while I was holding a Tytus Fellowship at the University of Cincinnati in May 2003. Thanks in particular to Christiane Sourvinou-Inwood for discussion. Contiguous themes are covered in three other papers: Rutherford 1995 on myths and pilgrimage; Rutherford 2003 on *theôria* and song, and Rutherford forthcoming-a on the initiatory pilgrimage in Philostratus' *Heroicus*. In this chapter the following abbreviations are used: FGrHist: *Die Fragmente der griechischen Historiker* (Leiden, 1923–); ID: *Inscriptions de Délos*; IG: *Inscriptiones Graecae*; LSCG: F. Sokolowski, *Lois sacrées des cités grecques* (Paris, 1969); SEG: *Supplementum Epigraphicum Graecum*.
[1] For the cult, see Younger 2002; for Greek *theôria* and Hindu pilgrimage, see also Rutherford 2000. For Hindu pilgrimage in general, cf. Eck 1985.
[2] Turner 1973.

Ian Rutherford

observes, the pilgrimage "renews [the participants'] sense of identity as South Indians and provides them with perspective on the narrow focus in which their daily life is normally lived."[3]

Secondly, pilgrimage can provide a framework for a *rite de passage*. This can happen in a very general way, in so far as the culmination of pilgrimage, when the pilgrims are deemed to transcend their normal social status, could be mapped onto the segregation-stage of a classic *rite de passage* (Turner again),[4] and also in the narrower sense in so far as a pilgrimage can function as a maturation ritual. At Sabarimalai, the majority of the pilgrims are "first-timers" (*kaṇṇis*), and in their case the pilgrimage in many ways resembles a maturation ritual: they make the journey accompanied by their families and led by a ritual guide (*periyaswami*), who instructs them in ritual acts required on the journey; they wear a distinctive black outfit and observe a number of ritual requirements relating to diet, sexual abstinence and personal grooming; when they reach the town of Erumeli, which is on the edge of the forest, thirty miles from the sanctuary, they perform a wild dance, and then they enter the forest to make the final stage of the pilgrimage.

A crucial factor in creating the initiatory ethos of the pilgrimage is the character of the deity Ayappan himself. In the cult myth the god was originally the mortal Manikantha, whose divine transformation came about as the result of a hunting expedition in search of tiger's milk. In imitation of the young hunter, the young pilgrims set aside their normal social identity and names during the pilgrimage, and refer to themselves by the communal name "Ayappan," suggesting that they are temporary incarnations of the deity. Another important factor in generating the initiatory ethos of the pilgrimage is the representation of its final stage, the journey through the forest, as fraught with danger:

> . . . the initiates are warned that the forest is full of tigers and wild elephants and reminded that the trip involves the climbing of steep slopes and the swimming of turbulent rivers, so that only those spiritually prepared are likely to live.[5]

Taking my cue from the Sabarimalai-pilgrimage I want in this chapter to investigate the question of what sort of significance "pilgrimage," defined in a very general sense, might have had for young people in ancient Greece, and in particular whether or not a case can be made for seeing it as a framework for "rite de passage."

[3] Younger 2002:17–25.
[4] Turner, above; for *rite de passage*, van Gennep 1960; Calame 2003.
[5] Younger 2002:18.

2. Pilgrimage and Young People in Ancient Greece

The most common form of pilgrimage in Greece was the state-delegation to a sanctuary, "*theôria*," as it is called, and one of the most complete accounts of *theôria* comes from a surprising source, the *Aithiopika*, a late Greek novel by Heliodorus of Emesa in Syria. According to Heliodorus, a *theôria* was regularly sent to Delphi by the Thessalian state of Ainis, a member of the Delphic Amphictiony. There, it performed a procession and a sacrifice in honor of the hero Neoptolemus, the son of Achilles, whose career culminated in a journey to Delphi where he died somehow, either because he confronted Apollo for helping to kill his father, or in a quarrel over the division of sacrificial meat. Heliodorus tells us quite a lot about the composition of the *theôria* as it made its procession towards the Delphic altar: there were fifty ephebes, who rode horses, peasants who drove bulls for sacrifice, and a chorus of *parthenoi*, who sang a hymn to Thetis. On the particular occasion Heliodorus describes, the *theôria* was led by a certain Theagenes, who claimed to be descended from Neoptolemus.

It is striking that the majority of the participants in the ritual were young people. It is perhaps questionable whether or not Heliodorus had direct experience of *theôria*, but he is a good authority at least for how *theôria* is represented in the Greek imagination, which is perhaps just as important. Although Heliodorus is the only source for an Ainianian *theôria* to honor Neoptolemus, there is some confirmation of the general pattern in a much older text, Pindar's Sixth Paean,[6] which seems to imply that young men come from the island of Aegina to worship Neoptolemus on the occasion of the Theoxenia festival at Delphi.[7] Choruses of young men occur in other Delphic *theôriai* as well. Herodotus tells of a Chian *theôria* to Delphi, comprised of one hundred young men, all but two of whom were carried off by the plague. Similarly, the Athenian *theôria* to Delphi known as the Pythais is well documented from the Hellenistic period by inscriptions which show that the participants included numerous young men called Pythaistai, who seem to have taken part in choral singing, and a dedication made on behalf of four Pythaistai from the deme of Ikarion in the early 4th century BCE shows four boys.[8] Young people, both boys and girls, are also a feature of *theôriai* to Delos: the Athenians sent young unmarried men, *êitheoi*, there in the time of Aristotle;[9] the narrative of Akontios and Kudippe, told by

---

[6] Suarez de la Torre 1997 is positive about historicity; see Rutherford forthcoming-a.
[7] Rutherford 2001; 334–335.
[8] IG 2.2.2816; Boethius 1918:27ff. and 148 and Testimonium 12. Cf. also "the daughters of the Argives," mentioned by Kallisthenes of Olynthus ap. Athenaeus *The Deipnosophists* 13.560c.
[9] ID 1 1869; IG 2.3, 3491; IG2.3, 3519.

Ian Rutherford

Callimachus but apparently reproduced from an earlier source, presupposes that choruses of both young men and women from the Cycladic islands of Keos and Naxos visited Delos;[10] *theôriai* from Kos to Delos around 300 BCE may have included a group of young women, the so-called *agretai*.[11] A Hellenistic inscription from Claros records that a young man called Polemaios visited Smyrna as a *theôros*.[12] Inscription on the walls of a shrine of the local deities "Anna and the Paides" at Akrai some distance from Syracuse (1st century BCE/1st century CE) attest pilgrimage there by groups which include children.[13] And in the second century CE the oracle of Claros attracted from a religious network spanning the whole of Asia Minor sacred delegations which included choruses of young people, sometimes boys alone, sometimes boys and girls.[14]

With these we may compare certain other rituals in which the performers are ephebes and the performance involves a round-trip journey, but which would not normally be placed in the same category as *theôria*. In general, De Polignac has tried to argue for the importance in the development of the Greek city-state of sanctuaries located outside the *polis* and associated with kourotrophic deities. These extra-*polis* sanctuaries are frequented by the young men of the city.[15] More specifically, among various journeys that the Athenian ephebes are attested as having made round Attica, at least from the second century BCE, is one to the island of Salamis, where they celebrated the Aianteia in honor of Ajax. This ritual is attested only in the Hellenistic period, but may well have been held right back to the fifth century BCE.[16] Surviving ephebic inscriptions indicate that the ephebes were praised for their stay by the Salaminians in language reminiscent of honorific inscriptions for *theôroi*.[17] We normally think of Salamis as within the territory of the Athenian state,

[10] Keos is known to have sent a group of *paides* to Delos in the early 4th century: IG 12.5.544A240.

[11] Cf. LSCG 156b. Strabo *Geography* 10.5.2 attests visiting choruses of *parthenoi*.

[12] Robert and Robert 1989, *Insc.Clar.* 1, Col.I, lines 28ff. Unlike *theôroi*, who return soon, Polemaios "remained there, associating with the best teachers" (ἐπέμει(νε) δὲ κἀκεῖ συνὼν τοῖς ἀρίστοις παιδευταῖς). The same pattern has been detected over a century earlier in an Athenian inscription (IG II² 886), dating from the reign of Attalus 1, which has been reconstructed to say that a young man from Pergamon who came as a *theôros* to the Panathenaia in Athens stayed on many years there so that he could study philosophy; it mentions an Evander, who was probably the Academic philosopher.

[13] SEG 42 (1992), 825–836, especially 833; Manganaro 1992:458n3.

[14] Lane-Fox 1986. Delegations from Heracleia Salbyke to Claros in the second century CE usually contained a *khoros* of nine boys, as well as a handful of adult officials; those from Tabai more often had seven.

[15] De Polignac 1995.

[16] Parker 1996, 153–154; Taylor 1997:187. The cleruchy on Salamis is already attested in the first century BCE: see IG 1.3.1.

[17] IG 2.2.1006, 22–23; IG 2.2.1011, 53–63.

326

but for ritual purposes Salamis may have been conceived as foreign territory, so this is indeed a form of a long-distance ritual activity conceptually almost indistinguishable from *theôria*.[18]

Indirect evidence for a practice in some respects similar comes from late archaic Crete. Excavation of the sanctuary of Hermes and Aphrodite at Hiera Syme have yielded bronze plaques from the archaic and classical period representing young men in various poses, many of them offering animals.[19] These have been interpreted as dedications made by Cretan ephebes at some point during the long and involved Cretan institutions of male maturation on Crete, which involved a period of communal living in an *agelê* or troop, and in some cases an erotic abduction by an older man leading to a two month period of feasting and hunting in the wilds.[20] In what context the dedications were made remains uncertain, but Angelos Chaniotis has recently suggested that we should imagine an amphictiony (comprising nearby towns such as Lato, Olous, Hierapytna, and Lyktos), in which ephebes from different cities, perhaps arranged in their ephebic troops (*agelai*), made a sort of communal pilgrimage from their towns to the sanctuary, possibly on the occasion of a festival there.[21] Similar patterns may have occurred elsewhere in Crete; for example, there seems to have been another amphictiony based round the sanctuary of Zeus Diktaios in the East of Crete, where the Cretan hymn to the Kouros was performed by representatives from a number of Cretan cities.[22]

3. The Problem: *Theôria* and Rites of Maturation

The question I want to ask is, why were young people involved to such an extent in *theôria*? One part of the answer may be that city-states were concerned to make a good impression at interstate venues, and sending their young people was a good way of doing this.[23] But it is also likely that taking part in interstate *theôria* may have played a part in the ritual articulation of maturation, the *rites de passage* that

---

[18] Salamis as foreign territory: Strabo *Geography* 9.1.11 (priestess of Athene Polias and cheese); it may not be a coincidence that the principal theoric ship in Athens is called the *Salaminia*; for antiquity. Jordan 1975:170 suggested that one of the roles of the sacred *genos* of the *Salaminioi* may have been to man it, and that its original function having been to take Salaminians transplanted to Attica (the *Salaminioi*) back to Salamis for the purpose of taking part in sacred festivals there.

[19] Lempese 1985:188–198.

[20] For the Cretan *ephêbeia*, Strabo 10.4.20 = Ephorus FGrHist 70F149; Willetts 1955:11–13.

[21] Chaniotis 1991; 1996:128–130.

[22] Chaniotis 1991.

[23] Cf. Rutherford 2004.

governed the transition from childhood to adulthood, and it is this issue that I want to explore in this paper.[24]

First of all, we will have to try to get some sense of how we would recognize a maturation ritual. There is no single formula, but rather an open-ended range of typical components.[25] These include:

- a mapping of rite of passage onto space, in such a way as the transition is coded as a period of segregation away from the home-community, in an area remote both spatially and conceptually from civilization, an area referred conventionally to as "wild space." The classic examples from ancient Greece are the *krupteia* in Sparta, the erotic abduction of ephebes in Crete, and the border-patrols of the ephebes in Attica. The complete form of this ritual has three stages, as van Gennep argued: separation from the original community, segregation, and reintegregation;[26]

- the transition may also be coded as a temporary loss of identity, which can be symbolized by change of clothing (e.g. transvestitism, as for example in the Athenian Oschophoria; the black cloaks of the Athenian ephebes),[27] change of name, rituals which rely on the fiction that the initiant has died; rituals in which the participants impersonate someone or something (the Bears at Brauron, for example), and so on.

- key ritual acts, such as (perhaps) dedication of the young man's hair, as Achilles boasts in the *Iliad* that he dedicated his hair to the River Spercheios before leaving for Troy.[28] Certain types of communal song and dance may belong here as well, as in the famous case of Alcman's Partheneion as illuminated by Calame. We would expect these rituals to be conducted in the name of deities who have a specialized function of looking after young people, i.e. the function known as "kourotrophic."[29]

---

[24] This issue seems worth exploring because it has not, as far as I can see, been addressed in any of the standard treatments of *rite de passage*. Brelich 1969 touches on it when he cites Layard 1951 concerning *rite de passage* in the New Hebrides, in which a group of young men sail together from one island, Atchin, to another, Oba, where the *rite de passage* occurs, involving initiation into the mysteries of sex, and one of the things that happens is a pretend conflict between visitors and locals; Brelich begins to address the issue of panhellenic festivals in an appendix 439 ff.

[25] See in general van Gennep 1960; Brelich 1969; Vidal-Naquet 1986. For applications of *rite de passage* framework see the articles in Padilla 1999. The reader is also referred to Dodd and Faraone 2003, a very stimulating collection which came to my attention only after I had completed this essay.

[26] Crete: see above; Athenian ephebes: Pélékidis 1962, Vidal-Naquet 1986.

[27] Black cloaks: Vidal-Naquet 1986.

[28] Homer *Iliad* 23.144–151; Cf. L. Sommer, "Haaropfer," *RE* 14.2105–2109.

[29] Song: Calame 1996:258–263; kourotrophic deities: e.g. De Polignac 1995:63.

On the face of it, these features are not present in the examples of young people escorting *theôriai* listed above. A *theôria* does indeed leave its home community, but not for "wild space"; the participants in the civic ritual do not lose their civic identity; rather, they go out of their way to flaunt it in a very public way. (The only qualification that needs to be made to this statement is that *theôroi* in a panhellenic or regional festival also take on, at least to some extent, a broader identity which transcends the narrower *polis*-identity the representation of which is their main concern); and most *theôriai* include no obvious rituals that seem specially connected with maturation.

The most that can be done here is to put forward a range of possibilities, such as the following:

1. The deities and heroes involved seem to be kourotrophic: in most of the cases given here, the primary deity being visited is Apollo, linked in the case of Delos to Artemis. Apollo is appropriate here in two ways. For one thing, he is the god of music, and most of these young people seem to have made up choruses, who must have performed at the sanctuary. But secondly, one of Apollo's primary roles is that of *kourotrophos*, protector of the *kouroi*. That idea is represented graphically in the dedication by the four *Puthaistai Paides* from the Attic deme of Ikarion.[30] Similarly, the hero Neoptolemus at Delphi, who seems to be the focus of Pindar's Aeginetans and Heliodorus' Ainianes, may be credited with a kourotrophic role, as indeed Ajax of Salamis presumably had a kourotrophic role for the Athenian ephebes.[31]

2. It is at least possible that young people sometimes made dedications of hair at sanctuaries. For Delphi, our evidence is ambiguous: hair-shearing rituals were no longer performed there regularly in historical times, but there was a perception that they had been once, and perhaps in exceptional circumstances still could be.[32] As for Delos, Herodotus (4.33 ff.) tells us that Delian girls consecrated their hair to the Hyperborean maidens, and Calame has taken this as one reason to believe that the Delia, embodied "a great seasonal festival for the propitiation for the growth of children and adolescents."[33] But although he acknowledges that the sending of choruses

---

[30] Above, page 000.

[31] See Suarez de la Torre 1997, especially 173.

[32] Plutarch *Theseus* 5, says that Athenians believed that in the time of Theseus it had been customary to dedicate adolescent hair at Delphi, indicating that it was not the normal custom then, and Theophrastus *Characters* 21, indicates that for a father to perform his son's hair-shearing ritual at Delphi was a sign of "petty ambition."

[33] Cf. also Callimachus *Hymn to Delos* 296–299; Pausanias 1.43.4; Calame 1997:108. Other elements Calame draws attention to are: first, the celebration of the birth of Apollo; second, the cult of honoring Eileithyuia; third, the sense of renewal implied in the offering of the first fruits.

to Delos from surrounding islands implies that the kourotrophic function of the festival involved the whole region,[34] he argues that the role of the Delians is primary, and foreign participation is secondary. But we could equally argue that for visitors to Delian cults had a marked kourotrophic and initiatory significance, particularly since they were in a state of separation from their communities, and it is not impossible that some of these groups made hair-offerings as well.

3. Certainly, a common feature of *theôria* was the performance of song and dance by choral escorts, particularly (but not exclusively) choruses of young people; the content of the songs is, unfortunately, usually unknown.[35] On Delos we know of a special form of dance, the so-called *Geranos* or Crane-Dance, performed around the Keraton altar, apparently on the occasion of the Aphrodisia festival there. This is supposed to have been established by Theseus, and the original performers are supposed to have been the *dis hepta* on their return journey from Crete. The possibility arises that on some occasions when Athenian *theôriai* visited Delos, choruses of young people performed the Crane-Dance. But what evidence there is seems to indicate that Athenian *theôriai* visited on the occasion of the Delia and perhaps other festivals of Apollo, not the Aphrodisia.[36]

4. In the case of Hiera Syme in Crete, if the bronze plaques found there do indeed attest the pilgrimage of delegations of ephebes in the context of an amphictionic network based round surrounding towns, then it is likely that some sort of ritual activities with significance for maturation took place there. One of these will have been the dedication of the bronze plaques themselves, another may have been offerings (and sacrifice, presumably) of animals, perhaps animals captured during the two month period of hunting associated with the Cretan *ephêbeia*. And there may well have been other activities as well, such as dedications of hair and/or choral performance.

That, however, is the most we can say about rituals. Is there anyway forward here?

---

[34] Calame 1997:108–109.
[35] See Rutherford 2004.
[36] See Calame 1997:158–162; the major evidence is Callimachus *Hymn to Delos* which passes directly from the *Geranos* to the Athenian *theôria*. Plutarch *Theseus* 21 says that the Delians danced it.
[37] See Sourvinou-Inwood 1990:297.
[38] Brauron: Brelich 1969:270; Sourvinou-Inwood 1988:21–22; Kahil 1977; Locrian Maidens: Graf 1978.

4. The Delphic Septerion: Rite of Passage or/and *Theôria*

Let us return to the issue of "segregation." The separation from the home-community involved in *theôria* is not complete, because a *theôria* represents its *polis*, and it is not true segregation, because the young men are not wandering in wild space but are the guests of the local sanctuary authorities.[37] Nor is it very long; and here we may contrast the case of the Attic *parthenoi* who (probably) spend a whole year separated from their home communities at Brauron, or the more radical segregation of the Locrian Maidens at Ilion.[38] If one wanted an example of a pilgrimage-type activity involving segregation, one might consider the ritual from Thebes, described by Pausanias (9.17.4–5), in which men from Tithoreia in Phocis, about fifty miles away, make a clandestine journey to the tomb of Amphion and Zethus in order to scrape off earth, while the Thebans tried to prevent them. Another such case of clandestine behavior is the Thessalian *theôria* to the tomb of Achilles in the Troad described in the *Heroicus* of Philostratus, which happens by night and has all sorts of chthonic associations; but unfortunately there is a good chance that this fascinating ritual is to a very large extent fabricated by Philostratus.[39]

A more complex case in which *theôria* and "wild space" seem to come together is to be found in a ritual from Delphi, the mysterious Septerion, and its sequel, which facilitated the fetching of laurel for the Pythian Games from the Vale of Tempe in Thessaly.[40] Every eight years, a hut was built in the precinct at Delphi, and then set fire to by members of the sacred guild of the Labyadai, accompanied by a boy; after this drama, the participants fled, and the boy made his way North to the valley of Tempe in Thessaly, where he purified himself, apparently in the River Peneius. Here is Plutarch's elliptical account (*De defectu oraculorum* [On the decline of oracles] 15, 418a–c):

> For the structure which is erected here near the threshing-floor every eight years is not like a nest-like serpent's den, but a copy of the dwelling of a despot or king. The onset upon it, which is made in silence through the way called "Dolon's Way," by which the Labyadae with lighted torches conduct the boy, who must have two parents living, and, after applying fire to the structure and upsetting the table, flee through the doors of the temple without looking back; and finally the wanderings and servitude of the boy and the purifications that take place at Tempe—all prompt a suspicion of some great and unholy deed of daring.

[39] See Rutherford forthcoming-a. A classical example of a dangerous pilgrimage from a different culture is the peyote-pilgrimage of the Huichol Indians, discussed by Meyerhoff 1976.

[40] Septerion: see Burkert 1983:127–130; Rutherford 2001:200–205.

Ian Rutherford

The boy could be seen as a sort of scapegoat, taking the blame for the burning of the hut.[41] His journey north is represented as traumatic, characterized by flight, wanderings, and servitude. Ancient authorities seem to be of the opinion that the boy represented the young Apollo at the point when he killed the Delphic Dragon, so that the myth reenacts the violent origins of Apolline rule at Delphi, and the first occasion when Apollo purified someone of blood-guilt, an occasion when the party purified was none other than himself.

Recent scholars who have worked on the Septerion have tended to stress the first account and have seen it as a canonical *rite de passage* articulating in ritual terms the transition from boy to adult male, with the standard stages of separation, segregation in "wild-space," and reintegration; on one level, the boy kills a symbolic foe, then is purified after a long journey, and reintegrated into the community as an adult; on another level, as Brelich argues in his fundamental work *Paides e Parthenoi*, the journey to Tempe, and the period spent there, resembles a rite of segregation in "wild-space," analogous to the more famous *krupteia*-ritual in Sparta, and these associations are reinforced by the chthonic associations of the Peneius river, which may reflect the liminal status of the initiant.[42] It should also be noticed that because only one boy goes through the ritual, while it is the city as a whole which organizes the ritual, the boy's initiation is symbolic, and represents the initiation of all boys of his age.

A view of the journey to and from Tempe which is, prima facie, at odds with the above is provided by the historian Theopompus,[43] who represents it as a much more elaborate ritual, in fact a *theôria*, but in the reverse direction we would expect a *theôria* to move, away from Delphi and then back again.[44]

Here [in Tempe], as the people of Thessaly report, Pythian Apollo purified himself on the orders of Zeus, when he had slaughtered the snake

---

[41] For the scapegoat interpretation, Fontenrose 1959: 453–61.
[42] Brelich 1969:426; "hiketes, obbligato al digiuno, presso un fiume collegato agli inferi, il pais delfico rappresenta le condicioni dell' iniziando allntanato della propria communità e precipitato in uno stato di crisi nell' angoscioso ambiente del non-abitato." For the chthonic associations of the river, cf. also Pindar, Paean 10, with Rutherford 2001:202. Claude Calame also points to a similar laurel-carrying ritual from Thebes, the Daphnephoria, in which one of the main participants is again a child. There may even have been a direct connection, if the procession from Delphi actually passed through Thebes. Perhaps the Theban Daphnephoria imitates the Delphic rite. In the Theban Daphnephoria, a procession is led by a young man, a laural-bearer or *daphnêphoros*, and a group of girls walks behind, singing hymns to Apollo to supplicate the god, presumably to protect the young man. So the Theban Daphnephoria was kourotrophic, and if it was, the argument goes, then Septerion was also.
[43] FGrHist 115H80, cited by Aelian (*Varia Historia* 3.1).
[44] On *theôria* in general, Rutherford 2002.

Pytho that still guarded Delphi, the oracle still being in the control of
Earth. He made himself a crown from the laurel of Tempe, and, carrying
a branch [from the same laurel] in his right hand he went to Delphi to
take over the oracle as the son of Zeus and Leto. There is an altar at the
very spot, where he put on the crown and removed the branch. Even now,
every eight years the Delphians send here the children of noble families
accompanied by someone to head the *theôria (arkhitheôrôn hena)*. They
arrive, make a lavish sacrifice in Tempe, and return with crowns woven
from the same laurel from which the god took branches for his crown on
the earlier occasion. They take the route known as the Pythian, which
carries them through Thessaly, Pelasgia, Oeta, and the territory of the
Aenianes, the Melians, the Dorians, and the Western Locrians.

So here there is no flight or wanderings. The journey to and from Tempe takes
the form of a sacred delegation, a highly organized *theôria*, composed of not one but
many Delphic children, from noble families, and a leader.[45] Having reached its destination, the *theôria* does what *theôriai* normally did: it carries out a major sacrifice on
behalf of the city that sent it. Theopompus does not say that one or all of the
Delphian *paides* purified themselves in the river, although he comes close to
implying it when he says that their model, Apollo, did so. Notice also that there is a
hint that the return journey is more elaborate than the journey out, because it is on
the return that the pilgrims carry the all important laurel crowns, and on the return
that they follow the "Pythian" route, which takes them though several member states
of the Delphic Amphictiony, moving from North to South;[46] it seems to me that this
emphasis on the return allows us scope to speculate that on the journey out the
performance of Theopompus' *theôria* was somewhat less formal, and perhaps shared
some features in common with the "wandering" in Plutarch's account. Nevertheless,
the differences between the accounts are striking: on the one hand, an isolated
wandering, on the other hand a well-staffed and very public *theôria*. It is enough to
make you suspect either that Theopompus is not referring to the same ritual as
Plutarch,[47] or that the form of the ritual may have changed considerably in the
interval between the time of composition of the two texts.

<hr/>

[45] Plutarch *De musica* 14, 1136a, speaks of an *aulêtes* acccompanying the *pais* on the journey back,
which would suit the model of a *theôria* also. Plutarch, *De defectu oraculorum* 418a says that "the city
[of Delphi] has marched as far as Tempe, initiating all Greeks beyond Thermopylae," which seems
to imply agency on the part of the *polis*: see further Burkert 1984:129.
[46] Except that the Western Locrians seem out of place.
[47] So Mommsen 1873:296 ff.

But I think the apparent discrepancy between the two texts admits of other solutions. One approach would be to think of the procession to Tempe as a ritual-complex with at least two components: first, that of the boy or boys undergoing the *rite de passage* and second a civic frame, represented by the *arkhitheôros*, which has the function of supervising and protecting.[48] That is at most a partial solution, because the activities of the boy(s) would still be relatively limited within the confines of an official *theôria*. Alternatively—and this is perhaps the solution to be preferred—two accounts may be interpreted as different ways of representing the ritual-complex. The account of Theopompus perhaps comes closest to reflecting the outline of the ritual as it happened, whereas Plutarch is talking about its symbolic and mythical significance: the reenactment of the Apollo's atonement for the murder of Python. And both solutions could, perhaps, be true at the same time. So here, then, we have a partial solution to the apparent absence of elements sugges-tive of *rite de passage* in *theôria*: the same ritual might be a *theôria* on an institutional level, but to some extent imagined as a journey through wild space, in which the participants take on the identities of their mythological forebears.

5. Myth and Cultic Mimesis.

The foregoing prompts me to ask more generally whether, even if the *theôria* or the rituals accompanying the *theôria* do not themselves involve obviously initiatory elements, there may be an accompanying myth which does.

Let us begin with Delphi, and specifically with *theôria* focused on the cult of Neoptolemus at Delphi. Whichever version of the myth of Neoptolemus' death we take, the lesson is essentially the same: pilgrimage to Delphi is dangerous; young men (similar in age to Neoptolemus) must approach Apollo with reverence, and not quarrel about the division of the sacrifice. For young men, pilgrimage to Delphi resembles a rite of passage precisely because they must take care to avoid the fate of Neoptolemus.[49]

In the Athenian *theôria* to Delphi, and important role is played by Theseus. Plutarch says that Theseus went to Delphi and dedicated his hair there, for which reason an area at Delphi called the Theseia was named after him. In the opening of the *Eumenides* Aeschylus describes the Athenians who conveyed the young

---

[48] For civic frame, see Rutherford forthcoming-b.

[49] For Neoptolemus, Rutherford 2001:313. Myerhoff 1976, reports that among the Huichol Indians pilgrimage to Wirikuta is perceived as particularly dangerous for young people ("primeros") attempting it for the first time.

Apollo to Delphi as "road-makers" (*keleuthopoioi*), and according to accompanying scholion:[50]

> Theseus cleared the road of robbers. And when [the Athenians] send a *theôria* to Delphi, some people walk in front holding axes, as if they are intending to pacify the land

What is being referred to is clearly the land route through Boeotia, and Theseus' well-known achievements eliminating local highwaymen on his journey to Athens (achievements actually represented on the pediments of the Athenian Treasury at Delphi)[51] are here related to free access to Delphi. Although some Athenian *theôriai* to Delphi went by sea, the land route seems to have been preferred, at least for the highly traditional Pythais,[52] and we have to infer that the leaders of these processions, perhaps the Pythaistai themselves, carried axes. The axes are a mythological throwback, creating the illusion that a present-day *theôria* is every bit as dangerous as the journey to Delphi was in the heroic age. Thus, an Athenian *theôria* connects with Theseus the ephebe in two ways: both because Theseus cleared the roads of robbers and dedicated his hair at Delphi, and for Athenian ephebes the young Theseus is, of course, the ultimate model.[53]

Theseus is also a model for the Athenian *theôria* to Delos, at least the one[54] which is etiologically connected with the myth of Theseus' Cretan voyage and the *dis hepta*, being a ritual obligation that was supposedly imposed by the vow that Theseus made before the expedition, and, to make the connection as vivid as it could possibly be, it was generally supposed that the sacred ship used in the Athenian *theôriai* was precisely the same one used by Theseus and the *dis hepta*.[55] Whether or not it is legitimate to see the Cretan episode as an initiatory myth is a matter of some debate at the moment. In favor of it are the following points:

[50] Aeschylus *Eumenides* 12 and Σ, cited by Boethius 1919:154; Smith 1993:1.43, 18–20 (reading θεωρίαν rather than θεωρίδα) Boethius 1919:31–33, suggests that the axes might originally have been a symbol of Apollo and carried as a first-fruit offering, and only later reinterpreted as a symbol of clearing the road. On the axes, also Parsons 1943:236.

[51] See Hoffelner 1988.

[52] Aristophanes *Birds* 189.

[53] Calame 1996:432 ff.; Ieranò 1987; Walker 1995:83–111. Axes occur in the iconography of Apollo Kareios in Phrygia: see Ceylan and Ritti 1997.

[54] The issue of Athenian *theôriai* to Delos is much vexed. Calame 1996:160, thinks it coincided with the Delia and took place in Hieros, in the spring. Calame does not believe that the Delian Aphrodisia (Theseus' foundation of the Crane Dance) in Hekatombaion coincided with an Athenian *theôria* to Delos, though Bruneau 1970:13 and Mineur 1984:238, disagree. Robertson 1992:128–131, argues that the *theôria* associated with Theseus took place in Mounikhion and Puanopsion, and he distinguishes this from another in Thargelion (Hieros, he believes, was no time for *theôria*).

[55] Callimachus *Hymn* 4, 314–315; Plato *Phaedo* 58b; Calame 1996:159–160.

1. Theseus' Cretan expedition is the etiological backdrop for two Athenian rituals that have been related to maturation: the Oschophoria in Pyanopsion, which supposedly originated upon the return of Theseus,[56] and in the preceding month of Mounikhion the the propitiation by Athenian girls in the Athenian Delphinion,[57] as well as the Delian Crane-Dance around the Keraton altar on the occasion of the Aphrodisia festival there;[58]

2. The Cretan narrative also includes a number of episodes suggestive of *rite de passage*, above all the celebrated voyage of Theseus, the theme of Bacchylides' Seventeenth Dithyramb;[59]

3. The primary theme of the narrative is the salvation of boys and girls;

4. Theseus has ephebic associatons in Athens (see above).

On the basis of this, it would seem a short step to seeing the whole myth of the Cretan expedition as concerned with the themes of initiation and maturation (as indeed was argued by Jeanmaire, Brelich, and others),[60] and in turn to seeing the Delian *theôria* as reflecting this ethos, reviving on a symbolic level the dangers that the *dis hepta* faced in Minion times. In his book on Theseus Claude Calame expresses doubt about this interpretation of the myth, pointing out that many details of the story do not fit this hypothesis, and in particular that Theseus is not himself an ephebe at the time of the events.[61] Calame is right to insist that we apply the highest standards of logical rigor to our analysis of the myth, but I suspect that he is being a little too cautious here. Theseus would tend to retain his initiatory associations, even though from the point of view of narrative diachrony he has achieved adult status by this point in the story.

---

[56] Oschophoria: Robertson 1992:121–124. This connection is all the more striking in so far as the Oschophoria was organized by the *Salaminioi*, and the *Salaminioi* would be expected to have had a role in organising Athenian *theôriai*, in view of the fact that the name of the main Athenian *theôris* was Salaminia. For the role of the Salaminioi, see Jordan 1975:170, cited above.

[57] Plutarch *Theseus* 18; Deubner 1932:201; Graf 1979:17–18.

[58] Calame 1997:81; Calame 1996:158–159; Callimachus *Hymn to Delos* 304 ff. With this ritual Calame associates the myth of Theseus, who is supposed to have founded the Crane-Dance on Delos "there is little doubt that the Theseus myth . . . gave the festival an initiatory value." Theseus, however, may be more associated with the Aphrodisia festival, where the Crane-Dance was performed.

[59] Jeanmaire 1939; Brelich 1969:444 ff. and 472, form the important point that the Cretan adventure articulates a "'tematica' a sfondo iniziatico"; Calame 1996:461n77 for bibliography.

[60] Cf. Roberston 1992:131–133.

[61] Calame 1996:432–435, with useful bibliographical note on 461–462 n78.

From the myth we move to the *theôria*. There is a chance, as I suggested earlier on, that young people accompanying Athenian *theôriai* performed ritual acts suggestive of initiation at Delos (the Crane-Dance, dedication of hair). But even if they did not, a major contribution may have been made by myth, which provides a symbolic context and sets an expectation. Thus, even if we cannot say that young men engaging in *theôria* in fact experience the "wild space" characteristic of rites of passage, nevertheless we could say that the accompanying myths create an imaginary or virtual wild space, which serves a similar purpose. This suggestion incidentally helps with the problem drawn attention to in section 3 about the incompatibility of *rite de passage* and the expression of identity function. We can now see that we can have both at the same time: on the level of ritual institution, the participants in the *theôria* express their civic identity as representatives of their city-state, but on the level of imagination and symbolism, they take on the identity of the heroes of the mythological past, and play out a drama which enacts a rite of passage, a crisis to be overcome, and a return and reaggregation into the city.

It is in the area of representation rather than of ritual that the Sabarimalai pilgrimage provides a parallel for the Greek *theôria*. Just as the boys in the Septerion represent the young Apollo, and young Athenians embarking on the *theôria* to Delos take on the role of the *Dis Hepta*, so Keralan pilgrims identify themselves with the young hunter deity. And just as the Greek cases I have discussed, the hazards-to-be-overcome which we expect in an initiation-ritual existed primarily on the level of mythology, so the Keralans imagine the final stage of the pilgrimage to be a dangerous trial. Thus the modern Indic pilgrimage illuminates the ancient Greek.

Twenty

Ritual Dreams and Historical Orders:
Incubation between Paganism and Christianity*

Charles Stewart

The practice of "incubation," which involves a person sleeping at a temple or church in order to have dreams of a god or a saint, has been documented in the eastern Mediterranean at every historical stage from classical antiquity to the present.[1] That the Turkish Director of Religious Affairs should recently have sent a directive to be posted at all saints' tombs in the country instructing that no one be permitted to sleep at these shrines indicates that the practice continues among Muslims in the region.[2] In Greece many Orthodox Christian saints' day pilgrimages entail sleeping overnight at churches, thereby creating a situation where incubation dreams may always occur. Outside of ritual contexts, and beyond church precincts, dreams of saints are entirely common throughout Greece. I have collected numerous cases from the island of Naxos where saints appear to people in dreams and heal them, or tell them where to find buried icons or treasures.[3]

Alongside ritual funeral lamentation, incubation presents one of the clearest examples of a cultural continuity from ancient to modern Greece. Our understanding of such continuities has been expanded by comprehensive studies that pay careful attention to Byzantine and modern variations of the ancient tradition.[4] The majority of continuity studies, however, demonstrate little interest in the changes and transformations that inevitably accompany continuity. A symptom of this is the rapidity with which they pass over the early Christian period.

Below I shall focus my attention entirely on the transition from pagan to Christian proprietorship of the practice of incubation in order to consider more

* *Acknowledgements.* I am grateful to David Brakke, Adam Kamesar, Sarah Morris, Simon Price, Claudia Rapp, Emma Scioli, and Jeremy Tanner for generously contributing comments and references that enriched this essay.
1 Deubner 1900; Hamilton 1906.
2 David Shankland, personal communication.
3 Stewart 1997; 2001.
4 See especially Alexiou 2002a.

closely the challenges which conversion posed to the continuity of incubation. Neither the early Christians nor the pagans thought of their incubation practices as continuous with one another. Christian rejections of continuity, and the alterations to incubation practice that they directed, remind us that Hellenic cultural practices carried over into later historical periods haphazardly, often only after undergoing modification. No transcendental *Volksgeist* guarded the rite of incubation to ensure its intact transmission. On the contrary, the practice of cultivating dreams was re-crafted by the Christians precisely in order to engineer changes in the religious imagination. Beneath the superficial continuity of incubation in late antiquity—and the practice of soliciting therapeutic dreams from holy figures by sleeping at their shrines did continue—there raged a struggle for possession of the "sign."[5] That sign was a ritual of healing that acted upon the unconscious in order to produce powerful effects upon popular consciousness.

As Aline Rousselle has contended, and as will be seen in examples below, healing was a metaphor for conversion.[6] Healing rituals such as those formulated by Zulu Zionist Christians in South Africa, or by the Native American Church in the U.S.A., often come to the fore precisely during moments of cultural change. Such rituals offer a means of making sense in the face of changing circumstances; they articulate assured identities at moments when traditional assumptions have become destabilized.[7] Although the practice of incubation continued over the *longue durée*, this did not happen because it occupied a remote corner of social life insulated from the effect of events. Incubation was, rather, in a front line position in the mediation of social change. In this respect it differed from ritual lamentation, which Christianity absorbed less problematically.[8] Late antiquity represented a period of conjuncture during which the meaning of ritual incubation underwent transformations while still retaining structural continuity with its past.[9]

Dreaming for cures was a prophetic enterprise and the intention to pronounce on temporal issues—the way things have been, are now, and will be—lent such dreams a synoptic, historicizing form. The people dreaming, or those writing on their behalf, often constructed scenarios, unconsciously and consciously, in which their religion would be maintained in the future. According to Patricia Cox Miller, dreams in late antiquity "formed a distinctive pattern of imagination which brought

[5] Comaroff 1985:196ff.
[6] Rousselle 1990.
[7] Kiernan 1994; Csordas 1999; Chirassi Colombo 1975:97.
[8] Alexiou 2002a:33.
[9] Marshall Sahlins has adapted the idea of the "conjuncture" from Braudel to capture the way in which Hawaiian rituals both continued and underwent transformation in the wake of Cook's visit (Sahlins 1985:xiv, 152).

visual presence and tangibility to such abstract concepts as time, cosmic history, the soul, and the identity of one's self. Dreams were tropes that allowed the world . . . to be represented."[10]

Consider, for example, the dream vision described by the Alexandrian poet Palladas after the destruction of the Sarapeion in 391 CE:

> I was amazed to see Zeus' bronze son [Herakles] who was once called upon in prayers but now cast aside. I said: "Averter of evils, offspring of three moons, you were never defeated but are today prostrate." But the god stood by me in the night and said: "Even though a god, I have learned to serve the times."[11]

Below I will consider similar dreams that formulated historical orderings, and influenced the social understanding of these orders, much as standard historiography does. Particular images in the dreams, such as statues, served as "chronotropes"—images that enabled thinking about historical periodization. This study thus amplifies Leach's observation that rituals modulate the social perception of time by suggesting that rituals may also influence, and even induce, social perceptions of history.[12]

The Last Pagan Dream?

I begin by considering a dream from the waning days of pagan Hellenism. The year is 484 CE. The Goths had already destroyed numerous Greek temples during their invasion in 396. Meanwhile Theodosius II's decree (435 CE) that any still intact pagan temples should be destroyed and purified by the erection of a cross was slowly converting any remaining structures to Christian churches.[13] Proclus, the Head of the Academy of Athens, Plato's *diadokhos* (successor), was 72 years old. He would die in the following year, having devoted his life to resisting Christianity, and to serving the goddess Athena. From the moment of his arrival in Athens Proclus had lived near Athena's shrine at the Parthenon. According to his disciple Marinus:

> The goddess herself acknowledged his devotion just after her statue—the one earlier erected in the Parthenon—was removed by those who even move immovables (καὶ ἀκίνητα κινούντων). The philosopher had a dream in which an attractive (εὐσχήμων) lady appeared to him and told

---

[10] Miller 1994:3.
[11] *Greek Anthology* 9.41, trans. Trombley 2000:35.
[12] Leach 1961. On ritual and history, see Lambek 1998.
[13] Frantz 1965:187.

him that he should prepare his house quickly. "Because the Mistress of Athens (κυρία 'Αθηναΐς)," she said, "wishes to live with you."[14]

No more is said about this event. Marinus moves on immediately to another dream in which Asclepius heals Proclus, and which I shall consider below.

The disappearance of the statue of Athena from the Parthenon spelled the end of ancient Greek religion on the Acropolis, but the statue promptly resurfaced in the dream of the last great pagan philosopher. Paganism thus did not definitively disappear; rather, it went into symbolic suspension pending definitive interpretation. Ancient Greek religion was interrupted, but the possibility remained that it might resume, much as contemporary Greek folk traditions hold that the liturgy being sung in Hagia Sophia when the Ottomans overran Constantinople will one day be completed. Similarly, after the Christians defiled the sacra of the Serapeion of Alexandria by exposing them to public view, the stalwart Olympius rallied his dejected fellow pagans. He assured them that the statues themselves were just material objects destined to vanish, but that the powers that had infused them had flown to heaven where they still existed.[15]

This example begins to reveal how dreams of gods can offer an historicizing representation of events. Proclus' dream reacted to the removal of the chryselephantine statue of Athena during the Christianization of Athens. The removal or destruction of the cult statues of an ancient city marked the end of a civic order. A civic statue of Athena known as the Palladium, for example, protected Troy until its removal by Odysseus permitted the sack of the city. Statues of the domestic gods could play a similar foundational role. After the fall of Troy, Aeneas transferred figurines of the hearth gods, the *Penates*, to Rome as part of the process of establishing a new order.[16] During Alexander's siege of Tyre some people in the city experienced panic dreams that their god Apollo would betray them and go over to Alexander's side. To prevent this they strapped down the civic statue of Apollo with ropes and nailed the sculpture to its pedestal so that the god could not desert them.[17]

The removal of cult statues was like lowering the flag. Images of statues of Marx and Lenin being removed from central squares in eastern Europe, or the destruction of the enormous stone Buddhas of Bamiyan (Afghanistan) in 2001, provide more contemporary illustrations of the linkage between monumental

[14] Marinus *Life of Proclus* 30, Masullo 1985; Trombley 2000:34ff.
[15] Sozomen *Ecclesiastical History* 7.15, MPG, vol. 67, col. 1455.
[16] Virgil *Aeneid* 3.12 (Penates), 2.166 (Palladium). See Faraone 1992:4, 7.
[17] Plutarch *Life of Alexander* 24.3. See also Diodorus Siculus 17.41.8; cf. Herodotus 8.64 where images of the gods are brought to the encampment at Salamis to protect the Greek forces.

sculpture and political change. The demolition and erection of statues after a change in political or religious regimes reflect new views of history governed by emerging "chronologies of desire."[18]

Once the statues of the ancient gods were removed there were unlikely to be very many more incubation dreams involving the ancient gods. Alterations to the architectural and artistic environment affected interior imagination. The Parthenon, for example, would eventually become a church of the Virgin Mary. Granted this changing context, Proclus' dream was potentially the dream to end all pagan dreams.

In picturing the transfer of Athena's image from a public to a personal space, Proclus' dream represented a reversal of the process of religious development as conceptualized by Fustel de Coulanges. In Fustel's view, ancient religion began as a domestic religion of the hearth and then expanded until it encompassed the entire sphere of the polis. In this example religion proceeds in the opposite direction.[19] From a psychoanalytical perspective, Proclus' dream would be classed as a dream of mourning. Freud applied mourning to the loss of one's country, or the loss of an ideal, as well as to the loss of a beloved person.[20] The signal feature of mourning, in his view, was the attempt by the ego to incorporate the lost figure. In taking the statue of Athena into his private sphere Proclus was engaging in the most characteristic mourning practice, which involved, in the words of Melanie Klein: "the individual's setting up [of] the lost loved object inside himself."[21] In difficult cases of mourning, according to the psychoanalysts Abraham and Torok, individuals transferred painful realities into inner psychic enclaves, or "crypts," where they were both entombed and encoded within the self.[22] Christianity had begun as a crypto-religion and now paganism entered its own crypt in the minds of those unwilling to relinquish it.

The Limits of Incubation

It could be objected that the dream of Proclus was not an incubation dream because it occurred in his own home, but I don't think it necessary to be so strict in our appreciation of incubation. Incubation literally means sleeping in/at a shrine with the intention of cultivating a dream, but a number of intermediate possibilities such as dreaming of a god/saint while traveling as a pilgrim to or from the shrine need

[18] Nixon (unpublished ms).
[19] Fustel de Coulanges n.d:132.
[20] Freud 1991:252.
[21] Klein 1975:362.

to be considered as part of the same concept. The magical papyri and theurgical texts circulating in the Roman Imperial period provided instructions on how to cultivate dreams at home, even how to fashion personal devotional statues of Hecate from rue.[23] It may, therefore, be inaccurate to draw too sharp a distinction between a house and a temple.

Proclus had devoted his entire life to serving the pagan gods. As a child the patron goddess of Byzantium[24] appeared to him in a dream and exhorted him to study philosophy, and when he became dissatisfied with his studies in Egypt he remembered this advice and moved to Athens, "in order that the succession from Plato might be preserved without adulteration."[25] At Athens he lived near the foot of the Acropolis, close to the Parthenon. He followed strict neoplatonic precepts, abstaining from eating living things, and performing sacrifices regularly. This exemplary level of devotion meant that dreams of gods might easily occur to him almost anytime, inside or outside of temples. In any case, Proclus did have healing dreams of the classic incubation variety.

Proclus' dream of Athena, considered above, followed another story relating how he had prayed at Asclepius' temple on behalf of a sick girl, Asclepigeneia, who immediately recovered her health. The temple of Asclepius, located at the southern foot of the Acropolis, was even closer to Proclus' home than the Parthenon. This healing event occurred slightly earlier than the dream of Athena and Marinus makes the contrastive remark that "at that time the whole city was fortunate in having the shrine of the Saviour [Asclepius] still unvandalized (ἀπόρθητον)."[26] In other words, divine care could be expected when temples still housed their statues, and particularly if one had a temple nearby (γείτονα).[27] Another time Proclus suffered a sudden paralysis that his "neighbor," Asclepius, cured. According to Marinus, "In a state between sleeping and waking he saw a snake entwining around his head. Then the paralysis began to disappear starting from his head downwards."[28] On yet another occasion he was cured of arthritis of the foot when a sparrow[29] flew down and snatched away his bandage. Subsequently when he dreamt that "someone from

[22] Abraham and Torok 1994:135; Gross 1992:36.
[23] Eitrem 1991:179.
[24] Festugière identifies her as Athena (Festugière 1966:1584).
[25] *Life of Proclus* 6, 9 (trans. Edwards 2000).
[26] *Life of Proclus* 29. See also Frantz 1965:195.
[27] In a contemporary dream narrative that I collected on Naxos the Virgin Mary appeared to a woman and proclaimed that she was her "neighbor" (γειτόνισσα), meaning that she was the manifestation of the Virgin Mary from the main icon of the neighborhood chapel. See Stewart 1997:884. For similar ideas about neighboring heroes in classical antiquity, see Rusten 1983; Brillante 1991:95.
[28] *Life of Proclus* 30.
[29] Sparrows could be sacred to Asclepius. See Aelian *Varia Historia* 5.17 collected in E. and L. Edelstein 1998:vol. 1, 378.

Epidaurus" kissed his knees he knew that he would not be further troubled by arthritis, which was congenital in his family.[30]

At the height of the Roman Empire there were hundreds of temples of Asclepius scattered throughout the Greco-Roman world. Asclepius was a compassionate healer of the sick, a miracle worker, child of a divine father and a mortal mother. Like Christ, he was often called simply *Sôtêr*—Savior. Even the early iconography of Christ seemed to draw on representations of Asclepius.[31]

Neoplatonists like Proclus and his predecessors incorporated Asclepius into their theology as a transcendental deity located in the sun, holding the cosmos in balance.[32] These Platonic formulations had the effect of creating an abstract, celestial conception of the god which converged on conceptions of God that developed within Christian theology (also under the influence of Platonism). In his *Sacred Tales* (second century CE) the rhetorician Aelius Aristides dreamt that he was walking late at night with a Platonist friend who directed Aristides, who was skeptical about Platonism, to look at the night sky, perhaps at the dawn star. He instructed, "This, as far as you are concerned, is what Plato calls the soul of the Universe." Aristides gazed up and claimed to see "Asclepius of Pergamum established in heaven."[33]

For the most part Aristides' *Sacred Tales* chronicled his illnesses, sufferings, and the therapies recommended by Asclepius in dreams. This pagan text thus arrived at a correlation between physical suffering and divine redemption very similar to the rising Christian genre of martyrs' stories.[34] There was only one major difference between Christ and Asclepius. Christ could raise the dead, but Asclepius could not. According to legend, he accomplished this feat once but it so outraged Zeus that he slew Asclepius and his resurrected patient with a thunderbolt.[35]

Despite this minor inadequacy the cult of Asclepius still represented one of the greatest challenges to the spread of Christianity, and Asclepius was one of the last pagan gods to lose currency.[36] The Christians attacked the institution of incubation head on. Tatian, a contemporary of Aristides, declared incubation cures to be cynical public relations exercises carried out by demons. These demons first made people ill and then disclosed their identities through dreams in order to receive praise before departing and terminating the illness.[37] A couple of generations

---

[30] *Life of Proclus* 31.
[31] For a comparison of Asclepius and Christ in iconography see Mathews 1999:69ff.
[32] E. and L. Edelstein 1998:vol. 2, 107.
[33] Aelius Aristides *The Sacred Tales* 4.56 (trans. Behr 1968:266).
[34] Behr 1968:46; Perkins 1995:189.
[35] Pindar *Pythian* 3.56ff.
[36] E. and L. Edelstein 1998:vol. 2, 257.
[37] Tatian *Oratio ad Graecos* 18. (Whittaker 1982).

later Tertullian also attributed incubation to demonic manipulation, adding the radical assertion that no one really dreamt at incubation shrines. It was, all, he said, just a demonic ploy to mislead people who were, by the way, just as vulnerable at home in their bedrooms as they were at incubation shrines.[38] These objections did not, of course, stop incubation practice at the grassroots level but it is worth bearing in mind that the early Christians would have liked to do just that. Ultimately they grudgingly contented themselves with modifying the external architecture and the theological underpinnings of incubation.

Dreams and Materiality

In the Introduction to his impressive study of local religious cults between Christianity and Islam, F.W. Hasluck speculated that there would probably have been more continuity from paganism to early Christianity than from Christian Byzantium into the Islamic Ottoman period.[39] He plausibly contended that beliefs are more likely to be maintained in circumstances when a population remains largely the same and converts, as opposed to situations where invaders espousing a new/different religion populate an area. Hasluck further advocated a distinction between "material" as opposed to "spiritual" continuity. Was a later religion just using the buildings of the former religion, or was it also appropriating spiritual ideas?[40] In the case of incubation, however, such a distinction may be misleading. The material and the spiritual dimensions were not independent, but integrally related to one another.

As we have seen in the case of Proclus, the removal of the cult statues of ancient deities directly affected the imaginary world of dreamers. Gods often appeared in dreams as statues of themselves. Aristides, for example, frequently dreamt of the various gods as statues (Asclepius, Zeus, Athena) and in other dreams he found it significant to report that he saw himself standing beside statues of the gods even though these were just background props.[41] In one dream a statue apparently crossed the divide between inanimate and animate right before his eyes: "Next we worshippers stood by it [a statue of Asclepius] just as when the paean is sung, I almost among the first. At this point, the God, now in the posture in which he is represented in statues, signaled our departure . . . [a]nd the God, with his hand, indicated for me to stay. And I was delighted by the honor and the extent to which I was preferred to the others, and I shouted out, 'The One,' meaning the God. But

---

[38] Tertullian *De Anima* 46, (Waszink 1947).
[39] Hasluck 1929:4.
[40] Hasluck 1929:5.

he said, 'It is you.'[42] Aristides' close relation to Asclepius—some would say his own megalomania—gave rise to another dream in which he saw a statue of himself morph into a statue of Asclepius. He considered this dream "very honorable."[43]

As Artemidorus wrote: "It makes no difference whether we see the goddess herself as we have imagined her to be or a statue of her. For whether the gods appear in the flesh or as statues fashioned out of some material, they have the same meaning." Except for the fact, he goes on to add, that "when the gods have been seen in person, it signifies that the good and bad fulfillments will take place more quickly than they would have if statues of them had been seen."[44] Brillante has contended that as dreams were themselves images, the gods appearing in them ultimately also became images—representations of gods, but not the actual gods. Whether the gods appeared as statues or directly in dreams was thus a moot point since either way they would be flattened into images.[45] The latter part of the passage from Artemidorus suggests, on the contrary, that the ancients made a subtle distinction here.

In any case, the important question of whether a god had really appeared or not, did not depend on whether the god appeared unmediated by symbolic representations (images) such as statues or dreams. *Epiphaneiai*, "divine manifestations," could occur in mental states, or via images, that we would today variously classify as phantoms, illusions, hallucinations, or dreams.[46] Artemidorus considered that some gods such as Pan and Ephialtes (nightmare) mainly manifested as emotional states in dreams, such as excitement, fear, or panic. They did not assume visual (or cognizable) form as did the majority of gods. Asclepius exceptionally bridged both possibilities. He could manifest himself to the senses and to the intellect.[47]

Artemidorus' opinion that dreams of statues fashioned from precious materials such as gold, silver, or amber were more auspicious than dreams of terra cotta, plaster, or wax statues returns our attention to the conditioning effects that the aesthetic environment exerted upon dreams.[48] Statues and effigies of Asclepius were fashioned in all these media but the principal public statue at Epidaurus, as at many other major temples, was of ivory and gold and thus very good to dream. According to Pausanias, the god was depicted "seated on a throne, grasping a staff, while holding the other hand over the head of a serpent; and a dog, lying by his side, is

---

[41] *Sacred Tales* 2.41, 3.47, 4.46f., 1.11.

[42] *Sacred Tales* 4.50.

[43] *Sacred Tales* 1.17; see also 4.49.

[44] Artemidorus *Oneirocritica* (The Interpretation of Dreams) 2.35, (see also 1.5, 2.44), (trans. White 1975). See also Scholia Pindar *Pythian* 3.137b cited in van Straten 1976:15; Gordon 1996.

[45] Brillante 1991:97.

[46] Versnel 1987:48; Pfister 1924:281.

[47] Artemidorus *Oneirocritica* 2.34.

[48] Artemidorus *Oneirocritica* 2.39.

also represented."[49] Pilgrims would encounter this statue as they entered the shrine, perhaps some would stop to meditate upon it at length, and its iconography evidently conditioned the subsequent dream narratives.[50]

Contemporary psychological studies help to clarify how effective incubation might have been for fostering particular types of dreams. In one study, a sample of American college students were asked to set themselves the mental task of solving a problem of their own choosing in their dreams. Approximately fifty percent of the students reported having dreams related to the topic. Of these subjects fifty percent (i.e. twenty-five percent of the original sample) felt that they had been able to solve their problem in the dream. Unrelated judges evaluated the dream transcripts and largely corroborated the dreamers' assessments of success in problem solving. These results were obtained in a secular society after only briefly exposing the subjects to the concept of incubation.[51] The percentage of successful incubation dreams would surely have been much higher in antiquity amongst faithful pilgrims conditioned by more elaborate, socially sanctioned preparations and exposed through ritual performance to impressive religious imagery.

The Christians' removal of these images and the prohibition of pagan public rituals would have interrupted the imaginary circuit between dream and artistic representation. Granted that artists often sculpted statues of gods after dream visions, or were commissioned to do so by patrons who had had such visions,[52] the destruction of material iconography instigated a vicious circle. Fewer images meant fewer dreams and thus the probability that still fewer images would creatively be produced in the future. Proclus' dream can thus be seen as a desperate cry against a vanishing world of ancient iconography; a last expression of the ancient religious imagination.

New World Orders

Around the same time as the statue of Athena was removed from the Parthenon, the temple of Asclepius, where Proclus had prayed for Asclipigeneia, was also pillaged and soon destroyed—whether by Christians, earthquake, or natural decay we cannot be certain. Not long afterwards, a church dedicated to Saint Andrew, a

---

[49] Pausanias *Description of Greece* 2.27.2, in E. and L. Edelstein 1998:345; Lapatin 2001:109ff.
[50] E. and L. Edelstein 1998:vol. 2, 151.
[51] Barrett 1993. Within the discipline of psychology the term "incubation" primarily means the activity of intentionally solving a particular problem in one's dreams. Work on this subject generally falls under the broader category of "creativity." For reports on current incubation exercises visit the website set up by Henry Reed, one of the foremost contemporary exponents of incubation: www.creativespirit.net/healingdreams.
[52] Van Straten 1976:15

Charles Stewart

healing saint, was constructed over the site of the former Asclepieion. Incubation continued at this church, which contained an additional aisle, perhaps a porch, such as was found in the earlier temple and at other churches designed for incubation. Indications are that at least some of St. Andrew's congregation had been born into pagan families devoted to Asclepius. Tombstones in the precinct of the church bear names such as Asklepiarion, and Asklepia.[53] In other words, the gap between the destruction of the temple and the building of the church was not so long that people would have been oblivious to the earlier god and form of worship.

The surprising thing is that these events occurred so late in Athens. Perhaps we may put this down to the conservative presence of the Academy in Athens, which did not close until well into the sixth century. At Aigai in Cilicia, on the other hand, the temple of Asclepius was torn down in the early fourth century at the order of Constantine the Great to prevent people being deflected from recognition of the true Savior. In Eusebius' view, "[w]ith it (fell) the one lurking there, not a demon or a god, but a kind of deceiver of souls."[54] According to the Byzantine commentator Zonaras, this was not the end of the story. When Julian the Apostate passed through Cilicia (363 CE) the priest of Asclepius from Aigai prevailed upon him to restore the temple. Julian agreed to retrieve the pillars of the original structure, which had been incorporated into a nearby church. Ultimately the task proved too difficult. After extracting the pillars the workers were unable to transport them to the site of the Asclepius temple. When Julian departed these pillars were left lying close to the church and the bishop easily reincorporated them into his building.[55]

Recognizing the pagan conviction in the animate power of their statues and temple structures the Christians frequently incised crosses on these to neutralize them. Some contemplated a policy of totally obliterating ancient temples so that no index of pagan worship would be left.[56] The precedent of events at the temple of Zeus Marnas in Gaza would have supported the case for such a policy. With the backing of Empress Eudoxia the local bishop, Porphyry, razed this temple to the ground in 402 CE Some of the sacred marble stones from the Marneion were then used to construct a paved walkway (πλατεῖαν) around the Christian basilica subsequently erected on the site. The fact that humans and animals alike were now treading on these sacred stones, "[c]aused greater grief to the idol-worshippers than the burning of the temple. Hence, the majority of them, especially the women, do

[53] Gregory 1986:239f.
[54] Eusebius *Life of Constantine* 3.56 in E. and L. Edelstein 1998:vol. 1, 420.
[55] Zonaras *Epitome Historiarum* 12c-d in E. and L. Edelstein 1998:vol. 1, 421.
[56] Zacharias *Life of Severus* 18f, cited in Trombley 1993–4:vol. 2, 7.

348

not step on these marbles to the present day."[57] It was difficult to be certain what recently converted Christians would revere in putatively Christian contexts. A similar situation was observed in highland Guatemala. There, Christian catechists, some of whom were also shamans in the traditional religion, came to church willingly. Their devotional attention did not, however, focus on the figure of Christ crucified set in raised position before the faithful, but rather on the spirits of the dead buried beneath the floor of the church.[58]

Granted the continued practice of incubation by Christians, the best that could be done was to try to make certain that people were contacting the right God in their dreams, and that they understood the basic theological principles behind incubation. In the latter part of the fourth century Athanasius, Bishop of Alexandria, perceived the need to correct local Christians who apparently held that Christian martyrs (saints) healed people by marshalling power over the demons of the lower air.[59] The idea that saints needed to resort to demons in order to be effective obviously allotted a theologically unacceptable role to pagan cosmology. In an Easter letter to his local priests, Athanasius declared: "[I]f they [the Christian populace] understood, they would believe that the martyrs are in Christ, not in the demons, and they would call upon Christ who is in them and wait until he reveals to them what they are seeking, either in a dream or by speaking in their heart, and they would not run to demons."[60]

Theological suspicions about the role of dreams in the popular devotion to martyrs can also be seen in canon 83 of the Council of Carthage, which opposed the construction of *marturia* (martyrs'/saints' shrines) founded on the basis of revelations in dreams.[61] There were, of course, legitimate dreams of martyrs. On his way to visit his sister, Macrina, Gregory of Nyssa dreamt three times in succession that he seemed to hold the "relics of the martyrs" in his hands and that a light shone from them as from a mirror held up to the sun. This dream predicted the impending death of Macrina.[62]

Shrines to the Christian martyrs where people came to be healed represented a counter balance to the old incubation temples of the pagans. Faced with the

[57] Mark the Deacon *Life of Porphyry, Bishop of Gaza* 76, Grégoire and Kugener 1930. (English translation: Rapp 2000. See also Trombley 1993–4:vol. 2, 166.

[58] D. Tedlock 1983. Visitors to the University of Thessaloniki in northern Greece might also find themselves worshipping a pavement. The University is located on the site of the old Jewish cemetery and some of the tombstones were incorporated as flagstones in campus walkways. The inscriptions on some of these gravestones may still be read.

[59] Brown 1995:74.

[60] Athanasius *Festal Letters* 42 (370 CE) (trans. in Brakke 1998:480).

[61] Dagron 1985;40.

[62] Gregory of Nyssa *Life of Macrina* 15 (Maraval 1971).

continuing success of the cult of Isis at Menouthis (near Alexandria), Cyril, Patriarch of Alexandria, had the relics of Saints John and Cyrus translated there to establish a Christian healing center. Perhaps the political need for such sites explains his defense of Christian incubation against Julian's charge that Christians "slept on tombs in order to have dreams."[63] Cyril did not fully approve of the cultivation of prophetic dreams. When the shrine of John and Cyrus was founded he asserted that people could now come to the "true and uncommercialized infirmary where no one has false dreams" (ἀληθινὸν καὶ ἀκαπήλευτον ἰατρεῖον· οὐ γὰρ ἡμῖν ὀνείρατα πλάττεται).[64] Accounts of dream visions of Saints John and Cyrus nonetheless figured prominently in the stories of cures that occurred at the shrine in Menouthis, and which were eventually recorded in the collection of miracles of SS. John and Cyrus.[65]

Julian's objection to Christian practice expressed revulsion at the idea of sleeping at a gravesite. To the pagan mind this must have seemed a singularly polluting and thus demented thing to want to do.[66] Pagans excluded birth and death from incubation temple precincts such as those of Asclepius at Epidaurus or Amphiaraus at Oropus, but often performed animal sacrifice before and/or after incubation. The Christians forbade blood sacrifice, but preferred to cultivate dreams in proximity to the tombs or relics of deceased saints. Pagan incubation involved expenditure on offerings, while Christian healing was advertized as free of charge—hence Cyril's quip that the shrine of John and Cyrus was "uncommercialized," or the epithet *anarguroi* (penny-less) for the healing saints Cosmas and Damian. The basic action of receiving a healing dream from a deity or saint was the same, but the ritual contexts and assumptions underlying pagan and Christian incubation were quite different.

Although they had begun by branding pagan incubation as demonic, the Christians ultimately settled into their own correlation of demons with healing. Demons went from cosmological principles mediating the transmission of dreams, to evil forces involved in the causation of illness. The pagans' refusal to reject their demons (gods) and embrace Christ could provoke illness, likewise lapses and sins on the part of Christians could invite in demons, momentarily breaking the protec-

---

[63] Cyril of Alexandria *Against Julian* 10, MPG, 76, c. 1024, cited in Dagron 1985:41. For an account of Cyril's politico-religious position see, Takács 1994.

[64] Cyril of Alexandria *Collected Sermons* 18, MPG, 77, c. 1105; Athanassiadi 1993:125. Another example of direct competition between pagan and Christian healing cults during this period would be the shrine of St. Thecla, which displaced the cult of Apollo Sarpedonios in Cilicia. See Dagron 1978:87.

[65] Fernández Marcos 1975.

[66] See Brown 1981:7.

tive seal of the Holy Spirit imparted at baptism. The way to heal such pathogenic demonic infestation was by exorcism, or baptism (a rite that included several exorcisms). The Church Fathers, and especially ascetic writers like Evagrius and Cassian, promoted the view of dreams as windows onto the true condition of the self. Whereas Aristides' dreams revealed the protection of Asclepius, and a set of physical therapies to undertake, Augustine's dreams two centuries later provoked reflection on the purity of his soul.[67] The Christian suppression of dreams as prophetic encouraged a compensatory shift to seeing them as expressions of the inner self for which one was responsible.[68] To be healed as a Christian thus potentially involved embracing a new structure of "self" where individual willpower contributed to the success of the cure.[69]

At first Christians did not produce very extensive public iconography or architecture. Not only did they face periodic state persecution, but they also initially adhered to the Jewish precept that one should not worship graven images.[70] By the time of Proclus, however, the average Christian shrine would very likely have been adorned with images, and this new iconography supplanted the religious imagery of the pagans.[71] The new churches could be likened to theaters where images told the life of Christ, or the saints, and architecture placed one in a Christian microcosm suspended between the present and the world to come. Visits to these places conditioned the dreams of the faithful just as surely as images of Asclepius had influenced pagan dreams in the preceding centuries. At Menouthis, St. John appeared to a paralytic pilgrim "in the form of a monk, not in a dream (ὄναρ) but in a waking vision (ὕπαρ) just as he was, and as he is represented in paintings (γράφεται)."[72] In a seventh-century account, St. Artemios appeared in a vision to a girl stricken with a bubonic tumor and healed her. She related that, "He resembled the icon standing on the left side of the . . . church [where she was cured]."[73] The growing popularity of portable icons—and their effectiveness in colonizing the imagination—can be seen in the case of a soldier who carried an image of Cosmas and Damian painted on a special cloth while stationed far away from the saints' church. His local-born wife became familiar with the saints strictly through this image and then had a healing dream where the saints appeared to her "in the form

---

[67] Dulaey 1973.

[68] Stroumsa 1999:204.

[69] Rouselle 1990:255.

[70] Bevan 1940:47, 86.

[71] Lane Fox 1987:676.

[72] *Miracles of SS. John and Cyrus* 52, in Fernández Marcos 1975:365. See also miracle 70, where the author of the collection, Sophronios, sees both saints, "in the forms which they had and in which they are represented in paintings," in Fernández Marcos 1975:397.

[73] *Miracles of St. Artemios* 34, (Crisafulli 1997:181).

in which they are represented" (ἐν ᾧ ἐκτυποῦνται σχήματι).[74] The circular relationship that held between pagan statues and dreams now seems to have transferred to a circular relationship between dreams and Christian iconography. This relationship would be further cultivated and disseminated by icon painters who painted their personal dream visions of the saints, thereby giving the collective a fund of images which they, in turn, could dream.[75]

Some of the first representations of Christ already in the third century depicted him performing healing miracles such as curing the woman with an issue of blood, or healing the leper. Healing was clearly destined to become a point of competition between paganism and Christianity; it was an issue across which converts would either be won or lost. Two accounts from the *Miracles of Cosmas and Damian* further illustrate how incubation narratives expressed the relationship between healing and conversion.

Renowned Christian healers (from Cilicia), Cosmas and Damian were martyred under Diocletian (287 CE). Churches dedicated to them had sprouted throughout the eastern Mediterranean by the mid-sixth century. During this period a set of stories reporting their miracles also accumulated.[76] One of these accounts related that the pagans habitually referred to Cosmas and Damian as Castor and Pollux. In one instance, a pagan man fell gravely ill and his friends counseled him to attend the clinic of Cosmas and Damian. Each day when they made their rounds among the sick he would call out for Castor and Pollux to attend to him, but they avoided him. Finally, stricken with pain he cornered the two doctors and they explained that they only answered to the names Cosmas and Damian and that their power came from Christ. If the man would recognize Christ then he could be healed. The pagan man accepted, was healed, and then, after being baptized a Christian, he returned to the pagan community to spread the good news. None of this is said to happen in a dream, but it sets the stage for the next miracle story.

A pagan man accompanied a Christian friend to a church of Cosmas and Damian. He was contemplating converting to Christianity and he thought that he might have a dream that would guide him. He spends a long time in the narthex of the church praying to Christ to give him a "vision" (ὀπτασία) or "divine illumination" (θεία ἔλλαμψη).[77] He then has a dream of three children eating morsels

---

[74] *Miracles of Cosmas and Damian* 13 (Deubner 1907:133); on the three-ply cloth "icon," called τριματαρία, see Festugière 1971:125n52.

[75] Dagron 1991:31.

[76] The stories of the miracles of Cosmas and Damian were certainly in circulation before 630 CE when Sophronios shows an awareness of them. See Festugière 1971.

[77] Although it is not said explicitly, he is quite probably contemplating an image of Christ. Compare Miracle 30 (in Deubner 1907:174) where a sick man contemplates images of the Virgin, Christ, and Cosmas and Damian before having a dream of the last two

of bread dipped into wine. He experiences a great desire to partake of this food, but the children refuse his request and he is overcome with fear that he will be killed. He realizes, even in his dream, that he has discovered the secret of the Eucharist and he also knows that Christians kill non-Christians who violate their mysteries. But Cosmas and Damian appear and give him bread to eat and he awakens confirmed in his intention to convert to Christianity.[78]

Conclusion: Dreams and the Desire for Chronology

Taken together these last two accounts narrate the final dissolution of pagan incubation, indeed of paganism itself. Just as Proclus' dream of Athena scripted a possible continuation of paganism, the Cosmas and Damian accounts narrated its impending absorption into Christianity. In this respect both of these dreams could be called historicizing—they are not just the reports of rituals or dreams but of historical orderings. The appearance of the statue of Athena in Proclus' dream no doubt reflected a response to changing times but I think we can also read it as a periodizing device; it offered a way of thinking about history, rather than solely a reaction to events.

The example of Nebuchadnezzar's dream in the Old Testament Book of Daniel (chap. 2) helps to clarify how a statue might offer a chronology. In this episode, Nebuchadnezzar, in fact, forgets his dream, and Daniel reminds him that he dreamt of a huge statue with a head of gold, chest of silver, midriff of bronze, legs of iron, and feet partly of iron and partly of clay. As he looked upon the statue a stone was thrown against it and toppled it. This stone remained and filled the whole earth. Daniel offered that the head represented Nebuchadnezzar's current Babylonian kingdom, which would be replaced by inferior and still more inferior kingdoms until a final collapse.

At the point of its delivery to Nebuchadnezzar this dream was prophetic, but for subsequent centuries it presented a ready-made periodizing framework within which ancient peoples could locate themselves.[79] The Jewish historian Josephus (first century CE), retold the story of Nebuchadnezzar's dream, reducing it to four kingdoms. The belly and thighs of bronze were clearly Alexander's empire, and the legs and feet of iron (no mention of clay) apparently represented Rome. He shied away from giving a meaning to the boulder—"I am expected to write of what is past and done," he wrote, "not of what is to be"—because he probably thought it signified

---

[78] These two stories follow each other as Miracles 9 and 10 in Deubner 1907:113–121, French trans. in Festugière 1971:110ff.
[79] Pomian 1980:607.

the Jewish Messiah but did not wish to risk offending his Roman readers.[80] The Christian theologian Hippolytus (third century CE), interpreted the iron legs as the Romans and the mixed toes of the statue as representing ten future democracies. These democracies would disagree with one another and ultimately Christ would descend from heaven, like the boulder in the prophecy, and install "the heavenly kingdom of the saints."[81] The identification of the boulder with the Second Coming remained standard for most Christian writers.

The Neoplatonist, anti-Christian philosopher Porphyry contended that the Book of Daniel was not actually composed around the time of the Babylonian captivity, but rather four centuries later (ca. 165 BCE).[82] At this time the Seleucid king Anitochus Epiphanes ruled Judaea and pursued a harsh policy of Hellenizing the Jews. At the time of its composition then, the dream of Nebuchadnezzar was already largely history—the Babylonians, Medes, and Persians had all come and gone. The purpose of this history/dream was to give hope to a second-century Jewish audience that the Seleucid rule would soon give way and the period of suffering would be over. No messianic reading of the boulder seems to have figured, simply a welcome change of rule. Eusebius and Jerome poured scorn on this offensive reading of the dream of Nebuchadnezzar and it is perhaps unsurprising that the volume in which Porphyry wrote these ideas, *Against the Christians*, survives only in fragments, mainly the citations of its critics.[83] Today, however, most scholars accept Porphyry's dating of the Book of Daniel. H. H. Rowley has argued that an earlier writer would not have made so many historical mistakes, such as considering Darius to be a Mede rather than a Persian. Nebuchadnezzar's dream, then, was historically erroneous rather than prophetically accurate.[84]

This example relates to the present study of incubation not only because it suggests that Proclus and his contemporaries may well have been familiar with the figure of the statue as a chronotrope. It also helps to address the question of the relationship between "real" dreams and their narration in texts. For a dream to be known publicly it must be represented by the person who experienced it. In the transition from experience to narration there is plenty of room for fabrication and in the case of important dreams such as those of Proclus, or the faithful at healing shrines, we might concede that we do not have accurate transcriptions of the original phenomenological dreams. What we do have, rather, are narratives that have themselves been "incubated" over generations, even centuries, in the imaginations

[80] Josephus *Jewish Antiquities* 10.210.
[81] Hippolytus *Commentary on Daniel* 2.13, *Kommentar zu Daniel* (Bonwetsch 2000).
[82] Cited in Jerome *Commentary on Daniel* Prologue, MPL, 25, 491.
[83] Harnack 1916.
[84] Rowley 1959:175ff.

of those re-telling the stories. These dreams thus come to look more like the Book of Daniel—tales composed at a later date specifically for political purposes such as offering hope to those in straitened circumstances, or to wage triumphalist polemic. The temporality of these narratives is consequently highly convoluted. As prophecies these dreams involve looking into the future from a point in the past, while from the perspective of the telling, everything that they relate is already historical.

Certainly the practice of incubation provoked contest between pagans and Christians in late antiquity and this imbued the dream accounts with, perhaps, more polemical overtones than are found in the dream cures of Asclepius recorded in the fourth century BCE.[85] The idea of dreaming to gain (healing) visions continued, yet few agreed on how and why it should carry on. This chapter has compiled evidence that would allow one to argue for either the continuity or discontinuity of incubation. Rather than treat the two as alternatives, it might be more productive, and realistic, to consider both to occur simultaneously.

This chapter also alerts present-day scholars interested in writing the history of incubation that some of the data which they seek to use also attempts the very same project of presenting a "history." Those who told stories of incubation often interpolated their partisan historical assessments right into the dreams themselves. The right dream might decide the struggle and change the course of events. In this respect, incubation in late antiquity can be viewed as a form of history in the guise of ritually induced dream.

[85] E. and L. Edelstein 1998:vol. 1, 221ff.; also LiDonnici 1995.

Twenty-One

The Ritual of Petition

Ruth Macrides

Petition is a multi-disciplinary and inter-disciplinary subject. To study petition is to study language and gesture, liturgy, images, inscriptions, documents, and orations. Petition was ubiquitous in the mediaeval West, where it has been the object of study,[1] and in the mediaeval East, where it has not. It was central to the lives of the Christian subjects of the Byzantine emperor in their devotional and penitential practices, in their business and legal affairs.

But was there a ritual of petition, the performance of a more or less invariable sequence of formal acts and utterances?[2] Although imperial rituals or ceremonies are an essential and defining characteristic of Byzantium, petition is elusive. The tenth-century *Book of Ceremonies* fails to provide prescriptions for the practice, although the work contains descriptions of both religious and civil imperial events, regular and irregular in occurrence. These ceremonies, which involved movement within the capital, a specified language and dress for participants who were also specified, and a banquet, were public performances which took place on a large number of days of the year.[3] It remains to be demonstrated for the practice of petition that it was a public performance, a formal and patterned practice, that it had a protocol and a personnel. The procedure has to be pieced together, its form and content determined through a reading of images and texts, chronologically scattered and disparate in nature.

Liturgical petition can provide a starting point in the search for the ritual of petition. Liturgical petition is the most visible and accessible form of petition. It was and is an integral part of the liturgies of St Basil of Caesarea and St John

---

[1] Koziol 1992.

[2] Ritual is etymologically and traditionally a term associated with religious practices. See "Ritual" in Bowersock et al. 1992:670–671. See, also, "ritual" in Levinson and Ember 1996:III, 1120–1123; Rappaport 1999:1–68, especially 24, 38.

[3] See Cameron 1987; McCormick 1985.

[4] For the stational liturgy in Constantinople and the *synaptē* and *ektenē* forms of litanic prayer ideally suited to the supplicatory character of processions there, see Baldowin 1987.

Chrysostom. In the middle ages these liturgies began with a processional litany,[4] a series of petitions to the Lord for peace, salvation, temperate seasons, abundant crops, prayers made on behalf of individuals and the community. The liturgy begins with the command, "Let us entreat the Lord," τοῦ Κυρίου δεηθῶμεν. Another litany takes place after the placing of the Holy Gifts on the altar. These prayers are introduced by the command, "Let us complete our petition to the Lord," πληρώσωμεν τὴν δέησιν ἡμῶν τῷ Κυρίῳ.[5]

Liturgical petition shares elements common to the prescriptions for court ceremonial: movement and utterances for particular places and moments during the ceremony, performed by particular participants.[6] The language of petition is the language of prayer and the word *déēsis* (δέησις) is central to it.

Déēsis provides the link between liturgical petition and petitioning the emperor. The word appears most prominently in the title of an imperial official, ὁ ἐπὶ τῶν δεήσεων, "the one in charge of the petitions," sometimes rendered as "the master of the petitions."[7] His existence is one of the strongest indications that there was a procedure for petitioning. Lead seals dating from the seventh century onwards survive for this official[8] and the lists of court hierarchy of the ninth-tenth century and of the fourteenth century mention him. In the former he is classed together with judges: "Those who are considered judges are three in number, that is, the eparch of the city, the koaistor, and the person in charge of petition."[9] Unlike the other two, however, ὁ ἐπὶ τῶν δεήσεων did not head a court.

From references to the men who held this title, in written sources and from inscriptions on their seals, it can be ascertained that the "master of the petitions" grew in prominence in the eleventh and twelfth centuries when he often combined the function with a high honorary title, such as *prōtopróedros*, and came from a leading family.[10] Furthermore, staff was attached to the "master of the petitions" as can be surmised from a lone seal of the tenth-eleventh centuries belonging to a "notary of the petitions."[11]

It is therefore possible to establish a list of those who held the title, a prosopography for the "master of the petitions,"[12] but to give substance to this official's

---

[5] Goar 1730:52.62; 59.114 (St. John Chrysostom), 135K; 139D (St. Basil).
[6] Cameron 1987:112.
[7] Guilland 1965. See now, Morris forthcoming. For the ecclesiastical *epí tōn deēseōn*, about whom even less is known, see Darrouzès 1970:378–379.
[8] Laurent 1981:II, 110–123.
[9] Oikonomides 1972:107.4–7; 322.
[10] *The Oxford Dictionary of Byzantium*, s.v. *epí tōn deēseōn*.
[11] Laurent 1981:II, no. 255.
[12] See Guilland 1965:112–118.

duties, to give him a job description, we need to go to the fourteenth-century treatise on court hierarchy by Pseudo-Kodinos. This work gives the following definition: "The one who is in charge of the petitions receives the petitions (ἀναφοράς)
of those who make requests and have been unjustly treated, when the emperor
passes by on horseback (καβαλλαρίου διερχομένου τοῦ βασιλέως)."[13] Seeing
this reference to a mounted emperor, the nineteenth-century historian of Roman
law, Zachariae von Lingenthal, understood the text to mean that the "master of
the petitions" operated in the military camp when the emperor was on campaign.[14]
A confirmation of his assumption could be derived from the example of a Leo, ὁ
ἐπὶ τῶν δεήσεων, "distinguished in speech and learning," who died at the battle
of Manzikert in 1071.[15] Furthermore, a treatise on military expeditions ascribed
to the tenth-century emperor Constantine Porphyrogennetos gives certain evidence
that the "master of the petitions" was engaged in his work while on campaign.
During marches,

> two *kandidátoi* or *spathárioi*, to the right and left of the emperor, ride
> along at a given distance with shields; and they receive those who
> approach and lead them to the emperor. These are asked by him what
> they are petitioning about and their petitions (τὰ δεητικά) are handed
> over and the *kandidátoi* give them to the "master of the petitions."[16]

Thus, from these references to the "master of the petitions" it appears that
Zachariae von Lingenthal was justified in his assumption: the field was the scene of
this official's activities. Yet, he cannot have been at work only there. He must have
been wherever the emperor was, and that was Constantinople mainly.

The capital retains traces of petitioning in an indirect way, through a place-
name which occurs in two parts of the city. *Ta Pittákia*, "briefs" or "petitions" is a
toponym for an area on the ancient acropolis, near the church of Hagia Eirene, and
for another near the Blachernai, along the Golden Horn.[17] Sources explain how the
name came to be associated with the sites. The *Patria*, a collection of sources about
the foundation of Constantinople and its monuments, records that the emperor
Leo I (457–474) would go every week to a column called *the Pittákia*, where all

---

[13] Verpeaux 1966:183.24–27.
[14] Von Lingenthal 1955:356n250: "während der Feldzüge."
[15] Bekker 1853:167.11–13.
[16] Reiske 1829:I, 485.9–15; new edition by Haldon (Haldon 1990:124.491–126.495). I have adopted
the editor's translation with slight variation.
[17] For the east end of the city: Mango 1993, Addenda to Study I, 3. For the west end: Magdalino
1996:69.

those who were suffering an injustice, be they from the city or the provinces, would deposit their petitions (*pittákia*). Subordinates of the prefect would guard these and, when the emperor came, they would give them to him and forthwith all there would receive their decisions (λύσεις). "Whence the place was called *Pittákia*."[18]

The *Patria* gives information about petitioning, by the way, in order to explain the meaning of the place-name. Other sources also only incidentally shed light on the other place in Constantinople called *The Pittákia*, situated near the Blachernai, along the Golden Horn. These texts set out to illustrate the attention to matters of justice by the ninth-century emperor Theophilos (829–842). Theophilos, the last Iconoclastic emperor, reviled in the sources for this, also received a lasting reputation as an emperor who gave above-the-ordinary attention to justice.[19] His wife, the empress Theodora, commissioned a work to rehabilitate his memory, and this, together with the less enthusiastic report of the chronicler George the Monk, tells of Theophilos' dispensing of justice on the move. In all the stories, in both sources, Theophilos was on his way to the Blachernai church, "as was his custom,"[20] when he was accosted by the petitioner. "He would come out of the palace every Friday of the year, ride (καβαλλικεύων) from the Daphne through the Hippodrome and go through the portico of the forum to the Blachernai."[21] Petitioners would come to the emperor at various points along this route which took the emperor from one end of the city to the other. Nuns who wished to supplicate him on behalf of their monastery were advised to wait at the portico of Maurianos where the emperor turned off the main road, the *Mésē*, up towards the Golden Horn.[22] A man came before the emperor "as he was going in the direction of the Blachernai," saying "the horse on which your Majesty is riding is mine."[23] A widow spoke to him at the Blachernai itself, proclaiming that she was treated unjustly by the brother of the Augusta: "he makes his houses taller with the buildings which he adds and he overshadows my dwellings, casting them in darkness and reducing them to nothing, as I am a scorned widow."[24]

---

[18] Preger 1901:166–167.

[19] For the reputation, acquired in the tenth century, see Markopoulos 1998:37–49. The twelfth-century *Timarion* features Theophilos as one of the judges in Hades (Romano 1974:78.804–812). See below, also, for a later reference to this emperor in connection with petitioning.

[20] Cont. George the Monk, in Bekker 1837:17–18; Regel 1891–98:41.15–16: κατὰ πᾶσαν Παρασκευὴν τοῦ χρόνου ὅλου. For discussion of these sources, see Laiou 1994, especially 151–153, 156.

[21] Regel 1891–98:41.15–18.

[22] Regel 1891–98:41.10–14; Cont. George the Monk, 809.3–21.

[23] Cont. George the Monk (Bekker 1837), 803.17–804.18.

[24] Ibid.: 793.15–794.1.

Justice was thus dispensed all along the emperor's route. There was not one fixed place.[25] Theophilos' movement from the palace to a specified church, from profane to sacred space, punctuated by fixed stopping places where petitioners could wait for the emperor, is reminiscent of the liturgical petition with its processional litany but also of protocols for imperial ceremonies.[26]

A memory of Theophilos' habit of receiving petitions on horseback in Constantinople is preserved in the fourteenth-century treatise on the court hierarchy by Pseudo-Kodinos. In a description of the preparations for the emperor when he rides on horseback (καβαλλικεύει), it is said that seven horses should be put at his disposal, for the following reason:

> They say that the emperor Theophilos was a lover of justice. Once, then, when he was mounted on a horse, they say, he encountered a woman who shouted that the horse on which the emperor was riding was hers. When the matter was examined, the woman was found to be telling the truth. The horse was hers but the eparch, having taken it, gave it as a gift to the emperor, as if it were his. When this became clear, the emperor dismounted straightway from the horse, as he was, and gave it to its owner. Since at that time there were no imperial horses in tow, the emperor was in need of a horse and he mounted whatever was at hand. The suite of horses was instituted so that, if something should happen, imperial horses would be ready for the emperor to mount.[27]

Although the story told differs from George the Monk's version in its details—a man and not a woman confronted the emperor[28]—it is significant that the memory of the emperor Theophilos' practice is preserved in this context. For the emperors Leo and Theophilos, attention to petition is reported as routine, a weekly event: "he used to go," "he was accustomed." For the third emperor about whom something is known in this capacity, Alexios I Komnenos (1081–1118), the event, or some aspect of it, would appear to have been exceptional. The chronicler Zonaras describes an occasion around 1116, towards the end of Alexios' reign, when the emperor returned to Constantinople from an expedition because of the illness of his wife.

---

[25] *Tà Pittákia* at the Golden Horn could have received its name because of an intensive association with petitions at that spot. See Wilson and Darrouzès 1968:25.45–55 (text); 23 (commentary); Magdalino 1996:69.

[26] See above, pages 356–357, and Cameron 1987:112.

[27] Verpeaux 1966:170.6–171.7.

[28] See above, page 359 and n. 23.

And while she regained strength, he was engaged in administrative matters, spending his time for the most part at Philopation. This was conducted by him in the following manner. He ordained appointed days on which he would sit there in public, facing onto the broad open space. Access to him was granted to anyone who wished, and each of the petitioners proffered a supplicatory memorandum (δεητήριον) of what he wanted. He instructed the secretaries to read what was placed before him and to acquaint him with their individual requests, and he then ordered a rescript (ἀντιγραφήν) to be made to each and confirmation to be provided to the petitioners. This was maintained by the emperor for a considerable time.[29]

Alexios made himself available to petitioners at Philopation, a palace and a park outside the city walls. Zonaras mentions the occasion, it seems, because it was unusual and not routine. In all three cases, that of Leo, Theophilos, and Alexios, whether the emperor received petitions on the move—a process reminiscent of the processional litany of the liturgy—or in a specific open area, he was accessible to his subjects and, directly accessible. There were no middlemen to go through before eventually, if ever, coming into the emperor's presence. In none of these cases is the "master of the petitions" mentioned.

Many of the above characteristics of Byzantine petitioning can be seen also in the example of a western ruler renowned for his exacting care for justice, the thirteenth-century king of France, Louis IX. Jean de Joinville, who wished to illustrate the ideal qualities of this monarch, gives an extensive account of Louis' practice in this area.

> In summer, after hearing mass, the king often went to the wood of Vincennes, where he would sit down with his back against an oak, and make us all sit round him. Those who had any suit to present could come to speak to him without hindrance from an usher or any other person. The king would address them directly, and ask: "Is there anyone here who has a case to be settled?" . . . I have sometimes seen him in summer, go to administer justice to his people in the public gardens in Paris, dressed in a plain woollen tunic, a sleeveless surcoat of linsey-woolsey, and a black taffeta cape round his shoulders, with his hair neatly combed, but no cap to cover it, and only a hat of white peacock's feathers on his head. He would have a carpet laid down so that we might sit around him, while all those who had any case to bring before him stood round about. Then he would pass judgement on each case, as I have told you he often used to do in the wood of Vincennes.[30]

---

[29] Büttner-Wobst 1897:III, 753.1–12.
[30] De Wailly 1874:34. Translation from Shaw 1963:177. For Louis' attention to justice, see Richard 1983; Bartlett 1981.

For Louis, as for the Byzantine emperors Leo and Theophilos, hearing petitions in an open space was a regular event. Like these emperors, Louis dispensed justice directly, face to face with the petitioners; like the emperor Alexios, he gave judgment in a park. As in Constantinople, in Paris also sites were named after the activity: the "Gate of the Requests" in Paris was comparable to *Ta Pittákia* in Constantinople.[31]

Thus, the sources for Byzantium reveal a kind of procedure for petitioning the emperor but only in the case of a few emperors. There is an official in charge of petitions but we know him from seals and treatises and not from his actions in specific cases.[32] Was petitioning so much an experience of everyday life that it rarely and only for specific reasons surfaces in the sources?[33] Does the fact that some emperors are reported as receiving petitions out of doors and while in motion preclude more regular petition sessions in the palace?

An indication is given in a letter of the emperor Theodore II Laskaris (1254–1258) in which he gives a summary of his daily activities:

> Attention to my troops rouses us from bed at dawn. The care for ambassadors, both their reception and their dismissal [occupies us], as the sun rises. While the sun is still climbing, we draw up the order of the battle lines. At midday, consideration of those who have brought petitions is attended to and prepared and we mount a horse to hear those who are not able to enter the doors of the palace. We judge the cases of our subjects when the sun is declining. . . .[34]

Theodore II refers to going out on horseback to receive the petitions of those who had been unable to come to the palace. In this case then, outdoor petitioning took place in addition to, and not in place of, petitioning in the palace. Theodore's palace was not, however, in Constantinople but rather at Nymphaion. Extraordinary times may have called for unusual measures. Can we be certain that the practice he describes with regard to petitions also held in Constantinople before 1204 and after 1261?

Later evidence for petitioning, from the thirteenth and fourteenth centuries, shows the emperor riding out to hear petitions. Two texts lay down the procedure in great detail: a *próstagma* of Michael VIII for his son Andronikos II, issued in 1272 when Andronikos became co-emperor, and the treatise of Pseudo-Kodinos. A

---

[31] Ed. de Wailly, 32.
[32] See Morris forthcoming.
[33] See the comments of McCormick 1985:7–8, on this point.
[34] Letter to Nikephoros Blemmydes, no. 44, in Festa 1898:58, 63–75.

new term appears in these texts which describes the practice: *kavalíkeuma*. In the *próstagma*, Michael VIII gives detailed instructions to his son about his riding out to hear petitions, both when he is with the emperor in Constantinople and when he is alone, outside the capital.

> If you are without my Majesty, let the horns and trumpets sound in your riding out [*kavalíkeuma*]. When you are with my Majesty, if you ride out privately, trumpets do not sound. For the sound of these [instruments] in the riding out of the emperors was devised for no other [thing] than in order that the advance of the emperor be announced to those who have been treated unjustly, so that those who need help from this source can approach the Imperial Summit. If you are with my Majesty, this announcement of the horns and trumpets in my Majesty's riding out will suffice for those who need this help. If you are away, this must be done in your riding out for the help of the unjustly treated.[35]

From this document, then, it would appear that the *kavalíkeuma* was an activity which took place both in Constantinople and outside the capital, although no indication is given how far away that might be.

Pseudo-Kodinos provides more discussion of the sounding of trumpets:

> When the emperor is ready and mounted, the cymbal players strike the cymbals, the trumpeters likewise blow the trumpets and the horn players play their silver instruments. The trumpets used for this service are not the same as the other trumpets but have a different shape. The sound of these organs makes manifest that if one of the people has a demand or is being unjustly treated, hearing these he (can) run and bring his demand.[36]

On the basis of this evidence from the Palaiologan period it has been suggested that the "*kavalíkeuma*, which played such an important part in late Byzantine ceremonial" was anticipated by Theodore II's practice in the "Empire of Nicaea."[37] This statement implies that the *kavalíkeuma* was a new ceremony whose origins can be traced to the court of the emperors of Nicaea "in exile" in Asia Minor. However, when the late evidence is put next to the earlier examples discussed above, it appears that Theodore II, Michael VIII, and later emperors were doing what previous emperors had done. Indeed, the anonymous author of the

[35] Heisenberg 1920, here, 39.32–44.
[36] Verpeaux 1966:172.3–173.15.

fourteenth-century treatise, Pseudo-Kodinos, indicates that in his time the practice was understood to be a continuation from much earlier times. This is demonstrated by the incident he cites from the emperor Theophilos' reign, giving it as the reason why so many horses accompany the emperor on his riding out to receive petitions.[38] What is different about the later practice is that it has become codified, prescribed in an imperial law (*próstagma*) and in a treatise on court hierarchy. It has also been given a name, *kavalíkeuma*.

It appears, then, that the outdoor reception of petitions by the emperor was a ritual practice long before its thirteenth–fourteenth century codification. In describing court hierarchy, the dress of officials, and the ceremonies of the court, Pseudo-Kodinos, the anonymous author of the treatise written in the mid-fourteenth century, sought, like Constantine Porphyrogennetos in his *Book of Ceremonies*, to make connections with the past, to restore a sense of order. In the case of the later treatise, the compiler was working at a time of great political dislocation and disorder.[39]

Up to now, the discussion has concentrated on outdoor petitioning. Yet, as we have seen, petitioning also took place at the palace, although references to this too are few and far between. The impression the sources give is that this practice was a great deal more time-consuming and complicated. In the early fifth century, Synesios described in a letter the large and thick Egyptian carpet—more like a mattress than a cover—that he had brought with him and used when "he was obliged to sleep in front of the Prefecture" in Constantinople while waiting to petition the emperor on behalf of the city of Cyrene.[40] Even when the emperor had given orders for petitioners to come into his presence, *silentiárioi* at the door could stop them because of their appearance, as was the case for St Sabbas, coming from Jerusalem to supplicate the emperor Anastasios in ragged clothes.[41] In the palace too, however, the "master of the petitions," is conspicuous by his absence.

Just as acclamations in imperial ceremonies were specified, so too written petitions were fixed and formal. For the written petition, as for the ceremony of petition itself, it is first in the late Byzantine period that a codified form appears: a late Byzantine collection of notarial formulae preserves a formulaic petition. However, surviving petitions from earlier periods show that the form of the petition had already been in place centuries before and varied little over time. Petitions begin

---

[37] Angold 1975:169–170.
[38] See above, p. 360.
[39] Cameron 1985:136; See also the comments of Shepard 2001:20, 22; Verpeaux 1966:39–40.
[40] Garzya 2000: II, no. 61, 76–78, 168–171. Synesios waited in front of τὰ μεγάλα ἀρχεῖα, a phrase which could refer to the palace. Cf. Garzya 2000:168.
[41] *Life of Sabbas*, in Schwartz 1939:141–143.

The Ritual of Petition

with the participial form of the verb τολμῶ, "I dare" or "I am bold" and the verb ἀναφέρω, "I mention," "I bring to your attention."[42] Here there is a striking similarity with the liturgical prayer recited just before the Lord's Prayer. The same verb, τολμῶ is used in an address to God: "Make us worthy, O Lord, to dare to call upon you (τολμᾶν ἐπικαλεῖσθαι), the heavenly God, Father, with frankness of speech and without blame."[43]

The formulaic opening and concluding phrases of petitions give an indication of the attributes of petitioners and emperor. The petitioner is made small and humble, the addressee is exalted: "Daringly I, the servant and fervent suppliant of your mighty and holy Majesty, mention, my holy Lord, God-crowned, God-promoted, God-directed holy emperor."[44] The concluding words repeat the statement that the petition was boldly made by the unworthy servant of his Majesty.

The petitions themselves give no indication of the gestures petitioners made when delivering their requests. To learn about these we have to go to descriptions[45] in chronicles, letters, romances, and to images of petitioning. Those who sought a favor might kneel or prostrate themselves, stretching their hands toward the person being entreated. But those who supplicated the emperor for pardon made, not surprisingly, much more dramatic gestures. The wife of Alexios Axouch fell at the emperor's feet, begging him for her husband's life, while beating herself.[46] The hero of the romance *Livistros and Rhodamne* was given the following advice on how to entreat the angry ruler, Eros:

> Bend your neck and make yourself small,
> make your eyes terrible as if frightened,
> clasp your hands tightly and
> fall to the ground before him
> and cry from your heart and entreat him.[47]

In images, the word *Déēsis* has come to be attached to compositions of the Theotokos and John the Baptist on either side of Christ, with their hands extended toward Him.[48] Was this the gesture of petition? It appears that the iconographic

[42] Ferrari 1912:no. 33, 21.
[43] Goar 1730:148.
[44] From an anonymous collection of letters of the fourteenth century in Vaticanus gr. 1891, 55v. But see also Michael Choniates' petition to the emperor Alexios III with reference to the taxes imposed on Athens (Lampros 1879/80:307, 311).
[45] For a collection of sources which describe postures of entreaty, see Koukoules 1948:I, 2:105–110. For the West, see Koziol 1992:59–63.
[46] Van Dieten 1975:145.95.
[47] Agapitos 1999:Appendix, 133: N 260–265.
[48] *Oxford Dictionary of Byzantium*: s.v. *deesis*; Walter 1968; Cutler 1987; Bale 1995.

subject called *Déēsis* today was not given this name by the Byzantines. The only case where the word is associated with an image is when a petition is presented to Christ in the name of the donor of the image. The best known example is that of George of Antioch in his church of St. Mary in Palermo, prostrate, with arms extended to the Theotokos who intercedes on his behalf before Christ. The inscription above the donor reads, "Petition (δέησις) of thy servant (δοῦλος) George, the emir."[49]

Surviving petitions show that they were written in varying styles and levels of Greek and, therefore, not always subjected to a uniform language or style of a secretary or notary. They appear to be in the words of the petitioners themselves. This is obviously the case in a *déēsis* of 1288 from the inhabitants of the island of Kos, from the clergy, the military, and the common people. This document which is preserved in the original in the monastery of Patmos is the only original petition to have survived. It contains many linguistic peculiarities, such as στάλβοι for σκλάβοι, "slaves," and ἰνέφερεν instead of ἀνέφερεν "mentioned."[50]

In some cases the petition refers to a previous petition and decision of an earlier emperor which now requires further attention. Thus the Jew who had become a Christian in the reign of John II Komnenos, petitioned John's son Manuel to send an order to the local imperial agent in Attaleia to resolve a dispute with the Jews there over property. The Jews were circumventing the earlier imperial order by bribing the *práktōr*. If the emperor Manuel were to reward the converted Jew with a response to his petition, he would not cease his entire life from praying for his Majesty, "whom I, the unworthy servant, have boldly petitioned." Manuel's decision has been preserved together with the petition. It instructs the petitioner to "show this *lýsis* of my Majesty to the doux of the Kibyrraioton so that he may summon the Jews."[51]

Another petition of the monks of Patmos to Manuel Komnenos refers to the gift of twelve peasants made by his grandfather Alexios I. Now the monks petition for an imperial order to stop the *práktōr* from Samos from disturbing them on account of these peasants. But they make a further request:

> We entreat that the mercy of your Majesty be extended still more over us and that you award us also other peasants. And we will not cease to make each day a *triságion* on behalf of your Majesty and to pray fervently for you.[52]

---

[49] Kitzinger 1990:plates 119, xxii, xxvi; der Nersessian 1960. The Theotokos as petitioner to Christ on behalf of the unjustly treated is too large a subject for this paper. For her representation as such in *Apócrypha*, see the discussion by Baun 2000.

[50] Nystazopoulou-Pelekidou 1980:II, no. 75, 224–235; here 227.4, 227.6

[51] J. and P. Zepos 1931:I, 373–375. See, too, Sharf 1971:156–157; Jacoby 1993:122 and n. 26.

[52] Vranouse 1980:I, no. 19, 190–192, 191.11–14.

In both the above cases, the petition was accompanied by the emperor's response. This response, it has been suggested, would have been written on the petition itself, at the bottom or on the back, and returned to the petitioner after it had been registered in the appropriate bureau of the administration.[53] Again, the role of the "master of the petitions" is hidden in all of this. If it were not for a letter of Theophylact, archbishop of Ochrid, to a bishop of Triaditza, we might not learn that the "master of the petitions" was involved in writing up the imperial decision. The bishop of Triaditza had accused this particular "master of the petitions" of accepting a pound of gold coins to rewrite the emperor's response, making it more favorable to the petitioner.[54] Theophylact was most indignant at the suggestion but the fact remains that we do not know what a petitioner had to pay to lodge a petition, to whom the payment was made, what the success rate was, how often one might have to petition before being heard. It emerges however from this letter, but also from other sources, that the *epí tōn deéseōn* was a person in the confidence of the emperor, an official very close to him (*oikeiótatos*).[55]

The above petitioners, the converted Jew and the monks of Patmos, also mention a gift in return for a successful response, prayers for the emperor. Eustathios of Thessalonike, writing to a newly appointed "master of the petitions," a member of the Doukas family, also offers a gift, "Persian apples," his own produce, which he gives together with his request for reconciliation, and the pardon of the official's brother.

> You have, o *pansévastos* lord, the first petition of Eustathios. I inaugurate the office happily for you, for I will make petition and my petition will be satisfied. And this will be for me auspicious, a good omen. And what is the entreaty? I happened upon your excellent brother on the road. And since I do not have very inquisitive eyes, and besides, because I was walking on an unsure road, I could not determine if this was the most excellent of men, Doukas. Whence I passed him unremarked, inclining my head slightly as to an unknown and I acquitted myself of obeisance as to a stranger. When my little house—as you would say—held me shortly thereafter and I was reclining at the table and my hand was dipping into the food and the quails which I bought from you were fluttering under the table, the eunuch John, as if in ambush, came close to me and attacked me sharply. He shouted why did I not address

[53] Dölger and Karayannopulos 1968:83–84; Nystazopoulou-Pelekidou 1980:230.
[54] Gautier 1980–86:345.40–53.
[55] See, also, Niketas Choniates (van Dieten 1975:270.27–29).

Doukas. . . . I am entreating you to ask for me reconciliation and pardon and to strive to achieve this for me. God is my witness. I became distressed with myself that I was so careless in the matter.[56]

The twelfth century is the period when the "master of the petitions" rises in prestige and importance, to judge from the higher honorary titles he holds and the distinguished families from which he comes.[57] This is also the period when petitions appear in new forms—the literary petition, written by men of high intellectual achievement and in an elaborate language. Eustathios' letter is a playful example of private business, but he also addressed a petition to the emperor Manuel "as from the city when a drought was oppressing it." This petition describes the state of the city "afflicted by a drought in the middle of winter."

For this reason we, the entire city, pour out our hearts before your imperial benefaction, and we seek the pouring forth of your mercy upon us, and we pour forth warm tears. Stretch out your holy arm and order in this way the restoration of water in the land, not for a day, as in Scripture, but for all eternity. There is no water for the people to drink. "Give us water that we may drink." But that is what a stiff-necked people said to the servant of God, Moses. . . . But we are a grateful people, servants well-exercised in faith, a people mindful of benefactions. . . . Become, most generous of emperors, like the Paktolos, pouring forth the gold, in this way a comforting Nile for the summer heat; rather both, gushing forth gold and water for your city.[58]

Eustathios tells the emperor that only he can give the solution, that he comes as a suppliant to the only one able, after God, to save the city. The emperor's God-given power is on the line.

Another petition, an anonymous appeal to the emperor John II, concerning the dire state of a stretch of the main road in Constantinople, is even more explicit about the emperor's position, the merging of the heavenly and earthly courts.

Listen to my words—for it is for this you are emperor—and, doing just things, receive a just embassy on behalf of the fatherland—so that you might justly, not unjustly, be called emperor which is the same as saying, God on earth and in heaven.[59]

[56] Migne, *Patrologia Graeca* 136, 1272–1273.
[57] Guilland 1965.
[58] Wirth 2000:291.72–83, 292.93–96.
[59] Mercati 1897:140–142.

In the twelfth century also, side by side with the literary petition, there are encomia which end with a request from the author. This combination of panegyric and petition is a mixing of genres that is a hallmark of twelfth-century literature.[60] The encomia give evidence of the confidence of the writer, a strong sense that his learning and eloquence place him on an even footing with his lord. These authors, Theophylact, Michael Italikos, and Theodore Prodromos lobby on behalf of education and rhetoric but also on behalf of themselves. Their confidence shows through in the playfulness with which they treat serious themes. They invert the relationship of master and servant, the petition's formula of humble slave and all-powerful lord.[61] Theodore Prodromos, in verses praising the emperor John II, returning victorious from a campaign against the Turks, concludes,

> You have hungered, O emperor, for the sake of me
> your slave. The emperor hungered, while I stuffed
> myself. He shivered while I was warm.
> The mighty great Komnenos was suffering, while
> humble, unfortunate Prodromos was living it up.
> What virtue of an emperor could be greater than these?[62]

This literary development culminates in the poems of Ptochoprodromos, poor Prodromos. The boldness of the petitioner, the τολμῶν first-word opening of the petition, becomes the center-point. The boldness is embodied literally in the content and form of the verses. These poems innovate not only in their use of the vernacular but also in turning an address to the emperor into a rhetoric of poverty.[63] In each poem the author adopts a different persona—the hen-pecked husband, the poor father of a large family, the monk looking for a secure place, the starving intellectual. And each poem ends with an elaborate plea for help. The petitioner is center stage:

> Such were my dread sufferings, almighty crowned lord,
> my sore tribulations caused by a warring wife,
> when she saw me coming home with empty hands.
> Unless your loving mercy reaches unto me, sole ruler,

---

[60] For the mixing of genres, see Macrides 1985. For a thirteenth-century example of an encomium with a request (ἀξίωσις) at the end, see George Akropolites (Heisenberg 1903:188.25–27).

[61] Magdalino 1993:425–441. The same can be seen in the sermons of the *didáskaloi* of the "Patriarchal School," addressed usually to the patriarch and often including an encomium of the patriarch with a request for a better salary or position. See Loukaki 1998:434.

[62] Hörandner 1974:310–316, here 315.185–191.

[63] Alexiou 1986; Beaton 1987; Magdalino 1993:341–342, 399, 429.

unless you satisfy her lust with gifts and favors,
I tremble, terror-stricken, lest untimely murder,
deprive you of your Prodromos, your best suppliant.[64]

The literary development of the petition is perhaps the best evidence that there was in Byzantium a ritual of petition. In the twelfth century it became an art form. Petition has been shown to share the recognizable features of court rituals. The practice, it seems, was so familiar that it was mentioned only sporadically by narrative sources and then only when something unusual made it worth noting.[65] As with other court rituals, protocols for petitioning exist, one from the tenth-century military treatise of Constantine VII, the other from the fourteenth-century treatise of court hierarchy by Pseudo-Kodinos. They describe a public performance involving movement of the emperor on horseback through the city or the countryside. The latter treatise gives the practice a name—*kavalíkeuma*—and describes its festive character, in the sounding of trumpets and horns. The late text likewise reiterates the traditional aspect of the ceremony by referring to continuity with past practice. Although, however, Pseudo-Kodinos is at pains to provide an historical background for particular elements of the procedure, the very example he gives shows that the ceremony changed and evolved, responding to events.[66] In petitioning, perhaps more than in other rituals, the sacred and the secular are fused: petition in prayer and petition before the emperor share language and gesture; there is a processional element in liturgical petition as in petitioning the emperor: the emperor moves from the imperial palace to specific churches in Constantinople, with fixed stopping places along the route.[67] Thus, there is movement between sacred and profane contexts, as in the protocols for other court ceremonies. Above all, the emperor who receives a petition and listens to the words of his supplicating subjects is "God on earth and in heaven."[68]

---

[64] *Ptochoprodromos* (Eideneier 1991, 135.274–279). See Alexiou 1999. I have adopted Alexiou's translation (Alexiou 1986:102) for all but the last word, εὐχέτης, which she translates as "congratulator." I prefer "suppliant" especially in combination with the name Prodromos. He is the emperor's "best suppliant" as someone who prays to God on the emperor's behalf and as one who beseeches the emperor on his own behalf.

[65] McCormick 1985:8. See, above, the case of Alexios I.

[66] Both Cameron and McCormick (see note 3) stress the changing nature of ceremony. See above, p. 360, for the example from Pseudo-Kodinos.

[67] Cameron 1987:112.

[68] See p. 368 above.

Twenty-Two

Rites of Spring:
Ritual, Resistance, and Taxonomic Regimentation
in Greek Cultural History

Michael Herzfeld

Some Preliminaries

The ritual practices associated in Greece with the so-called "swallow songs" (χελιδονίσματα), which welcome those avian harbingers of springtime, constitute a textbook demonstration of one of the pet theories of Victorian evolutionism: the survival of ancient custom (from what E. B. Tylor saw as the "childhood of mankind"[1]) as a practice conducted exclusively by children in the modern age. The lingering effects of this "allochronism"—the relegation of exotic "others" to a different kind of time, cultural phylogeny reduced to biological ontogeny—persist in anthropological writings until relatively recently, as Johannes Fabian has observed.[2] In Greece, local political realities led to the internalization of this perspective.[3] In this view, the peasantry were the living childhood of the nation, their customs a repository of practices from the dawn of their civilization. By turning the tables on scholarly practice and treating the classification of Greek folksongs as a form of ritualized bureaucracy, comparable in important respects to the ritualization of state-citizen relationships through the agencies of the national government and its offices, we can take an area long marginalized in the interests of most anthropologists—folklore—and demonstrate its relevance to how we understand the state's treatment of the citizenry. The point is an urgent one at this very general level, because the rise of social anthropology in Greece and the critiques of folklore as an outdated nationalist enterprise have together relegated folklore, if I may slightly recast a familiar phrase, to the dustbin of historiography.

[1] Tylor 1865.
[2] Fabian 1983:32 et passim.
[3] See the discussion in Danforth 1984.

In order to pursue this argument, I first want to make three interrelated points. First, the "childhood of civilization" argument did not wholly accord with what Margaret Hodgen rightly identified as an important modification of evolutionism when it was applied to European societies[4]: whereas the Tylorian paradigm was progressivist in its universal applications, Europeans—and especially the Greeks and their philhellenic admirers and tormentors—saw "survivals" as the basis for a return to a glorious and superior past, to which the elites of more powerful European nations now held the key. Second, the dialectic between paganism and Christianity implied in such folkloric restorations should be read, not merely as religious adaptation, but—as Charles Stewart has cogently argued[5]—as a politically motivated syncretism. Folklorists themselves (particularly J. C. Lawson) recognized that the re-use of pagan temples as Christian churches, and of pagan rituals as popular Christianized rites, was a smart move in the struggle for the allegiance of the peasantry to the new religion and its political embodiment in the Byzantine polity; when nineteenth-century writers like Spyridon Zambelios and Constantine Paparrhegopoulos laid down the principles of "Hellenic-Christian civilization"— those same principles that the Papadopoulos regime was to invoke so grotesquely— they too were engaged in a process of mythologization aimed at transforming early religious conflict into ahistorical political unity.[6]

A third point concerns the "swallow songs" specifically. The textual processes through which these songs became the focus of a children's ritual should be seen, not solely as a product or effect of cultural change, but as an integral component of Church and state political control. There is a direct analogy between the paternalism of state and Church on the one hand (one need only think of all the jokes about "father Papadopoulos"[7] and about the use of πάτερ (father) as a standard form of address to priests), and that implied in the survivalist thesis about the childhood of mankind, on the other. At some moment of which all historical testimony is now lost, the Church and its representatives apparently had children, already under the control of their parents and teachers (the latter a strong presence in the medieval and modern texts), perform what had hitherto been an Apollonian rite, and do so in a way that ostensibly represented the collective will of the community that its members should conform to a code of generous reciprocity. In so doing, they transformed the swallow song into an intentional act of what, borrowing from Shawn Malarney's notion of state functionalism, I shall call "church function-

---

[4] Hodgen 1936:48n1.
[5] Stewart 1994.
[6] Lawson 1910:45–46; Paparrhegopoulos 1853; Zambelios 1852; 1859. On nationalist historiography as myth in the Lévi-Straussian sense, see Herzfeld 1985a.
[7] Orso 1979:3–4.

alism."[8] And when, with the achievement of national independence, education passed into the rigid hands of the state bureaucracy, these rituals became an integral part of the elite's culturally and politically hierarchical teleology: they modeled in public but extremely local spaces the drafting of a fractious populace in the service of a polity in which all were expected to respect common values.

Such a reading contains, necessarily, a considerable degree of speculation. Yet the work of Margaret Alexiou, in particular, has shown that cultural continuity, even (or perhaps especially) when dissociated from its current ideological moorings, is a worthy object of study. Moreover, as she points out in an important and unjustly neglected article,[9] its early treatment as purely literary, rather than as embodied in music and dance (and, we might add, other social practices), has obscured the very basis on which continuity is maintained. Anthropologists who have refused even to consider the potential relevance of cultural continuity have flattened the historical depth of their analyses and, despite some recent exceptions,[10] have replaced crass evolutionism with a scarcely less reductionist and atemporal structuralism, itself ironically a form of survivalism in its lack of attention to the specificity of historical process.

One important exception to this pattern is Stanley J. Tambiah,[11] whose work on religious and political process in Thailand has led him to consider processes of continuity and transformation as processes the evidence for which particularly undercuts conventional survivalism, with its literal readings of such concepts as tradition and modernity. His argument can similarly be deployed in critical assessment of the timeless myths of essential culture promulgated by authoritarian states. By seeing tradition and modernity as rhetorical constructs, moreover,[12] we can more easily understand how the apparent teleologies of ritual practice are embedded in carefully constructed notions of common sense. Common sense is a classificatory device;[13] so is much of folklore research; and the meeting of the two in implicit (and therefore hard-to-challenge) assertions that children must both learn the values of social harmony and represent them for the community as a whole reproduces on local stages the paternalism of a Western-dominated world in

---

[8] See Malarney 1996.

[9] Alexiou 1985:54.

[10] See Seremetakis 1991, especially pp. 124–125.

[11] Tambiah 1976.

[12] See the especially useful discussions of tradition and modernity as contextual constructs by David Sutton (Sutton 1994) and Vassos Argyrou (Argyrou 1996).

[13] This is the thrust of much of Mary Douglas's work (especially Douglas 1966 and 1975), and her influence informs my own discussions of bureaucracy (Herzfeld 1992), as does earlier work on the relationship among ritual, bureaucracy, and classification by Don Handelman (see especially Handelman 1998).

which nation-states, successors as paternalistic as the churches to whose temporal power they succeeded, inculcate models of law and order into their citizenries.

The Material

I conducted research on the swallow songs over three decades ago.[14] At the time, having just emerged from a period of intense exposure to the nationalistic folk-lorism of the colonels' Greece as a non-degree student at the University of Athens (1969–70), I was both skeptical of the uses to which the colonels' academic syco-phants were trying to put cultural continuities and interested in trying to develop a more dynamic understanding of what those continuities might signify in the larger historical sense. Part of the research entailed fieldwork on the islands of Rhodes and Nisyros, and I also conducted a computer analysis of the song texts in order to identify the principal factors influencing the similarities and differences among them. In addition, I considered the sole surviving ancient "variant," which is preserved by Athenaeus in the *The Deipnosophists*;[15] he attributed it in turn to the Rhodian poet Theognis, who appears to have been writing in approximately the sixth century BCE. I also considered two versions of a medieval text allegedly sung by Byzantine schoolboys.[16]

The ancient text appears as part of an Apollonian rite from Lindos. We have no historical evidence that specifically charts the transformation of this religious exercise into a children's spring ritual, but the effect was to combine two separate ancient ritual moments—the beginning of the new year (1 March) and an autumn rite devoted to Apollo—into a segment of the local ritual sequence in which the passage from Carnival to Easter is reinforced by a parallel celebration of seasonal transition. This sequence is clearly demarcated by the children's collecting of undyed (white) eggs and the scattering of white daisies on 1 March, the linking period marked by wearing a red-and-white thread called "March" (μάρτης) and the closure symbolized by the red flowers decorating the Ἐπιτάφιος (bier of Christ) and the red-dyed eggs collected by the children on Easter Sunday.[17] It is clear that rites of seasonal transition have here been assimilated to a Christian ritual sequence. The pagan rituals were effectively declawed through their refashioning as children's rites, especially as these, already in the Byzantine texts and certainly in

---

[14] See Herzfeld 1972.
[15] *Deipnosophistae* viii, 360b–d (in Page 1962:450–451).
[16] The two medieval texts are in the Bibliothèque Nationale in Cambrai (Auguste Molinier, *Catalogue général des bibliothèques publiques de France—Départements* vol. 17 [Cambrai, 1891], p. 211: ms. No. 554 [512] and the Vallicelliana in Rome (ms. F-73; see Fabre 1890).
[17] Herzfeld 1977. See also Herzfeld 1973.

modern times, were organized by local priests and teachers and were thus subject to the decorum of Christian morality. When I observed the 1 March procession in Rhodes in 1972, for example, my request to take a photograph of the children had them scrambling to stand in separate groups of boys and girls, respectively, while their teacher looked benignly on. The corporal and spatial discipline of gender segregation underscored the complete absorption of the ritual into officially approved practices. It mattered little that its antecedents were pagan: it seems possible that in antiquity it had even been performed in autumn despite its vernal implications because the month of Boedromion, roughly corresponding to September, was dedicated to Apollo. Indeed, its double deracination—from autumn to spring and from Apollo to Christ—perhaps then more effectively assured its assimilation to the new religion than the most rigid ban could have guaranteed its complete disappearance.

In some places, this absorption into Christian ritual cycles is more dramatic. On Nisyros, in the island capital of Mandraki, it is Lazarus Saturday into which a version of the χελιδονίσματα—the closest extant version to the Byzantine texts—has been built. The resurrection of Lazarus anticipates the greater Resurrection of Easter, and this also ensures that anything remotely "pagan" will be viewed as subordinate to the larger, Christian schema.[18] Authority is confirmed at all levels, and the involvement of schoolchildren dramatically and synecdochically enacts the authority of the Church over the people as a whole—this association being furthered by particularly strong local traditions of the κρυφὸ σχολειό (the clandestine school conducted by local Christian clergy in defiance of the Ottoman authorities), intimating that all villagers are as schoolchildren before the authority of the Church.

Questions of Authority

Here, however, we begin to see another side of the material, one in which the absoluteness of authority comes seriously into question. It has been customary to "explain" the subversive elements in these rituals as carnivalesque safety valves that, by releasing the desire for insubordination, reaffirm each year the permanence of authority. Such functionalist explanations will only work, however, when we have historical evidence to show that those in power deliberately encouraged such inbuilt teleologies—as, for example, happens in some totalitarian regimes.[19] Here, such evidence is neither present nor, in my view, likely to appear. Rather, I suspect, the rituals reflect an

[18] I include some brief descriptive materials in Herzfeld 1977.
[19] For discussions of state-orchestrated ritual teleologies, see especially Binns 1979–1980; Handelman 1998; Malarney 1996.

irrepressible dimension of Greek rural society that reflects the fact that, Church and state authorities notwithstanding, it remains the local people who actually fashion the ritual practices—which consequently reflect their values and attitudes.

In pursuing this point, I am building on some much more recent research that I conducted with craft apprentices in Crete. Space does not permit extended treatment here,[20] so suffice it to say that boys who work in various craft trades as apprentices confront authoritarian masters whose goal is not to teach them—indeed, they may prefer to avoid the potential competition that such instruction could bring in its train—but simply to exploit their labor. The few who do succeed in mastering the crafts in questions in the face of their masters' unwillingness to teach them, however, may end up as the business partners of the latter: having survived the obstacle course of apprenticeship, they have shown themselves to possess the agonistic cunning necessary to survive in a highly competitive male social environment.

With this in mind, we find that the local texts of the swallow songs exhibit plentiful signs of a similar rebelliousness. Again, a functionalist explanation might simply treat the rituals as ways of chasing insubordination away[21]—much as the children formulaically chase the vermin away in their songs (ὄξω ψύλοι καὶ κοριοί, / μικροί, μεγάλοι ποντικοί, "out, fleas and bugs, / mice and rats!")—thereby diverting the rebellious energy away from potentially dangerous channels. But a more persuasive explanation, I suggest, is to be sought in the possibility that these rituals instead reflect the social reality of Greek village life, and that, even for the Church and state, some rebelliousness was perhaps to be encouraged and even engaged.

That Greek children are deliberately goaded into agonistic attitudes is well established.[22] My research with craft apprentices in Crete suggests this pattern in a somewhat extreme degree: some masters appear to go out of their way to *obstruct* rather than *instruct* their apprentices—but they also show every sign of delight when the more enterprising of their young charges succeed in thwarting their secretive behavior.

At the same time, one might assume that the bureaucratic nation-state and what some puristic "neo-Orthodox" theologian-philosophers regard as the "Protestant" (because bureaucratic and disenchanted) national Orthodox Church would oppose such a deliberate embedding of insubordination in the very practices

[20] Herzfeld 1995. For a fuller account see Herzfeld 2003. The research in question was supported by the Spencer Foundation, the National Endowment for the Humanities, the National Science Foundation, the J. S. Guggenheim Memorial Foundation, and the American Philosophical Society, none of which is responsible for my conclusions.

[21] As an example of the so-called "equilibrium model," the theoretical framing in question here, see Gluckman 1955.

[22] On the inculcation of agonistic attitudes in Greek children, see especially Friedl 1962:78–81; Hirschon 1992.

ostensibly designed to maintain authority.[23] We should not forget, however, that, whatever the theory behind such structural considerations, they are translated into actual practice by social beings: bureaucrats and priests are drawn from the society they serve, and thus understand and share in its social norms even when these appear to contravene official norms. Moreover, the state itself is relatively young, while the disenchanting of the national Church—if its critics are right in this regard—is an even more recent development.

Most important of all, this is the key issue of legitimacy that the Greek state, like its American counterpart, must face. Neither state has yet completely managed to deal with the fact that a nation based on ideals of liberty, individuality, and spontaneous self-expression will, almost by definition, be unruly; its citizens can always invoke national stereotypes in defense of their errant ways—for example, when Cretan sheep-thieves invoke what nationalist historiography has made the hero-guerrillas (κλέφτες, thieves) of the War of Independence.[24] In much the same way, communists, deemed "anti-hellenic" by their royalist foes, invoked these same proto-types of national liberty.[25] Never, perhaps, was "possessive individualism" more determinedly wrested from the property-owning classes than in the first 130 years or so of Greek statehood.[26] And the debates continue, if only because even today there are "traditional acts" that, despite the idealizations of Eurocentric conservatives, contravene the official image of a rational, "European," and "civilized" nation.

So deeply entrenched is this model that even official attempts to tame it can be coopted in unexpected ways. I well remember, for example, how a Cretan friend who had invited me to dinner in a restaurant brought along his own guitarist to liven things up and generate *kéfi*.[27] As the evening got under way, he raised his glass, eyed everyone with stern cheerfulness, and in a stentorian bellow ordered, "Be happy (ευτυχεῖτε)!" The routinization of spontaneity is one effect of the state's response to the everyday phenomenon of the spontaneous disruption of routines: essentializing structures breed essentializing responses.

The relationship among the state, ideals of free-spiritedness, and the forms of authority is thus complex and represents a palimpsest of responses to the processes whereby modern Greece has emerged as a nation-state. It is in this context that I want to consider how the spring rituals associated with the swallow songs, while certainly representing an unusually clear case of continuity with the ritual past, also

---

[23] See especially Giannaras 1972 and other works by the same author.
[24] On κλέφτες as a prototype of "national" unruliness, see especially Herzfeld 1985b:28–33.
[25] See Lambrinos 1947; also Kordatos 1924.
[26] On "possessive individualism," see Macpherson 1962:196; also Handler 1988 for an account of its adoption by a European-derived nationalism.
[27] On the social dimensions of *kéfi*, see Cowan 1990:105–112; Papataxiarchis 2001:156–179.

represent processes of transformation that have to do with this play of power. As Tambiah has shown for Thailand, ideas about the nature of authority are deeply embedded in ritual practices, which provide a matrix for modifying as well as preserving them and a context in which local practices respond to encompassing visions of order.

With Tambiah,[28] too, we should beware of trying to read too much referential content into these highly formulaic texts. This is the danger of simply treating them as "survivals," a view in which they are either seen as elements of the childish past or literal texts that have been "corrupted" from the high worship of ancient deities—a favorite tactic of literal-minded nineteenth-century folklorists. Rather than reading them as timeless but damaged relics of the past, "fragments" of a partially lost "high culture" in the then dominant Romantic tradition, I prefer to see them as carriers of etymological hints about the transformations that the societies that produce them have undergone. This approach avoids the teleological implications of saying that these rituals license "rebellion" in order to divert the risk of "revolution,"[29] while acknowledging the likelihood, already noted here, that at various times some officers of Church and state would have recognized the possibility of investing them deliberately with precisely that teleological function.

Historical Antecedents

It is probably no coincidence that the fullest elaborations of the ritual texts occur close to sources of monastic authority—in Constantinople (and possibly Rome) in medieval times, and today in Mandraki, the town on Nisyros where the monastery of Panayia Spiliani is located. Indeed, it is noteworthy that, while the other three villages of Nisyros (Nikia, Emborio, and Pali) are home to related ritual forms, these are already considerably simpler in form and content than those of Mandraki. In other words, the evidence suggests—although it is tenuous—that these supposedly pagan rites are actually strengthened when they come into direct contact with the regnant Christian authority. As Charles Stewart reminds us, syncretism can be as much about the politics of culture as it is about religious doctrine.[30]

With these observations in mind, let us now turn to the medieval texts. These form part of what folklorists call a *quête*—a custom in which the children of the community visit all the houses, demanding some symbolic gift and threatening

---

[28] Tambiah 1968; 1979.
[29] The approach owes much to Giambattista Vico's *Principij di Scienza Nuova* (Vico 1744) and Austin's "A Plea for Excuses" (Austin 1971); but it also extends the notion of etymology beyond the purely verbal to images and conceptual schemata; on teleological models, see n. 19, above.
[30] See n. 5, above.

violence against the persons and property of any who might dare to refuse. No doubt the fact that, with few exceptions, the violence is largely hypothetical led earlier scholars to view these practices in functionalist terms: symbolic violence as a release mechanism, order reaffirmed, the community's internal solidarity renacted and thereby crafted anew.

The commentary accompanying the medieval text, however, shows us that sometimes the violence could be real (if relatively harmless). The text itself is explicit about the threats involved.[31] Some of the formulae are repeated, with minor variations, in the modern songs: ν' ἀγοράζουμεν ἐφτά, νὰ πουλοῦμε δεκαεφτά ("to buy seven, to sell seventeen"), and so on. The medieval versions do not help us in our search for clarification of these rather obscure incantations; here indeed it seems that ritual language "works" more through its redundancy and its diagrammatic qualities than through any recoverable referentiality.[32] One might speculate that the phrase reflects local profiteering, but it could equally reflect concerns with the fertility of chickens (itself also an economic issue, be it said); or, again, it may have an entirely different and now unrecoverable origin.

Other phrases suggest the displacement of the violence: δῶστε μας τὸν κόπο μας, / μὴ μᾶς δείρει ὁ δάσκαλος, / κ' ἔχετε τὸ κρῖμα μας / καὶ τὴν ἁμαρτία μας ("give us the reward for our effort, / so the teacher won't beat us/ and you be responsible for our sorrow / and our wrongdoing"). The term κόπος, usually translated as "effort," is in fact its reciprocal here: it means "the reward for our effort." But note how the threat of violence has been displaced to the teacher-pupil relationship, in a manner that suggests training for a highly agonistic society: the children will not be punished for their own dereliction of duty, but for their failure to place the blame elsewhere—an outcome that, in their singing, they represent as entirely predictable.

While one might see this as a way of putting moral pressure on the entire community to conform to custom, which indeed it may also be, it also fits the common pattern, described by Renée Hirschon,[33] of training children to expect deceit, unfairness, and abuse at the hands of those who wield power but with whom, at the same time, they expect to enjoy some measure of reciprocal affection (this being the fundamental model of paternalism). The attitude enshrined in these

---

[31] An example from the village of Kattavia, Rhodes, ends, ὄξω ψύλλοι καὶ κοριοί, / μέσα Μάρτης καὶ Λαμπρή ("out, fleas and bugs; in, March and Easter"). When a householder refuses to offer a gift, the children significantly reverse the formula: ὄξω Μάρτης καὶ Λαμπρή, / μέσα ψύλλοι καὶ κοριοί ("out, March and Easter; in, fleas and bugs") (Herzfeld 1972:105–106).

[32] Here, in addition to Tambiah's work on ritual (Tambiah 1968; 1979), we should take note of Roman Jakobson's extremely apposite essay, "Linguistics and Poetics" (Jakobson 1960).

[33] Hirschon 1992.

Michael Herzfeld

songs also accustoms the children to placing the blame for their failures on those same powerful forces: "you" will be responsible for our failure, just as an unspecified "they" is always said "not [to have] let us" be a free nation, build our house as we wished, and so on. This is the corollary of deceit at the domestic level as well. It is clearly enshrined in the text. It does not really matter whether we know what is being collected, or whether it was, more specifically, once supposed to be a set of seven eggs. What matters is that, if we fail to collect "it," we will be in trouble—and it will be your fault. This stance encapsulates the concept known in Greek as εὐθυνοφοβία (literally, "fear of responsibility") and widely regarded as the pragmatic basis of all citizen-bureaucrat interaction.[34] Here the source of authority does seem to be sanctioning a practice that makes authority itself bear the brunt of the blame: the state or the Church is fashioning its members to be fiercely rebellious but under cover of a cunning (πονηριά) that allows the authority to deny all responsibility for the rebellious behavior, thereby reproducing that behavior in turn. In other words, we see here historical traces of a pattern that characterizes family relationships, attitudes of and toward the national bureaucracy, and socialization in work and business styles alike. It is hard to be sure, of course: we are reading social values from modern ethnographic sources into what are, for the most part, fully decontextualized texts.

In the case of one of the villages on Rhodes that have yielded such texts, however, I have done conventional social-anthropological fieldwork two years after my 1971 folklore research there. The problems I encountered in the field there, which I have described elsewhere,[35] attest to a high degree of institutionalized indirection (some would call it deviousness) in which a formally polite manner masked complex and ramified techniques of social exclusion and competition. It was also a village in which, in an unwitting evocation of Foster's "image of limited good,"[36] one resident confirmed the agonistic quality of local social relations by remarking, "The wealth of your vines is the poverty of mine," and described how important it was for him to be evasive as a means of protecting his interests—a clear indication that the structures of blame and responsibility are strategically deployed in the pursuit of pragmatic self-interest (Greek συμφέρον).[37]

[34] Herzfeld 1992:143–147.
[35] Herzfeld 1983.
[36] Foster 1965. Although Foster's model of "limited good" may be both less widely applicable than he may originally have intended (in terms of peasant societies specifically), but also more generalizable to a wide variety of situations involving limited resources, it does describe a situation to which this villager's gnomic remark corresponds with remarkable precision.
[37] On the concept of συμφέρον and related concepts of obligation, see particularly Campbell 1964:213–262; Loizos 1975:65–66.

380

Another View of Continuity: The Undisciplined Alternative

The image that emerges here is very different from the Enlightenment recreation of the Hellenic rationalist spirit. While it would be inappropriate to generalize from this case to the entirety of Greek folklore, we have a case in which the social context and the textual tradition are both documented and seem to extract persuasive echoes from other ethnographic evidence. Since much of Hirschon's work was conducted with Asia Minor refugees, for example, there is at least a strong possibility that communities in which swallow songs were performed in much of the eastern part of the Greek world—including Constantinople—might once have exhibited suggestive links between songs and the style of local social interaction in much the same way as I have tried to indicate here for the Dodecanese. Both the local teachers and the national classification of folklore support an image of these songs as an expression of social harmony and conformism that is suggestively belied by these hints of insubordination and quarrelsomeness as well as of the evasion of responsibility—features of the familiar world of Greek everyday life rather than of the idealized portrait that Greek officialdom promotes in the defense of a "European" and "modern" identity inspired by the rationality that nationalistic philosophers and philologists read back into the ancient texts.

One reason for which these less respectable aspects of the ritual do not emerge in the classic commentaries in Greek folklore, I suggest, is the assumption that the divisive aspects of Greek society were of Turkish origin. Given that the swallow songs were among the most amply documented folkloric relics of classical antiquity, along with laments for the dead, official folklore would not have wished to see them besmirched by such associations. Yet we know that continuity does not necessarily follow the logic wished for it by nationalists. Margaret Alexiou's demonstration of continuity in the lament tradition, unlike that of Zambelios, does not attempt to sweep the Church's opposition to these practices under the carpet by claiming that the senior religious hierarchy was "foreign" to the Greek spirit, but shows how this poetic tradition expressed a subaltern, highly localized, and yet immensely pervasive set of ideas.[38] Similarly, we now see that the swallow songs express, not the continuity of a glorious ancient spirit as defined by the Enlightenment, but instead a continuity of cheeky insubordination that would constitute a major embarrassment for the nationalist framers of state ideology, with their generally moralistic vision of unbroken continuity with the ancient world.

That alternative view of continuity with the ancient world would have been particularly embarrassing to them because it would have revealed that their own

---

[38] Alexiou 2002a; Zambelios 1859.

bureaucratic practices, including those of the production and use of folklore classification, were deeply implicated in the same tension between authority and insubordination. They dragooned folksong texts into a format that appeared to suppress the insubordinate character of some of those texts, exercising stringent moral censorship over the interpretation of all texts that appeared to be historical in character. Nevertheless, even in the austere taxonomy of N. G. Politis,[39] we encounter, in the categories of "Akritic" and "kleftic" songs—which allegedly reflected the lives of the Byzantine border barons and of the heroes of the struggles against Turkish rule, respectively—an attempt to insulate from the moral contamination of both these categories the larger and more literal category of historical songs. If those categories that spoke to the national historiography most directly were not "historical," what were they? Saying that they were mythological overlooks the awkward fact that, in Greek as much as in English, "myth" means "fabrication." Yet to recognize these heroic texts as historical would have been to admit to the canon the celebration of disobedience to the law of the land. This is a dilemma that reproduces in the classification of songs the central conundrum of any country—the U.S. is another example—founded by "rebels" wielding "frontier justice."

The inventors of this taxonomy could not afford to suppress all evidence of the insubordinate, or intimate,[40] side of their cultural heritage, because to do so would in effect have been to deny that Greeks were those free-spirited people who preferred death to servitude. Instead, they mythologized the evidence. Much as the shepherds of mountain Crete would tell strangers that animal-theft was a thing of the past, associated with their resistance to the Turkish oppressor, the folklorists—members of an educated elite that would forever dissociate itself from such disreputable matters—used their taxonomy to suggest that the disruptive behavior of swashbuckling guerrillas and questing children alike were marginal, a thing of the past,[41] and appropriate only to the benighted conditions of a time now banished by the return in modern times to the status of a truly European, orderly, and respectable civilization. In other words, they mythologized in order to assert control—to deny the contradiction that lay at the heart of their polity and their cultural claims.

---

[39] Politis 1914.

[40] See Herzfeld 1997a.

[41] Danforth 1986, makes this point by using the argument that Johannes Fabian developed about "allochronism" in anthropology but deploying it instead as a critique of nationalist folklore studies. On the supposedly "European" character of Greek culture in its modern setting, see especially Kozyris 1993.

Twenty-Three

How to Do Things with Things: Architecture and Ritual in Northern Greece

Laurie Kain Hart

Ritual, as a kind of event, occupies time and space, and its location is integral to its meaning and effectiveness. Because rituals involve images, display—and a panoply of senses—our conceptions of meaning based in language are not enough to solve the problems of ritual meaning. Theorists have noted that visual cues are configurational and simultaneous: language selects particular properties for conceptual attention, but the visual or haptic cue is "constitutive" not "referential"—and says both more and less than you want to say. Location is, in the same way, indeterminate: ritual makes places, but places may both support and disturb ritual assignments. In what follows here I discuss this lability with reference to the paradoxical meanings associated with houses in a border area of Greece that has suffered successive displacements of population. While the anthropological (and folkloric) literature on rural Greece (including my own earlier work in the Peloponnese)[1] has rightly, I believe, emphasized the central role of the house in the context of domestic and ecclesiastical rituals that mobilize forms of social continuity (and in literature the metaphorical senses of the house also follow from this ritual function) it is also possible to track another career of the house in which it takes on the role of an idiosyncratic, and ambivalent historical cipher. Freud's intuitions about the spatial nature of the uncanny; the architect Le Corbusier's acerbic attacks on ritual in relation to architecture; and Bourdieu's sense of an insidious misrecognition naturalized in architectural form, point us in a direction more in tune with the unsettling qualities of the house that are conveyed in ethnographic testimony.

A second inspiration for these comments is the essay written by Jack Goody in the 1970s as a protest against anthropology's overplaying of the "key to culture" role of rituals. Given that, on the one hand, the "formality [and] repetitiveness [of rituals] also means culture lag and loss of meaning"[2] (as Le Corbusier argued) and

---

[1] Hart 1992; see also Kyriakidou-Nestoros 1975.
[2] Goody 1977:30

that, on the other, the nuances of ritual performances often "require exegesis even for the main participants,"[3] Goody doubts that (quoting Monica Wilson), "rituals reveal values at their deepest level . . . men express in ritual what moves them most, and since the form of expression is conventionalized and obligatory, it is the values of the group that are revealed."[4] Rather, Goody insists, ceremonial behaviors are only one type of action which ought to be seen in the context of other genres; and, finally, "the function of 'ritual' can be better elucidated under changing rather than static conditions."[5] What this means for my purposes here is that to understand something of the peculiar part played by the house in social experience, we need to explore the forces in counterpoint to the rituals of habitation.

1

In the summer of 2000, I asked an elderly Greek couple I knew about how they came to live in their house in the former Muslim quarter of one of the villages in the Prespa area in Western Greek Macedonia. Like many stories about houses, this one was about a family history. However it did not trace the story of the house in the way one might expect, with the familiar (if always complicated and often ad hoc) justifications of the rules of inheritance, marriage, and exchange.[6] In answer to my question, the householder told me about how his mother was deceived by her second husband.

> I was born at A., in Pontus. My family arrived in 1923 in Greece. My father died, and my mother, a widow with a child, met a man when she got to Thessaloniki, in Kalamaria [the refugee quarter]. She sent me to D. [a village in the Prespa area] to an uncle, and went with the new husband near the border with Bulgaria. After a while, she sent for me. She had asked her new husband: do you have any children? He said no; but it wasn't the truth. He had an infant, and he threw him away when he left Turkey. An Armenian who had no children took the baby. He cradled him in goose down, he loved him. Later, the Armenian got in touch with the father. He told him the boy was there, that he could

---

[3] Ibid.:31.
[4] Ibid.:32.
[5] Ibid.:34.
[6] See, e.g. Just 2000:194. As Just observes, Lévi-Strauss' concept of the house as an entity that endures socially through time by holding on to certain kinds of property and titles and prerogatives might seem inapplicable to the Mediterranean peasant household with its constant fragmentations (see also Sutton 1994.). However, as Just notes: "if [such a house] had to rip itself apart in order to spawn its own likenesses, the dreams and aspirations of its members—at least of its oldest members—were often of its perpetuation and continuity"(Just 2000:192).

always visit him, that he was always welcome at the Armenian's house—but don't take the boy, he said. The father took him though, and six months later the boy died. That father should not have taken him back.

In that town near the Bulgarian border where my mother lived they wove silk. One morning my mother washed her hair and bathed before we set off for market at Florina to buy some thread for weaving. She took cold, and had a fever for thirteen days and then she got up and died. She never would have married that man had she known he'd lied and had children.

His wife, listening, agreed and described the experience of coming to Greece: *"It was, thrown out of this house, thrown out of the other."* This refugee, still a boy, was expelled from his stepfather's house, and returned to Prespa. The story was repeated to me more times than I can count: losing one parent was generally enough to make a child an "orphan;" having two was no guarantee of protection in these conditions. Discussions concerning houses repeatedly detailed the insecurities of kinship and place: there was never only one experience of exile but always a series of expulsions. As a refugee, this man eventually claimed entitlement, in state land redistributions, to a portion of the abandoned "Turkish" properties near the village of his uncle, and there he settled. The house in which he now lived was inseparable from the biographical history of the houses from which he had been expelled: to say this in the language of ritual theory, it functioned as an index of social insecurity as well as iconically and pragmatically as a measure against it. Houses here appeared as the debris of events—from which they were perceptually inseparable—and, despite their often massive size and the durability of their materials, as fragile and provisional.

Although we can convincingly argue that geographies are cultural, the relationship between ritual and architecture or landscape is as elusive as it is obvious. Rituals are said to be, in a dependent sense, embedded in places, and places are shaped by ritual action. In the agro-pastoral societies of the Balkans and the Mediterranean, social selves are importantly constituted by the rituals of inclusion and exclusion relating to the house.[7] Even more than the village,[8] the house serves

---

[7] The "house" here is better understood as a domain and not as a single structure. I would argue that while the central domestic dwelling tends to remain as the sign of its existence when a "house society" ossifies, in agro-pastoral societies generally, the house is constituted by a complex of domestic and other structures scattered in a landscape (see Clarke 2000.) On the other hand it would also miss the point to say that the house is an institution rather than a thing. Rather, the institution is apprehended through the thing/s, phenomenologically (as Gell notes [1982:62], the "fetish"—or any socially significant made thing—is "the visible knot which ties together an invisible skein of relations, fanning out into social space and social time. These relations are not referred to symbolically as if they could exist independently of their manifestation in this particular form. . . .")

[8] Sutton 1994.

in the pursuit of cultural ideals and social mastery. If this is the case then as do all social constructions, houses—and this is what I want to explore here—carry the experience of social alienation. It is as though the house is an institution that can never keep its promises, and the extreme example of communities subject to forced displacement only makes this obvious.

The house understood as an institution has instrumental and communicative functions in the local and regional setting, critical functions in the operations of kinship and inheritance, and it persists in the landscape as a kind of sign of past claims, declines, and resurrections. Charles Piot, in a study of Kabre houses in West Africa, quotes one of his informants who explained to him that certain houses were especially "heavy with history"—the history of settlement, wars, witches, and emigrations. "These houses," Piot's informant says, "meet all this history with their rituals, and tame it for us. . . . [a *history with the outside*] is where we find our power and why they are the big houses . . ." (Piot 1999:130). Kabre emphasis on a "history with the outside" draws our attention to the external sources of power and energy that are transformed into the artifacts of a village; the house is more than what Lefèbvre, referring to modern commodifications of shelter, calls a genitalized container. Displacement produces with reference to the house an oscillation between a complete evacuation of meaning and an intensification of meaning. While anthropology has produced a body of literature on the built environment as a reflection of cosmological order, in what follows I want to explore the flip side of this architectural order, namely the disturbing history that needs to be "tamed" and the object that is potentially empty—both of which inspire efforts to ritualize place.

2

If ritual is a genre of routinization, as important to the organization of the individual psyche as it is to the reproduction of the social group, it can be understood as a kind of counter-entropic technique. The extraordinary and traumatic are non-ritual, but so also are the texture and the excess of what Malinowski called "the imponderabilia of everyday life."[9] If ritual is a technique, it is applied to some material, and that material is also the source of the entropy against which it operates— the body, the psyche, social interactions, etc. The built environment is entropic in this way. The built environment as an assemblage of things is an unruly spatio-temporal storehouse whose surplus—or deficit—of meanings is controlled by

---

[9] Malinowski 1984.

ritual. The experience of involuntary displacement—or displacement and return—uncovers the unruliness of these semiotics of place.[10]

In the Prespa lake district of northwestern Greece, at the borders of Greece, Albania, and the former Yugoslavian Republic of Macedonia, the history of village life in the course of the last century has been one of social inversions, population displacements, and political hazard. At the end of the nineteenth century, these villages were composed of Muslim landlords and Christian Slav-Macedonian-speaking agricultural laborers; after the second Balkan War the area was incorporated into the Greek state. With the flight of Muslims before and after 1923 (the date of the Lausanne agreement on the exchange of populations between Greece and Turkey), the Slav-Macedonians took possession of local land and refugees of Greek descent from Anatolia were settled by the government in homesteads abandoned by Muslims. With World War II and the Greek civil war (1944–1949) local development was arrested and thousands of residents (children and adults) were forced into exile. The postwar landscape was characterized by villages destroyed or minimally repopulated by, in some cases, the remnants of indigenous families, and in others, exogenous populations, including formerly transhumant Aromanians (Vlachs) and families of refugee descent (Orthodox Christians, from the exchange of populations with Turkey) who moved to Prespa from locations elsewhere in Greece. Economic migrations in the 1960s and 1970s contributed further to depopulation.

One important element of this picture of a locality is the presence of a group of remarkable—large, distinctive, often expertly crafted—buildings, mostly built between 1920 and the late 1930s, some of which have been abandoned and some of which are lived in and restored. The transition from mud brick to stone house, or from bare mud to beaux-arts plaster in the Greek Macedonian houses of the 1920s signified the consolidation of the family and its fortune. These houses represented the accumulated work and capital of their inhabitants; stone houses were, more often than not, financed by labor abroad, in America, from 1900 to the mid 1930s. The house was an expression of social mastery. Men acquired both autonomy and community as heads of houses. In the rural Balkans, "master" also evokes the persona of the master builder (μάστορας), the skilled craftsman who

---

[10] Gell's argument that the visual index in art—and by extension also in architecture—is not the same as the linguistic sign is well taken. Accepting his notion of "abduction" as the process of inference related to the visual sign, we could say that I am concerned here with the ritual routinization of "abductions" and conversely with disruptions in customary processes of abduction—inferences concerning the social agency of makers, users, observers. ("Any artifact, by virtue of being a manufactured thing, motivates an abduction which specifies the identity of the agent who made or originated it" [Gell 1998:23].)

knows how to build an enduring structure and is the master of his team of apprentices and laborers (μπλουκιά). Furthermore these houses of the prewar period express the brief ascendancy of local Slav-Macedonian farmers over Turks and Albanians. In the writings of travelers in Macedonia in the first half of the century types and qualities of housing are read as the codes of a hierarchical, ethnic system of architecture.[11]

Two of the villages in the Prespa group are under architectural preservation regulations; the rest are not, and in fact government construction loans through earthquake relief programs have provided incentives for the demolition of older mud-brick houses. Even in houses that have been continuously inhabited by the family of the original inhabitants and builders, substantial changes have occurred in the use of space. The most notable of these concerns the shift from residential groups of brothers (and their spouses and children) to residential groups of nuclear or stem families. Where there is more than one heir, this has meant the partitioning of large houses into segments or the destruction of large houses and their replacement by individual bungalows or apartments. In some cases, the multiplicity of heirs has meant that title remains unresolved and buildings crumble. In many cases, new owners have occupied houses emptied of their former inhabitants and they have reconfigured the buildings for their own purposes.

The built environment also contains some impressive churches dating from the tenth to the late nineteenth centuries, some which have also been subject to various forms of reuse and revision. In some of these new constructions and revisions, conscious efforts have been made to exploit messages of style: a basilica-plan, pitch-roofed church belongs to a now out of date or "traditional" Macedonian style, native to the periphery, while a cross-plan, domed church explicitly imitates the modern Greek national style of the metropolitan center. Similarly, the domestic rural ideal-types of the 1920s and 1930s are gradually replaced by the bungalows of the late twentieth century. This pattern of rural "development" or change also stakes particular claims in the face of the disruptions caused by the political history and conflicts of this border zone.[12]

Radical changes in the semiotics of architecture over the course of the last century extend to the materials and processes of construction even where this is not at first obvious. Stories about the masons who formerly built the houses in Prespa tend to be grandiose and heroic—much like the legends told in Northern Greece about Byzantine and Ottoman arched bridges said to have been built by Alexander

---

[11] Bérard 1911. For a fuller discussion of the codes of architecture, see Hart 2000.
[12] Arguably, national border zones are always semiotically supercharged with the expectation of some visible proof of the claims of sovereignty and national difference. See Hart 1999.

the Great or Heracles. While some new buildings of stone are built now, the stone is not the same as it was in the twenties, when it was quarried locally or brought from the riverbeds. The masons are no longer local masons or householders or itinerant guilds, but low status migrants from Albania, and they are expected to work anonymously, not signing their buildings with their inscribed faces or insignia as their predecessors often did.

The masons of the 1930s worked in well-established teams and were respected craftsmen. Present day Albanian masons, by contrast, have a hard time of it. They cross the border on foot over the mountains and they are periodically expelled in police sweeps. Now some have permits to work, but they need patrons to acquire them.

Recently, on a holiday, one of the masons dressed up in his fine clothes and went to the café for a beer. As he sat there the men at the next table put a lit cigarette in his pocket and another down the back of his shirt. They laughed and went back to their beers. In tears and confusion, he came to the contractor who employed him. The contractor was scandalized but the abuse was indicative of the changed meaning of the craft: these builders are understood to be laborers from the underclass.

While I had earlier thought of the landscape and the built environment as resources for ritual actions "making sense of" life histories, stories I gathered from local residents pointed toward extraordinary events: the front lines of the Balkan wars, sudden land redistributions, evacuations, unresolved disputes. Family histories all involved great travels and long distances, dispersions and consolidations. Often the construction of a house appears in stories as a kind of biographical moment of order, a hiatus between the prelude of labor migration and the destructive intrusion of a global cataclysm.[13]

The spatio-temporal work of orientation that we call ritual—we could take the example of the foundation ritual performed in the construction of houses in Greece—thus does its work against the material recalcitrance of the physical world and of history.[14] *Because* houses constitute glaring evidence of the real fragility and accident of social constructions, the house is a powerful implement in social rituals.

Ritual theory in anthropology, especially since van Gennep, has liberally used architectural analogies. Van Gennep's architectural theory of ritual and his less

---

[13] The narrative of one family history gives some indication of this. I offer an extended version of this narrative in the endnote to this chapter.

[14] For a definition of ritual I will take Rappaport's—"performance of more or less invariant sequences of formal acts and utterances not entirely encoded by the performer." The entailments of ritual according to Rappaport are: "convention, social contract, morality, time, creation, sacredness, the divine, meaning" (Rappaport 1999).

explicit ritual theory of architecture are now part of our disciplinary intuition. *Rites of Passage* (1909) understands symbolic action as a structuring of space.[15] Van Gennep conceives of territorial passages on the model of houses, with conditions of interiority, exteriority, and liminality; and ritual passages on the model of territory. For van Gennep, the house is both a ritual object (as the subject itself of ritual performance, often as a surrogate for persons) and a site for ritual (as a space and a place for ritual performance). Even more generally, van Gennep imagines society as a kind of house, of specific architectural character.

Van Gennep points out that there are rituals to the construction of houses— laying the foundations, opening doors, etc.—that are simultaneously rites of passage for both household and house as structure.[16] Where the house is not developed as a surrogate, as a ritual object, still it functions as a site for rituals—for example, for the betrothal of a daughter. Houses as sites for rituals may involve the house accidentally—as a mere space for the accomplishment of a ritual; or indexically— as when the locating of a ritual in the house indexes the hospitality of the ritual sponsor. Both of these are conceptually different from the house as ritual object, although the house can be used as a prop when it is used as a site—e.g. when mock thieves fight their way into a house in a betrothal ceremony.[17]

Van Gennep conflates architecture and ritual in such a way that it is hard to imagine life except as a series of exits and entrances, or to imagine an architecture divorced from ritual control. At the same time he envisions modernity as thin in ritual and unobstructed in space: the "free space" of modernity is counterposed to the ritualized "mass" of tradition. In "semi-civilized" society, space is densely

---

[15] Van Gennep 1960.

[16] Suzanne Blier's work on the Batammaliba house in Togo and Benin (Blier 1987) is a stellar demonstration of the complexly iconic and symbolic process of house building and deconstruction: both the process of building and the thing itself underscore the literalism of the parallel between architecture and humans. (If Roman houses failed in reality to conform to the libertarian ideals of Fustel de Coulanges, the Batammaliba house with its altars and resting places for deceased elders and emphasis on the independence of the self-reliant household is more than a perfect exemplar!). The Batammaliba house is human body, "cosmological model, paradise referent, temple, social diagram, psychological complement, protective fortress, and theater." (Blier 1987:24.) Foundation and construction rituals "encapsulate" these features. The house serves in accomplishing rites of transition: the Batammaliba architect opens the doorway in a ritual linking the new house to the deceased family elders, divides exterior from interior space and assures the safety of the interior for occupation, confirms the identity of the house and the mortal body of its owner. The house serves as a surrogate of a deceased man or woman in rituals, houses must be fed, and houses die. In other words, there are among the Batammaliba, and certainly elsewhere in the ethnographic record in less virtuoso versions, extensive rituals which involve the construction and manipulation of the house itself as a ritual object.

[17] Van Gennep 1960:122.

controlled by the blockades of ritual.[18] Van Gennep's model is essentially static, a hierarchy of types. There is nothing in van Gennep resembling the struggle within ol between types of spatial order, or the scramble for control of space that we find in Lefèbvre ("whatever is not invested in an appropriated space is stranded"[19]) nor is there any sense of the perdurance of material orders beyond or outside of their ritual functionality.

Van Gennep gives us a model for thinking about the saturation of places by ritual, and this model works very well for understanding the mechanisms through which the body is organized in a social space—a *habitus*. What is not stated but also important here is an analysis of that against which these organizational efforts are undertaken: the potential loss or confusing surplus of meaning, disorienting changes in spatial assignments, the recalcitrance or dissolution of the material world within which rituals are situated. These things are especially evident under conditions of social disruption but it is also the case that in as much buildings are "things" and not only "structures" there are problems inherent in our social relations in and to space that need to be accounted for to understand the mythologies and desires we invest in houses.

4

In understanding the peculiar kinds of meanings and influences carried by buildings and settlements in a landscape a theory about the nature of things can be helpful (because buildings are things). As we have seen, the founding of and living in buildings is saturated with indexical and symbolic communicative acts, but buildings exceed, in their being things and not acts and words, the domestication of ritual. Buildings are not semiotically very "sticky"; and so they rely on constant interpretation. Where architectures travel (as in imperial architectures) they have to make their messages short and simple (for example, they declare themselves to be "big" or "expensive" or "eternal"; they may also use writing to identify themselves more clearly).[20] Nevertheless, as acts that physically endure, they can stop making

---

[18] "A society," he writes, " is similar to a house divided into rooms and corridors. The more a society resembles ours in its form of civilization, the thinner are its internal partitions and the wider and more open are its doors of communication. In a semicivilized society, on the other hand, sections are carefully isolated, and passage from one to another must be made through formalities and ceremonies which show extensive parallels to (. . .) rites of territorial passage" (1960: 26). Curiously, this is the reverse of what he knew of actual buildings, hallways being quite unknown in the Iroquois long house, and a veritable blight, according to Le Corbusier, in the French house of 1908.
[19] Lefèbvre 1994.
[20] Or, as Robert Venturi put it (et al. 1972), buildings may communicate as "ducks" (through iconic form) or "sheds" (as neutral props for signs).

sense and still require detours and command a place in consciousness; hence the confusing fact that buildings both matter greatly and may not matter at all.[21]

Ritual operations—socially prescribed sets of more or less invariant words and actions—are necessary to elicit meaning from landscape.[22] As Margaret Kenna demonstrated in her analysis of Greek landscape, kinship, and mortuary ritual, ritual establishes connections among villages, houses, chapels, graves, and the identities and prerogatives of persons, connecting the living to the dead, the physical to the immaterial.[23] The central role of the house in the organization of Greek cultural and social life is incontestable, whether that house be an apartment in an urban πολυκατοικία (apartment block), a πατρικὸ σπίτι (patrilineally transferred house), a matrilineal dowry house as in the uxorilocal islands, or, as it has been among agro-pastoralists especially in the north, a kind of *zadruga* or shared fraternal residence.

Buildings, like landscapes, are part of systems of property, and struggles over the division and reclamation of landed property are pervasive in unsettled zones such as the border areas of northern Greece. Nancy Munn writes that Australian aborigines observe ritual interdictions that create a set of shifting "excluded or restricted regions" for each person throughout life;[24] these interdictions produce transient boundaries that compel people to make what she calls "detours."[25] This business of being "still there" (enduring visibility) makes property what it is— whether aboriginal or western.[26] Citing legal philosophy Munn notes: "the very claim of property is that it is something lasting."[27] It is lasting, and, of course, exclu-

---

[21] Whether or not the man-madeness of buildings makes them very different as social shelter from elements of the "natural" landscape is a debated question. This question has two parts: whether or not the domestication of the human species separates us from our animal builder similars like the beaver, and whether or not house-dwelling, relatively sedentary, humans become quite different from those who erect no shelter or flimsy ones. Shelter of any kind is part of a system of preferential concealments, but Wilson (1988) argues that among forager peoples systems of discretion and avoidance are qualitatively different from those implicated in solid permanent dwellings. This is an appealing thesis because it emphasizes the fluidity and presentness of the forager social world, but I doubt the ethnographic record supports a firm distinction between permanent and impermanent or solid dwellings (see, for example, Descola 1996 for an intermediate sort of case). Munn's essay problematizes a classic distinction made by Tambiah (1985b), Wilson, and others, between center-oriented and bounded spaces: the useful distinction can be preserved, but Munn seems correct in showing the salience of boundary zones to even center-oriented spatial orientations.

[22] Cf. Myers 1986:67.

[23] Kenna 1976.

[24] Munn 1996:448.

[25] Ibid.:452.

[26] "Places" are the "topographic remnants of the centered fields of ancient actors. . . . (t)hus the ancestors' spatiocorporeal or action fields turn into enduring 'bases' for the future transient action fields of others." Munn 1996:454–455.

[27] Rose 1994:272 (cited in Munn 1996:456).

sionary, as long as it is connected with the corpus of interdictions sanctioned by ritual action. Access, exclusion, and protection are always part of the work of buildings.[28] This "claim" summons up an obvious counterclaim—the all too visible evidence of property that dissolves, outlasts its fields of action, or is appropriated.

Austin, Searle, and others helped us to understand how words, far from being merely descriptive and referential, could function as the demiurges of their own domain of social, institutional reality: they could count as events or they could make things happen. As Tambiah demonstrated in his analysis of Malinowski's presentation of Trobriand ritual,[29] words can take on the force of things—"verbal missiles"—in magical operations. Conversely, the tactile manipulation of things helps in persuasive magical transfers, the bruteness of things being borrowed, so to speak, in support of the task of persuasion. The performative nature of ritual goes beyond "mere statement" in part because of the physical nature of display.[30]

But if ritual derives support from things, it can be destabilized by them. Magical or ritual performances specify the qualities of things that are to be mobilized in magical operations—limiting their meanings as things to those sought out by the performance. It is equally true that things always exceed, in their manner of existing, these metaphorical predications, and some ritual theorists have emphasized this aspect in understanding the synesthetic and emotional impact of ritual.[31] So we have another question to answer: not only "How to do things with words," but an equally complex, "How to do things with things": how do people control things so that things bend to their task, and not to some other, and what is the impact of their surplus of possible meanings as they endure beyond their ritual functions.

How do we behold things? In their analysis of the photography of William Eggleston, Mike Weaver and Anne Hammond cite Karl Jaspers' distinction between an "essentialist symbol and the existentialist *chiffre* or cypher." A "symbol" is produced by a syllogism involving reductions from the thingness of things. Weaver and Hammond observe: "the symbol and metaphor employ a recognizable set of relations between different objects; the cipher or metonymy uses heterogeneous relations between objects for ends that are not easy to describe, but yet seem meaningful."[32] Buildings, like visual images, are always, though often awkwardly, in a context. As in a photograph, in a landscape the contiguity of things is enforced

[28] Delaney 1998.
[29] Tambiah 1968.
[30] Rappaport 1999:143
[31] Langer 1953; Turner 1967.
[32] Weaver and Hammond 1993:56.

simply by shared space: the element of inexplicit meaning that belongs to the nature of things as opposed to the order of ritual predication is well expressed in Weaver and Hammond's phrase "unresolved contiguity."[33] But without the photographer's art that asserts a boundary and an inner coherence to the spectacle of juxtaposition, this non-specific meaning might better be called anarchic dispersal (I owe this insight to Stephan Feuchtwang). Ritual specification makes things what they are, but it cannot eliminate the excess quality of things as ciphers.

Ritual theorist Roy Rappaport argues that buildings communicate their own autonomous set of assertions. The endurance of a thousand-year-old cathedral "demonstrates" the endurance of liturgy, place, and people as a totality. The very age and invariance of objects such as religious buildings, monuments, and sacra, exemplify the endurance and propriety of liturgical orders; hence the tribute of nationalism to archaeology. In sum: "indexical messages are made heavy by material representation in ritual." Such buildings would seem to be extremely reliable devices. A second look, however, might make us reconsider this. In architecture we have two flows of meaning in opposite directions: a ritually predicated set of assertions and exclusions (of meanings and persons) and a kind of uncontrolled and unresolved perdurance in space and time.

5

Are buildings really so transparently self-referential as the example of the cathedral might imply? Lévi-Strauss argues, to the contrary, that the social and physical entity of the house is "formed at the intersection of incompatible perspectives that threaten to break apart at any moment."[34] The house is a form of social organization balancing contradictory forces of blood and soil, affinity and descent, kin and class, in the formation of identity. As such the house projects a taken-for-granted durability on a foundation of radical instability. The extravagance of the trust demanded by this institution is matched by the depth of the bitterness its disappointments engender. Effort is required to keep the house in its place and to specify and control its qualities. It might be the case that houses drain ritual repertoires as much as stock or replenish them.[35]

---

[33] Weaver 2000. Places, as the philosopher Edward Casey notes, gather contradictory things into "one area of common engagement" and in doing this gathering, place, Casey argues, ". . . is deconstructive of [those] oppositions that it brings and holds together within its own ambience" (Casey 1996).

[34] Lévi-Strauss 1982; also Carsten and Hugh-Jones 1995.

[35] Lévi-Strauss introduced the term "house society" (*societé à maison*) to supplement those of tribe, village, clan, and lineage, where the latter terms did not seem adequate to express the combination of undifferentiated, matrilineal, and patrilineal strategies of collective continuity found in such societies as the Kwakiutl of the NW Coast and medieval European noble families.

What Lévi-Strauss stressed was the way in which the house acted not only to mediate but also to suspend and contain the incompatible perspectives of various actors in the system of social reproduction.[36] The creation of a "house" in this sense is a naturalization of power through obscuring its dependence on exchange. Lévi-Strauss' exposé of the house is also only one part of a more general questioning of appearances with regard to semiotics of the material world. Lévi-Strauss describes the deceptions that non-discursive forms can engender precisely by their apparently self-referential nature: the spatial symmetry of a Bororo village tells a false story about dual organization, and hides the operation of hierarchical castes. Thus houses need ritual to say what they are and to resist the fragmentation of their antagonistic components, just as rituals exploit the bruteness of the house to enforce their predications; their autonomous communicative potential is not self-evident.

6

Stories from Prespa, like the story of Iannis I recounted at the beginning of this chapter, seem to support Lévi-Strauss' sense of the instability of topological and architectural readings. Sometimes this sense is quite explicitly described. At lunch one day in one of the villages, a visiting émigré from Australia told a story to the local people about something she remembered from her childhood: A man came from elsewhere to Prespa for the first time. Descending from the mountains, and gazing for the first time at the snow covered Small Prespa lake with the island of Hagios Akhillios in the middle, he marveled at this amazing expanse of fields that surrounded the cluster of houses and churches. Of course he was mistaking the lake for fields. The company politely listened: they all know it in several of its variants—

[36] " . . . the father, as wife taker, sees in his son a privileged member of his lineage, just as the maternal grandfather, as wife-giver, sees in his grandson a full member of his own. It is at the intersection of these antithetical perspectives that the house is situated, and perhaps is formed. After which, as in opposite mirrors, the initial tension is reflected throughout all levels of social life" (Levi-Strauss 1982:186). For Levi-Strauss, this is the result of a situation in which "political and economic interests, on the verge of invading the social field, have not yet overstepped the 'old ties of blood,' as Marx and Engels used to say," i.e. they borrow the language of kinship but do not in some sense adhere to the crucial distinction between descent and affinity as indexing identity versus exchange. Without a proper notion of exchange, he seems to say, culture loses its key function, which is to heal the rift introduced by exogamy through a new kind of continuity, the system of exchange. Descent, Levi-Strauss implies, implies natural continuity; affinity implies cultural continuity. If descent and affinity are simply two strategies of reproducing the house, culture loses its proper domain and is modeled after nature (a "second nature": history). "By gluing together real interests and mythical pedigrees, it procures for the enterprises of the great a starting point endowed with absolute value" (1982:187). This is how the invention of a "House" naturalizes power. But Levi-Strauss' argument for the aristocracy is only the extreme case of a more general argument.

the version set in antiquity, the one that features Byzantine emperors, and the versions in which local people are named and play the roles. The story is popular because it tells how outsiders are fooled by what they see, and because it also talks about how some insiders are disappointed by what they have: just a big shallow lake, not broad plains of fertile, easily worked, and profitable, land.

7

Deception is a possibility of symbolic communication in general, and in fact the possibility of something being deceptive turns it from being a thing into being a sign. Ritual language is not discursive explanation: as Bloch, following Rappaport, Austin, and others, notes, it may lose in "meaning" what it gains in influence.[37] (For Bloch, the lack of meaning of formalized language/ritual is not accidental to its function, which is more or less to "hide reality": the arbitrariness of social hierarchy, for example, or the real fertility of women). Rappaport also emphasizes the potential of all symbolic systems to lie because a sign can occur in the absence of its signification or referent.[38]

Architectural designers have been aware of the problem of how to "fix" the meaning of material things. In small societies these meanings are encoded in ritual (although Goody and others suspect we have exaggerated the precision or democracy of that encoding). In societies with literacy and academies, the codes are reproduced by specialized means, although to function adequately architecture relies on popular ritual. It is then possible for these codes to lose touch with or be out of synch with their ritual anchors, as appears to have happened in late nineteenth-century Europe. In this crisis of representation ambitious builders sought an eternal code which is a code without ritual: modernist architects of this period thought they could find it in "pure form." In their pursuit of truth in architecture, architectural theorists such as Le Corbusier aimed to eliminate all indexical and iconic referentiality in buildings: "The 'styles' are a lie."[39] Le Corbusier wanted a new style—a no-style—generated by a way of life, an elimination of all "dead concepts in regard to the house." While we throw away old tools, we insist on living in old houses. "Why?," Le Corbusier asks. Because men love home, and develop a "cult of the home." We are attached to our household gods. Le Corbusier compares the

---

[37] Bloch 1989. "It is not there to report facts but to influence people" (Austin 1975:234 quoted in Bloch 1989:32).
[38] Rappaport, however, seems to think that ritual "ameliorates" the problem of the possible deceitfulness of language.
[39] Le Corbusier 1927:3.

house to a cult, a dogma, a religion. Because it has remained the same, it will crumble. Le Corbusier paints an unfortunate picture of the modern trapped in his unworthy and pestilential house, demoralized and furtive.[40] For Le Corbusier there is a problem about the way people think about the house. "The right state of mind does not exist":[41] the dream of making a home of one's own continues to provoke "an actual state of sentimental hysteria." Against this desire for the house as a monument and ritually saturated legacy Le Corbusier protests: "A house will no longer be this solidly built thing which sets out to defy time and decay; it will be a tool as the motor car is becoming a tool."[42]

Le Corbusier's conception of the deceptiveness of the European house was comprehensively damning: first, it was deceptive because it was historical (decorative, referential) and ritualistic (not transparent with reference to function, full of symbolic, conventional, and imitative elements). Second it was deceptive because it was the locus of transcendental sentimentality and individualism and the will to status. It pretended, in other words, *to exist* (here his observations are not so different from those of Lévi-Strauss) when in fact it really could not.

What Le Corbusier was suggesting was not so much that houses could never be ritually integrated with social life; rather, he was stating the fact—as he saw it—

---

[40] "Truth to tell, the modern man is bored to tears in his home; so he goes to his club. The modern woman is bored inside her boudoir; she goes to tea parties. The modern man and woman are bored at home: they go to nightclubs. But lesser folk who have no clubs gather together in the evening under the chandelier and hardly dare to walk through the labyrinth of their furniture which takes up the whole room and is all their fortune and their pride" (Le Corbusier 1927:121–122).

[41] Ibid.:229.

[42] Ibid.:237. Le Corbusier felt the threat of a serious danger: "The problem of the house is the problem of the epoch" (ibid.:227); "society is an unstable thing and is cracking under the confusion caused by fifty years of progress which have changed the face of the world more than the last six centuries have done." At the same time he felt that no one had quite grasped the real nature of the crisis: "The problem of the house has not yet been stated" (ibid.:4). Jean Giradoux, writing a preface to Le Corbusier's writings in the midst of WWII, seems to regard this compulsoriness of the contemporary less as liberation, and more in light of populist frustration: ". . . the prime factor of the longevity of a people is this: a people must be exactly as old as its times. No civilization, no matter how deeply rooted, no matter how regenerative, can consent to be outclassed or outdated by younger civilizations, even in fields of minor importance. At no time may it overlook or shrink from the increase of ease and facility by which mechanical or social progress enlist the citizen, and risk estranging him from his very nature. If the civilization does not grant him, unstintingly and in a form befitting its genius, the rewards of life that other civilizations enjoy, it will turn those rewards into lures, and no sooner will he have suspected their existence than they will entice him away from himself and alienate him from his civilization. . . . once he has been made aware of privileges dealt out to others, he will never again ascribe their absence from his own life to a mere delay but to an incapacity. Little by little, as he confronts those who enjoy a mode of life with a high rate of exchange, he will adopt the scoffing, renunciatory attitude of the citizen whose currency is cheap" (Giradoux 1973:xviii).

that in his milieu they were not, and when they were no longer ritually integrated, but persisted as if they were, they were inauthentic, even pestilential, objects.

8

Le Corbusier wrote about the houses of the turn of the twentieth century as labyrinths and of the behavior of their inhabitants as furtive; he believed that this was a question of a certain kind, even "style," of dwelling. Others see the habits and values of concealment as coterminous with dwelling itself. The archaeologist Peter Wilson argues that permanent dwellings played a revolutionary role in human prehistory in establishing and setting up an opposition between domestic intimacy and neighborly uncertainty.

Freud in his reflections on the uncanny made a not dissimilar connection between the house and what is hidden.[43] In Freud's argument *heimlich* or homely and *unheimlich* or uncanny are not really opposites but just the same phenomenon regarded from the inside and the outside of the house. "Home" has a second meaning of "concealed," or "covert." Actions at home are obscure or concealed, so while home relieves the strains described by Wilson for forager societies as "watching and being watched" it engenders the new strains of opaque social barriers.[44] Freud's citations dwell on the territorial and collective dimensions of *un/heimlich*: he quotes: "The protestant landowners do not feel . . . *heimlich* among their catholic followers." The uncanny, as Freud puts it, concerns some confusion about the nature of the presuppositions on which the world is based, an instability of self-knowledge.

As Freud tells us, what is uncanny is the "unintended recurrence" of things familiar to us but alienated from the mind through a process of repression. The German word centers on "home" and on the slippage between the familiar and unfamiliar. The English word is etymologically related to skill and knowledge ("can," "cunning"): "canny" means wise, wary, and endowed with occult powers, and "uncanny" means unsafe to trust, and again, supernatural, occult. Both German and English usages specifically concern subversion. The English "uncanny"

---

[43] An example from the nineteenth century: "Starving out the English as the canny Scotch has so often done." And from the same period: "These gipsies were a queer uncanny folk." The romance languages and Greek seem to have no such special word, apart from *strange* or *foreign*. The German word especially seems related to the rise of a mentality of domesticity from the seventeenth century on. The English *canny* is also of relatively recent coinage; it would not be illogical to guess that canny is a modification of *uncanny* rather than the reverse.

[44] Social life in primate groups "depends in large part on each individual person paying attention to others, on watching and being watched" (Wilson 1988:20).

attaches to unquiet people or places, especially stones, nests, or visions of landscape. Both canny and uncanny may mean clear-sighted, meaning seeing things that others miss.

Freud's examples of the uncanny stress the insecurity engendered by the theoretical, sign-like convergence between home and kinship, kinship and ethnicity. Freud compares the *unheimlich* to walking over a buried spring or dried up pond and feeling that water might come up there again.[45] The watery image is especially apt for the Prespa example.[46]

9

The disruptive experience of the Greek civil war was not unique to the Prespa area or to Macedonian exiles but rather common to many such rural areas. Remembering her return in 1950 to her village in central Greece, a woman interviewed by anthropologist Anna Collard testified that

> nothing was the same anymore, there were houses burnt and others without their roofs. . . . There were grasses and weeds growing everywhere, out of the cracks in the walls, right up to the doors, from inside the windows. It was so high where there should have been paths, and all over the square. . . . We saw people we knew, neighbors we'd come with

---

[45] In support of his conception of the double nature of the uncanny Freud cites a conversation from literature. A certain family, the Zecks, are said to be all "heimlich." "'Heimlich' . . . What do you understand by 'heimlich'?" "Well . . . they are like a buried spring or a dried-up pond. One cannot walk over it without always having the feeling that water might come up there again." "Oh, we call it 'unheimlich': you call it 'heimlich' . . ." . In my understanding, the Great Prespa lake has some of these qualities. The lake is internally divided by the borders of the three neighboring states but the border is not visible although the territories of fishermen are known. The lake rises and falls and these changes are said to predict the coming of war; it has been recently falling dramatically, which is locally explained as the consequence of an underground fissure.

[46] The following citation from testimonies of the Bosnian war gives concreteness to the anxiety Freud describes. ". . . the Croats from Letnica . . . feel highly embarrassed occupying the dwellings and using the furniture of people that have fled their homes too. For most of them, the fact that they themselves have abandoned their homes and possessions does not offer much emotional consolation. They feel like intruders in the personal domains of other people whose presence can be felt in every corner of the house, and in the objects and the big gardens that they left behind. In the beginning, a woman told me, she would often 'hear' voices or knocks on the door in the middle of the night, expecting the previous inhabitants to return (there have been many accounts about Serbs crossing the Serbo-Croatian lines at night, to find out what happened to their villages and houses). Above all, to enter somebody else's home is considered dishonourable. This will in the end cause misfortune: Somebody else's property has never brought luck to anybody, . . . they often say. Ideally, the Croats from Letnica would prefer to build new houses for themselves. But for the moment this is not feasible. . . ," (Ger Duijzings in Povrzanović and Jambrešić Kirin 1996:160–161).

but grew afraid of them. You could never tell anymore, who belonged to
whom. Each family kept its secrets to itself. That was the worst, not
knowing anymore.[47]

Not only who belonged to whom, but what belonged to whom was in question. "Evacuation," Collard writes, " meant that the actual physical continuity of
these villages was broken for the first time since their settlements hundreds of years
before."[48] The suddenness of evacuation was often remembered by means of a
housekeeper's images: the washing left wet on the line, bread ready to be baked,
trousseaux left behind.

Placelessness was indeed the antithesis of Greek order, which is an order of
villages (even if their stability is illusory). A woman speaking of her husband, who
went missing in the war, laments: "he was a family man and now he's died a gypsy
without family or house."[49] Greek use of the counterexample of the gypsy—like
that of the Scythian nomad counterposed to the polis-dweller in antiquity—dramatizes all that the house is meant to stand for as the means towards and proof of
civilization. (The Zagorochorian woman—the mountain woman par excellence—
is approvingly said "never to leave her village.")

The stories people tell about such disrupted places in the aftermath of war are
made up of metonymical detail and idiosyncratic events. The unresolved contigui-
ties of these pieces of narration express the irresolution of contiguity on the ground.
The house is present but the metaphor of the house, so active in the construction
of everyday social reality in Greece, is depleted.

Pierre Bourdieu observed that "inhabited space—starting with the house—is
the privileged site of the objectification of . . . generative schemes."[50] "Property," he
tells us, "appropriates its owner, embodying itself in the form of a structure generating practices perfectly conforming with its logic and demands";[51] ". . . socialization instills a sense of the equivalences between physical space and social space."[52]
The built environment of a village or a homestead is a monument that testifies to
ambitious, even organic premises about dwelling. But the landscape of villages
subjected to forced disruption does not sustain the fictions of equivalences between
physical and social space; instead, it undermines the distinction between κλῆρος,

[47] Collard 1990:230.
[48] Ibid.:233.
[49] Ibid.:240.
[50] Bourdieu 1990:76
[51] Ibid.:57.
[52] Ibid.:71.

"lot" (as in "drawing lots") and the closely related but socially distinct κληρονομιά, "inheritance." While inheritance is a drawing of equal portions among legitimate heirs within a closed space of reproduction, the κλῆρος takes place in a space cleared of its attachments by fiat: place returned to the abstraction of space. These successive lotteries figure prominently in local narratives of justice and injustice: it was by lot that in the Macedonian border area nominally empty houses and fields were distributed to relocated populations, that land reform was carried out periodically through the 1930s to the early 1960s, that small plots are today given by village communities to young families. Invocations of the closely related concepts, lot, fate, portion, and legacy, point to the estranged or uncertain ties between owners and possessions and subjects and futures.

I asked a woman living, on her own, in a small, traditional χαγιάτι (a wooden verandah common to northern architecture) style house in an old agnatic compound in one of the villages, how she came to live in this house which seemed only hanging on by a thread.

My grandfather was the only son—there were five girls, but daughters didn't have a right to the property when they married. So he had all the property, and he went to America, and in 1928 he came back and built the house. The war came; my father died on the Greek front in 1941. He died for Greece. The αντάρτες [fighters in the Democratic Army] came, the planes [of the government forces] started bombardments. They came and took us, with my mother and the children of my mother's brother by truck to one village and then another near Prilep. I spent a year in this village. There had been some Vlachs there but they'd gone to Thessaloniki. We worked tending pigs. But we were children, and in the afternoon we fell asleep, and the pigs fell in the water and drowned.

After a year we moved to Prilep and went to school. My mother married a man from Prespa there. In 1954 I'd gone as far as the 1st year of middle school. The Red Cross came. My mother had remarried and the new husband didn't want us children, she'd given birth to new children. So I went back with my two brothers. My grandmother was paralyzed when we got home, and there was a cobbler in the house, an outsider [ξένος], who knows what he was. The police had to help us to get him out. We brought grandmother back from Florina and looked after her until she died in 1956. Then my brother married and I couldn't stay in this house any longer so I went to live with Anthoula. When I arrived from abroad I didn't know how to make a living, if you go to school you don't know anything but letters. The Vlachs here looked after me and gave me bread and milk. When they first came here the Vlachs destroyed the houses, they took out the windows and the doors. They were wild and lived with their animals, but now they are educated and the same as us, or more so. So when we returned we worked in other peoples' fields like the Albanians do now; they [αὐτοί] had given our fields away. [At that point she offered me some walnut cake, and told me that the walnuts were given to her by her neighbors, who now owned the walnut trees of her grandfather.]

My husband was from K., I married him in 1958. At 16 he went with the ἀντάρτες, was caught, and spent 10 years in jail, Thessaloniki, Makronissos. He came to live with me at Anthoula's because he had a house in K., but they [αὐτοί] had given it to Vlachs. In 1964 I went to Skopje. My aunt kept the house here when my brothers left otherwise they [αὐτοί] would have taken it. My mother couldn't do much for us; my father in law gave us a room in the public housing apartment he had. We had a little work here and there, but things are bad now. I am making my papers for this house. They say since my father was killed for Greece it shouldn't be any problem. My two brothers are in Canada; they came back in 1994, but in 1998 when they arrived they couldn't get into the country, someone here must have said something. Skopje is heavy, and I have heart problems. It's better here. I don't want to have anything to do with politics; I'm born here. The house will stand as long as I do and then who cares after that.

In this story relations between the person and the house are unsteady, and the forms of instability are also starkly gendered. This native daughter tries to make sense of the course of her life in a kind of homecoming and at the same time takes refuge from that ambition in a utilitarian way of speaking: the return involves the pragmatic considerations of clean air, and a house with no future.[53] As a woman, she takes up the domestic operations that routinize, if not ritualize, habitation in

---

[53] Again, testimony from ex-Yugoslavia bears out the importance of the house and street rather than broader frames of identification: "The space they [exiles] narrate about is thus not the national territory negotiated in the current 'territorial claims,' but primarily home territory encompassing one's own bedroom, kitchen, garden, and street. Home is a place of security, one's 'life-work' and the symbol of the success of the family. The loss of the house and everything it stood for represents one of the fundamental motifs in all our testimonies. The meaning of the house as the irreplaceable symbol and the guideline of identity is evident from the fact that many informants saved or at least tried to save the photographs of their houses which they showed to me on their own initiative. . . . Some informants who have no photographs keep amateur drawings of them." quoted in Povrzanović and Jambrešić Kirin 1996:14.

the context of a present unclearly situated with reference to the past or future. Cooking cheese pies, offering hospitality to strangers, going from the house to church and back, sitting, in the evening, with her neighbors on the wall of the road across from the house, waiting for the grandchildren to spend a few days of their summer holidays, her social world is still ruled by the conventions of the νοικοκυρά (mistress of the house).

It is impossible to finish a set of thoughts about architecture and ritual in Greece without thinking of Greece's most famous story about building, *The Bridge of Arta*.[54] The story or ballad—common throughout the Balkans—involves the attempt of builders and apprentices to build a bridge over the river in the town of Arta. They labored each day only to find that during the night, the bridge had collapsed. They learn, by means of a bird or a spirit, that the bridge will only stand if the wife of the master builder is walled up within it. In some variants, any one of the wives of the master masons will do; in others it is a daughter. Some versions make it clear that the masons do everything they can to prevent their own wives from responding to the message. In other versions they make an agreement among themselves to leave the choice to chance, but only one unlucky brother does not secretly warn his wife. In most variants, they stall: they dispatch a bird, who is to tell the wife or wives to come very slowly to meet them, but the bird itself inverts the message and tells her to come in all haste. A reading of the tale as simple misogyny overlooks the sadness with which the predicament of the masons is rendered, and that where the husband does appear indifferent to the sacrifice of his wife this is glossed as extraordinary cruelty.[55] This poem is a tragedy, not a celebratory tale.[56] This extraordinary ritual of immolation is also a confession about the more banal entropy of things, about the frustration of the objectives of labor and the illusion of local social reproduction. More generally the rituals of architecture might better be thought about as attempts to rein in the unruly coexistence of recalcitrant things in space than as simple devices for the expression and reproduction of cultural order.

---

[54] For a fuller discussion, see Hart 1998.

[55] In Albanian novelist Ismail Kadare's version (*The Three Arched Bridge*) it is not a woman who is sacrificed but rather a local mason, a laborer drafted into the wage economy by the itinerant *équipe*. In fact, his wife and family profit from his sale or sacrifice.

[56] Mandel glosses the *Bridge of Arta* as a reproduction of Greek cosmology and specifically of woman's role as mediator between "households and the worlds of the living and the dead," of woman as concurrently "an instantiation of both nature and culture" (Mandel 1983:173). By this reading woman in the tale is the classic liminal figure—dominated and immured in the bridge but threatening to shatter the structure because and by means of her grief and anger (she desists from shaking the foundations only for the sake of a beloved brother who might pass over). However, if we compare the variants we are led in a different direction. The woman in the *Bridge of Arta* is marked less, perhaps, by her femininity and more by her locality, or to be more precise, localism. She is, ironically, at least the icon of the ends for which the builders enter into the means of labor, the circuit of imperial production.

Laurie Kain Hart

Endnote

A Family History *(continued from note 13)*

Petros tells me that his grandfather was a ντόπιος (a "local," which in this region can signify a person of Slav-Macedonian descent, or, depending on context, simply a local resident). They were very poor; they gathered the chaff of the wheat of others. He married a woman from home but she left, "turned Moslem and married a Turk." He went to Asia Minor, across from Mytilini, in 1892 and married a Greek. They had sheep and lived in a village of all Greeks, no Turks—by contrast to home, which was a mixed population. He returned to Greece in 1913—the Greeks in Asia Minor, Petros said, were importing arms for an uprising, the Turks found out and threw them out. They arrived in Thessaloniki and worked in tobacco for a year before they returned to Prespa. His mother was a Greek who didn't know ντόπικα (Slav-Macedonian) and could only speak to the teacher. She became ill and died, and the children remained "orphans." In 1915 they had war with Bulgaria and Serbia: the Bulgarians came to the frontiers. Then there was the 1916 war with Austria, Germany, France, Italy, England. "The King Constantine was a Germanophile. The Bulgarians went as far as Olymbos and the French fought them. When we went to collect wood we saw some of the opposition: they called us Bulgars." The story after 1916 continues in the same vein: wars, evacuations, epidemics, starting over again after each devastation. The family exploits its Asia Minor connection and get some reparations, increasing their land holdings. Petros marries a local girl from Y., and buys land with the dowry money from his father-in-law working in Detroit. They are still hungry but now they are millers. In 1935 they build the house: the builders come from Sphika (a now abandoned local village of masons) and from near the Albanian border. The house has a "history," a story, he tells me: "in the old days we paid the παπάς [priest] ourselves, and for this we kept the gold in the house. Someone came to steal the gold. They riffled the chests, but they didn't find the wallet hidden in there among the folded shirts." The second World War was not unlike the first: "everybody was naked again and there was no food." The Italians, the Germans, the Serbs: expulsions. Either as ντόπιοι (of Slav-Macedonian descent) or as Mikrasiates (Greek refugees from Asia Minor) they were accused of being communists. In 1945 the army came, in 1947 the police, and after that the αντάρτες (partisans, guerillas). Markos and Zachariades (communist partisan leaders) lived in this house. Thirty families petitioned for a Greek language (not Slav-Macedonian) school. They had to hide from the planes then. "Someone said that if you put sugar in your tobacco you turn yellow and they won't know what's the matter with you and they won't take you." But Petros ended up in Albania, in the flight from government forces in 1949. It was poor in Prespa when he came back: a woman from K. came to ask for clothes—they'd taken all the clothes to the provincial town controlled by the government. When Petros tells his stories, he uses all the old names of the hills and neighborhoods: not the Macedonian names, but the Turkish ones. His other relatives went to Poland and Russia with the war, and then to Australia. Returning from Australia, the foreign relatives are reclaiming portions of the houses which remain in their families, and then they are razed so that each family has a bungalow to itself. Petros however still lives, with his brother and his brother's wife, in the house his father built.

Twenty-Four

Little Soldiers for/against the State: Embodied Repositionings in a Male Rite of Passage in Northern Greece[1]

Jane K. Cowan

Structure, Agency and "the Body"

If the literature on "the body" is most visibly presented as a debate about culture versus nature, the "essential" versus the "constructed," it is equally enmeshed in a debate about structure versus agency. Michel Foucault's accounts of the production of bodies through a focus on discursive formations constituted a theoretical move, consistent with his intellectual project as a whole, determined to challenge conceptions of a unified, self-knowing subject and the voluntaristic model of social action they entailed. In the context of historically-specific and changing if, in Foucault's hands, somehow "ideal-typical" institutions ("the insane asylum," "the prison," "the clinic"), he persuasively documented how particular disciplinary practices have produced the "docile" and ultimately self-monitoring bodies of modernity.[2] Foucault not only alerted us to the fact that the body is shaped through and expressive of power relations; he also offered new ways to think about power, and the relations between power and pleasure.[3] Yet whether as a result of theoretical fiat or empirical lacuna, Foucault had little to say about the body as a material entity or as an acting, experiencing subject.

As witnesses to cross-cultural variations in what Marcel Mauss called "les techniques du corps" anthropologists, intermittently but over a long period, had also pondered "the body."[4] Many followed Mary Douglas' structuralist musings on the

---

[1] An earlier version of this chapter appeared as Cowan 1998. I am grateful to Keith Brown, Marie-Bénédicte Dembour, David Sutton, and Richard Wilson for comments.
[2] Foucault 1965; Foucault 1979; Foucault 1973.
[3] Foucault 1978.
[4] Mauss 1935.

metaphorization of society as a body, and conversely, the mapping of social bound-aries onto individual bodies.[5] But it was the advent of "practice anthropology" in the 1970s which helped to move anthropology beyond a hermeneutics of metaphor, a closed system endlessly reproducing itself, toward a focus on the dialectic of struc-ture and agency.[6] When, in the early 1980s, I was attempting to develop a theoret-ical approach for a study of social dancing in Greece as a site for the articulation and negotiation of gender relations, I found inspiration in Pierre Bourdieu's attempts to theorize processes of "embodiment" in the context of the reproduction of social systems, while also recognizing the creativity of agents.[7] His attention to such issues as practical knowledge, "habitus," the distinction between rules and strategies, and the role of improvisation and the manipulation of tempo and timing was, at the time, revelatory.[8] Bourdieu's acknowledgment of the significance of "trivial" everyday gestures of power and deference, which contrasted with the exclusive preoccupation with ritual among many anthropologists, encouraged a tracing of the production of embodied subjectivities *across contexts* without unduly privileging any one of them, a principle I was later to follow in my analyses. His "outline of a theory of practice" went a long way toward taking account of the actor as agent, even if "the actor" persisted as a somewhat abstract category. Yet it remained a rationalist account, priv-ileging logic and virtually ignoring emotion, and thereby working with a truncated model of the human desires and needs which inform and motivate action. As a theory for grappling with the subjective, as well as objective, aspects of embodi-ment—embodiment as an affective yet always culturally and socially patterned expe-rience—it was incomplete.[9]

From Ethnography to Theory and Back Again

His theoretical ideas apart, Bourdieu's inclusion of ethnographic examples from his Algerian (Kabyle) fieldwork to illustrate and explore his theoretical propositions were suggestive to me in demonstrating the specific potential contribution which

[5] Douglas 1970.
[6] Ortner 1984.
[7] Bourdieu 1977.
[8] There are certain striking parallels here with Anthony Giddens' attempted reformulation of the notion of structure through "structuration theory," developed in the same period. These are elabo-rated in Giddens 1976. Note, for example, Giddens' emphasis on the importance of "practical consciousness." Ironically, Giddens' work is vulnerable to many of the same criticisms as is Bourdieu's with respect to an overly rationalist and voluntarist conception of social action. See Karp 1986.
[9] Here, anthropological work in the tradition of the Oxford School on social experience and collec-tive representations was extremely helpful. See e.g. Lienhardt 1961, and Karp 1980. Feminist work on women's complex and contradictory experiences of power relations was also inspiring. See e.g. Abu-Lughod 1986, and Vance 1984.

anthropologists can make to work on "the body." Among them, one of the most important, in my view, is their capacity to provide theoretically-informed analyses of processes of embodiment in situ, in relation to the historical, cultural, social, political, and economic specificities of the contexts under investigation. I am making here a stronger claim for this than Bourdieu did, for his text is somewhat ambiguous about the relation between theory and ethnography. The title marks it as a theoretical text (*Outline of a Theory of Practice*) and throughout he is at pains to insist that social analysts must show greater awareness of the effects of theoretical "knowing" upon what it seeks to know. Following this logic, one should probably read the Kabyle materials as apprehended and reworked in terms of a theoretical model which they then serve to illustrate. But it is intriguing to wonder about the extent to which the Kabyle incidents *generated* the model, by virtue of failing to make sense in terms of previous models.

The tentative, unfinished nature of the project ([an] *Outline . . .*) points to this more dialectical relation between theory and ethnography, but it is not explicitly explored. Questions like: *How much does the fluidity of Kabyle political and social organization and the subsequent requirement to be always ready to improvise inform Bourdieu's emphasis on strategy, improvisation, negotiation?* and moreover, *How much does the "fit" between Kabyle dispositions toward negotiation and those of contemporary Western European market societies reinforce this emphasis?* pose the issue of the relation between indigenous models of social action and so-called "social scientific" (i.e. ostensibly, universally-applicable) analytical models. They also illuminate, by displacing and making visible, the unavoidable "culturality" of analytical language. This particular Pandora's Box remains firmly closed, though, as Bourdieu goes no further than most treatises in addressing the question of whether *any* social theory, by its very definition, can withstand a critique of ethnocentrism, since any social theory assumes, if not advocates, *particular* models of human nature and of sociality and makes their elaboration the primary criterion for analytical adequacy in sociological accounts.

Serious acknowledgment of "local" specificities and their implications within particular studies ought to provoke more skepticism among anthropologists toward the more grandiose theoretical claims of our era's theory gurus, such as the usefulness of generalized concepts ("discourse," "the body," even "the modern body"). It may also require more modest conclusions. Anthropologists' groundedness in empirical material need not render us the data-collecting drones of the social sciences, however, nor are the resulting accounts necessarily of only parochial interest. This groundedness can be, epistemologically, both a brake to grand theory's wildest excesses and a spur to retheorization (apart from Bourdieu, witness Marilyn Strathern's reconceptualization of persons in some societies as "dividuals" as an answer to conundrums posed by her New Guinea fieldwork data).[10] Yet the nature of fieldwork, where evidence is gathered through observing, talking to, and living with people—a mode of research that involves, in relation to other episte-mological activities, an unusually intimate access to ordinary people's everyday lives—perpetually reminds the anthropologist not only of the importance of keeping "locality" theoretically in view. It also forces her to grapple with the rela-tionship between "discourses" (properly pluralized) and human subjects, as a "lived" quotidian process.

Investigating "Real" Bodies in Real Places

How, then, does one explore "real" bodies in a way that marshals the best insights of "theory"? A very cursory description of my own attempt to develop an approach adapted to a specific context, through brief reference to just two of the discursive fields I had to take into account, those of "dance" and of "tradition," will show one possible strategy, while also providing background information for the case study to follow. In the years 1983-85 I chose to investigate the issue of embodiment as a dimension of the production, reproduction, and negotiation of social relations, especially of gender, in the context of social dancing in Sohos, a small town in northern Greece.[11] Finding no single theoretical model adequate in enabling me to indulge my numerous analytical curiosities, I was compelled to become bricoleuse, constructing an approach which drew insights and ideas from many different soci-ological and anthropological traditions. Like Bourdieu, Foucault, and others I was interested in the ways social meanings (or "discourses" or "collective representa-tions") became literally *incorporated* in the flesh and sinews of our being. Yet having chosen to investigate this primarily within social dancing I had to deal more directly with the specifically *performative* aspects of bodily acts as claims about identity, rela-tionship, and experience, and its implications for issues of reflexivity. I was intrigued with the duality intrinsic to our bodily nature—that people both *have* bodies and *are* bodies. The social concomitants of this fact directed me, on the one hand, toward *the body as sign*, as a material object which may be read or deciphered, and on the other hand, toward *the body as agent and material locus of subjectivity*, as a site of desires, emotions, and experiences.

As I have insisted above, these theoretical concerns could not be investigated in the abstract. "Discourses of the body" were—as they always are—enmeshed with other social, moral, political, and historical discourses (and, of course, prac-

---

[10] Strathern 1988. Strathern uses the concept of "dividual" coined, and developed, by McKim.
[11] Cowan 1990.

tices) and these needed to be traced out. The vivid intensities and confusing tensions that I encountered on dance floors from Athens to Chania to the agricultural villages of Thrace and Macedonia in the late 1970s, and that convinced me that social dancing deserved sociological scrutiny, were a product of quite specific, historically-rooted cultural meanings and social arrangements. If multiple issues coalesced at the dance floor in contemporary Greece—sociability, sexuality, morality, identity, power—this was not necessarily intrinsic to dance universally, nor true for all other times and places. I needed to take account of the particular cultural and historical resonances of dance itself as it had developed as a concept and practice within this society. It was critical thus to stress at the outset that dance had traditionally been at the *literal and metaphorical center* of social life in Greek communities. At the weddings and feast days of the rural peasant communities that were the norm until the mid-twentieth century, families joined together, and in that central space—the neighborhood churchyard, the village square—all the rich, contradictory dimensions of communal coexistence were likely to be "danced out." Thus, in a society where publicly-demonstrated bodily mastery and control (of self and sometimes of others, of space and of symbolic capital) have been necessary conditions for prestige, honor, and reputation, dancing inevitably involves constant assertion and contestation, even as it gives vent to desires for, and experiences of, sensuality, sociability, and solidarity. Indeed, since dancing is associated with multiple and contradictory imperatives, sentiments, and experiences, it operates within Greek popular culture as both an instantiation and a metaphor for the ambiguities of social action more generally.

While dancing remains even today a primarily *participatory* rather than *spectator* sport, and thus is still in the grip of a popular culture and consciousness (including their locally variable manifestations), for over a century it has also been subjected to ideological transformation through discourses of "tradition" established and disseminated by a "patriotic" national discipline of folklore. Thus, in the mid-1980s, Sohoians who danced regularly for pleasure and out of duty "knew" that *some* of their local dances were properly-speaking *folk dances*, associated with the past and a long-enduring "tradition," a suitable subject for "folklorists" like myself. Other dances—waltz, foxtrot, bunny hop, which people danced at fundraising dances—were usually believed to hold no special interest to people like me, since as European imports they could not reveal anything about the distant ancient Greek past.

In sum, an ethnographic exploration of the embodiment of gender (my primary research problem) required taking account of a range of discourses and practices, as well as considerable methodological and analytical flexibility. In the remainder of this chapter, I explore an event, a three-day celebration commemorating the departure of some twenty youths for military service in 1983, as a dramatization of social transition involving changes in gender identity, status, and citizenship for young men. For readers familiar with my previous publications, it can be read alongside the other events I have already analyzed— especially weddings and the pre-Lenten Carnival—since the celebratory forms use the same rhetorical (bodily and verbal) vocabulary and rehearse many of the same themes.[12] However, the questions I pose here to this material are subtly different than they were a decade ago, for in responding to the ongoing discussions about gender and location, I have been enabled to make new kinds of sense from my material.

Little Soldiers

Still in my nightclothes, shivering next to a woodstove I had struggled a quarter of an hour to light, and clasping for warmth a mug of coffee, I heard it. The frigid bleakness of that first day of December, 1983, was disturbed by a faint and distant rhythmic thumping. *Daoúlia!* But it was Thursday—not a wedding procession, surely, since these always commenced on Saturday. I opened the sliding glass door to my tiny balcony, which overlooked one of the market's winding streets, and leaned over the railing. Though nearly 10 a.m., the street was quiet. Bitter cold had dissuaded all but the improvident to venture to market. Yet a few buildings down the road, Nitsa—her hair in curlers under a scarf—was leaning over the rail of her second-floor balcony, on the pretext of shaking out a rug. "Good morning, Nitsa!" I shouted. "What's happening?" She tossed her head gaily in the direction of the sound: "*Fadarákia!*"[13] The "little soldiers" were celebrating their last days of freedom before departing for the army.

It was a telling introduction to an event that turned out to be among the most dramatic and emotionally charged, yet strikingly, least talked about (to me), of my fieldwork. No one had thought to warn the "folklorist," the professional label by which I was generally known, resident in their midst since the previous spring, of this impending event. Evidently, it was not deemed (and thus redeemed as) a "custom" of that truly authentic "tradition" which many townspeople considered to be my only legitimate concern. Other ritual practices tended to be marked as either "traditional" (such as the wedding and the pre-Lenten *Karnavalia*) or, within the same symbolic economy, as "European" and "modern" (such as the local civic association's fund-raising dances). Such practices were imbued with an extreme self-

---

[12] See Cowan 1990; 1988; 1994.
[13] Meaning "little soldiers."

consciousness about traditionality and modernity, the past and the present: the major symbolic poles in terms of which identities were forged. The departure of the *fadarákia*, though exhibiting a familiar ritual structure, was noticeably "unmarked" in relation to a discourse of tradition, a feature whose implications I shall explore in the final part of the chapter.

Greek ethnographies contain no references to the social or ceremonial commemoration of young men's departure for the army. Nonetheless, a number of ethnographers have stressed that for men, military service, rather than marriage, is considered the event that transforms youths into men.[14] In Sohos, in the 1980s, young men customarily were inducted at age nineteen, and they never married, and rarely became engaged, until after completing the two-year period of service. Military service is mandatory under Greek law, although it may be deferred for reasons of education or of unusual family responsibilities. Often his first extended absence from home and community (certainly the case for most of the Sohoian youths) the shock was intensified by a disciplinary regime which is notoriously gruelling—physically, mentally, and emotionally. Even today, and despite certain changes over the past decade in its disciplinary practices, a primary means by which the military institution attempts to *incorporate* into new recruits its preferred model of adult masculinity is a continuous and often brutal and humiliating "testing" of the youth's "manhood" (ἀνδρισμός). This may commence with the preliminary physical examination, when a roomful of new recruits, stripped naked, is forced to bend over so that their anuses can be examined for signs of penetration, to identify "passive" (thus, in cultural terms, feminized) homosexuals.[15] It continues through subjection to a range of practices in which they must confront and learn to deal with extreme regulation of their bodies (its rhythms, functions, capacities, postures), time and movement in space, mind-numbing labor, boredom, capricious exercises of power by their superiors, and situations of danger and even death.

From an anthropological perspective, military service in the Greek army is a classic example of a *rite de passage*, with parallels to male initiation rites throughout the world. However, a primary difference between it and the initiation rites of so-called tribal societies is that in the latter, it is community elders who conduct and control the initiation process undergone by their children. In the Greek case, it is

---

[14] The anthropologist David Sutton, confirming that he, too, knew of no references in the ethnographic literature on this subject, noted that on the island of Kalymnos, the two primary reasons for dynamite-throwing outside of the Easter period, when it is traditional, are the arrival of a visiting dignitary, and the departure of a youth for the army (personal communication, September 18, 1997).

[15] I was alerted to this practice through a presentation by Evthymios Papataxiarchis at an anthropological conference commemorating the establishment of the Department of Social Anthropology at the University of the Aegean in Mytilene, Lesvos, in August 1986. See also Loizos 1994:71.

the State that assumes this role. An additional step is thus involved: boys are transformed into men, but they are also, literally and metaphorically, removed from their homes and stripped of the insignia of all the identities which locate them. Sent for training to army installations in distant regions, and for active service to yet other—often border—sites, they trace the boundaries of their nation-state with their bodies as they meet other recruits, also displaced, and engage in a common project based on a shared nationality. The architects of this policy arguably intended that through this bodily habitus they would come to internalize a sense of Greek national identity and a loyalty toward the nation-state they were charged with defending.[16]

In the following analysis of the structure and content of the three-day celebrations which constitute a prelude to the military exile (and, for ease, using the "ethnographic present-tense"), I focus on these two primary arenas of renegotiation of identity and affiliation: the transition from a juvenile to an adult masculinity, and the transition from a subordinate local to a subaltern of the state. I will try to show that with respect to both arenas, the celebrations articulate—in large part through a language of the body—*identities in formation*, enacting emotional ambivalences, status ambiguities and including gestures of both accommodation and contestation. Implicitly, I am taking up the challenge posed by recent criticisms that, a few prescient exceptions notwithstanding, the analysis of men and masculinity in Mediterranean societies is only beginning to catch up with feminist-inspired work on women in demonstrating the range, variability, and complexity of gender identities and practices.[17] Similarly, persuaded by arguments that local social processes need to be better contextualized in relation to national and global frameworks, I hope to demonstrate what reframing a *rite de passage* beyond the immediate community can reveal about the imbrication of gender with other identities which "locate" the self. Throughout, I intend to show how much the social and emotional power of this event depends on both the rhetorical force and the experiential sensitivity of young men's bodies.

---

[16] In recent years, the policy of sending military recruits far away from home has changed, and young men are often posted fairly near to home. The period of service has also been reduced. David Sutton (personal communication, 1997) suggests that this indicates that the authorities deem, rightly in general, that the inculcation of a national consciousness in the young men has been by now broadly achieved, through institutions like mass media and the education system.

[17] The criticism is articulated by Loizos 1994. Some works which did address the performance of masculinity and, implicitly or explicitly, acknowledge its multiplicity, include Herzfeld 1985b and Papataxiarchis 2001. More recently, the theme has been taken up by others; see e.g. Faubion 1993, and Sutton 2000.

Day 1: Coercive Pleasures and Confrontation with State Authority

When I caught up with the *fadarákia* late on Thursday morning, I found eighteen young men carrying bottles of ouzo and slowly dancing on the uphill road to the central square in a spirited and disorderly procession, whistling, clapping, interjecting "ehhh-IH!" and "áide!" and stepping to the quick-quick-quick-slow beat of the *patináda* dance played by a troupe of Gypsy musicians. They were dressed in the everyday uniform of male youths; their faded jeans, sweaters, and denim jackets unremarkable except for their flimsiness in the windy, below-freezing weather, this being itself a sign of their "hot blood." However, in addition, they all wore Hawaiian-print flowered hats. "That's for 'flower children,'" quipped a male acquaintance, who noted that these sorts of hats were worn every year in jokey "peacenik" protest to the state's call for cannon fodder. A young woman remarked: "In moments like this, they are bound together, they become 'one.'" The boys knew they shared a common fate (a common misfortune!) and were not only marking it but literally embodying it through their dress, gestures and consumption. "It is a bit like Carnival in that way, and like our weddings," she added. "These boys are real party animals (γλευτζέδες). Just give them *daoúlia* and they go nuts!"

Most of the hats we saw had a small placard of paper pinned to them, marked "167" (the administrative code for this group of inductees) and above it, in smaller letters, "Sparta" or "Thebes" (the military base to which the youth was assigned). Some placards had "SOS" marked in Latin script, but most had skull-and-crossbones scrawled on them. "God Save Us!" remarked my companion. "Today we die! Not forever, of course, but for two years," explained one of the celebrants.

The small bottles of ouzo which the youths carried were offered, usually wordlessly and without greeting, to people who had stepped outside the shops and houses to watch the procession. The person receiving the "treat" (κέρασμα) accepted the bottle, raised it and offered the conventional wish given to a person about to depart on a journey: "May the good go with you, and return with you" (μὲ τὸ καλὸ νὰ πᾶς καὶ μὲ τὸ καλὸ νὰ γυρίσεις). One of the youths carried a ten-liter jug to which a funnel was attached by a greasy string. This was used to refill the smaller bottles for offering the public, but also in jovial, coercive horseplay among themselves.

The youths moved in a loose group, shifting easily to accommodate the different rhythms of the songs played by the Gypsies. The latter, a troupe known as "the *daoúlia*" and consisting of one ντaoύλι or drum plus, on this occasion, three ζουρνάδες or double-reeded shawms (very unusually, an extra ζουρνά had been hired to increase the sound!) played both folk and popular tunes, but

413

predominantly songs about love and exile. For example, they repeatedly played a song called "Anastáki" a folksong of the local region of Macedonia but popularized by the nationally famous singer, Charis Alexiou, which recounted a mother's grief for her absent son. Marking out the rhythm with their bodies, the boys sang along:

Δὲν θέλω ἐγὼ παινέματα
παρηγοριὲς καὶ ψέματα.
Θέλω τὸ γιό μου, τὸν 'Αναστάκη
ποὺ εἶναι στὴν ξενιτειά.
Αὐτὸ μικρό μου καπετανάκι
ποὺ δὲν μοῦ γράφει πιά.
Χαρεῖτε τὰ καράβια σας,
τὰ πλούτη μὲς στ' ἀμπάρια σας
δὲν θὰ τὰ λιμπιστῶ.
Θέλω τὸ γιό μου, τὸν 'Αναστάκη,
ποὺ δὲν θὰ τὸν ξαναδῶ.

I don't want laments,
Sympathy, lies.
I want my son, Anastákis,
Who is in the foreign land.
The one, my little captain,
Who doesn't write to me anymore.
Enjoy your ships,
Your wealth, your high-living
They don't interest me.
I want my son, Anastákis,
Who I'll never see again.

Frequently, as they processed very slowly up the hill, eight to ten youths would spontaneously form a huddle, squatting on the ground, arms around each other, facing inwards and singing with and to each other, one or two of them marking out the beat forcefully with their arms. After a verse or two they would rise and resume the dancing. In the final ten meters of incline before the road peaked and flattened out, the boys turned and faced downhill, toward the people watching them from the marketplace and toward the *daoúlia*, and slowly danced backwards up the hill. Then, one of the boys picked up the ten-liter bottle of ouzo, and began to pour its contents into the mouth of a fellow celebrant, as other celebrants held the latter in place, supporting or constraining (it wasn't clear to me). As the boy being "treated" drank, ouzo running down his cheeks, the *daoúli* player leaned back slightly, beating the *daoúli* strapped to his chest with rapid, even strokes, creating a dramatic stretching of the musical tempo, and rhythmically imitating the gushing of the ouzo. After a few seconds, signaled by the release of the boy from his forced "treating," the *daoúli*, still facing the celebrants, hit a forceful downbeat and returned the tune to its original tempo. A few moments later, another youth dropped to his knees, waving his arms in the air to the *daoúli's* beat, and others quickly joined him, sitting spread-eagled with arms waving, piled together. A minute or two passed, and the boys rose and continued to the central square, to dance the more sedate line dances. A little later, the group, the musicians, and myself stopped for a meal at a pizza restaurant, then continued through the streets, and whenever reaching one of the boys' family houses, dancing with his family.

In this celebration which was never referred to as a "ritual" but which had a clear ritual structure and purpose, the *fadarákia* drew on a repertoire of bodily gestures, postures, and poses—both individual and collective—familiar and practiced from other local, ritual contexts, in particular, the wedding and the Carnival. The scenes described above, which were repeated many times during that first day, especially, are typical of the boisterous antics of the groom's male relatives on their long, slow processions to and from the bride's house.[18] Like the groom's relatives, the *fadarákia* appropriate the major roads, slowly and noisily encircling and multiply criss-crossing the town, demanding the attention of the townspeople, whom they ritually host through their proffered bottles of ouzo, while cultivating a soulful, intoxicated camaraderie with each other. Their first day of celebration was largely preoccupied with creating this sensory intensification of the young men's presence, both for others (they are noisier and more unruly; they impose sharp, burning tastes and tediously slow tempos on everyone else; they refuse to move out of the way) but also for themselves (they expose their bodies to the cold and wind; they drink to intoxication; they embrace, lean on, stumble over each other; they laugh, bellow, weep). However, in two encounters that first morning, the boys' playful domineering slipped into a more serious altercation. Both cases involved outsiders, and these outsiders were both, in some sense, representatives of the state.

The first occurred early in the morning, when the mob of young men with their hats and their musicians, entered the central grounds of the lycée, much as they would during the Carnival with their goatskins and masks, to "show off for their girlfriends." Though this entrance consequently had a quality of ritualized confrontation, the school principal—strict, humorless, and intensely disliked by

[18] See Cowan 1990, chapter 4.

many; also, significantly, an "outsider"—would not tolerate such a disruption to the school routine and refused to play along. Within a few minutes of their arrival she demanded that they depart. When the boys persisted in their singing and dancing, defiantly ignoring her demands, she phoned the local gendarmerie who, belatedly arriving on the scene, rather sheepishly moved the boys on.

A second incident involved a bus driver from Salonika, an employee of the regional transport system with a schedule to keep, who became annoyed when made to wait momentarily while a celebrant obstructed the main road. As he was maneuvering around the young man, several of the other celebrants provocatively banged the sides of the bus, whereupon the bus driver halted the vehicle, opened the door and began to argue with them. Although vociferous, the argument seemed to end amicably, and the bus eventually continued up the hill. However, when it returned down the hill a quarter of an hour later, the celebrants got their revenge. The bus was made to wait another fifteen minutes, perched on a dangerous incline with a full load of passengers, while three boys lay down in front of the bus, joined later by a fourth. A few of the other celebrants tried to persuade their companions to get up but they refused. The driver was forced to back up, but when he repositioned the bus on the side of the road, he was again harassed by the youths, who wiped his windshield with a dirty shirt, and whooping noisily, clambered in and out of the bus through the back doors. The incident ended only when, having forced their way on again, they persuaded the driver to accept a long drink of ouzo. He was then allowed to depart.

In the two instances above, the confrontation concerned not only persons differentiated by age, gender, and location (youthful male "locals" to older "outsiders"). It also revealed a clash between two different temporalities and symbolic economies. The boys obstreperously disregarded the rational use of time and respect for authority on which both the school and the transport system depend.[19] The representatives of both these state institutions, in turn, resisted being drawn into the ritually redefined moment, refusing the boys' presence, their hospitality, and their theatrically-gestured claims to dominance.

---

[19] There is an explicit awareness of the control of time and tempo as an expression of power in many Greek contexts (for Sohos, see Cowan 1990:123). The symbolic importance of time in negotiations between the locality and the state, and between Greece and "Europe," was reiterated a few years ago when the Greek government tried to enforce a rule that nightclubs (μπουζούκια) close at 2 a.m. rather than 4 a.m. It was argued that Greeks were not productive enough, partly because they did not get enough sleep, and that they ought to become more hard-working like their European neighbors. This provoked an intense debate on Greek modernization and how "European" the Greeks really are.

Day 2: House-Visiting: Deference and Emerging Autonomy

The *fadarákia* were not visible on the second day. They spent the day together, visiting in turn the houses of each young man, and receiving that family's hospitality of drink and food. I was not present for these visits, but did hear reports about them; and I had also observed on Day 1 several examples of the ritualized encounter between the boy, his cohort, and his family. The symbolic logic of these visits was very familiar. What was unusual, and striking, was their aura of indeterminacy, such that it was often possible to observe the renegotiation of the young man's status through the dance.

To illustrate the sort of transformation that was occurring, I need to say a few words about the everyday embodiment of adolescent masculinity. I remember watching in fascination, over the period of a year, the gradual transition of a spontaneous and sensitive twelve-year-old boy to the studied "cool," nonchalance, and toughness which constituted the typical repertoire of public poses of adolescent youths in this community. Youths hung around the games rooms and *kafetéries*, smoking cigarettes and drinking beer, or went visiting other villages in cars driven by older cousins, watching and flirting with girls and arranging secret rendezvous. It was expected, if not always approved, that youths now moved around more freely than before and pursued their own interests and desires. They were generally viewed as "crazy" and "irresponsible," though also pitied for their dependency. The youths were, in fact, compelled to rehearse publicly a model of autonomous masculinity while simultaneously remaining almost completely dependant on their father and mother for all their material needs.

In the street celebrations of the *fadarákia*, the youths adopted a swagger that was more than usually ostentatious, pressing ouzo on the drivers of trucks and cars, in particular. Remarkably, older men in these vehicles and on the street tended to tolerate these excesses with equanimity and rarely scolded or quarreled with the young celebrants. In those moments in the celebration when the young man, accompanied by his friends, returned to his parental house, however, the dynamics of the encounter between younger and older men, and in particular, between son and father, visibly altered. As on other ritual occasions (such as Carnival), it was incumbent upon the young men, as socially subordinate, to travel to the homes of their parents or other older relatives, who as socially superior, had the privilege of "sitting" ("like a Pasha") and waiting for them.

The boy's arrival with his cohort and the musicians initiated a formalized set of exchanges which, in sharp contrast to their comportment on the road, elicited upright, restrained, and deferential postures. The mother, and sometimes father, emerged from the house with a tray of food, followed by a tray of tiny shot glasses of ouzo, offering these to the visitors. After this, the son would wait while his father ordered a song from the musicians, and "gifted" them for it while placing initially his wife, then later his son, at the head of the dance line. The son later usually gifted the musicians so that his mother could dance, but only sometimes on these occasions did he gift them for his father. To do so was to claim a degree of autonomy from paternal authority and to redefine the father-son relationship on a less hierarchical, more reciprocal basis. Even though "gifting" expresses the donor's pleasure and pride in the person thereby entitled to assume the honored lead position in the dance, only some are granted the prerogative to gift. Obviously, certain fathers found the transition posed by their son's coming of age as threatening, and the sons did not always insist on this public gesture.

However, for other fathers, this moment of the son's public claims to adulthood in the dance evoked a fierce joy and pride. One father of two sons, both recently finished with the army, recited to me the scene when his second son, at the departure celebrations, gifted the *daoúlia* and placed him in the first position. Overwhelmed with emotion, the father danced with great energy and flair. "My God, Papa! You're incredible! What a dance!" the son exclaimed, throwing down bill after bill, until his entire wallet was emptied. The father was extremely moved by the son's recognition of the father's pleasure in him and by the son's reciprocal pleasure in his father, expressed in his unrestrained gifting. Through the dance and its gifting the father and son performatively redefined their relationship in ways which, happily, seem to have been sustained. Father and sons (with their respective wives) live together in an extended household, and appear to enjoy an unusually amicable and cooperative relationship.

Day 3: Departure as Death

On Saturday morning the *fadarákia* reappeared in the marketplace, winding around, then through, the town. At the beginning they were not consolidated as a group. Boys drifted away (and later returned) to greet friends and relatives, among them, the proprietors of the market shops, who would offer the boy a blessing and gift him with money, and refill the perpetually emptying bottles of ouzo. Gradually, the *fadarákia* group solidified; they moved in procession through the streets, and marked the intersections with circling line dances. In contemplative moments in the musical pace, they signaled and honored one of their cohort's engagement in the emotions provoked by the situation, drawing the bell of the *zourná* to the friend's ear and corporeally echoing his engrossment.

Girls and women came out today, the girls just watching, the older women also accepting drinks from the proffered bottles of ouzo. The boys seemed tired; they stood out of dances sometimes, and many had lost their hats. Still, as the crowd gradually gathered in the central square—women on the upper level by the church, men on the road below, children running everywhere in between—the energy began to rise. At nearly noon, a young man nicknamed Tsaousis ("Boss") arrived, and assumed easily his role as central figure and most flamboyant (often lead) dancer. As the *daoúlia* played, the dance line grew. Girls and women began to join the line without hesitation, and when it became too long, it broke into four or five smaller lines. For a while, there was a line of just mothers; sons would dramatically gift the musicians for their mothers to dance, then join their own peers dancing separately. But then fathers joined in, then sisters, girlfriends, brothers. As the multiple lines of dancers circled past each other, there was continuous greeting, joking, flirting, horseplay. Money was tossed into the air, the denominations rising steadily-from 100 to 500, then to 1000, and finally to 5000. As time passed, more originated from the boys' pockets than from their fathers'.

At 1 p.m. the taxis arrived. The church bells chimed mournfully, "as for a funeral," many remarked. The *daoúlia*, manipulating the pace, slowed down dramatically, and began to play a song heard at weddings and at funerals. The sorrowful response was palpable:

Μιὰ φορά 'ναι ἡ λεβεντιά
μιὰ φορὰ εἶναι νιάτα.
Μὲ ζήλευε ἡ γειτονιὰ κι ὅλοι οἱ κοτζαμπάτζηδες.
Μὲ ζήλευε καὶ ἡ μάνα μου
καὶ ἤθελε νὰ μὲ διώξει.
Διῶξε με, μάνα μ', διῶξε με
πολὺ μακριὰ στὰ ξένα,
ξένες νὰ κάνω ἀδερφές,
ξένες καὶ παραμάνες,
ξένες νὰ πλένουν τὰ ροῦχα μου.
Μία φορά, τρεῖς καὶ πέντε,
καὶ ὕστερα τὰ παίρνουν καὶ
τὰ διώχουν στὰ σοκκάκια.
"Πάρε, παιδί μ', τὰ ροῦχα σου,
στὴ μάνα σ' νὰ τὰ πλένει."
""Ἂν εἶχα μάνα κι ἀδερφές,
δὲν βρίσκομαι στὰ ξένα."

Manly vigor does not last,
Youth passes quickly.

My neighbors and the town's rich men were all jealous of me.
Even my mother was jealous of me
And wanted to drive me away.
Drive me away, mother,
Far away to the foreign lands.
I'll take foreigners as sisters,
Foreigners as stepmothers.
Foreign women will wash my clothes.
Once, three times, five times,
After that, they take them and throw them in the streets.
"Here, my boy, take your clothes, and
Send them to your mother for washing."
"If I had mother or sister,
I wouldn't have come to the foreign land."

The long lines of dancers collapsed as fathers, mothers, siblings, girlfriends, moved in to say goodbye. Money, as well as hats, were tossed wildly into the air, and sometimes carried away by the wind as the crowds cheered.

The *fadarákia* huddled together now, hugging each other, piling on top of each other, placing their ear to the *zourná* and weeping. The crowd, finally, moved toward the taxis. More hats, more money, shot up through the crowd. Kissed, held, wept over, the boys entered the taxis. One boy climbed onto the roof, on a second a flowered hat was secured with brown tape, and the taxis departed, honking wildly. Many women, overcome with grief, entered the church to light candles.

It would be hard to invent a scene with greater Durkheimian "collective effervescence" than this one. And in terms of a van Gennepian ritual structure it is almost embarassingly neat.[20] On this final day, one saw the emotional and embodied manifestations of the "binding" between the recruits, and also the more spontaneous (in relation to the previous two days) signaling, through the joining and leaving of the dance, of the range of relationships they held with others (relatives, sweethearts, friends). The arrival of the entire town on the central square marked it as a genuinely communal event and a recognition of the community's loss, rather than merely that of individual families. With the relationships between the young men as a collectivity, and between each young man and his "significant others," visibly and emphatically marked, the army recruits departed for the last time as boys (παιδιά), to return as men.

---

[20] Van Gennep 1960.

Evading "Tradition"

Considering their social, emotional, and sensory intensity, the celebrations marking the departure of the *fadarákia* are surprisingly "unmarked" in Sohoian local discourse. They are hardly talked about as an "event," a "tradition," or a "ritual." Though I was known to be interested in documenting the town's particular way of life, I was given no advance warning of the young men's impending departure in 1983. Both before and after that event, narratives about "young men leaving for army service" were relatively rare and fragmentary. Rather than being a story about "the way our young men live in Sohos" (like the conventionalized "set pieces" I often heard about "our wedding" or "our Sohoian Carnival") these were always reminiscences of particular personal experiences.

It took over a decade before I came to see this *absence of elaboration* as significant in itself. Yet it is indisputably so in a context where the discourse of modernization was (and to a large degree, still is) the major organizing framework in terms of which people understood themselves in relation to the national community and to the world at large. This remains especially true for those living in rural communities, who feel compelled constantly to measure themselves against their "more modern" compatriots in the cities. Through the education system, the media, and public discourses generally, rural inhabitants have learned that their "traditional" ways are a mark both of authenticity and of backwardness. Few objects and practices are able to evade the relentless, if ambivalent, valuations of the symbolic economy of traditionality versus modernity.

It is all the more surprising, then, that the celebratory departure of the *fadarákia* does so. Yet clearly it was not, and is not, regarded (either by lay people or by folklore scholars) as falling within the category of "morals and traditions" (ἤθη καὶ ἔθιμα), as elaborated, for instance, by the Greek folklorist, Nikolaos Politis. This may account for its absence in the folkloric, as well as the anthropological, corpus. But why exactly does it fail to fit? Is it because it is considered as a purely "secular" rite with no religious connotation? Or because it is somehow too "modern" (dating no earlier than the establishment of Greek sovereignty in Macedonia in 1912)? Or because it violates a conception of an autonomous village society (the implicit model in folklore, as in its sibling discipline, anthropology, until only a few decades ago) by making reference to the relation between powerful centers and their rural peripheries? At the same time, the celebration is not regarded as particularly "modern," either. The symbolic idiom it adopts is quite the opposite. Even so, it appears to be a practice of some longevity. Although I did not systematically collect stories about the *fadarákia* and its history, I learned that these sorts of celebrations had been undertaken by the fathers of the young men, too. Indeed,

I now suspect that, from the time that the Greek state began to induct men regularly into military service, Sohoians have marked such departures with celebrations.

With respect to the historical moment of the data of the present analysis, however—that is, the mid-1980s—the ambiguity and in some sense, *invisibility*, of the ritual celebration in terms of the symbolic poles of traditionality and modernity allowed it to elude the objectification, appropriation, and commodization that had already befallen many analogous practices, here in Sohos and throughout Greece. Folklorists working for the national universities and folklore academies, anthropologists, journalists, and television crews, as well as local and national politicians, had followed Sohoian Carnivals scrupulously for many years, and Sohoians had learned to expect them and even to anticipate their questions. Nobody had ever come from outside the town to interview them or make a documentary about the *fadarákia*'s departure, however—until I, by virtue of living in the town, stumbled upon and recorded it. The celebration was performed *by locals, for locals* and this, I would argue, is largely what it was *about*: that is, *locality* and young men's *location* here, *in this place*, with its particular tempos, tastes, ties, and sentiments which, in certain ways, contravene modern national ideals. Indeed, the fact that the young men chose to celebrate their departure using primarily an idiom of Sohoian "tradition"—*daoúlia*, ouzo, laments of death and exile, the dances, postures, gestures, bodily states, and ritual etiquette familiar from wedding celebrations and Carnival—*and chose to do this knowing that the powerful outsiders were not watching*, indicates a mastery of, and attachment to, local repertoires of symbolic practices. These the young men used, easily and with pleasure, for their own purposes. The use of this idiom constitutes, moreover, a statement of local identification among young men who might have highlighted other identifications (for instance, by using national symbols or those of international youth culture). Drawing upon the Sohoian repertoire the young men, on the brink of giving themselves and their bodies over to the State, momentarily defied its rationalities, disciplines, and standardizations.

Conclusion

The body is a semiotic field which invites many problematics, many readings. Foucault's identification of the body as the primary object of modern regimes of power offers the most general of starting points, while Bourdieu's suggestions toward an analysis of the dialectical relation between the body and the world constitute an only slightly more detailed methodological imperative. To trace definitively the operations of discourses and power it is important to examine *specific* case studies of bodily action, and this necessarily must make reference to specific cultural, social, and political forms and to the discourses they both incorporate and partially evade. The *fadarákia*'s departure celebrations and the postures and poses they adopted within them can be interpreted as the initial phase of a rite of passage where male youths become men, necessitating a dramatized refiguring of relations within the family and between themselves and the community. It can further be interpreted as the *fadarákia*'s, and the community's, ritualized—and to some degree, resistant—response to the state's appropriation of local young men for national projects, an appropriation which entails the completion of the project (initiated most intensively by the educational system) of transforming them from locals to citizens.

Significantly, the renegotiations at the level of family and community, as well as of the community vis-à-vis the state, were *performatively invoked*—much as in J. L. Austin's "performative utterance" wherein a performance can change the world—*using a Sohoian expressive and bodily idiom.*[21] Young men drew on the repertoire of gestures, postures, stances, bodily states, intoxicants, songs, and dances used in and familiar to them from wedding celebrations and Carnival, although they also added symbols and accoutrements which made the event distinctive: flowers and multicolored Hawaiian hats with cross-bones and state administrative codes. Echoing certain Carnival shenanigans, these celebrations included ritualized confrontation between the young men and individuals representing the state's authority. Indeed, in both ritual contexts, the confrontation was not that of two parties sharing similar social and moral values. To the contrary, it involved a confrontation between individuals representing opposing rationalities, aesthetics, and spatio-temporal orientations, associated, respectively, with the locality and the nation-state system.

The *fadarákia*'s departure celebrations were able symbolically to exploit that clash between the local and the national more than was usually possible in other Sohoian celebrations. Unlike both the Carnival and the wedding festivities, the departure celebrations were not imbued with an aura of traditionality. The ritually-framed performance of a local aesthetic as well as of a local "structure of feeling" consequently eluded domestication by the statist folkloric and other folkloricizing discourses.[22] The very disinclination of Sohoians to draw attention to its "authenticity" was a measure, paradoxically, of that same quality, in the sense that it remained a locally-defined and locally-controlled event, rather than one objectified in terms of a nationally-oriented discourse of tradition.[23] Sending off their little

---

[21] Austin 1975.
[22] On the notion of a "structure of feeling," see Williams 1977.
[23] As described, for instance, in Handler 1988.

Jane K. Cowan

soldiers with a town-wide celebration to which outsiders were not invited, Sohoians quietly resisted the national appropriation of local symbols, as well as the state appropriation of local persons.

The dancing, drinking, fighting body of the *fadaráki* (a ritual role as well as a social persona) negotiated multiple repositionings: as a male, a family member, a Sohoian townsman, a Greek citizen. His use of a particular bodily mode of celebration can be anthropologically read at other levels, too: not only as an expression of local affinities and identifications but, in addition, as a subtle *performative comment* on the relation between the locality and the nation-state, and between tradition and "tradition." In exploring several dimensions of complex processes of embodiment, I have tried to give a sense of the ways competing, intersecting worlds lay claim to human bodies, as well as how bodies make claims about those different worlds.

Bibliography

Abraham, N. and Torok, M. 1994. "Mourning *or* Melancholla: Introjection *versus* Incorporation," in Abraham, N. and Torok, M., *The Shell and the Kernel: Renewals of Psychoanalysis*, trans. and ed. N. Rand. Chicago: University of Chicago Press, 125–138.

Abu-Lughod, L. 1986. *Veiled Sentiments: Honor and Poetry in a Bedouin Society*. Berkeley: University of California Press.

Adler, M. A. and Wilshusen, R. H. 1990. "Large-Scale Integrative Facilities in Tribal Societies: Cross-Cultural and Southwestern U.S. Examples," *World Archaeology* 22:133–146.

Adorno, Th. 1991. *Notes to Literature, I.* New York: Columbia University Press.

Agapitos, P. A. 1998. "Narrative, Rhetoric and 'Drama' Rediscovered: Scholars and Poets Interpret Heliodorus," in R. Hunter (ed.), *Studies in Heliodorus*. Cambridge: Cambridge Philological Society, Supplementary vol. 21, 125–156.

——— 1999. "Dreams and the Spatial Aesthetics of Narrative Presentation in *Livistros and Rhodamne*," *Dumbarton Oaks Papers* 53:111–147.

Alexiou, M. 1975. "The Lament of the Virgin in Byzantine Literature and Modern Greek Folksong," *Byzantine and Modern Greek Studies* 1:111–140.

——— 1985. "Τί εἶναι—καὶ ποῦ βαδίζει—ἡ ἑλληνικὴ λαογραφία," in S. Skartsis (ed.), Πρακτικὰ Τέταρτου Συμποσίου Ποίησης—᾽Αφιέρωμα στὸ Δημοτικὸ Τραγούδι. Athens: Γνώση, 43–60.

——— 1986. "The Poverty of Écriture and the Craft of Writing: Towards a Reappraisal of the Prodromic Poems," *Byzantine and Modern Greek Studies* 10:1–40.

——— 1990. "Οἱ γυναῖκες σὲ δύο μυθιστορήματα τοῦ Στράτη Μυριβήλη — μῦθος, φαντασία καὶ βία," Νέα ῾Εστία 128:67–88.

——— 1993. "Writing Against Silence: Antithesis and Ekphrasis in the Prose Fiction of Georgios Vizyenos," *Dumbarton Oaks Papers* 47:275–285.

——— 1999. "Ploys of Performance: Games and Play in the Ptochoprodromic Poems," *Dumbarton Oaks Papers* 53:92–109.

——— 2002a. *The Ritual Lament in Greek Tradition*, 2nd ed. revised by D. Yatromanolakis and P. Roilos. Lanham, Md.: Rowman and Littlefield.

——— 2002b. *After Antiquity: Greek Language, Myth, and Metaphor*. Ithaca, N.Y.: Cornell University Press.

Alexiou, M. and Dronke, P. 1971. "The Lament of Jephta's Daughter: Themes, Traditions, Originality," *Studi Medievali*, 3rd ser., 12.2:819–863.

Allott, P. 2001. "Globalization from Above: Actualizing the Ideal Through Law, " in K. Booth et al. (eds.), *How Might We Live? Global Ethics in the New Century*. Cambridge: Cambridge University Press, 61–79.

And, M. 1987. *Karagöz. Turkish Shadow Theatre*. Istanbul: Dost Yayinlari.

Andrewes, A. 1982. Chapter 44, in I. E. S. Edwards et al. (eds.), *The Cambridge Ancient History*, II:3, 2nd ed. Cambridge: Cambridge University Press.

Andrić, I. 1977. *The Bridge on the Drina* [1945], trans. L. F. Edwards. Chicago: University of Chicago Press.

Angold, M. 1975. *A Byzantine Government in Exile: Government and Society under the Laskarids of Nicaea (1204–1261)*. Oxford: Oxford University Press.

Antoniades, S. 1939. *La place de la liturgie dans la tradition des lettres grecques*. Leiden: A. W. Sitjthoff.

Aretz, S. 1999. *Die Opferung der Iphigeneia in Aulis. Die Rezeption des Mythos in antiken und modernen Dramen*. Beiträge zur Altertumskunde 131. Stuttgart: Teubner.

Argyriadi, M. 1993. "The Influences of Christian Ritual and Tradition on Children's Play: Religious Toys and Games," Ἐθνογραφικά 9:213–222.

Argyrou, V. 1996. *Tradition and Modernity in the Mediterranean: The Wedding as Symbolic Struggle*. Cambridge: Cambridge University Press.

Athanassiadi, P. 1993. "Dreams, Theurgy and Freelance Divination," *Journal of Roman Studies* 83:115–130.

Austin, J. L. 1971. "A Plea for Excuses," in C. Lyas (ed.), *Philosophy and Linguistics*. London: Macmillan, 79–101.

—— 1975. *How to Do Things with Words*, 2nd ed. Cambridge, Mass.: Harvard University Press.

Babbitt, F. C. 1936. *Plutarch: Moralia*, V. Cambridge, Mass.: Harvard University Press, Loeb Classical Library.

Babcock, B. A. (ed.). 1978. *The Reversible World: Symbolic Inversion in Art and Society*. Ithaca, N.Y. : Cornell University Press.

Babiniotis, G. 1991. "Ποιητικὴ μεταγλώσσα καὶ μεταγλωσσικὴ ποίηση στὸν Ἐλύτη," Ἡ Λέξη 106:733–749.

Bakhtin, M. M. 1981. *The Dialogic Imagination: Four Essays*. Austin: University of Texas Press.

—— 1984. *Rabelais and His World*. Bloomington: Indiana University Press.

—— 1986. *Speech Genres and Other Late Essays*, trans. V. W. McGee; eds. C. Emerson and M. Holquist. Austin: University of Texas Press.

Bakic-Hayden, M. and Hayden, R. 1992. "Orientalist Variations on the Theme 'Balkans': Symbolic Geography in Recent Yugoslav Cultural Politics," *Slavic Review* 51.1:1–15.

Bakker, E. J. 1997. *Poetry in Speech: Orality and Homeric Discourse*. Ithaca, N.Y.: Cornell University Press.

Bakker, E. J. et al. (eds.) 2002. *Brill's Companion to Herodotus*. Leiden: Brill.

Bakker, W. F. and Philippides, D. 2000. "The Lament of the Virgin by Ephraem the Syrian," in S. Kaklamanes et al. (eds.), Ἐνθύμησις Νικολάου Μ. Παναγιωτάκη. Herakleion: Πανεπιστημιακὲς Ἐκδόσεις Κρήτης, 39–55.

Baldowin, J. F. 1987. *The Urban Character of Christian Worship: The Origins, Development, and Meaning of Stational Liturgy*. Rome: Pontificium Institutum Studiorum Orientalium.

Bale, A. M. 1995. "Ἡ παράσταση τῶν δεομένων στὴν παλαιοχριστιανικὴ τέχνη," Κληρονομία 27:215–237.

Bank, A. 1977. *Byzantine Art in the Collections of the Soviet Museums*. New York/ Leningrad: H. N. Abrams and Aurora Art Publishers.

Barrett, D. 1993. "The 'Committee of Sleep': A Study of Dream Incubation for Problem Solving," *Journal of the Association for the Study of Dreams* 3:115–122.

Barthes, R. 1974. *S/Z: An Essay*, trans. R. Miller. New York: Farrar, Strauss and Giroux.

—— 1987. *Criticism and Truth*, trans. K. Keuneman. London: Athlone.

Bartlett, R. 1981. "The Impact of Royal Government in the French Ardennes: The Evidence of the 1247 Enquête," *Journal of Medieval History* 7: 83–96.

Basso, E. B. 1985. *A Musical View of the Universe: Kalapalo Myth and Ritual Performances.* Philadelphia: University of Pennsylvania Press.

Bateson, G. 1955. "A Theory of Play and Fantasy," *Psychiatric Research Reports* 2: 39–51.

——— 1958. *Naven.* Stanford: Stanford University Press.

Bauman, R. 1977. *Verbal Art as Performance.* Rowley, Mass.: Newbury House.

——— 1992. "Contextualization, Tradition, and the Dialogue of Genres: Icelandic Legends of the *kraftaskáld*," in A. Duranti and C. Goodwin 1992, 127–145.

———1993. "The Anthropology of Theater and Spectacle," *Annual Review of Anthropology* 22: 369–393.

Bauman, R. and Sherzer, J. 1974. *Explorations into the Ethnography of Speaking.* Cambridge: Cambridge University Press.

Baun, J. 2000. "Middle Byzantine 'Tours of Hell': Outsider Theodicy?," in D. C. Smythe (ed.), *Strangers to Themselves: The Byzantine Outsider.* Aldershot: Ashgate, 47–60.

Beaton, R. 1980. *Folk Poetry of Modern Greece.* Cambridge: Cambridge University Press.

——— 1987. "The Rhetoric of Poverty," *Byzantine and Modern Greek Studies* 11:1–28.

——— 1994. *An Introduction to Modern Greek Literature.* Oxford: Clarendon Press.

——— 1996. *The Medieval Greek Romance,* 2nd revised ed. London: Routledge.

Beazley, J. D. 1955. "Hydria Fragments in Corinth," *Hesperia* 24:305–319.

——— 1963. *Attic Red-Figure Vase-Painting,* 2nd. ed. Oxford: Oxford University Press.

——— 1971. *Paralipomena: Additions to Attic Black-Figure Vase-Painters and to Attic Red-Figure Vase-Painters.* Oxford: Clarendon Press.

Beck, H.-G. 1969. "Antike Beredsamkeit und byzantinische Kallilogia," *Antike und Abendland* 15:91–101.

Beckwith, J. 1962. *The Veroli Casket.* London: H.M. Stationery Office.

Beeman, W. 1979. "Cultural Dimensions of Performance Conventions in Iranian Ta'ziyeh," in P. J. Chelkowski (ed.), *Ta'ziyeh: Ritual and Drama in Iran.* New York: New York University Press, 24–31.

Behr, C. A. 1968. *Aelius Aristides and the Sacred Tales.* Amsterdam: Hakkert.

Bekker, I. 1837. *Theophanes continuatus, Ioannes Comeniata, Symeon Magister, Georgius Monachus.* Bonn: Weber.

——— 1853. *Michael Attaleiates. Historia.* Bonn: Weber.

Belezinis, A. 1999. Ὁ ὄψιμος Ἐλύτης. Athens: Ἴκαρος.

Bell, C. 1992. *Ritual Theory, Ritual Practice.* New York: Oxford University Press.

——— 1997. *Ritual: Perspectives and Dimensions.* New York: Oxford University Press.

Ben-Amos, D. 1976. "Analytical Categories and Ethnic Genres," in D. Ben-Amos (ed.), *Folklore Genres.* Austin: University of Texas Press, 215–242.

Bennett, C. 1994. "Concerning 'Sappho Schoolmistress'," *Transactions of the American Philological Association* 124:345–347.

Benson, P. 1993. *Anthropology and Literature.* Urbana: University of Illinois Press.

Bérard, C. 1974. *Anodoi: Essai sur l'imagerie des passages chthoniens.* Bibliotheca Helvetica Romana 13. Neuchâtel: Attinger.

Bérard, V. 1911 [1896]. *La Turquie et 'l'Hellénisme Contemporain': La Macédoine.* Paris: Félix Arcan.

Bernand, A. and Masson, O. 1957. "Les inscriptions grecques d'Abou-Simbel," *Revue des Études Grecques* 70:1–46.

Bevan, E. 1940. *Holy Images: An Inquiry into Idolatry and Image-Worship in Ancient Paganism and Christianity.* London: George Allen and Unwin.

Bichler, R. 2000. *Herodots Welt: Der Aufbau der "Historie" am Bild der fremden Länder und Völker, ihrer Zivilisation und ihre Geschichte.* Berlin: Akademie Verlag.

Binns, C. 1979–80. "The Changing Face of Power: Revolution and Development of the Soviet Ceremonial System," *Man* (n.s.) 14:585–606 and 15:170–187.

Birdwell-Pheasant, D. and Lawrence-Zuniga, D. (eds.) 1999. *House Life: Space, Place, and Family in Europe.* Oxford: Berg.

Biris, K. 1952. "Ὁ Καραγκιόζης, Ἑλληνικὸ λαϊκὸ θέατρο," Νέα Ἑστία.

—— 1957. "Ἡ λεβεντιὰ τῆς Ρούμελης στὸ ἑλληνικὸ λαϊκὸ θέατρο," Νέα Ἑστία 661–668.

Bjelić, D. I. and Savić, O. (eds.) 2002. *Balkan as Metaphor: Between Globalization and Fragmentation.* Cambridge, Mass.: MIT Press.

Bjelić, S. 2002. "Introduction: Blowing Up the Bridge," in Bjelić and Savić 2002, 15–16.

Blackburn, S. H. et al. (eds.) 1989. *Oral Epics in India.* Berkeley: University of California Press.

Blech, M. 1982. *Studien zum Kranz bei den Griechen.* Berlin: de Gruyter.

Blier, S. 1987. *The Anatomy of Architecture: Ontology and Metaphor in Batammaliba Architectural Expression.* Cambridge: Cambridge University Press.

Bloch, M. 1974. "Symbols, Song, Dance and Features of Articulation: Is Religion an Extreme Form of Traditional Authority?," *European Journal of Sociology* 15.1:55–81.

—— 1989. *Ritual, History, Power: Selected Papers in Anthropology.* London: The Athlone Press.

—— 1992. *Prey into Hunter: The Politics of Religious Experience.* Cambridge: Cambridge University Press.

Blundell, M. W. 1989. *Helping Friends and Harming Enemies: A Study in Sophocles and Greek Ethics.* Cambridge: Cambridge University Press.

—— 1990. *Sophocles' Oedipus at Colonus.* Newburyport, Mass.: Focus Classical Library.

Blundell, S. 1995. *Women in Ancient Greece.* London: British Museum Press.

Bonwetsch, G. N. 2000. *Kommentar zu Daniel,* 2nd ed. revised by M. Richard. Berlin: Akademie Verlag.

Boose, L. 1982. "The Father and the Bride in Shakespeare," *Publications of the Modern Language Association of America* 97:325–347.

Borecky, B. 1963. "The Primitive Origin of the Greek Conception of Equality," in L. Varcl and R. F. Willetts (eds.), *Geras: Studies Presented to George Thomson on the Occasion of his 60th Birthday.* Prague: Charles University, 41–60.

Bourdieu, P. 1977. *Outline of a Theory of Practice,* trans. R. Nice. Cambridge: Cambridge University Press.

—— 1990. *The Logic of Practice,* trans. R. Nice. Oxford: Polity Press.

Bourke, A. 1988. "The Irish Traditional Lament and the Grieving Process," *Women's Studies International Forum* 11:287–291.

Bowersock, G. W. et al. (eds.) 1992. *Late Antiquity: A Guide to the Postclassical World.* Cambridge, Mass.: Harvard University Press.

Bowie, A. M. 1993. *Aristophanes: Myth, Ritual and Comedy.* Cambridge: Cambridge University Press.

—— 1997. "Tragic Filters for History; Euripides' *Supplices* and Sophocles' *Philoctetes*," in C. Pelling (ed.), *Greek Tragedy and the Historian.* Oxford. Clarendon Press, 39–62.

—— forthcoming. "Fate May Harm Me, I Have Dined Today: Near-Eastern Royal Banquets and Greek Symposia in Herodotus," in Ch. Orphanos (ed.), *Symposium: Banquet et représentations en Grèce et à Rome.* Toulouse: Presses Universitaires du Mirail.

Brady, I. 1991. *Anthropological Poetics.* Savage, Md.: Rowman and Littlefield.

Brakke, D. 1998. "'Outside the Places, Within the Truth': Athanasius of Alexandria and the Localization of the Holy," in D. Frankfurter (ed.), *Pilgrimage and Holy Space in Late Antique Egypt.* Leiden: Brill, 445–481.

Brelich, A. 1969. *Paides e parthenoi, I.* Incunabula Graeca 36. Rome: Edizioni dell'Ateneo.

Brett, G. 1954. "The Automata in the Byzantine Throne of Solomon," *Speculum* 29:477–487.

Briant, P. 1996. *Histoire de l'empire perse de Cyrus à Alexandre.* Paris: A. Fayard.

Brillante, C. 1991. "Metamorfosi di un'immagine: le statue animate e il sogno," in idem, *Studi sulla rappresentazione del sogno nella Grecia Antica.* Palermo: Sellerio, 95–111.

Brommer, F. 1937. *Satyroi.* Würzburg: Triltsch.

—— 1944. *Satyrspiele.* Berlin: De Gruyter.

Brown, P. 1981. *The Cult of Saints: Its Rise and Function in Latin Christianity.* Chicago: University of Chicago Press.

—— 1995. *Authority and the Sacred: Aspects of the Christianization of the Roman World.* Cambridge: Cambridge University Press.

Brubaker, L. 1999. *Vision and Meaning in Ninth-Century Byzantium: Image as Exegesis in the Homilies of Gregory of Nazianzus.* New York: Cambridge University Press.

Brueckner, A. and Pernice, E. 1893. "Ein attischer Friedhof," *Athenische Mitteilungen* 18:73–191.

Bruneau, P. 1970. *Recherches sur les cultes de Delos à l'époque hellénistique et à l'époque impériale.* Bibliothèque des Écoles Françaises d'Athènes et de Rome 217. Paris: Éditions de Boccard.

Bruner, E. M. 1991. "Introduction: The Ethnographic Self and the Personal Self," in Brady 1991, 1–26.

Budelmann, F. 2000. *The Language of Sophocles: Communality, Communication and Involvement.* Cambridge: Cambridge University Press.

Burian, P. 1972. "Supplication and Hero Cult in Sophocles' *Ajax*," *Greek, Roman, and Byzantine Studies* 13:151–156.

Burke, E. 1757. *A Philosophical Enquiry into the Origin of Our Ideas of the Sublime and Beautiful.* London: R. and J. Dodsley.

—— 1989 [1960]. *The Philosophy of Edmund Burke,* ed. L. I. Bredvold and R. G. Ross. Ann Arbor, Mich.: University of Michigan Press.

Burkert, W. 1966. "Greek Tragedy and Sacrificial Ritual," *Greek, Roman, and Byzantine Studies* 7:87–121, repr. in Burkert 2001:1–36.

—— 1976. "Opfertypen und antike Gesellschaftsstruktur," in G. Stephenson (ed.), *Der Religionswandel unserer Zeit im Spiegel der Religionswissenschaft.* Darmstadt: Wissenschaftliche Buchgesellschaft, 168–187.

—— 1983. *Homo Necans: The Anthropology of Ancient Greek Sacrificial Ritual and Myth*, trans. P. Bing. Berkeley: University of California Press.

—— 1985a. *Greek Religion*, trans. J. Raffan. Cambridge, Mass.: Harvard University Press.

—— 1985b. "Opferritual bei Sophokles. Pragmatik—Symbolik—Theater," *Der altsprachliche Unterricht* 28:5–20.

—— 1987. *Ancient Mystery Cults*. Cambridge, Mass.: Harvard University Press.

—— 2001. *Savage Energies: Lessons of Myth and Ritual in Ancient Greece*. Chicago: University of Chicago Press.

Burnett, A. P. 1971. *Catastrophe Survived: Euripides' Plays of Mixed Reversal*. Oxford: Oxford University Press.

—— 1983. *Three Archaic Poets: Archilochus, Alcaeus, Sappho*. London: Duckworth.

Buschor, E. 1937. *Feldmäuse: Sitzungsberichte*. Bayerische Akademie der Wissenschaften, Philosophisch-Historische Klasse. Munich: Beck.

Büttner-Wobst, Th. 1897. *Ioannis Zonarae, Epitomae Historiarum*, Books XIII-XVIII Bonn: Weber.

Buxton, R. G. 1987. "Euripides' *Alkestis*: Five Aspects of an Interpretation," in L. Rodley (ed.), *Papers Given at a Colloquium on Greek Drama in Honour of R. P. Winnington-Ingram. Journal of Hellenic Studies*, Supplementary Paper 15, London: Society for the Promotion of Hellenic Studies, 17–31.

Byron, George Gordon (Lord) 1885. *Childe Harold's Pilgrimage: A Romaunt*, ed. W. J. Rolfe. Boston: Houghton, Mifflin and Company.

—— 1899. *The Works of Lord Byron. Poetry: Volume II*, ed. E. H. Coleridge. London: John Murray; New York: Charles Scribner's Sons.

Caccamo Caltabiano, M. and Radici Colace, P. 1992. *Dalla Premoneta alla Moneta: Lessico monetale greco tra semantica e ideologia*. Pisa: ETS Editrice.

Cairns, F. 1972. *Generic Composition in Greek and Roman Poetry*. Edinburgh: Edinburgh University Press.

Calame, C. 1974. "Réflexions sur les genres littéraires en Grèce archaïque," *Quaderni Urbinati di Cultura Classica* 17, 113–128.

—— 1991. "'Mythe' et 'Rite' en Grèce: Des catégories indigènes?," *Kernos* 4: 179–204.

—— 1996. *Thésée et l'imaginaire athénien: Légende et culte en Grèce antique*, 2nd revised ed. Lausanne: Éditions Payot.

—— 1997. *Choruses of Young Women in Ancient Greece: Their Morphology, Religious Role, and Social Function*, 2nd ed., trans. D. Collins and J. Orion. Lanham, Md.: Rowman and Littlefield.

—— 1998. "Mort héroïque et culte à mystère dans l'Oedipe à Colone de Sophocle," in Graf 1998:326–356.

—— 2003. "Le rite d'initiation tribale comme catégorie anthropologique (Van Gennep et Platon)," *Revue de l'histoire des religions* 220:6–62.

Calinescu, M. 1987. *Faces of Modernity: Avant-Garde, Decadence, Kitsch*. Durham, N.C.: Duke University Press.

Calotychos, V. 1997. "Thorns in the Side of Venice? Galanaki's *Pasha* and Pamuk's *White Castle* in the Global Market," in Tziovas 1997a, 243–260.

Cameron, A. 1987. "The Construction of Court Ritual: The Byzantine Book of Ceremonies," in D. Cannadine and S. Price (eds.), *Rituals of Royalty: Power and Ceremonial in Traditional Societies*. Cambridge: Past and Present Publications, 106–136.

Campbell, D. A. 1982. *Greek Lyric I,* Cambridge, Mass.: Harvard University Press, Loeb Classical Library.

Campbell, J. K. 1964. *Honour, Family, and Patronage: A Study of Institutions and Moral Values in a Greek Mountain Community.* Oxford: Clarendon Press.

Canivet, P. and Leroy-Molinghen, A. 1977. *Théodoret de Cyr: Histoire des Moines de Syrie,* I. Paris: Éditions du Cerf.

Cantarella, R. 1942. *Poeti Bizantini,* 2 vols. Milan: Vita e Pensiero.

Carey, C. 1986. "Archilochus and Lycambes," *Classical Quarterly* (n.s.) 36:60–67.

Carlyle, Th. 1908. *Sartor Resartus: On Heroes, Hero-Worship and the Heroic in History.* London: J. M. Dent.

Carpentier, A. 1995. "The Baroque and the Marvelous Real," in L. P. Zamora and W. Faris 1995, 89–117.

Carson, A. 1990. "Putting Her in Her Place: Woman, Dirt and Desire," in D. M. Halperin et al. (eds.), *Before Sexuality.* Princeton: Princeton University Press, 135–169.

Carsten, J. and Hugh-Jones, S. (eds.) 1995. *About the House: Lévi-Strauss and Beyond.* Cambridge: Cambridge University Press.

Casey, E. 1996. "How to Get from Space to Place in a Fairly Short Stretch of Time: Phenomenological Prolegomena," in S. Feld and K. Basso (eds.), *Senses of Place.* Santa Fe: School of American Research Press, 13–52.

Ceylan, A. and Ritti, T. 1997. "A New Dedication to Apollo Kareios," *Epigraphica Anatolica* 28:57–67.

Chadwick, H. 1974. "John Moschus and His Friend Sophronius the Sophist," *The Journal of Theological Studies* 25:41–74.

Chaniotis, A. 1991. "Von Hirten, Krautsammlern, Epheben und Pilgern: Leben auf dem Bergen in antiken Kreta," *Ktema* 16:93–109.

—— 1996. *Die Verträge zwischen kretischen Poleis in der hellenistischen Zeit.* Stuttgart: Frank Steiner Verlag.

Chanos, D. 1991. Τὸ παιδικὸ λαϊκὸ φυλλάδιο, περιοδικό, βιβλίο. Athens: Αἴολος.

Chantraine, P. 1968–80. *Dictionnaire étymologique de la langue grecque.* Paris: Klincksieck.

Chernenko, E. V. 1991. "Eisengepanzerte 'Ritter' der skythischen Steppe," in Rolle et al. 1991, 131–135.

Chirassi Colombo, I. 1975. "Acculturation et cultes thérapeutiques," in F. Dunand and P. Lévêque (eds.), *Les syncrétismes dans les religions de l'antiquité: Colloque de Besançon (22–23 Octobre 1973).* Leiden: Brill, 96–111.

Chryssanthopoulos, M. 1994. Γεώργιος Βιζυηνός. Μεταξὺ φαντασίας καὶ μνήμης. Athens: Ἀναγνώσεις.

Clarke, M., 2000. "Changing House and Population Size on Methana, 1880–1996: Anomaly or Pattern?," in S. B. Sutton (ed.), *Contingent Countryside: Settlement, Economy, and Land Use in the Southern Argolid Since 1700.* Stanford: Stanford University Press, 107–124.

Claus, P. J. 1989. "Behind the Text: Performance and Ideology in a Tulu Oral Tradition," in Blackburn et al. 1989, 55–74.

Clethero, S. 2000–01. "An Exploration into Creativity," *Gap* 1.2:2–7 and 2.1:45–51.

Clifford, J. 1986a. "Introduction: Partial Truths," in Clifford and Marcus 1986, 1–26.

—— 1986b. "On Ethnographic Allegory," in Clifford and Marcus 1986, 165–193.

Clifford, J. and Marcus, G. E. 1986. *Writing Culture: The Poetics and Politics of Ethnography*. Berkeley: University of California Press.

Cocchiara, G. 1981. *Il mondo alla rovescia*. Torino: Boringhieri.

Coldstream, J. N. 1968. *Greek Geometric Pottery: A Survey of Ten Local Styles and Their Chronology*. London: Methuen.

Collard, A. 1990. "The Experience of Civil War in the Mountain Villages of Central Greece," in M. Sarafis and M. Eve (eds.), *Background to Contemporary Greece*. London: Merlin Books, 223–254.

Collard, C. 1975. *Euripides Supplices*. Gröningen: Bouma's Boekhuis.

Comaroff, J. 1985. *Body of Power, Spirit of Resistance: The Culture and History of a South African People*. Chicago: University of Chicago Press.

Conca, F. 1989. "Scribi e lettori dei romanzi tardo antichi e bizantini," in A. Garzya (ed.), *Atti del Primo Convegno di Studi Tardoantichi: "Metodologie della ricerca sulla tarda antichità."* Naples: D'Auria, 223–246.

—— 1990. *Nicetas Eugenianus, De Drosillae et Chariclis amoribus*. Amsterdam: J. C. Gieben.

Connor, W. R. 1987: "Tribes, Festivals, and Processions; Civic Ceremonial and Political Manipulation in Archaic Greece," *Journal of Hellenic Studies* 107:40–50.

Coros, M. 1983. "Sousta," *Reflections in Phenomenology* 4:14–27.

Cowan, J. 1988. "Folk Truth: When the Scholar Comes to Carnival in a 'Traditional' Community," *Journal of Modern Greek Studies* 6:2:245–260.

—— 1990. *Dance and the Body Politic in Northern Greece*. Princeton: Princeton University Press.

—— 1992. "Japanese Ladies and Mexican Hats: Contested Symbols and the Politics of Tradition in a Northern Greek Carnival Celebration," in J. Boissevain (ed.), *Revitalising European Rituals*. London: Routledge, 172–197.

—— 1994. "Women, Men and Pre-Lenten Carnival in Northern Greece: An Anthropological Exploration of Gender Transformation in Symbol and Practice," *Rural History* 5:2:195–210.

—— 1998. "Piccoli soldati per e contro lo Stato. Incorporazione e riposizionamento in un rito di passaggio maschile nella Grecia settentrionale," *Etnosistemi* 5:5:111–120.

Crapanzano, V. 1977. "Introduction" in V. Crapanzano and V. Garrison (eds.), *Case Studies in Spirit Possession*. New York: John Wiley and Sons, 1–40.

—— 1980. *Rite of Return: Circumcision in Morocco*. Psychoanalytic Study of Society 9. New York: Library of Psychological Anthropology.

—— 1986. "Herme's Dilemma: The Masking of Subversion in Ethnographic Description," in Clifford and Marcus 1986, 51–76.

Crisafulli, V. 1997. "Commentary" in V. Crisafulli and J. Nesbitt, *The Miracles of St. Artemios*. Leiden: Brill, 227–291.

Csordas, Th. 1999. "Ritual Healing and the Politics of Identity in Contemporary Navajo Society," *American Ethnologist* 26:3–23.

Culler, J. 1975. *Structuralist Poetics: Structuralism, Linguistics, and the Study of Literature*. Ithaca, N.Y.: Cornell University Press.

Cutler, A. 1987. "Under the Sign of the Deesis: On the Question of Representativeness in Medieval Art and Literature," *Dumbarton Oaks Papers* 41:145–156.

Dagron, G. 1978. *Vie et miracles de Saint Thècle*. Brussels: Société des Bollandistes.

—— 1985. "Rêver de Dieu et parler de soi. Le rêve et son intreprétation d'après le sources Byzantines," in T. Gregory (ed.), *I Sogni nel Medioevo: Seminario internazionale, Roma, 2–4 ottobre 1983.* Rome. Edizioni dell'Ateneo, 37–55.

—— 1991. "Holy Images and Likeness," *Dumbarton Oaks Papers* 45:23–33.

Daley, L. W. 1939. "An Inscribed Doric Capital from the Argive Heraion," *Hesperia* 8:165–169.

Danforth, L. 1982. *The Death Rituals of Rural Greece.* Princeton: Princeton University Press.

—— 1984. "The Ideological Context of the Search for Continuities in Greek Culture," *Journal of Modern Greek Studies* 2:53–87.

—— 1989. *Firewalking and Religious Healing: The Anastenaria of Greece and the American Firewalking Movement.* Princeton: Princeton University Press.

d'Angour, A. 1997. "How the Dithyramb Got Its Shape," *Classical Quarterly* 47:2:331–51.

Darrouzès, J. 1970. *Recherche sur les OFFIKIA de l'église byzantine.* Paris: Institut Français d'Études Byzantines.

Dawkins, R. M. 1950. *Forty-Five Stories from the Dodekanese.* Cambridge: Cambridge University Press.

—— 1953. *Modern Greek Folktales.* Oxford: Oxford University Press.

de Boor, C. [1904]. *Georgii Monachi, Chronicon,* Leipzig: Teubner, revised ed. by P. Wirth. Stuttgart: Teubner, 1978.

Delaney, D. 1998. *Race, Place, and the Law, 1836–1948.* Austin: University of Texas Press.

Demas, E. 1992. "The Social Factors and the Folk Dance Reforms in Metsovo and Melia in Epirus," in *Dance Studies* 16:9–33.

Demetracopoulos, Ph. 1979. "The Exegeses of the Canons in the Twelfth Century as School Texts," *Diptycha* 1: 143–157.

Dent, E. 1928. *Foundations of English Opera: A Study of Musical Drama in England During the Seventeenth Century.* Cambridge: Cambridge University Press.

Depew, M. and Obbink, D. 2000. "Introduction," in M. Depew and D. Obbink (eds.), *Matrices of Genre: Authors, Canons, and Society.* Cambridge, Mass.: Harvard University Press, 1–14.

de Polignac, F. 1995. *La naissance de la cité grecque,* 2nd ed. Paris: Éditions la découverte.

der Nersessian, S. 1960. "Two Images of the Virgin in the Dumbarton Oaks Collection," *Dumbarton Oaks Papers* 14:81–85.

Descola, Ph. 1996. *The Spears of Twilight: Life and Death in the Amazon Jungle,* trans. J. Lloyd. London: Harper Collins.

Detienne, M. 1996. *The Masters of Truth in Archaic Greece,* trans. J. Lloyd. New York: Zone Books.

—— 2000. *Comparer l'incomparable.* Paris: Seuil.

—— 2001. "Back to the Village: A Tropism of Hellenists?," *History of Religions* 41.2:99–113.

Deubner, L. 1900. *De incubatione.* Leipzig: Teubner.

—— 1907. *Kosmas und Damian.* Leipzig: Teubner.

—— 1932. *Attische Feste.* Berlin: H. Keller.

de Wailly, N. 1874. *Jean Sire de Joinville, Histoire de Saint Louis,* 2nd ed. Paris: Firmin Didot Frères.

Diamandaras, A. 1892. "Καστελλοριζιακὰ Παραμύθια," Δελτίον τῆς ʿΙστορικῆς καὶ ʾΕθνολογικῆς ʿΕταιρείας τῆς ʿΕλλάδος 4:696-721.

Diamond, S. (ed.) 1986. "A Special Issue on Poetry and Anthropology," *Dialectical Anthropology* 11:2–4.

Diehl, E. 1942. *Anthologia Lyrica Graeca. Supplementum: Addenda et corrigenda fasciculorum I-VI editionis alterius*. Leipzig: Teubner.

Diggle, J. 1984. *Euripidis Fabulae, I.* Oxford: Clarendon Press.

Dillehay, T. 1990. "Mapuche Ceremonial Landscape, Social Recruitment and Resource Rights," *World Archaeology* 22:223–241.

Dillery, J. 1992. "Darius and the Tomb of Nitocris," *Classical Philology* 87:30–38.

Dillon, M. 1997. *Pilgrims and Pilgrimage in the Greek World*. London: Routledge.

—— 2002. *Girls and Women in Classical Greek Religion*. London and New York: Routledge.

Dodd, D. B. and Faraone, C. A. (eds.) 200. *Initiation in Ancient Greek Rituals and Narratives: New Critical Perspectives*. London: Routledge.

Dodds, E. R. 1960. *Euripides, Bacchae*, 2nd ed. Oxford: Oxford University Press.

Dölger, F. and Karayannopulos, J. 1968. *Byzantinische Urkundenlehre*. Munich: C. H. Beck.

Doody, M. 1998. *The True Story of the Novel*. London: Fontana.

Douglas, M. 1966. *Purity and Danger. An Analysis of Concepts of Pollution and Taboo*. London: Routledge and Kegan Paul.

—— 1970. *Natural Symbols*. New York: Vintage.

—— 1975. *Implicit Meanings: Essays in Anthropology*. London: Routledge and Kegan Paul.

Dowden, K. 1989. *Death and the Maiden: Girls' Initiation Rites in Greek Mythology*. London: Routledge.

du Boulay, J. 1974. *Portrait of a Greek Mountain Village*. Cambridge: Cambridge University Press.

Duffy, J. 1992. *Michael Psellus. Philosophica Minora*, I. Leipzig: Teubner.

Duijzings, G. 1996. "The Exodus of Letnica, Croatian Refugees from Kosovo in Western Slavonia. A Chronicle," in R. Jambrešić Kirin and M. Povrzanović (eds.), *War, Exile, Everyday Life: Cultural Perspectives*. Zagreb: Institute of Ethnology and Folklore Research, 147–170.

Dulaey, M. 1973. *Le rêve dans la vie et la pensée de saint Augustin*. Paris: Études Augustiniennes.

Dundes, A. (ed.) 1996. *The Walled-Up Wife: A Casebook*. Madison: University of Wisconsin Press.

Dunn, F. 1996. *Tragedy's End: Closure and Innovation in Euripidean Drama*. Oxford: Oxford University Press.

Duranti, A. 1997. *Linguistic Anthropology*. Cambridge: Cambridge University Press.

Duranti, A. and Goodwin, Ch. 1992. *Rethinking Context: Language as an Interactive Phenomenon*. Cambridge: Cambridge University Press.

Dutoit, E. 1936. *The thème de l'adynaton dans la poésie antique*. Paris: Belles Lettres.

Dyck, A. 1986. *Michael Psellus–The Essays on Euripides and George of Pisidia and on Heliodorus and Achilles Tatius*. Vienna: Verlag der Österreichischen Akademie der Wissenschaften.

Easterling, P. E. 1981. "The End of the *Trachiniae*," *Illinois Classical Studies* 6:56–74.

—— 1988. "Tragedy and Ritual. Cry 'Woe, Woe,' But May the God Prevail," *Mètis* 3:87–109.

—— 1993. "Tragedy and Ritual," in R. Scodel (ed.), *Theater and Society in the Classical World*. Ann Arbor: University of Michigan Press, 7–23. (Shorter version of Easterling 1988.)

Eck, D. T., 1985. *Darsán: Seeing the Divine Image in India,* revised ed. Chambersburg, Penn.: Anima Books.

Edelstein, E. and Edelstein, L. 1998. *Asclepius: Collection and Interpretation of the Testimonies, I.* Baltimore: Johns Hopkins University Press.

Edmonds, J. M. 1928. *Lyra Graeca I,* revised and augm. ed. London: Heinemann, New York: Putnam, Loeb Classical Library.

Edmunds, L. 1996. *Theatrical Space and Historical Place in Sophocles'* Oedipus at Colonus. Lanham, Md.: Rowman and Littlefield.

Edwards, M. 2000. *Neoplatonic Saints: The Lives of Plotinus and Proclus by their Students.* Liverpool: Liverpool University Press.

Eide, T. 1999. "Reformulated Repetitions in Homer," *Symbolae Osloenses* 74:97–139.

Eideneier, H. 1979. "Ein byzantinischen Kalendergedicht in der Volksprache," *Hellenika* 31:368–419.

—— 1991. *Ptochoprodromos.* Cologne: Romiosini.

Eitrem, S. 1988. "The Necromancy in the *Persai* of Aischylos," *Symbolae Osloenses* 6:1–16.

—— 1991. "Dreams and Divination in Magical Ritual," in C. Faraone and D. Obbink (eds.), *Magika Hiera: Ancient Greek Magic and Religion.* Oxford: Oxford University Press, 175–187.

Elytis, O. 1939. Προσανατολισμοί. Athens: Πυρσός.

—— 1959. Τὸ ῎Αξιον 'Εστί. 6th ed., 1970. Athens: ῎Ικαρος.

—— 1971. Τὸ φωτόδεντρο καὶ ἡ δέκατη τέταρτη ὀμορφιά. Athens: ῎Ικαρος.

—— 1974. Τὰ 'Ετεροθαλῆ. Athens: ῎Ικαρος.

—— 1982. Τρία ποιήματα μὲ σημαία εὐκαιρίας. Athens: ῎Ικαρος.

—— 1984. Τὸ ἡμερολόγιο ἑνὸς ἀθέατου 'Απριλίου. Athens: ῎Ικαρος.

—— 1985. 'Ο μικρὸς ναυτίλος. Athens: ῎Ικαρος.

—— 1987. 'Ανοιχτὰ χαρτιά, definitive edition. Athens: ῎Ικαρος.

—— 1991. Τὰ ἐλεγεῖα τῆς 'Οξώπετρας. Athens: ῎Ικαρος.

—— 1992. 'Εν λευκῷ. Athens: ῎Ικαρος.

—— 1995. *Open Papers,* trans. O. Broumas and T. Begley. Port Townsend, Wash.: Copper Canyon Press.

—— 1997. *The Collected Poems of Odysseus Elytis,* trans. J. Carson and N. Sarris. Baltimore: Johns Hopkins University Press.

—— 1998. 'Εκ τοῦ πλησίον. Athens: ῎Ικαρος.

Evelyn-White, H. G. 1914. *Hesiod, the Homeric Hymns, and Homerica.* London: Heinemann and New York: Macmillan, Loeb Classical Library.

Fabian, J. 1983. *Time and the Other: How Anthropology Makes its Object.* New York: Columbia University Press.

Fabre, P. 1890. "Le polyptique du chanoine Benoît à la Vallicelliane," *Mélanges d'archéologie et d'histoire* 10:384–388.

—— 1905. *Le "Liber Censuum" de l'église romaine.* Bibliothèque des Écoles Françaises d'Athènes et de Rome, 2nd series, 6. Paris: A. Fointemoing, Mai.

Faraone, C. 1992. *Talismans and Trojan Horses.* Oxford: Oxford University Press.

Farinou-Malamatari, G. 1987. 'Αφηγηματικὲς τεχνικὲς στὸν Παπαδιαμάντη, 1887-1910. Athens: Κέδρος.

Faris, W. 1995. "Scheherazade's Children: Magical Realism and Postmodern Fiction," in L. P. Zamora and W. Faris 1995:163–190.

Faubion, F. 1993. *Modern Greek Lessons: A Primer in Historical Constructivism.* Princeton: Princeton University Press.

Fernandez, J. 1972. "Persuasions and Performances: Of the Beast in Every Body and the Metaphors of Everyman," *Daedalus* 101.1:39–60.

—— 1974. "The Mission of Metaphor in Expressive Culture," *Current Anthropology* 15.2:119–145.

—— 1976–77. "Poetry in Motion: Being Moved by Amusement, Mockery, and Mortality in the Asturian Mountains," *New Literary History* 8:459–483.

—— 1981. "The Order of Discourse," in R. Young (ed.), *Untying the Text: A Post-Structuralist Reader.* New York: Routledge and Kegan Paul, 48–78.

Fernandez Marcos, N. 1975. *Los Thaumata de Sofronio: Contribución al Estudio de la Incubación Cristiana.* Madrid: Instituto Antonio Nebrija.

Ferrari, G. 1990. "Figures of Speech: The Picture of *Aidos*," *Métis* 5:185–200.

—— 1997. "Figures in the Text: Metaphors and Riddles in the *Agamemnon*," *Classical Philology* 92:1–45.

—— 2002. *Figures of Speech.* Chicago: The University of Chicago Press.

Ferrari dalle Spade, G. 1912. *Formulari notarili inediti dell'età bizantina.* Rome: Tipografia del Senato.

Festa, N. 1898. *Theodori Ducae Lascaris Epistulae CCXVII.* Florence: G. Carnesecchi e figli.

Festugière, A.-J. 1966. "Proclus et la religion traditionnelle," in R. Chevallier (ed.), *Mélanges d'archéologie et d'histoire offerts à André Piganiol,* vol. 3. Paris: SEVPEN, 1581–1590.

—— 1971. *Sainte Thècle, Saints Côme et Damien, Saints Cyr et Jean (Extraits), Saint Georges.* Paris: A. et J. Picard.

Fitzgerald, A. 1930. *The Essays and Hymns of Synesius of Cyrene.* London: H. Milford.

Fleming, K. E. 2000. "*Orientalism*, the Balkans, and Balkan Historiography," *American Historical Review* 105:1218–1233.

Flueckiger, J. 1996. *Gender and Genre in the Folklore of Middle India.* Ithaca, N.Y.: Cornell University Press.

Foley, H. P. 1985. *Ritual Irony: Poetry and Sacrifice in Euripides.* Ithaca, N.Y.: Cornell University Press.

—— 1992. "*Anodos* Dramas: Euripides' *Alcestis* and *Helen*," in R. Hexter and D. Selden (eds.), *Innovations of Antiquity.* New York and London: Routledge, 133–160.

—— 1993. "The Politics of Tragic Lamentation," in A. H. Sommerstein et al. (eds.), *Tragedy, Comedy and the Polis.* Bari: Levante Editori, 101–143.

—— 1994. *The Homeric Hymn to Demeter.* Princeton: Princeton University Press.

—— 2001. *Female Acts in Greek Tragedy.* Princeton: Princeton University Press.

Foley, J. M. 1991. *The Immanent Art: From Structure to Meaning in Traditional Oral Epic.* Bloomington: Indiana University Press.

Fontenrose, J. 1959. *Python; A Study of Delphic Myth and Its Origins.* Berkeley: University of California Press.

Ford, A. 2002. *The Origin of Criticism.* Princeton: Princeton University Press.

Forster, E. M. 1927. *Aspects of the Novel.* New York: Harcourt Brace.

Foster, G. M. 1965. "Peasant Society and the Image of Limited Good," *American Anthropologist* 67:293–315.

Foucault, M. 1965. *Madness and Civilization*. New York: Pantheon.

—— 1972. *The Archaeology of Knowledge*. New York: Harper and Row.

—— 1973. *The Birth of the Clinic*. New York: Pantheon.

—— 1978. *The History of Sexuality, Vol. 1: An Introduction*. New York: Pantheon.

—— 1979. *Discipline and Punish: The Birth of the Prison*. New York: Random House.

—— 1981. "The Order of Discourse," in R. Young (ed.), *Untying the Text: A Post-Structuralist Reader*. New York: Routledge and Kegan Paul, 48–78.

Fox, J. 1974. "'Our Ancestors Spoke in Pairs': Rotinese Views of Language, Dialect, and Code," in Bauman and Sherzer 1974, 65–85.

Fraenkel, E. 1950. *Aeschylus Agamemnon*. Oxford: Clarendon Press.

Frantz, A. 1965. "From Paganism to Christianity in the Temples of Athens," *Dumbarton Oaks Papers* 19:185–205.

Freeman, K. 1948. *Ancilla to the Pre-Socratic Philosophers*. Cambridge, Mass.: Harvard University Press.

Freud, S. 1991. "Mourning and Melancholia," in idem, *On Metapsychology*. London: Penguin, 251–268.

Friedl, E. 1962. *Vasilika: A Village in Modern Greece*. New York: Holt, Rinehart and Winston.

Friedrich, R. 1996. "Everything to Do with Dionysos? Ritualism, the Dionysiac, and the Tragic" in M. S. Silk (ed.), *Tragedy and the Tragic*. Oxford: Clarendon Press, 257–283.

Fustel de Coulanges, n.d. *The Ancient City. A Study on the Religion, Laws, and Institutions of Greece and Rome*, trans. W. Small. Garden City, N.Y.: Doubleday.

Gaisford, Th. 1820. *Poetae Minores Graeci*, 3. Oxford: Clarendon Press. Oxford: Clarendon Press.

Galanaki, Rh. 1987. Ὁ Βίος τοῦ Ἰσμαΐλ Φερὶκ Πασᾶ – *Spina nel cuore*. Athens: Ἄγρα.

—— 1996. *The Life of Ismail Ferik Pasha: Spina nel Cuore*, trans. and foreword K. Cicellis. London and Chester Springs, UNESCO Publishing: Peter Owen.

Gale, N. H. et al. 1980. "Mineralogical and Geographical Silver Sources for Archaic Greek Coinage," *Metallurgy in Numismatics*. Royal Numismatic Society Special Publication 13, 1:3–49.

Garber, M. 1992. *Vested Interests*. New York: Harper Perennial.

Garitte, G. 1966. "'Histoires Édifiantes' Géorgiennes," *Byzantion* 36:396–423.

Garland, R. 1985. *The Greek Way of Death*. London: Duckworth.

—— 1992. *Introducing New Gods: The Politics of Ancient Religion*. London: Duckworth.

Garner, R. 1988. "Death and Victory in Euripides' *Alcestis*," *Classical Antiquity* 7:58–71.

Garvie, A. F. 1986. *Aeschylus, Choephori*. Oxford: Clarendon Press.

—— 1998. *Sophocles, Ajax*. Warminster: Aris and Phillips.

Garzya, A. 1973. "Literarische und rhetorische Polemiken der Komnenenzeit," *Byzantinoslavica* 34:1.14:7–8.

—— 2000. *Synésius de Cyrène, Correspondance*, trans. D. Roques. Paris: Les Belles Lettres.

Gautier, P. 1986. *Théophylacte d'Achrida*. Thessalonike: Association de Recherches Byzantines.

Geertz, C. 1972. "Deep Play: Notes on the Balinese Cockfight," *Daedalus* 101:1–37.

—— 1973a. *The Interpretation of Cultures: Selected Essays by Clifford Geertz*. New York: Basic Books.

—— 1973b. "Person, Time, and Conduct in Bali," in C. Geertz 1973a, 360–411.

—— 1980. *Negara: The Theater State in Nineteenth-Century Bali.* Princeton: Princeton University Press.

Gell, A. 1998. *Art and Agency: An Anthropological Theory.* Oxford: Clarendon Press and New York: Oxford University Press.

Genette, G. 1969. *Figures II.* Paris: Seuil.

Gentili, B. 1982. "Archiloco e la funzione politica della poesia del biasimo," *Quaderni Urbinati di Cultura Classica* (n.s.) 11:7–28.

—— 1988. *Poetry and Its Public in Ancient Greece: From Homer to the Fifth Century,* trans. A. T. Cole. Baltimore: Johns Hopkins University Press.

Gernet, L. 1917. "Hypothèses sur le contrat primitif en Grèce," *Revue des Études Grecques* 30.(139):249–293 (part I), (140):363–383 (part II).

—— 1928. "Fraires antiques," *Revue des Études Grecques* 41:313–59.

—— 1968. *Anthropologie de la Grèce antique.* Paris: Maspero.

Giangrande, G. 1962. "On the Origins of the Greek Romance: The Birth of a Literary Form," *Eranos* 60:132–159.

Giannaras, Ch. 1972. Ὀρθοδοξία καὶ Δύση. Ἡ θεολογία στὴν Ἑλλάδα σήμερα. Athens: Ἀθηνᾶ.

Gibert, J. 2003. "Apollo's Sacrifice: The Limits of a Metaphor in Greek Tragedy," *Harvard Studies in Classical Philology* 101:159–206.

Giddens, A. 1976. *New Rules of Sociological Method: A Positive Critique of Interpretive Methodologies.* London: Hutchison.

Giraudoux, J. 1973 [1943]. "Introduction" in Le Corbusier, *The Athens Charter.* New York: Grossman Publishers, xv–xix.

Giusti, A. 1993. "Nota a Niceta Eugeniano," *Studi Italiani della Filologia Classica* 11:216-223.

Gladigow, B. 1998. "Ritual Komplexes," in H. Cancik et al. (eds.), *Handbuch religionswissenschaftlicher Grundbegriffe,* vol. 4. Stuttgart: W. Kohlhammer, 458–460.

The Glory of Byzantium, Art and Culture of the Middle Byzantine Era A.D. 843-1261. The Metropolitan Museum of Art. New York: H. N. Abrams, 1997.

Gluckman, M. 1955. *Custom and Conflict in Africa.* Oxford: B. Blackwell.

—— 1962. "Les Rites de Passage," in idem (ed.), *Essays on the Ritual of Social Relations.* Manchester: Manchester University Press, 1–52.

Gluckman, M. and Gluckman, M. 1977. "On Drama, and Games and Athletic Contests," in Moore and Myerhoff 1977a, 227–243.

Goar, J. [1730]. *Euchologion,* 2nd ed., Venice: B. Javarinus, repr. Graz: Akademische Druck-u. Verlagsanstalt, 1960.

Gödde, S. 2000. *Das Drama der Hikesie: Ritual und Rhetorik in Aischylos' Hiketiden. Orbis Antiquus* 35. Münster: Aschendorff.

Goffman, E. 1956. *The Presentation of Self in Everyday Life.* Garden City, N.Y.: Doubleday.

—— 1967. *Interaction Ritual: Essays on Face-to-Face Behavior.* Garden City, N.Y.: Doubleday.

—— 1974. *Frame Analysis: An Essay on the Organization of Experience.* Cambridge, Mass.: Harvard University Press.

Gomme, A. W. 1956. *A Historical Commentary on Thucydides, II.* Oxford: Oxford University Press.

Goodwin, C. and Duranti, A. 1992. "Rethinking Context: An Introduction," in Duranti and Goodwin 1992, 1–42.

Goody, J. 1977. "Against 'Ritual': Loosely Structured Thoughts on a Loosely Defined Topic," in Moore and Myerhoff 1977a, 25–35.

Gordon, R. 1996. "The Real and the Imaginary. Production and Religion in the Graeco-Roman World," in idem, *Image and Value in the Graeco-Roman World. Studies in Mithraism and Religious Art*. London: Variorum, 5–34.

Gould, J. 1994. "Herodotus and Religion," in S. Hornblower (ed.), *Greek Historiography*. Oxford: Oxford University Press, 91–106; reprinted in idem 2001, 359–377.

—— 1996. "Tragedy and Collective Experience," in M. Silk (ed.), *Tragedy and the Tragic: Greek Theatre and Beyond*. Oxford: Clarendon Press, 217–243.

—— 2001. *Myth, Ritual Memory, and Exchange: Essays in Greek Literature and Culture*. Oxford: Oxford University Press.

Gourgouris, S. 2002. "Hypnosis and Critique (Film Music for the Balkans)," in Bjelić and Savić 2002, 323–350.

Graf, F. 1978. "Die lokrischen Mädchen," *Studi Storico-Religiosi* 2:61–79.

—— 1979. "Apollon Delphinios," *Museum Helveticum* 36:2–22.

—— 1996. "Ritual," in S. Hornblower and A. Spawforth (eds.), *The Oxford Classical Dictionary*, third ed., Oxford: Oxford University Press, 1318-1320.

—— (ed.). 1998. *Ansichten griechischer Rituale. Geburtstags-Symposium für Walter Burkert*. Stuttgart: B. G. Teubner.

Gramit, D. 1985. "The Music Paintings of the Cappella Palatina in Palermo," in T. Seebass (ed.), *Imago Musicae II*, International Yearbook of Musical Iconography. Durham, NC, 9–49.

Grayson, A. K. 1975. *Assyrian and Babylonian Chronicles*. Locust Valley, N.Y: J. J. Augustin.

Green, J. R. 1985. "A Representation of the *Birds* of Aristophanes," in *Greek Vases in the J. Paul Getty Museum*. Occasional Papers on Antiquity 3. Malibu: J. Paul Getty Museum, 95–118.

Grégoire, H. and Kugener, M.-A. 1930. *Vie de Porphyre, évêque de Gaza*. Paris: Belles Lettres.

Gregory, T. 1986. "The Survival of Paganism in Christian Greece: A Critical Essay," *American Journal of Philology*, 107:229–242.

Grene, D. and Lattimore, R. 1991. *The Complete Greek Tragedies, I.* Chicago: University of Chicago Press.

Griffin, A. 1982. *Sikyon*. Oxford: Oxford University Press.

Griffin, J. 1980. *Homer on Life and Death*. Oxford: Clarendon Press.

Griffith, M. 1999. *Sophocles, Antigone*. Cambridge: Cambridge University Press.

Grimal, P. 1985 [1951]. *The Dictionary of Classical Mythology*, trans. A. R. Maxwell-Hislop. Oxford: B. Blackwell.

Grimes, R. 1990. *Ritual Criticism*. Columbia, S.C: University of South Carolina Press.

Grinker, R. R. 1994. *Houses in the Rainforest: Ethnicity and Inequality among Farmers and Foragers in Central Africa*. Berkeley: University of California Press.

Grosdidier de Matons, J. 1977. *Romanos le Mélode et les origines de la poésie réligieuse à Byzance*. Paris: Éditions Beauchesne.

Gross, K. 1992. *The Dream of the Moving Statue*. Ithaca, N.Y.: Cornell University Press.

Guarducci, M. 1930. "Pandora o i Martellatori," *Monumenti Antichi* 33:6–38.

—— 1944/45. "Tripodi, Lebeti, Oboli," *Rivista di Filologia e di Istruzione Classica* 22:3:171–80.

Bibliography

—— 1961. "Epigraphical Appendix," in G. M. A. Richter, *The Archaic Gravestones of Attica*. London, Phaidon Press, 155–172.

Guépin, J. P. 1968. *The Tragic Paradox: Myth and Ritual in Greek Tragedy*. Amsterdam: A. M. Hakkert.

Guilland, R. 1965. "Études sur l'histoire administrative de l'empire byzantin: Le maître des requêtes. Ὁ ἐπὶ τῶν δεήσεων," *Byzantion* 35:97–118.

Gumperz, J. J. 1982. *Discourse Strategies*. Cambridge: Cambridge University Press.

—— 1992. "Contextualization and Understanding," in Duranti and Goodwin 1992, 230–252.

Guralnick, E. 1978. "Proportions of Kouroi," *American Journal of Archaeology* 82:461–72.

Gurevich, A. I. 1988. *Medieval Popular Culture: Problems of Belief and Perception*, trans. J. Bak and P. Hollingsworth. Cambridge: Cambridge University Press; Paris: Maison des Sciences de l'Homme.

Hadjipantazis, Th. 1984. Ἡ εἰσβολὴ τοῦ Καραγκιόζη στὴν Ἀθήνα τοῦ 1890. Athens: Στιγμή.

—— 1991. "The Silk Route Blocked: Theories on the Origin of the Greek Shadow Theatre," in *Cultural and Commercial Exchanges between the Orient and the Greek World*. Athens: Centre for Neohellenic Research, National Hellenic Research Foundation, 139–147.

Hägg, T. 1983. *The Novel in Antiquity*, revised ed. Oxford: B. Blackwell.

Haldon, J. F. 1990. *Constantine Porphyrogenitus: Three Treatises on Imperial Military Expeditions*. Vienna: Verlag der Österreichischen Akademie der Wissenschaften.

Halkin, F. 1957. *Bibliotheca Hagiographica Graeca*, 3 vols. Brussels: Société des Bollandistes.

—— 1984. *Novum Auctarium Bibliothecae Hagiographica Graeca*. Brussels: Société des Bollandistes.

Hall, E. 1989. *Inventing the Barbarian: Greek Self-Definition Through Tragedy*. Oxford: Oxford University Press.

—— 1996. *Aeschylus, Persians*. Warminster: Aris and Phillips.

—— 1999. "Sophocles' *Electra* in Britain," in J. Griffin (ed.), *Sophocles Revisited, Essays Presented to Sir Hugh Lloyd-Jones*. Oxford: Oxford University Press, 261–306.

Hall, E. et al. (eds.) 2000. *Medea in Performance 1500–2000*. Oxford: European Humanities Research Centre of the University of Oxford.

Halleran, M. R. 1988. "Text and Ceremony at the Close of Euripides' *Alkestis*," *Eranos* 86:123–129.

Hamilton, M. 1906. *Incubation, or, the Cure of Disease in Pagan Temples and Christian Churches*. St. Andrews: W. C. Henderson.

Handelman, D. 1998. *Models and Mirrors: Towards an Anthropology of Public Events*, repr. ed. Oxford: Berghahn Books.

Handler, R. 1988. *Nationalism and the Politics of Culture in Quebec*. Madison: University of Wisconsin Press.

Hansen, P. A. 1983. *Carmina epigraphica graeca saeculorum VIII–V A. CHR. N.* Berlin and New York: de Gruyter.

—— 1989. *Carmina epigraphica graeca saeculi IV A.CHR. N.* Berlin: de Gruyter.

Hardy, Th. 1912. *Tess of the d'Urbervilles: A Pure Woman*. repr. 1920. London: Macmillan.

Harris, D. 1995. *The Treasures of the Parthenon and Erechtheion*. Oxford: Oxford University Press.

Harrison, A. R. W. 1968. *The Law of Athens. I.* Oxford: Clarendon Press.

Harrison, J. F. 1900. "Pandora's Box," *Journal of Hellenic Studies* 20:99–114.

—— 1922. *Prolegomena to the Study of Greek Religion.* Cambridge: Cambridge University Press.

Hart, L. K. 1992. *Time, Religion, and Social Experience in Rural Greece.* Lanham, Md.: Rowman and Littlefield.

—— 1998. "Does the Bridge Have a Sex?" Paper presented at the 1998 Meetings of the American Anthropological Association, Washington, D.C.

—— 1999. "Culture, Civilization, and Demarcation at the North-West Borders of Greece," *American Ethnologist* 26 (1):196–220.

—— 2000. "The Occupation of Houses: The Legacy of Displacement in Northwest Greece." Paper presented to the Hellenic Studies Program, Princeton University.

Hartog, F. 1988. *The Mirror of Herodotus: The Representation of the Other in the Writing of History,* trans. J. Lloyd. Berkeley: University of California Press.

Harvey, A. E. 1955. "The Classification of Greek Lyric Poetry," *Classical Quarterly* 5:157–175.

Hasluck, F. W. 1929. *Christianity and Islam Under the Sultans, I.* Oxford: Clarendon Press.

Heisenberg, A. 1903. *Georgii Acropolitae Opera, I.* Leipzig: Teubner, repr. by P. Wirth, Stuttgart: Teubner, 1978.

—— 1920. "Aus der Geschichte und der Literatur der Palaiologenzeit," *Sitzungsberichte der Bayerischen Akademie der Wissenschaften. Philosophisch-philologische und historische Klasse.* Munich, 10:33–51.

Henrichs, A. 1983. "The 'Sobriety' of Oedipus: Sophocles *OC* 100 Misunderstood," *Harvard Studies in Classical Philology* 87:87–100.

—— 1991. "Namenlosigkeit und Euphemismus: Zur Ambivalenz der chthonischen Mächte im attischen Drama," in H. Hofmann and A. Harder (eds.), *Fragmenta dramatica: Beiträge zur Interpretation der griechischen Tragikerfragmente und ihrer Wirkungsgeschichte.* Göttingen: Vandenhoeck und Ruprecht, 161–201.

—— 1993. "The Tomb of Aias and the Prospect of Hero Cult in Sophokles," *Classical Antiquity* 12:165–180.

—— 1994/95. "Why Should I Dance? Choral Self-Referentiality in Greek Tragedy," *Arion* 3.1:56–111.

—— 1998. "Dromena und Legomena: Zum rituellen Selbstverständnis der Griechen," in Graf 1998, 33–71.

—— 2000. "*Drama* and *Dromena*: Bloodshed, Violence, and Sacrificial Metaphor in Euripides," *Harvard Studies in Classical Philology* 100:173–188.

—— forthcoming. "Wie ein Rind zur Schlachtbank: Zur Problematisierung der Opferthematik in der griechischen Tragödie," to be published in R. Schlesier (ed.), *Mythos und Interpretation.*

Herington, J. 1985. *Poetry into Drama: Early Tragedy and the Greek Poetic Tradition.* Berkeley: University of California Press.

Herzfeld, M. 1972. *The Khelidonisma: A Study in Textual and Ritual Variation,* University of Birminham: M.A. thesis.

—— 1973. "Προφορική παράδοση καὶ πολιτιστικὴ συνέχεια στὶς ἀνοιξιάτικες τελετὲς τῶν νοτιοροδίτικων χωριῶν," Δωδεκανησιακὰ Χρονικά 2:270–288.

441

Bibliography

—— 1977. "Ritual and Textual Structures: The Advent of Spring in Rural Greece," in R. Jain (ed.), *Text and Context: The Social Anthropology of Tradition*, A.S.A. Essays in Social Anthropology 2. Philadelphia: Institute for the Study of Human Issues, 29–50.

—— 1980. "Social Borderers: Themes of Ambiguity and Conflict in Greek Folk Song," *Byzantine and Modern Greek Studies* 6:1–80.

—— 1982. *Ours Once More: Folklore, Ideology and the Making of Modern Greece*. Austin: University of Texas Press.

—— 1983. "Categories of Inclusion and Exclusion and 'Looking Both Ways: The Ethnographer in the Text,'" *Semiotica* 46-2/4:151–166.

—— 1985a. "Lévi-Strauss in the Nation-State," *Journal of American Folklore* 98:191–208.

—— 1985b. *The Poetics of Manhood: Contest and Identity in a Cretan Mountain Village*. Princeton: Princeton University Press.

—— 1992. *The Social Production of Indifference: Exploring the Symbolic Roots of Western Bureaucracy*. Oxford: Berg.

—— 1995. "It Takes One to Know One: Collective Resentment and Mutual Recognition among Greeks in Local and Global Contexts," in R. Fardon (ed.), *Counterworks: Managing the Diversity of Knowledge*. London: Routledge, 124–142.

—— 1997a. *Cultural Intimacy: Social Poetics in the Nation-State*. New York: Routledge.

—— 1997b. *Portrait of a Greek Imagination: An Ethnographic Biography of Andreas Nenedakis*. Chicago: University of Chicago Press.

—— 2003. *The Body Impolitic: Artisans and Artifice in the Global Hierarchy of Value*. Chicago: University of Chicago Press.

Hesseling, D. C. and Pernot, H. 1910. *Poèmes Prodromiques en grec vulgaire*. Amsterdam: J. Müller.

Hirschon, R. 1989. *Heirs of the Greek Catastrophe*. Oxford: Oxford University Press.

—— 1992. "Greek Adults' Play, or, How to Train for Caution," *Journal of Modern Greek Studies* 10:35–56.

Hock, R. F. 1997. "The Rhetoric of Romance," in S. Porter (ed.), *Handbook of Classical Rhetoric in the Hellenistic Period 330 B.C.–A.D. 400*. Leiden: Brill, 445–465.

Hodgen, M. T. 1936. *The Doctrine of Survivals: A Chapter in the History of Scientific Method in the Study of Man*. London: Allenson.

Hoessly, F. 2001. *Katharsis: Reinigung als Heilsverfahren. Studien zum Ritual der archaischen und klassischen Zeit sowie zum Corpus Hippocraticum*. Hypomnemata 135. Göttingen: Vandenhoeck und Ruprecht.

Hoffelner, A. 1988. "Die Metopen des Athener-Schatzhauses. Ein neuer Rekonstruktionsversuch," *Athenische Mitteilungen* 103:77–117.

Holst-Warhaft, G. 1992. *Dangerous Voices: Women's Laments and Greek Literature*. London and New York: Routledge.

—— 2000. *The Cue for Passion: Grief and its Political Uses*. Cambridge, Mass.: Harvard University Press.

Holt, P. 1989. "The End of the *Trachiniai* and the Fate of Heracles," *Journal of Hellenic Studies* 109:69–80.

Hörandner, W. 1974. *Theodoros Prodromos, Historische Gedichte*. Vienna: Verlag der Österreichischen Akademie der Wissenschaften.

Huber, M. 1915. *Johannes Monachus: Liber de Miraculis*. Heidelberg: Carl Winter's Universitätsbuchhandlung.

Hull, D. B. 1972. *Digenis Akritas: The Two-Blood Border Lord.* Athens, Ohio: Ohio University Press.

Humphreys, S. C. 1980. "Family Tombs and Tomb Cult in Ancient Athens: Tradition or Traditionalism?," *Journal of Hellenic Studies* 100:96–126.

Hunger, H. 1972. "Aspekte der Griechischen Rhetorik von Gorgias bis zum Untergang von Byzanz," *Sitzungsberichte der Österreichischer Akademie der Wissenschaften, philos.-histor. Klasse,* 277:3: 6–7.

—— 1978. *Die hochsprachliche profane Literatur der Byzantiner.* Munich: Beck.

—— 1981. "The Importance of Rhetoric in Byzantium," in M. Mullett and R. Scott (eds.), *Byzantium and the Classical Tradition.* Birmingham: Centre for Byzantine Studies, University of Birmingham, 35–47.

Hunt, E. 1977. "Ceremonies of Confrontation and Submission: The Symbolic Dimension of Indian-Mexican Political Interaction," in Moore and Myerhoff 1977a, 124–147.

Hunt, L. A. 1984. "Comnenian Aristocratic Palace Decorations," in M. Angold (ed.), *Byzantine Aristocracy.* Oxford: British Academy Publications, 138–157.

Hunt, Y. 1993. *Traditional Dance in Greek Culture.* Athens: Center for Asia Minor Studies.

Hunter, R. L. 1999. *Theocritus. A Selection.* Cambridge: Cambridge University Press.

Huntington, R. and Metcalf, P. 1979. *Celebrations of Death: The Anthropology of Mortuary Ritual.* Cambridge: Cambridge University Press.

Hutchinson, G. O. 1985. *Aeschylus, Septem contra Thebas.* Oxford: Clarendon Press.

Hymes, D. H. 1975. "Breakthrough into Performance," in D. Ben-Amos and K. Godstein (eds.), *Folklore: Performance and Communication.* The Hague: Mouton, 11–74.

—— 1981. *"In Vain I Tried to Tell You": Essays in Native American Ethnopoetics.* Philadelphia: University of Pennsylvania Press.

I. K. 1989. Ἔρωτος Ἀποτελέσματα. Ἱστορίαι ἠθικοερωτικαί, 1792, ed. M. Vitti. Athens: Ὀδυσσέας.

Ieranò, G. 1987. "Osservazioni sul Teseo di Bacchilide (Dith.18)," *Acme* 40:87–103.

Immerwahr, H. R. 1966. *Form and Thought in Herodotus.* Cleveland: Western Reserve University Press.

Innes, D. C. 1995. *Demetrius: On Style,* in *Aristotle: Poetics,* ed. and trans. S. Halliwell, *Longinus: On the Sublime,* ed. and trans. W. H. Fyfe, revised by D. Russell, *Demetrius: On Style,* ed. and trans. D. C. Innes, based on the translation by W. R. Roberts, Cambridge, Mass.: Harvard University Press, Loeb Classical Library.

Ioannou, Y. 1978. Ὁ Καραγκιόζης. Athens: Ἑρμῆς.

Iordanova, D. 2001. *Cinema of Flames: Balkan Film, Culture and the Media.* London: British Film Institute.

Iser, W. 1974. *The Implied Reader.* Baltimore: Johns Hopkins University Press.

—— 1978. *The Act of Reading: A Theory of Aesthetic Response.* Baltimore: Johns Hopkins University Press.

—— 1989. *Prospecting: From Reader Response to Literary Anthropology.* Baltimore: Johns Hopkins University Press.

Jacoby, D. 1993. "Les Juifs de Byzance: une communauté marginalisée," in Ch. Maltezou (ed.), Οἱ περιθωριακοὶ στὸ Βυζάντιο. Athens: Ἵδρυμα Γουλανδρῆ-Χόρν, 103–154.

Jakobson, R. 1971. "Shifters, Verbal Categories and the Russian Verb," in idem, *Selected Writings,* II. The Hague, 130–147.

—— 1960. "Linguistics and Poetics," in T. A. Sebeok (ed.), *Style in Language*. Cambridge, Mass.: MIT Press, 350–377.

—— 1987. *Language and Literature*. Cambridge, Mass.: Harvard University Press.

Janowitz, N. 2002. *Icons of Power: Ritual Practices in Late Antiquity*. University Park, Penn.: Pennsylvania State University Press.

Jauss, H. R. 1982a. *Aesthetic Experience and Literary Hermeneutics*, trans. M. Shaw. Minneapolis: University of Minnesota Press.

—— 1982b. *Toward an Aesthetic of Reception*. Minneapolis: University of Minnesota Press.

Jeanmaire, H. 1939. *Couroi et courètes; essai sur l'éducation spartiate et sur les rites d'adolescence dans l'antiquité hellénique*. Lille: Bibliothèque Universitaire.

Jeffreys, E. 1980. "The Comnenian Background to the Romans d'Antiquité," *Byzantion* 10:455–486.

Jenkins, R. 1963. "The Hellenistic Origins of Byzantine Literature," *Dumbarton Oaks Papers* 17:37–52.

Jobst, W. 1970. *Die Höhle im griechischen Theater des 5. und 4. Jahrhunderts v. Chr.* Vienna: Böhlaus.

Jordan, B. 1975. *The Athenian Navy in the Classical Period: A Study of Athenian Naval Administration and Military Organization in the Fifth and Fourth Centuries B.C.* Berkeley: University of California Press.

Josephus, F. 1998. *Jewish Antiquities*, trans. H. St. J. Thackeray; eds. R. Marcus, A. Wikgren. Cambridge, Mass.: Harvard University Press, Loeb Classical Library.

Jouanna, J. 1992. "Libations et sacrifices dans la tragédie grecque," *Revue des Études Grecques* 105:406–434.

Jurenka, H. 1902. "Die neuen Bruchstücke der Sappho und des Alkaios," *Zeitschrift für die Österreichischen Gymnasien* 53:289–298.

Jusdanis, G. 1987. "Is Postmodernism Possible Outside the 'West'? The Case of Greece," *Byzantine and Modern Greek Studies* 11:69–92.

Just, R. 1989. *Women in Athenian Law and Life*. London: Routledge.

—— 2000. *A Greek Island Cosmos: Kinship and Community on Meganisi*. Oxford: James Currey and Santa Fe: School of American Research Press.

Kadare, I. 1997. *The Three-Arched Bridge*. New York: Vintage Books.

Kafandaris, K. 1988. Ἑλληνικὰ Λαϊκὰ Παραμύθια, 2 vols. Athens: Ὀδυσσέας.

Kahil, L. 1977. "L'Artémis de Brauron: Rites et Mystère," *Antike Kunst* 20:86–98.

Kakavoulia, M. 1997. "Interior Monologue: Recontextualizing a Modernist Practice in Greece," in Tziovas 1997a, 135–149.

Kalavrezou, I. 2003 (ed.). *Byzantine Women and Their World*. Cambridge, Mass.: Harvard University Art Museums.

Kalavrezou, I. and Trahulia-Sabar, N. 1993. "Critique of the Emperor in the Vatican Psalter 752," *Dumbarton Oaks Papers* 47:195–219.

Kamerbeek, J. C. 1984. *The Plays of Sophocles. Commentaries. Part VII: The Oedipus Coloneus*. Leiden: E. J. Brill.

Kannicht, R. 1969. *Euripides, Helena*. Heidelberg: Carl Winter. Universitätsverlag.

Karakallinos, V. 1954. "Diegesis," Ἁγιορείτικη Βιβλιοθήκη 19:219–22.

Karp, I. 1980. "Beer Drinking and Social Experience: An Essay in Formal Sociology," in I. Karp and C. Bird (eds.), *Explorations in African Systems of Thought*. Bloomington: Indiana University Press, 83–119.

—— 1986. "Agency and Social Theory: A Review of Anthony Giddens," *American Ethnologist* 13.1:131–137.

Kassis, K. 1985. Παραλογοτεχνία στην Ελλάδα: 1830-1980, Λαϊκά Φυλλάδια. Ὁ γραφτὸς Καραγκιοζης. Athens: Ἰχώρ.

Kazantzakis, N. 1973. Βίος καὶ πολιτεία τοῦ Ἀλέξη Ζορμπᾶ. Athens: Ἐκδόσεις Ἑ. Καζαντζάκη.

Kazhdan, A. 1967. "Bemerkungen zu Niketas Eugenianos," *Jahrbuch der Österreichischen Byzantinischen Gesellschaft* 16:101–117.

—— 1983. "Certain Traits of Imperial Propaganda in the Byzantine Empire from the Eighth to the Fifteenth Centuries," in G. Makdisi et al. (eds.), *Preaching and Propaganda in the Middle Ages*. Paris: Presses Universitaires de France, 13–27.

Kazhdan, A. and Epstein, A. 1985. *Change in Byzantine Culture in the Eleventh and Twelfth Centuries*. Berkeley: University of California Press.

Keil, B. 1889. "Die Monatscycklen der byzantinischen Kunst in spätgriechischer Literatur," *Wiener Studien* 11:94–142.

Kelly, J. and Kaplan, M. 1990. "History, Structure, and Ritual," *Annual Review of Anthropology* 19:119–150.

Kenna, M. 1976. "Houses, Fields and Graves: Property and Ritual Obligation on a Greek Island," *Ethnology* 15:62–76.

Kent, R. G. 1953. *Old Persian: Grammar, Texts, Lexicon*. New Haven: American Oriental Society.

Kertzer, D. I. 1988. *Ritual, Politics, and Power*. New Haven: Yale University Press.

Kierkegaard, S. 1983. *Fear and Trembling; Repetition*, trans. and ed. H. V. Hong and E. H. Hong. Princeton: Princeton University Press.

Kiernan, J. 1994. "Variation on a Christian Theme: The Healing Synthesis of Zulu Zionism," in C. Stewart and R. Shaw (eds.), *Syncretism/Anti-Syncretism: The Politics of Religious Synthesis*. London: Routledge, 69–84.

Kiourtsakis, Y. 1981. Προφορικὴ παράδοση καὶ ὁμαδικὴ δημιουργία. Τὸ παράδειγμα τοῦ Καραγκιόζη. Athens: Κέδρος.

—— 1985. Καρναβάλι καὶ Καραγκιόζης. Οἱ ρίζες καὶ οἱ μεταμορφώσεις τοῦ λαϊκοῦ γέλιου. Athens: Κέδρος.

Kirk, G. S. 1985. *The Iliad: A Commentary, I, Books 1–4*. Cambridge: Cambridge University Press.

Kitzinger, E. 1991. *The Mosaics of St. Mary's of the Admiral in Palermo*. Washington, D.C.: Dumbarton.

Klein, M. 1975. "Mourning and its Relation to Manic-Depressive States (1940)," in eadem, *Love, Guilt and Reparation, and Other Works 1921–1945*. London: Hogarth and the Institute of Psychoanalysis, 344–369.

Kligman, G. 1988. *The Wedding of the Dead: Ritual, Poetics, and Popular Culture in Transylvania*. Berkeley: University of California Press.

Knox, B. 1993. *The Oldest Dead White European Males and Other Reflections on the Classics*. New York: W. W. Norton.

Komines, A. 1960. "Γρηγορίου τοῦ Κορινθίου, ἐξηγήσεις εἰς τοὺς ἱεροὺς λειτουργικοὺς κανόνας τοῦ Δαμασκηνοῦ καὶ Κοσμᾶ τοῦ Μελῳδοῦ," *Akten des 11 Intern. Byzantinistenkongress*, Munich, 248–53.

Kopidakis, M. Z. 1991. "Υ. Τὸ πιὸ ἑλληνικό." Ἡ Λέξη 11:768–773.

Kordatos, Y. 1924. Ἡ κοινωνικὴ σημασία τῆς ἑλληνικῆς ἐπαναστάσεως τοῦ 1821. Athens: Γ. Βασιλείου.

Korg, J. 1995. *Ritual and Experiment in Modern Poetry.* London: Macmillan.

Koukoules, Ph. 1944–49. Βυζαντινῶν βίος καὶ πολιτισμός, 5 vols., repr. Athens: Παπαζήσης, n.d.

Koziol, G. 1992. *Begging Pardon and Favor: Ritual and Political Order in Early Medieval France.* Ithaca, N.Y. : Cornell University Press.

Kozyris, J. Ph. 1993. "Reflections on the Impact of Membership in the European Economic Community on Greek Legal Culture," *Journal of Modern Greek Studies* 11:29–49.

Kraay, C. M. 1976. *Archaic and Classical Greek Coins.* London: Methuen.

Krikos-Davis, K. 1996. "Seferis and the Myth of Adonis," in P. Mackridge (ed.), *Ancient Greek Myth in Modern Greek Poetry: Essays in Memory of C. A. Trypanis.* London: F. Cass, 53–66.

Kroll, J. H. and Waggoner, N. M. 1984. "Dating the Earliest Coins of Athens," *American Journal of Archaeology* 88:325–340.

Krummen, E. 1998. "Ritual und Katastrophe: Rituelle Handlung und Bildersprache bei Sophokles und Euripides," in Graf 1998, 296–325.

Kryzhickij, S. D. 1991. "Antike Stadtstaaten im nördlichen Schwarzmeergebiet," in Rolle et al. 1991, 187–200.

Küchler, S. 1987. "*Malangan*: Art and Memory in a Melanesian Society," *Man* 22:238–55.

——1992. "Making Skins: *Malangan* and the Idea of Kinship in Northern New Ireland," in J. Coote and A. Shelton (eds.), *Anthropology, Art and Aesthetics.* Oxford: Oxford University Press, 94–112.

Kuhn, T. 1962. *The Structure of Scientific Revolutions.* Chicago: University of Chicago Press.

Kuhrt, A. 1982. "Assyrian and Babylonian Traditions in Classical Authors: A Critical Synthesis," in H.-J. Nissen and J. Renger (eds.), *Mesopotamien und seine Nachbarn: Politische und kulturelle Wechselbeziehungen im alten Vorderasien vom 4. bis 1. Jahrtausend v. Chr.,* I. Berlin: D. Reimer, 539–554.

—— 2002. "Babylon" in Bakker et al. 2002, 475–496.

Kurke, L. 1991. *The Traffic in Praise.* Ithaca, N.Y.: Cornell University Press.

Kurtz, D. C. and Boardman, J. 1971. *Greek Burial Customs.* London: Thames and Hudson.

Kustas, G. 1970. "The Function and Evolution of Byzantine Rhetoric," *Viator* 1:55–73.

Kyriakidou-Nestoros, A. 1975. Λαογραφικὰ Μελετήματα. Athens: Ὀλκός.

—— 1978. Ἡ Θεωρία τῆς Ἑλληνικῆς Λαογραφίας. Athens: Ἑταιρεία Σπουδῶν Νεοελληνικοῦ Πολιτισμοῦ καὶ Γενικῆς Παιδείας.

Kyrieleis, H. 1996. *Der grosse Kuros von Samos.* Bonn: Habelt.

Lachenaud, G. 1978. *Mythologies, religion et philosophie de l'histoire dans Hérodote.* Lille: Atelier réproduction de thèses Université de Lille, iii.

Lada-Richards, I. 1999. *Initiating Dionysus: Ritual and Theatre in Aristophanes' Frogs.* Oxford: Clarendon Press.

Lafitau, J. F. 1997. *Customs of the American Indians Compared with the Customs of Primitive Times, II,* trans., eds. W. Fenton and E. Moore. Toronto: The Champlain Society.

Laiou, A. 1986. "The Festival of Agathe: Comments on the Life of Constantinopolitan Women," Βυζάντιον· Ἀφιέρωμα στὸν Ἀνδρέα Ν. Στράτο, *Vol. I.* Athens , 111–122.

—— 1994. "Law, Justice, and the Byzantine Historians: Ninth to Twelfth Centuries," in
A. E. Laiou and D. Simon (eds.), *Law and Society in Byzantium, Ninth–Twelfth
Centuries*. Washington, D.C.: Harvard University Press, 151–185.

Lambek, M. 1998. "The Sakalava Poiesis of History: Realizing the Past Through Spirit
Possession in Madagascar," *American Ethnologist* 25:106–127.

Lambrinos, G. 1947. Τὸ δημοτικὸ τραγούδι. Athens: Τὰ Νέα Βιβλία.

Lambropoulos, V. 1988. *Literature as National Institution: Studies in the Politics of Modern
Greek Criticism*. Princeton: Princeton University Press.

Lampros, P. 1879–80. Μιχαὴλ 'Ακομινάτου τοῦ Χωνιάτου τὰ Σωζόμενα, I.
Athens, repr. Gröningen: Bouma's Boekhuis, 1968.

Lanata, G. 1960. "L'ostracon fiorentino con versi di Saffo. Note paleografiche ed
esegetiche," *Studi Italiani di Filologia Classica* (n.s.) 32:64–90.

Lane Fox, R. 1987. *Pagans and Christians*. San Francisco: Harper and Row.

Langer, S. 1953. *Feeling and Form: A Theory of Art*. New York: Scribner's.

Lapatin, K. 2001. *Chryselephantine Statuary in the Ancient World*. Oxford: Oxford
University Press.

Lardinois, A. 1994. "Subject and Circumstance in Sappho's Poetry," *Transactions of the
American Philological Association* 124:57–84.

—— 1996. "Who Sang Sappho's Songs?," in E. Greene (ed.), *Reading Sappho:
Contemporary Approaches*. Berkeley: University of California Press, 150–172.

—— 2001. "Keening Sappho: Female Speech Genres in Sappho's Poetry," in A. Lardinois
and L. McClure (eds.), *Making Silence Speak: Women's Voices in Greek Literature
and Society*. Princeton: Princeton University Press, 75–92.

Laum, B. 1924. *Heiliges Geld*. Tübingen: Mohr.

Laurent, V. 1981. *Le corpus des sceaux de l'Empire byzantin*. Paris: Éditions du Centre
National de la Recherche Scientifique.

Lausberg, H. 1960. *Handbuch der literarischen Rhetorik: Eine Grundlegung der
Literaturwissenschaft*. Munich: M. Hueber.

Lavecchia, S. 2000. *Pindari Dithyramborum Fragmenta*. Rome and Pisa: Ateneo.

Lawson, J. K. 1910. *Modern Greek Folklore and Ancient Greek Religion*. Cambridge:
Cambridge University Press.

Layard, J. 1951. "The Pilgrimage to Oba. An Atchin Sex-Initiation Rite," *Südseestudien,
Études sur l'Océanie*, 331–357.

Layoun, M. (ed.) 1990. *Modernism in Greece? Essays on the Critical and Literary Margins of
a Movement*. New York: Pella.

Lazarev, V. N. 1966. *Old Russian Murals and Mosaics: From the 11th to the 16th Century,*
trans. B. Roniger, revised by N. Dunn. London: Phaidon.

Le Corbusier (Charles-Eduard Jeanneret) 1927. *Towards a New Architecture*. New York:
Brewer, Warren, and Putnam.

Leach, E. 1961. "Two Essays Concerning the Symbolic Representation of Time," in idem,
Rethinking Anthropology. London: Athlone, 124–136.

—— 1966. "Ritualization in Man in Relation to Conceptual and Social Development."
Philosophical Transactions of the Royal Society of London 251(722):403–408.

—— 1988. *Culture and Communication*. Cambridge: Cambridge University Press.

Leduc, C. 1990. "Come darla in matrimonio? La sposa nel mondo greco, secoli IX-IV a.C.," in G. Duby et al. (eds.), *Storia delle donne in Occidente, Vol. 1: L'Antichità*. Bari: Laterza, 246–314.

Lefèbvre, H. 1994. *The Production of Space*, trans. D. Nicholson-Smith. Oxford: B. Blackwell.

Lemos, I. S. 2002. *The Protogeometric Aegean: The Archaeology of the Late Eleventh and Tenth Centuries B.C.* Oxford: Oxford University Press.

Lempese, A. 1985. Τὸ ἱερὸ τοῦ Ἑρμῆ καὶ τῆς Ἀφροδίτης στὴν Σύμη Βιάννου. Athens: Ἡ ἐν Ἀθήναις Ἀρχαιολογικὴ Ἑταιρεία.

Leone, P. A. M. 1968. *Ioannis Tzetzae Historiae*. Naples: Librena Scientifica Editrice.

Leontis, A. 1999. "The Bridge Between the Classical and the Balkan," *The South Atlantic Quarterly* 98.4:633–654.

Levinson, D. and Ember, M. (eds.) 1996. *Encyclopedia of Cultural Anthropology*. New York: Henry Holt.

Lévi-Strauss, C. "Histoire et Ethnologie." *Annales* 38.6:1217–1231.

——— 1982. *The Way of the Masks*. Seattle: University of Washington Press.

LiDonnici, L. 1995. *The Epidaurian Miracle Inscriptions: Text, Translation and Commentary*. Atlanta: Scholars Press.

Lienhardt, L. 1961. *Divinity and Experience: The Religion of the Dinka*. Oxford: Clarendon Press.

Lindberg, G. 1977. *Studies in Hermogenes and Eustathios*. Lund: Lindell.

Lloyd, G. E. R. 1971. *Polarity and Analogy*. Cambridge: Cambridge University Press.

Lloyd-Jones, H. 1970. *Aeschylus, The Eumenides*. Englewood Cliffs, N.J.: Prentice-Hall.

——— 1996. *Sophocles, Fragments*, Cambridge, Mass.: Harvard University Press.

——— 1998. "Ritual and Tragedy," in Graf 1998, 271–295.

Lobel, E. and Page, D. 1955. *Poetarum Lesbiorum Fragmenta*. Oxford: Clarendon Press.

Lodge, D. 1966. "Tess, Nature and the Voices of Hardy," in idem (ed.), *Language of Fiction: Essays in Criticism and Verbal Analysis of the English Novel*. London: Routledge and Kegal Paul, 164–188.

Loeb, E. H. 1982. Review of *Die Geburt der Götterin der griechischen Kunst der klassischen Zeit* (Jerusalem: Shikmona, 1979), *Gnomon* 54:783–786.

Loizos, P. 1975. *The Greek Gift: Politics in a Cypriot Village*. Oxford: B. Blackwell.

——— 1994. "A Broken Mirror: Masculine Sexuality in Greek Ethnography," in A. Cornwall and N. Lindisfarne (eds.), *Dislocating Masculinity: Comparative Ethnographies*. New York: Routledge, 66–81.

Lombardo, S. 1997. *Homer, Iliad*. Indianapolis: Hackett Publishing.

Longford, E. 1975. *Byron's Greece*. New York and London: Harper and Row.

Longinović, T. 2002. "Vampires Like Us: Gothic Imaginary and the Serbs," in Bjelić and Savić 2002, 39–60.

Lonsdale, S. 1993. *Dance and Ritual Play in Greek Religion*. Baltimore: Johns Hopkins University Press.

Loraux, N. 1990. *Les mères en deuil*. Paris: Seuil.

——— 1998. *Mothers in Mourning*. Ithaca, N.Y.: Cornell University Press.

Lord, A. B. 1960. *The Singer of Tales*. Cambridge, Mass.: Harvard University Press.

——— 1991. *Epic Singers and Oral Tradition*. Ithaca, N.Y.: Cornell University Press.

——— 1995. *The Singer Resumes the Tale*. Ithaca, N.Y.: Cornell University Press.

Loukaki, M. 1998. "Remarques sur le corps de douze didascales au XIIe siècle," in ΕΥΨΥΧΙΑ. *Mélanges offerts à Hélène Ahrweiler*, II. Paris: Publications de la Sorbonne, 427–438.

Loutzaki, I. 1991. "Structure and Style of an Implement Dance in Neo Monastiri, Central Greece," *Studia Musicologica Scientiarum Hungaricae* 33:439–448.

Lowe, N. J. 2000. *The Classical Plot and the Invention of Western Narrative.* Cambridge: Cambridge University Press.

Maas, P. and Trypanis, C. 1963. *Sancti Romani Melodi Cantica.* Oxford: Clarendon Press.

Macpherson, C. B. 1962. *The Political Theory of Possessive Individualism: Hobbes to Locke.* Oxford: Clarendon Press.

Macrides, R. J. 1985. "Poetic Justice in the Patriarchate: Murder and Cannibalism in the Provinces," in L. Burgmann et al. (eds.), *Cupido Legum.* Frankfurt am Main: Löwenklau Gesellschaft, 137–168. Repr. in Macrides, R. J., *Kinship and Justice in Byzantium, 11th–15th centuries.* Aldershot: Ashgate, 1999.

Magdalino, P. 1981. "The Byzantine Holy Man in the Twelfth Century," in S. Hackel (ed.), *The Byzantine Saint.* London: Fellowship of St. Alban and St. Sergius, 51–66.

—— 1990. "Constantinople and the 'ἔξω χῶραι' in the Time of Balsamon," in N. Oikonomides (ed.), *Byzantium in the 12th Century.* Athens: Society of Byzantine and Post-Byzantine Studies.

—— 1993. *The Empire of Manuel I Komnenos, 1143–1180.* Cambridge: Cambridge University Press.

—— 1996. *Constantinople médiévale. Études sur l'évolution des structures urbaines.* Paris: Éditions de Boccard.

Magdalino, P. and Nelson, P. 1982. "The Emperor in Byzantine Art of the Twelfth Century," *Byzantinische Forschungen* 8:123–83.

Maguire, E. D. 1999. *The Rich Life and the Dance. Weavings from Roman, Byzantine and Islamic Egypt.* Champaign, Ill.: Krannert Art Museum and University of Illinois Urbana-Champaign.

Maguire, H. 1981. *Art and Eloquence in Byzantium.* Princeton: Princeton University Press.

Malarney, S. K. 1996. "The Limits of 'State Functionalism' and the Reconstruction of Funeral Ritual in Contemporary Northern Vietnam," *American Ethnologist* 23:540–560.

Malinowski, B. 1984. *Argonauts of the Western Pacific: An Account of Native Enterprise and Adventure in the Archipelagoes of Melanesian New Guinea.* Prospect Heights, Ill.: Waveland Press.

Malnati, A. 1993. "Revisione dell'ostrakon fiorentino di Saffo," *Analecta Papyrologica* 5:21–22.

Maltese, E. V. 1982. *Sofocle, Ichneutae.* Firenze: Gonnelli.

Mandel, R. 1983. "Sacrifice at the Bridge of Arta: Sex Roles and the Manipulation of Power," *Journal of Modern Greek Studies* 1.1:173–183.

Manganaro, G. 1992. "Iscrizioni 'rupestri' di Sicilia," in L. Gasperini (ed.), *Rupes Loquentes. Atti del convegno internazionale di studio sulle iscrizioni rupestri di età romana in Italia.* Rome: Instituto Italiano per la Storia Antica, 447–501.

Manganaro, M. (ed.) 1990. *Modernist Anthropology.* Princeton: Princeton University Press.

Mango, C. 1993. *Studies on Constantinople.* Aldershot: Variorum.

Maraval, P. 1971. *Grégoire de Nysse, Vie de Sainte Macrine.* Sources Chrétiennes 178. Paris: Éditions du Cerf.

Marcovich, M. 1992. *Theodori Prodromi, de Rhodanthes et Dosikles amoribus libri IX.*
    Stuttgart: Teubner.
Marcus, G. E. and Fischer, M. J. 1986. *Anthropology as Cultural Critique.* Chicago:
    University of Chicago Press.
Marinetti, F. 1971. *Selected Writings*, trans. R. W. Flint and A. A. Coppotelli. New York:
    Farrar, Strauss and Giroux.
Markopoulos, A. 1998. "The Rehabilitation of the Emperor Theophilos," in L. Brubaker
    (ed.), *Byzantium in the Ninth Century: Dead or Alive?* Aldershot: Ashgate, 37–49.
Marriot, M. 1976. "Hindu Transactions: Diversity Without Dualism," in B. Kapferer
    (ed.), *Transaction and Meaning: Directions in the Anthropology of Exchange and
    Symbolic Behavior.* A.S.A. Essays in Social Anthropology 1. London and
    Philadelphia: Institute for the Study of Human Issues, 109–142.
Martin, R. P. 1989. *The Language of Heroes: Speech and Performance in the Iliad.* Ithaca,
    N.Y.: Cornell University Press.
Martlew, I. 2000. *Studies in the Byzantine Novel*, University of Western Australia, thesis
    presented for degree of Ph.D.
Mastoraki, J. 1983. 'Ιστορίες γιά τά βαθιά. Athens: Κέδρος.
Mastronarde, D. 1994. *Euripides, Phoenissai.* Cambridge: Cambridge University Press.
——— 2002. *Euripides, Medea..* Cambridge: Cambridge University Press.
Masullo, R. 1985. *Vita di Proclo.* Napoli: M. D'Auria.
Mathews, T. 1999. *The Clash of the Gods: A Reinterpretation of Early Christian Art*, revised
    ed. Princeton: Princeton University Press.
Mauss, M. 1935. "Les Techniques du Corps," *Journal de Psychologie Normale et
    Pathologique* 35:271–293.
Mazower, M. 2000. *The Balkans: A Short History.* New York: The Modern Library,
    Chronicle Books.
McCormick, M. 1985. "Analyzing Imperial Ceremonies," *Jahrbuch der Österreichischen
    Byzantinistik* 35:1–20.
McDaniel, L. 1998. *The Big Drum Ritual of Carriacou: Praise Songs in Ceremony of Flight.*
    Gainesville, Fla.: University Press of Florida.
McNeal, R. A. 1988. "The Brides of Babylon: Herodotus 1.196," *Historia* 37:54–71.
Meiggs, R. and Lewis, D. M. 1969. *A Selection of Greek Historical Inscriptions to the End of
    the Fifth Century B.C.* Revised ed., Oxford: Oxford University Press, 1988.
Meineke, A. 1836. *Ioannis Cinnami Epitome Rerum ab Ioanne et Alexio Comnenis Gestarum.*
    Bonn: Weber.
Melas, S. 1952–53. "Μιὰ διασκεδαστικὴ ἔρευνα. Ὁ Καραγκιόζης," in the news-
    paper 'Ακρόπολις, October 30, 1952–January 7, 1953, November 23, 1952
Melville Jones, J. R. 1993. *Testimonia Numaria.* London: Spink.
Meraklis, M. G. 1984. Ἑλληνικὴ Λαογραφία. Κοινωνικὸ Συγκρότημα. Athens:
    Ὀδυσσέας.
Mercati, G. 1897. "Gli aneddoti d'un codice Bolognese," *Byzantinische Zeitschrift* 6:126–143.
Merkelbach, R. 1957. "Sappho und ihr Kreis," *Philologus* 101:1–29.
——— 1962. *Roman und Mysterium.* Munich: Beck.
Meyerhoff, B. G. 1974. *Peyote Hunt: The Sacred Journey of the Huichol Indians.* Ithaca,
    N.Y.: Cornell University Press.

Michalopoulou, A. 1996. Γιάντες. Athens: Καστανιώτης.

Migne, J. P. 1857–66. *Patrologia Graeca*. Paris: Migne.

Milionis, Ch. 1985. Καλαμᾶς καὶ 'Αχέροντας. Athens: Στιγμή.

1996. *Kalamas and Acheron*, trans. M. Chambers. Athens: Kedros, Modern Greek Writers Series.

——— 1992. "Ὁ Παπαδιαμάντης καὶ ἡ ἠθογραφία (ἤ ἠθογραφίας ἀναίρεσις)," Γράμματα καὶ Τέχνες, 59–65.

Miller, P. C. 1994. *Dreams in Late Antiquity: Studies in the Imagination of a Culture*. Princeton: Princeton University Press.

Mineur, W. H. 1984. *Callimachus, Hymn to Delos*. Mnemosyne, Bibliotheca Classica Batava, Supplement 83. Leiden: E. J. Brill.

Mioni, E. 1951. "Il Pratum Spirituale di Giovanni Mosco: Gli Episodi inediti del Cod. Marciano Greco II, 21," *Orientalia Christiana Periodica* 17:61–94.

Moerman, D. 1979. "Anthropology of Symbolic Healing," *Current Anthropology* 20.1:59–80.

Molinier, A. 1891. *Catalogue général des bibliothèques publiques de France—Départements*, vol. 17. Cambrai.

Mommsen, A. 1878. *Delphika*. Leipzig: Teubner.

Moore, S. 1977. "Political Meetings and the Simulation of Unanimity," in Moore and Myerhoff 1977a, 151–172.

Moore, S. and Myerhoff, B. G. (eds.) 1977a. *Secular Ritual*. Assen, Amsterdam: Van Gorcum.

——— 1977b. "Introduction: Secular Ritual: Forms and Meanings," in Moore and Myerhoff 1977a, 3–24.

Morinis, E. A. 1992. *Sacred Journeys: The Anthropology of Pilgrimage*. New York: Greenwood Press.

Morris, I. 1993. "Poetics of Power. The Interpretation of Ritual Action in Archaic Greece," in C. Dougherty and L. Kurke (eds.), *Cultural Poetics in Archaic Greece: Cult, Performance, Politics*. Cambridge: Cambridge University Press, 15–45.

——— 2000. *Archaeology as Cultural History: Words and Things in Iron Age Greece*. Oxford: B. Blackwell.

Morris, R. forthcoming. "What Did the ἐπὶ τῶν δεήσεων Actually Do?," in D. Feissel and J. Gascou (eds.), *La petition à Byzance*. Paris: Travaux et Memoires du Centre de Recherche d'Histoire et Civilisation de Byzance, Monographies.

Morrison, T. 1972. *The Bluest Eye*. New York: Simon and Schuster.

——— 1988. *Beloved*. New York: Knopf.

Mosino, F. 1977. "Lirico corale a Reggio: Una notizia trascurata," *Quaderni Urbinati di Cultura Classica* 26:117–119.

Moskof, K. 1980. Δοκίμια, I. Athens: Ἐξάντας.

Moyer, I. S. 2002. "Herodotus and the Egyptian Mirage: The Genealogies of the Egyptian Priests," *Journal of Hellenic Studies* 122:70–90.

Müller, C. 1988. *Kindheit und Jugend in der griechischen Frühzeit: Eine Studie zur pädagogischen Bedeutung von Riten und Kulten*. Giessen: Focus.

Mullett, M. 1984. "Aristocracy and Patronage in the Literary Circles of Comnenian Constantinople," in M. Angold (ed.), *The Byzantine Aristocracy, IX to XIII Centuries*. Oxford: British Archaeological Reports, International Series 221, 173–201.

Mullett M. and Scott, R. (eds.) 1981. *Byzantium and the Classical Tradition*. Birmingham: Centre for Byzantine Studies, University of Birmingham.

Munn, N. 1996. "Excluded Spaces: The Figure in the Australian Aboriginal Landscape," *Critical Inquiry* 22:446–465.

Murray, O. (ed.) 1990. *Sympotica: A Symposium on the* Symposion. Oxford: Clarendon Press.

—— 1993. *Early Greece*, 2nd ed. London: Fontana.

Myers, F. 1986. *Pintupi Country, Pintupi Self: Sentiment, Place, and Politics Among Western Desert Aborigines*. Washington, D.C.: Smithsonian Institution Press.

Myrivilis, S. 1943. Ὁ Βασίλης ὁ Ἀρβανίτης. Athens: Πήγασος.

—— 1949. Ἡ Παναγιὰ ἡ Γοργόνα. Athens: Ἑστία.

—— 1983. *Vasilis Arvanitis*, trans. P. Andronikos. Armidale, N.S.W.: University of New England.

Myrsiades, L. S. 1976. "The Karaghiozis Performance in Nineteenth-Century Greece," in *Byzantine and Modern Greek Studies* 2:83–97.

—— 1980. "The Female Role in the Karaghiozis Performance," in *Southern Folklore Quarterly* 44:145–163.

Myrsiades, L. and Myrsiades, K. 1988. *The Karagiozis Heroic Performance in Greek Shadow Theater*. Hanover, N.H.: University Press of New England.

Mystakidou, Aik. 1982, *Karagöz:* Τὸ θέατρο σκιῶν στὴν Ἑλλάδα καὶ στὴν Τουρκία. Athens: Ἑρμῆς.

Nagy, G. 1989. "Early Greek Views of Poets and Poetry," in G. Kennedy (ed.), *Cambridge History of Literary Criticism*, I: *Classical Criticism*. Cambridge: Cambridge University Press, 1–77.

—— 1990. *Pindar's Homer: The Lyric Possession of an Epic Past*. Baltimore: Johns Hopkins University Press.

—— 1992. "The 1991 Presidential Address, Chicago, Illinois: Homeric Questions," *Transactions of the American Philological Association* 122:17–60.

—— 1994/95a. "Transformation of Choral Lyric Traditions in the Context of Athenian State Theater," *Arion* 3.3.1:41–55.

—— 1994/95b. "Genre and Occasion," *Métis* 9/10:11–25.

—— 1996a. *Homeric Questions*. Austin: University of Texas Press.

—— 1996b. *Poetry as Performance: Homer and Beyond*. Cambridge: Cambridge University Press.

—— 1999. *The Best of the Achaeans: Concepts of the Hero in Archaic Greek Poetry*, revised ed. Baltimore: Johns Hopkins University Press.

—— 2001a. "Homeric Poetry and Problems of Multiformity: The 'Panathenaic Bottleneck,'" *Classical Philology* 96:109–119.

—— 2001b, "The Sign of the Hero: A Prologue," in J. K. Berenson Maclean and E. B. Aitken (eds.), *Flavius Philostratus, Heroikos*. Atlanta: Society of Biblical Literature, xv-xxxv.

Naiden, F. S. 2000. *Greek Supplication Prior to 300 BCE*. Ph.D. dissertation. Cambridge, Mass.: Harvard University.

Nissen, Th. 1938. "Unbekannte erzählungen aus dem pratum spirituale," *Byzantinische Zeitschrift* 38:351–376.

—— 1939. "Zu den ältesten Fassungen der Legende vom Judenknaben," *Zeitschrift für französische Sprache und Literatur*, 62.7–8:393–403.

Nixon, L. "Eflatun Pinar, Çatal Höyük and Chronologies of Desire," unpublished ms.
Nolan, S. 1994. *From Lamentation to Law: The Development of Legal Discourse in the Oresteia, Electras, and Orestes*. Ph.D. dissertation. Cambridge, Mass.: Harvard University.
Nystazopoulou-Pelekidou, M. 1980. Βυζαντινὰ ῎Εγγραφα τῆς Μονῆς Πάτμου, ΙΙ. Athens: ᾽Εθνικὸν "Ιδρυμα ᾽Ερευνῶν.
Oakley, J. H. 1982. "The Anakalypteria," *Archäologischer Anzeiger*, 113–118.
Oakley, J. H. and Sinos, R. H. 1993. *The Wedding in Ancient Athens*. Madison, Wis.: University of Wisconsin Press.
Odo of Deuil, 1948. *De profectione Ludovici VII in orientem*, trans. and ed. V. G. Berry. New York: Columbia University Press.
Oikonomides, N. 1972. *Les listes de préséance byzantines des IXe et Xe siècles*. Paris: Éditions du Centre National de la Recherche Scientifique.
—— 1977. "John VII Palaeologus and the Ivory Pyxis at Dumbarton Oaks," *Dumbarton Oaks Papers* 31:329–337.
Oliver, G. 2000. "Athenian Funerary Monuments: Style, Grandeur and Cost," in G. Oliver (ed.), *The Epigraphy of Death: Studies in the History and Society of Greece and Rome*. Liverpool: Liverpool University Press, 59–80.
O'Neill, O. 2002. *A Question of Trust* (The BBC Reith Lectures). Cambridge: Cambridge University Press.
Orso, E. G. 1979. *Modern Greek Humor: A Collection of Jokes and Ribald Tales*. Bloomington: Indiana University Press.
Ortner, S. 1984. "Theory in Anthropology Since the Sixties," *Comparative Studies in Society and History* 66:126–166.
Osborne, R. 1988. "Death Revisited, Death Revised: The Death of the Artist in Archaic and Classical Greece," *Art History* 11:1–16.
—— 1994. "Archaeology, the Salaminioi, and the Politics of Sacred Space in Archaic Attica," in S. E. Alcock and R. Osborne (eds.), *Placing the Gods: Sanctuaries and Sacred Space in Ancient Greece*. Oxford: Oxford University Press, 143–160.
—— 1997. "Men Without Clothes: Heroic Nakedness and Greek Art," *Gender and History* 9:504–28.
The Oxford Dictionary of Byzantium, 3 vols. New York: Oxford University Press, 1991.
Padel, R. 1995. *Whom the Gods Destroy: Elements of Greek and Tragic Madness*. Princeton: Princeton University Press.
Padilla, M. W. (ed.) 1999. *Rites of Passage in Ancient Greece: Literature, Religion, Society*. London: Bucknell University Press.
Page, D. L. 1955. *Sappho and Alcaeus: An Introduction to the Study of Ancient Lesbian Poetry*. Oxford: Clarendon Press.
—— 1959. *History and the Homeric Iliad*. Berkeley: University of California Press.
—— 1962. *Poetae Melici Graeci*. Oxford: Clarendon Press.
Papadiamandis, A. 1981–88. ῎Απαντα, ed. 5 vols. N. Triandafyllopoulos. Athens: Δόμος.
Papadopoulos-Kerameus, A. 1912. *Noctes Petropolitanae*. St. Petersburg: V. F. Kirshbaum.
Papagiotopoulou, A. 1992. "Relations Between the Leading Dancer and the Co-Dancers in Neo-Hellenic Dance: A Case Study," *Dance Studies* 6:9–27.
Paparrhegopoulos, C. 1853. ῾Ιστορία τοῦ ῾Ελληνικοῦ ῎Εθνους ἀπὸ τῶν ἀρχαιοτάτων χρόνων μέχρι τῆς σήμερον. Athens: ᾽Α. Κορομηλᾶς.

Papataxiarchis, E. 2001. "Friends of the Heart: Male Commensality, Gender, and Kinship in Aegean Greece," in P. Loizos and E. Papataxiarchis (eds.), *Contested Identities: Gender and Kinship in Modern Greece.* Princeton: Princeton University Press, 156–179.

Parke, H. W. 1977. *Festivals of the Athenians.* London: Thames and Hudson.

Parker, H. N. 1993. "Sappho Schoolmistress," *Transactions of the American Philological Association* 123:309–351.

Parker, R. 1983. *Miasma: Pollution and Purification in Early Greek Religion.* Oxford: Clarendon Press.

——— 1996. *Athenian Religion: A History.* Oxford: Clarendon Press.

Parsons, A. W. 1943. "Klepsydra and Paved Court of Pythion," *Hesperia* 12:191–267.

Parsons, P. J. 2001. "'These Fragments We Have Shored against Our Ruin,'" in D. Boedeker and D. Sider (eds.), *The New Simonides: Contexts of Praise and Desire.* New York: Oxford University Press, 55–64.

Pasquato, O. 1976. *Gli spetacoli in S. Giovanni Crisostomo: Paganesimo e Cristianesimo ad Antiochia e Constantinopoli nel IV secolo.* Rome: Pontificium Institutum Orientalium Studiorum.

Patala, Z. 1996. "Les chants grecs du Liber Politicus du chanoine Benoit," *Byzantion* 66:512–530.

Pélékides, Ch. 1962. *Histoire de l'Éphebie attique des origines à 31 av. J.-C.* Paris: Éditions de Boccard.

Pelling, C. 1997. "Conclusion," in C. Pelling (ed.), *Greek Tragedy and the Historian.* Oxford: Clarendon Press, 213–235.

——— 2000. *Literary Texts and the Greek Historian.* London and New York: Routledge.

Pentzikis, N. G. 1963. Ἀρχιτεκτονικὴ τῆς σκόρπιας ζωῆς. Thessaloniki: ΑΣΕ.

——— 1987. Ὁ πεθαμένος καὶ ἡ ἀνάσταση, 3rd ed. Athens: Ἄγρα.

Perkins, J. 1995. *The Suffering Self.* London: Routledge.

Perry, E. B. 1967. *The Ancient Romances: A Literary-Historical Account of their Origins.* Berkeley: University of California Press.

Petropoulos, J. C. B. 1994. *Heat and Lust: Hesiod's Midsummer Festival Scene Revisited.* Lanham, Md.: Rowman and Littlefield.

Pfister, F. 1924. "Epiphanie," in Pauly-Wissowa, *Paulys Real-Encyclopädie der classischen Altertumswissenschaft,* Supplementband IV. Stuttgart: J. B. Metzlersche, 277–323.

"Pherraios," R. [1790]. Σχολεῖον τῶν ντελικάτων ἐραστῶν, ed. P. S. Pistas. Athens: Ἑρμῆς, 1971.

Pickard-Cambridge, A. [1968]. *The Dramatic Festivals of Athens.*

Pignani, A. 1983. *Niceforo Basilace, Progimnasmi e monodie.* Byzantina et neo-hellenica Neapolitana 10. Naples: Bibliopolis.

Pitts, W. 1991. "Like a Tree Planted by the Water: The Musical Cycle in the African-American Baptist Ritual," *Journal of American Folklore* 104:318–340.

Platnauer, M. 1938. *Euripides' Iphigenia in Tauris.* Oxford: Clarendon Press.

Plepelits, K. 1989. *Hysmine und Hysminias.* Stuttgart: Hiersemann.

Poe, J. P. 1989. "The Altar in the Fifth-Century Theater," *Classical Antiquity* 8:116–139.

Poggioli, R. 1968. *The Theory of the Avant-Garde.* Cambridge, Mass.: Harvard University Press.

Polignac, F. de 1995. *La naissance de la cité grecque: cultes, espace et société, VIIIe–VIIe siècles.* 2nd revised ed. Paris: Éditions la Découverte.

Politis, N. G. 1914. Ἐκλογαὶ ἀπὸ τὰ τραγούδια τοῦ ἑλληνικοῦ λαοῦ. Athens: Ἑστία, repr. Athens: Βαγιωνάκης, 1978.

Polyakova, S. V. 1971. "Ekfrasa 12 mesjatev Evmatija Makremvolita," *Palestinskii Sbornik* 23;114–124.

Pomian, K. 1980. "Periodizzazione," in *Enciclopedia Einaudi*, vol. 10. Torino: Einaudi, 603–650.

Popham, M. R. et al. 1982. "The Hero of Lefkandi," *Antiquity* 56:169–74.

—— et al. 1993. *Lefkandi II.2. The Protogeometric Building at Toumba: The Excavation, Architecture and Finds.* London: British School at Athens.

Porta, F. R. 1999. *Greek Ritual Utterances and the Liturgical Style.* Ph.D. dissertation. Cambridge, Mass.: Harvard University.

Povrzanović, M. and Jambrešić Kirin, R. 1996. "Negotiating Identities? The Voices of Refugees Between Experience and Representation," in R. Jambrešić Kirin and M. Povrzanović (eds.), *War, Exile, Everyday Life: Cultural Perspectives.* Zagreb: Institute of Ethnology and Folklore Research, 3–19.

Preger, Th. (ed.) 1901. *Scriptores Originum Constantinopolitanarum.* Leipzig: Teubner, repr. 1989.

Price, R. M. 1985. *A History of the Monks of Syria by Theodoret of Cyrrhus.* Kalamazoo, Mich.: Cistercian Publications, 85.

Pritchard, J. B. (ed.) 1969. *Ancient Near Eastern Texts Relating to the Old Testament*, 3rd ed. Princeton: Princeton University Press.

Pritchett, W. K. 1993. *The Liar School of Herodotos.* Amsterdam: J. C. Gieben.

Propp, V. 1968. *Morphology of the Folktale*, trans. L. Scott. 2nd revised ed. Austin: University of Texas Pres.

—— 1984. *Theory and History of Folklore*, trans. A. Martin and R. Martin. Minneapolis: University of Minnesota Press and Manchester: Manchester University Press.

Puchner, W. 1976/78. "Σύντομη ἀναλυτικὴ βιβλιογραφία τοῦ θεάτρου σκιῶν στὴν Ἑλλάδα," *Λαογραφία* 31:294–324.

—— 1979/81. "Συμπλήρωμα στὴν ἀναλυτικὴ βιβλιογραφία τοῦ θεάτρου σκιῶν στὴν Ἑλλάδα," *Λαογραφία* 32:370–378.

—— 1985. Οἱ βαλκανικὲς διαστάσεις τοῦ Καραγκιόζη. Athens: Στιγμή.

Pulleyn, S. 1997. *Prayer in Greek Religion.* Oxford: Clarendon Press.

Rabe, H. 1896. *Anonymi et Stephani in Artem Rhetoricam Commentaria.* Berlin: G. Reimer.

—— 1913. *Hermogenis Opera.* Leipzig: Teubner.

Rabinow, P. 1986. "Representations Are Social Facts: Modernity and Post-Modernity in Anthropology," in Clifford and G. E. Marcus 1986, 234–261.

Race, W. H. 1997. *Pindar*, II. Cambridge, Mass.: Harvard University Press, Loeb Classical Library.

Ralles, G. A. and Potles, M. 1852–59. Σύνταγμα τῶν θείων καὶ ἱερῶν κανόνων, 6 vols. Athens: Γ. Χαρτοφύλαξ.

Rankin, H. D. 1978. "Telestagoras of Naxos and the Lycambes Story," *L'Antiquité Classique* 47:149–152.

Rapp, C. 2000. "Mark the Deacon, *The Life of Porphyry of Gaza*," in T. Head (ed.), *Medieval Hagiography: An Anthology.* New York: Garland, 53–75.

Rappaport, R. A. 1984. *Pigs for the Ancestors.* New Haven: Yale University Press.

—— 1999. *Ritual and Religion in the Making of Humanity.* Cambridge: Cambridge University Press.

Rauk, J. 1989. "Erinna's *Distaff* and Sappho Fr. 94," *Greek, Roman, and Byzantine Studies* 30:101–116.

Reardon, B. 1991. *The Form of Greek Romance.* Princeton: Princeton University Press.

Redfield, J. 1985. "Herodotus the Tourist," *Classical Philology* 80:97–118.

Reeder, E. D. 1995. *Pandora: Women in Classical Greece.* Baltimore and Princeton: Walters Art Gallery and Princeton University Press.

Regel, W. 1891. "De Theophili imperatoris benefactis," in *Analecta Byzantino-Russica* 41:15–16.

Rehm, R. 1988. "The Staging of Suppliant Plays," *Greek, Roman, and Byzantine Studies* 29:263–307.

—— 1994. *Marriage to Death.* Princeton: Princeton University Press.

—— 2002. *The Play of Space.* Princeton: Princeton University Press.

Reinach, T. 1902. "Nouveaux Fragments de Sappho," *Revue des Études Grecques* 15:60ff.

Reiske, J. J. 1829–30. *Constantine Porphyrogennitus, De Cerimoniis aulae Byzantinae.* Bonn: E. Weber.

Renfrew, C. and Cherry, J. (eds.) 1986. *Peer Polity Interaction and Socio-Political Change.* Cambridge: Cambridge University Press.

Richard, J. 1983. *Saint Louis.* Paris: A. Fayard.

Richardson, N. J. 1974. *The Homeric Hymn to Demeter.* Oxford: Clarendon Press.

Richter, G. M. A. 1960. *Kouroi, Archaic Greek Youths: A Study of the Development of the Kouros Type in Greek Sculpture.* London: Phaidon.

Riffatere, M. 1983. *Text Production.* New York: Columbia University Press.

Robbins, E. 1984. "Intimations of Immortality: Pindar, *Ol.* 3.34–35," in D. Gerber (ed.), *Greek Poetry and Philosophy: Studies in Honor of Leonard Woodbury.* Chico, Calif.: University of California Press, 219–228.

—— 1990. "Who's Dying in Sappho fr. 94?," *Phoenix* 44:111–121.

Robert, C. 1912. "Aphoristische Bemerkungen zu Sophokles' IXNEYTAI," *Hermes* 47:536–561.

—— 1914. "Pandora," *Hermes* 49:17–38.

Robert, L. and Robert, J. 1989. *Claros I: Décrets hellénistiques.* Paris: Éditions Recherche sur les Civilisations.

Roberts, D. 1988. "Sophoclean Endings: Another Story," *Arethusa* 21:177–196.

Robertson, Noel. 1992. *Festivals and Legends: The Formation of Greek Cities in the Light of Public Ritual.* Toronto: University of Toronto Press.

Robinson, Ch. 1981. "The Greekness of Modern Greek Surrealism," *Byzantine and Modern Greek Studies* 7:119–137.

Rohde, E. 1914. *Der griechische Roman und seine Vorläufer*, 3rd ed. Leipzig: Breitkopf und Härtel.

Roilos, P. 1998. "Ὁ νεκρὸς ὡς δέντρο στὰ ἑλληνικὰ μοιρολόγια. Ἡ μεταφορὰ στὴν παραδοσιακὴ προφορικὴ ποίηση τελετουργικοῦ χαρακτῆρα," Ἑλληνικά 48:61–85.

—— 2000. "'*Amphoteroglossia*': The Role of Rhetoric in the Medieval Greek Learned Novel," in P. Agapitos and D. Reinsch (eds.), *Der Roman im Byzanz der Komnenzeit.* Frankfurt am Main: Beerenverlag, 109–126.

—— 2002a. "Orality and Performativity in the *Erotokritos*," *Cretan Studies* 7:213–230.

—— 2002b. "Ἡ ἀφηγηματική εἰρωνία στὰ ἱστορικὰ μυθιστορήματα τοῦ Παπαδιαμάντη," *Σύγκριση/Comparaison* 13:32–51.

—— 2003. "The Poetics of Mimicry: Iakovos Pitzipios' Ὁ Πίθηκος Ξούθ and the Beginnings of the Modern Greek Novel," in G. Nagy and A. Stavrakopoulou (eds.), *Modern Greek Literature: Critical Essays*. New York: Routledge.

—— 2004. "The Politics of Writing: Greek Historiographic Metafiction and Maro Douka's *A Cap of Purple*," *Journal of Modern Greek Studies*.

—— forthcoming, 2004. *Amphoteroglossia: Toward a Poetics of the Medieval Greek Novel*. Cambridge, Mass.: CHS/Harvard University Press.

Rolle, R. 1989. *The World of the Scythians*, trans. G. Walls. London: Batsford.

Rolle, R. et al. (eds.) 1991. *Gold der Steppe: Archäologie der Ukraine*. Neumünster: K. Wachholtz.

Röllig, W. 1969. "Nitokris von Babylon," in R. Stiehl and H. E. Stier (eds.), *Beiträge zur alten Geschichte und deren Nachleben. (Festschr. F. Altheim)*. Berlin: de Gruyter, 127–135.

Romano, R. 1974. *Timarione*. Naples: University of Naples.

Rosaldo, R. 1968. "Metaphors of Hierarchy in a Mayan Ritual," *American Anthropologist* 70 (3):524–536.

Rose, C. 1994. *Property and Persuasion: Essays on the History, Theory, and Rhetoric of Ownership*. Boulder: Westview Press.

Rose, H. J. 1950. "Ghost Ritual in Aeschylus," *Harvard Theological Review* 43:257–280.

Rösler, W. 1990. "*Mnemosyne* in the *Symposion*," in Murray 1990, 230–237.

—— 1992. "Homoerotik und Initiation: Über Sappho," in T. Stemmler (ed.), *Homoerotische Lyrik. 6. Kolloquium der Forschungsstelle für europäische Lyrik des Mittelalters an der Universität Mannheim*. Tübingen: Narr, 43–54.

Rossellini, M. and Saïd, S. 1978. "Usages des femmes et autres nomoi chez les "sauvages" d'Hérodote: Essai de lecture structurale," *Annali della Scuola Normale Superiore di Pisa* 8:949–1005.

Rossi, L. E. 1971. "I generi letterari e le loro leggi scritte e non scritte nelle letterature classiche," *Bulletin of the Institute of Classical Studies* 18:69–94.

Roueché, C. 1993. *Performers and Partisans at Aphrodisias in the Roman and Late Roman Periods*. London: Society for the Promotion of Roman Studies.

Rouget, G. 1985. *Music and Trance: A Theory of the Relations between Music and Possession*, trans. and rev. by B. Biebuyck and G. Rouget. Chicago: The University of Chicago Press.

Rousselle, A. 1990. *Croire et guérir: La foi en Gaule dan l'antiquité tardive*. Paris: A. Fayard.

Roux, G. 2001. "Semiramis: The Builder of Babylon," in J. Bottéro (ed.), *Everyday Life in Ancient Mesopotamia*. Edinburgh: Edinburgh University Press, 141–161.

Rowley, H. H. 1959. *Darius the Mede and the Four World Empires in the Book of Daniel: A Historical Study of Contemporary Theories*. Cardiff: University of Wales Press.

Rusjaeva A. S. and Vinogradov, J. G. 1991. "Der 'Brief des Priesters' aus Hylaia," in Rolle et al. 1991, 201–202.

Russell, Ch. 1985. *Poets, Prophets, and Revolutionaries: The Literary Avant-Garde from Rimbaud through Postmodernism*. New York: Oxford University Press.

Russell, D. A. 1993. *Plutarch: Selected Essays and Dialogues*, Oxford: Oxford University Press.

Russell, D. A. and Wilson, N. G. 1981. *Menander Rhetor*. Oxford: Oxford University Press.

Rusten, J. 1983. "ΓΕΙΤΩΝ ΗΡΩΣ: Pindar's Prayer to Heracles (N. 7.86–101) and Greek Popular Religion," *Harvard Studies in Classical Philology* 87:289–297.

Rutherford, I. 1994/45. "Apollo in Ivy. The Tragic Paean," *Arion* 3.3.1:115–135.
—— 1995. "Theoric Crisis: The Dangers of Pilgrimage in Greek Religion and Society," *Studi e Materiali di Storia delle Religioni* 61:276–292.
—— 2000. "Theoria and Darsvan: Pilgrimage and Vision in Greece and India," *Classical Quarterly* 50:133–46.
—— 2001. *Pindar's Paeans. A Reading of the Fragments with a Survey of the Genre.* Oxford: Oxford University Press.
—— 2002. "Theoria," in *Der Neue Pauly.* Stuttgart: J. B. Metzler, 12/1:398–399.
—— 2004. "Χορὸς εἷς ἐκ τῆσδε τῆς πόλεως: State-Pilgrimage and Song-Dance in Athens," paper delivered at the Warwick conference on Music and the Muses, April 1999, forthcoming in the Proceedings of the Conference (Oxford: Oxford University Press).
—— forthcoming a. "Blacks Sails to Achilles. Pilgrimage and Initiation in Philostratus' Heroicus."
—— forthcoming b. "Theoria and the Olympic Games: A Neglected Aspect of Ancient Athletics."
Sacks, O. 1985. *The Man Who Mistook His Wife for a Hat.* London: Duckworth.
Sahlins, M. 1985. *Islands of History.* Chicago: University of Chicago Press.
Said, E. 1983. *The World, the Text, and the Critic.* Cambridge, Mass.: Harvard University Press.
Salanitro, G. 1992. "Orazio e Niceta Eugeniano," *Sileno* 18:247–8.
Salisbury, R. F. 1965. "The Siane of Eastern Highlands," in P. Lawrence and M. J. Meggitt (eds.), *Gods, Ghosts, and Men in Melanesia; Some Religions of Australian New Guinea and the New Hebrides.* London: Oxford University Press, 50–77.
Savrami, K. 1992. "Two Diverse Versions of the Dance Zeimbekiko," *Dance Studies* 16:57–103.
Savvopoulos, D. 1981. Ἡ ρεζέρβα. Athens: Ἰθάκη.
Schechner, R. 1985. *Between Theater and Anthropology.* Philadelphia: University of Pennsylvania Press.
—— 1988. *Performance Theory.* London: Routledge.
—— 1993. *The Future of Ritual.* London: Routledge.
Schibli, H. S. 1990. *Pherekydes of Syros.* Oxford: Clarendon Press.
Schlesier, R. 1990. "Apopompe," in H. Cancik et al. (eds.), *Handbuch religionswis-senschaftlicher Grundbegriffe,* vol. 2. Stuttgart: Verlag W. Kohlhammer, 38–41.
Schmitt-Pantel, P. 1990. "Sacrificial Meal and *Symposion*: Two Models of Civic Institutions in the Archaic City?," in Murray 1990, 14–33.
Schöne, A. 1987. *Der Thiasos: Eine ikonographische Untersuchung über das Gefolge des Dionysos in der attischen Vasenmalerei des 6. und 5. Jhs. v. Chr.* Göteborg: P. Aström.
Schreckenberg, H. 1960. ΔΡΑΜΑ: *Vom Werden der griechischen Tragödie aus dem Tanz.* Würzburg: Konrad Triltsch.
Schwartz, E. 1939. *Kyrillos von Skythopolis.* Leipzig: J. C. Hinrichs.
Scodel, R. (ed.) 1993. *Theater and Society in the Classical World.* Ann Arbor: University of Michigan Press.
Seaford, R. 1987. "The Tragic Wedding," *Journal of Hellenic Studies* 107:106–130.
—— 1990. "The Imprisonment of Women in Greek Tragedy," *Journal of Hellenic Studies* 110:76–90.

—— 1994a. *Reciprocity and Ritual: Homer and Tragedy in the Developing City-State.* Oxford: Oxford University Press.

—— 1994b. "Sophokles and the Mysteries," *Hermes* 122:275–288.

—— 1996. *Euripides, Bacchae.* Warminster: Aris and Phillips.

—— 1977/78. "The 'Hyporchema' of Pratinas," *Maia* 29:81–94.

—— 1998. "Tragic Money," *Journal of Hellenic Studies* 108:119–39.

—— 2000. "The Dionysiac Don Responds to Don Quixote: Rainer Friedrich on the New Ritualism," *Arion* 8.2:74–98.

—— 2003. "Tragic Tyranny," in K. Morgan (ed.), *Popular Tyranny.* Austin: Texas University Press.

—— forthcoming 2003. "Dionysos, Money and Drama," *Arion.*

—— forthcoming 2004. *Money and the Early Greek Mind.* Cambridge.

Seebass, T. 1973. *Musikdarstellung und Psalterillustration im frühen Mittelalter. Studien ausgehend von einer Ikonologie der Handschrift Paris Bibliothèque Nationale Fonds Latin 1118,* 2 vols. Bern: Francke.

—— 1991. "Iconography and Dance Research," *Yearbook for Traditional Music.* New York, International Council for Traditional Music, 23:37–40.

Segal, C. 1981a. "Griechische Tragödie und Gesellschaft," in E. Wischer (ed.), *Propyläen Geschichte der Literatur: Literatur und Gesellschaft der westlichen Welt.* Berlin: Propyläen Verlag, 1.198–217, 546–547.

—— 1981b. *Tragedy and Civilization: An Interpretation of Sophocles.* Cambridge, Mass.: Harvard University Press.

—— 1986. *Interpreting Greek Tragedy: Myth, Poetry, Text.* Ithaca, N.Y.: Cornell University Press.

—— 1993. *Euripides and the Poetics of Sorrow: Art, Gender and Communication in Alcestis, Hippolytus, and Hecuba.* Durham, N.C.: Duke University Press.

—— 1995. *Sophocles' Tragic World.* Cambridge, Mass.: Harvard University Press.

—— 1997. *Dionysiac Poetics and Euripides' Bacchae,* 2nd ed. Princeton: Princeton University Press.

Seidensticker, B. 1979. "Sacrificial Ritual in the *Bacchae,*" in G. W. Bowersock et al. (eds.), *Arktouros: Hellenic Studies Presented to Bernard M. W. Knox on the Occasion of his 65th Birthday.* Berlin: W. de Gruyter, 181–190.

Seremetakis, C. N. 1991. *The Last Word: Women, Death, and Divination in Inner Mani.* Chicago: University of Chicago Press.

Shapiro, H. A. 1991. "The Iconography of Mourning in Athenian Art," *American Journal of Archaeology* 95:629–656.

Sharf, A. 1971. *Byzantine Jewry from Justinian to the Fourth Crusade.* London: Routledge and Kegan Paul.

Shaw, M. R. B. 1963. *Joinville and Villehardouin, Chronicles of the Crusades.* Harmondsworth: Penguin, repr. 1977.

Shepard, J. 2001. "Courts in East and West," in P. Linehan and J. L. Nelson (eds.), *The Medieval World.* London: Routledge, 14–36.

Sherzer, J. 1990. *Verbal Art in San Blas.* Cambridge: Cambridge University Press.

Shieffelen, E. 1976. *The Sorrow of the Lonely and the Burning of the Dancers.* New York: St. Martin's Press.

Shilstone, F. W. 1988. *Byron and the Myth of Tradition.* Lincoln, Nebr.: University of Nebraska Press.

Sifakis, G. 1984. 'H παραδοσιακή δραματουργία τοῦ Καραγκιόζη. Πρώτη προσέγγιση. Athens: Στιγμή.

Simon, E. 1959. *Die Geburt der Aphrodite.* Berlin: De Gruyter.

—— 1982a. "Satyr-Plays on Vases in the Time of Aeschylus," in D. Kurtz and B. Sparkes (eds.), *The Eye of Greece: Studies in the Art of Athens.* Cambridge: Cambridge University Press, 123–148.

—— 1982b. "Review of H. Loeb, *Die Geburt der Götter in der griechischen Kunst der klassischen Zeit,* " *Gnomon* 54:785-786.

—— 1983. *Festivals of Attica: An Archaeological Commentary.* Madison: Wisconsin University Press.

—— 1989. "Hermeneutisches zur Anodos von Göttinnen, " in G. Bauchhenss (ed.), *Festschrift Nikolaus Himmelmann,* Mainz am Rhein: von Zabern, 197-203.

Sinos, R. 1998. "Divine Selection," in C. Dougherty and L. Kurke (eds.), *Cultural Poetics in Archaic Greece.* Oxford: Oxford University Press, 73–91.

Smith, J. 1982. *Imagining Religion: From Babylon to Jonestown.* Chicago: The University of Chicago Press.

Smith, M. S. 1975. *Petronii Cena Trimalchionis.* Oxford: Clarendon Press.

Smith, O. L. 1993. *Scholia Graeca in Aeschylum quae exstant omnia.* Leipzig: Teubner.

Snodgrass, A. M. 1986. "Interaction by Design: The Greek City State," in Renfrew and Cherry 1986, 47–58.

Sokolowski, F. 1962. *Lois sacrées des citées grecques. Supplément.* Paris: Éditions de Boccard.

—— 1969. *Lois sacrées des citées grecques.* Paris: Éditions de Boccard.

Sommerstein, A. H. 1989. *Aeschylus, Eumenides.* Cambridge: Cambridge University Press.

Sourvinou-Inwood, Ch. 1983. "A Trauma in Flux: Death in the 8th Century and After," in R. Hägg (ed.), *The Greek Renaissance of the Eighth Century B.C.: Tradition and Innovation.* Stockholm: Skrifter utgivna av Svenska Institutet i Athen, 33–48.

—— 1987/88. "Antigone 904–20: A Reading," *Annali,* Istituto Universitario Orientale, Napoli. Sezione filologica 9–10:19–35.

—— 1988. *Studies in Girls' Transitions: Aspects of the Arkteia and Age Representation in Attic Iconography.* Athens: Kardamitsas.

—— 1989a. "Assumptions and the Creation of Meaning: Reading Sophocles' *Antigone,*" *Journal of Hellenic Studies* 109:134–148.

—— 1989b. "The Fourth Stasimon of Sophocles' *Antigone,*" *Bulletin of the Institute of Classical Studies* 36:141–165.

—— 1990. "What is *Polis* Religion?," in O. Murray and S. Price (eds.), *The Greek City: From Homer to Alexander.* Oxford: Oxford University Press, 295–322.

—— 1991. *'Reading' Greek Culture: Texts and Images, Rituals and Myths.* Oxford: Clarendon Press.

—— 1994. "Something to Do with Athens: Tragedy and Ritual," in R. Osborne and S. Hornblower (eds.), *Ritual, Finance, Politics: Athenian Democratic Accounts Presented to David Lewis.* Oxford: Oxford University Press, 269–289.

—— 1995a. *'Reading' Greek Death.* Oxford: Clarendon Press.

—— 1995b. "Male and Female, Public and Private, Ancient and Modern," in E. Reeder (ed.), *Pandora.* Princeton: Princeton University Press, 111–120.

—— 1997a. "Reconstructing Change: Ideology and Ritual at Eleusis," in M. Golden and P. Toohey (eds.), *Inventing Ancient Culture? Historicism, Periodization and the Ancient World*. London: Routledge, 136–164.

—— 1997b. "Medea at a Shifting Distance: Images and Euripidean Tragedy," in J. J. Clauss and S. I. Johnston (eds.), *Medea: Essays on Medea in Myth, Literature, Philosophy and Art*. Princeton: Princeton University Press, 253–296.

—— 2003. *Tragedy and Athenian Religion*. Lanham, Md.: Lexington Books.

Speck, P. 1984. "'Interpolations et non-sens indiscutables: Das erste Gedicht der Ptochoprodromika," *Poikila Byzantina* 4 *(Varia I)*: 273–309.

Staal, F. 1989. *Rules Without Meaning: Ritual, Mantras, and the Human Sciences*. New York: P. Lang.

Stavrakopoulou, A. 1994. *The Theme of Marriage in the Karaghiozis Recorded Performances of the Whitman/Rinvolucri Collection*, Doctoral dissertation, Harvard University.

—— 1999. "Ἡ συμβολὴ τῆς συλλογῆς *Whitman/Rinvolucri* στὴ μελέτη τοῦ Καραγκιόζη," in the newspaper Καθημερινή, Sunday, January 3, 1999.

Stehle, E. 1997. *Performance and Gender in Ancient Greece: Nondramatic Poetry in its Setting*. Princeton: Princeton University Press.

Steiner, G. 1984. *Antigones*. Oxford: Oxford University Press.

Steingress, G. 2000. "New Flamenco: The Hybrid Construction of Identity by Performance," presentation at a workshop on hybridization in popular music, Barcelona. (Publication forthcoming.)

Steinrück, M. 2000. "Neues zu Sappho," *Zeitschrift fürPapyrologie und Epigraphik* 131:10–12.

Stengel, P. 1915. "ΛΟΥΤΡΑ. ΧΕΡΝΙΒΕΣ," *Hermes* 50:630–635.

—— 1920. *Die Griechische Kultusaltertümer*. 3rd ed. Munich: C. H. Beck.

—— 1922. "Opferspenden," *Hermes* 57:539–550.

Steppan, Th. 1997. "Tanzdarstellungen der mittel-und spätbyzantinischen Kunst," *Cahiers archéologiques* 45:141–168.

—— 2000. "The Artukid Bowl: Courtly Art in the Middle Byzantine Period and its Relation to the Islamic East," in O. Z. Pevny (ed.), *Perceptions of Byzantium and Its Neighbors (843-1261)*. New York: Metropolitan Museum of Art, 84–101.

Stevenson, H. M. 1888. *Theodori Prodromi Commentarios in Carmina Sacra Melodorum Cosmae Hierosolymitani et Ioannis Damasceni*. Rome: Ex Bibliotheca Vaticana.

Stewart, A. 1990. *Greek Sculpture: An Exploration*, 2 vols. New Haven: Yale University Press.

—— 1997. *Art, Desire and the Body in Ancient Greece*. Cambridge: Cambridge University Press.

Stewart, Ch. 1991. *Demons and the Devil: Moral Imagination in Modern Greek Culture*. Princeton: Princeton University Press.

—— 1994. "Syncretism as a Dimension of Nationalist Discourse in Modern Greece," in C. Stewart and R. Shaw (eds.), *Syncretism/Anti-Syncretism: The Politics of Religious Synthesis*. London: Routledge, 127–144.

—— 1997. "Fields in Dreams: Anxiety, Experience and the Limits of Social Constructionism in Modern Greek Dream Narratives," *American Ethnologist* 24:877–894.

—— 2001. "Οἱ ὀνειρευάμενοι. Τὰ γεγονότα τοῦ 1930 στὴν Κόρωνο," Ἀρχαιολογία καὶ Τέχνες, 80:8–14.

Stinton, T. C. W. 1986. "The Scope and Limits of Allusion in Greek Tragedy" in M. Cropp et al. (eds.), *Greek Tragedy and Its Legacy: Essays Presented to D. J. Conacher.* Calgary: University of Calgary Press, 67–102.
—— 1990. *Collected Papers.* Oxford: Oxford University Press.
Stokes, W. 1890. *Anecdota Oxoniensia: Lives of Saints from the Book of Lismore.* Oxford: Clarendon Press.
Strange, J. 1851. *Caesarii Heisterbacensis Monachi Dialogus Miraculorum,* 2 vols. Cologne: H. Lempertz and Co.
Strathern, M. 1988. *The Gender of the Gift: Problems with Women and Problems with Society in Melanesia.* Berkeley: University of California Press.
Stroumsa, G. 1999. "Dreams and Visions in Early Christian Discourse," in D. Shulman and G. Stroumsa (eds.), *Dream Cultures: Explorations in the Comparative History of Dreaming.* Oxford: Oxford University Press, 189–212.
Strzygowski, J. 1888. "Die Monatscyklen der byzantinischen Kunst," *Repertorium für Kunsturischenschaft* 11:22–46.
Suarez de la Torre, E. 1997. "Neoptolemos at Delphi," *Kernos* 10:153–176.
Sugarman, J. 1997. *Engendering Song: Singing and Subjectivity at Prespa Albanian Weddings.* Chicago: University of Chicago Press.
Sulimirski, T. and Taylor, T. 1991. "The Scythians," *Cambridge Ancient History,* vol. 3, 2nd ed. Cambridge: Cambridge University Press, 552–555.
Sutton, D. 1994. "'Tradition' and 'Modernity': Kalymnian Constructions of Identity and Otherness," *Journal of Modern Greek Studies* 12:239–260.
—— 2000. *Memories Cast in Stone.* Oxford: Berg.
Sutton, D. F. 1973. "Satyric Elements in the *Alcestis,*" *Rivista di Studi Classici* 21.3:84–91.
—— 1975a. "The Staging of Anodos Scenes," *Rivista di Studi Classici* 23:347–355.
—— 1975b. "Sophocles' *Iambe,*" *Eos* 63:245-48.
Sutton, R. F., Jr. 1989. "On the Classical Athenian Wedding: Two Red-Figure Loutrophoroi in Boston," in idem (ed.), *Daidalikon: Studies in Memory of Raymond V. Schoder, S.J.* Wauconda, Ill.: Bolchazy-Carducci, 334–351.
Sutton, S. B. 1994. "Settlement Patterns, Settlement Perceptions: Rethinking the Greek Village," in P. N. Kardulias (ed.), *Beyond the Site: Regional Studies in the Aegean Area.* Lanham, Md.: University Press of America, 313–335.
Tachtsis, K. 1977. "Ζεϊμπέκικο, 1964. "Ένα δοκίμιο," in G. Holst (ed.), Δρόμος γιὰ τὸ ρεμπέτικο. Athens: Denise Harvey, 202–209.
Takács, S. 1994. "The Magic of Isis Replaced, or, Cyril of Alexandria's Attempt at Redirecting Religious Devotion," *Poikila Byzantina (Varia V)* 13:491–507.
Tambiah, S. J. 1968. "The Magical Power of Words," *Man* (n.s.),175–208.
—— 1976. *World Conqueror and World Renouncer: A Study of Buddhism and Polity in Thailand against a Historical Background.* Cambridge: Cambridge University Press.
—— 1981. "A Performative Approach to Ritual," *Proceedings of the British Academy* 65:113–169.
—— 1985a. *Culture, Thought, and Social Action: An Anthropological Perspective.* Cambridge, Mass.: Harvard University Press
—— 1985b. "The Galactic Polity in Southeast Asia," in idem 1985a, 254–286.
Tannery, P. 1887. "Théodore Prodrome sur le grand et le petit (a Italicos)," *Annuaire de l'association pour l'encouragement des études grecques en France* 21:104–19.

Taplin, O. 1977. *The Stagecraft of Aeschylus: The Dramatic Use of Exits and Entrances in Greek Tragedy*. Oxford: Clarendon Press.

Taylor, M. C. 1997. *Salamis and the Salaminioi. The History of an Unofficial Athenian Demos*. Amsterdam: J. C. Gieben.

Tedlock, B. 1983. "A Phenomenological Approach to Religious Change in Highland Guatemala," in C. Kendall et al. (eds.), *Heritage of Conquest: Thirty Years Later*. Albuquerque: University of New Mexico Press, 235–246.

Tedlock, D. 1983. *The Spoken Word and the Work of Interpretation*. Philadelphia: University of Pennsylvania Press.

—— 1991. "The Speaker of Tales Has More Than One String to Play on," in Brady 1991, 309–340.

Theotokas, G. 1973 [1929]. 'Ελεύθερο Πνεῦμα, ed. K. Th. Dimaras. Athens: 'Ερμῆς.

—— 1986. *Free Spirit*, trans. S. Stavrou. *University of Minnesota Modern Greek Studies Yearbook* 2, 153–200.

Thomas, R. 1995. "The Place of the Poet in Archaic Society," in A. Powell (ed.), *The Greek World*. London: Routledge, 104–129.

Thompson, F. 1973. *Lark Rise to Candleford*. London: Penguin Modern Classics.

Thomson, G. 1941. *Aeschylus and Athens: A Study in the Social Origins of Drama*, 3rd ed. London: Lawrence and Wishart, 1966.

—— 1949. *Studies in Ancient Greek Society, I: The Prehistoric Aegean*, 2nd ed. London: Lawrence and Wishart, 1954.

Thomson, M. H. 1955. *Textes grecs inedits relatifs aux plantes*. Paris: Les Belles Lettres.

—— 1960. *Le jardin symbolique: Texte grec tiré du Clarkianus XI*. Paris: Les Belles Lettres.

Tobin, J. 1998. "Tango and the Scandal of Homosocial Desire," in Washabaugh 1998a, 79–102.

Todorov, T. 1973. "Le discours de la magie," *L'Homme* 13 (4):38–65.

—— 1977. *The Poetics of Prose*, trans. R. Howard. Oxford: B. Blackwell.

—— 1981. *Introduction to Poetics*, trans. R. Howard. Minneapolis: University of Minnesota Press.

Todorova, M. 1995. *Imagining the Balkans*. New York and London: Oxford University Press.

Torp, L. 1988. "The Dance Event and the Process of Transformation: A Case Study of the Anastenaria in Lagadha, Greece," in L. Torp (ed.), *The Dance Event: A Complex Cultural Phenomenon*. Copenhagen: ICTM Study Group, 74–80.

—— 1992. "'It's All Greek to Me': The Invention of Pan-Hellenic Dances—and Other Stories," in M. Chestnut (ed.), *Telling Reality*. Copenhagen: NIF Publications, 273–294.

Trigger, B. 1990. "Monumental Architecture: A Thermodynamic Explanation of Symbolic Behaviour," *World Archaeology* 22:119–32.

Trilling, J. 1997. "Daedalus and the Nightingale: Art and Technology in the Myth of the Byzantine Court," in H. Maguire (ed.), *Byzantine Court Culture from 829 to 1204*. Washington, D.C.: Dumbarton Oaks, 217–30.

Trombley, F. 1994. *Hellenic Religion and Christianisation, c. 370–529*, 2 vols. Leiden: Brill.

—— 2000. "Religious Experience in Late Antiquity: Theological Ambivalence and Christianization," *Byzantine and Modern Greek Studies* 24:2–60.

Trypanis, C. (ed.) 1968. *Fourteen Early Byzantine Cantica*. Vienna: Wiener byzantinistische Studien, Bd. 5.

—— 1971. *The Penguin Book of Greek Verse*. Harmondsworth: Penguin.

Tsouni, D. 1987. "Music and Dance at Greek Wedding Receptions in Adelaide," *Chronico* 7:99–108.

Turner, E. 1991. "Experience and Poetics in Anthropological Writing," in Benson 1993, 27–47.

Turner, V. 1967. *The Forest of Symbols: Aspects of Ndembu Ritual.* Ithaca, N.Y.: Cornell University Press.

—— 1968. *The Drums of Affliction: A Study of Religious Processes Among the Ndembu of Zambia.* Oxford: Clarendon Press.

—— 1969. *The Ritual Process: Structure and Anti-Structure.* Chicago: Aldine.

—— 1973. "The Center Out There: Pilgrim's Goal," *History of Religions* 12.3:191–230.

—— 1974a, *Dramas, Fields, and Metaphors; Symbolic Action in Human Society.* Ithaca, N.Y.: Cornell University Press

——1974b. "Pilgrimages as Social Processes" in idem 1974a, 166–239.

—— 1977. "Variations on a Theme of Liminality," in Moore and Myerhoff 1977a, 36–52.

—— 1982a. *Celebration: Studies in Festivity and Ritual.* Washington, D.C.: Smithsonian Institute.

—— 1982b. *From Ritual to Theatre: The Human Seriousness of Play.* New York City: Performing Arts Journal Publications.

—— 1987. *The Anthropology of Performance.* New York: Performing Arts Journal Publications.

Tylor, E. B. 1865. *Researches into the Early History of Mankind and the Development of Civilization.* London: John Murray.

Tziovas, D. 1986. *The Nationism of the Demoticists and its Impact on Their Literary Theory.* Amsterdam: Hakkert.

—— 1989. "Residual Orality and Belated Textuality in Greek Literature and Culture," *Journal of Modern Greek Studies* 13:296–305.

—— (ed.) 1997a. *Greek Modernism and Beyond: Essays in Honor of Peter Bien.* Lanham, Md.: Rowman and Littlefield.

—— 1997b. "Mapping out Greek Literary Modernism," in Tziovas 1997a, 25–39.

Ucciardello, G. 2001. "Sapph. frr. 88 e 159 V. in POxy. LXIV 4411," *Zeitschrift für Papyrologie und Epigraphik* 136:167–168.

Urquhart, J. 1993. *Away: A Novel.* Toronto: McClelland and Stewart.

Vance, C. (ed.) 1984. *Pleasure and Danger: Exploring Female Sexuality.* Boston: Routledge, Kegan and Paul.

van der Burg, N. M. H. 1939. Ἀπόρρητα—Δρώμενα—Ὄργια· *Bijdrage tot de kennis der religieuze terminologie in het Grieksch.* Amsterdam: H. J. Paris.

van der Weiden, M. J. H. 1991. *The Dithyrambs of Pindar.* Amsterdam: J. C. Gieben.

van Dieten, J. L. 1975. *Nicetae Choniatae Historia.* Berlin and New York: Walter de Gruyter.

van Gennep, A. 1960. *The Rites of Passage*, trans. M. Vizedom and G. Caffee, intr. S. Kimball. Chicago: University of Chicago Press.

—— 1981 [1909]. *Les rites de passage.* Paris: Éditions A. et J. Picard.

van Straten, F. T. W. 1976. "Daikrates' Dream. A Votive Relief from Kos, and Some Other κατ' ὄναρ Dedications," *Bulletin Antieke Beschaving (Babesch)* 51:1–38.

—— 1995. Ἱερὰ καλά: *Images of Animal Sacrifice in Archaic and Classical Greece.* Religions in the Graeco-Roman World 127. Leiden: E. J. Brill.

Vasilevskii, V. 1886. Θεοδώρου τοῦ Προδρόμου βίος Μελετίου τοῦ νέου. *Pravoslavnyi Palestinskij Sbornik* 17:40–69.

Vayenas, N. 1997. "Hellenocentrism and the Literary Generation of the Thirties," in Tziovas 1997a, 43–48.

Venturi, R. et al. 1972. *Learning from Las Vegas.* Cambridge, Mass.: MIT Press.

Vérilhac, A.-M. and Vial, Cl. 1998. *Le mariage grec du VIe siècle av. J.-C. à l'époque d'Auguste. Bulletin de Correspondance Héllénique,* Supplément 32. Athens: École Française d'Athènes.

Vernant, J.-P. 1972. "Ambiguité et renversement. Sur la structure énigmatique de l' 'Oedipe roi'," in J.-P. Vernant and P. Vidal-Naquet, *Mythe et tragédie en Grèce ancienne.* Paris: Maspero, 99–131.

Verpeaux, J. 1966. *Pseudo-Kodinos, Traité des Offices.* Paris: Éditions du Centre National de la Recherche Scientifique.

Versnel, H. S. 1987. "What Did Ancient Man See When He Saw a God? Some Reflections on Greco-Roman Epiphany," in D. van der Plas (ed.), *Effigies Dei: Essays on the History of Religions.* Leiden: Brill, 42–55.

——— 1996. "Teletê," in S. Hornblower and A. Spawforth (eds.), *The Oxford Classical Dictionary,* third ed., Oxford: Oxford University Press, 1480.

Vico, G. 1744. *Principij di Scienza Nuova.* Naples: Stamperia Muziana.

Vidal-Naquet, P. 1972. "Chasse et sacrifice dans l'Orestie d'Eschyle," in Vernant, J.-P. and Vidal-Naquet, P., *Mythe et tragédie en Grèce ancienne.* Paris: Maspero, 133–158.

——— 1986. "The Black Hunter and the Origin of the Athenian *Ephebia,*" in P. Vidal-Naquet, *The Black Hunter: Forms of Thought and Forms of Society in the Greek World,* trans. A. Szegedy-Maszak. Baltimore: Johns Hopkins University Press, 106–128.

Vitti, M. 1977. Ἡ γενιὰ τοῦ τριάντα. Athens: Ἑρμῆς.

——— 1984. Ὀδυσσέας Ἐλύτης. Athens: Ἑρμῆς.

——— 1991. Ἰδεολογικὴ λειτουργία τῆς νεοελληνικῆς ἠθογραφίας, 3rd ed. Athens: Κέδρος.

Vizyenos, G. 1980. Νεοελληνικὰ Διηγήματα. ed. P. Moullas. Athens: Ἑρμῆς.

——— 1988. *My Mother's Sin and Other Stories,* trans. W. F. Wyatt, Jr. Hanover, N.H.: University Press of New England.

——— 1995. Ἡ φιλοσοφία τοῦ καλοῦ παρὰ Πλωτίνῳ, ed. P. Kalligas. Athens: Ἀρμός.

Vogt, A. 1967. *Constantine Porphyrogenitus, Le Livre des Cérémonies.* Paris: Les Belles Lettres.

Vogt, E. Z. and Abel, S. 1977. "On Political Rituals in Contemporary Mexico," in Moore and Myerhoff 1977a, 173–188.

Voigt, E.-M. 1971. *Sappho et Alcaeus.* Amsterdam: Athenaeum/Polak and Van Gennep.

von Harnack, A. (ed.) 1916. *Porphyrius, "Gegen die Christen."* Berlin: Verlag der König. Preuss. Akademie der Wissenschaften.

von Lingenthal, D. K. E. Z., 1955. *Geschicte des griechisch-römischen Rechts,* repr. ed. Aalen: Verlag Scientia.

Vranouse, E. L. 1980. Βυζαντινὰ Ἔγγραφα τῆς Μονῆς Πάτμου, *I.* Athens: Ἐθνικὸν Ἵδρυμα Ἐρευνῶν.

Vryonis, S. 1978. "Recent Scholarship on Continuity of Culture: Classical Greeks, Byzantines, Modern Greeks," in S. Vryonis (ed.), *The "Past" in Medieval and Modern Greek Culture.* Malibu, Calif.: Undena Publications, 237–256.

—— 1981. "The *Panegyris* of the Byzantine Saint: A Study in the Nature of a Medieval Institution, Its Origins and Fate," in S. Hackel (ed.), *The Byzantine Saint.* London: Fellowship of St. Alban and St. Sergius, 196–226.

Waanders, F. M. J. 1983. *The History of* τέλος *and* τελῶ *in Ancient Greek.* Amsterdam: Grüner.

Walker, H. J. 1995. *Theseus and Athens.* New York: Oxford University Press.

Wallace, R. 1962. "The Early Coinages of Athens and Euboea," *Numismatic Chronicle* 7.2:23–42.

Walter, Ch. 1968. "Two Notes on the Deesis," *Revue des Études Byzantines* 26:311–336.

Walz, C. 1832–6. *Rhetores Graeci.* Stuttgart: J. G. Cottae.

Washabaugh, W. (ed.). 1998a. *The Passion of Music and Dance: Body, Gender, and Sexuality.* Oxford: Berg.

—— 1998b. "Fashioning Masculinity in Flamenco Dance," in idem 1998a, 39–50.

Waszink, J. H. 1947. *Tertullian, De Anima.* Amsterdam: J. M. Meulenhoff.

Weaver, M. 2000. "William Eggleston: From Meaning to Being," lecture at Haverford College, Penn., April 28.

Weaver, M. and Hammond, A. 1993. "William Eggleston: Treating Things Existentially," *History of Photography* 17.1:54–61.

Webb, R. 1997. "Salome's Sisters: The Rhetoric and Realities of Dance in Late Antiquity and Byzantium," in L. James (ed.), *Women, Men, and Eunuchs: Gender in Byzantium.* London: Routledge, 119–146.

Webster, T. B. L. 1970. *The Greek Chorus.* London: Methuen.

Weitzmann, K. 1951. *Greek Mythology in Byzantine Art.* Princeton: Princeton University Press.

—— 1979. *Age of Spirituality, Late Antique and Christian Art, Third to Seventh Century.* New York: The Metropolitan Museum of Art and Princeton University Press.

—— 1981. *Classical Heritage in Byzantine and Near Eastern Art.* London: Variorum.

Welcker, F. G. 1816. *Sappho von einem herrschenden Vorurtheil befreyt.* Göttingen: Wanderhoek [=*Kleine Schriften. Zweyter Theil.* Bonn: E. Weber, 1845, 80–144].

West, M. L. 1970. "Burning Sappho," *Maia* 22:307–330.

—— 1974. *Studies in Elegy and Iambus.* Berlin: de Gruyter.

West, R. 1941. *Black Lamb and Grey Falcon.* New York: Penguin.

West, S. R. 2002. "Scythia," in Bakker et al. 2000, 437–456.

White, H. 1978. *Tropics of Discourse: Essays in Cultural Criticism.* Baltimore: Johns Hopkins University Press.

White, R. J. 1975. *Artemidorus. The Interpretation of Dreams.* Park Ridge, N.J.: Noyes Press.

Whittaker, M. 1982. *Tatian, Oratio ad Graecos and Fragments.* Oxford: Clarendon Press.

Widnäs, M. 1966. "Les synaxaires slavo-russes des «Fragments Findlandais»," *Commentationes Humanarum Litterarum* 38.1:1–214.

Wilamowitz-Moellendorff, T. von 1917. *Die dramatische Technik des Sophokles. Aus dem Nachlass herausgegeben von Ernst Kapp. Mit einem Beitrag von Ulrich von Wilamowitz-Moellendorff.* Berlin: Weidmannsche Buchhandlung.

Willetts, R. F. 1955. *The Aristocratic Society in Ancient Crete.* London: Routledge.

William, Archbishop of Tyre 1948. *A History of Deeds Done Beyond the Sea,* trans. and ed. E. Babcock and A. C. Krey. New York: Columbia University Press.

Williams, R. 1977. *Marxism and Literature*. Oxford: Oxford University Press.

Wilson, N. and Darrouzès, J. 1968. "Restes du cartulaire de Hiéra-Xérochoraphion," *Revue des Études Byzantines* 26:5–47.

Wilson, P. 2000. *The Athenian Institution of the Choregia*. Cambridge: Cambridge University Press.

Wilson, P. J. 1988. *The Domestication of the Human Species*. New Haven: Yale University Press.

Winkler, J. J. 1990. "The Education of Chloe: Hidden Injuries of Sex," in idem, *The Constraints of Desire*. London and New York: Routledge, 101–126.

Wirth, P. 2000. *Eustathii Thessalonicensis Opera Minora*. Berlin: Walter de Gruyter.

Wissowa, G. 1903–1980. *Paulys Real-Encyclopädie der classischen Altertumswissenschaft. Supplement 4*. Stuttgart: J. B. Metzler.

Wolf, G. and Andraschko, F. M. 1991. "'. . . und heulen vor Lust.' Der Hanf bei den Skythen," in Rolle et al. 1991, 157–160.

Wolff, C. 1992. "Euripides' 'Iphigenia among the Taurians': Aetiology, Ritual, and Myth," *Classical Antiquity* 11:307–334.

Wolff, H. J. 1944. "Marriage Law and Family Organization in Ancient Athens: A Study on the Interrelation of Public and Private Law in the Greek City," *Traditio* 2:43–95.

Wolter, E. 1879. *Der Judenknabe (5 Griechische, 14 Lateinische und 8 Französische Texte)*. Halle: Max Niemeyer.

Woronoff, W. 1978. "Structures parallèles de l'initiation des jeunes gens en Afrique noire et dans la tradition grecque," in *Afrique noire et monde méditerranéen dans l'antiquité: Colloque de Dakar, 19–24 Janvier 1976*. Université de Dakar: Nouvelles Éditions Africaines, 237–234.

Wortley, J. 1992. *The Spiritual Meadow (Pratum Spirituale) by John Moschus*. Kalamazoo, Mich.: Cistercian Publications.

Yannakakis, E. 1997. "Fragmentation of Consciousness in Pentzikis' *Pragmatognosia*," in Tziovas 1997a, 151–162.

Yatromanolakis, D. 1998. "Simonides Fr. Eleg. 22 W^2: To Sing or to Mourn?," *Zeitschrift für Papyrologie und Epigraphik* 120: 1–11 (reprinted in G. Nagy (ed.), *Greek Literature, 3: Greek Literature in the Archaic Period, The Emergence of Authorship*. New York and London: Routledge 2001).

—— 1999a. "Alexandrian Sappho Revisited," *Harvard Studies in Classical Philology* 99:179–195.

—— 1999b. "When Two Fragments Meet: Sapph. fr. 22 V.," *Zeitschrift für Papyrologie und Epigraphik* 128:23–24.

—— 2000. "Healing Sounds: Music and Medicine in Greek Antiquity," keynote lecture delivered at the Theoretical and Diagnostic Histopathology Conference, University of Thrace, Alexandroupolis, August.

—— 2001a. "Visualizing Poetry: An Early Representation of Sappho," *Classical Philology* 96:159–168.

—— 2001b. "Toward an Archaeology of Sounds," lecture delivered at Harvard University, Cambridge, Mass., December.

—— 2001c. "To Sing or to Mourn? A Reappraisal of Simonides 22 W^2," in D. Boedeker and D. Sider (eds.), *The New Simonides: Contexts of Praise and Desire*. New York and Oxford: Oxford University Press, 208–225.

Bibliography

—— 2002. "Έτερογλωσσικοὶ διάλογοι καὶ ἀνα-σύνθεση στὴ Σαπφὼ τοῦ Ὀδυσσέα Ἐλύτη," Σύγκριση/*Comparaison* 13:60–72.

—— 2004. "Contrapuntal Inscriptions: Music, Image, Text," forthcoming.

—— forthcoming. *Sappho in the Making: An Anthropology of Reception.*

Yatromanolakis, D. and Roilos, P. 2003. *Towards a Ritual Poetics.* Athens: Foundation of the Hellenic World.

Younger, P. 2002. *Playing Host to the Deity: Festival Religion in South Indian Tradition.* New York: Oxford University Press, 17–25.

Zagagi, N. 1999. "Comic Patterns in Sophocles' *Ichneutae,*" in J. Griffin (ed.), *Sophocles Revisited: Essays Presented to Sir Hugh Lloyd-Jones.* Oxford: Oxford University Press, 177–218.

Zambelios. S. 1852. ˇΑισματα δημοτικὰ τῆς Ἑλλάδος. Μετὰ μελέτης ἱστορικῆς περὶ μεσαιωνικοῦ ἑλληνισμοῦ. Corfu: ˇΑ. Τερζάκης καὶ Θ. Ρωμαῖος.

—— 1859. Πόθεν ἡ κοινὴ λέξις τραγουδῶ. Σκέψεις περὶ ἑλληνικῆς ποιήσεως. Athens: Ἐ. Σούτσας καὶ ᾿Α. Κτενᾶς.

Zamora, L. P. and Faris, W. B., 1995. *Magical Realism: Theory, History, Community.* Durham, N.C.: Duke University Press.

Zeitlin, F. I. 1965. "The Motif of the Corrupted Sacrifice in Aeschylus' *Oresteia,*" *Transactions and Proceedings of the American Philological Association* 96:463–508.

—— 1966. "Postscript to Sacrificial Imagery in the *Oresteia* (Ag. 1235–37)," *Transactions and Proceedings of the American Philological Association* 97:645–653.

—— 1970. *The Ritual World of Greek Tragedy.* Ph.D. dissertation. New York: Columbia University.

—— 1996. *Playing the Other: Gender and Society in Classical Greek Literature.* Chicago: University of Chicago Press.

Zepos, J. and P. 1931. *Jus Graecoromanum,* I. Aalen: Scientia, repr. 1962.

Zijderveld, C. 1934. Τελετή: *Beijdrage tot de kennis der religieuse terminologie in het Grieksch.* Purmerend, Netherlands: J. Muusses.

Ziolkowski, J. 1986. *Nigel of Canterbury: Miracles of the Virgin Mary, in Verse.* Toronto: Pontifical Institute of Mediaeval Studies.

Žižek, S. 1999. "'You May!' Slavoj Žižek Writes About the Post-Modern Superego," *London Review of Books,* 18 March 1999, 21:6, 3/6.

Zografou, M. 1993. "The Role of Dance in the Progression of a Pontic Wedding," *Dance Studies* 17:49–60.

Contributors

MARGARET ALEXIOU is Professor Emerita in the Department of the Classics, Harvard University, where she held the George Seferis Chair of Modern Greek Studies (1985–2000). She previously taught at the University of Birmingham. Her major publications are *The Ritual Lament in Greek Tradition*, second edition revised by Dimitrios Yatromanolakis and Panagiotis Roilos (2002), and *After Antiquity: Greek Language, Myth, and Metaphor* (2002). She has written on ancient Greek death ideologies, the medieval Greek novel, Renaissance Greek, and nineteenth and twentieth-century Greek literature and culture. She is currently working on a critical edition of the twelfth-century Byzantine poems *Ptochoprodromika*.

ANGUS M. BOWIE is Lobel Praelector and Fellow in Classics at the Queen's College, University of Oxford. He held his first post as a Research Fellow at Emmanuel College, Cambridge, before becoming Lecturer in Greek at Liverpool University. His major research interests include literary theory, Herodotus, Greece and Persia, ancient Greek comedy, and ancient Greek anthropology. His publications include *The Poetic Dialect of Sappho and Alcaeus* (1981), *Aristophanes: Myth, Ritual and Comedy* (1993), and numerous articles on comedy, tragedy, historiography, Virgil and religion. He is currently bringing to a conclusion a commentary on Herodotus Book 8.

VANGELIS CALOTYCHOS is Assistant Professor of Comparative Literature and Hellenic Studies at New York University. He previously taught at Harvard University. His *Modern Greece: A Cultural Poetics* (2003) is a consideration of modernity in Greece. He has edited two interdisciplinary volumes on contemporary Cyprus. He is currently co-translating Menis Koumandareas's short stories and writing a set of essays on Balkan narrative and film.

JANE K. COWAN is Senior Lecturer and Chair in the Department of Anthropology at the University of Sussex at Brighton, England. Her publications include *Dance and the Body Politics in Northern Greece*, *Macedonia: The Politics of Identity and Difference*, and (with M. Dembour and R. Wilson) *Culture and Rights: Anthropological Perspectives*. She has written on dance and ritual performance, identity, gender relations, and minority politics in contemporary Greece. She is currently examining minority petitions to the League of Nations, and the international practices of making minorities and states.

JOHN DUFFY holds the Dumbarton Oaks Professorship of Byzantine Philology and Literature at Harvard University. His teaching and research interests range from the Cappadocian Fathers in the fourth to Michael Psellos in the eleventh century. His major publications are critical editions of Byzantine texts (six to date and three more in progress), including two volumes in the Teubner series of philosophical and theological writings of Psellos. He has written numerous articles on Byzantine Greek literature and culture.

PAT EASTERLING is an Honorary Fellow of Newnham College, University of Cambridge, and a Fellow of the British Academy. She was Regius Professor of Greek at Cambridge from 1994 to 2001, and before that Professor of Greek at University College, London. She edited Sophocles' *Trachiniae* (1982), (with B. M. W. Knox) Volume I of the *Cambridge History of Classical Literature* (1985), *The Cambridge Companion to Greek Tragedy* (1997), and (with Edith Hall) *Greek and Roman Actors* (2002). She is currently writing a commentary on Sophocles' *Oedipus at Colonus* for Cambridge Greek and Latin Classics.

GLORIA FERRARI is Professor of Classical Archaeology and Art at Harvard University. She previously taught at Wilson College, Bryn Mawr College, and at the University of Chicago. Her publications include *Il commercio dei sarcofagi asiatici* (1966), *Materiali dei Museo Archeologico Nazionale di Tarquinia XI: I vasi attici a figure rosse del periodo arcaico* (1988), and *Figures of Speech: Men and Maidens in Ancient Greece* (2002). Her article on the miniature frieze from the West House at Thera (forthcoming in the *American Journal of Archaeology*) deals with geographical description as both a visual and a literary genre, and with the Iron Age reception of Bronze Age traditions.

LAURIE HART is Associate Professor and Chair, Department of Anthropology, Haverford College. She holds a Master of Architecture degree from the University of California at Berkeley and a PhD in Anthropology from Harvard University. She is the author of *Time, Religion, and Social Experience in Rural Greece* (1992) and "Culture and Civilization at the Northwest Borders of Greece" (*American Ethnologist* 1999.) Her research interests include the anthropology of the Mediterranean, religion, architecture, art, kinship, and collective conflict.

ALBERT HENRICHS is Eliot Professor of Greek Literature at Harvard University. He has written extensively on ancient Greek literature, religion, and myth. Major areas of research include the Greek god Dionysos and his modern reception; the representation of ritual in literature and art; the religious self-awareness of the ancient Greeks; and the history of classical scholarship since 1800. In 1990 he delivered the Sather Lectures on "Gods and Rituals in Greek Tragedy" at the University of California in Berkeley. Among other books, he is the author of *Die Götter Griechenlands: Ihr Bild im Wandel der Religionswissenschaft* (1987), and

Warum soll ich denn tanzen? Dionysisches im Chor der griechischen Tragödie (1996). His most recent articles on ritual include "Drama and Dromena: Bloodshed, Violence, and Sacrificial Metaphor in Euripides" (2002), and "Wie ein Rind zur Schlachtbank: Zur Problematisierung der Opferthematik in der griechischen Tragödie" (forthcoming). He is currently working on the status of writing and the role of written texts in ancient Greek religion.

MICHAEL HERZFELD, Harvard University, conducts anthropological research in Greece, Italy, and Thailand. He previously taught at Vassar College and Indiana University and has held visiting appointments in Australia, Britain, France, and Italy. Author of nine books (of which *The Body Impolitic: Artisans and Artifice in the Global Hierarchy of Value* appeared in fall, 2003) and recipient of the J. I. Staley Prize and the Rivers Memorial Medal, he has served as editor of *American Ethnologist* and as president of the Modern Greek Studies Association and the Society for the Anthropology of Europe.

GAIL HOLST-WARHAFT is an Adjunct Professor in the Departments of Classics and Comparative Literature and Interim Director of the Institute for European Studies at Cornell University. She has written numerous articles on twentieth-century Greek literature, music, and culture. Among her recent books are *The Classical Moment: Views from Seven Literatures* (co-edited with D. R. McCann, 1999), and *The Cue for Passion: Grief and its Political Uses* (2000).

IOLI KALAVREZOU is Dumbarton Oaks Professor of Byzantine Art in the Department of History of Art, Harvard University. She has taught at the University of California, Los Angeles, and the University of Munich. Her major publications include *Byzantine Icons in Steatite* (1985) and numerous articles on ivory carving, imperial art, and manuscript illumination. She is the editor of *Byzantine Women and Their World* (2003). Her current research focuses on imperial symbols and relics in the hands of the empire, and on secular objects in the everyday world of Byzantium. She is completing a book on the iconography of a tenth-century illustrated Psalter.

RUTH MACRIDES is Lecturer in Byzantine Studies at the University of Birmingham, England. She has published on legal and literary subjects as well as the nineteenth-century reception of Byzantium in Greece and Britain. Her studies on Byzantine law are collected in *Kinship and Justice in Byzantium, 11th–15th Centuries* (1999). She is also the editor of *Travel in the Byzantine World* (2002).

GREGORY NAGY is the Francis Jones Professor of Classical Greek Literature and Professor of Comparative Literature at Harvard University. He is the author of

The Best of the Achaeans: Concepts of the Hero in Archaic Greek Poetry (1979; 2nd ed. 1999), which won the Goodwin Award of Merit, American Philological Association, in 1982. Other publications include *Comparative Studies in Greek and Indic Meter* (1974), *Greek Mythology and Poetics* (1990), *Pindar's Homer: The Lyric Possession of an Epic Past* (1990), *Homeric Questions* (1996), *Poetry as Performance: Homer and Beyond* (1996), and *Plato's Rhapsody and Homer's Music: The Poetics of the Panathenaic Festival in Classical Athens* (2002). Since 2000, he has been the Director of the Harvard Center for Hellenic Studies in Washington DC, while continuing to teach at the Harvard campus in Cambridge, Mass.

ROBIN OSBORNE is Professor of Ancient History at the University of Cambridge and a Fellow of King's College. He was previously a Professor of Ancient History in the University of Oxford. He has published widely in both Greek history and archaeology, including *Classical Landscape with Figures: The Ancient Greek City and Its Countryside* (1987), *Greece in the Making, c.1200–479 B.C.* (1996) and *Archaic and Classical Greek Art* (1998). He is co-editor with P. J. Rhodes of *Greek Historical Inscriptions 404–323 B.C.* (2003), a replacement for M. N. Tod's volume of that name. His own current work concerns the changing iconography of Athenian vase painting during the period 520–450, and Athenian social and political history. He is also director of a project funded by the Arts and Humanities Research Board (UK), "The Anatomy of Cultural Revolution: Athenian Art, Literature, Language and Politics 430–380 BC."

PANAGIOTIS ROILOS is Associate Professor of Modern Greek Studies in the Department of the Classics, Harvard University. He was previously Assistant Professor of Byzantine and Renaissance Greek literature at the Ohio State University. His book *Amphoteroglossia: Toward a Poetics of the Medieval Greek Novel* is to appear soon. He has written on oral poetics, metaphor and ritual, medieval Greek poetics, Renaissance Greek poetry, and nineteenth- and twentieth-century Greek literature and culture. He is currently writing a book on the reception of the classical tradition in the period of the Greek Enlightenment (late eighteenth–early nineteenth centuries).

IAN RUTHERFORD is Professor of Classics, University of Reading. His major publications are *Pindar's Paeans* (2001) and *Canons of Style in the Antonine Age: Idea-theory in Its Literary Context* (1998). His research interests and other publications focus on Greek lyric poetry, ancient religion, particularly pilgrimage, relations between Greece and the Near East, and Ancient Anatolia. He is currently working on a book on state pilgrimage (*theôria*) in ancient Greece and a study of the Hesiodic Catalogue of Women.

Contributors

RICHARD SEAFORD is Professor of Greek Literature at the University of Exeter. He is the author of numerous articles on Greek literature and Greek religion from Homer to the New Testament, of commentaries on Euripides' *Cyclops* (1984) and on Euripides' *Bacchae* (1996), and of *Reciprocity and Ritual: Homer and Tragedy in the Developing City-State* (1994). He is co-editor of *Reciprocity in Ancient Greece* (1998). Forthcoming is *Money and the Early Greek Mind: Homer, Philosophy, Tragedy* (2004). He is currently writing a book on Dionysos.

CHRISTIANE SOURVINOU-INWOOD has been a Junior Research Fellow at St. Hugh's College, University of Oxford, University Lecturer at Liverpool University, Senior Research Fellow at University College, Oxford, and Reader at Reading University. She the author of the following books: *Theseus as Son and Stepson* (1979); *Studies in Girls' Transitions* (1988); *'Reading' Greek Culture: Texts and Images, Rituals and Myths* (1991); *'Reading' Greek Death* (1995); *Tragedy and Athenian Religion* (2003); *Hylas, the Nymphs, Dionysos and Others: Myth, Ritual, Ethnicity* (2004), and articles on Greek archaeology, ancient Greek religion, and social history.

ANNA STAVRAKOPOULOU is a Lecturer in the Department of Greek Philology at the University of Thessaloniki. She has taught at NYU, Yale, and the University of Crete. She is currently completing an Ilex Foundation sponsored project on the impact of written sources on orally composed texts. She is the co-editor of *Modern Greek Literature: Critical Essays* (2003), and has written articles on Greek shadow theater.

CHARLES STEWART is Reader in Anthropology at University College London. He is the author of *Demons and the Devil: Moral Imagination in Modern Greek Culture* (1991), and co-editor of *Syncretism/Anti-Syncretism: The Politics of Religious Synthesis* (1994). His major research interests include indigenous and academic perspectives on cultural mixture, especially syncretism and creolization; and the ethnography, politics, and modern history of Greece, the Balkans, and Europe. He is currently working on an historical and ethnographic study of dreams in Greece.

DIMITRIOS YATROMANOLAKIS is Assistant Professor in the Department of Classics, Johns Hopkins University. A former Junior Fellow in the Society of Fellows, Harvard University, he has written on archaic Greek poetry and cultural history, Greek vase-painting, and Greek literary papyri. He is the author of *Parchments of Sappho* (forthcoming) and *Sappho in the Making* (forthcoming). He is currently writing a book on the institution of poetic and musical contests (*mousikoí agônes*) in the archaic, classical, and hellenistic periods.

473

Index of Subjects

bb

objects, and ritual 18, 38, 43–48,
　393–94
onomatopoiia, 132
opposition, in ritual, 91
oral literature (orality), 19–20, 105–9,
　112, 139–48
order, 10

paganism, and Christianity, 338–55,
　371–82
paradigm, 56–59
paradox, 217–25
parody, 210–26
partheneia, 57, 328
parthenoi, 325, 331
paternalism, 372–73
performance, 5–8, 12
　and poetry, 139–48
performance studies, 8
performative transmission, 65
petition
　in literature, 369–70
　ritual of, 356–370
phonestheme, 135
pilgrimage, 323–37, 338
poeta vates, 127–28
poeticity, 17, 18
politics, 16, 27–28, 227–42
　ritual and, 39–42, 75–76, 371–82
Polynesia, 9
postmodernism, 111–12, 123
power, display of, 38, 405
practice, 4, 20–21
　anthropology, 405
progumnasma, 104–5, 115, 211–26
propemptikon, 69
purification, 169–70, 195–97

rationalism, 4, 125
reciprocity, 9, 97–98
recreation, 7, 9–10
reflexivity, 8–10, 408
refugees, 384–96, 399–402
repetition
　poetry and, 139–48
　ritual and, 139
repetitiveness, 11, 22
revelry, 10
reversal of ritual, 181–88, 189–98,
　256, 258–60
rhetoric, 172–78, 210–26
Rhodes, 374–75
rigidity, 10–11
rites of passage, 5, 6, 57, 128,
　245–60, 323–37, 410–24
rites of maturation, 323–37
ritual
　abnormality and, 181–88, 189–98
　Arabian, 270–72
　Babylonian, 267–70
　children's, 100–102, 371–82
　definition of, 11–12
　discourse, 55, 66–67, 121–36
　gender and, 161–88
　historiography and, 261–78
　imagery, 63
　Indian, 270–72, 323–24
　language, 36, 121, 151
　legislation and, 164–81
　literature and, 94–120, 121–36
　offerings, 43–48, 76–77, 327, 328
　Persian, 261–67
　poetics, 3–34
　poetry, 9, 18
　religious, 261–78

Index of Names